This Book Is the Property of:

State _____   Book No. _____

Province _____

County _____

Parish _____

School District _____

Other _____

Enter information in spaces to the left as instructed.

| Issued to | Year Used | Condition | |
		Issued	Returned

PUPILS to whom this textbook is issued must not write on any page or mark any part of it in any way; consumable textbooks excepted.

1. Teachers should see that the pupil's name is clearly written in ink in the spaces above in every book issued.
2. The following terms should be used in recording the condition of the book: New; Good; Fair; Poor; Bad.

CENTURY 21® 11e
Computer Skills and Applications

Lessons 1–88

Jack P. Hoggatt, Ed. D.

Professor of Business, Emeritus
University of Wisconsin - Eau Claire
Eau Claire, Wisconsin

James R. Smith, Jr., Ed. D.

Director, Quality Enhancement Plan
Wake Technical Community College
Raleigh, North Carolina

Jon A. Shank, Ed. D.

Professor of Education, Emeritus
Robert Morris University
Moon Township, Pennsylvania

Australia • Brazil • Canada • Mexico • Singapore • United Kingdom • United States

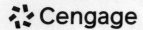

Century 21 Computer Skills and Applications Lessons 1–88: Keyboarding, **11th Edition**

Jack P. Hoggatt, James R. Smith, Jr., and Jon A. Shank.

SVP, GM Skills & Global Product Management: Jonathan Lau

Product Director: Lauren Murphy

Product Manager: Amanda Lyons

Product Assistant: Anna Goulart

Executive Director, Content Design: Marah Bellegarde

Director, Learning Design: Leigh Hefferon

Associate Learning Designer: Courtney Cozzy

Marketing Director: Trish Bobst

Marketing Manager: Abigail Hess

Director, Content Delivery: Patty Stephan

Senior Content Manager: Anne Orgren

Digital Delivery Lead: Noah Vincelette

Senior Designer: Diana Graham

Cover image(s): antishock/Shutterstock.com

For product information and technology assistance, contact us at
**Cengage Customer & Sales Support, 1-800-354-9706
or support.cengage.com.**

For permission to use material from this text or product, submit all requests online at **www.copyright.com**.

Library of Congress Control Number: 2018947224

ISBN: 978-1-337-91030-9

Cengage
200 Pier 4 Boulevard
Boston, MA 02210
USA

Cengage is a leading provider of customized learning solutions with employees residing in nearly 40 different countries and sales in more than 125 countries around the world. Find your local representative at: **www.cengage.com.**

To learn more about Cengage platforms and services, register or access your online learning solution, or purchase materials for your course, visit **www.cengage.com.**

Notice to the Reader

Publisher does not warrant or guarantee any of the products described herein or perform any independent analysis in connection with any of the product information contained herein. Publisher does not assume, and expressly disclaims, any obligation to obtain and include information other than that provided to it by the manufacturer. The reader is expressly warned to consider and adopt all safety precautions that might be indicated by the activities described herein and to avoid all potential hazards. By following the instructions contained herein, the reader willingly assumes all risks in connection with such instructions. The publisher makes no representations or warranties of any kind, including but not limited to, the warranties of fitness for particular purpose or merchantability, nor are any such representations implied with respect to the material set forth herein, and the publisher takes no responsibility with respect to such material. The publisher shall not be liable for any special, consequential, or exemplary damages resulting, in whole or part, from the readers' use of, or reliance upon, this material.

Printed in Mexico
Print Number: 04   Print Year: 2023

CONTENTS

Cycle 1   Learn and Build Your Skills

Chapter 1   Mastering the Alphabetic Keys   1-1

Lesson 1	Home Keys (asdf jkl;)	**1-2**
Lesson 2	Review	**1-6**
Lesson 3	New Keys: h and e	**1-9**
Lesson 4	New Keys: i and r	**1-12**
Lesson 5	Review	**1-14**
WP Applications 1		1-16
Basic Technology Skills 1		1-18
Lesson 6	New Keys: o and t	**1-23**
Lesson 7	New Keys: n and g	**1-25**
Lesson 8	New Keys: Left Shift and . (period)	**1-27**
Lesson 9	Review	**1-29**
WP Applications 2		1-31
Basic Technology Skills 2		1-32
Lesson 10	New Keys: u and c	**1-37**
Lesson 11	New Keys: w and Right Shift	**1-39**
Lesson 12	New Keys: b and y	**1-41**
Lesson 13	Review	**1-43**
WP Applications 3		1-45
Basic Technology Skills 3		1-46
Lesson 14	New Keys: m and x	**1-51**
Lesson 15	New Keys: p and v	**1-53**
Lesson 16	New Keys: q and , (comma)	**1-55**
Lesson 17	Review	**1-57**
WP Applications 4		1-59
Basic Technology Skills 4		1-60
Lesson 18	New Keys: z and : (colon)	**1-65**
Lesson 19	New Keys: Caps Lock and ?	**1-67**
Lesson 20	New Keys: Backspace, Tab, and Quotation Mark (")	**1-69**
Lesson 21	New Keys: Apostrophe (') and Hyphen (-)	**1-73**
WP Applications 5		1-75
Basic Technology Skills 5		1-77
Communication Skills 1		1-84
Chapter Review		1-86

Chapter 2   Learning the Numeric Keypad   2-1

Lesson 22	Numeric Keypad 4, 5, 6, 0	**2-2**
Lesson 23	Numeric Keypad 7, 8, 9	**2-4**
Lesson 24	Numeric Keypad 1, 2, 3	**2-5**
Lesson 25	Subtraction and Multiplication	**2-6**
Lesson 26	Division	**2-8**
Skill Builder 1		2-10
WP Applications 6		2-12
Basic Technology Skills 6		2-19
Chapter Review		2-24

Chapter 3   Accessing Help for Answers   3-1

Lesson 27	Help Basics	**3-1**
Lesson 28	Special Features	**3-5**
Skill Builder 2		3-9
Basic Technology Skills 7		3-11
Chapter Review		3-21

Chapter 4   Communicating and Scheduling at School and Work   4-1

Application Guide		**4-1**
Lesson 29	Format Email Messages	**4-8**
Lesson 30	Create, Format, and Manage Email Messages	**4-9**
Lesson 31	Contacts, Calendar, Tasks, and Notes	**4-11**
Skill Builder 3		4-16
Basic Technology Skills 8		4-18
Communication Skills 2		4-25
Chapter Review		4-28

Chapter 5   Communicating Clearly with Letters   5-1

Application Guide		**5-1**
WP Applications 7		5-4
Lesson 32	Personal-Business Letters	**5-10**
Lesson 33	Business Letters, Additional Letter Parts, and Envelopes	**5-14**
Lesson 34	Modified Block Personal-Business Letters	**5-18**
Assessment 1 – Email and Letters		5-21
Skill Builder 4		5-24
Advanced Technology Skills 1		5-27
Chapter Review		5-33

Chapter 6   Creating Effective Reports   6-1

Application Guide		**6-2**
WP Applications 8		6-7
Lesson 35	MLA Reports	**6-11**
Lesson 36	Outlines and MLA Reports with Citations	**6-15**

Contents

Lesson 37   Reports in Standard, Unbound Format   **6-20**
Lesson 38   Multicolumn Documents with Text Boxes
and Pictures   **6-24**
Skill Builder 5   6-30
Advanced Technology Skills 2   6-32
Communication Skills 3   6-37
Chapter Review   6-39

Chapter 7   Organizing Information
in Tables   **7-1**
Application Guide   **7-2**
WP Applications 9   7-2
Lesson 39   Basic Tables   **7-11**
Lesson 40   Tables: Merging and Splitting Cells   **7-14**
Lesson 41   Tables: Changing Row Height, Borders,
and Shading   **7-21**
Lesson 42   Sort and Convert Tables   **7-24**
Assessment 2 – Reports and Tables   7-27
Skill Builder 6   7-32
Advanced Technology Skills 3   7-34
Chapter Review   7-38

Chapter 8   Presenting with Electronic
Presentations   **8-1**
Application Guide   **8-1**
Lesson 43   Slide Layout and Design Themes   **8-8**
Lesson 44   Add Graphics to Slides   **8-12**
Lesson 45   Tables, Graphs, and Charts   **8-20**
Lesson 46   Use Designer to Enhance Slides   **8-25**
Lessons 47–48   Create and Deliver a Presentation   **8-28**
Assessment 3 – Presentations   8-33
Skill Builder 7   8-35
Advanced Technology Skills 4   8-38
Chapter Review   8-44

Chapter 9   Preparing Worksheets   **9-1**
Application Guide   **9-1**
Lesson 49   Workbook and Worksheet Basics   **9-4**
Lesson 50   Format and Print Worksheets   **9-8**
Lesson 51   Using Formulas and Functions   **9-12**
Lesson 52   Editing Worksheets   **9-17**
Lesson 53   Enhancing Worksheet Skills   **9-21**
Lesson 54   Worksheets with Charts   **9-25**
Assessment 4 – Worksheets   9-30
Skill Builder 8   9-33
Advanced Technology Skills 5   9-35
Communication Skills 4   9-38
Chapter Review   9-41

Chapter 10   Learning Database Basics   **10-1**
Application Guide   **10-1**
Lesson 55   Create a Database   **10-10**

Lesson 56   Create a Database Form   **10-17**
Lesson 57   Add Fields, Delete Fields,
and Edit Records   **10-22**
Lesson 58   Work with Database Queries, Filters,
and Sorts   **10-27**
Lesson 59   Work with Database Reports   **10-31**
Assessment 5 – Database Basics   10-35
Skill Builder 9   10-38
Advanced Technology Skills 6   10-40
Communication Skills 5   10-45
Chapter Review   10-47

Integrated Project   Newhouse
Realty   Newhouse-1

Cycle 2   Enhance and Master Your Skills

Chapter 11   Managing Communications
and Schedules   **11-1**
Application Guide   **11-1**
Lesson 60   Create and Edit Contact Groups   **11-6**
Lesson 61   Organize and Manage Emails   **11-10**
Lesson 62   Schedule Meetings and Print Calendars   **11-12**
Skill Builder 10   11-16
Planning for Your Career 1   11-18
Chapter Review   11-21

Chapter 12   Managing Written
Communication   **12-1**
Application Guide   **12-1**
Lesson 63   Business and Personal-Business
Letters Review   **12-2**
Lesson 64   Mail Merge and Data Source Files   **12-3**
Lesson 65   Main Document Files and Mail Merge
Management   **12-9**
Lesson 66   Mail Merge Labels and Directories   **12-13**
Assessment 6 – Enhanced Email and Letters   12-16
Skill Builder 11   12-22
Planning for Your Career 2   12-25
Communication Skills 6   12-30
Chapter Review   12-33

Chapter 13   Reporting with Style   **13-1**
Application Guide   **13-1**
Lesson 67   Unbound and MLA Report Review   **13-5**
Lesson 68   Bound Report with Footnotes   **13-8**
Lesson 69   Collaborative Report with Footnotes   **13-12**
Lesson 70   Two-Column Reports with Pictures   **13-15**
Skill Builder 12   13-18
Planning for Your Career 3   13-20
Chapter Review   13-22

Chapter 14 Enhancing Information
in Tables **14-1**

Application Guide **14-2**
Lesson 71 Table Tabs, Indentations, and Lists **14-5**
Lesson 72 Tables with Repeated Headings **14-8**
Lesson 73 Table Calculations and Analysis **14-12**
Assessment 7 – Enhanced Reports and Tables 14-17
Skill Builder 13 14-23
Planning for Your Career 4 14-25
Communication Skills 7 14-28
Chapter Review 14-30

Integrated Project Central Valley
Education Foundation CVEF-1

Chapter 15 Communicating Effectively
with Enhanced Presentations **15-1**

Application Guide **15-1**
Lesson 74 Enhance Slide Show Presentations with
Screen Clippings **15-7**
Lesson 75 Enhance Slide Show Presentations with
Graphics, Animations, and Transitions **15-15**
Lesson 76 Enhance Slide Show Presentations
with Audio **15-22**
Lesson 77 Deliver an Effective Presentation **15-27**
Assessment 8 – Enhanced Presentations 15-29
Skill Builder 14 15-34
Planning for Your Career 5 15-36
Communication Skills 8 15-39
Chapter Review 15-41

Chapter 16 Preparing and Analyzing
Financial Worksheets **16-1**

Application Guide **16-1**
Lesson 78 Formatting and Worksheet Skills **16-4**
Lesson 79 Cell References **16-10**
Lesson 80 "What If" Questions, IF Function,
and Formatting **16-15**
Lesson 81 Integrating Worksheet and
Word Processing Documents **16-21**

Lesson 82 Spreadsheet Applications **16-24**
Assessment 9 – Enhanced Worksheets 16-26
Skill Builder 15 16-30
Planning for Your Career 6 16-32
Chapter Review 16-37

Chapter 17 Using a Database to Create,
Analyze, and Distribute
Information **17-1**

Application Guide **17-1**
Lesson 83 Database Review and Reinforcement **17-3**
Lesson 84 Data Mining and Analysis Using
Computed Fields **17-8**
Lesson 85 Using a Database to Create
a Mail Merge **17-10**
Lesson 86 Data Mining and Analysis Using
Computed Fields and Column Totals **17-14**
Lesson 87 Using Queries Created from Multiple
Tables to Create Word Documents **17-18**
Lesson 88 Using a Database to Create Form
Letters, Envelopes, and Labels **17-22**
Assessment 10 – Enhanced Database Skills 17-27
Skill Builder 16 17-30
Planning for Your Career 7 17-32
Communication Skills 9 17-38
Chapter Review 17-41

Integrated Project HPJ Communication
Specialists **HPJ-1**

Glossary **G-1**
Index **I-1**

Online Appendices

visit login.cengage.com
A Numeric Keys
B Leadership Development
C Reference Guide

DIGITAL AND PROFESSIONAL SKILLS CHARTS

Digital Skill	Page No.
Computer Basics **Basic and Advanced Technology Skills** **Modules**	
Close Button	1-61
Cloud Computing	8-38
Computer and System Maintenance	5-28
Computer Ethics	4-18
Computer Safety and Security	5-30
Copy and Move Files and Folders	1-82
Desktop	1-47
Digital Citizenship	4-18
Encrypt Files	5-27
Ethics	4-18
Evaluating Search Results	6-33
Files and Folders	1-80
Help	3-1
Internet	2-19
Menu Bar	1-61
Mouse Skills	1-48
Netiquette	4-18
New Document	1-45
Open Application	1-60
Operating System	1-46
Password	5-29
Phrase Searching	3-18
Print	1-45
Rename and Delete Files and Folders	1-81
Ribbon Path	1-61
Save/Save As	2-14
Search the Web	3-13
Shut Down	1-50
Start Button	1-47
Task Bar	1-60
Tool Bar	1-64
Validating and Fact Checking	6-35
Window (Maximize, Minimize, Restore)	1-62
Workplace Safety	5-32

Digital Skill	Page No.
Email **Chapters 4 and 11**	
Add/Remove Contacts	11-7, 11-8
Attach File	4-2
Calendar	4-4
Categorize/Email Tags	4-2
Contact Groups	11-6
Contacts	4-4
Create an Email	4-9
Create Folders	11-10
Create Meetings	11-12
Editing Email	4-2
Junk Email Filter	11-10
Manage Email	4-11
Notes	4-7
Search People	4-3
Tasks	4-6
Word Processing **Chapters 1, 5, 6, 7, 8, 12, 13, 14**	
Adjusting Column Width and Row	7-8
Bold	1-17
Bullets and Numbering	5-8
Centering Tables	7-6
Clip Art and Pictures	6-6
Cover Page	13-4
Cut, Copy, Paste	1-31
Decimal Tab	14-2
Envelopes	5-7
Find and Replace	5-4
Font Group	5-4
Format Painter	7-5
AutoCorrect	1-16
Hyphenation	5-5
Indentations	6-8
Insert	1-16
Insert Date and Time	5-6
Insert Footnote	6-10
Insert Tables	7-2

Digital Skill	Page No.
Insert/Delete Rows and Columns in Tables	7-6
Italic	1-17
Line and Page Breaks	6-7
Line and Paragraph Spacing	1-59
Mail Merge	12-1
Mail Merge Labels, Badges, and Directory	12-13
Margins	1-59
Merge and Split Cells in Tables	7-7
Overtype	1-16
Page Break	6-7
Page Numbers	6-8
Portrait/Landscape Orientation	7-8
Print Preview and Print	1-45
Remove Space after Paragraph	5-7
Select Text	1-31
Select and Format Table Cell Content	7-4
Shading and Borders in Tables	7-9
Shapes	8-14
Show/Hide ¶	5-10
Sort Tables	7-10
Spelling and Grammar	5-5
Styles	6-9
Table Styles	7-9
Tabs	1-75
Templates	13-4
Text Boxes	6-5
Text Inserted from File	6-10
Text Wrapping Break	5-7
Thesaurus	5-6
Underline	1-17
Undo/Redo	1-45
Vertical Alignment	7-6
Zoom	1-45

Presentations Chapters 8 and 15	
Animations	15-1
Audio	15-5
Bulleted List Slide	8-9
Designer	15-2
Design Theme	8-2
Hyperlinks	15-2
Navigation Shortcuts	15-3

Digital Skill	Page No.
Notes Page	8-6
Outline View	8-6
Pictures and Videos	15-4
Screen Clippings	15-5
Slide Layouts	8-4
Slides	8-1
Slide Show	8-7
Slide Sorter View	8-7
Slides with Graphics	8-12
Slides with Tables, Graphs (Bar, Line), and Charts (Pie)	8-20
Timing	15-5
Title and Content Layout	8-9
Title Slide	8-9
Transitions	15-6
Variants	15-10
View Options	8-5

Spreadsheets Chapters 9 and 16	
Cells, Columns, and Rows	9-2
Chart Layout and Styles	9-27
Chart Type	9-26
Charts (Column, Bar, and Pie)	9-25
Cut, Copy, and Move	9-10
Cell Content and Format—Clear and Delete	9-10
Cell Content—Format	9-10
Cell Content—Select and Edit	9-17
Format Numbers	9-12
Formulas	9-13
Functions this should be (Sum, Average, Count, Max, Min)	9-15
Gridlines and Column and Row Headings—View and Print	9-7
Integrating Worksheet and Word Documents	16-21
Labels and Values	9-5
Move Around in a Worksheet	9-4
Range of Cells—Select	9-10
Rows and Columns—Insert and Delete	9-21
Worksheet Window	9-3
Worksheets and Workbooks	9-2
"What If" Function	16-15

Digital Skill	Page No.
Database **Chapters 10 and 17**	
Add Fields	10-22
Add Records	10-14
Computed Fields	17-9
Create Form Letters, Envelopes, and Labels Using a Database	17-22
Database Mail Merge	17-22
Data Mining	17-8
Data Type (Number, Text, Currency, Date and Time)	10-4
Datasheet View	10-3
Design View	10-4
Fields	10-2
Filter	10-8
Forms	10-5
Move in Tables and Forms	10-8
Multiple Table Queries	00
Primary Key	10-4
Print a Table	10-16
Queries	10-5
Records	10-5
Reports and Report Wizard	10-7
Sorts (Multiple)	10-8
Sorts (Primary and Secondary)	10-8
Tables	10-2

Professional Skill	Page No.
Planning for Your Career **Chapters 11, 12, 13, 14, 15, 16, 17**	
Application Form	15-36
Career Advancement	17-35
Career Portfolio	11-18
Digital Resume	12-27
Employer Expectations	16-32
Employment and Application Letter	13-20
Follow-up Letter	15-38
Interview	14-25
Lifelong Learning	16-33
Mentor	17-34
Networking	17-36
Print Resume	12-25
Professionalism	17-35
Reference Lists	11-19
Resume Tools	12-29

FEATURES

Unique Unit Features	Pages
21st Century Skills	1-8, 3-8, 4-7, 6-17, 7-20, 9-29, 11-11, 12-15, 13-8, 14-15, 15-20, 16-20, 17-17
Advanced Technology Skills	5-27, 6-32, 7-34, 8-38, 9-35, 10-40
Application Guide	4-1, 5-1, 6-2, 7-2, 8-1, 9-1, 10-1, 11-1, 12-1, 13-1, 14-2, 15-1, 16-1, 17-1
Assessment	5-21, 7-27, 8-33, 9-30, 10-35, 12-16, 14-17, 15-29, 16-26, 17-27
Basic Technology Skills	1-18, 1-32, 1-46, 1-60, 1-77, 2-19, 3-11, 4-18
Chapter REVIEW	1-86, 2-24, 3-21, 4-28, 5-33, 6-39, 7-38, 8-44, 9-41, 10-47, 11-21, 12-33, 13-22, 14-31, 15-41, 16-37, 17-41
checkpoint	1-5, 1-10, 1-11, 1-14, 1-26, 1-29, 1-43, 1-81, 1-83, 2-3, 2-9, 2-13, 3-15, 5-12, 5-13, 5-18, 5-20, 5-31, 6-13, 6-19, 6-28, 7-15, 7-20, 7-22, 7-24, 7-25, 7-26, 7-36, 9-16, 9-19, 9-24, 10-14, 10-17, 10-20, 10-22, 10-24, 10-29, 10-31, 10-34, 13-17
COLLABORATION	1-10, 1-11, 1-20, 1-22, 1-30, 1-34, 1-44, 1-85, 2-6, 2-7, 2-9, 3-3, 3-8, 4-7, 4-15, 4-19, 5-12, 5-13, 5-14, 5-20, 6-13, 6-17, 6-19, 6-20, 6-28, 6-36, 7-23, 7-25, 7-26, 8-31, 9-16, 9-19, 9-20, 9-24, 9-35, 9-37, 10-9, 10-14, 10-24, 11-9, 11-11, 12-5, 12-15, 13-8, 14-15, 14-16, 15-28, 15-40, 16-15, 17-17, 17-39
Communication Skills	1-84, 4-25, 6-37, 9-38, 10-45, 12-30, 14-28, 15-39, 17-38
Digital Citizenship and Ethics	3-3, 4-15, 5-14, 6-20, 7-23, 9-20, 10-9, 11-9, 12-5, 14-16, 16-15
Planning for Your Career	11-18, 12-25, 13-20, 14-25, 15-36, 16-32, 17-32
Skill Builder	2-10, 3-9, 4-16, 5-24, 6-30, 7-32, 8-35, 9-33, 10-38, 11-16, 12-22, 13-18, 14-23, 15-34, 16-30, 17-30
Timed Writings	2-11, 3-10, 5-26, 10-35, 12-16, 14-17, 16-31, 17-31, A-2, A-6, A-9
WP Applications	1-16, 1-31, 1-45, 1-59, 1-75, 2-12, 5-4, 6-7, 7-2

Century 21

Computer Skills and Applications, 11e

Give your students the best in computing education from the proven business education leader! The Eleventh Edition of *Century 21 Computer Skills and Applications* helps prepare students for a lifetime of keyboarding and computer success with pioneering solutions updated to reflect everyday business challenges. Trust the leader who has taught more than 90 million people to type—bringing nearly a century of educational experience and innovations together in one inclusive product.

CENTURY 21
Computer Skills and Applications
Eleventh Edition
LESSONS 1-88
sam
HOGGATT • SMITH • SHANK

The Right Approach, with the Right Coverage

▶ Combined our best content from the *Century 21 Keyboarding and Computing and Skills* series—three books in one!

▶ Streamlined and more focused units of instruction

▶ Clean breakout of keying drills and introductions to the Microsoft *Office* Suite

Increased emphasis on building **Communication Skills**.

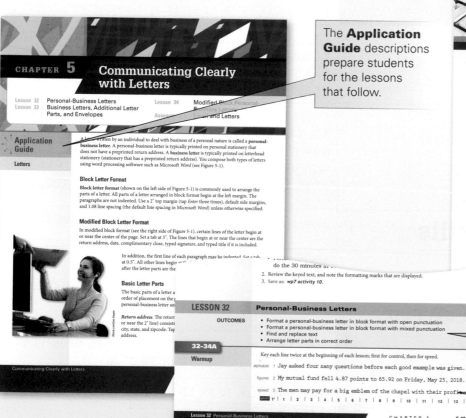

The **Application Guide** descriptions prepare students for the lessons that follow.

Learning Outcomes mapped to lesson activities.

Warmup drills support keyboard skills.

Career Planning and Technology Skills Provide Real-World Context

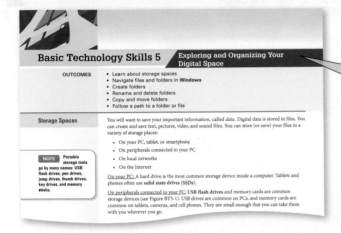

Basic Technology Skills 5 — Exploring and Organizing Your Digital Space

OUTCOMES
- Learn about storage spaces
- Navigate files and folders in Windows
- Create folders
- Rename and delete folders
- Copy and move folders
- Follow a path to a folder or file

Storage Spaces

You will want to save your important information, called *data*. Digital data is stored in files. You can create and save text, pictures, video, and sound files. You can store (or save) your files in a variety of storage places:

- On your PC, tablet, or smartphone
- On peripherals connected to your PC
- On local networks
- On the Internet

NOTE — Portable storage tools go by many names: USB flash drives, pen drives, jump drives, thumb drives, key drives, and memory sticks.

On your PC: A hard drive is the most common storage device inside a computer. Tablets and phones often use **solid state drives (SSDs)**.

On peripherals connected to your PC: **USB flash drives** and memory cards are common storage devices (see Figure BT5-1). USB drives are common on PCs, and memory cards are common on tablets, cameras, and cell phones. They are small enough that you can take them with you wherever you go.

Basic Technology Skills reinforce and improve students' foundational understanding of computing concepts.

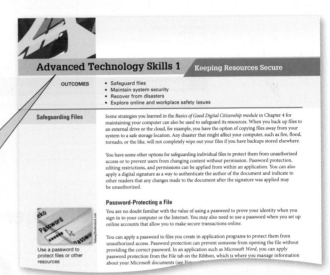

Advanced Technology Skills 1 — Keeping Resources Secure

OUTCOMES
- Safeguard files
- Maintain system security
- Recover from disasters
- Explore online and workplace safety issues

Safeguarding Files

Some strategies you learned in the *Basics of Good Digital Citizenship* module in Chapter 4 for maintaining your computer can also be used to safeguard its resources. When you back up files to an external drive or the cloud, for example, you have the option of copying files away from your system to a safe storage location. Any disaster that might affect your computer, such as fire, flood, tornado, or the like, will not completely wipe out your files if you have backups stored elsewhere.

You have some other options for safeguarding individual files to protect them from unauthorized access or to prevent users from changing content without permission. Password protection, editing restrictions, and permissions can be applied from within an application. You can also apply a digital signature as a way to authenticate the author of the document and indicate to other readers that any changes made to the document after the signature was applied may be unauthorized.

Password-Protecting a File

You are no doubt familiar with the value of using a password to prove your identity when you sign in to your computer or the Internet. You may also need to use a password when you set up online accounts that allow you to make secure transactions online.

You can apply a password to files you create in application programs to protect them from unauthorized access. Password protection can prevent someone from opening the file without providing the correct password. In an application such as Microsoft *Word*, you can apply password protection from the File tab on the Ribbon, which is where you manage information about your Microsoft documents (see Figure...

Use a password to protect files or other resources

Advanced Technology Skills build on students' knowledge and help them apply their understanding to more challenging topics.

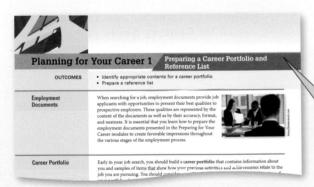

Planning for Your Career 1 — Preparing a Career Portfolio and Reference List

OUTCOMES
- Identify appropriate contents for a career portfolio
- Prepare a reference list

Employment Documents

When searching for a job, employment documents provide job applicants with opportunities to present their best qualities to prospective employers. These qualities are represented by the content of the documents as well as by their accuracy, format, and neatness. It is essential that you learn how to prepare the employment documents presented in the Preparing for Your Career modules to create favorable impressions throughout the various stages of the employment process.

Career Portfolio

Early in your job search, you should build a **career portfolio** that contains information about you and samples of items that show how your previous activities and achievements relate to the job you are pursuing. You should consider...

Planning for Your Career connects computing concepts with key skills needed to develop professionally, from preparing for an interview to creating a career portfolio.

The Cycle Approach

CONTENTS

Cycle 1 — Learn and Build Your Skills

Chapter 1 — Mastering the Alphabetic Keys
- Lesson 1 Home Keys (asdf jkl;)
- Lesson 2 Review
- Lesson 3 New Keys: h and e

Skill Builder 1 — 2-10
WP Applications 6 — 2-12
Basic Technology Skills 6 — 2-19
Lesson 41 Tables: Changing Row Height, Borders, and Shading — 7-21
Lesson 42 Sort and Convert Tables — 7-24
Assessment 2 - Reports and Tables — 7-27
Skill Builder 6 — 7-32
Advanced Technology Skills 3 — 7-34
Chapter Review — 7-38

Chapter 8 — Presenting with Electronic Presentations — 8-1
Application Guide — 8-1
Lesson 43 Slide Layout and Design Themes — 8-8

Cycle 2 — Enhance and Master Your Skills

Chapter 11 — Managing Communications and Schedules — 11-1
Application Guide — 11-1
Lesson 60 Create and Edit Contact Groups — 11-6
Lesson 61 Organize and Manage Emails — 11-10
Lesson 62 Schedule Meetings and Print Calendars — 11-12
Skill Builder 10 — 11-16

A unique cycle approach reinforces keyboarding skills by breaking out instruction into two cycles. Students begin with a foundation in the **basics**, then revisit content to **improve** skills. Students return to content again to **enhance** abilities, and then finally learn to **build** upon the knowledge already developed. Each cycle ends with an integrated business simulation project.

Formative and Summative Assessments and Applications

Chapter Reviews test mastery of chapter concepts. **Checkpoints** offer real-time opportunities for assessment and reflection while progressing through the chapter.

Assessments test students' mastery of software applications.
WP Applications put software features into practice within the chapters. Comprehensive

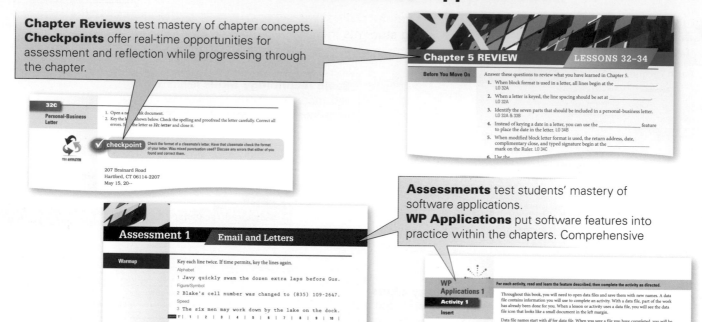

Integrated Learning for Stronger Results

Digital Citizenship and Ethics and **21st Century Skills** add interesting and relevant topics for classroom discussion.

The **Collaboration** icon highlights opportunities for group activities and discussion topics.

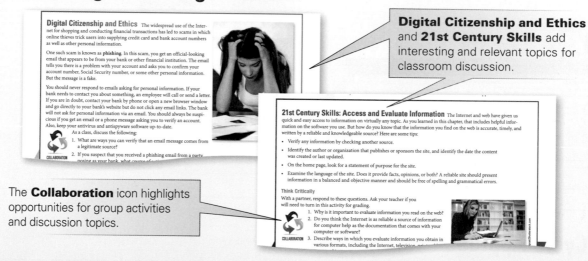

A Proven Approach for Mastering Keyboarding Skills

Triple control guidelines for timed writings and skill building include three factors—syllabic intensity, average word length, and percentage of high–frequency words—for the most accurate evaluation of students' keying skills.

Tested and proven pedagogy provides sound new key learning, skill building, model document illustrations, and triple-controlled timed writings to ensure that assessments are reliable and consistent.

LA all letters used

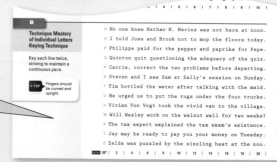

Computer Applications and Beyond!

Core computer application skills are taught and reinforced so that students are prepared for life! Instead of teaching students the entire application, the critical components are emphasized and mastered.

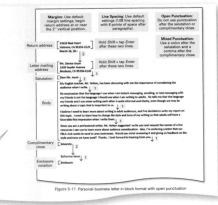

Figure 5-11 Personal-business letter in block format with open punctuation

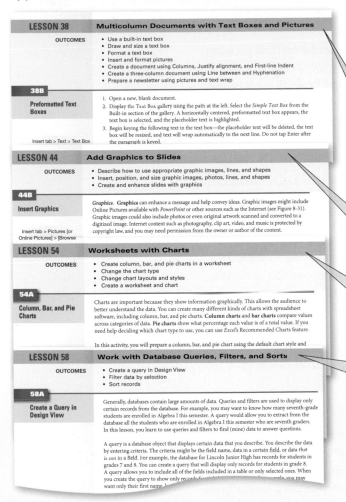

Word processing skill is enhanced by the model documents provided for letters, tables, reports, and special documents.

Presentations coverage includes creating slides, graphics, tables, charts, and slide shows—and learning the appropriate way to present.

Spreadsheet activities include basic functions as well as working with formulas and charts to help resolve numeric problems for business, education, and personal use.

Database coverage includes adding/deleting records and fields, sorting, and reports.

Meet SAM (Skills Assessment Manager) sam

SAM's online learning environments enable students to learn keyboarding and computer concepts essential to academic and career success. Students observe and practice, then apply their skills in the live application. Auto-graded assignments save time and energy.

For this edition of *Century 21 Computer Skills and Applications*, SAM replaces MicroType as an optional digital companion to the print text. With SAM, the keying drills, timed writings, skill buildings, and other activities can be completed and submitted online.

If your course is using SAM, visit **http://sam.cengage.com** to find out more about how to use SAM with this textbook.

Visit Us Online!

To access data and solution files, as well as a wealth of teaching and learning resources, visit us at **login.cengage.com** today!

PREFACE

The eleventh edition of *Century 21® Computer Skills and Applications* provides a high degree of flexibility for moving between traditional and new content areas. This flexibility permits the structuring of courses to meet the needs of students, school districts, and the community.

The eleventh edition presents choices in word processing, database, spreadsheet, and presentation software features. It also presents keyboarding, computer concepts, Digital Citizenship and Ethics topics, and 21st Century career skills. Additionally, the Integrated Projects are business simulations for real-world practice. Appendix B (available online) on leadership development provides activities on leadership topics that can be taught as a unit or distributed throughout the course.

New special features highlight Basic and Advanced Technology Skills as well as Communication Skills and Planning for Your Career to take classroom learning into the real world.

The *Century 21* family includes a full range of high-quality supplementary items to enhance your courses, including a website at login.cengage.com. Thank you for choosing *Century 21*. Whether you are a new instructor, new to *Century 21*, or simply updating your *C21* materials, we know that you will find this edition an exciting solution for your classes.

How to Use this Book

There are a number of ways that the many available digital and print resources can be used in a classroom/lab.

Student Edition

The **student text** (ISBN 9781337910309) provides features designed to meet your instructional needs. Each application chapter opens with an **Application Guide** that introduces concepts and shows thumbnail model documents. Some guides have activities for reinforcement. Within each chapter, a series of lessons provides plenty of hands-on activities with step-by-step instructions.

Each lesson begins with a list of learning outcomes and warmup drills that prepare students for lesson activities. Lessons contain computer applications for learning and applying skills and documents to format. Tips and notes in the margins provide helpful hints, and data files assist with the completion of longer activities. Marginal Ribbon paths summarize important task steps.

All chapters end with a Chapter Review. **Communication Skills** activities hone grammar, spoken communication, and more. **WP Applications** put software features into practice.

Basic and Advanced Technology Skills introduce students to technology concepts, while **Planning for Your Career** connects computing concepts with key skills needed to develop professionally, from preparing for an interview to creating a career portfolio.

Certain activities, indicated by the Collaboration icon, are identified as suitable for **teamwork** projects. Special features within the chapters include **21st Century Skills** and **Digital Citizenship and Ethics**. These two features cover topics such as media literacy, personal responsibility and initiative, plagiarism, and identity theft, along with questions for critical thinking and discussion.

Special **Skill Builder** sections containing skill building and timed writings provide opportunities for students to improve their keying techniques and productivity. **WP Applications** put software features into practice. **Assessments** test students' mastery of software skills. There are three **integrated business simulation projects**: one after Chapter 14, and one at the end of each cycle.

These projects require students to use their critical-thinking/decision-making skills as they work in a simulated business environment.

Instructor Resources

In addition to the textbook, the complete instructional program includes an Instructor Companion website, which contains an instructor's manual, *PowerPoint* presentations, Cognero web-based assessment with testing and questions, solution files, and more.

To access the Instructor Companion site and Cognero test bank, sign in to http://login.cengage.com and add this text to your instructor dashboard.

Student Resources

The data files needed to complete this text's activities are found on the free student companion website for this text along with other resources. To access the student companion site, visit http://login.cengage.com and search for this text.

Skills Assessment Manager (SAM)

SAM is the software that teaches and reinforces keyboarding skills. Instructors may teach the course using the print book only, the print book plus SAM, or SAM only. If your course is using SAM, visit http://sam.cengage.com to find out more about how to use SAM with this textbook.

To purchase SAM with a print textbook, talk to your Cengage Learning Consultant.

Alternative Purchase Options
There are also available e-Book versions of the text; call for more information on these (800-354-9706) or talk to your Cengage Learning Consultant.

About the Authors

Dr. Jack P. Hoggatt is a Professor Emeritus of Business at the University of Wisconsin-Eau Claire. While at UWEC, he served as Chair of the Department of Business Communication, Assistant Dean of Student Affairs, and CADE Director for the University of Wisconsin-Eau Claire. He has taught courses in Business Writing, Advanced Business Communications, and the communication component of the university's Masters in Business Administration (MBA) program. Dr. Hoggatt has held offices in several professional organizations, including president of the Wisconsin Business Education Association. He has served as an advisor to local and state business organizations, has been named the Outstanding Post-Secondary Business Educator for Wisconsin, and is a member of the Wisconsin Phi Beta Lambda Hall of Fame.

Courtesy of Dr. Jack P. Hoggatt

Dr. James R. Smith, Jr. is the Director of the Quality Enhancement Plan at Wake Technical Community College. His work there focuses on reducing online learning barriers and supporting student learning, persistence, and success in online learning. Previously, he was the Undergraduate and Graduate Program Coordinator for the Business and Marketing Teacher Education Program at North Carolina State University. He has been a secondary business and marketing teacher, a State Consultant for Business and Information Technology, and a local school system Career and Technical Education Administrator. Dr. Smith has held offices in professional organizations, and he has received the Outstanding Leadership Award from the National Association of Supervisors of Business Education and the Outstanding Career and Technical Educator from the North Carolina Career and Technical Education Association—Business Education Division. In 2014, he was inducted into the Educators Hall of Fame at East Carolina University.

Courtesy of Dr. James R. Smith, Jr.

Note from the Authors

This text will serve as a solid foundation upon which you can build your course to meet the varying needs of your students. It contains an appropriate balance between new-key learning, building input skill, and formatting frequently used documents using features from various software application packages. Each software application is presented in the breadth and depth needed for students to be able to use their software competencies, as well as their keyboarding skills and formatting knowledge, to enhance their productivity as they continue their education, carry out their personal affairs, and enter the workplace. The chapter activities, including the Basic Technology, Advanced Technology, and Planning for Your Career activities, provide teachers with many opportunities to connect computer skills and applications to other curricular goals valued by administrators, other teachers, employers, and the community.

Reviewers

Anna Olivas
Hornedo Middle School
El Paso, Texas

Tana Askins
Evans Middle School
Lubbock, Texas

CYCLE 1

Learn and Build Your Skills

LESSONS 1–59

In Cycle 1 (Chapters 1 through 10), begin with learning the basics to form a foundation, then apply the basics to content to build your skill.

CHAPTER 1 — Mastering the Alphabetic Keys

Lesson 1   Home Keys (asdf jkl;)
Lesson 2   Review
Lesson 3   h and e
Lesson 4   i and r
Lesson 5   Review
Lesson 6   o and t
Lesson 7   n and g
Lesson 8   Left Shift and . (period)
Lesson 9   Review
Lesson 10   u and c
Lesson 11   w and Right Shift
Lesson 12   b and y
Lesson 13   Review
Lesson 14   m and x
Lesson 15   p and v
Lesson 16   q and , (comma)
Lesson 17   Review
Lesson 18   z and : (colon)
Lesson 19   Caps Lock and ?
Lesson 20   Backspace, Tab, and Quotation Mark (")
Lesson 21   Apostrophe (') and Hyphen (-)

LESSONS 1–21

We live in the *Information Age* (also called the *Digital Age*). We use computers to gather, create, and share information for personal, educational, and business uses. Information that once took days or even weeks to create and distribute can now be created and shared very quickly. Using a computer and various types of software programs, you can create spreadsheets, databases, presentation visuals, emails, and other documents such as reports, letters, and tables. Once created, you can send these documents to another person almost anywhere in the world in a matter of seconds.

The higher your level of keyboarding skill, the faster you can complete the software application. Plus, the keyboard is used not only to input information into the computer but also to extract information. The more skilled you are at the keyboard, the faster you can gather, create, and share information.

Andrey_Popov/Shutterstock.com

LESSON 1   Home Keys (asdf jkl;)

OUTCOMES

- Learn control of home keys (**asdf jkl;**)
- Learn control of the **Space Bar** and **Enter** key

1A

Work-Area Arrangement

Arrange your work area as shown in Figure 1-1.

- Keyboard directly in front of chair
- Front edge of keyboard even with edge of desk
- Monitor placed for easy viewing
- Book at right of monitor

Figure 1-1 Work-area arrangement

Keying Position

The way you sit when you use the keyboard is important. You can key more accurately when you sit correctly.

The features of correct keying position are shown in Figure 1-2 and listed below.

- Fingers curved and upright over home keys
- Wrists low, but not touching keyboard
- Forearms parallel to slant of keyboard
- Body erect
- Feet on floor for balance
- Eyes on copy

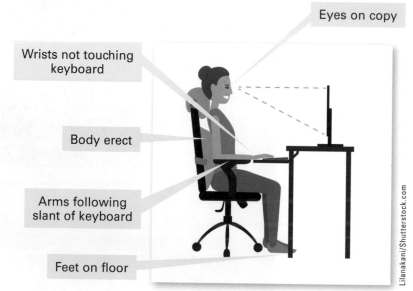

Eyes on copy

Wrists not touching keyboard

Body erect

Arms following slant of keyboard

Feet on floor

Lilanakani/Shutterstock.com

Figure 1-2 Keying position at the computer

Home-Key Position

The keys on which you place your fingers to begin keying are called the **home keys**. The home keys are **a s d f** for the left hand and **j k l ;** for the right hand.

1. Find the home keys on the keyboard illustration shown in Figure 1-3.
2. Locate and place your fingers on the home keys on your keyboard.
3. Keep your fingers well curved and upright (not slanting).
4. Remove your fingers from the keyboard. Place them in home-key position again. Curve and hold your fingers lightly on the keys.

Figure 1-3 Home-key position

Keystroking and Space Bar

When you key, tap each key lightly with the tip of the finger. Keep your fingers curved as shown in Figure 1-4. The **Space Bar** is used to place a space between words. Tap the Space Bar with the right thumb. Use a quick down-and-in motion (toward the palm). Avoid pauses before or after spacing.

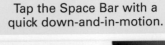
Curve fingers and tap the keys.

Tap the Space Bar with a quick down-and-in-motion.

Figure 1-4 Keying and spacing technique

NOTE Software programs such as those in the Microsoft *Office* suite interact with your computer to make it possible for you to create documents, worksheets, databases, and electronic visuals.

Keyboarding skills are critical in order to operate software programs efficiently.

1. Place your fingers in home-key position.
2. Key the line below. Tap the Space Bar once at the point of each arrow.
3. Review proper position at the keyboard (1B). Key the line again.

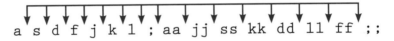
a s d f j k l ; aa jj ss kk dd ll ff ;;

Enter Key

The Enter key is used to return the insertion point to the left margin and to move it down one line. The **margin** is the blank space between the edge of the paper and the print. Tap the Enter key once to **single-space (SS)**. This moves the insertion point down one line. Tap the Enter key twice to **double-space (DS)**. This moves the insertion point down two lines. Study the illustration at the left.

1. Place your fingers on the home-row keys.
2. Reach the little finger of the right hand to the Enter key.
3. Tap the Enter key.
4. Return the finger quickly to home-key position.
5. Practice tapping the Enter key several times.

Enter-key reach

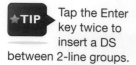

1F

Home Keys and Space Bar

TIP Tap the Enter key twice to insert a DS between 2-line groups.

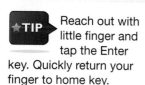

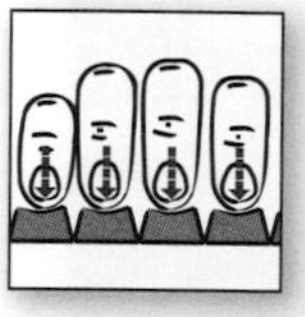

Keep fingers curved and upright

Key each line once single-spaced. Double-space between 2-line groups. Do not key the line numbers.

```
1  a aa s ss d dd f ff j jj k kk l ll ; ;; asdf jkl;

2  a aa s ss d dd f ff j jj k kk l ll ; ;; asdf jkl;
```

Tap the Enter key twice to double-space (DS)

```
3  f ff d dd s ss a aa ; ;; l ll k kk j jj fdsa ;lkj

4  f ff d dd s ss a aa ; ;; l ll k kk j jj fdsa ;lkj
```
DS

```
5  sj sj ld ld a; a; jf jf lj da k; fs ksj dla ;f ja

6  sj sj ld ld a; a; jf jf lj da k; fs ksj dla ;f ja
```
DS

1G

Enter Key

TIP Reach out with little finger and tap the Enter key. Quickly return your finger to home key.

Key each line once single-spaced. Double-space between 2-line groups.

```
1  ;; dd aa jj

2  ;; dd aa jj

3  ll ss kk ff dd j

4  ll ss kk ff dd j

5  sa sa jd jd lk lk f;f

6  sa sa jd jd lk lk f;f

7  da da jk jk s; s; fl fl kk

8  da da jk jk s; s; fl fl kk
```

✓ checkpoint Does your **J** finger remain in place as you tap the Enter key? If not, make an effort to improve your reach technique.

LESSON 2   Review

OUTCOMES
- Review control of home keys (**asdf jkl;**)
- Review control of the **Space Bar** and **Enter** key

2A

Work-Area Arrangement and Keying Position

Arrange your work area as shown in Figure 1-5.

- Keyboard directly in front of chair
- Front edge of keyboard even with edge of desk
- Monitor placed for easy viewing
- Book at right of monitor

Figure 1-5 Work-area arrangement

MSSA/Shutterstock.com

Figure 1-6 Keying position

Review Figure 1-6 for keying position.

- Fingers curved and upright over home keys
- Wrists low, but not touching keyboard
- Forearms parallel to slant of keyboard
- Body erect
- Feet on floor for balance
- Eyes on copy

2B

Home-Key Position

1. Find the home keys on the chart: **a s d f** for the left hand and **j k l ;** for the right hand.
2. Locate and place your fingers on the home keys on your keyboard with your fingers well curved and upright (not slanting).
3. Remove your fingers from the keyboard; then place them in home-key position again, curving and holding them lightly on the keys.

Home Keys and Space Bar

Keying technique

Spacing technique

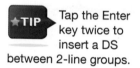
★TIP Tap the Enter key twice to insert a DS between 2-line groups.

When you key, remember to tap each key lightly with the tip of the finger. Tap the Space Bar with the right thumb. Use a quick down-and-in motion (toward the palm). Avoid pauses before or after spacing.

Key each line once single-spaced. Double-space between 2-line groups. Do not key the line numbers.

```
1  a s d f dd aa ff ss j k l ; ll jj ;; kk fd as j;kl
2  a s d f dd aa ff ss j k l ; ll jj ;; kk fd as j;kl
```
Tap the Enter key twice to double-space (DS)

```
3  ll aa jj dd ;; ss kk ff jj aa ll ;; ss dd kk ff ll
4  ll aa jj dd ;; ss kk ff jj aa ll ;; ss dd kk ff ll
```
DS

```
5  ka ls ;f jd ak sl f; dj lf jd ka ;s fl dj ak s; js
6  ka ls ;f jd ak sl f; df lf jd ka ;s fl dj ak s; js
```
DS

```
7  sjs kak f;f ldl jsj aka ;f; dld sjs a;a fsf kdk ll
8  sjs kak f;f ldl jsj aka ;f; dld sjs a;a fsf kdk ll
```
DS

2D

Enter Key

Enter *Right little* finger

Use the correct reach for the Enter key. Reach the little finger of the right hand to the Enter key. Tap the key. Return the finger quickly to home-key position.

Key each line once single-spaced. Double-space between 2-line groups.

```
1  s ss l ll;
2  s ss l ll;

3  f ff j jj d dd;
4  f ff j jj d dd;

5  k kk a aa l ll s ss;
6  k kk a aa l ll s ss;

7  j jj f ff d dd ; ;; a aa;
8  j jj f ff d dd ; ;; a aa;

9  s ss l ll a aa k kk s ss f ff;
10 s ss l ll a aa k kk s ss f ff;
```

Key each line once single-spaced. Double-space between 2-line groups. Do not key the red lines between groups of words.

 TIP ¶ Click the **Show/ Hide ¶** button in the Paragraph group on the Home tab to display formatting marks for spaces and paragraphs.

```
1  as; as;|ask ask|ad; ad;|add add|all all|fall fall;

2  as; as;|ask ask|ad; ad;|add add|all all|fall fall;

3  a sad lass; a sad lass;|all fall ads all fall ads;

4  a sad lass; a sad lass;|all fall ads all fall ads;

5  add a; add a;|ask a lad ask a lad|a salad a salad;

6  add a; add a;|ask a lad ask a lad|a salad a salad;

7  a lad ask dad a lad ask dad|a sad fall a sad fall;

8  a lad ask dad a lad ask dad|a sad fall a sad fall;
```

2F
End-of-Class Routine

At the end of each class period, complete the following steps.

1. If you have been asked to save the lesson(s), follow your instructor's directions for saving.
2. Exit the software.
3. Turn off equipment if directed to do so.
4. Store materials as your instructor directs.
5. Clean up your work area and push in your chair before you leave.

21st Century Skills: Initiative and Self-Direction

Initiative and self-direction are important skills and attributes to attain as you develop as a student and as a person. These skills and attributes will help you succeed in any task you set out to do in the course of your personal and professional life, including learning keyboarding and computer applications. Taking initiative means making the decision to do something—a job, a project, a specific task—without needing to be prompted by someone else. It means you don't need to have a teacher, parent, or friend tell you that you must do something. You see what needs to be done, and you do it. Self-direction means you are able to guide yourself and motivate yourself through the various steps of a job, project, or task. You make good decisions about what needs to be done next, and if necessary, you push yourself to do it. As with any other skill, learning to keyboard properly requires a certain amount of initiative and self-direction.

Think Critically

1. What prompted you to want to learn keyboarding and computer applications?
2. Now that you have worked through the first lessons of this book, how do you think you can demonstrate initiative and self-direction as you learn these skills?
3. Describe some ways in which you have demonstrated initiative and self-direction at home, at school, or on a job.

Konstantin Chagin/Shutterstock.com

LESSON 3   New Keys: h and e

OUTCOMES
- Learn reach technique for **h** and **e**
- Combine **h** and **e** smoothly with home keys

3A

Warmup

Key each line twice single-spaced. Double-space between 2-line groups.

All keystrokes learned

1 aa jj ss ;; ff kk dd ll jj aa ;; ss kk ff ll dd aa

2 ask; ask; sad; sad; lad; lad; all; all; fall; fall

3 a lad asks; ask a sad lass; all fall ads; a salad;

Tap Enter twice to double-space (DS) between lesson parts.

3B

Plan for Learning New Keys

All of the remaining keys that you learn will require your fingers to reach from the home keys to tap other keys. Follow the plan given below to learn the reach for each new key.

Standard Plan for Learning New Keys

1. Find the new key on the keyboard chart provided.
2. Look at your keyboard and find the new key on it.
3. Study the picture at the left of the practice lines for the new key. Note which finger is used for the key.
4. Curve your fingers and place them in home-key position (over **asdf jkl;**).
5. Watch your finger as you reach to the new key and back to home position a few times. Keep your finger curved.
6. Key the set of drill lines according to the directions provided, keeping your eyes on the copy as you key.

New Keys: h and e

h *Right index* finger

e *Left middle* finger

Use the *Standard Plan for Learning New Keys* (3B) for each key that you learn. Review the plan now. Relate each step of the plan to the illustrations and copy shown below. Then key each line twice. Do not key the line numbers, the vertical lines separating word groups, or the labels.

Learn h

```
1  h j h j|hj hj|j h j h|jh jh|had had|has has|shall;
2  jh jh|ash ash|hash hash|shad shad|half half|flash;
3  lash lash|dash dash|half half|hash hash|hall hall;
```

Learn e

```
4  e d e d|ed ed|d e d e|de de|feel feel|deeds deeds;
5  less less|feed feed|deal deal|fake fake|seal seal;
6  sale sale|keel keel|sell sell|desk desk|jade jade;
```

Combine h and e

```
7  she she|held held|shed shed|head head|shelf shelf;
8  he he|heal heal|shell shell|shade shade|jade jade;
9  heed heed|heel heel|flesh flesh|leash leash|he he;
```

Tap Enter twice to double-space (DS) between lesson parts.

Technique Check

COLLABORATION

Techniques are very important. In the early stages of learning to key, it is helpful to have others observe your techniques and tell you how you are doing. Sometimes your instructor will provide the feedback. Other times you will receive feedback from one of your classmates.

1. Open *df 3d check sheet*. Print the document. Close the file.
2. Work with a classmate. Ask your classmate to key lines 7–9 (above) as you watch for proper techniques. Mark notes on your check sheet. Share your comments with your classmate.
3. Ask your classmate to rate your techniques as you key lines 7–9. Discuss your ratings with your classmate.

✓ **checkpoint**   Check your classmate's technique.

Key Mastery

Key each line twice.

```
1 ask ask|seek seek|half half|leaf leaf|halls halls;
2 ask dad; he has jell; she has jade; he sells leeks
3 he led; she has; a jak ad; a jade eel; a sled fell
4 she asked a lass; she led all fall; she has a lead
5 he led; she had; she fell; a jade ad; a desk shelf
```

3F

Compose Sentences

Read the sentences below. From the list at the left, choose the word that best completes the sentence. Use all words. Key the word and tap the Enter key.

desk
fell
held
sad
salad
sale
seeds
she
shed
shelf

1. *Why are you so _____?*
2. *He _____ down the stairs.*
3. *She planted the grass _____.*
4. *Jack _____ the baby.*
5. *Did the _____ end on Saturday?*
6. *The antique _____ is quite expensive.*
7. *The lawn mower is in the _____.*
8. *When did _____ leave?*
9. *The book is on the _____.*
10. *What did you put in the _____?*

COLLABORATION

 **checkpoint** Trade places with a classmate. Check your classmate's answers.

LESSON 4 New Keys: i and r

OUTCOMES

- Learn reach technique for **i** and **r**
- Combine **i** and **r** smoothly with home keys

4A

Warmup

Key each line twice.

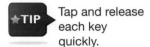

TIP Tap and release each key quickly.

Home keys	1 a f d s k j ; l ask fad all dad sad fall lass jj ;
h/e	2 j h ha has had ash hash d e led fed fled sled fell
All keys learned	3 she had a sale; ask a lad; she sells jade; a lake;

DS

4B

New Keys: i and r

Follow the plan for learning new keys shown in Lesson 3B. Key each line twice. If time permits, key lines 7–9 again.

i *Right middle* finger

r *Left index* finger

Learn i

1 k i|ki ki|is is|if if|ill ill|aid aid|kid kid|hail
2 ki ki|like like|jail jail|file file|said said|dial
3 if a kid; he did; a lie; if he; his file; a kid is

Learn r

4 f r|fr fr|far far|her her|are are|ark ark|jar jars
5 fr fr|jar jar|red red|her her|lark lark|dark dark;
6 a jar; a rake; read a; red jar; hear her; are free

Combine i and r

7 ride ride|fire fire|risk risk|hire hire|hair hairs
8 her hair; hire her; a fire; is she fair; is a risk
9 a ride; if her; is far; red jar; his are; her aide

Double-space (DS) between lesson parts.

Key each line twice.

Reach review

1 hj ed ik rf hj de ik fr hj ed ik rf jh de ki fr hj
2 he he|if if|all all|fir fir|jar jar|rid rid|as ask

h/e

3 she she|elf elf|her her|hah hah|eel eel|shed shelf
4 he has; had jak; her jar; had a shed; she has fled

i/r

5 fir fir|rid rid|sir sir|kid kid|ire ire|fire fired
6 a fir; is rid; is red; his ire; her kid; has a fir

All keys learned

7 jar jar|deal deal|fire fire|shelf shelf|lake lakes
8 he is; he did; ask her; red jar; she fell; he fled

All keys learned

9 if she is; he did ask; he led her; he is her aide;
10 she has had a jade sale; he said he had a red fir;

Unscramble the letters shown below to create ten words. If you have difficulty, key the letters in different orders to unscramble the words.

1. kas
2. arf
3. efra
4. arde
5. drak

6. arek
7. kile
8. rhei
9. rfei
10. lhefs

LESSON 5   Review

OUTCOMES
- Improve reachstroke control and keying speed
- Improve technique on **Space Bar** and **Enter**

5A

Warmup

TIP
- Keep your wrists low but not touching the keyboard.
- Keep your forearms parallel to the slant of the keyboard.

Key each line twice.

Home keys 1   `aa jj ff kk ss ll dd ;; aj fk sl d; dd ff jj ll kk`

h/e 2   `he fee she ash deed deaf shed held head half easel`

i/r 3   `fire rile risk hire rail dial rake like raid rider`

DS

5B

Space Bar Technique

TIP Quickly space after each word and immediately begin the next word.

Use a down-and-in motion for spacing

Key each line twice.

Short, easy words

1   `is as if he hi has ask had are her jar kid lad sad`

2   `jail half lake sail side rail leaf desk fade flair`

3   `his like reel fails laser seeks lease hired safari`

DS

Short-word phrases

4   `he is|if she|a jar|he did|as he is|has had|she did`

5   `red jar|a lake|red hair|her desk|as a lark|as dark`

6   `he said|she has had a|here he is|all fall|are free`

DS

 **checkpoint**   Are you sitting up straight in your chair with your feet on the floor as you key? If not, make an effort to improve your keying position.

Enter Key

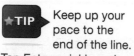

TIP Keep up your pace to the end of the line. Tap Enter quickly and immediately begin the next line.

Key each line twice.

1 if he is;

2 as if she is;

3 he had a fir desk;

4 she has a red jell jar;

5 he has had a lead all fall;

6 she asked if he reads fall ads;

7 she said she reads all ads she sees;

8 his dad has had a sales lead as he said;

9 he heard a leaf fall as a sad dad ask a lass;

10 a red sled fell; his airfare is free; risk a fall;

DS

5D

Key Mastery

Key each line twice.

1 he she heel shelf held heed shed heal hire herself

h/e 2 he had a sled; she hired a; he has had; she held a

3 he had half; a red shed; a sales desk; half a leaf

4 air sir fire liar hair iris ride fair dried desire

i/r 5 hire her; she is a risk; his airfare; he fired her

6 he hired her; hire her kids; a real ride; his ire;

7 he is; he has a red sled; like jade; if he is free

All keys 8 is a; he has a jar; a lake; she is safe; fried eel
learned
9 he is free; here she is; she has a jade; like her;

10 he had a; red jars; fire risk; fall ads; sled ride

DS

WP Applications 1

Activity 1

Insert

Throughout this book, you will need to open data files and save them with new names. A data file contains information you will use to complete an activity. With a data file, part of the work has already been done for you. When a lesson or activity uses a data file, you will see the data file icon that looks like a small document in the left margin.

Data file names start with *df* for *data file*. When you save a file you have completed, you will be given the file name to use.

The **Insert** feature is active when you open a software program. Move the insertion point to where you want to insert text; key the new text.

1. Open *df wp1 activity 1*.
2. Use the insert feature to insert the text highlighted in yellow.

   Tom said, "Did you hire John?"

   Mary has five red blocks.

   I will ask her for a jar of peaches.

   She hired a man to fix the desk last fall.

   She wore a dark red dress to the dance.

3. Save the file as *wp1 activity 1* by deleting the *df* at the beginning of the file name that appears in the File Name box when you click *File* and then *Save As*.

> ★**TIP** Most word-processing programs are in Insert mode by default.

> **NOTE** If you are using *Office 365* with AutoSave enabled, you will see "Save a Copy" instead of "Save As" in the File menu.

Activity 2

Overtype

Overtype allows you to replace (type over) current text with newly keyed text.

1. Open *df wp1 activity 2*.
2. Use the overtype feature to change the text highlighted in yellow.

   She had half a jar of red jam.

   Ask Chen if he has a file for sale.

   Felipe's ad is here at the lake.

   Kellee has a new desk and file.

   David heard a lark in his tree.

3. Save as: *wp1 activity 2*.

> ★**TIP** If your Overtype feature is not activated, your instructor will provide instructions if he/she wants you to complete this activity.

Activity 3

AutoCorrect

The **AutoCorrect** feature detects and corrects *some* typing, spelling, and capitalization errors for you automatically.

Key the following lines; note which errors are corrected automatically by the AutoCorrect feature.

   a redd file is heree;

   hirred a sadd lass;

   she is a rissk;

Activity 4

Underline

Home tab > Font >
Underline

★TIP Ctrl + U
<u>Underline</u>

The **Underline** feature underlines text as it is keyed.

1. Open *df wp1 activity 4*.
2. DS after the heading and the following lines DS.

   if <u>he</u> is;

   as if <u>she</u> is;

   <u>he</u> had a fir desk;

   <u>she</u> has a red jell jar;

   <u>he</u> has had a lead all fall;

3. Save as: *wp1 activity 4*.

Activity 5

Italic

Home tab > Font >
Italic

★TIP Ctrl + I
Italic

The **Italic** feature prints letters that slope up toward the right.

1. Open *df wp1 activity 5*.
2. DS after the heading and key the following lines DS.

   had *had* sad *sad* her *her* lake *lake* dad *dad* has *has*;

   if *he* is; as *he* fled; risk a *lead*; has a red *sled*;

   a *jade* fish; ask if *she* slid; *she* has asked a kid;

   as if *he* did; *he* asked a lad; *his* aide has a sled;

   he has a sled; if *he* has a jar; see if *he* is here;

3. Save as: *wp1 activity 5*.

Activity 6

Bold

Home tab > Font >
Bold

★TIP Ctrl + B
Bold

The **Bold** feature prints text darker than other copy as it is keyed.

1. Open *df wp1 activity 6*.
2. DS after the heading and key the following lines DS.

   a **red** jar;

   she said **half** a

   she asked if **he** had;

   a **red** desk; he fired **her**;

   a **kid** led; **he** is fair; ask **her**

3. Save as: *wp1 activity 6*.

Basic Technology Skills 1

Technology Impacts Our Lives

OUTCOMES
- Study the history of computers
- Describe how computers improve productivity
- Consider how computers are part of everyday life

History of Computers

Imagine a world without computers. Sort of hard to imagine isn't it? Computers have totally changed the way we work, live, and think. Computers have integrated themselves into all aspects of our lives and society. *Instagram*, *Twitter*, and *Facebook* have changed how we connect and communicate with each other. Logging onto a computer or "smart" device instantly connects us to the world. While most of these advancements have been positive, they have also presented challenges to personal privacy and to the ethical use of technology.

The first electronic computers were introduced in the mid-1900s. These computers were very big, as you can see in Figure BT1-1. Some computers were housed in large rooms and weighed hundreds of pounds.

Figure BT1-1 Early computers were large and heavy

Early computers could perform only basic operations. For example, they could add, subtract, divide, and multiply. They could do these tasks many times faster than a person could. However, they were painfully slow compared with today's computers.

Advances in computers came slowly at first. Once computers had a way to store information, the demand for them grew. People started building smaller computers. In 1977, the Apple personal computer was introduced. Since that time, computers have steadily changed and improved. Some important milestones in the history of computing include:

1946 The first large-scale electronic computer, called ENIAC, was created.
1951 UNIVAC, one of the first commercial computers, was bought by the U.S. Census Bureau.
1963 The computer mouse was developed by Douglas Engelbart.

(Continued)

1965   Minicomputers were introduced. These were the first computers to use integrated circuits.

1969   Small computers helped astronauts land on the moon.

1977   Apple PCs and IBM PCs were introduced. Personal computers
1981   became practical for business and personal use.

1983   Notebook computers were introduced.

1984   Apple introduced the Macintosh computer and the graphical interface using pictures, or icons, instead of text commands.

1991   The World Wide Web was developed. Internet use began to increase rapidly.

1993   PDAs were introduced, which were the first small, handheld computers. They gave inspiration to today's smart cell phones.

2001   Tablet PCs were introduced. Handwriting and speech continue to become more popular as input methods.

2007   Apple released the iPhone, which is both a handheld computer and a phone with wireless Internet capabilities. As an input tool on the iPhone, fingertips replace the mouse.

2008   Google released Google Chrome as a new and unique web browser.

2009   Google's Gmail was released and the Bing search engine was released by Microsoft.

2010   Apple unveiled the iPad, changing the way consumers view media and jump-starting the tablet computer market. The online photo and video sharing service *Instagram* was introduced as the newest form of social media.

2011   IBM's Watson supercomputer won *Jeopardy* in February.

2013   Connected TVs and tablets moved into the mainstream as media providers such as Netflix and Hulu rival broadcast and cable companies. Also, identity theft, data breaches, privacy issues, and national security topped headlines throughout the year.

2014   Seven new web domain names are released including .guru, .clothing, and .bike.

2015   Microsoft released *Windows 10*, featuring faster startup, integrated web apps, and improved support for digital media and cloud computing.

2015   Neuromorphic chips are introduced and are configured more like brains than traditional microprocessors. Car-to-car communication, a simple wireless technology, promises to make driving much safer.

2017   Self-driving cars and trucks may soon be commonplace on highways. Scientists are making remarkable progress at using digital brain implants to restore freedom of movement for those with spinal cord injuries.

From the 1970s, computer makers have been in intense competition. Each seeks to create faster, smaller, easier to use, and less expensive computers. The results have been a huge success. The power of computers has more than doubled every two years for the past 40 to 45 years. That is a lot!

Today's fast, tiny, and powerful computers are finding their way into the most unlikely places. Often without knowing it, we use dozens of computers every day (Figure BT1-2). They have become more important in our lives with every passing year. As a result, they now influence the way we work, live, and play.

QLED TV   iPhone   Video games

Figure BT1-2 Computers are part of many common devices

As we enter a new decade, what potential do computers and technology hold to help us in our daily lives? Current and future advances in technology offer us almost limitless opportunities to do much good in the world. Agricultural drones with advanced sensors and imaging capabilities are giving farmers new ways to increase yield and reduce crop damage. Gene therapy has promising potential to take on cancer, heart disease, and other common illnesses. Data and artificial intelligence are producing ultra-accurate forecasts that will make it feasible to integrate wind and solar power into the electrical grid.

With all great potential comes great challenges. Breakthroughs in genomics have the possibility to help millions but are also challenging our moral and ethical boundaries. The relentless push to add connectivity to personal and home gadgets can create dangerous side effects and threats to our personal identity and security. Advances in technology are threatening the way we do business and even our national security. How will we address these challenges in the future?

How Computers Improve Productivity

COLLABORATION

People worked and lived for thousands of years without computers. So why have we become so dependent on them now? The simple answer is that computers help us get more done. They increase our productivity. **Productivity** is a measure of how much work can be done in a certain amount of time.

1. Work in a group or team. Pick one member as a scribe to take notes. Brainstorm as many answers as you can to these three questions:
   a. How do computers make people more productive? List and explain your ideas.
   b. Can computers make people less productive? List and explain your answers.
   c. Can you get along without a computer, a smartphone, or other digital tools? List and explain your answers.

2. Present and discuss your answers with the class or with another team and compare your ideas. What answers and ideas did your group identify that other groups did not? What answers and ideas did other teams come up with that your group may have missed?

How Computers Are Part of Everyday Life

Imagine if all computers suddenly disappeared. As you go through your day today, think about how things would be different without computers.

School

Think about your school. Most likely the heating, cooling, emergency, and communication systems all use computers. Obviously, the computer labs would disappear. Most clocks would stop, and the lights would not turn on. Fire alarms might not work properly. In addition, your teacher could not enter your grades without the help of a computer. How many of your assignments require the use of a computer?

Transportation and Public Safety

Think about transportation. Without computers, most modern cars would stop working. Many of the safety, pollution control, and starter systems on cars use computers. Cars with onboard computers can now parallel park and anticipate movements of vehicles surrounding them to avoid accidents. Traffic lights and warning systems use computers. The Amber Alert system warns motorists to be on the lookout for missing children. Many lives have been saved as a result of computer alert systems.

Home

Think about your home. Most appliances, clocks, and other electronic devices would stop working. Your digital phone would not exist. Your televisions, radios, DVRs, and computer games would quit working, too! There would be no more Internet, texting, or social media.

Money and Shopping

Think about your money and shopping. Money transactions are routed and recorded by computers. All ATMs and online banking apps require computers to function. Credit card systems would cease to work. You would not be able to buy anything at the mall or online because businesses could not process transactions or payments. At brick-and-mortar stores, elevators and escalators would stop working. There would be no lighting, no air conditioning, and no security systems.

The Space Program

Think about the space program. Without computers, spaceships would never get off the ground. Satellites (Figure BT1-3) would quit working. The International Space Station would crash to Earth. We might not discover new opportunities in our expanding universe.

Figure BT1-3 Telecommunications satellite

COLLABORATION

You know how computers are used in many areas of people's everyday lives. You will explore some other areas where computers are important in this activity.

1. Work in a team with three or four classmates. Ask one team member to take notes and ask another to lead the discussion.

2. Brainstorm how computers are used in each of the following categories. Make a list of as many ideas as you can.

- Science
- Medicine
- Business and industry
- Arts and entertainment
- Protecting the environment

3. Discuss your list with the class or with another group of students in your class.

LESSON 6 New Keys: o and t

- Learn reach technique for **o** and **t**
- Combine **o** and **t** smoothly with all other learned keys

6A

Warmup

Keep fingers curved and upright

Key each line twice.

Home row 1 jskj; dlaf; sad fall; had a hall; a fall ad; ask a

3rd row 2 a fire; if her aid; he sees; he irks her; fish jar

All keys learned 3 he had half a jar; as she fell; he sells fir desks

6B

New Keys: o and t

o *Right ring* finger

t *Left index* finger

Follow the plan for learning new keys shown in Lesson 3B. Key each line twice.

Learn o

1 l o|l o|lo lo|do do|of of|so so|old old|fold fold;

2 fork fork|soak soak|hold hold|sold sold|joke joke;

3 a doe; old fork; solid oak door; old foe; oak odor

Learn t

4 f t|f t|it it|fat fat|the the|tied tied|lift lift;

5 ft ft|fit fit|sit sit|hit hit|kite kite|talk talk;

6 lift it; tie the; hit it; take their test; is late

Combine o and t

7 to to|too too|took took|hot hot|lot lot|tort tort;

8 hook hook|told told|fort fort|sort sort|jolt jolt;

9 told a joke; jot or dot; took a jolt; took a look;

★TIP
- Keep your fingers curved and upright.
- Use a down-and-in spacing motion.
- Keep your eyes on the copy as you key.

Key each line twice.

h/e

1 the the|lead lead|held held|hear hear|heart heart;

2 he heard|ask their|here the|has fled|hide the jars

i/t

3 its its|hit hit|tie tie|sit sit|kite kite|fit fit;

4 a tire|a fire|tied to it|it fits|it sits|it is fit

o/r

5 or or|for for|fort fort|oar oar|soar soar|rot rot;

6 three doors|a red rose|for a fort|he rode|for free

Space Bar

7 of he or it is to if do el odd off too are she the

8 off of it|does the|if she|to do the|for the|she is

All keys learned

9 if she is; ask a lad; to the lake; off the old jet

10 he or she; for a fit; if she did; the jar; a salad

6D

Enrichment Activity

Unscramble the letters shown below to create eight words. If you have difficulty, key the letters in different orders to unscramble the words.

1. otd
2. tej
3. erhe
4. ierd
5. aekl
6. satf
7. aodr
8. htroe

LESSON 7   New Keys: n and g

OUTCOMES

- Learn reach technique for **n** and **g**
- Combine **n** and **g** smoothly with all other learned keys

7A

Warmup

Key each line twice.

h/e 1 he has a hoe; he has her heart; her health; he had

o/t 2 took the toad; it is hot; a lot; her toes; dot it;

i/r 3 a tire; it is fair; their jar; their skis; ride it

7B

New Keys: n and g

n *Right index* finger

g *Left index* finger

Key each line twice. If time permits, key lines 7–9 again.

Learn n

1 j n|jn jn|an an|and and|end end|ant ant|land lands
2 jn jn|and and|den den|not not|end end|and and|sand
3 not a train; hand it in; near the end; nine or ten

Learn g

4 f g|fg fg|go go|jog jog|got got|frog frog|get gets
5 fg fg|get get|egg egg|dig dig|logs logs|golf golf;
6 good eggs; eight dogs; a frog; a goat; golf gadget

Combine n and g

7 gone gone|nag nag|ago ago|gnat gnat|dragon dragons
8 green grass; nine ants; need glasses; ten gallons;
9 go golfing; not again; long ago; ten frogs; a gang

7C

Enter Key Technique

Tap Enter quickly and start a new line without pausing

Key each line twice.

1 here she is;

2 he is at the inn;

3 she goes to ski there;

4 he is also to sign the log;

5 he left the egg on the old desk;

6 he took the old dog to the ski lodge;

✓ checkpoint Does your **J** finger remain in place as you tap the Enter key? If not, make an effort to improve your reach technique.

7D

Key Mastery

★TIP Keep your eyes on the copy as you key.

Key each line twice.

n/g
1 gone gone|sing sing|long long|song song|gang gangs

2 sing a song; log on; sign it; and golf; long songs

Space Bar
3 is is|go go|of of|or or|he he|it it|the the|and an

4 if it is a jar|he has a dog|like to go|to do signs

All keys learned
5 an old oak desk; a jade ring; at her side; of the;

6 he goes there at night; she has left for the lake;

7 he took her to the lake; take the hooks off; he is

8 the old jet; sign the list on the; go to the right

7E

Compose Sentences

desk

hired

lake

long

tires

Read the sentences below. From the list at the left, choose the word that best completes the sentence. Key the word and tap the Enter key.

1. Parker likes to swim at the _____.

2. Owen left his glasses in the _____.

3. The company _____ both of us for the summer job.

4. The _____ on the car need to be replaced.

5. The fish was over 20 inches _____.

LESSON 8 — New Keys: Left Shift and . (period)

OUTCOMES

- Learn reach technique for **Left Shift** and **.** (period)
- Combine **Left Shift** and **.** (period) smoothly with all other learned keys

8A

Warmup

Key each line twice.

Reach review 1 `rf ol gf ki hj tf nj ed fr lo fg ik jh ft jn a; de`

Space Bar 2 `as if go at it is in he or to of so do on jet lake`

All keys learned 3 `a jar; if an; or do; to go; an oak door; she told;`

8B

New Keys: Left Shift and . (period)

Left Shift *Left little* finger

. (period) *Right ring* finger

★TIP To use the Left Shift key:

1. Hold down the Left Shift key with the little finger on the left hand.
2. Tap the letter with the right hand.
3. Return finger(s) to home keys.

Key each line twice. If time permits, rekey lines 7–9.

Learn Left Shift

1 `a J|Ja Ja|Ka Ka|La La|Hal Hal|Kal Kal|Jan Jan|Jane`

2 `Jan did it; Kent took it; Ida said; Jane has a dog`

3 `I see that Kate is to aid Hans at the Oakdale sale`

Learn . (period)

4 `l .|l. l.|fl. fl.|ed. ed.|ft. ft.|rd. rd.|hr. hrs.`

5 `l. l.|fl. fl.|hr. hr.|e.g. e.g.|i.e. i.e.|in. ins.`

6 `a. s. d. f. j. k. l. ;. h. e. i. r. o. t. n. g. o.`

Combine Left Shift and . (period)

7 `I do. Ian is. Olga did. Jan does. Ken is gone.`

8 `Hal did it. I shall do it. Kate left on a train.`

9 `Jan sang a song. Linda read it. Ken told a joke.`

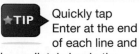

8C

Enter Key Technique

TIP ► Quickly tap Enter at the end of each line and immediately begin the next line.

Key each line twice.

1 I like the dog.

2 Janet is at the inn.

3 Jake is to take the test.

4 Hank and Jo left for the lake.

5 Hans took the girls to a ski lodge.

6 Jeff took the old desk to the ski lodge.

7 Jason and Jeff like to listen to those songs.

8 Jane and Lane took the train to the old ski lodge.

8D

Key Mastery

TIP ►
• Space once after . following abbreviations and initials.
• Space once after . at the end of a sentence except at the end of a line. There, tap Enter without spacing.

Key each line twice.

Abbreviations/
initials
1 He said ft. for feet; rd. for road; fl. for floor.

2 Lt. Hahn let L. K. take the old gong to Lake Neil.

Short
words
3 a an or he to if do it of so is go for got old led

4 go the off aid dot end jar she fit oak and had rod

Short
phrases
5 if so|it is|to do|if it|do so|to go|he is|to do it

6 to the|and do|is the|got it|if the|for the|ask for

All letters
learned
7 Ned asked Janet. He got the oak door at the lodge.

8 J. L. lost one of the sleds he took off the train.

8E

Enrichment Activity

Unscramble the letters shown below to create eight words. If you have difficulty, key the letters in different orders to unscramble the words.

1. gikn
2. noij
3. gsoe
4. ealt
5. oaltt
6. easdk
7. reith
8. ianga

LESSON 9   Review

OUTCOMES
- Improve use of **Space Bar**, **Left Shift**, and **Enter**
- Improve keying speed of words, phrases, and sentences

9A

Warmup

Key each line twice.

Reach review 1 ki fr lo de jn fg jh ft l. 1.lo i.o. r.e. n.g. h.t

Space Bar 2 a as ask|h he hen|n no not|t to too took|d do dot;

Left Shift 3 Keith left. Lana is not here. Jason sang the song.

9B

Key Mastery

Key each line twice.

n/g
1 jn jn|fg fg|slang slang|lingo lingo|jargon jargon;
2 Nate sang eight or nine songs; Lana sang one song.

o/t
3 lo lo|ft ft|to to|foot foot|lots lots|tooth tooth;
4 John has lost the list he took to that food store.

i/r
5 ki ki|fr fr|ire ire|risk risk|ring ring|tire tire;
6 Ida is taking a giant risk riding their old horse.

Left Shift/.
7 Jason K. Hanselt; Katie O. Higgins; Kirk N. Jones;
8 J. L. Johnson is going to Illinois to see her son.

9 jh jh|de de|he he|here here|hear hear|share share;
10 Helen and Jason sold eight of the heaters for Hal.

 checkpoint Did you space once after periods following initials?

9C

Enter Key Technique

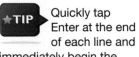 **TIP** Quickly tap Enter at the end of each line and immediately begin the next line.

Key each line twice.

1 Jon has gone to ski;

2 he took a train at eight.

3 Karen asked for the disk;

4 she is to take it to the lake.

5 Joe said he left the file that

6 has the data he needs at the lodge.

7 Janine said she felt ill as the ski

8 lift left to take the girls to the hill.

9 Joe and Lane had to take the train to Kansas.

10 Janel has the date for the girls to rehearse.

9D

Increase Speed

Key each line twice.

Key words (Think, say, and key the words.)

1 is and the if she of air did dog risk forks eight

2 rifle signs their then title ant aisle dials dish

3 shall signal tight shelf rigid right soaks island

Key phrases (Think, say, and key the phrases.)

4 is to|or do|to it|if he is|to do|it is|of an|if he

5 he did|of the|to all|is for|is a tie|to aid|if she

6 he or she|to rig it|if she did|is to sit|is to aid

Key sentences (Tap keys at a brisk, steady pace.)

7 Jake is to go to the lake to get her old red skis.

8 Hal asked for a list of all the old gold she sold.

9 Helen said she left the old disk list on his desk.

9E

Technique Review

COLLABORATION

Your techniques are an important part of learning to key. You should continue to work to refine your techniques.

1. Open **df 9e check sheet**. Print the document. Close the file.
2. Work with a classmate. Ask your classmate to key lines 7–9 (above) as you watch for proper techniques. Mark notes on your check sheet. Share your comments with your classmate.
3. Ask your classmate to rate your techniques as you key lines 7–9. Discuss your ratings with your classmate.

Activity 1

Select Text

> **TIP** ► Double-click to select a word; Ctrl-click to select a sentence.

For each activity, read and learn the feature described; then complete the activity as directed.

Once you have keyed text, you can make changes to it. To do so, you must select it first. The Select Text feature allows you to select (highlight) text to apply formatting changes or perform other actions. Text can be selected using the mouse or the keyboard. As little as one letter of text or as much as the entire document (Select All) can be selected.

Once selected, the text can be bolded, italicized, underlined, deleted, copied, moved, printed, saved, etc.

1. Open *df wp2 activity 1*.
2. Use the Select Text feature to select and add bold and italic to the text as shown below.

   John F. Kennedy: *"And so, my fellow Americans: ask not what your country can do for you—ask what you can do for your country."*

   Dwight D. Eisenhsower: *"Love of liberty means the guarding of every resource that makes freedom possible—from the sanctity of our families and the wealth of our soil to the genius of our scientists."*

   Franklin D. Roosevelt: *"I see a great nation, upon a great continent, blessed with a great wealth of natural resources."*

   Abraham Lincoln: *"Both parties deprecated war, but one of them would make war rather than let the nation survive, and the other would accept war rather than let it perish, and the war came."*

3. Save as: *wp2 activity 1*.

Activity 2

Cut, Copy, and Paste

Home tab > Clipboard > Cut, Copy, or Paste

> **TIP** ► Ctrl + X: Cut
> Ctrl + C: Copy
> Ctrl + V: Paste

After you have selected text, you can use the Cut, Copy, and Paste features. The **Cut** feature removes selected text from the current location; the **Paste** feature places it at another location. The **Copy** feature copies the selected text so it can be placed in another location (pasted), leaving the original text unchanged.

1. Open file *df wp2 activity 2*. Copy the text in this file and paste it a TS (tap Enter 3 times) below the last line of text.
2. In the second set of steps, use Cut and Paste to arrange the steps in order.

   Step 1. Select text to be cut (moved).

   Step 2. Click *Cut* to remove text from the current location.

   Step 3. Move the insertion point to the desired location.

   Step 4. Click *Paste* to place the cut text at the new location.

3. Save as: *wp2 activity 2*.

Basic Technology Skills 2

Hardware, Software, and Information Processing

- Discover various types of hardware
- Identify three types of software
- Learn the five steps of information processing

Hardware

Computer **hardware** includes all the parts of a computer that you can touch with your hands. Hardware can be found either inside of or connected to computers. For example, inside your computer you may find a **hard drive** that stores data. Computers also have **microprocessors**, as shown in Figure BT2-1, inside them. A microprocessor is a small circuit board that controls all the work a computer does. The microprocessor is the brain of the computer, which makes it the most important part. A microprocessor is also called a **processor** or a **CPU**, which stands for **central processing unit**. Hardware can also be connected to a computer. Examples of this type of hardware include a keyboard, mouse, or monitor.

Microprocessors are found in computers of all shapes and sizes. They are located in laptops, smartphones, cameras, home appliances, remote controls, and cars. They control streetlights and fire alarms, and they dispense money at ATMs.

Computers of all types are called digital communication tools, or **DigiTools**. Figure BT2-2 shows several different DigiTools.

Figure BT2-1
Microprocessors are the brains inside a computer

Stockbyte/Getty Images

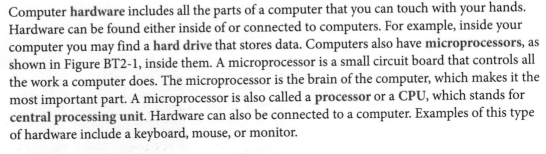

| Desktop | Laptop | Tablet |

Oleksiy/Shutterstock.com · Ksander/Shutterstock.com · Scanrail1/Shutterstock.com

Smartphones and handhelds · Wearable tech

12bit/Shutterstock.com · Anna Hoychuk/Shutterstock.com

Figure BT2-2 DigiTools come in a variety of sizes and shapes

NOTE

Microprocessors are digital. This means that they calculate with two digits—0 and 1. Stringing billions of digits together in just the right order, such as 01011101, will make a microprocessor jump into action and do what you want it to do.

Personal Computers

You probably own or have used a **personal computer**, or **PC**. A PC is designed for an individual user. It may be a desktop PC, a laptop PC, or a tablet PC. You also may use a handheld computer or smartphone.

A personal computer may have many parts. Examine the parts of the typical desktop PC in Figure BT2-3. Do you have all of these parts in your computer system?

Figure BT2-3 Parts of a desktop PC

Peripherals

A computer cannot do everything by itself! It needs help to perform various tasks. Other devices that work with a computer are called **peripherals** (see Figure BT2-4). Printers, digital tablets, scanners, virtual reality goggles, and headsets are examples of peripherals.

> **NOTE** DigiTools, which include computers and peripherals, are also called devices, electronic devices, and, consumer electronics.

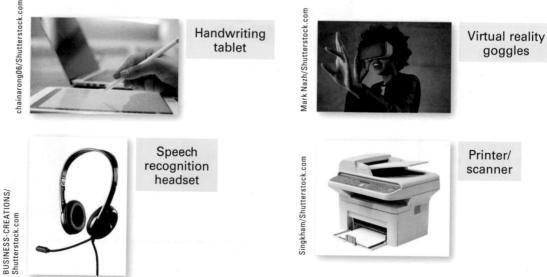

Figure BT2-4 Computer peripherals

COLLABORATION

1. Discuss with your class or team the many different DigiTools. Answer these questions:

   - What is the first thing you remember doing with a computer?

   - Which digital communication tools do you use most and why?

   - What peripherals have you used? Have you ever used a scanner, a speech or recording headset or microphone, an artist drawing or writing tablet, or a digital camera? If so, what work or activity did you do with these tools?

   - Have you used a smartphone (such as an iPhone or Android), digital video recorder, desktop PC, laptop PC, handheld computer, tablet PC, or global positioning system (GPS)?

   - Have you ever used a DigiTool such as an iPod or MP3 player, a digital video recorder, a cell phone, or a game console just for entertainment reasons?

   - If you have a smartphone, what games can you play on your phone? Can you download music, ringtones, and webpages on your phone? Does your phone have fingertip (multi-touch) control or a virtual keypad for text messaging? What do you like most about your phone? What do you dislike about your phone? What would you improve if you could?

2. Study the typical computer system shown in Figure BT2-3. Discuss these questions:

   - Is it nearly the same as the computer system you will be using at school?

   - In what ways might it be different?

   - Do you have a computer at home? If so, what is it like?

Software

Computers need instructions to work properly. These instructions are called **software**. Software gives instructions to a computer's microprocessor. It tells the computer hardware what to do.

Do you make calls, send text messages, or tweet? Do you visit websites? Do you download music or take pictures? If the answer is yes, then you are already using software. For example, if you play a video game like the one shown in Figure BT2-5, the game you play is the software program. (The game console is hardware.) Word processing, spreadsheet, and drawing programs are also examples of software.

Figure BT2-5 Video games are examples of software

There are three general types of software:

- **Operating systems (OSs)** control how computers communicate with the hardware and how they interact with you, the user.

- **Applications** allow you to complete a specific task. Applications let you create a report, browse the Internet, edit a multimedia video, or calculate a math problem. Applications are generally installed on a local computer.

- **Online apps** also let you complete specific tasks such as editing photos, playing games, and viewing multimedia. Online apps run over the Internet inside a web browser or on a smartphone. (See Figure BT2-6.)

★TIP Online apps work much like the applications on your PC. Online apps can create documents, publish webpages, send email, and post your personal calendar online.

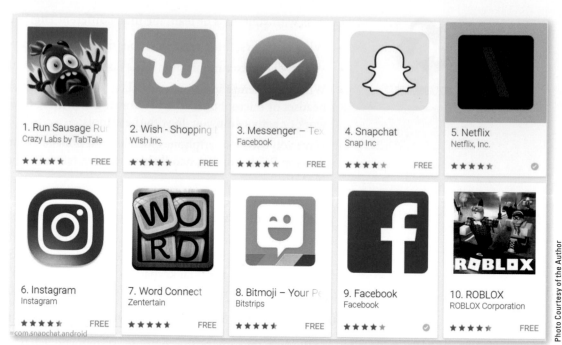

Figure BT2-6 Online apps for free or purchase run through a web browser or on a smartphone

Can you suggest to a friend the name of an application or online app he or she can use to solve specific problems? There are so many to choose from. You can often guess the use of a program from its name. A few commonly used applications and online apps are listed below. Match the program name with its use.

a. *Spider Solitaire*   _____ 1. Word processing

b. *Snapchat*   _____ 2. Webpage creation software

c. *Blogger*   _____ 3. Popular game

d. *Microsoft Word*   _____ 4. Drawing program

e. *Google Chrome*   _____ 5. Internet/web browser

f. *iTunes*   _____ 6. Social media

g. *Google Sites*   _____ 7. Image-editing software

h. *Paint*   _____ 8. Music downloading software

i. *Photoshop*   _____ 9. Post and publish online opinions and information

Information Processing

We interact with computers using a five-step process. This process is called **information processing** and is illustrated in Figure BT2-7. Information processing puts words, pictures, and numbers (called **data**) into forms we can use and understand.

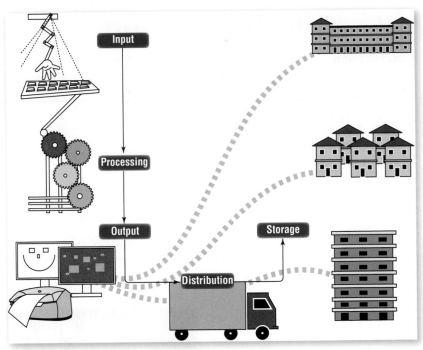

Figure BT2-7 The five steps of information processing

- **Input** lets you put data into a computer. You can use your fingers on a touch screen, an electronic pen on a drawing tablet, a keyboard, a speech headset, a scanner, a camera, and other tools to input data.

- **Processing** lets you change or manipulate data using software. You may add numbers, sort a list of names, and alter the colors on a picture.

- **Output** is the way you get data from a computer. You can read a text message, print a report, view your photos on a monitor, or listen through speakers or earphones.

- **Distribution** involves sharing information with the people who want it. For example, you may post a blog, build a website, and use a phone to send a picture to a friend.

- **Storage** lets you save data for later use. You can store on your local hard drive, save on a small flash drive, and save on the Internet.

When you transfer photos from a smartphone camera to your computer, you may do all five of the information processing steps. Match the tasks listed below with the five information processing steps.

a. Input	_____ 1. View your photo on the screen
b. Processing	_____ 2. Transfer your picture from a camera to a computer
c. Output	_____ 3. Save a copy of the photo in an online photo gallery
d. Distribution	_____ 4. Attach the photo to an email or text message and send it to a friend
e. Storage	_____ 5. Use software to enhance or improve the photo

LESSON 10 New Keys: u and c

OUTCOMES
- Learn reach technique for **u** and **c**
- Combine **u** and **c** smoothly with all other learned keys

10A

Warmup

Key each line twice.

Reach review
1 fg jn lo fr ki de 1. ft jh gf ij tf nj ed ol rf .1

Space Bar
2 if so to of no go is in it as see are art jet lake

Left Shift
3 Ken has a horse. Jan has a dog. He is going too.

10B

New Keys: u and c

Key each line twice. If time permits, rekey lines 7–9.

u *Right index* finger

c *Left middle* finger

Learn u

1 j u|ju ju|just just|rust rust|dust dust|used used;

2 ju ju|jug jug|jut jut|turn turn|hug hug|sure sure;

3 turn it; due us; the fur; use it; fur rug; is just

Learn c

4 d c|dc dc|can can|tic tic|catch catch|clock clock;

5 dc dc|ice ice|cat cat|car car|care care|dock docks

6 a can; the ice; she can; the dock; the code; a car

Combine u and c

7 cut cute duck clue cuff cure luck truck curd such;

8 such luck; a cure; to cut; the cure; for the truck

9 Janet and Jack told us to take four cans of juice.

Key Mastery

★TIP
- Reach up without moving your hands away from your body.
- Reach down without moving your hands toward your body.

Key each line twice.

3rd/1st rows
1 no to in nut run cue tot cot nun urn ten turn cute
2 Nan is cute; he is curt; turn a cog; he can use it

Left Shift and .
3 Jett had a lead. Kate ate the cake. Lane let us.
4 I said to use Kan. for Kansas and Ore. for Oregon.

Short words
5 if the and cue for end fit rug oak she fur due got
6 an due cut such fuss rich turn dock curl such hair

Short phrases
7 a risk|is fun|to rush|for us|a fit|the dog|such as
8 just in|code it|turn it|cure it|as such|is in luck

All keys learned
9 He told us to get the ice. Juan called her for us.
10 Hal is sure that he can go there in an hour or so.

Think and key by letter response.

One-hand words
11 data edge card race after great street states dear
12 Jill edge look race hill effects onion states look

Think and key by word response.

Balanced-hand words
13 Dick sign lake dial odor sick dish hair duck goal;
14 Diana is to go to the lake to do the audit for us.

10D

Critical Thinking Activity

The White House

President Abraham Lincoln

You have learned to key the letters shown below. Notice that only the letters keyed with the right hand are shown as capitals. Key as many U.S. presidents' last names as you can using only these letters.

a c d e f g H I J K L N O r s t U

LESSON 11 New Keys: w and Right Shift

OUTCOMES

- Learn reach technique for **w** and **Right Shift**
- Combine **w** and **Right Shift** smoothly with all other learned keys

11A

Warmup

Key each line twice.

Reach review 1 fr fg de ju ft jn ki lo dc ki rf 1. ed jh ol gf tf

u/c 2 luck used cure such cute cause lunch accuse actual

All letters learned 3 Jefferson just took the huge lead in the election.

11B

New Keys: w and Right Shift

w *Left ring* finger

Right Shift *Right little* finger

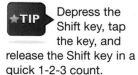 **TIP** Depress the Shift key, tap the key, and release the Shift key in a quick 1-2-3 count.

Key each line twice. If time permits, rekey lines 7–9.

Learn w

1 s w|sw sw|two two|wet wet|low low|how how|was was;

2 sw sw|were were|what what|snow snow|worker worker;

3 to show; to watch; to win; when we; wash and wear;

Learn Right Shift

4 ;A ;A;|A1 A1;|Dan Dan;|Ann Ann;|Ron Ron;|Gene Gene

5 Chicago; San Diego; Santa Fe; Atlanta; Eau Claire;

6 Richard left for San Diego; Fran left for Chicago.

Combine w and Right Shift

7 Charla and Wanda will watch the show with Willard.

8 We will want to show the award to Walt and Andrew.

9 Wes wished he was in Washington watching the show.

Key Mastery

Key each line twice.

w and Right Shift

1 Dr. Wade works here; Dr. Weeks left two weeks ago.

2 Will Whitt get a watch when his is in town on Wed.

n/g

3 sing a song|long gone|wrong sign|and got|a gallon;

4 Glenda signed the wrong check. Jen is gone again.

Short words

5 is and the she sir for rid cut got rug oak end dog

6 wet red oil ear inn gas ink car on ace look no sea

Short phrases

7 he did|a jet ride|she is|if she can go|take a look

8 as soon as|to go to|if it is|when he is|has done a

All keys learned

9 Jason and Chuck are going. Laurie thinks she can.

10 Frank worked eight hours; Linda worked four hours.

11D

Spacing with Punctuation

Key each line twice.

1 Dr. Hoag said to use wt. for weight; in. for inch.

2 J. R. Chen has used ed. for editor; Rt. for Route.

3 Sue said Jed Ford got an Ed.D. degree last winter.

4 Use i.e. for that is; cs. for case; ck. for check.

5 Sgt. Rusk said he told A. J. Nagai to take charge.

6 St. Cloud State; St. Olaf College; St. Louis State

11E

Critical Thinking

In this lesson, you learned the Right Shift key. There are 12 U.S. presidents' names that you can key using the Right Shift key and the letters you have learned that are shown below. See how many of the 12 you can key.

a c d e f g h i j k l n o r s t u w

LESSON 12

New Keys: b and y

- Learn reach technique for **b** and **y**
- Combine **b** and **y** smoothly with all other learned keys
- Learn to determine **gwam**

12A

Warmup

Keep fingers curved and upright

Key each line twice.

Reach review 1 ft. de lo ju sw ki fr dc jn jh l. fg rt ws ol ed.

c/n 2 nice coin cent cane niece dance ounce check glance

All letters learned 3 Jack Elgin had two hits in the first four innings.

12B

New Keys: b and y

b *Left index* finger

y *Right index* finger

Key each line twice. If time permits, rekey lines 7–9.

Learn b

1 f b f b|fb bf|fib fib|big big|book book|bank bank;

2 fb fb fb|bugs bugs|oboe oboe|label label|bird bird

3 Bob bid; Rob bunted; black rubber ball; brief job;

Learn y

4 j y|jy jy|jay jay|yes yes|eye eye|day day|rye rye;

5 yiy yiy|eye eye|only only|yellow yellow|your yours

6 why did you; yellow cycle; only yesterday; he says

Combine b and y

7 buy buy|boy boy|busy busy|buddy buddy|byway byway;

8 by the bay; you buy a; big burly boy; a yellow bus

9 Bobby went by way of bus to buy the big blue belt.

12C

Space Bar Technique

 **TIP** Space with a down-and-in motion immediately after each word.

Key each line once.

1 Jason will be able to take the bus to the concert.
2 Gary is to sign for the auto we set aside for her.
3 Rey is in town for just one week to look for work.
4 Ted is to work for us for a week at the lake dock.
5 June said he was in the auto when it hit the tree.
6 Dan has an old car she wants to sell at this sale.
7 Dr. Dent could say yes if Anna asks her for a job.
8 Only three of the eight girls finished their test.

12D

Enter Key Technique

Key each line once. At the end of each line, quickly tap the Enter key and start the next line.

1 Gary will hit first.
2 Jan will be the second hitter.
3 Nick will be second and bat after Jason.
4 Roberto will be the center fielder and hit eighth.

gwam 1' | 1 | 2 | 3 | 4 | 5 | 6 | 7 | 8 | 9 | 10 |

12E

Determine Number of Words Keyed

A **standard word** in keyboarding is five characters. These five characters can be letters, numbers, symbols, or spaces. Each group of five characters is shown by the number scale under lines you key. (See scale under line 4 in 12D above.) One measure used to describe keying skill is the number of words you key in a certain amount of time, such as a minute ('). The number of standard words keyed in 1' is called *gross words a minute* (**gwam**).

1. Key line 4 of 12D again as your instructor times you for 1'. Then follow the steps below to find 1' *gwam* for the timing.

   - Note on the scale the figure beneath the last word you keyed. That is your 1' *gwam* if you key the line partially or only once.

   - If you complete the line once and start over, add 10 to the figure you determined in step 1. The result is your 1' *gwam*.

2. Key line 4 of 12D again as your instructor times you for 30 seconds ("). Then follow the steps below to find 30" *gwam*.

   - Find 1' *gwam* (total words keyed).

   - Multiply 1' *gwam* by 2. The resulting figure is your 30" *gwam*.

LESSON 13   Review

OUTCOMES

- Improve spacing, shifting, and entering
- Increase keying control and speed

13A

Warmup

Key each line twice.

Reach review   1   ton only beat teen week rich used nice count B. J.

b/y   2   buy yes boy year obey eyes been yield debate Bobby

All letters learned   3   Jason knew the gift you held was for Dr. Jacobson.

13B

Space Bar and Shift Keys

TIP   Space with a down-and-in motion immediately after each word.

Key each line twice.

Space Bar (Space immediately after each word.)

1   in by we so do the and run yet ink low jet fun can

2   in the|when he|if she will|run to|yes you|can be a

3   Lance take a look at her car to see what is wrong.

4   Janet lost both of the keys to the car in the lot.

Shift keys (Hold down Shift key; tap key; quickly return finger(s) to home keys.)

5   Dr. Alou; Jose K. Casey; Sue A. Finch; Jon B. Bins

6   Della and I went to France in June to see her dad.

7   Roger and Carlos went to Salt Lake City on Friday.

8   The San Francisco Giants were in town on Thursday.

Balanced-hand words (Think and key by word response.)

9   keys odor rush sick dial girl half clay both signs

10   field cycle handy angle chair widow; works; burnt;

11   Diana and I did go to the social with Dick and Bo.

12   Their bicycle is in the cornfield by the big rock.

 **checkpoint**   Do you reach up to keys without moving your hands away from your body?

13C

Check Speed

★ TIP Keep the insertion point moving steadily across each line (no pauses).

Key each line once double-spaced. Key a 20" timed writing on each line. Your rate of gross words a minute (*gwam*) is shown below the lines.

1 I will see her.

2 Janet has a new job.

3 Jack will go to the lake.

4 Karl is to go skiing with her.

5 Kara has two old oak doors to sell.

6 Faye and I took the test before we left.

7 Jessie said she will be in school on Tuesday.

8 Jay will go to the city to work on the road signs.

gwam 20" | 3 | 6 | 9 | 12 | 15 | 18 | 21 | 24 | 27 | 30 |

13D

Speed Building

★ TIP
- Keep your fingers curved and upright.
- Space quickly without pausing between words.

Key each line once.

1 Judy had gone for that big ice show at Lake Tahoe.

2 Jack said that all of you will find the right job.

3 Cindy has just left for work at the big ski lodge.

4 Rudy can take a good job at the lake if he wishes.

5 Rob saw the bird on the lake by the big boat dock.

6 Ted knew the surf was too rough for kids to enjoy.

7 Jane and Gus wanted to take the corner shelf down.

8 Rodney and I hid the chair behind the closet door.

13E

Critical Thinking

COLLABORATION

Work with another student to complete this activity. Unscramble the letters shown below to create ten words. Work as quickly as you can. Raise your hand when you have all ten words.

1. eto
2. eht
3. cush
4. kjeo
5. gornw

6. kieal
7. oohtt
8. eehcr
9. wstae
10. ydnboe

WP Applications 3

Activity 1

Undo and Redo

Undo Redo

Use the **Undo** feature to reverse the last change you made in text. Undo restores text to its original location, even if you have moved the insertion point to another position. Use the **Redo** feature to reverse the last Undo action.

1. Create a new document and key the sentence below. Do not tap Enter when you reach the end of the first line. When a line is full, the next word will automatically wrap to the next line.

The final show featured the Brooklyn **Band** in concert at the Lincoln Center and the San Francisco **Band** at the Herbst Theatre in the Arts Center.

2. Change *Band* to *Orchestra* in both places.
3. Use the Undo feature to reverse both changes.
4. Use the Redo feature to reverse the last Undo action.
5. Save as: **wp3 activity 1**.

Activity 2

Zoom

View tab > Zoom

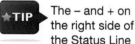
★TIP The – and + on the right side of the Status Line can also be used to zoom out and zoom in.

100%

Use the **Zoom** feature to increase or decrease the amount of the page appearing on the screen. As you decrease the amount of the page appearing on the screen, the print will be larger. Larger print is easier to read and edit. As you increase the amount of the page appearing on the screen, the print becomes smaller. Other options of the Zoom feature include viewing one page, two pages, or multiple pages on the screen.

1. Learn how to use the Zoom feature of your software.
2. Open the **df wp3 activity 2** file. Complete the steps given below. Keep the file open; you will use it in Activity 3.
   a. Step 1: View the document at 75% using the Zoom feature.
   b. Step 2: View the document as a whole page.
   c. Step 3: View the document at 200%.
   d. View the document at 100%.

Activity 3

Print Preview and Print

File tab > Print

Print

File tab > Print > Print

Quite often you will want to see the whole page on the screen to check the appearance (margins, spacing, graphics, tables, etc.) of the document prior to printing. You can display an entire page by using the **Print Preview** feature (see Figure 1-7). After previewing the document, you can return to it to make additional changes, or, if no additional changes are required, you can print the document.

1. Learn how to use the Print Preview feature of your software.
2. View the document as a whole page using Print Preview.
3. Print the document.
4. Close the file.

Figure 1-7 Print Preview

Basic Technology Skills 3 | Operating System Basics

OUTCOMES
- Learn about operating systems
- Study the **Windows** Start screen and menu
- Sharpen your mouse skills
- Turn off your computer

Operating Systems

An operating system (OS) is the most important software on any computer. It controls the hardware. The OS also makes it possible to run other types of software. Think of your operating system as a control center. An OS allows you to perform tasks such as:

- Entering your login name and password
- Helping you find applications and files
- Choosing among available printers
- Shutting down your computer

The most popular operating systems for computers today are *Windows* and *MacOS*. There are also operating systems for smartphones (Android and iOS) and other types of specialized devices. This text focuses on the *Windows* OS for computers.

Login Names and Passwords

As a police officer checks a driver's license when making a traffic stop, an OS checks for your login and password when you start a computer.

- A **login name** identifies you to a computer
- A **password** is a series of letters and/or numbers and symbols that you key to gain access

Your login name and password may be assigned by your school. However, you may be able to create your own password. If you do, choose it carefully. Your password is your main security device. Follow these password rules:

- Keep your password secure. Never share it with others.
- Respect others. Do not ask them for their passwords.
- Do not sneak to find someone else's password, even as a prank
- Think of a password you will remember
- Do not create a password that someone else can easily guess

The strongest passwords contain letters, symbols, and numbers. They are not words found in the dictionary. A password such as *secr375et* is an example of a strong password. A poor example is an obvious word such as *password* or a string of numbers such as *1234*.

If your computer is on a network or runs on a different operating system or version, login instructions may differ. To create your login account, user name, and/or password, check with your instructor for directions for your specific computer or network system.

> **NOTE** **Passwords protect** your data, files, pictures, email, websites, and other information from misuse by others.

Windows Start Screen and Menu

In *Windows*, after you sign in, you will see the **desktop**. From the desktop you can access the **Start screen** by clicking the Start button in the lower-left corner of the screen. The Start screen, shown in Figure BT3-1, is a collection of buttons and tiles, each representing a function or an application. Your Start screen may look different from the one shown in the figure.

The Start screen is a **graphical user interface (GUI)**. A **user interface (UI)** allows users, like you, to interact with the computer. From the Start screen you can open applications or "apps," check your mail or calendar, or go to a social media site. You can add apps to your Start screen so that you just need to click a tile to start that app.

Tiles can be static or dynamic. Live or dynamic tiles let you preview information about the associated application. For example, if you have a news app, you can see the latest news headlines in the tile without opening the application. Static tiles serve as a gateway to applications such as *Office* programs, the Internet, games, pictures, or videos you have stored on your computer.

Figure BT3-1 The *Windows 10* desktop and Start screen

Start button

The *Windows* Start button is a universal tool that can be accessed from anywhere no matter what you are doing or what application you are running. To access the Start menu, move the mouse pointer to the Start button and click. The Start menu appears on the left side of the screen (see Figure BT3-2).

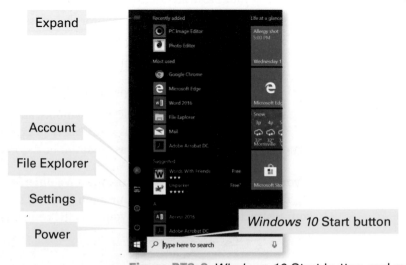

Figure BT3-2 *Windows 10* Start button and menu

There are five buttons on the Start menu. They are Expand, Account, File Explorer, Settings, and Power. Let's take a brief look at each of these buttons.

The **Expand** button expands to reveal the names of all menu items. The **Account** button allows you to change account settings, lock the computer screen, or sign out. The **File Explorer** button launches the File Explorer app that allows you to search to find files stored on your computer or external devices. The **Settings** button gives you access to settings for the network, time and language, devices, updates, and security, among other items. The **Power** button lets you shut down or restart your computer. The Sleep selection allows your PC to remain on but operate at low power. Your apps stay open so when your PC awakes, you can begin where you left off.

Mouse Skills

The mouse is a hovering and pointing device. It is a navigation tool that controls a pointer on your screen, which is used to control your OS. Just as a helicopter can hover above a city, a mouse can hover over any part of your *Windows* desktop. After you move your mouse into position, you can click one of its buttons to activate commands on your computer. A typical mouse is shown in Figure BT3-3.

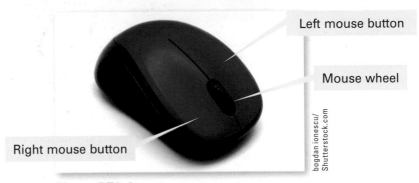

Left mouse button

Mouse wheel

Right mouse button

bogdan ionescu/
Shutterstock.com

Figure BT3-3 Parts of a typical mouse

> **NOTE** If you are using a digital pen, hover ¼ inch above the surface and move the pointer around the screen as you would with a mouse. If you have a multi-touch screen, use your fingers like a mouse pointer.

Many people use a digital pen in addition to a mouse. Laptop computers usually have a track pad that you can use instead of a mouse. On some computers, you can use your fingers as a pointing device. A variety of pointing devices are shown in Figure BT3-4.

Place your mouse on a mouse pad or hard surface. Slide your mouse (or a pen or your fingers, depending on your computer) to move the pointer around your desktop. If you are using a track pad on a laptop, touch the track pad and slide your finger in any direction to move the pointer on your screen.

As you move the mouse or other pointing device, watch the pointer move on the screen. It will move in the direction that you move your pointing device. The pointer often takes the shape of an arrow. At other times, the pointer looks like a hand. When using different applications, your pointer can change appearance to other shapes too. You can move your pointer to any spot on the desktop.

Track pad

Ergonomic mouse

Digital pen

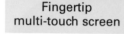

Fingertip
multi-touch screen

Game controls

Figure BT3-4 Other pointing devices

If your mouse cannot be moved any further, lift it off the surface on which you are sliding it. Move it a few inches and place the mouse back on the surface and continue. After positioning the pointer over the icon or object you wish to use, you can:

- Left-click to select something
- Double-click to open an application, a file, or an image
- Click and drag objects around the screen
- Right-click to open pop-up context menus

Turn Off the Computer

Start button > Power
icon > Shut down

Exiting a computer the proper way will help you avoid losing important information. Exiting is sometimes called "shutting down," "signing out," or "logging off." When *Windows* shuts down, it completes tasks such as:

- Closing any open applications
- Saving unsaved data
- Closing open connections to networks or the Internet
- Saving current settings

When your computer is on, your OS, applications, and data are stored in **memory** chips inside the computer. One type of memory is called **RAM**, or **random access memory**. Another type of memory is called **flash memory**. When the computer is turned off, the memory in RAM is erased or cleared. Any unsaved data will be lost.

After you have practiced with the mouse, follow these steps to turn off your computer.

1. Close any applications you have open—you may be prompted to save your work.
2. Display the Start menu by clicking the *Start* button and click the *Power* button.
3. Click *Shut down* (see Figure BT3-5).

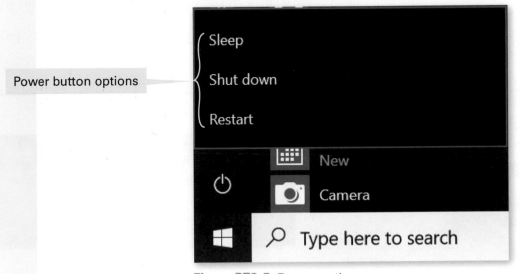

Power button options

Figure BT3-5 Power options

4. After the computer has shut down, turn off the power switch on the monitor and any peripheral devices you have been using.

LESSON 14

New Keys: m and x

OUTCOMES

- Learn reach technique for **m** and **x**
- Combine **m** and **x** smoothly with all other learned keys

14A

Warmup

Key each line twice.

Reach review 1 `fg jy lo fr jn de sw ft ki jh fb dc ju by us if ow`

b/y 2 `by bay buy big yes boy buy bit try bury ruby byway`

All letters learned 3 `Beth can win the gold if she will just key faster.`

14B

New Keys: m and x

Key each line twice. If time permits, rekey lines 7–9.

m *Right index* finger

x *Left ring* finger

Learn m

1 `j m|jm jm|jams jams|make make|mail mail|most most;`

2 `jm jm|me me|may may|moon moon|grim grim|mean meant`

3 `to them; meet me; make a mark; mail it; mean to me`

Learn x

4 `s x|sx sx|six six|fix fix|exit exit|extend extend;`

5 `sx sx|six six|tax tax|hex hex|fix fix|exact exact;`

6 `to excel; to exile; an exit; by six; an excise tax`

Combine m and x

7 `mix fox six jam men box hoax coax maxim axle taxi;`

8 `to fix; mix it; six men; make an exit; make a box;`

9 `Maxine Cox took the exit exams in Texas on Monday.`

14C

Key Mastery

TIP
- Reach up without moving your hands away from your body.
- Reach down without moving your hands toward your body.

Key each line twice.

3rd/1st rows
1 men box but now cut gem rib ton yet not meet mired
2 cub oxen torn went time were note court worn owned

Short words
3 and own she box fix city duck held hair name their
4 art gas face honk milk draw junk aware extra start

Short phrases
5 you want|if she is|one of the|that is|they are not
6 make the call|for all the|and is|able to|they may;

All keys learned
7 Jacki is now at the gym; Lexi is due there by six.
8 Stan saw that he could fix my old bike for Glenda.

14D

Spacing with Punctuation

TIP Do not space after an internal period in an abbreviation such as Ed.D.

Key each line twice.

1 He has an Ed.D. in music; I have an Ed.D. in math.
2 She may send a box c.o.d. to Ms. Cox in St. Louis.
3 Maxine will take a boat to St. Thomas in December.
4 Maria used Wed. for Wednesday and Mon. for Monday.

14E

Critical Thinking

California
Florida
Illinois
New York
Ohio
South Dakota
Texas
Utah
Washington
Wyoming

Key the sentences below. From the list at the left, choose the word that best completes the sentence. Do not key the numbers.

1. Mount Rushmore is located in _____.
2. The Devils Tower is located in _____.
3. San Antonio is located in _____.
4. The Statue of Liberty is located in _____.
5. San Francisco is located in _____.
6. Disney World is located in _____.
7. Mt. St. Helens is located in _____.
8. Bryce Canyon is located in _____.
9. The Rock and Roll Hall of Fame is located in _____.
10. The Lincoln Tomb is located in _____.

LESSON 15 · New Keys: p and v

OUTCOMES
- Learn reach technique for **p** and **v**
- Combine **p** and **v** smoothly with all other learned keys

15A

Warmup

Key each line twice.

One-hand words 1 gate link face moon extra hook base join beef milk

Phrases 2 if you will|take a look|when they|join us|to see a

All letters learned 3 Jo Buck won a gold medal for her sixth show entry.

15B

New Keys: p and v

Key each line twice. If time permits, rekey lines 7–9.

p *Right little* finger

v *Left index* finger

Learn p

1 ; p ;p|pay pay|put put|apt apt|kept kept|pack pack

2 ;p ;p|pain pain|paint paint|paper paper|soap soap;

3 a plan; a party cap; pick a place; a pack of paper

Learn v

4 f v f v|via via|live live|have have|vote vote|save

5 vf vf|van van|visit visit|liver liver|voice voice;

6 five vans; have a visit; very valid; vim and vigor

Combine p and v

7 pave hive open save plan jive soap very pain votes

8 apt to vote; pick a vase; pack the van; five pans;

9 Pam has a plan to have the van pick us up at five.

15C

Key Mastery

 TIP
- Reach up without moving your hands away from your body.
- Reach down without moving your hands toward your body.

Key each line twice.

Reach review
1 jn fr ki ft lo dc jh fg ju fb fv ;p sx jm de jy sw
2 just dear sweat jump fever decade injury swat hush

3rd/1st rows
3 born none mix bore curve more noon bunny comb vice
4 open exit were none trip crop brown money pine pin

Short phrases
5 go to a|they may keep|with your|and the|it will be
6 very much|sure to|a big|make a|too much|to view it

All letters learned
7 Kevin does a top job on your flax farm with Craig.
8 Dixon flew blue jets eight times over a city park.

15D

Shift and Enter Key Technique

 TIP
Keep eyes on copy as you shift and as you tap the Enter key.

Key each line once. At the end of each line, quickly tap the Enter key and immediately start the next line.

1 Dan took a friend to the game.

2 Jan had a double and a single.

3 Bob and Jose Hill will sing a song.

4 Sam and Jo took the test on Monday.

5 Laura sold her old cars to Sandra Smith.

6 Nicky left to play video games with Tim.

7 Jill gave him a good rate on state purchases.

8 Bob may go to the city to work for the firms.

gwam 30" | 2 | 4 | 6 | 8 | 10 | 12 | 14 | 16 |

15E

Critical Thinking Activity

1. To key the names of 13 U.S. states, you have to know the letter *m*. How many of the 13 states can you key?

2. Only three U.S. state names include the letter *p*. How many can you key?

3. Only five U.S. state names include the letter *v*. Can you key them?

4. Four U.S. state names begin with "New." Can you key them?

5. Four U.S. state names begin with either "North" or "South." Can you key them?

LESSON 16 New Keys: q and , (comma)

OUTCOMES

- Learn reach technique for **q** and **,** (**comma**)
- Combine **q** and **,** (**comma**) smoothly with all other learned keys

16A

Warmup

Key each line twice.

All letters learned 1 six buy jam ask dog call vote down fork crop there

p/v 2 five pups; to vote; pay for; very plain; her plan;

All letters learned 3 Jacki Farve played six games on Thursday with Ben.

16B

New Keys: q and , (comma)

q *Left little* finger

, (comma) *Right middle* finger

★TIP Space once after , (comma) used as punctuation.

Key each line twice. If time permits, rekey lines 7–9.

Learn q

1 a q a q|aqua aqua|quote quote|quad quad|quit quits
2 aq|queen queen|quake quake|equip equip|quick quick
3 a square; the quote; a quart; to acquire; is equal

Learn , (comma)

4 k , k , k, k, ,k,|a,b c,d e,f g,h i,j k,l m,n o,p,
5 Monday, Tuesday, Wednesday, Thursday, and Saturday
6 Rob took Janet, Pam, Seth, and Felipe to the game.

Combine q and , (comma)

7 Key the words quit, squad, square, and earthquake.
8 I have quit the squad, Quen; Raquel has quit, too.
9 Quit, quiet, and quaint were on the spelling exam.

16C

Key Mastery

TIP Reach up without moving your hands away from your body.

Key each line twice. If time permits, key lines 7–8 again.

Double letters
1 add egg ill books access three effect otter cheese
2 Betty and Ross will help cook the food for dinner.

q/comma
3 Marquis, Quent, and Quig were quite quick to quit.
4 Quin, Jacqueline, and Paque quickly took the exam.

Short phrases
5 a box|if the call|when you go|if we can|look for a
6 if we go|it is our|up to you|do you see|she took a

All letters learned
7 Jevon will fix my pool deck if the big rain quits.
8 Verna did fly quick jets to map the six big towns.

16D

Practice

Key each line twice. Try to key the line faster the second time.

Adjacent keys

1 df io sa lk er jk re po ds uy ew ui sa jh gf mn cv
2 Erin never asked Wes Ash to save paper; Perry did.

Long direct reaches

3 ym ec rb nu rg vr ny br mu ice nylon mug any dumb;
4 Bryce must bring the ice to the curb for my uncle.

Double letters

5 doll less food good noon call roof pool wall meet;
6 Ann will seek help to get all food cooked by noon.

16E

Critical Thinking

1. Key the sentences below. From the list at the left, choose the name that best completes the sentence.
2. Use the Internet to learn about these five U.S. presidents. Record the years that each person was president, his birth state, and his home state.

Thomas Jefferson

John F. Kennedy

Franklin Roosevelt

George Washington

Woodrow Wilson

1. *The president who drafted the Declaration of Independence was _____.*
2. *The president who was commander in chief of the Continental Army prior to becoming president was _____.*
3. *The president who called for new civil rights legislation in the sixties was _____.*
4. *The president who held office when Pearl Harbor was attacked was _____.*
5. *The president when the United States entered into World War I was _____.*

LESSON 17   Review

OUTCOMES
- Learn to key block paragraphs
- Improve keying technique and speed

17A

Warmup

Key each line twice.

All letters learned   1   Jared helped Maxine quickly fix the big wood vase.

Shift keys   2   Jake and Kathy went to New York City on Wednesday.

Easy   3   Pamela may hang the signs by the door in the hall.

17B

Block Paragraphs

Key each paragraph once. Tap Enter only at the end of the paragraph. Double-space between the paragraphs; then key the paragraphs again at a faster pace.

Paragraph 1

You already know that you can use the Enter key to
space down and start a new line. If you don't use the
Enter key, the insertion point will continue on the
same line until it reaches the right margin. Then it
will automatically space down to the next line.

Paragraph 2

Later in the textbook you will learn how to adjust
the right and left margins to vary the line length.
As you make the line length smaller, the margins
become larger. As you make the line length larger, the
margins become smaller.

 **★TIP** The paragraphs at the right are called "block" paragraphs. This is because all lines begin evenly at the left margin.

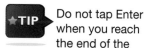 **★TIP** Do not tap Enter when you reach the end of the first line. When a line is full, the next word will automatically jump to the next line. This is called **wordwrap**.

17C

Check Keying Speed

Key a 30" timed writing on each line. Your rate in gross words a minute (*gwam*) is shown below the lines.

1 She owns all of the lake land.
2 The man with the sign may aid them.
3 I may make my goal if I work with vigor.
4 Six of the girls may make a bid for the gown.
5 Laurie and Orlando may make the map of the island.

gwam 30" | 2 | 4 | 6 | 8 | 10 | 12 | 14 | 16 | 18 | 20 |

17D

Build Speed

Key each line twice.

1 I may have six quick jobs to get done for low pay.
2 Vicky packed the box with quail and jam for Jason.
3 Max can plan to bike for just five days with Quig.
4 Jim was quick to get the next top value for Debby.
5 Jack B. Manly requested approval for extra weight.
6 Jacque may have plans for the big dance next week.

gwam 1' | 1 | 2 | 3 | 4 | 5 | 6 | 7 | 8 | 9 | 10 |

17E

Critical Thinking

1. Key the sentences below. From the list at the left, choose the name that best completes the sentence. Do not key the numbers.
2. Use the Internet to learn about these five U.S. presidents. Record the years that each person was president, his birth state, and his home state.

Ulysses S. Grant

Warren G. Harding

Andrew Jackson

Abraham Lincoln

Ronald Reagan

1. _____ *was a military commander in the Civil War prior to becoming president of the United States.*

2. _____ *was the only president to serve in two wars, the Revolutionary War and the War of 1812.*

3. *The Teapot Dome scandal took place when* _____ *was U.S. president.*

4. *He was an actor prior to becoming a public official.* _____ *served two terms as governor of California and two terms as President of the United States.*

5. *This president had no formal education. He was President at the start of the Civil War and was assassinated right before the end of the war. The name of this president was* _____ *.*

WP Applications 4

Activity 1

Margins

Layout tab > Page Setup > Margins

Use the **Margins** feature to change the amount of blank space at the top, bottom, right, and left edges of the paper (see Figure 1-8). The default margin settings are not the same for all software.

1. Open the *df wp4 activity 1* file.
2. Change the margins to the Wide margin option.
3. Change the left and right margins to 2.5" and the top margin to 2" using the Custom Margins option.
4. **Save as:** *wp4 activity 1*.

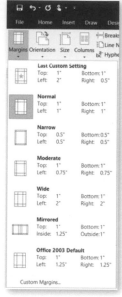

Figure 1-8 Setting margins

Activity 2

Line and Paragraph Spacing

Home tab > Paragraph > Line and Paragraph Spacing

Line and Paragraph Spacing

Use the **Line and Paragraph Spacing** feature to change the amount of white space left between lines of text and between paragraphs. Single spacing, one-and-a-half spacing, and double spacing are common to most software.

Microsoft *Word* adds a little more white space at the end of paragraphs. The amount of space added depends on the size of the type being used. This allows a little more white space between lines of type than a default setting of 1. The default is treated as single spacing.

1. Open the *df wp4 activity 2* file.
2. Move the cursor to the end of the file following the word *spacing*.
3. Change the line spacing to 1 and *Remove Space After Paragraph*.
4. Finish keying the first line and the next three lines shown below. (The line numbers will appear automatically; you will not need to key them.)

   1. Click the I-beam where you want the line spacing changed.
   2. Access the Line and Paragraph Spacing feature.
   3. Specify the line spacing.
   4. Begin or continue keying.

5. After keying the last line, copy and paste the four lines a triple space below the last line.
6. Select the last four lines and change the line spacing to 2.0.
7. **Save as:** *wp4 activity 2*.

Basic Technology Skills 4 — Windows OS Basics

OUTCOMES
- Open applications
- Learn the parts of a **Windows** application
- Resize, minimize, maximize, and restore windows
- Learn more about pointers

Open Applications

Your computer gives you several different ways of starting applications, depending on the operating system and version.

- The application you want may appear on the Start screen as a tile. Click the tile to start the application.

- Click the *Type here to search* box in the lower-left corner of the desktop. Key the name of the application you wish to open in the **search box**. In Figure BT4-1, we are searching for *PowerPoint*. As you start to key the word, application programs that contain the word appear on the list of results. Click the app to begin work.

- An application's icon may appear on the desktop or be pinned to the **taskbar** along the bottom of the screen (see Figure BT4-2). Double-click the shortcut icon or just click the taskbar icon to start the app.

Applications containing the words you type appear above the search box

Key application name here

Figure BT4-1 Search for apps

Shortcut icon on desktop

App pinned to taskbar

Figure BT4-2 Start apps from the desktop

Parts of a Windows Application

The *Windows* OS opens each application in a separate frame called a **window**. That is how the *Windows* OS got its name. Many windows look similar to each other even though they may contain different applications. In Figure BT4-3, look at the parts in an application called *PowerPoint*. Like many applications, it has a **Ribbon** where all the commands are displayed.

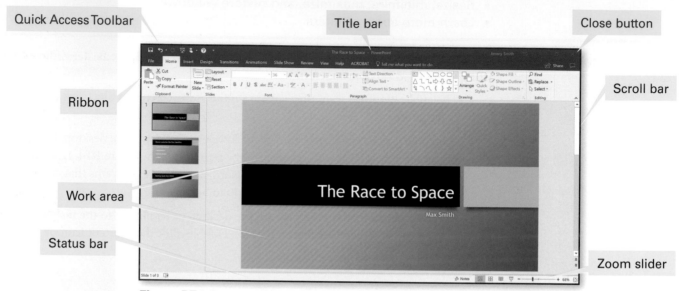

Figure BT4-3 *PowerPoint* application window

Other open windows may have slightly different parts. For example, an application used to edit photos has a menu bar and buttons for issuing commands as well as window control buttons. (See them in Figure BT4-4.)

NOTE **The Quick Access Toolbar** is always visible and provides one-click access to the Save, Undo, and Redo commands as well as the ability to optimize for Touch or Mouse interaction.

Figure BT4-4 An application window with menus and buttons

1. Start *Windows*, if necessary. Move the pointer to the *Type here to search* box.
2. Key *PowerPoint* in the search box.
3. Click *PowerPoint* in the list of results.
4. When the *PowerPoint* window opens, click *Blank Presentation*. In the new presentation, look for the parts shown in Figure BT4-3.
5. Click the *Click to add title* placeholder and key your name.
6. Click the minus (–) sign on the Zoom slider. Then click the plus (+) sign. Notice what happens to your name.
7. Close *PowerPoint* by clicking the *Close* button as shown in Figure BT4-3. (Do not save.)

Resize, Minimize, Maximize, and Restore Windows

Application windows can be different sizes and placed in different areas on the desktop. If a window does not cover the entire desktop, you can move it or resize it.

To move a window, click the title bar and drag the window. To resize a window, place the pointer on the top, bottom, or side edge of the window to display a double-sided arrow. Then drag in the direction you want to resize. To change the height and width of a window at the same time, hover the pointer over a corner. The pointer will change shape to a diagonal double-sided arrow as shown in Figure BT4-5. Click and drag the arrow in any direction until the application is the size you want it to be.

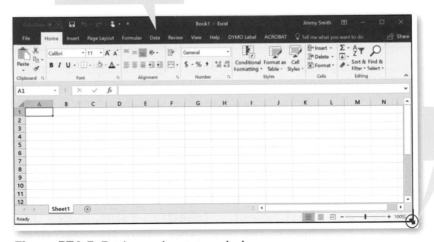

Figure BT4-5 Resize and move a window

You can "hide" an application window by clicking its **Minimize** button. (See Figure BT4-6.) This sends the window to the taskbar. This is called *minimizing* the window. When you minimize a window, its program does not close. It simply moves from the screen. To display the window again, click that program's icon on the taskbar.

To make the window fill the entire screen, click the **Maximize** button. To restore a window to its previous size, click the **Restore Down** button. Practice with these buttons in the next activity.

The Maximize and Restore Down buttons trade places depending on the size of the window. When a window is full size, the Restore Down button displays so you can reduce the size of the window. When the window is not full size, the Maximize button displays so you can make the window full size.

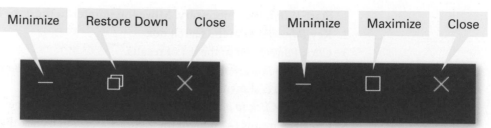

Figure BT4-6 Minimize, Maximize, Restore Down, and Close buttons

1. Start *Excel*.
2. If the program window does not cover the entire desktop, click the *Maximize* button. The window changes to full size.
3. Click the *Restore Down* button. The window is now smaller than full-screen size.
4. Hover the mouse pointer over the lower-right corner of the *Excel* window. When the pointer changes to a double-sided arrow, click and drag down and to the right to make the window bigger. (See Figure BT4-5 on page 1–62.)
5. Click the *Minimize* button shown in Figure BT4-6. The window disappears from the screen, but the *Excel* icon in the taskbar shows a colored bar under it to show there is an open file.
6. Restore *Excel* by clicking its icon on the taskbar.
7. Hover the mouse pointer over the lower-right corner of the window. Use the double-sided arrow to make the window smaller.
8. Click and drag the *Excel* title bar to move the window to the upper-right corner of the screen. Then move it to the lower-left corner of the screen.
9. Close *Excel*.

Learn More about Pointers

The pointer sometimes changes shape. The shape lets you know what you can do at a particular place on the desktop. Study Table BT4-1 to learn about the most common pointer shapes. You will discover a few new ones when you complete the next activity using the *Paint* application.

Table BT4-1 Mouse and pen pointer shapes

 Select or **Arrow**. Tells you where the mouse is located as you move it across the screen.

 Text Select or **Insertion Point**. Moves the insertion point (flashing line) to the exact spot where you need to key words or numbers. Also helps you select text.

 Spinning Circle. Tells you that the system is busy and that you need to wait.

 Double-Sided Arrow. Appears when you are hovering over a place where you can resize an object.

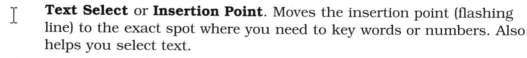 **Move** or **Four-Sided Arrow**. Lets you know when an object can be moved.

 Link Select or **Pointing Hand**. Appears when there is a link you can click.

 Handwriting or **Pen**. Used for handwriting recognition.

1. Start the *Paint* program and click the *Maximize* button if necessary.
2. Point to different icons on the Ribbon. Hesitate for a few seconds over each icon. The name and a brief description of each will appear. For example, Figure BT4-7 shows the pointer hovering over the Pencil tool so that its name and description appear.

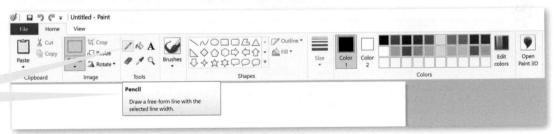

Point to icons to read description of tool

Figure BT4-7 Read the on-screen tip for each tool

3. Click the *Fill with color* tool; it looks like a bucket spilling paint. Move the pointer down to a blank part of the window. Notice how the pointer changes appearance to look like a bucket.
4. Next, click the *Magnifier* tool; it looks like a magnifying glass. Move back to the work area and see how your pointer changes to display the tool with which you are working.
5. Click the *Pencil* on the toolbar (see Figure BT4-7). Move the pointer to the work area. Click and hold the mouse button and drag the pencil pointer to write your first name. You can release the mouse button to add spaces between letters.
6. Choose a different color from the Colors tool palette and write your last name.
7. Click the *Eraser* on the Home tab. Drag it to erase one letter of your name.
8. Use *Paint* to practice drawing. Try many of the tools and colors on the tabs and tool palettes. Experiment!
9. Click the *Paint* window's *Close* button. (Do not save.)

LESSON 18 — New Keys: z and : (colon)

OUTCOMES

- Learn reach technique for **z** and **: (colon)**
- Combine **z** and **: (colon)** smoothly with all other learned keys

18A

Warmup

Key each line twice.

All letters learned 1 Max was a big star when he played for Jack Vasque.

Shift keys 2 Ramon Santos; Karl Jones; Kate Van Noy; Sue McMan;

Easy 3 Jan and Bob may work with the maid on the problem.

18B

New Keys: z and : (colon)

z Left little finger

: (colon) Right little finger + Left Shift

⭐TIP ▶ Space once after : used as punctuation.

Key each line twice. If time permits, rekey lines 7–9.

Learn z

1 a z az za za|zap zap|zoo zoo|zone zone|azure azure
2 zip zip|zinc zinc|quiz quiz|zera zero|Zelda Zelda;
3 speed zone; a zigzag; a zoology quiz; puzzle size;

Learn : (colon)

4 ; : ;: :; :;|a:b c:d e:f g:h i:j k:l m:n o:p q:r :
5 To: From: Date: Subject: To: Jason Drew Kummerfeld
6 To: Max Tobin|From: Jerry Duncan|Dear Mr. Maxwell:

Combine z and : (colon)

7 Please key these words: amazed, seize, and zigzag.
8 Hazel reads: Shift to enter: and then space twice.
9 Zane will use these labels: City: State: ZIP Code:

18C

Key Mastery

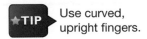

★TIP Use curved, upright fingers.

Key each line twice. If time permits, key lines 5–6 again.

q/z
1 quiz quartz amaze quote Amazon mosque muzzle quick
2 Zane amazed us all on the quiz but quit the squad.

x/comma
3 six, box, tax, axle, next, extra, exhibit, example
4 Lexi, Rex, and Felix went to Texas to the exhibit.

v/m
5 move save moon visit imply valve most vain improve
6 Melvin, Kevin, or Matt drove the van to Las Vegas.

18D

Key Block Paragraphs

1. Key each paragraph once. Tap Enter only at the end of the paragraph.
2. Key a 1' timed writing on each paragraph. Use the numbers and dots above the words to determine *gwam*. Each dot indicates one additional word. For example, if you key to the end of *average* in line 1, you have keyed nine words.

Paragraph 1

```
       •    2    •    4    •    6    •    8    •
The space bar is used frequently. On average,
   10    •   12    •   14    •   16    •   18
every fifth or sixth stroke is a space when you
 •    20    •   22    •   24    •   26    •   28
key. If you use good techniques, you will be able
 •    30    •   32    •
to increase your speed.
```

Paragraph 2

```
       •    2    •    4    •    6    •    8    •
Just keep the thumb low over the space bar. Move
 10    •   12    •   14    •   16    •   18    •
the thumb down and in quickly towards the palm of
 20    •   22    •   24    •   26    •   28    •
your hand to get the prized stroke you need to
   30    •   32
build top skill.
```

LESSON 19 — New Keys: Caps Lock and ?

OUTCOMES
- Learn reach technique for **Caps Lock** and **?**
- Combine **Caps Lock** and **?** smoothly with all other learned keys

19A

Warmup

Key each line twice.

Alphabet 1 Jack P. Hildo may buy five quartz rings next week.

x/z 2 excess zebra fixture zoology exact zest extra zero

Easy 3 Jay is to turn to the right when the signal turns.

gwam 1' | 1 | 2 | 3 | 4 | 5 | 6 | 7 | 8 | 9 | 10 |

19B

New Keys: Caps Lock and ?

The **Caps Lock** key is used to key a series of capital letters. To key capital letters, tap the Caps Lock key. Key the letters that are to appear in capitals. Then tap the Caps Lock key again to turn off this feature.

Key each line twice. If time permits, rekey lines 7–9.

Caps Lock *Left little* finger

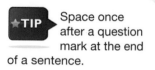

? (question mark) *Right little* finger + Left Shift

★TIP Space once after a question mark at the end of a sentence.

Learn Caps Lock

1 Put CUBS and CARDS and METS and EXPOS on the sign.
2 OHIO STATE plays INDIANA on Wednesday or Thursday.
3 Microsoft is MSFT; Intel is INTC; Coca Cola is KO.

Learn ? (question mark)

4 ; ? ; ? ;?|g?h i?j k?l m?n o?p q?r s?t u?v w?x y?z
5 Who? Who? What? What? When? When? Why? Why? Where?
6 Ask who? Are you sure? What time? Where is Glenda?

Combine Caps Lock and ?

7 What symbol is DIS? What symbol is YHOO? Did Bill?
8 What does CPA stand for? What does CFO stand for?
9 Did your mother use NB, NE, or NEBR. for NEBRASKA?

19C

Key Mastery

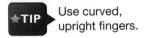

TIP Use curved, upright fingers.

Key each line twice. If time permits, key lines 5–6 again.

z/v
1 David and Zack Valdez zipped through both quizzes.
2 Vizquel, Alvarez, Chavez, and Gonzalez have voted.

q/p
3 Quincy quickly put the papers next to the puppies.
4 Paul quickly keyed: quota, opaque, parquet, equip.

x/c
5 Carl Drexler stood next to Connie Cox and Tex Cey.
6 Rex Cain and Max Carr paid the extra tax for Carl.

19D

Key Block Paragraphs

Key each paragraph once. Tap Enter only at the end of the paragraph. Key a 1' timed writing on each paragraph. Determine your *gwam*.

Paragraph 1

```
        •    2    •    4    •    6    •    8    •
Before long you will key copy that is written in
 10    •    12    •    14    •    16    •    18    •
script. Script copy is copy that is written with
  20    •    22    •    24    •    26    •    28    •
pen or pencil. With practice, you will be able
    30    •    32    •    34    •
to key script at a rapid rate.
```

Paragraph 2

```
        •    2    •    4    •    6    •    8    •    10
A rough draft is a draft that is not yet in final
    •    12    •    14    •    16    •    18    •
form. It is where the writer can get his or her
  20    •    22    •    24    •    26    •    28    •
thoughts down on paper. After the rough draft is
    30    •    32    •    34    •    36    •    38    •
completed, it is ready to be edited. It may take
    40    •    42    •    44    •    46    •    48
several edits before it is put in final form.
```

LESSON 20   New Keys: Backspace, Tab, and Quotation Mark (")

OUTCOMES

- Learn reach technique for **Backspace, Tab,** and **quotation mark**
- Combine **Backspace, Tab,** and **quotation mark** smoothly with all other learned keys

20A

Warmup

Key each line twice.

Alphabet   1   Quig just fixed prize vases he won at my key club.

Caps Lock   2   Find ZIP Codes for the cities in WYOMING and IOWA.

Easy   3   It may be a problem if both girls go to the docks.

gwam 1' | 1 | 2 | 3 | 4 | 5 | 6 | 7 | 8 | 9 | 10 |

20B

New Key: Backspace

Backspace *Right little* finger

★TIP This symbol means to delete. ℘

The **Backspace** key is used to delete characters. You should key the Backspace key with your right little finger. Keep your index finger anchored to the **J** key as you tap Backspace. Tap the Backspace key once for each letter to be deleted. Then return the finger to the **;** key. When you hold down the Backspace key, letters to the left of the insertion point will be deleted until the Backspace key is released.

Use the Backspace key to edit the sentence as instructed.

1. Key the following.

   The delete

2. Use the Backspace key to make the change shown below.

   The ~~delete~~ backspace

3. Continue keying the sentence as shown below.

   The backspace key can be

4. Use the Backspace key to make the change shown below.

   The backspace key ~~can be~~ is

5. Continue keying the sentence as shown below.

   The backspace key is used to fix

6. Use the Backspace key to make the change shown below.

   The backspace key is used to ~~fix~~ make

7. Continue keying the sentence shown below.

   The backspace key is used to make changes.

New Key: Tab

Tab key *Left little* finger

★TIP Click the **Show/Hide ¶** button in the Paragraph group of the Home tab to display nonprinting characters. Tab appears as a right arrow (→).

The **Tab** key is used to move the insertion point to a specific location on the line. For example, Tab can be used to indent the first line of a paragraph. Word processing software has preset tabs called *default* tabs. Usually, the first default tab is set 0.5" to the right of the left margin. This tab setting is used to indent paragraphs as shown below.

Key each paragraph once. If time permits, key them again.

Tab → The tab key is used to indent blocks of copy such as these.

Tab → It should also be used for tables to arrange data quickly and neatly into columns.

Tab → Learn how to use the tab key by touch; doing so will add to your keying skill.

Tab → Tap the tab key very quickly. Begin keying the line immediately after you tap the tab key.

New Key: Quotation Mark

Quotation Mark: Press Left Shift and tap " (shift of ') with the *right little* finger.

Key each line twice; DS between 2-line groups.

Learn " (quotation mark)

1 ;; "; "; ";" ";" "I believe," she said, "you won."

2 "John Adams," he said, "was the second President."

3 "James Monroe," I said, "was the fifth President,"

4 Alison said "attitude" determines your "altitude."

NOTE: On your screen, quotation marks may look different from those shown in these lines.

Tab and Backspace

Key each paragraph once. Use the Backspace key to correct errors as you key. If time permits, key the paragraphs again.

Tab → George Washington was the first president of the United States. Before becoming president, he played a key role in helping the colonies gain their freedom.

Tab → Washington was the commander of the Continental Army. Much has been written about the winter he and his army spent at Valley Forge.

Tab → Washington played a critical role in the history of the United States of America and is often referred to as the father of our country.

Check Speed

Key each paragraph once. Double-space between paragraphs. Key a 1' timed writing on each paragraph and then determine *gwam*.

E all letters used

```
        •    2    •    4    •    6    •    8    •
    How you key is just as vital as the copy you
  10    •   12    •   14    •   16    •   18    •
work from or produce. What you put on paper is a
  20    •   22    •   24    •   26    •   28
direct result of the way in which you do the job.
        •    2    •    4    •    6    •    8    •
    If you expect to grow quickly in speed, take
  10    •   12    •   14    •   16    •   18    •
charge of your mind. It will then tell your eyes
  20    •   22    •   24    •   26    •   28    •
and hands how to work through the maze of letters.
```

Critical Thinking

Delaware

Lake Michigan

Lake Superior

Mt. McKinley

Mt. Rainier

Rhode Island

Vermont

Wyoming

Yellowstone National Park

Zion National Park

Key the sentences below. From the list at the left, choose the word or words that best complete the sentence. Do not key the numbers.

1. The oldest national park in the United States is _____.
2. The highest mountain peak in the United States is _____.
3. The largest lake in the United States is _____.
4. The smallest state is _____.
5. The state with the least population is _____.

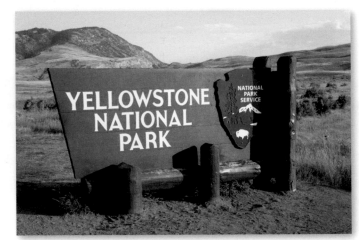

Zack Frank/Shutterstock.com

LESSON 21   New Keys: Apostrophe (') and Hyphen (-)

OUTCOMES

- Learn reach technique for ' (apostrophe) and - (hyphen)
- Improve and check keying speed

21A

Warmup

Key each line twice.

alphabet 1 Glenn saw a quick red fox jump over the lazy cubs.

caps lock 2 STACY works for HPJ, Inc.; SAMANTHA, for JPH Corp.

easy 3 Kamela may work with the city auditor on the form.

gwam 1' | 1 | 2 | 3 | 4 | 5 | 6 | 7 | 8 | 9 | 10 |

21B

**New Keys:
' (Apostrophe)
and - (Hyphen)**

★TIP On your screen, apostrophes may look different from those shown in these lines.

Key each line twice.

Learn ' (apostrophe)

1 ;' ;' ;' '; '; I've told you it's hers, haven't I.

2 I'm sure it's Ray's. I'll return it if he's home.

3 I've been told it isn't up to us; it's up to them.

Learn - (hyphen)

4 ;- ;- -;- -;- - on the up-and-up; play tug-of-war;

5 part-time job; attorney-at-law; my brother-in-law;

6 The sources are up-to-date. Joan works part-time.

Combine ' and -

7 ;' ;' ;- ;- ;-' ;-' -'; -'; up-to-date list; x-ray

8 Didn't he say it couldn't be done? I don't agree.

9 I told him the off-the-cuff comment wasn't needed.

10 That isn't a cause-and-effect relationship, is it?

11 The well-known guest is a hard-hitting outfielder.

12 Put an apostrophe in let's, it's, isn't, and don't.

Apostrophe *Right little*
finger

Hyphen Reach *up* to
hyphen with *right little*
finger

21C

Speed Check: Sentences

Key two 30" timings on each line. Your rate in *gwam* is shown word-for-word below the lines.

	gwam 30"
When do you think you will go?	12
Tara just finished taking her exam.	14
Nancy told the man to fix the car brake.	16
Val could see that he was angry with the boy.	18
Karen may not be able to afford college next year.	20

gwam 30" | 2 | 4 | 6 | 8 | 10 | 12 | 14 | 16 | 18 | 20 |

If you finish a line before time is called and start over, your *gwam* is the figure at the end of the line PLUS the figure above or below the point at which you stopped.

21D

Speed Building

1. Key each line twice.
2. Key a 1' writing on each line; determine *gwam* on each timing.

1 Pamela may make a profit off the land by the lake.

2 Eight of the firms may handle the work for Rodney.

3 Vivian may make a map of the city for the six men.

4 Helen held a formal social for eight of the girls.

5 He may work with the men on the city turn signals.

6 The dog and the girl slept in a chair in the hall.

gwam 1' | 1 | 2 | 3 | 4 | 5 | 6 | 7 | 8 | 9 | 10 |

21E

Speed Check: Paragraphs

Key two 1' timings on each paragraph; determine *gwam* on each timing.

 all letters used

         •   2   •   4   •   6   •   8   •
     Are you one of the people who often look from
10 • 12 • 14 • 16 • 18 •
the copy to the screen and down at your hands? If
20 • 22 • 24 • 26 • 28 •
you are, you can be sure that you will not build a
30 • 32 • 34 • 36 • 38 •
speed to prize. Make eyes on copy your next goal.
         •   2   •   4   •   6   •   8   •
     When you move the eyes from the copy to check
10 • 12 • 14 • 16 • 18 •
the screen, you may lose your place and waste time
20 • 22 • 24 • 26 • 28 •
trying to find it. Lost time can lower your speed
30 • 32 • 34 • 36 • 38 •
quickly and in a major way, so do not look away.

WP Applications 5

Activity 1

Tabs

 View tab > Show > Ruler

 Left tab

Right tab

Most software has left tabs already set at half-inch (0.5") intervals from the left margin. However, tabs can be set at intervals you determine. When you set a tab, the preset tabs are automatically cleared up to the point where you set the tab. Most software lets you set left tabs, right tabs, and decimal tabs. You will work with decimal tabs in a later chapter.

Left tabs align all text evenly at the left by placing the text you key to the right of the tab setting. Left tabs are commonly used to align words.

Right tabs align all text evenly at the right by placing the text you key to the left of the tab setting. Right tabs are commonly used to align whole numbers.

1. Open the *df wp5 activity 1* file.
2. DS after the heading and set a left tab at **2"** and at **4.5"**.
3. Key the four lines a DS below the heading using these tab settings. TS after keying the fourth line.

Left tab at 2"	Left tab at 4.5"
(Tab) Sheryl Ho (Tab)	Moorcroft (Enter)
Hector Lopez	Gillette
Pierre Pizarro	Upton
Janice Robinson	Sundance

4. Reset a left tab at **1"** and at **5"**; key the lines again.
5. Save as: *wp5 activity 1*.

Activity 2

Apply What You Have Learned

1. Create a new document and key lines 1–6, applying formatting as shown. Do not key the line numbers.

1. **Kennedy** was a *Democrat*; **Lincoln** was a *Republican*.
2. Is the correct choice <u>two</u>, <u>too</u>, or <u>to</u>?
3. Is *Harry Potter and the Deathly Hallows* still on the bestseller list?
4. There was an article on her in the *New York Times*.
5. Are the names to be **bolded** or <u>underlined</u> or **<u>bolded and underlined</u>**?
6. The <u>underscore</u> is being used less frequently than *italic*.

2. After keying the lines, make the following changes.
   line 1
   Change *Kennedy* to *Washington* and *Democrat* to *Federalist*.
   line 4
   Change *New York Times* to *Washington Post*.
   line 6
   Delete *frequently*. Insert or **bold** after *italic*.
3. Save as: *wp5 activity 2*.

Activity 3

Apply What You Have Learned

1. Open *df wp5 activity 3*.
2. Use the Select Text feature to select and change the formatting of the copy using bold and italic as shown below.
3. Use the copy and paste feature to arrange the presidents in the order they served: Roosevelt 1901–1909, Wilson 1913–1921, Truman 1945–1953, Reagan 1981–1989.
4. Save as: *wp5 activity 3*.

Harry S. Truman: *"The American people stand firm in the faith which has inspired this Nation from the beginning. We believe that all men have a right to equal justice under law and equal opportunity to share in the common good. We believe that all men have the right to freedom of thought and expression."*

Theodore Roosevelt: *"Much has been given us, and much will rightfully be expected from us. We have duties to others and duties to ourselves; and we can shirk neither."*

Ronald Reagan: *"We are a nation that has a government--not the other way around. And this makes us special among the nations of the Earth. Our government has no power except that granted it by the people. It is time to check and reverse the growth of government, which shows signs of having grown beyond the consent of the governed."*

Woodrow Wilson: *"We have built up, moreover, a great system of government, which has stood through a long age as in many respects a model for those who seek to set liberty upon foundations that will endure against fortuitous change, against storm and accident."*

Activity 4

Apply What You Have Learned

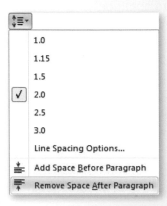

1. Open a new document.
2. Set the Line Spacing to 2.
3. Remove Space After Paragraph (see illustration at left).
4. Set left tabs at 2.5 and 5.
5. Key the following.

Please invite the following individuals to be our guests at the July 15 reception:

Mr. and Mrs. Jason Beckett	Dr. Michelle White	Ms. Faye Culver
Ms. Maria Ortiz	Ms. Maxine Aguilar	Ms. Alexandra Harper
Mr. Ashton Schumann	Dr. Theodore Benning	Mr. Mitchell Parizo
Mr. and Mrs. Paul Sorrento	Mr. and Ms. Jay Becker	Mrs. Stephen Chen
Mrs. Alison Greenfield	Mr. Felipe Nolan	Dr. Janette Ramirez

6. Save as: *wp5 activity 4*.

Basic Technology Skills 5 | Exploring and Organizing Your Digital Space

OUTCOMES
- Learn about storage spaces
- Navigate files and folders in **Windows**
- Create folders
- Rename and delete folders
- Copy and move folders
- Follow a path to a folder or file

Storage Spaces

You will want to save your important information, called *data*. Digital data is stored in files. You can create and save text, pictures, video, and sound files. You can store (or save) your files in a variety of storage places:

- On your PC, tablet, or smartphone
- On peripherals connected to your PC
- On local networks
- On the Internet

> **NOTE** Portable storage tools go by many names: USB flash drives, pen drives, jump drives, thumb drives, key drives, and memory sticks.

On your PC: A hard drive is the most common storage device inside a computer. Tablets and phones often use **solid state drives (SSDs)**.

On peripherals connected to your PC: **USB flash drives** and memory cards are common storage devices (see Figure BT5-1). USB drives are common on PCs, and memory cards are common on tablets, cameras, and cell phones. They are small enough that you can take them with you wherever you go.

Bomshtein/Shutterstock.com
ExaMedia Photography/Shutterstock.com
Blackboard/Shutterstock.com

Figure BT5-1 USB flash drives, memory cards, and the cloud are common storage locations

On local networks: You may be asked to save on your school's local network. This is often called a **LAN**, or **local area network**. To use a LAN, you need an account. Since many people can save to the same network, security is an issue. To keep networks safe, LAN accounts require login names and passwords. After you connect to your network, you can save your files in your own assigned folders. Local networks are managed by experts called **system administrators**.

On the Internet: The Internet is the biggest network of all. You can save your information to a storage service provider over the Internet instead of on your personal computer or on your school's LAN. This is called "saving to the **cloud**."

There are several advantages to saving files online. When you save on the Internet, you do not need to carry around a laptop, USB flash drive, CD, or memory card. You can access your files from any computer connected to the web. Also, if your hard drive crashes, you do not need to worry. Your files will still be safe online. Many Internet-based companies let you save online for free or for a small fee. Google, Amazon, Dropbox, and Apple will let you save to their cloud storage. Microsoft *Office 365* allows you to save to **OneDrive** using the Save As command on the File tab, as shown in Figure BT5-2. You can also turn on the AutoSave feature to automatically save your documents to OneDrive as you work. Subscriptions to *Office 365* include OneDrive storage. Using a login name and a password, you can open an account for these services. You can store word processing, spreadsheet, presentation, picture, video, email, and many other types of files.

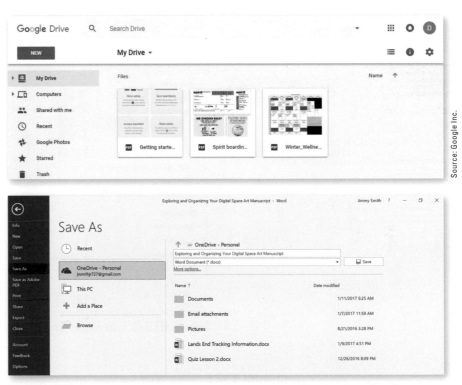

Source: Google Inc.

Figure BT5-2 Google and Microsoft let you save files in the cloud

1. Start *Word* and open the document *df bt5 saving spaces*.
2. Print the document and then close it.
3. Using information supplied by your instructor, complete the table. Keep this document as a reference guide to places you can store your files.

Navigate Files and Folders in File Explorer

Files are used to store digital information. Files can be stored inside **folders**. Think of a folder as a box in which you can put all of your files. Inside the box, you can put smaller boxes. System administrators often call these **subfolders**.

Good file organization begins with giving your files and folders names that are logical, relevant, and easy to understand. You can use *File Explorer* to see how files and folders are organized on your computer (see Figure BT5-3). This feature may be somewhat different on your computer, depending on your *Windows* version and setup.

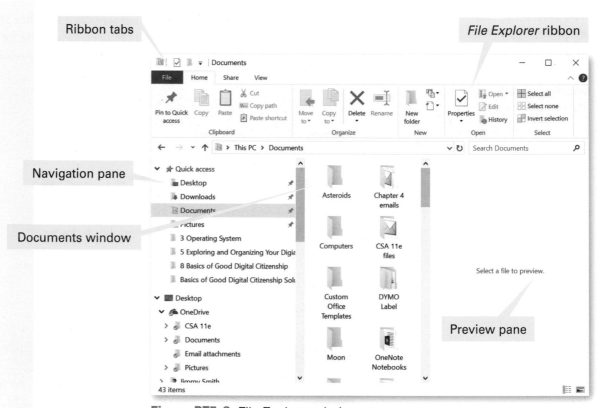

Figure BT5-3 *File Explorer* window

As in *Word*, *File Explorer* uses the Ribbon to organize common tasks, such as copying and moving, creating new folders, and changing the view. *File Explorer* has four tabs—File, Home, Share, and View. The File tab contains file and folder commands. The Home tab contains commands such as Copy, Paste, Move to, Delete, and Rename. The Share tab lets you email files or folders and even burn them to a disc. The View tab lets you specify how the *File Explorer* window is laid out, how files are displayed, and how *Windows* sorts your icons.

1. Start *Windows* if necessary.
2. Click *File Explorer* in the Start menu. *File Explorer* opens and displays the resources on your computer.

★TIP You can also open *File Explorer* by clicking the File Explorer icon on the taskbar.

3. Click a folder in the Navigation pane such as the Documents folder. The Home tab displays. Notice the various functions you can perform in the Home tab.
4. Click the *Share* and *View* tabs to see the functions you can perform in each.
5. In the Navigation pane, click *Desktop*. Notice the contents of the desktop are now displayed. Click other places in the Navigation pane to see what changes.
6. Click *This PC* in the Navigation pane. Click the triangle to the left of *This PC*. (If you don't see a triangle, hover the mouse over the Navigation pane.) Notice the folders that appear.
7. Click one of the folders. The contents of the folder are displayed.
8. Some of the folders displayed may have triangles beside them. Click right-facing triangles to display subfolders, and click downward-facing triangles to close the display of subfolders.
9. Within a subfolder, click one of the files inside. Click the *View* tab and then click *Preview pane* in the Panes group to see a preview of the contents of the file.
10. Close *File Explorer* by clicking the *File* tab and clicking *Close*.

Create Folders

Home tab > New >
New folder

NOTE For the following activities, your instructor may direct you to create your folders in a different place. Substitute with the directions that your instructor gives you.

You need to give each new folder a name. The name should tell you the type of information in the folder. This way you can find files more easily. For example, you can place a file called All about Moon Rocks in the Moon Rocks folder. (You would not place it in a folder called Maps to Mars.)

Let's take a closer look at the Home tab of File Explorer in Figure BT5-4. From the Home tab, you can create, rename, delete, copy, paste, and move folders.

Figure BT5-4 *File Explorer* Home tab

1. Open *File Explorer*. Click *This PC*.
2. Select the *Documents* folder.
3. Click *New folder* on the Home tab.
4. Where you see New folder, key *Computers* (see Figure BT5-5).

TIP You also may right-click the middle of the Documents window, click *New*, and then click *Folder* from the pop-up menu.

Figure BT5-5 Name a folder

5. Tap *Enter* or click outside the folder to have the computer accept the folder name you keyed in step 4.

6. Create eight new folders in your Documents folder. Use the following names for the folders:

Space	*Stars*
Moon Rocks	*Perfect Planets*
Maps to Mars	*Comets*
Saturn	*Asteroids*

 **checkpoint** Do you have nine new folders? One folder should be named Computers. The others should have the names shown in step 6.

Rename and Delete Folders

★TIP You can also rename a folder by right-clicking the folder and choosing *Rename* from the pop-up menu. Key the new name. You can also delete folders using the right-click method.

Sometimes you decide a different name would be better for a folder. Some folders are no longer needed and should be deleted. You can use the Rename and Delete commands on the *File Explorer* Home tab to accomplish these tasks.

1. Reopen *File Explorer* if necessary and select the *Documents* folder.
2. Click the *Perfect Planets* folder to select it.
3. Click *Rename* on the Home tab.
4. Key the new name **Planets** and tap *Enter* to confirm the new name.
5. Rename the *Moon Rocks* folder to the new name **Moon**.
6. Click the *Comets* folder to select it.
7. Click the *Delete* button on the Home tab.
8. Choose *Yes* if you see a Delete Folder dialog box to confirm that you want to send the folder to the Recycle Bin (see Figure BT5-6).

Figure BT5-6 Confirm delete

9. Delete the folders Maps to Mars and Asteroids. Click *Yes* to confirm that you want to send each folder to the Recycle Bin.

Copy and Move Folders

A folder that is inside another folder is called a *subfolder*. Subfolders hold information related to the topic of a main folder. In Figure BT5-7, the Space folder shows four subfolders: Moon, Planets, Saturn, and Stars. To create a subfolder, copy or move a folder into another folder.

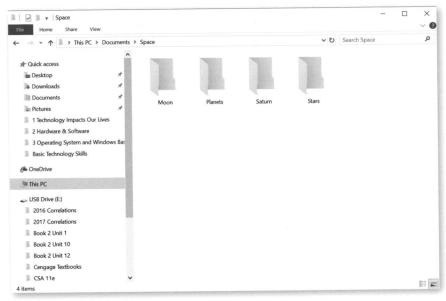

Figure BT5-7 Subfolders inside the Space folder

Move a Folder by Dragging

You can move folders into other folders by selecting and dragging them.

1. Reopen your Documents folder using *File Explorer* if necessary.
2. Click the *Moon* folder and drag it on top of the *Stars* folder as shown in Figure BT5-8.
3. Practice by dragging the *Stars* folder into the *Space* folder in the same way.

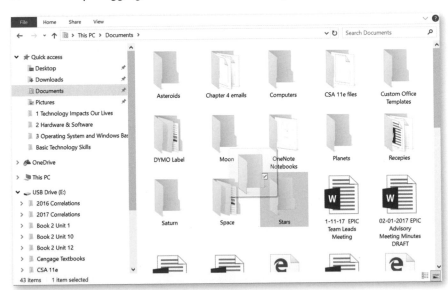

Figure BT5-8 Move a folder by dragging it to a new location

★TIP Another way to move a folder is to use the *Move to* command on the Home tab.
1. Select the folder to move.
2. Click the *Move to* button.
3. Click *Choose location* at the bottom of the drop-down menu.
4. In the Move Items dialog box, navigate to the folder you want to move into.
5. Click *Move* to complete the move.

Home tab > Clipboard > Copy, Cut, or Paste

Copy or Move a Folder Using Ribbon Commands

You can use the Copy or Cut and Paste commands to copy or move a folder.

1. Click the *Planets* folder.
2. Click the *Copy* button on the Home tab.
3. Double-click the *Space* folder to open it.
4. Finally, click *Paste* on the Home tab and the Planets folder is pasted into the Space folder.
5. Use the Up arrow to the left of the path box to move up a level (back to the Documents folder). Click the *Saturn* folder.
6. Click the *Cut* button on the Home tab.
7. Open the Space folder and then click *Paste* to move the Saturn folder into the Space folder.
8. Move up a level and double-click the *Computers* folder to open it.
9. Create 12 new subfolders inside the Computers folder. Create folders for Chapter 1, Chapter 2, Chapter 3, and so on, up to Chapter 17. Your instructor may ask you to use these folders to store files you work with in this course.
10. Close *File Explorer*.

 TIP To navigate to a higher level folder, click the Up arrow just to the left of the address bar that displays below the Ribbon.

 checkpoint Do you have four subfolders (Moon, Planets, Saturn, and Stars) in your Space folder?

Follow a Path to a Folder or File

As you work with applications, you will find that you sometimes must follow a precise path through your folders to the files you need. The **path** for a file is shown in the address box just below the Ribbon in *File Explorer*. You can also see the path at the top of dialog boxes such as Save As or Open.

A path statement can be written in a type of shorthand from folder to folder until you get to your file. For example:

Documents\Space\Planets\Saturn\All about Saturn.docx

NOTE The marks (\) between folder names are called *backslashes*.

1. Open *File Explorer*.
2. Follow this path to locate the Planets folder that you copied earlier to the Space folder: *Documents\Planets*.
3. Right-click the *Planets* folder in the Navigation pane and then click *Delete* on the shortcut menu.
4. If necessary, click *Yes* to confirm the deletion.
5. Close *File Explorer*.

Communication Skills 1

1. Study each of the eight rules.
   a. Key Learn line(s) beneath each rule, noting how the rule is applied.
   b. Key Apply line(s), using correct capitalization.

Rule 1: Capitalize the first word of a sentence, personal titles, and names of people.

Learn 1   Ask President Beck to invite Mr. Joseph Alexander to the meeting.

Apply 2   do you have name tags for mr. and mrs. justin van buren?

Rule 2: Capitalize days of the week and months of the year.

Learn 3   The next meeting will be on the first Friday of November.

Apply 4   the event was planned for the first monday of april, not may.

Rule 3: Capitalize cities, states, countries, and specific geographic features.

Learn 5   They visited the Napa Valley region near San Francisco, California.

Apply 6   when in france, we saw paris from atop the eiffel tower.

Rule 4: Capitalize names of clubs, schools, companies, and other organizations.

Learn 7   The Utah Leadership Conference was hosted by Logan High School.

Apply 8   she competed in the nike women's half marathon in san francisco.

Rule 5: Capitalize historic periods, holidays, and events.

Learn 9   The Fourth of July celebrates the signing of the Declaration of Independence.

Apply 10   is veterans day an official united states public holiday?

Rule 6: Capitalize streets, buildings, and other specific structures.

Learn 11   The address of the White House is 1600 Pennsylvania Avenue.

Apply 12   the texas school book depository is on elm street in dallas.

Rule 7: Capitalize an official title when it precedes a name and elsewhere if it is a title of high distinction.

Learn 13   Princess Diana of Wales was involved with many charities.

Learn 14   Michelle Rosario was elected our class president.

Apply 15   the president spoke to the nation after the las vegas tragedy.

Apply 16   mr. st. claire, our company president, spoke at the meeting.

Rule 8: Capitalize initials; also, letters in abbreviations if the letters would be capitalized when the words are spelled out.

Learn 17   The University of Wyoming offers both a Ph.D. and an Ed.D.

Apply 18   Does FBLA stand for Future Business Leaders of America?

Learn 19   the letter came from washington, d.c. from jon j. ortega.

Apply 20   cooper a. smith told us vfw stands for veterans of foreign wars.

(continued on next page)

2. Key Proofread & Correct, using correct capitalization.
   a. Check answers.
   b. Using the rule number(s) at the left of each line, study the rule relating to each error.
   c. Rekey each incorrect line, using correct capitalization.

Save as: **CS1 ACTIVITY1**

Proofread & Correct

Rules

1,6,8   1 mr. james r. jeffers has an office in the empire state building.

1,3,5   2 paco missed the fourth of july gala; he was in mexico city.

1,2   3 i made an appointment for felipe cruz with dr. jay in may.

1,4,6   4 holiday sweets, inc. is on the corner of sixth street and state.

1,2,6,7   5 will senator benson be at the lincoln center on friday?

1,2,3,4   6 chou took a job with intel in santa clara, california last may.

1,3   7 do you live in altoona, wisconsin, or altoona, pennsylvania?

1,2,5   8 veterans day is officially observed on november 11.

1,3,6   9 the statue of liberty is located on liberty island in new york.

1,2,6 10 you will receive your next dividend from ibm in june or july.

ACTIVITY 2: Word Choice

1. Study the definitions of the words.
2. Key all *Learn* and *Apply* lines, choosing the correct words in the *Apply* lines.

Save as: **CS1 ACTIVITY2**

know (vb) to be aware of the truth of; to have understanding of	**your** (adj) of or relating to you or yourself as possessor
no (adv/adj/n) in no respect or degree; not so; indicates denial or refusal	**you're** (contr) you are

Learn 1 Did she **know** that there are **no** exceptions to the rule?

Apply 2 I just (know, no) that this is going to be a great year.

Apply 3 (Know, No), she didn't (know, no) that she was late.

Learn 1 When **you're** on campus, be sure to pick up **your** schedule.

Apply 2 (Your, You're) mother left (your, you're) keys on the table.

Apply 3 When (your, you're) out of the office, notify (your, you're) supervisor.

ACTIVITY 3: Composing

1. Read the quotations.
2. Choose one and make notes of what the quotation means to you.
3. Key a ¶ or two indicating what the quotation means to you.
4. Proofread, revise, and correct.

Save as: **CS1 ACTIVITY3**

1. "A teacher affects eternity; he can never tell, where his influence stops." (Henry B. Adams)

2. "Every man I meet is in some way my superior." (Ralph Waldo Emerson)

3. "I'm a great believer in luck, and I find the harder I work the more I have of it." (Thomas Jefferson)

4. "Success is not final, failure is not fatal; it is the courage to continue that counts." (Winston Churchill)

5. "I destroy my enemy when I make him my friend." (Abraham Lincoln)

ACTIVITY 4: Speaking

COLLABORATION

Save as: **CS1 ACTIVITY4**

When asked what their greatest fear is, people often rank the "fear of public speaking" higher than they do the "fear of death." In other words, many people would rather die than get up and make a presentation in front of an audience. With a group of your classmates, develop suggestions for overcoming this fear and being able to speak with confidence in front of the public. Be prepared to present these ideas to your classmates.

Before You Move On

Answer these questions to review what you have learned in Chapter 1.

1. Describe how you should arrange your work area. LO 1A

2. List five points that describe proper keying position. LO 1B

3. What are the home keys for the left hand? What are the home keys for the right hand? LO 1C

4. Tap the Enter key with your _____ finger. LO 1E

5. Space _____ after a semicolon used as punctuation. LO 3C

6. When keying, keep your wrists low but not _____ the keyboard or desk. LO 1B

7. Keep your _____ on the copy as you key. LO 2A

8. How many times should you space after a period at the end of a sentence? LO 8D

9. To key a capital of the letter *P*, hold down the _____ key. LO 8B

10. To key a capital of the letter *S*, hold down the _____ key. LO 11B

11. The number of standard words keyed in 1' is called _____ (*gwam*). LO 12E

12. To key a series of capital letters, use the _____ key. LO 19B

13. How many times should you space after a question mark at the end of a sentence? LO 19B

14. Word processing software has preset tabs called _____ tabs. LO 20C

15. When you hold down the _____ key, letters to the left of the insertion point will be deleted. LO 20B

Learning the Numeric Keypad

Lesson 22   Numeric Keypad 4, 5, 6, 0
Lesson 23   Numeric Keypad 7, 8, 9
Lesson 24   Numeric Keypad 1, 2, 3
Lesson 25   Subtraction and Multiplication
Lesson 26   Division

LESSONS 22–26

NOTE Instruction on top-row numeric keys is available in Appendix A, Numeric Keys.

Numbers—how would people communicate without them? Numbers tell time, dates, distances, and amounts. They allow you to see how much you must pay for a new computer game. They let you give an exact street address. They tell you how to reach a friend on a cell phone. They let you know how you scored on an exam. They tell you how much a gallon of gas costs and how many miles per gallon your vehicle gets.

People use numbers to analyze and share information. Because numbers are precise, keying them accurately is important. In this chapter, you will learn to key numbers using the numeric keypad. In later chapters, you will use this skill to input numbers into *Excel* worksheets (spreadsheets) and *Access* databases to store, organize, and manipulate data that can be used to make important decisions.

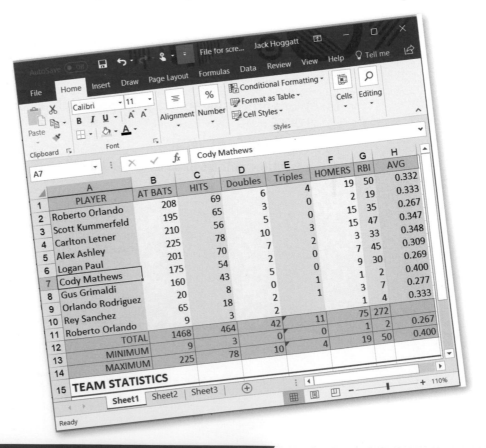

LESSON 22   Numeric Keypad 4, 5, 6, 0

OUTCOMES
- Learn numeric keypad operating position
- Learn to access the Calculator program
- Learn reachstrokes for **4**, **5**, **6**, and **0**

22A

Numeric Keypad Operating Position

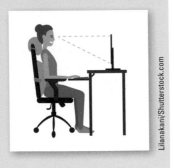

Lilanakani/Shutterstock.com

Position yourself at the keyboard as shown at the left. Sit in front of the keyboard with the book at the right—body erect, both feet on the floor.

Curve the fingers of your right hand and place them on the numeric keypad. Use the little finger for the Enter key as indicated in Figure 2-1. To key the numbers, place the:

- Index finger on **4**
- Middle finger on **5**
- Ring finger on **6**
- Thumb on **0**

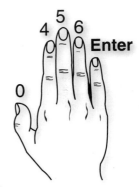

Germán Ariel Berra/Shutterstock.com

Figure 2-1 Home keying position for numeric keypad

22B

Access the Calculator

Use the Calculator on your computer to learn and practice the numeric keypad. Follow these instructions to access the Calculator.

1. Start *Windows* if necessary.
2. Click in the *Type here to search* box located in the lower left-hand area of the screen.

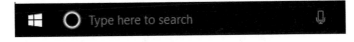

3. Key **Calculator** in the Search box. Then select *Calculator* in the list of search results.
4. The Calculator window opens, as shown in Figure 2-2.

Figure 2-2 Calculator

22C

Home Keys 4, 5, 6, and 0

 TIP You may need to tap the Num Lock (number lock) key (located above the 7 on the numeric keypad).

Germán Ariel Berra/Shutterstock.com

 TIP
- Tap each key quickly with the tip of the finger.
- Keep the fingers curved and upright.
- Use the side of the right thumb to tap the 0 similar to the way you tap the Space Bar.

Use the Calculator to complete the addition drills following these steps:

1. Key the first number with the proper finger(s) and tap the + key with the little finger of the right hand.
2. Key the next number and tap the + key.
3. After entering the last black number in the column and tapping the + key, verify your answer with the answer shown in color.
4. Tap *Esc* on the main keyboard to clear the number. Then do the next problem.

Drill 1

A	B	C	D	E
4	5	6	4	6
4	5	6	5	4
8	10	12	9	10

Drill 2

A	B	C	D	E
44	55	44	45	56
55	66	66	46	45
99	121	110	91	101

Drill 3

A	B	C	D	E
45	54	46	44	64
56	64	65	56	46
64	56	45	65	55
165	174	156	165	165

Drill 4

A	B	C	D	E
40	40	60	506	504
50	60	50	406	406
60	50	40	540	560
150	150	150	1,452	1,470

Drill 5

A	B	C	D	E
54	504	405	605	450
50	605	506	406	406
56	406	604	540	605
160	1,515	1,515	1,551	1,461

 **checkpoint** Did you check each answer against the book?

LESSON 23   Numeric Keypad 7, 8, 9

OUTCOMES
- Learn reachstrokes for **7**, **8**, and **9**
- Combine the **7**, **8**, and **9** keys with other keys

23A

Warmup

Germán Ariel Berra/Shutterstock.com

Use the Calculator to complete these addition drills.

A	B	C	D	E
4	56	406	440	546
5	45	504	506	664
6	64	650	605	654
15	165	1,560	1,551	1,864

23B

New Keys 7, 8, and 9

Germán Ariel Berra/Shutterstock.com

7 *Index* finger
8 *Middle* finger
9 *Ring* finger

Drill 1   7

A	B	C	D	E
577	607	747	667	756
774	575	70	75	707
757	740	675	757	574
2,108	1,922	1,492	1,499	2,037

Drill 2   8

A	B	C	D	E
808	680	884	458	800
484	584	480	684	68
586	868	856	880	548
1,878	2,132	2,220	2,022	1,416

Drill 3   9

A	B	C	D	E
459	954	496	944	964
596	609	965	596	469
964	596	459	659	595
2,019	2,159	1,920	2,199	2,028

Drill 4   **All numbers learned**

A	B	C	D	E
409	740	695	509	594
507	964	570	476	807
608	850	409	840	560
1,524	2,554	1,674	1,825	1,961

LESSON 24   Numeric Keypad 1, 2, 3

OUTCOMES

- Learn reachstrokes for **1**, **2**, and **3**
- Combine the **1**, **2**, and **3** keys with other keys

24A

Warmup

Use the Calculator to complete these addition drills.

A	B	C	D	E
549	596	406	740	479
670	408	809	596	809
486	758	750	805	957
1,705	1,762	1,965	2,141	2,245

24B

New Keys 1, 2, and 3

1 *Index* finger
2 *Middle* finger
3 *Ring* finger

Drill 1   1

A	B	C	D	E
171	916	147	415	156
814	151	811	611	417
151	110	901	718	901
1,136	1,177	1,859	1,744	1,474

Drill 2   2

A	B	C	D	E
202	289	722	290	256
425	524	208	724	728
726	262	526	282	249
1,353	1,075	1,456	1,296	1,233

Drill 3   3

A	B	C	D	E
453	453	303	734	368
396	309	963	583	493
363	396	357	639	735
1,212	1,158	1,623	1,956	1,596

Drill 4   **All numbers learned**

A	B	C	D	E
429	710	195	325	914
537	264	570	176	827
608	350	432	840	360
1,574	1,324	1,197	1,341	2,101

COLLABORATION

Using the Calculator, work with a classmate to solve the math problems shown below.

1. Parker wrote five checks this week. Check No. 216 was for $38.91, Check No. 217 was for $17.42, Check No. 218 was for $56.20, Check No. 219 was for $3.95, and Check No. 220 was for $16.74. What was the total amount of the five checks?

2. Karen bought items costing $1.98, $3.65, $2.74, $2.05, $.97, $3.68, and $1.40. What was the amount she owed excluding tax?

3. Kimberly accumulated these points during this grading period for quizzes (10, 10, 8.5, 9.5, 7, and 8), projects (48, 25, 16, 23, and 17), and tests (90, 95, and 87). How many points did she accumulate for quizzes? For projects? For tests? How many total points did she accumulate this grading period?

4. Tim, Jane, Chen, and Felipe each bowled three games. Tim's scores were 98, 175, and 126. Jane's scores were 127, 145, and 129. Felipe's scores were 145, 127, and 140. Chen's scores were 136, 114, and 169. What were the total pins for each person, and what were the total pins for their team?

LESSON 25   Subtraction and Multiplication

OUTCOMES

- Learn subtraction on the numeric keypad
- Learn multiplication on the numeric keypad

25A

Warmup

German Ariel Berra/Shutterstock.com

Use the Calculator to complete these addition and subtraction drills.

A	B	C	D	E
102	938	476	517	147
289	304	560	976	359
854	391	208	645	275
1,245	1,633	1,244	2,138	781

A	B	C	D	E
813	836	938	712	468
− 492	− 104	− 726	− 254	− 107
321	732	212	458	361

Subtraction

German Ariel Berra/Shutterstock.com

– *Little* finger

Use the Calculator to complete these subtraction drills. Key the first number and tap the – key. Key the second number and tap the Enter key.

Drill 1

	A	B	C	D	E
	907	872	614	730	756
	− 489	− 312	− 459	− 583	− 621
	418	560	155	147	135

Drill 2

	A	B	C	D	E
	509	847	625	913	810
	− 293	− 764	− 501	− 264	− 398
	216	83	124	649	412

Multiplication

German Ariel Berra/Shutterstock.com

* *Ring* finger

Use the Calculator to complete these multiplication drills. Key the first number and tap the * key. Key the second number and tap the Enter key.

Drill 3

	A	B	C	D	E
	96	75	84	40	132
	× 40	× 46	× 73	× 28	× 19
	3,840	3,450	6,132	1,120	2,508

Drill 4

	A	B	C	D	E
	405	697	803	467	371
	× 208	× 50	× 32	× 140	× 62
	84,240	34,850	25,696	65,380	23,002

Drill 5

	A	B	C	D	E
	803	526	377	420	130
	× 92	× 19	× 28	× 52	× 62
	73,876	9,994	10,556	21,840	8,060

Math Problems

COLLABORATION

Using the Calculator, work with a classmate to solve these math problems.

1. Owen bought four cups @ $3.98 each, six plates @ $4.50 each, and four saucers @ $4.25 each. How much was the purchase Owen made? How much was the total purchase before tax? How much was the total purchase with a 5 percent sales tax included?

2. Miles missed 12 points on the first exam, which was worth 125 points. He lost 23 points on the second exam, which was worth 150 points, and he lost 15 points on the third exam, which was also worth 150 points. What were the total points available on the three exams? What were the total points that Miles got on the three exams?

3. One of the plates Owen purchased (problem 1) was chipped. He decided to return the damaged plate. How much did the dishes cost him after the return of the damaged plate? Include the 5 percent sales tax in the total cost.

4. During the week, Sharon purchased five beverages @ $1.50 each, three sandwiches @ $3.25 each, two cups of soup @ $1.98 each, three bags of chips @ $.90 each, and two desserts @ $1.25 each. How much did Sharon spend this week if there is no tax on the food she purchased?

LESSON 26   Division

OUTCOMES

- Learn division on the numeric keypad
- Learn to complete math problems on the numeric keypad

26A

Warmup

Germán Ariel Berra/Shutterstock.com

Use the Calculator to complete these addition and subtraction problems.

Drill 1

A	B	C	D	E
821	673	276	401	972
309	540	809	823	108
547	189	305	576	354
1,677	1,402	1,390	1,800	1,434

Drill 2

A	B	C	D	E
711	253	841	395	926
− 254	− 196	− 290	− 503	− 755
457	57	551	− 108	171

26B

Division

Germán Ariel Berra/Shutterstock.com

/ *Middle* finger

Use the Calculator to complete the division drills shown here. Key the dividend and tap the / key. Key the divisor and tap the Enter key. Round answers to two decimal places.

Drill 1

A	B	C	D	E
120.6	79	90.33	119	70.8
5/603	11/869	6/542	8/952	10/708

Drill 2

A	B	C	D	E
21.65	64.49	197.51	95.56	134.58
23/498	79/5,095	43/8,493	62/5,925	67/9,017

Math Problems

COLLABORATION

 TIP A deposit is an addition to a bank account. A check or service charge is a subtraction from a bank account.

Using the Calculator, work with a classmate to solve these math problems.

1. Rebecca made four deposits last month. They were for $37.28, $15.91, $45.76, and $50.37. How much money did she deposit for the month?

2. Sarah bought two CDs for $15.99 each. She bought two video games for $59.95 and $49.75. The state sales tax is 5.5 percent. How much did she spend?

3. Yukio is paid each week. His last four checks were for $49.78, $35.97, $53.76, and $28.73. What did he average per week over this period?

4. Antonio is paid $6.25 per hour. Last week he worked 4 hours on Monday, 3½ hours on Tuesday, 5 hours on Wednesday, 2 hours on Thursday, and 4½ hours on Friday. How much did he make last week?

5. At the end of last month, Brandon had an ending bank balance of $153.37. During the month, he made one deposit for $97.68. He wrote five checks ($7.98, $15.83, $38.53, $17.21, and $49.76). His service charge this month was $3.25. What is his current balance after recording these amounts?

✓ **checkpoint** Compare your answers with a classmate's answers. If they do not agree, do the problem again to find the correct answer.

Skill Builder 1

A

Warmup

Key each line twice. If time permits, key the lines again.

Alphabet

1 Before leaving, Jexon quickly swam the dozen laps.

Caps Lock

2 JACK, CHARLA, and JANA all ran for VICE PRESIDENT.

Speed

3 Hal and I may go to the social held on the island.

gwam 1' | 1 | 2 | 3 | 4 | 5 | 6 | 7 | 8 | 9 | 10 |

B

Improve Keying Technique

Key each line twice, striving to maintain a continuous pace.

Balanced-hand words

1 go if am us to by of he an so is do it go me be or

2 is and the may did man due big for box but oak six

3 with when make such work city down they them their

Balanced-hand phrases

4 big box|pay for|and the|own them|to the end|he may

5 if they|make a|the right|by the|wish to|when did I

6 sign the|for them|make them|when is|and then|to it

Balanced-hand sentences

7 Nancy and I may go to the city for the audit form.

8 Enrique may make a map of the island for the firm.

9 Orlando may work with the men on the bus problems.

gwam 30" | 2 | 4 | 6 | 8 | 10 | 12 | 14 | 16 | 18 | 20 |

★TIP Keep your eyes on the copy.

C

Keying Handwritten (Script) Copy

Key each line twice.

1 Script is copy that is written with pen or pencil.

2 Copy that is written poorly is often hard to read.

3 Read script a few words ahead of the keying point.

4 Doing so will help you produce copy free of error.

5 Leave proper spacing after punctuation marks, too.

6 With practice, you can key script at a rapid rate.

D

Speed Forcing Drill

Key a 30" timed writing on each line, striving to key more on each attempt. Your *gwam* is shown below the lines.

1 Pamela may be able to go.

2 You can see the next game too.

3 Mike will be out of town on Friday.

4 Shawn and I can take the exam next week.

5 Nancy will bring your new computer next week.

6 The new version of the video game will be on sale.

gwam 30" | 2 | 4 | 6 | 8 | 10 | 12 | 14 | 16 | 18 | 20 |

E

Timed Writing

1. Key three 1' timed writings on each paragraph, striving to key more on each timing; determine *gwam*.

2. Key a 2' timed writing on both paragraphs combined, striving to maintain your highest 1' *gwam*.

 all letters used

gwam 1' 2'

Each president since George Washington has   8   4

had a cabinet. The cabinet is a group of men and   18   9

women selected by the President. The Senate must   28   14

approve them. Usually, it is a rare exception   37   19

rather than the rule for the person selected by   47   24

the president to be rejected by this branch of the   56   28

government. In keeping with tradition, most of   66   33

the cabinet members belong to the same political   75   38

party as the president.   <u>80</u>   40

    The purpose of the cabinet is to provide advice   10   45

to the president on matters pertaining to the job   20   50

of president. The person holding the office, of   29   55

course, may or may not follow the advice. Some   38   59

presidents have frequently utilized their cabinet.   48   64

Others have used it little or not at all. For   57   69

example, President Wilson held no cabinet meetings   67   74

at all during World War I.   <u>73</u>   76

gwam 1' | 1 | 2 | 3 | 4 | 5 | 6 | 7 | 8 | 9 | 10 |
2' | 1 | 2 | 3 | 4 | 5 |

WP Applications 6

Activity 1

Explore the Word Ribbon

This activity teaches you the basics of using a key feature of *Word* and other Microsoft *Office* applications, the Ribbon. The Ribbon displays most of *Word*'s commands in **Ribbon tabs** along the top of the screen. Figure 2-3 shows the *Word* Home tab.

Ribbon tabs   Dialog box launcher   Drop-down arrow

Group   More button

Figure 2-3 Commands on the *Word* Home tab

When you open a document in *Word*, the commands on the Home tab display by default. To view more commands, click the tabs at the top of the Ribbon. Commands are organized into *groups*. The Home tab has five groups: Clipboard, Font, Paragraph, Styles, and Editing.

You can display additional commands and options using other features of the Ribbon (refer to Figure 2-3):

- Click a *dialog box launcher* arrow, at the lower-right corner of a group, to display a dialog box that contains additional commands relating to that group
- Click a *More* button for a gallery such as the Styles gallery to display the entire gallery
- Click a drop-down arrow on a command button to see additional commands for that button

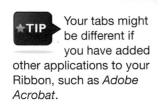

★TIP Your tabs might be different if you have added other applications to your Ribbon, such as *Adobe Acrobat*.

1. Start *Windows.* Key **Word** in the *Type here to search* box located in the lower-left area of the screen and tap *Enter.* Then select *Word 2016* from the list of search results.
2. Click *Blank document* to open a new document. The Home tab is selected by default.
3. Click the *Insert* tab to display the tab shown in Figure 2-4. Note the ten groups in which the commands are organized.

Insert tab

Figure 2-4 Insert tab commands

4. Display the hundreds of commands available by clicking each of the remaining tabs: *Draw, Design, Layout, References, Mailings, Review, View,* and *Help*. You can also click the *File* tab. Unlike the other tabs, the File tab shows its commands in a vertical menu.

5. Return to the *Home* tab and view the groups on this important tab. Find the following commands or features in each group. If you are not sure what some commands do, hover your pointer over them for a brief description.

   • *Clipboard*: Find the Cut and Copy commands. They are light gray, indicating they are not currently active.

   • *Font*: Find the Font Color button and click the small drop-down arrow on the button to display the Font Color palette. Click anywhere on the screen to close the palette.

   • *Paragraph*: Click the Paragraph group's dialog box launcher to open the Paragraph dialog box. Click the *Cancel* button in the dialog box to close it.

   • *Styles*: Click the *More* button at the lower-right corner of the Styles gallery to see all the styles in the gallery.

   • *Editing*: Locate the Find and Replace commands, and then click the drop-down arrow on the Find button to see additional commands.

6. Close *Word* by clicking the *Close* (X) button in the upper-right corner of the *Word* window. (Do not save.)

Activity 2

Key and Edit Text in Word

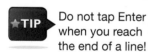
TIP Do not tap Enter when you reach the end of a line! When a line is full, the next word will automatically wrap to the next line.

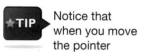
TIP Notice that when you move the pointer around the work area of a *Word* document, it changes in appearance to the pointer called an *I-beam*. This pointer tells you that you can click to insert text.

To key text, tap each key on the keyboard or other input device that you are using. If you press a wrong key, you can use the Backspace key to delete your mistakes. As you key text, remember to:

• Tap the Space Bar once to space between words.

• Tap the Space Bar once after a comma (,)

• Tap the Space Bar once after a period (.), a question mark (?), an exclamation mark (!), and a colon (:)

• Hold down the Shift key while tapping a letter key to create a capital letter

• Tap Enter only at the end of a paragraph

1. Start *Word* and create a new blank document.

2. Key the following text in the document. Tap Enter only at the end of paragraphs.

   Space Exploration

   <your name>

   The Russians were the first to send someone into space. The Russians called their astronauts by the name cosmonauts. The first cosmonaut left Earth on April 12, 1961.

3. Move the mouse pointer so that it is positioned to the left of the first word in your document (right before *Space Exploration*). Click once to place the insertion point (blinking line) before this line.

4. Key the first change (the text marked in yellow) as shown here.

   The History of Space Exploration

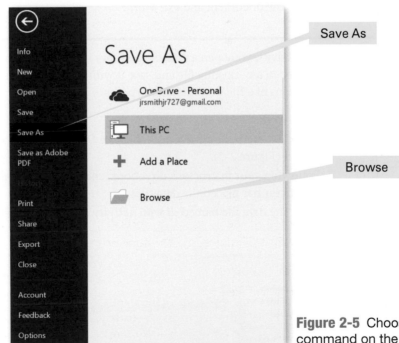

5. Position the insertion point at the end of your name and tap Enter. Key the changes shown below that are marked in yellow.

> The Russians
>
> The Russian and the American space programs were in competition. The Russians were the first to send someone into space. The Russians called their astronauts by the name cosmonauts. The first cosmonaut, Yuri Gagarin, left Earth on April 12, 1961.
>
> The Americans
>
> The Americans were eager to catch up. The United States sent their first astronaut, Alan Shepard, into space on May 5, 1961.

Activity 3

Save a Document

File tab > Save As
(or Save a Copy)

As soon as you create a new file, you should save it. A file that has been saved can be opened again so you can edit the text. Use the Save As command on the File tab to begin the process of saving a file. You will then have to navigate to the location on your computer or other storage area where you want to save the file.

1. Click the *File* tab on the Ribbon. Then click *Save As* as shown in Figure 2-5.

Figure 2-5 Choose the Save As command on the File tab

2. Click *Browse*. The Save As dialog box opens.

3. Without unmarking the name that automatically appears, key **wp6 activity 3** as shown in Figure 2-6.

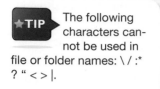

TIP The following characters cannot be used in file or folder names: \ / :* ? " < > |.

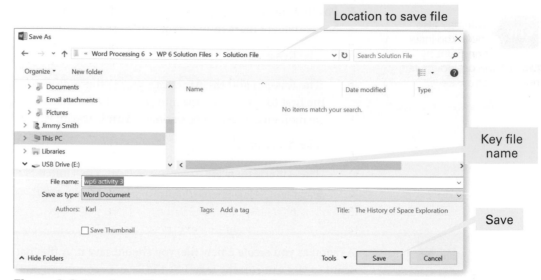

Location to save file

Key file name

Save

Figure 2-6 Naming a file in the Save As dialog box

4. Follow your instructor's request to find and open the folder where you will store the file.
5. Click the *Save* button.
6. Close the document and exit *Word*.

Activity 4

Open an Existing File and Save with New Name

In this activity, you open a data file and save it with a new name. You could use this same procedure to open any existing file and save it with a new name, such as when you want to save different versions of a file for different purposes.

1. Start *Word*.
2. In the *Word* opening screen, click *Open Other Documents* in the lower-left corner of the screen (Figure 2-7).
3. Following your instructor's directions, choose the network or local folder where your instructor has placed the data files.
4. Click the data file named *df wp6 activity 4* as shown in Figure 2-8.

Figure 2-7 Open Other Documents command in *Word* start window

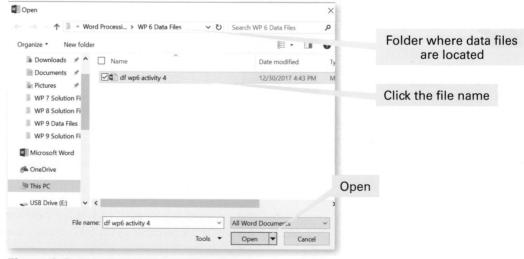

Folder where data files are located

Click the file name

Open

Figure 2-8 Select and open a data file

File tab > Save As or
Save a Copy> Save

TIP Triple-click
{*Enter Your
Name*} to
quickly highlight the entire
line.

5. Click *Open*. The document appears on the screen.
6. Read the document. You may need to use the scroll bar to scroll to the bottom.
7. Drag your insertion point over {*Enter your name*} to highlight this text, and then release the mouse button. Key your name. It will replace the highlighted text.
8. Replace {*Enter your class name*} and {*Enter your instructor's name*} with the appropriate information.
9. Scroll to the bottom of the document and click the insertion point in the blank space for the first similarity. Key the first similarity.
10. Key the rest of your answers in the appropriate spaces.
11. Click the *File* tab and click *Save As*.
12. Find the folder where your instructor has told you to save your files.
13. Key **wp6 activity 4** in the File name box and click *Save*.
14. Close the document and exit *Word*.

Activity 5

Preview and Print a Document in Word

File tab > Print > Print

Sometimes you need a printed copy of your work. Print by clicking the File tab followed by the Print command. This command opens the Print screen shown in Figure 2-9. On this screen, you can choose your printer, select the number of copies to print, and choose other options. You can also preview your document to check for any last-minute errors or formatting issues before you print.

1. Start *Word* if it is not already open.
2. Open the **wp6 activity 3** file you created earlier.
3. Click the *File* tab on the Ribbon.
4. Click *Print*. The screen to the right of the Print command changes as shown in Figure 2-9.

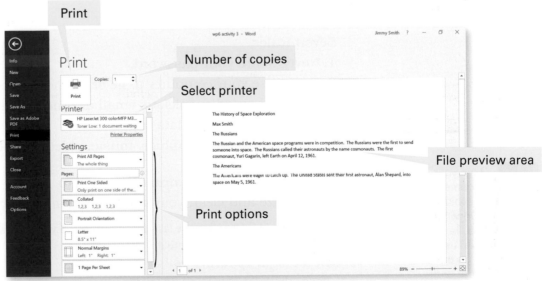

Figure 2-9 Printing options

5. Make sure the number of copies is set to **1**. If it is not, use the arrow keys to change it. You can also highlight the number in the box and key the number you want.
6. Choose the printer assigned by your instructor.

7. Review the other options in the list.

8. Look at the picture of your document to the right. If you catch a last-minute mistake, click the *Back* button at the top left of the screen and make changes to the document. Save the changes and then go back to step 3.

9. Click the *Print* button near the upper-left corner of the screen.

10. Close the document and exit *Word*.

Activity 6

Numbered Lists and Acceptable-Use Policies

When you are using a computer, you need to follow certain rules. Chances are your school has rules you should follow. These rules are called acceptable-use policies, or AUPs. In this activity, you will key an AUP using a numbered list.

Numbered lists can be used to track steps of instruction, lists of items, and more. When you key a list where each item is preceded by 1, 2, 3, 4, and so on, you are creating a numbered list. When creating a numbered list:

- Key the number 1
- Key a period
- Tap the Space Bar once
- Key text for the numbered item and then tap Enter

★TIP Compare the rules in this activity to the ones you must follow at your school.

If *Word*'s automatic numbering feature has been turned on, the remaining numbers in your list should be automatically added each time you tap Enter. If automatic numbering has been turned off, just type the numbers.

1. Start *Word* if it is not already open. In a new, blank document, key the following AUP:

   Acceptable-Use Policy
   <your Name>
   Seven Rules
   1. Never share your password.
   2. Never use your computer to lie or offend others.
   3. Do not forward suspicious email or other messages.
   4. Do not steal digital data from others.
   5. Do not download graphics, music, videos, or other data from the Internet without permission.
   6. Do not bring food or drink into the lab.
   7. Organize and clean your workstation area every day.

★TIP Save your document often to avoid losing your work. Once you have saved a file with a name, you can use the Save button on the Quick Access Toolbar or the File tab.

2. When you tap Enter after the last line, a number 8 will appear if automatic numbering is on. Simply tap Backspace to delete it.

3. Save the file as **wp6 activity 6**.

4. Change the color of the first rule to blue.
   a. First, highlight the line with your pointer. (If automatic numbering is turned on, the number and the period following it will not be highlighted.)
   b. Next, if necessary click the *Home* tab and, in the Font group, click the drop-down arrow on the right side of the *Font Color* button. See Figure 2-10.
   c. In the palette that displays, choose any blue color, such as Blue in the Standard Colors.

If you click the *Font Color* button instead of its drop-down arrow, the current color shown in the button (such as Red) will be applied to the selected text.

5. Change the color of the other rules in your document using colors from the Font Color palette. Make each rule a different color.

6. Select the title *Acceptable-Use Policy* and click the *Bold* button in the Font group on the Home tab.

7. Select your name and click the *Italic* button in the Font group on the Home tab.

8. Select the heading *Seven Rules* and click the drop-down arrow on the *Underline* button to display the palette of underline styles. Click the *Double underline* style.

9. Click the *Save* button on the Quick Access Toolbar (shown in Figure 2-10) to quickly save the file.

10. Print and close the file. Exit *Word* and shut down the computer unless your instructor tells you otherwise.

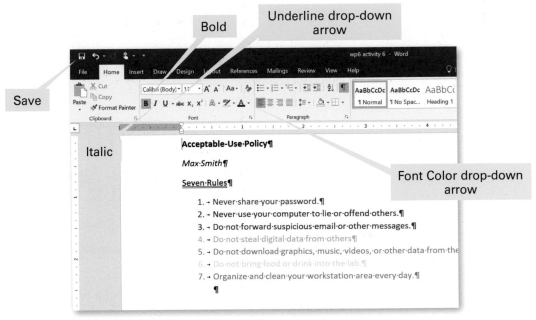

Figure 2-10 Apply colors and Font group formats

Basic Technology Skills 6

Internet Basics

OUTCOMES

- Learn about networks and the Internet
- Learn about connecting to the Internet
- Explore the parts of a web browser window
- Access and navigate webpages

Networks and the Internet

Networks

When one computer links to another computer, a **network** is created. A small network may have only a few computers. A large network can include thousands of computers. A network with computers located within a short distance (such as within the same school) is called a *local area network (LAN)*.

When many LANs link to one another, a web of networks is created (see Figure BT6-1). The **Internet** is a web of computer networks that spans the Earth. Files on the Internet are stored on powerful computers called **servers**.

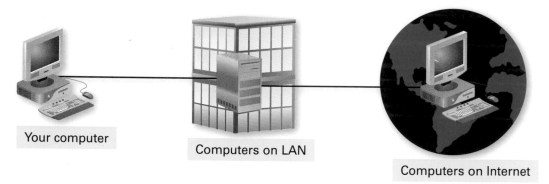

Your computer

Computers on LAN

Computers on Internet

Figure BT6-1 Using your computer, you can find information on a LAN or on the Internet

The Internet

The Internet created new ways for people to communicate. People use the Internet to research topics, exchange messages, buy and sell products, and promote organizations and ideas.

Electronic mail, commonly called email, is a popular use of the Internet. **Email** is the electronic transfer of messages. It allows users to exchange information quickly and easily. Blogs and instant messaging also are popular uses of the Internet. A **blog** allows users to post messages for others to read. Blogs are usually organized around a particular topic, such as music or sports, or around people's lives. There are blogs for millions of different topics and people. **Instant messaging** allows users who are online to key text messages. The messages are displayed almost instantly for the person you are chatting with.

An important part of the Internet is the World Wide Web. It is often called simply *the web*. The **World Wide Web** is a system of computers that can handle documents formatted in a special language. This language is called *HTML (Hypertext Markup Language)*. HTML documents, called *webpages*, can display text as well as graphics. They allow users to move from one document to another using hyperlinks. A group of related webpages is called a *website*.

Websites are created for many reasons. One reason is to sell products. The selling and buying of products on the Internet is called **e-commerce**. Billions of dollars' worth of products are sold each year through e-commerce. Clothes, cars, groceries, medicine, movie tickets, books, and music are just a few of the items that customers can buy online. See Figure BT6-2.

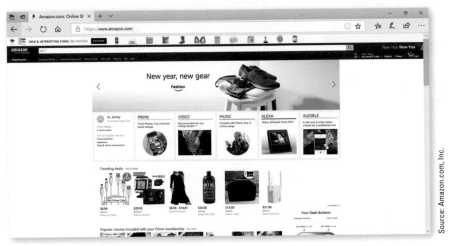

Figure BT6-2 People can search for and buy products of all kinds online

Websites are also used by people, companies, governments, and other groups to provide information. For example, you can access a website provided by the Supreme Court of the United States. On this site, you can find articles about current news events related to the federal judicial system. You also will find information about our government, the latest news and updates, and you can blog on current events. See Figure BT6-3.

Figure BT6-3 Information about our judicial system can be found on the Supreme Court website

Connecting to the Internet

To access the Internet from a home computer, you may need to set up an account with an Internet service provider. An **Internet service provider (ISP)** is a company that provides customer connections to the Internet. AT&T, Verizon, Spectrum, and Comcast are examples of popular ISPs. Many schools provide ISP service through their LANs.

In the past, most computers were connected to their networks by wires. This has limited us as to how and where we connect to the Internet. Wireless Internet connections now allow freedom of movement. Computers and other digital devices can be linked to the Internet without wires through a device called an *access point*. The area around an access point is called a *hotspot*. With the proper equipment, you can connect to the Internet when you are in a hotspot. Hotspots can be created in schools, restaurants, airports, hotels, and even public parks. Another way of connecting wirelessly to the Internet is using the cellular (phone) network.

Parts of a Web Browser Window

A **web browser** is a program that lets you find and view webpages. Microsoft *Edge*, Google *Chrome*, Apple *Safari*, and *Firefox* are popular web browsers. Look at the Google *Chrome* window shown in Figure BT6-4. You see a title bar, tabs, and control buttons like those you have learned about in other *Windows* programs. A Microsoft *Edge* browser window is shown in Figure BT6-2. Notice the similarities between Microsoft *Edge* and Google *Chrome*.

Figure BT6-4 The Google *Chrome* browser window

Source: Google Inc.

Access and Navigate Webpages

Web Addresses

In the previous *Basic Technology Skills* module, *Exploring and Organizing Your Digital Space*, you learned to follow a path to locate a file on your computer. In a similar way, you must locate webpages you want to view. A **uniform resource locator (URL)** is an address for a website. You can key a URL into the address bar of a web browser. After you key a URL and give the appropriate command, the browser will look for the address and display the site's webpage.

URLs contain **domain names**. For example, the domain name *nasa.gov* is part of the address for the National Aeronautics and Space Administration website. The *.gov* at the end of the URL stands for *government*. Domain names can give you some insight into the purpose of the sites you visit. Table BT6-1 shows a few examples:

Table BT6-1 Example domain names

.edu	Educational	.gov	Governmental
.mil	Military	.net	Network providers
.org	Organizational	.us	Country code for the United States
.biz	Business	.mx	Country code for Mexico
.com	Commercial	.ca	Country code for Canada
.pro	Professional	.jp	Country code for Japan
.info	Informational	.cn	Country code for China

In this activity, you will use a URL to find the NASA welcome page. Instructions given are for Microsoft *Edge*. If you have a different browser, the directions will be similar.

1. Follow your instructor's directions to log on to the Internet.
2. Start Microsoft *Edge* (or another browser). Click the address bar. The current address should be highlighted. If it is not, click and drag over the address to select it. In the address bar, key **www.nasa.gov** as shown in Figure BT6-5.

https://www.nasa.gov/

Figure BT6-5 Microsoft *Edge* address bar

3. Tap Enter. The characters *http://* (or sometimes *https://*) will be automatically added to the beginning of the address. A welcome page similar to the one shown in Figure BT6-6 should appear.

Source: Nasa.gov

Figure BT6-6 The NASA welcome page

TIP In a URL, **http://** is short for Hypertext Transfer Protocol. HTTP is the means by which information is shared over the web. **https://** stands for HTTP Secure, indicating that communications to and from this website are encrypted, thus more secure.

TIP The first page you visit on a website is called a *welcome page*. Welcome pages change often. Your page may look different from the one in Figure BT6-6.

4. Use the scroll bar to move down the NASA welcome page.
5. To visit another website, key **www.airandspace.si.edu** in the address bar and tap Enter. The Smithsonian National Air and Space Museum welcome page should display.
6. Using the scroll bars, examine the welcome page. Click the *Close* button on the browser window to close Microsoft *Edge*.

Hyperlinks

TIP When the pointer passes over a hyperlink, it becomes a hand with a pointing finger.

Many webpages have hyperlinks. A **hyperlink** can be text, a button, or a graphic. When you click a hyperlink, you are taken to a new location. Not all of the pictures or words on a webpage are hyperlinks. How can you find hyperlinks on a webpage? Simply move the pointer (usually an arrow) around the page with your mouse, finger, or digital pen. When the pointer changes to a hand with a pointing finger, you have found a hyperlink.

When you click a hyperlink, the browser moves to a new location. If you want to return to the previous page, click the **Back button** in the browser window. To return to the page you just left, click the **Forward button**. To return to your home page or starting point, click the **Home button**.

TIP You do not have to key www to access a webpage. You can save time by just keying the domain name.

1. Log on to the Internet. Start Microsoft *Edge* or another browser. In the address bar, key **msn.com**.
2. Move the mouse pointer around the welcome page. Watch the pointer become a pointing finger when it passes over a hyperlink.
3. Click a hyperlink such as *Entertainment*. Quickly scan the new page. Click the *Back* button (see Figure BT6-7). This will take you back to the previous page.

Back/Forward   Home   Close

Figure BT6-7 Microsoft *Edge* buttons

4. Click the *Forward* button. This will take you to the page you just left.
5. Click the *Home* button. This will take you to your starting home page.
6. Click the *Close* button on the browser window to close Microsoft *Edge*.

Chapter 2 REVIEW

Before You Move On

Answer these questions to review what you have learned in Chapter 2.

1. When using the Calculator, you may need to tap the _____ key (located above the 7 on the numeric keypad). LO 22C

2. Explain how you access the Calculator. LO 22B

3. The key used for division on the numeric keypad is the _____ . LO 26B

4. Use the _____ finger of the right hand to tap the key for division. LO 26B

5. Use the _____ finger of the right hand to key the – for subtraction. LO 25B

6. When using the numeric keypad, use your _____ to tap the 0 key. LO 22A

7. List the steps for using the Calculator to do a subtraction problem. LO 45B

8. The key used for multiplication on the numeric keypad is the _____ . LO 25C

9. Use the _____ finger of the right hand to tap the key for multiplication. LO 25C

10. Describe home-keying position for the numeric keypad. LO 22A

CHAPTER 3

Accessing Help for Answers

Lesson 27   Help Basics
Lesson 28   Special Features

LESSON 27   Help Basics

OUTCOMES
- Gain an overview of software Help features
- Learn to use software Help features

27A

Overview

Application software offers built-in Help features that you can access directly in the software as you work. **Help** is the equivalent of a user's manual on how to use your software. Most software Help includes the following features:

- Search for topics

- Point to screen items for a concise explanation of their use

- Access technical resources, training/tutorials, free downloads, and other options at the software developer's website

Word Help

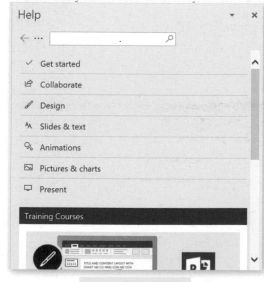

PowerPoint Help

Figure 3-1 Similar Help screens

The Help features work the same way for each software application in the Microsoft Office suite. For example, the Microsoft Help feature works the same in *Word* or *Excel* as it does in *PowerPoint* or *Access* (see Figure 3-1). The software's Help features can be accessed by tapping F1 (on some computers, you may have to tap the *Fn* key before tapping F1) or by clicking the *Tell me what you want to do* box above the Ribbon (see Figure 3-2). As you key in the *Tell me* box, a smart list anticipates what you might want help with. If you see what you want to do appear below the box, then click and it will take you to directions on how to perform the task. If you do not see the task you want to perform, you can click the question mark symbol (?) (see Figure 3-3) and a Help Viewer panel similar to the ones pictured in Figure 3-1 displays. The *Tell me* box can be closed by clicking anywhere on the screen outside the box. The Help Viewer panel can be closed by clicking the **Close button** located at the upper-right of the Help feature.

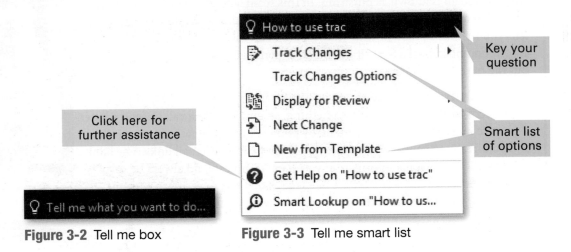

NOTE To access all functions of Help, you must be connected to the Internet.

Figure 3-2 Tell me box

Figure 3-3 Tell me smart list

27B

Accessing Help

1. Click in the *Tell me what you want to do* box above the Ribbon.
2. Click outside the list to close the *Tell me* list.
3. Access Microsoft Office *Word* Help (see Figure 3-4).
4. Click the *Close* button on the Help Viewer.

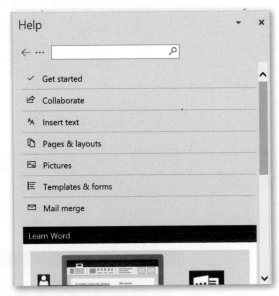

Figure 3-4 *Word* Help

Digital Citizenship and Ethics

The widespread use of the Internet for shopping and conducting financial transactions has led to scams in which online thieves trick users into supplying credit card and bank account numbers as well as other personal information.

One such scam is known as **phishing**. In this scam, you get an official-looking email that appears to be from your bank or other financial institution. The email tells you there is a problem with your account and asks you to confirm your account number, Social Security number, or some other personal information. But the message is a fake.

You should never respond to emails asking for personal information. If your bank needs to contact you about something, an employee will call or send a letter. If you are in doubt, contact your bank by phone or open a new browser window and go directly to your bank's website but do not click any email links. The bank will not ask for personal information via an email. You should always be suspicious if you get an email or a phone message asking you to verify an account. Also, keep your antivirus and antispyware software up-to-date.

COLLABORATION

As a class, discuss the following:

1. What are ways you can verify that an email message comes from a legitimate source?

2. If you suspect that you received a phishing email from a party posing as your bank, what course of action would you take?

27C

Using the Help Panel

1. Access Microsoft Office *Word* Help.
2. Study the Help panel features shown in Figure 3-5.

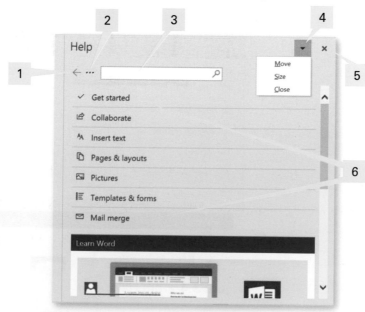

1. Back button
2. Home button
3. Search online help
4. Drop down to Move (the Help panel to a different location), Size (increase or decrease size of the Help panel), or Close
5. Close button
6. Help categories (prepopulated for each Office application)

Figure 3-5 Help panel features

3. Click *Pages & layouts* in the Help categories list. Use the scroll bar to scroll down to see what is included with *Pages & layouts*.
4. Use the Back button to return to the *Word* Help screen.
5. Click *Pictures* in the Help categories list.
6. Use the Home button to return to the Home screen.
7. Use the drop-down menu to adjust the size of the Help screen.
8. Use the drop-down menu to move the Help screen to the left side of the screen.
9. Close the Help feature.

27D

Exploring Help

1. Access Help and follow the instructions below.
2. Click the first category, *Get started* (see Figure 3-6). The selections open to an overview video of the *Word* application.

Figure 3-6 Exploring Help

3. Click *Explore new Word training* near the bottom of the screen. Scroll through the videos to see what is available.
4. Explore Help further by viewing a topic that interests you. Help contains many resources that will be helpful in the future. The list of Help topics varies depending on the application you are using.
5. Close the Help feature.

> **NOTE** Because Help is an online resource, topics and information are likely to change. If your screen choices do not match the steps shown here, be flexible by exploring the options that are available to you and searching for the information you need.

LESSON 28 Special Features

- Learn to use the pop-up description feature
- Access additional software support on the Internet

28A

Learning about ScreenTips

1. Read the information about pop-up descriptions after these steps.
2. Learn how to use the pop-up description feature of your software.
3. Take a pop-up description tour of your screen. Use the feature to learn what unfamiliar screen items do.

A valuable Help feature for new users is the pop-up description box. This feature may be called ScreenTips, Quick Tips, or something similar. It allows you to use the mouse to point to commands or other objects on the screen. After a brief period of time, a pop-up box appears, giving a concise description of the feature.

Figure 3-7 shows what happens when you point at the **Format Painter** command found in the **Clipboard** group on the Home tab. For this particular command, the pop-up box tells you:

- The name of the command (for some commands, the shortcuts to activate the command are also given)

- What it is used for

- How to use it

To find out more about a pop-up, click *Tell me more* at the bottom of the pop-up box. The Help Viewer panel opens to reveal more information about the command (see Figure 3-8). When you are finished reading the information in a pop-up, move the pointer away from the command to close the pop-up.

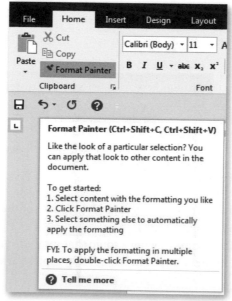

Figure 3-7 Pop-up box information

Figure 3-8 Help description

1. Use the pop-up description to learn about each of the features shown in Figure 3-9.
2. Key a sentence or two explaining the purpose of each feature.

Thesaurus (Review tab)

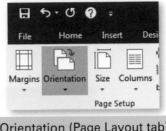
Orientation (Page Layout tab)

Copy (Home tab)

Figure 3-9 Using ScreenTips

1. Access *http://office.microsoft.com/en-us/* (see Figure 3-10) or the manufacturer's website of the software you are using.
2. Spend some time browsing what is available online from the software manufacturer. Click the following:

   - *Products* to view information about Microsoft's latest Office products and applications
   - *Resources* to view frequently asked questions, open the Office blog, and find out information about security and compliance, as well as system requirements
   - *Templates* to browse available templates for business and personal documents
   - *Support* to access training videos for each of the Office applications

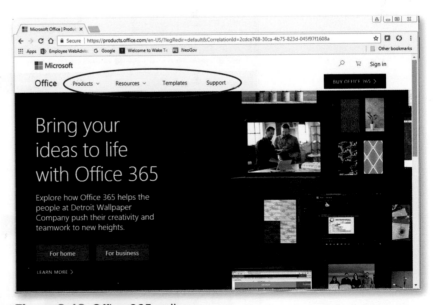

Figure 3-10 Office 365 online

1. Access *http://office.microsoft.com/en-us/*.
2. Click *Support* at the top of the screen; then click *Training* at the top of the Support menu (see Figure 3-11).

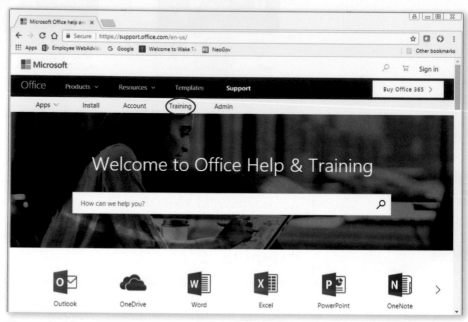

Figure 3-11 Support menu

3. At the Office 365 Training Center, click the *Word* icon (see Figure 3-12).

Figure 3-12 Office 365 Training Center

4. A video training library opens, providing you video training on several *Word* topics (see Figure 3-13).

Figure 3-13 *Word* video training center

5. Click *Create documents*. A video display appears along with written instructions and a list of suggested topics for more training. Click on the video to begin your training.
6. After viewing the video, click *Apps* at the upper-left to explore other applications that interest you. Similar instructional materials are available for each Office application.

21st Century Skills: Access and Evaluate Information
The Internet and web have given us quick and easy access to information on virtually any topic. As you learned in this chapter, that includes helpful information on the software you use. But how do you know that the information you find on the web is accurate, timely, and written by a reliable and knowledgeable source? Here are some tips:

- Verify any information by checking another source.
- Identify the author or organization that publishes or sponsors the site, and identify the date the content was created or last updated.
- On the home page, look for a statement of purpose for the site.
- Examine the language of the site. Does it provide facts, opinions, or both? A reliable site should present information in a balanced and objective manner and should be free of spelling and grammatical errors.

Think Critically
With a partner, respond to these questions. Ask your teacher if you will need to turn in this activity for grading.

COLLABORATION

1. Why is it important to evaluate information you read on the web?
2. Do you think the Internet is as reliable a source of information for computer help as the documentation that comes with your computer or software?
3. Describe ways in which you evaluate information you obtain in various formats, including the Internet, television, print publications, and in person.

lightpoet/Shutterstock.com

Skill Builder 2

Warmup

Key each line twice. If time permits, key the lines again.

Alphabet

1 Jasper amazed Hank by quickly fixing two big vans.

-/'/"

2 "Did Kate need 'one-half' or 'two-thirds' to win?"

Speed

3 Laurie may fish off the big dock down by the lake.

gwam 1' | 1 | 2 | 3 | 4 | 5 | 6 | 7 | 8 | 9 | 10 |

B

Technique Mastery of Individual Letters

Key each line twice, striving to maintain a continuous pace.

★TIP Keep your fingers curved and upright.

A Abe ate banana bread at Anna's Cafe at 18 Parkway.

B Bob Abbott bobbled the baseball hit by Barb Banks.

C Cecelia can check the capacities for each cubicle.

D Dan added additional games and divided the squads.

E Emery recently developed three new feet exercises.

F Jeff Florez offered the fifty officials free food.

G Gregg gingerly gave the giggling girl a gold ring.

H Herb shared his half of the hay with his neighbor.

I I will live in Illinois after leaving Mississippi.

J Jay, Jet, and Joy enjoyed the jet ride to Jamaica.

K Kay Kern took the kayak to Kentucky for Kent Kick.

L Will lives in Idaho; Lance Bell lives in Illinois.

M Mary Mead assumed the maximum and minimum amounts.

C

Speed Forcing Drill

Key two 30" timed writings on each line.

1 Sarah may take us to the game.

2 Did the boys make the signs for us?

3 Ann and Jay may be able to take the car.

4 Yoko started a new job on Thursday or Friday.

5 Jo needs to key two words a minute faster to pass.

gwam 30" | 2 | 4 | 6 | 8 | 10 | 12 | 14 | 16 | 18 | 20 |

D

Speed Forcing Drill

Key a 30" timed writing on each line. Your *gwam* is shown below the lines.

 TIP Reach out with your little finger and tap the Enter key quickly. Return your finger to its home key.

1 Jan left to go home.
2 They won their last game.
3 Kay's test score was terrible.
4 The four games may not be canceled.
5 The hurricane struck Florida on Tuesday.
6 The teacher said Jane could make up the exam.
7 She may be able to catch a later flight on Friday.

gwam 30" | 2 | 4 | 6 | 8 | 10 | 12 | 14 | 16 | 18 | 20 |

E

Technique: Capital Letters

Key the paragraph at the right twice; try to increase your speed the second keying.

 TIP
1. Hold down the shift key.
2. Tap the letter with the finger on the opposite hand.
3. Return fingers to home keys.

Rockefeller Center in New York City is named after John D. Rockefeller, Jr. The center includes such things as the General Electric Building, NBC Studios, and Radio City Music Hall. Nearby attractions include St. Patrick's Cathedral, The Museum of Modern Art, Harvard Club of New York City, Princeton Club of New York, and Times Square.

F

Timed Writing

Key three 1' timed writings on the paragraph, striving to key more on each timing; determine *gwam*.

 A all letters used

```
          •      2      •      4      •      6      •      8      •     10
        John D. Rockefeller was one of the richest people
     •     12      •     14      •     16      •     18      •     20
in the world. He accumulated most of his wealth from
  •     22      •     24      •     26      •     28      •     30      •
the oil company he started. He is not only known for
  32      •     34      •     36      •     38      •     40      •
his money, but also for his philanthropy. He was a
  42      •     44      •     46      •     48      •     50      •     52
person who provided extra large quantities of money to
     •     54      •     56      •     58      •     60      •     62      •
worthwhile organizations. His gifts were made to such
  64      •     66      •     68      •     70      •     72
areas as medicine, education, and research.
```

Basic Technology Skills 7

Browser and Search Features

OUTCOMES

- Use the History and Favorites features of the browser
- Use the Search feature on a website
- Employ techniques to search the entire web
- Improve search techniques
- Use power search techniques to find information

Browser History and Favorites

Browser programs such as *Edge*, *Internet Explorer*, *Chrome*, *Safari*, and *Firefox* have features that can help you find and revisit websites. The **History** feature shows you a list of links for sites you have visited recently. Some browsers let you change the display of sites in the History list to show sites visited by date, by order, or by frequency. You may also be able to use the browser's address bar to view links to sites you have recently visited.

The **Favorites** feature allows you to create a list of links for sites you visit often. (Some browsers call these links Bookmarks rather than Favorites.) You can use the links to move quickly to a site. You can organize them into folders to make it easier to locate the link you want.

Activity 1

1. Log on to the Internet and start Microsoft *Edge* or your default browser.

2. Locate and display your History list. (In *Edge*, click the *Hub* icon and then click the *History* icon. See Figure BT7-1.)

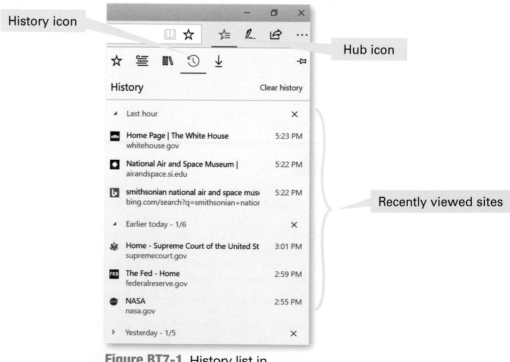

Figure BT7-1 History list in Microsoft *Edge*

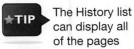
3. On the History list, click the link for the NASA site (nasa.gov) that you visited earlier.

4. Display the History list again. If you are using *Edge*, click the expansion arrow to the left of *Last hour* (or *Earlier today*) if necessary, and view the websites you have most recently viewed.

5. Click the *National Air and Space Museum* link.

6. Click anywhere in the address bar to see a list of sites you have most frequently viewed. (See Figure BT7-2.)

Figure BT7-2 Frequently viewed websites in Microsoft *Edge*

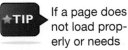
7. You also can open a previously viewed page by keying the first part of the URL. Start keying **msn** in the address bar. *Edge* automatically fills in the .com/ part of the address, and the full URL appears in the drop-down list with a History icon as shown in Figure BT7-3.

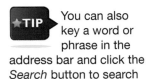
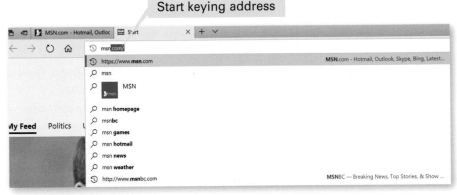

Figure BT7-3 Previously accessed website in Microsoft *Edge*

8. You can either tap *Enter* to accept the filled-in URL or click the link for *https://www.msn.com* that appears below the address bar. Your browser displays this site. Leave your browser open for the next activity.

★TIP To save articles or sites you want to look at later without cluttering your favorites list, you can use the Microsoft *Edge* reading list feature. After clicking the star icon on the address bar, click the *Reading list* tab in the drop-down dialog and save the site similarly to saving a favorite.

1. The msn.com website contains the latest headlines from around the world, weather, sports, and other information that you can use every day. To make visiting the site easy, you can add it to your Favorites list. Click the *Add to favorites or reading list* icon at the right end of the address bar (in *Edge* it looks like a star) to display a Favorites drop-down (see Figure BT7-4) or a bookmark dialog box.

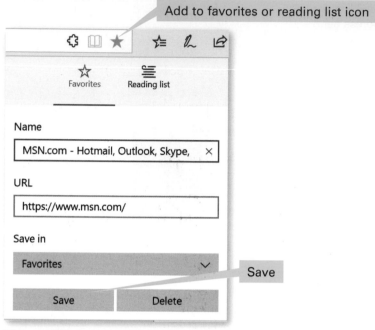

Figure BT7-4 Adding to Favorites or Reading list in Microsoft *Edge*

2. To add a favorite, make sure the *Favorites* tab is selected and the Name for the site is what you want. Click *Save*.
3. Click the *Home* button to go to your home page. Then click the *Hub* icon. (Use Bookmarks in *Firefox* or *Chrome*.) Click the *Favorites* icon.
4. Locate the link on your Favorites list for the msn.com site. Click the link to go to this site.
5. Use any method to display the NASA site you visited earlier and then add the NASA site to your Favorites list.

Search for Information on a Website

You can use a **search** feature to find information. Services such as Google and Yahoo! search the entire web. Other search tools search a single site, such as NASA or the Library of Congress.

To search either the web or a single site, key a word (called a **keyword**) into a search text box and tap *Enter* or click the *Search* or *Go* command. An example of the search box from the NASA site is shown in Figure BT7-5.

NASA's search box

Figure BT7-5 The NASA website search feature

Each time you search for something on the web, you are conducting a **query**. A query is a problem you want the search tool to resolve. Search tools use mathematical logic to satisfy a query based on the keyword(s) you enter.

Answers to a query are called **results**. When the search is complete, a list of results (also called *hits*) appears. Scroll through the results and choose the one that seems to have the information you need.

Sample search results for a NASA search on the word "satellites" are shown in Figure BT7-6. To access an item from the list, click the link. If you want to go back to the list to try another link, use the Back button. Some search engines list the results in pages. To see more results, click the page number or *Next*.

Activity 3

1. Log on to the Internet and start your browser. Use the Favorites link to go to the NASA website at http://www.nasa.gov.
2. Look for a search box similar to the one shown in Figure BT7-6.
3. Key the term **satellites** in the search box. Click the *Search* (magnifying glass) button to begin the search.

Links to more pages of results

Figure BT7-6 Search results on the NASA website

4. Scroll through the results to find an item that interests you. Click the link and read the first paragraph of the article. If your browser supports the reading list feature, save the article to your reading list. Use the Back button to return to the main list and read parts of one or two other articles, and save them to your reading list.

5. Open *Word* and start a new, blank document. Summarize in a paragraph what you read in the three articles. Save the document as *bt7 nasa* and close it.

1. If necessary, log on to the Internet and start your browser. In the address bar, key **nps.gov**. This is the URL for the U.S. National Park Service website.

2. On the welcome screen, look for a search box. Key the name of a U.S. national park in the search box. For example, you could key **Yosemite** or **Yellowstone**. Click *Search* or the button provided to start the search.

3. Scroll through the hits to find an item that interests you. Click the link and read the first paragraph of the article. Use the Back button if desired and read one or two more articles.

4. Open a new, blank *Word* document. Write a short statement summarizing what you read in each of your three articles from this exercise. Save the document as *bt7 nps* and close it.

1. If necessary, log on to the Internet and start Microsoft *Edge*. Use the History feature to go to the U.S. National Park Service website (http://www.nps.gov).

2. Add this site to your Favorites list.

3. In the site's search box, key **Yellowstone**. Click *Search* or the button provided to start the search.

4. Open a new, blank *Word* document.

5. Read the items in the search results as needed and answer the following questions in your document:

   - In what state(s) is the park located?

   - What is the size of the park?

   - When was the park established as a park?

   - What are some of the main attractions of the park?

6. Save the document as *bt7 questions* and close it.

✓ **checkpoint**

Compare your answers with those of a classmate. If the first two answers differ, check the website again for accurate information.

Search the Entire Web

It is one thing to search a site such as NASA with thousands of pages of information. It is quite another to search the entire Internet containing billions of possible results. Articles and reports can be found on almost any topic from millions of sites. Finding the exact information you need can be a challenge.

Web-based search engines can help you meet this challenge. A search engine is a program that performs keyword searches to pinpoint the Internet content you need.

To use a search engine, log on to the Internet and open your browser. Key the URL of any search engine in the address bar. The addresses of some common search tools are listed here:

- Google   google.com
- Yahoo!   yahoo.com
- Bing   bing.com

Narrow a Search

You will often need to narrow your search results by adding keywords to your search phrase.

1. If necessary, start your browser and key **google.com** (or pick another search tool) in the address bar; then tap *Enter*.
2. Key the words **hiking trails** in the search window shown in Figure BT7-8 and tap *Enter*.

Figure BT7-7 Google search engine in the Google *Chrome* web browser

3. Open a new, blank *Word* document. Save the document as ***bt7 search***. Record the number of results you received. As illustrated in Figure BT7-8, the results probably number in the millions.

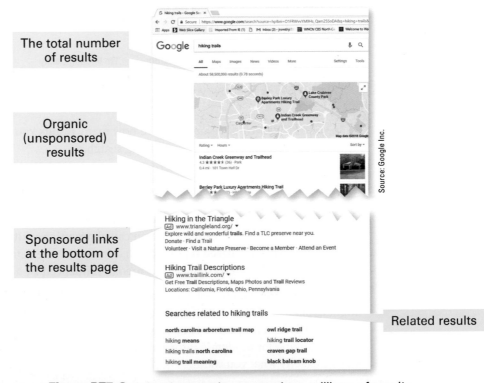

The total number of results

Organic (unsponsored) results

Sponsored links at the bottom of the results page

Related results

Figure BT7-8 A few keywords can produce millions of results

★TIP A web browser is a program used to visit websites, while a search engine is a tool that allows you to look for specific websites or information based on keywords, dates, and other criteria. Common examples of web browsers include *Edge*, *Safari*, *Firefox*, and *Chrome*. Common examples of search engines are Google, Bing, and Yahoo!.

NOTE **You will see** *sponsored links* **at the right side (or sometimes at the top) of your results. These links are advertisements sponsored by companies that want to sell products. Unless you plan on buying something, do not click sponsored links or you'll see an advertisement.**

4. Scroll down and review the organic, or unsponsored, results that have been returned. Notice that they can encompass any hiking and/or hiking trail–related topics. For example:

- State Park trails
- Hiking trails directory
- Day hiking trails
- Trails for all-terrain vehicles
- Dog-friendly trails

Since these results are so broad, we will narrow the search geographically.

5. Key the search words **hiking trails north carolina** and tap *Enter*.
6. In your *bt7 search* document, record how many results you received when you limited the search by geographical location.

These results are still a little broader than you may need. So we will narrow the search further to include only information on trails you can hike in North Carolina parks.

7. Key **hiking trails north carolina parks** as shown in Figure BT7-9 and tap *Enter*.

Source: Google Inc.

Figure BT7-9 Narrow your search

8. In your *bt7 search* document, record how many results you received. Compare the total number of results with each succeeding search.
9. Close your browser. Save the *Word* document and close it.

Analyze Search Results

Search results may contain dozens, thousands, hundreds of thousands, or even millions of entries. The main lists of results are often called **organic results**. (See Figure BT7-8.) These results occur naturally based on the search criteria and the detailed mathematics applied by Google or another search engine. They are *not* influenced by advertising dollars.

Depending on the search tool, you may see **sponsored links**. (See Figure BT7-8.) These links might appear shaded in color or marked as "Ad," flanking the results on the side and/or near the top. Advertisers have paid to list these sites. They may not be the most relevant to your search if you are looking for academic information. However, if you are looking to buy something, they may be exactly what you want.

Improve Search Techniques

★TIP Results are sorted by order of relevance. This means that the websites or documents most likely to contain the information you want are listed first. But if you do not get the information you want, you may need to improve your keyword choices and try again.

As you surf the Internet looking for information, remember some of these important search tips.

- Search engines such as Google find the **stem** of a word (for example, *hike*) and include related words with different endings or tenses in the search (for example, *hiking*, *hiker*, and *hiked*).

- Do not worry about capitalization. *North Carolina* is the same as *north carolina*.

- If you use multiple words such as *hiking trail parks*, you will receive a list of results that correlates with all three words. But the correlation may be random. For example, you may be taken to a web article that contains information about *locations you can mountain bike*, *parks that allow use of all-terrain vehicles*. This may not be at all what you are seeking.

- You can turn individual words into phrases by using quotation marks; for example, *appalachian trail*. This is called **phrase searching**. The quotation marks force a search for the exact sequence of words enclosed within the marks.

- Search engines throw out small or insignificant words such as *and*, *I*, *it*, *the*, and *or* and single digits such as *1* and *7*. This helps speed up the search, so do not bother entering them.

- If a normally insignificant word is absolutely essential to the success of a search, put a + directly in front of it preceded by a space; for example, *+1*.

Activity 7

★TIP Use the exact name, **Solitude Mountain Resort**, to narrow your search further. Did you find http:// www.skisolitude .com?

★TIP The *I'm Feeling Lucky* option on Google will take you directly to Google's most relevant website result for your query.

In this activity, you will use phrase searching to locate a specific Utah ski resort high in the Wasatch Mountains east of Salt Lake City (SLC), Utah. Imagine that you can recall only the vaguest details but do remember that it is in *Big Cottonwood Canyon*.

Figure BT7-10 Finding what you are looking for is easy online

1. Start your browser if necessary and key the address **google.com**.
2. Key the words **big cottonwood canyon** within quotation marks following your other search words:

   ski snowboard utah "big cottonwood canyon"

3. In your *bt7 search* document, record how many results came from your query. Did Google return results and links that mention the Solitude Mountain Resort? If so, record a few samples in your notes.
4. Save and close the document.

Power Search Techniques

Searches are much easier, more powerful, and more fun than they were in the past. In this next activity, you will try some powerful search techniques. You will:

- Search for the types of books you like to read
- Query for a definition by entering the **define** operator

Angela Waye/Shutterstock.com

- Search for a street map by entering an address along with the city and state
- Query a stock quote by entering the appropriate ticker symbol
- Conduct queries to find the weather in a city or at an airport
- Search for great places to eat in Utah
- Use the negative operator (−) to exclude things you do not want in your search
- Pose queries in the form of natural questions

Activity 8

1. Start a new, blank *Word* document and save it as ***bt7 power search***; then start your browser if necessary. Go to **google.com**.
2. Search for the following:

   books about skiing

   books on snowboarding

3. Conduct a search for the types of books you like to read. List the top three results in your ***bt7 power search*** document.
4. Find a map for a location near Solitude Mountain Resort by keying the following:

   12000 e big cottonwood canyon rd ut

   or

   12000 e big cottonwood canyon rd 84121

5. Click the map to expand it. Use the zoom control to move out from the location until you see the entire state of Utah.
6. Use your street address and zipcode to find a map that zooms in on your street in your community.
7. Conduct a query to find the current stock price for Google, Apple, and Microsoft. Use the following ticker symbols:

   goog

   aapl

   msft

   Record the price of all three stocks in the ***bt7 power search*** document.
8. Find the weather in Salt Lake City, which is about 30 miles from Solitude Mountain Resort. Key the following:

   weather slc

   or

   weather slc airport

   Record the current conditions in the ***bt7 power search*** document.
9. Find a list of great restaurants in Utah, but exclude Italian food. Key the following: **utah restaurants-Italian**.

   Record the three top results in the ***bt7 power search*** document.

10. Find a list of restaurants in your area, but exclude fast-food restaurants. How complete a list did you obtain? Key the number in the *bt7 power search* document.

11. Use a natural question to find answers to the following queries:

What is the population of Utah?

Who is the governor of Utah?

Record the answers to those questions in the *bt7 power search* document.

12. Define and record three words you do not know the meaning of. Use the define operator followed by the word. For example:

define: snowboarding

define: skiing

13. Save your answers and notes in the *bt7 power search* document and close it.

Before You Move On

1. What are the three things the Help feature allows you to do? follows 27A

2. List two ways you can access Help when you have a question. follows 27A

3. List two of the three things the dropdown arrow on the Help screen allows you to do. LO 27C

4. Explain how the pop-up description box (ScreenTips) can help you learn how to use an application or create a document. LO 28A and 28B

5. Name the four types of information you can access at Office 365 Online. LO 28C

6. Explain how Microsoft's Online Training Center can help you now and on the job in the future. LO 28D

Apply What You Have Learned

Accessing Help

1. Access the Help viewer by tapping the F1 key.

2. Click the *Tell me what you want to do* box.

3. Describe how the help you are provided by each method of access is different.

Using ScreenTips

1. Access the Home tab in *Word*.

2. View the pop-up description box for the Styles group on the Home tab.

3. In two to three sentences, explain the information the pop-up description box provides you.

CHAPTER 4

Communicating and Scheduling at School and Work

Lesson 29   Format Email Messages
Lesson 30   Create, Format, and Manage Email Messages
Lesson 31   Calendaring, Contacts, and Tasks

Application Guide

What Is Personal Information Management Software?

We live in a fast-paced world. Our schedules are filled with school, work, family, and extra-curricular activities. We are constantly communicating with others. The latest technological advances allow us to exchange more information faster than ever before. We are inundated with information. We schedule appointments and exchange addresses, telephone numbers, cell phone numbers, email addresses, etc.

It is critical to be organized if we are to survive in this fast-paced world. Today's personal information manager software (PIMS) provides the solution to manage this abundance of information and to be personally and professionally organized. As shown in Figure 4-1, most PIMS has:

- An **Email** feature to send, receive, and manage emails

- A **Calendar** feature to keep track of schedules

- A **People (Contacts)** feature to maintain information needed to contact others

- A **Tasks** feature to record items that need to be done

- A **Notes** feature to provide reminders

JPC-PROD/Shutterstock.com

| Email | Calendar | People | Tasks | Navigation Options including Notes, Folders, and Shortcuts |

Figure 4-1 Components of PIMS

Email

Mail > Home tab > New > New Email

Message tab > Include > Attach File

Email (electronic mail) is used in most business organizations. Because of the ease of creating and the speed of sending, email messages have nearly replaced the memo and the letter. Generally, delivery of an email message takes place within seconds, whether the receiver is in the same building or in a location across the globe. An email message is illustrated in Figure 4-2.

Email heading. The format used for the email heading may vary slightly, depending on the program used for creating email. The heading generally includes who the email is being sent to (**To**), what the email is about (**Subject**), and who gets copies of the email (**Cc**). The name of the person sending the email and the date the email is sent are automatically included by the software. If you don't want the person receiving the email to know that you are sending a copy of the email to another person, the blind copy (**Bcc**) feature can be used.

Email body. The paragraphs of an email message all begin at the left margin and are SS with a DS between paragraphs.

Email attachments. Attachments can be included with your email by using the Attachment feature of the software. Common types of attachments include word processing, database, and spreadsheet files as well as graphics and PDF (Portable Document Format) files.

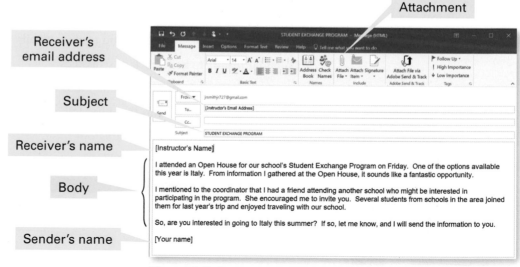

Figure 4-2 Email message

Home tab > Tags

 In order to see or use the Categorize feature, you must have a Microsoft *Exchange* email account. Otherwise, this feature is not active.

Email tags. Tags (reminders) can be placed on your email messages to mark them as unread or read, to categorize them, or to mark them for follow-up. This provides reminders for you to deal with specific emails at a later date or to easily find and access emails that have been categorized. The Tags group is located on the Home tab (see Figure 4-3).

The Unread/Read icon is used to mark a message that you have read as unread or to mark a message that you haven't read as read. The Categorize tag is used to mark messages as high importance or low importance or as another category that you create. If you wanted to mark all the messages that you receive from a particular person or a particular firm, you can rename a color tag with the name of the person or the name of the company. The Follow Up tag is used to mark messages that you plan on taking care of at a later time.

Figure 4-3 Email tags

Home tab > Find >
Search People

Search People. Use the Search People feature to quickly access email address information about any person included in your contacts by clicking the Search People box and keying the name. This feature is located on the Home tab in the Find group (see Figure 4-4).

Figure 4-4 Search People

Email Inbox—Search and Arrange By. The email Inbox receives all incoming email messages. To find specific email messages you can use the Search feature (see Figure 4-5).

The Search feature finds specific messages based on a word, phrase, or other text. Once you enter text in the Search box, the Search Tools context tab appears on the Ribbon (see Figure 4-6). Here you can filter search results by different criteria, such as From a specific person, or Unread messages. You can also use the Arrange By feature to organize your Inbox. Access this feature by clicking the *All* drop-down list arrow (shown in Figure 4-5) and selecting *Arrange By*. The more common arrangements are by Date, From, To, and Size.

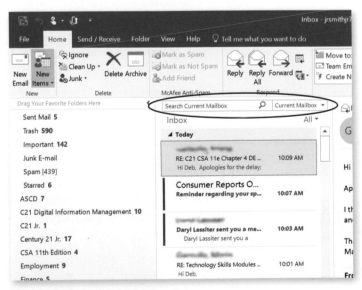

Figure 4-5 Search email

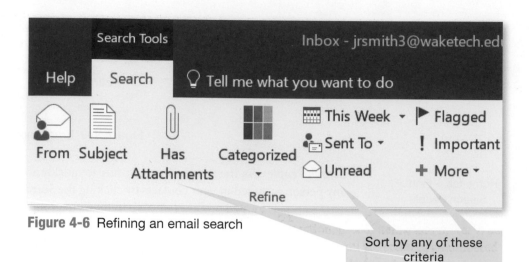

Figure 4-6 Refining an email search

Sort by any of these criteria

Calendar

Calendar > Home tab >
New > New Appointment

The Calendar feature is used to record and display appointments electronically. The calendar can be displayed and printed in a variety of ways (daily, weekly, or monthly), depending on how it will be used. The daily display is illustrated in Figure 4-7.

Appointments can be scheduled by clicking *New Appointment* on the Home tab of the Ribbon (Ctrl + N) or by selecting the day and then clicking in the location where you want to key the information. Recurring appointments (those that occur repeatedly) can also be scheduled. For example, if you had a music lesson every Monday at 4 p.m., you could use the Recurrence feature to automatically place the music lesson on the calendar each Monday at 4 p.m.

Figure 4-7 Daily calendar with appointments

Contacts

People > Home tab >
New > New Contact

The Contacts feature is used to store information about your associates. Generally, the person's name, business address, phone number, and email address are recorded. The Notes portion can be used to record additional information about the person. Click *New Contact* on the Home tab of the Ribbon or use the quick keys (Ctrl + N) to access the New Contact dialog box (see Figure 4-8).

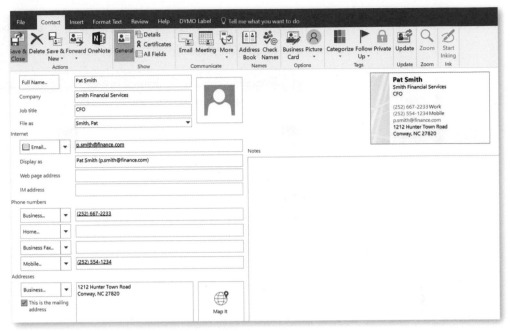

Figure 4-8 New Contact information

Information recorded in Contacts can be viewed electronically in several different views:

- People
- List
- Business Card
- Phone
- Card

The Business Card view is illustrated in Figure 4-9.

Figure 4-9 Contacts in Business Card view

Use the alphanumeric search list on the left of the contacts to quickly access the person you are looking for by clicking the first letter of their last name. As contact information changes, the cards can be edited by double-clicking the business card.

Contact information can also be printed in a variety of styles, including card style, small booklet style, medium booklet style, memo style, and phone directory style. Card style is illustrated in Figure 4-10.

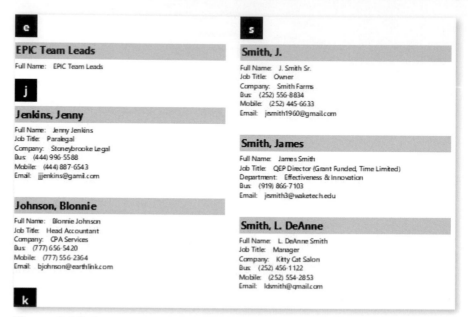

Figure 4-10 Contacts printed in card style

Tasks

Tasks > Home tab >
New > New Task

The Tasks feature allows you to record tasks that you are responsible for completing (see Figure 4-11). When a task is recorded, it is less likely to be forgotten. Completion dates and reminders can be set for each task. Once the task has been completed, it can be checked off, as shown in Figure 4-11. Click *New Task* on the Home tab of the Ribbon, or use the quick keys (Ctrl + N) to access the Tasks dialog box. Use the Current View feature to display different views of the tasks that have been entered.

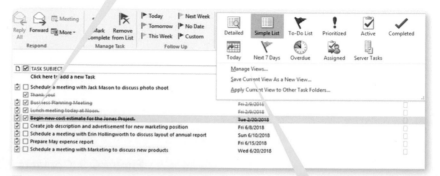

Figure 4-11 Tasks (To-Do/Did list)

Notes

Navigation Options >
Notes > Home tab >
New > New Note

★ TIP
1. You can create a note from any Outlook folder by pressing *Ctrl + Shift + N*.
2. Type the text in the note.
3. To save and close the note, click the note icon in the upper-left corner of the note window, and then click *Save & Close*.

Notes are the electronic equivalent of paper sticky notes. Use Notes to jot down questions, ideas, reminders, and anything you would write on paper. You can leave Notes open on the screen while you work. This is convenient when you are using notes for saving information you might need later, such as directions or text you want to reuse in other items or documents.

To create a note, click the Navigation Options button (…) in the Navigation bar and click *Notes*. Then click *New Note* in the Home tab to open a "sticky note" where you can type your note (see Figure 4-12).

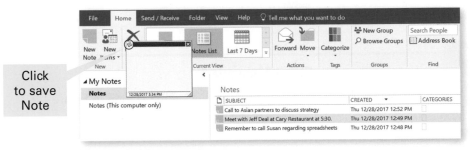

Figure 4-12 Notes feature

21st Century Skills: Communicate Clearly
As you learned in this chapter, email has become one of the most common ways for computer users to communicate, both personally and for business purposes. Although email is considered less formal than other business communications, it is still important to articulate your thoughts and ideas effectively in an email message. You should:

- Write in complete, active sentences

- Proofread and check your spelling

- Avoid "bells and whistles," such as writing in all caps or inserting emoticons, that detract from your message

Most importantly, you should always know your audience and understand that your message could be shared either intentionally or by mistake with someone else.

Think Critically

With a partner, respond to these questions. Ask your instructor if you will need to turn this activity in for grading.

COLLABORATION

1. What perception might you form of a person who sends an email that has spelling and grammatical errors?
2. Under what circumstances in a business setting might email *not* be the best form of communication?
3. Give an example of how you could use email at work to instruct others on a topic.

Rawpixel.com/Shutterstock.com

LESSON 29

Format Email Messages

OUTCOME

- Learn to format email messages

alphabet 1 Jordan placed first by solving the complex quiz in one week.

spacing 2 When you get to the game, save two seats for Ron and Felipe.

speed 3 Jan paid the big man for the field work he did for the firm.

gwam 1' | 1 | 2 | 3 | 4 | 5 | 6 | 7 | 8 | 9 | 10 | 11 | 12 |

29B

Email Messages

★TIP Email can be saved using the same process used to save a *Word* document.

Email Message 1

1. Study the model email illustration in Figure 4-2.
2. Format and key the model illustration.
3. Proofread your copy; correct all errors.
4. Send the email to your instructor's email address, or your instructor may assign a classmate's email address to use instead.
5. **Save as: *29b email1*.**

Email Messages 2 and 3

1. Format and key the email messages 2 and 3 shown below and on the next page.
2. Proofread your copy; correct all errors.
3. Send the email messages to your instructor's email address, or your instructor may assign a classmate's email address to use instead.
4. **Save as: *29b email2*** and ***29b email3*.**

Email Message 2

Subject: HELP

Hopefully, my sister told you that I would be emailing you. I'm writing a report on Mark Twain for my English class. Last weekend when Katherine was home, we were talking about this assignment. She mentioned that you were an English major and seemed to think that you had completed a course that focused on Mark Twain. She suggested that I contact you to see if you would be able to suggest some sources that I might use for this assignment.

As part of the report project, we have to read two of his books. I've already started reading *Life on the Mississippi*. Could you offer a suggestion as to what other book I should read for this assignment?

Katherine said that you are planning on coming home with her during spring break. I'll look forward to meeting you.

[Your Name]

ASDF_MEDIA/Shutterstock.com

Email Message 3

Subject: WEBPAGE CREATION

As we develop our webpage, we may want to review some of those developed by other symphonies. I have already looked at several. San Francisco's was one that I felt we could model ours after.

Theirs is clear, concise, and easy to navigate. In addition to the normal sections, they have a section called "More about the San Francisco Symphony." Here they include such things as:

1. A brief history
2. The mission statement
3. Community programs
4. News items about the Symphony

To view their webpage, go to www.sfsymphony.org. I'll look forward to working with you at our next committee meeting.

[Your Name]

LESSON 30 — Create, Format, and Manage Email Messages

OUTCOMES
- Learn to create email messages
- Learn tips for evaluating email messages
- Learn tips for managing email messages

30B

Create Email Message

You have narrowed down to three the number of schools that you are considering attending when you graduate. A friend of yours started school this fall at one of your final three choices. Send an email to your friend to gather additional information about the school he/she is attending to help you decide on which of the three schools to attend. Before starting the email, think about all the things that are important to you in selecting a school to attend.

After completing your email, print a copy of it, exchange it with one of your classmates, and complete 30C.

30C

Evaluate Email Message

1. Read the email your classmate created for 30B.
2. Read the following Tips for Creating Effective Email Messages.
3. Evaluate your classmate's email based on these tips, using the Email Evaluation Form (*df 30c eval form*).

Tips for Creating Effective Email Messages

1. **Subject lines are important; use them**. A subject line entices the receiver to open and read the message immediately. Messages that aren't opened immediately often get overlooked. At a later date, a subject line allows the receiver to quickly find and access emails. Consider the subject line to be like the wrapping on a package. The package with the best wrapping attracts more attention than the other packages.

2. **The length of the message should be considered; keep them short**. The number of emails a person receives has steadily increased. Keep your message short. By keeping your message short, you won't waste the time of the person you are sending it to, and the receiver is more likely to understand the main points you are making. Longer messages tend to be disorganized.

3. **Your emails reflect you; make a good impression**. An email may be the first impression that the receiver has of you and your organization. The same care given to memos and letters should be given to emails. Make a good impression by having a well-organized message.

4. **Proofread your email message before sending; errors are unacceptable**. Most email messages require editing during writing and after they have been created. Proofread for correct spelling, punctuation, grammar, sentence structure, and capitalization. If you don't, you are either telling the receiver they are not important or that you lack the ability to create an error-free message.

5. **Respond to emails quickly; if you don't, you are still sending a message**. If you are not in a position to respond to an email immediately, let the sender know when they can expect to receive an answer. Doing so builds goodwill.

6. **Be careful of sending negative messages; you can't retract them**. Often people say things in anger that they later regret. It is a good idea to write down your ideas to release your anger but wait until the next day to send the email. A very high percentage of those messages are either never sent or revised considerably before being sent.

7. **Consider bullet points to emphasize specifics; they are easier to follow**. Important information can be lost in a long sentence using commas to separate points. A bullet list of points makes it easy to see exactly what you are requesting. If you have multiple questions, a bullet list may result in getting all questions answered.

8. **Consider whether email is the best form of communication; often it is not**. Don't get in the habit of communicating everything with email. There are times when face-to-face communication or a phone call will get you the desired result. Remember, it is much easier to say no in an email than it is when the person is talking to you in person.

9. **Double-check dates and times; otherwise, you may have a surprise party**. Date errors are common; for example, keying Tuesday, January 20, when January 20 is really on Wednesday. This results in confusion or the possibility of a person showing up on the wrong date. Always double-check dates.

10. **Make it clear what you want; make it as easy as possible for the receiver to provide what you want**. After creating an email, read it as though you were receiving it. Ask the question, "What does this person want?" If you are not sure, the reader definitely won't be. Another question you should ask is whether you have made it easy for the person to do what you want. The easier it is, the more likely the person will accommodate you.

Phovoir/Shutterstock.com

30D

Manage Email

 TIP You will learn more about how to manage and organize your email in Chapter 11.

Read the following tips for managing email.

Tips for Managing Email

✓ Set up separate accounts for personal and business email messages.

✓ Set aside specific times each day to respond to emails. Don't let incoming emails take your attention away from important tasks that you are working on.

✓ Respond to an email when you read it unless doing so will take too much time. Not responding clutters your mind as well as your inbox. Reading an email a second time that could have been quickly dealt with in the first reading is a waste of time.

✓ Delete emails after responding to them unless a record is needed. Large emails with attachments take up a lot of storage space.

✓ Use shortcuts:
- Ctrl + D (Delete current email)
- Ctrl + R (Reply to current email)
- Ctrl + F (Forward current email)

✓ Use the Junk Email feature to block spam as well as to block individuals you don't want to receive email messages from.

✓ Delete older messages that are no longer of value to you.

✓ Use the phone rather than email for topics that require a great deal of discussion.

✓ Create separate folders for persons you correspond with frequently or for topics where you want to keep related emails together.

✓ Try to leave the office each day with an empty inbox.

30E

Create Email

Your instructor is having trouble managing his or her email. Send an email message to your instructor offering suggestions for managing email. You can use the tips shown in 30D as a basis for your email, or you can come up with your own tips. Keep the message brief. Offer only three to five tips in the message.

LESSON 31   Contacts, Calendar, Tasks, and Notes

OUTCOME

- Learn to use the Contacts, Calendar, Tasks, and Notes features

31B

Contacts

People > Home tab > New > New Contact

Home tab > Current View > Business Card

1. Open *Outlook*.
2. Create new contacts with the information from the six business cards on pages 4-12 and 4-13.
3. Ask your instructor to screen check that you have successfully created the new contacts. (Your instructor may assign a classmate to complete the screen check.)

Jackson W. Farrell
Local Sales Agent

2701 Standord Avenue
Dallas, TX 75225
jwfarrell@yah-oo.com

Phone: 469-405-3288
Fax: 469-405-3290

www.AguilarRealty.com

Aguilar Realty
COMPANY

Old Home Studio

Maria Santos

381 Hilltop Drive
Longmont, CO 80501

970-923-1655
msantos@microsoft.com

Fax: 970-923-1600

Jason Finnimore
Director of Human Resources

731 Chadwick Circle
Kissimmee, FL 34746
407-382-1832 ph
407-382-1838 fax
jpfennimore@translink.com

Global Technologies

Printing Unlimited

Gary L. Bergeron

Design Associate

316 Huntington Avenue
Minneapolis, MN 55416

Phone (612) 901-7815
Fax (612) 901-7823

bergerongl@yahoo.com

Katrina A. Lopez
Freelance Presenter

Team Building to Go!
200 Vista Lane, San Diego, CA 92073

TEL | 619-333-0118
EMAIL | kalopez@g-mail.com
WEB | www.teambuildtogo.com

EZ Printing

Kaitlin A. Dixon
Marketing Representative
489 Melrose St. W
Chicago, IL 60657

Phone 708.515.0689
dixonka@g-mail.com

www.EZPrintxx.com

31C

Calendar

Calendar > Home tab >
New > New Appointment

1. Open *Outlook*.
2. Record the appointments shown below for June of the current year.
3. Print a copy of the month of June and turn it in to your instructor for grading.

1. Board Meeting on June 18, (current year) from 8 to 11:30 a.m. in the Lincoln Conference Room.
2. Board Luncheon on June 18, (current year) from 12:00 to 1:30 p.m. at Bartorolli's.
3. Jamison Russell, Vice President of Riley Manufacturing, on June 17, (current year) from 1:30 to 2:30 p.m.
4. Vivian Bloomfield, Manager of Garnett Enterprises, on June 27, (current year) from 8:30 to 9:30 p.m.
5. Chamber of Commerce meeting on June 13, (current year) from 5:30 to 7:30 p.m.

31D

Tasks

Tasks > Home tab > New
> New Task

1. Open *Outlook*.
2. Record the tasks shown below using the Tasks feature.
3. Print a copy of the task list and turn it in to your instructor for grading.

1. Schedule an appointment with Jack Mason to discuss photo shoot.
2. Schedule a meeting with Marketing to discuss new products (Due Date: June 20).
3. Prepare May expense report (Due date: June 15).
4. Schedule meeting with Erin Hollingsworth to discuss layout of annual report (Due Date: June 10).
5. Create job description and advertisement for new marketing position (Due Date: June 8).

31E

Notes

Navigation Options >
Notes > New Note

1. Open *Outlook*.
2. Record the notes shown below using the Notes feature.
3. **Save as: *31e notes*.**

1. Get agenda ready for the June 23 opening meeting with branch managers.
2. Call Brookstone Travel Agency to discuss discounts for volume travel.
3. Check with Paul to discuss his role at the branch managers meeting.
4. Schedule meeting with Ms. St. Claire to finalize board luncheon.
5. Call Jamal Carter to get report on the Gender Communication seminar.

1. Look in the Contacts you created in 31B; open *Word* data file **df 31f answers**.
2. Answer the following questions in the *df 31f answers* file.
3. Save as: **31f answers**.

1. What company does Jackson Farrell work for?
2. What is Kaitlin Dixon's email address?
3. What is the Fax No. where Maria Santos works?
4. What is Gary Bergeron's title?
5. What is Ms. Lopez's first name?

Ana Blazic Pavlovic/Shutterstock.com

Digital Citizenship and Ethics
Bullying comes in many forms, from teasing and name-calling to pushing and hitting to excluding others from a group. Technology has provided new ways for people to bully each other. Cyberbullying—or using online communications technology to harass or upset someone—has become increasingly common as more and more people gain access to cell phones and the Internet.

Now, cell phones, email, and social media can be used to send hateful messages or to share humiliating images. Threatening messages can be sent via chat rooms, message boards, and social networking sites. Name-calling and abusive remarks are thrown at players on gaming sites. What can you do about cyberbullying? As a class, discuss the following.

COLLABORATION

Think Critically

1. What are three things you can do so that you do not become a victim of cyberbullying?
2. If you've been the victim of cyberbullying, what course of action should you take?

Skill Builder 3

Warmup

Key each line twice. If time permits, key the lines again.

Alphabet

1 Wesley Van Jantz quickly proofed the biology exam.

Bottom Row

2 Nancy Mann will move six zinc boxes from the cave.

Speed

3 Pamela may hand signal to the big tug by the dock.

gwam 1' | 1 | 2 | 3 | 4 | 5 | 6 | 7 | 8 | 9 | 10 |

Technique Mastery of Individual Letters Keying Technique

Key each line twice, striving to maintain a continuous pace.

★TIP Fingers should be curved and upright.

N No one knew Nathan N. Nevins was not here at noon.

O I told Jose and Brook not to mop the floors today.

P Philippe paid for the pepper and paprika for Pepe.

Q Quinton quit questioning the adequacy of the quiz.

R Carrie, correct the two problems before departing.

S Steven and I saw Sam at Sally's session on Sunday.

T Tim bottled the water after talking with the maid.

U He urged us to put the rugs under the four trucks.

V Vivian Von Vogt took the vivid van to the village.

W Will Wesley work on the walnut wall for two weeks?

X The tax expert explained the tax exam's existence.

Y Jay may be ready to pay you your money on Tuesday.

Z Zelda was puzzled by the sizzling heat at the zoo.

gwam 30" | 2 | 4 | 6 | 8 | 10 | 12 | 14 | 16 | 18 | 20 |

C

Speed Forcing Drill

Key a 30'' timed writing on each line, striving to key more on each attempt.

 TIP Keep your eyes on the copy as you reach out and tap the Enter key quickly.

1 Paula went out for track.

2 Jan told me to see that movie.

3 Which search engine did Carmen use?

4 Paul bought the video game last weekend.

5 Sandy had a meeting with Mr. Sanchez at noon.

6 My coach told me to be ready for a difficult game.

gwam 30" | 2 | 4 | 6 | 8 | 10 | 12 | 14 | 16 | 18 | 20 |

D

Speed Building

1. Key three 1' timed writings on each paragraph, striving to key more on each timing; determine *gwam*.

2. Key a 2' timed writing on both paragraphs combined, striving to maintain your highest 1' *gwam*.

A all letters used

	gwam	1'	2'

The Bill of Rights includes the changes to — 8 — 4

the Constitution that deal with human rights of — 18 — 9

all people. The changes or amendments were designed — 28 — 14

to improve and correct the original document. They — 38 — 19

were made to ensure the quality of life and to — 47 — 24

protect the rights of all citizens. — 54 — 27

One of the changes provides for the right to — 9 — 32

religious choice, free speech, and free press. — 18 — 36

Another addresses the right to keep and bear fire- — 28 — 41

arms. Another provides for the rights of the people — 39 — 47

with regard to unreasonable search and seizure — 48 — 51

of person or property. Two others address the — 57 — 56

right to have an immediate and public trial by a jury — 67 — 61

and the prevention of excessive bail and fines. — 77 — 66

gwam 1' | 1 | 2 | 3 | 4 | 5 | 6 | 7 | 8 | 9 | 10 |

2' | 1 | 2 | 3 | 4 | 5 |

Basic Technology Skills 8

Basics of Good Digital Citizenship

OUTCOMES

- Learn about ethics and netiquette rules
- Learn about computer crime
- Learn about safety issues related to using the Internet
- Learn about copyright issues

Ethics and Netiquette

Computer users must be concerned with ethics related to information and networks. **Ethics** are moral standards or values. They describe how people should behave. **Netiquette** is a term often used to describe rules for proper online behavior.

To communicate successfully, you follow certain rules of ethical behavior. For example, you would not answer your cell phone and start shouting at someone. That would be considered rude. You also should follow rules of polite behavior when communicating online. The word *netiquette* is formed from the words *etiquette* (the requirements for proper social behavior) and *net* (from the word *Internet*).

Some netiquette rules relate to email and instant messages. For example, do not key or text in ALL CAPS. That is like shouting your message and is considered rude. Here are some other netiquette rules that you should know.

- Do not give out phone numbers or other personal information unless you are sure the site is safe.
- Never give out personal information about other people without their permission.
- Do not forward messages from other people without their permission.
- Send information only to those who need it. Busy people do not want to spend time reading messages that do not relate to them.
- Do not send spam. **Spam** includes any unsolicited or unwanted message.
- Be courteous to others in all online messages and on webpages. Do not use offensive or biased language.
- Respect the privacy of others. Do not read email or other material that is meant for someone else.
- Assume that messages (email, instant messages, phone conversations, blog postings, and social media postings) are not secure. Do not include private information.
- Be ethical. Do not copy material from the web and use it as your own without paying for it and listing it as a source.
- Do not use another person's computer or cell phone without his or her permission.
- Do not use the Internet for anything that is illegal.

1. Start *Word*. Open the document **df bt8 opportunity**. Read the email message contained in this document.
2. Work with one or two classmates to evaluate the email message. Does the message follow netiquette rules? On a separate sheet of paper, make a list of any rules this message violates.

COLLABORATION

3. Can your team identify any potential problems with the offer being made in this message? If so, list them.

4. Compare your team's responses to other teams in your class. Discuss any differences in team responses.

Computer Crime

Individuals and businesses alike can be victims of computer-related crime. People and companies must be careful to protect their private data. They also must protect the data gathered from others. For example, companies may have medical records or credit card numbers of customers. Those records are often stored on computers. This makes the records vulnerable to computer crime.

Computer Viruses and Hackers

One type of illegal activity related to computing is spreading computer viruses. A **computer virus** is a destructive program. A virus can be loaded onto a computer and run without the computer owner's knowledge. Viruses are dangerous. They can destroy data quickly. They also can cause a computer or network to stop working properly. Some viruses can travel across networks and get past security systems. Antivirus programs can find and remove viruses before they do harm. To protect their data, users should back up (make a copy of) important data and keep it in a safe place.

Another computer crime is called **hacking**. Hacking is accessing computers or networks without permission. People who do this are called **hackers**. Hacking is both unethical and illegal. Penalties for hacking can be up to 20 years in prison!

Hackers may be able to access and misuse information that belongs to others. For example, a hacker might steal a customer's credit card number to buy products over the Internet. This is an example of computer fraud.

Figure BT8-1 Computer hacked by ransomware

Phukan/Shutterstock.com

Another computer crime is committed through the use of **ransomware**. Ransomware is a type of malicious software that threatens to publish the victim's data or permanently deny access to it unless a "ransom" is paid (see Figure BT8-1). While some simple ransomware may lock the system in a way that is not difficult for a knowledgeable person to reverse, more advanced malware uses a technique called *crypotoviral extortion* in which it encrypts victim's files, making them inaccessible, and demands a ransom payment to decrypt them.

Ransomware attacks are typically carried out using a **Trojan**, a program that is disguised as a legitimate file that the user is tricked into downloading or opening. However, one high-profile example, the "WannaCry worm," traveled automatically between computers without user interaction.

Beginning in 2012, the use of ransomware scams has grown internationally. Individuals and companies falling victim to this type of computer crime can lose money and permanent access to their data. In businesses such as hospitals, hackers can block access to patient records, putting lives in danger.

Identity Theft

Sometimes a criminal may steal more than a credit card number. He or she may steal a person's identity. The criminal will find as much personal information about a victim as possible. For example, bank account numbers, Social Security numbers, job information, family information, and spending records may be hacked. Personal information also may come from a stolen purse or wallet.

Once a criminal has this type of information, he or she can pretend to be the person who owns that information. This is called **identity theft**. Money may be moved out of the victim's bank account. A new credit card account, using the victim's name, may be opened. Vacations, cars, and other expensive items may be charged to the victim's credit card. When the credit card bills are not paid, the overdue account is reported on the victim's credit report. The victim may be turned down for loans or may not be hired for jobs because of the bad credit report.

Millions of Americans have been victims of identity theft. Individuals and businesses have lost billions of dollars to this type of crime. The U.S. Federal Trade Commission (FTC) provides resources for victims of identity theft (see Figure BT8-2). The FTC also provides tips for reducing this crime. To reduce the chances of being a victim of identity theft, you can:

- Request and review a copy of your credit report every year
- Use strong passwords on credit card, bank, and phone accounts
- Avoid giving out personal information on the phone, through the mail, or over the Internet unless the site is reputable
- Shred charge receipts, credit records, checks, and bank statements before throwing them away
- Keep your Social Security card and number in a safe place
- Protect access to home computers and guard against computer viruses

Figure BT8-2 The U.S. Federal Trade Commission provides resources for identity theft victims

Scams

Some criminals run scams on the Internet. A **scam** is a scheme used to take money under false pretenses. For example, someone may want to sell you stolen music or will take your money without sending you the product you bought. To avoid being the victim of a scam, buy only from reputable companies. Do not give out personal information or credit card numbers unless you are certain the company is honest and the website is safe.

In this activity, you will access a website that has information about computer crimes. You will follow hyperlinks to find an article about one crime case and print the article.

1. If necessary, log on to the Internet and start Google *Chrome* or another browser. In the address bar, key **cybercrime.gov**. This site is hosted by the U.S. Department of Justice. (If you are using a different browser, follow the appropriate steps to complete this activity.)
2. Click hyperlinks related to computer crime and computer crime cases. Read about one computer crime case. Ask your instructor or a classmate for help if you cannot find an article.
3. Right-click and then click *Print* from the shortcut menu to see how the document will appear when printed. Scroll through the print preview and note the page numbers that include the article you chose.
4. In the left pane select your printer if needed. Choose to print 1 copy of only the pages on which your article appears. Click *Print*.
5. Read the case again from your printed copy. Use a marker or pen to highlight the main points of the article. Be prepared to share these points with the class.

Internet Safety

Beware of sharing personal information

Using the Internet is a great way to communicate and interact with other people. As in the real world, many people you meet will be honest and kind. They will have no intention of harming you or cheating you. However, as in the real world, some people in the virtual world try to cheat or harm others. For this reason, computer users must be concerned about safety.

Personal Safety

As a computer user, you should be concerned about your personal safety. When you meet someone on the Internet, you have only this person's word about who he or she is. You probably cannot see the person. The person may say that his or her age is 14 when it is really 40. The person may claim to be a woman when he is really a man. The person may pretend to be interested in the things that interest you to gain your trust. The person's real motive may be to deceive you or harm you.

To protect yourself, never give out your full name, personal address, phone number, school address, or other private information to individuals you do not know personally. Never send your picture to someone you do not know personally. Never agree to meet in person someone you have met on the Internet unless you have a parent or guardian present.

The person you meet might really be your age and share your interest in a hobby or sport. In that case, Mom or Dad can wait at the next table while you and your new friend talk and enjoy pizza. Your new friend probably brought Mom or Dad along, too. If the person you meet turns out to be different than you expected, you will be glad you have Mom or Dad nearby.

Safety of Data

Computer users should be concerned about the safety of their private data. Many people buy products from websites. Doctors have patients fill out medical history forms online. Bank customers make transactions online. All of those situations require entering personal information. How can you make sure your data will be safe when you use these kinds of websites?

Reputable companies take measures to ensure that the data will be safe. Internet browsers have built-in features that can help protect your personal information and identity. Settings in your browser help identify unsafe sites and let you set the security levels for trusted sites. A secure site address begins with https://, and a lock icon appears next to the site name in the address bar (see Figure BT8-3).

Lock icon

https:// means the site is secure

Welcome to the CIA Web ×

← → C ⬤ Central Intelligence Agency [US] | https://www.cia.gov/index.html

Source: Google Inc.

Figure BT8-3 Address bar of a secure website

A **digital certificate** verifies the identity of a person or indicates the security of a website. These certificates are issued by trusted companies such as VeriSign. Clicking the lock icon reveals security information about the website (see Figure BT8-4). The address bar is color-coded to let you know that your transactions are over a secure connection. For example, red means the certificate is out of date. Green is the most secure. Yellow means the certification authority cannot be verified and there might be a problem.

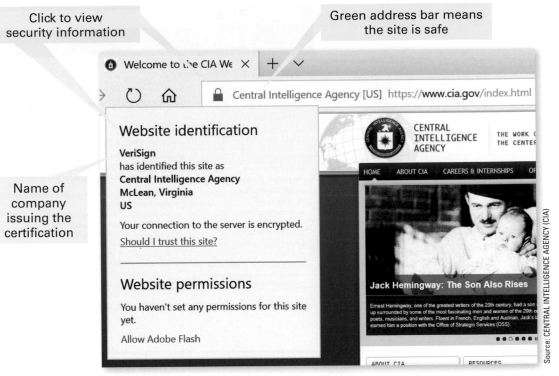

Figure BT8-4 Information about a website's certification

Once a company has your private data, it should take measures to keep it safe. Companies can use special hardware and software called **firewalls** to help prevent unauthorized users from getting to your data.

You should be aware of what a company plans to do with your data. Many companies post a privacy policy on their websites. A **privacy policy** is a document that tells how personal data will be used. A link such as *Privacy Statement* or *Privacy Policy* is often shown at the bottom of a site's welcome page. The first part of a typical privacy statement is shown in Figure BT8-5. Before entering your data, read the site's privacy policy to see if you approve of how your data will be used.

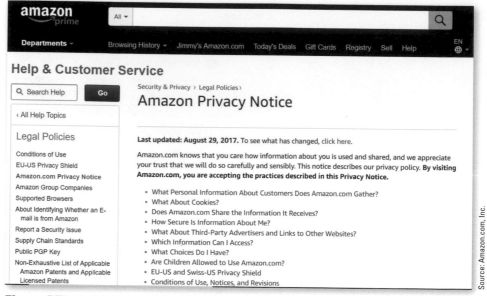

Figure BT8-5 Privacy statement for a website

Copyright Issues

People or companies that create works that are new, useful, and potentially profitable may be granted a copyright for those works. A **copyright** is a form of protection granted by the U.S. government. Copyright laws and rules tell how copyrighted works can be legally used. Works such as books, articles, music, plays, movie scripts, and artwork can be copyrighted. Copyrighted material may carry the © symbol. However, you should assume that material is copyrighted even if you do not see the symbol.

As a general rule, you may not use copyrighted material legally unless you have the owner's permission. However, you may be able to use a small portion of a copyrighted work for educational purposes. The rules that relate to this type of use are called the **fair use doctrine**.

Fair use doctrine does not allow plagiarism. The term **plagiarism** refers to using material created by another person and claiming it as your own. For example, suppose you find a report on the Internet that fits the assignment you were given. You print the report and turn it in with your name as the writer. This is plagiarism. Plagiarism in schoolwork may result in suspension or another serious punishment.

Copyright rules also affect what you can do with some works after you purchase them. For example, movies and music are often sold with certain terms and conditions. These terms may limit how you can use the movie or music. You may be able to make one or two copies of a song for backup purposes or to play on your personal devices. However, you may not be allowed to make copies of the song to give to friends.

Karramba Production/Shutterstock.com

Communication Skills 2

ACTIVITY 1: Number Expression

1. Study each of the eight rules shown at the right.
   a. Key the *Learn* line(s) beneath each rule, noting how the rule is applied.
   b. Key the *Apply* line(s), expressing numbers correctly.

Rule 1: Spell a number that begins a sentence even when other numbers in the sentence are shown in figures.

Learn   1   Eleven of the team members are 18 years old.

Apply   2   15 books on the reading list were mysteries; 20 were romance.

Rule 2: Use figures for numbers above ten and for numbers from one to ten when they are used with numbers above ten.

Learn   3   Blake sold 13 dahlias, 8 begonias, and 12 lilies on Friday.

Apply   4   There were eleven poodles, six collies, and twelve beagles.

Rule 3: Use figures to express date and time (unless followed by o'clock).

Learn   5   Flight 384 left San Francisco at 10:50 a.m. on May 26.

Apply   6   The parade will start at ten thirty a.m. on Monday, June one.

Rule 4: Use figures for house numbers except house number One.

Learn   7   The address of the hospital is One State Street, not 11 State Street.

Apply   8   The last two addresses were 1 York Lane and 2358 Lake Road.

Rule 5: Use figures to express measures and weights.

Learn   9   Jason, our son, is 5 ft. 2 in. tall and weighs 103 lbs. 9 oz.

Apply   10   The desk is five ft. long and three feet wide and weighs 48 lbs.

Rule 6: Use figures for numbers following nouns.

Learn   11   Read Chapter 6 and answer questions 1, 3, and 6 on page 153.

Apply   12   Amendment six on page thirteen was proposed by Senator Chen.

Rule 7: Spell (and capitalize) names of small-numbered streets (ten and under).

Learn   13   Maria delivered the papers on 36th Street and Second Avenue.

Apply   14   Madison Square Garden is located at four Pennsylvania Plaza.

Rule 8: Spell indefinite numbers.

Learn   15   I own almost twenty percent; she owns about ten percent.

Learn   16   Nearly sixty delegates were women; that is nearly a third.

Apply   17   Over 30 percent of the voters were from Casper.

Apply   18   About 1/2 of the voters cast ballots for Marshall Jamison.

(continued on next page)

2. Key Proofread & Correct, expressing numbers correctly. Then follow the steps below.
   a. Check answers.
   b. Using the rule number at the left of each line, study the rule relating to each error you made.
   c. Rekey each incorrect line, expressing numbers correctly.

Save as: **CS2 ACTIVITY1**

Proofread & Correct

Rules

1	1	30 students signed up for the test, sixteen are still undecided.
2	2	Rubio scored thirty points, Mitchell 28, and Ingles seven.
3	3	Do you know if Flight 718 is still scheduled for nine thirty a.m.?
3, 4	4	Your interview is scheduled for eight thirty at 1 State Street.
5	5	The picture is two ft. six in. tall and four ft. wide.
5	6	The container is five ft. square and weighs fifty lbs. three oz.
6	7	Mr. Ramirez assigned pages 66 to 78 of Chapter Three for Monday.
7	8	We were assigned the area between 3rd Street and 6th Avenue.
8	9	Nearly 1/4 of the coins on display were dated before 1910.
8	10	My commission averaged about 15 percent for July.

ACTIVITY 2: Word Choice

1. Study the definitions of the words.
2. Key the *Learn* line, noting the correct usage of each word.
3. Key the *Apply* lines, inserting the correct word(s).

Save as: **CS2 ACTIVITY2**

cite (vb) to quote; use as support; to commend; to summon	**their** (pron) belonging to them
sight (n/vb) ability to see; something seen; a device to improve aim; to observe or focus	**there** (adv/pron) in or at that place; word used to introduce a sentence or clause
site (n) the place something is, was, or will be located	**they're** (contr) a contracted form of *they are*

Learn 1 He will **cite** the article from the web**site** about improving your **sight**.

Apply 2 You need to (cite, sight, site) five sources in the report due on Friday.

Apply 3 The (cite, sight, site) he chose for the party was a (cite, sight, site) to be seen.

Learn 1 **There** is the car **they're** going to use in **their** next play production.

Apply 2 (Their, there, they're) making (their, there, they're) school lunches.

Apply 3 (Their, there, they're) is the box of (their, there, they're) tools.

ACTIVITY 3: Composing

1. Read the quotations.
2. Choose one and make notes of what the quotation means to you.
3. Key a paragraph or two indicating what the quotation means to you.
4. Proofread, revise, and correct.

Save as: **CS2 ACTIVITY3**

1. "Man does not live by words alone, despite the fact that sometimes he has to eat them." (Adlai Stevenson)

2. "No man is rich enough to buy back his past." (Oscar Wilde)

3. "It is not fair to ask of others what you are unwilling to do yourself." (Eleanor Roosevelt)

4. "it is amazing what you can accomplish if you do not care who gets the credit." (Harry Truman)

5. "Success is not the key to happiness. Happiness is the key to success. If you love what you are doing, you will be successful." (Albert Schweitzer)

Community Service is helping others by giving of your time, talents, and effort. People perform community service to make a difference in society, to help those less fortunate, to learn skills that can be transferred to future jobs, and because "it is the right thing to do."

Research service learning opportunities in or near the community where you live. Prepare a brief talk to deliver to four or five of your classmates explaining several of the community service opportunities in your area and trying to convince them to join you in one of the service learning opportunities.

Save as: CS2 ACTIVITY4

Before You Move On

1. Name the five components of PIMS. LO 29B

2. The three parts of an email are _____, _____, and _____. LO 29B

3. Copies of an email can be sent by using the _____ feature of email. LO 29B

4. Which feature helps you find the correct email address for a contact? LO 34C

5. Which feature allows you to record and display appointments electronically? LO 34B

6. Which feature helps you record projects and activities you are responsible for completing? LO 32D

7. This feature allows you to record reminders of things you need to remember. LO 32E

8. Which email feature allows you to record information about your friends and business associates? LO 32B

9. Email messages have partially replaced these two types of business documents. LO 29B

10. Name two of the four pieces of information that can be included in the email heading. LO 30C

Apply What You Have Learned

Email Message

1. Open *Outlook* and key the following information as an email. Use your instructor's email address or the email address provided by your instructor.

   SUBJECT: MATH REASONING SKILLS CHALLENGE
   A meeting to discuss the Math Reasoning Skills Challenge has been set. The meeting will be on Tuesday, April 17, in Room 23 at 2:30 p.m. Vice Principal Arlo Rome will join us.

   The main purpose of the meeting is to discuss the rules for taking part in this competition. We also will talk about program awards and future meeting dates.

2. Carefully proofread the email before you send it.

Appointments, Contacts, Tasks, and Notes

1. Open *Outlook* and perform the following activities using your personal/school account:
   a. Create these appointments:
   - Birthday party at Doris' Grill at 1:00 p.m. on July 27
   - Volleyball Game at South Central Park at July 15

b. Record these new contacts:
- Beverly House, Owner, Beverly's Fabric World, 225 Winning Way, Raleigh, NC 27603, 919-669-2288 (cell), 919-662-5353 (business)
- Bob Sopko, Dentist, 2929 Ridge Road, Durham, NC 27517, 919-555-3111 (business)

c. Create this task list:
- Pick up dry cleaning on the way home from work
- Drop off prescriptions to be filled at pharmacy
- Stop by grocery store for hamburger, tomatoes, and lettuce

d. Create these notes:
- Call Sherri in the morning to remind her to send her resume
- Ask Becky Peters to contact Marvin Brooks for a meeting

2. When you have completed each item, ask your instructor to screen check that you have performed each item correctly.

3. Once your instructor has verified your work is correct, delete or remove these items from *Outlook*.

Communicating Clearly with Letters

Lesson 32   Personal-Business Letters
Lesson 33   Business Letters, Additional Letter
            Parts, and Envelopes

Lesson 34   Modified Block Personal-
            Business Letters
Assessment 1   Email and Letters

Application Guide

Letters

A letter written by an individual to deal with business of a personal nature is called a **personal-business letter**. A personal-business letter is typically printed on personal stationery that does not have a preprinted return address. A **business letter** is typically printed on letterhead stationery (stationery that has a preprinted return address). You compose both types of letters using word processing software such as Microsoft *Word* (see Figure 5-1).

Block Letter Format

Block letter format (shown on the left side of Figure 5-1) is commonly used to arrange the parts of a letter. All parts of a letter arranged in block format begin at the left margin. The paragraphs are not indented. Use a 2" top margin (tap *Enter* three times), default side margins, and 1.08 line spacing (the default line spacing in Microsoft *Word*) unless otherwise specified.

Modified Block Letter Format

In modified block format (see the right side of Figure 5-1), certain lines of the letter begin at or near the center of the page. Set a tab at 3". The lines that begin at or near the center are the return address, date, complimentary close, typed signature, and typed title if it is included.

In addition, the first line of each paragraph may be indented. Set a tab at 0.5". All other lines begin at the left margin. The spacing before and after the letter parts are the same as for block format.

Basic Letter Parts

The basic parts of a letter are described below and on the next page in order of placement on the paper. Differences between the parts of a personal-business letter and a business letter are identified.

Return address. The return address on a personal-business letter (start at or near the 2" line) consists of a line for the street address and one for the city, state, and zipcode. Tap *Shift + Enter* once after each line of the return address.

iStock.com/Lise Gagne

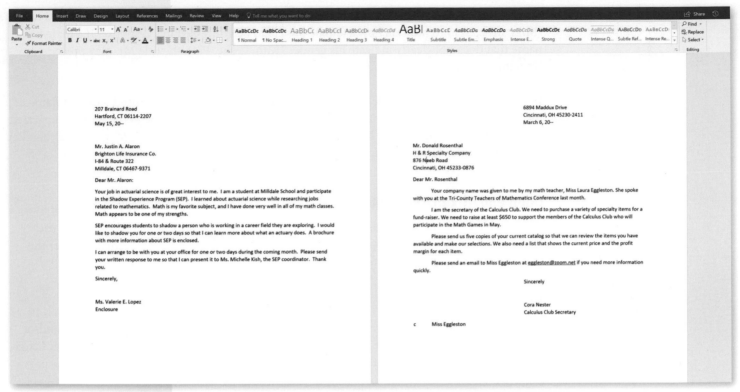

Figure 5-1 Letters in *Word*: Block format (left) and modified block format (right)

The return address on a business letter need not be keyed if the street, city, state, and zipcode are preprinted on letterhead stationery. In addition, the company name, phone numbers, and/or website are usually part of the letterhead.

Date. When keying a personal-business letter, key the month, day, and year on the line below the city, state, and zipcode and then tap *Enter* twice to begin the letter address.

Letter address. Key the first line of the letter (delivery) address below the date. A personal title (Miss, Mr., Mrs., Ms.) or a professional title (Dr., Lt., Senator) is keyed before the receiver's name. Tap *Shift + Enter* to move from line to line within the mailing address. Tap *Enter* once after keying the last line of the mailing address to begin the salutation.

Salutation. Key the **salutation** (greeting). Include a courtesy title with the person's name, for example, Dear Ms. Jones. Tap *Enter* after keying the salutation.

Body. Key the letter body (message) using the default line spacing, and tap *Enter* once after each paragraph and after the last line of the last paragraph in the body to begin the complimentary close.

Complimentary close. Key the **complimentary close** (farewell), and then tap *Enter* twice to key the name of the writer. Capitalize only the first word in the complimentary close.

TIP Holding the Shift key when you tap *Enter* inserts a line break that removes the 8 points of space after a paragraph.

Name of the writer. Key the name of the writer. The name may be preceded by a personal title (Miss, Mrs., Ms.) to indicate how a female prefers to be addressed in a response. If a male has a name that does not clearly indicate his gender (Kim, Leslie, Pat), the title Mr. may precede his name.

In many letters, a position title (Manager, President, Salesperson, etc.) is used with the name of the writer. The position title may be keyed on the same line as the name of the writer (separated with a comma) or on the next line. If placed on the next line, tap *Shift + Enter* once and then key the position title. Tap *Enter* once to begin the next letter part, if any.

Open and Mixed Punctuation

When **mixed punctuation** is used, place a colon after the salutation and a comma after the complimentary close. When **open punctuation** is used, do not key any punctuation after the salutation and complimentary close.

Additional Letter Parts

The following letter parts are frequently included in letters following the writer's name and/or position title. If more than one of these parts is included in a letter, key them in the order listed below. To properly place each part, tap *Enter* once at the end of the line that precedes the part you are including.

Reference initials. If someone other than the originator of the letter keys it, his/her initials are keyed in lowercase letters at the left margin below the writer's name and/or title.

Attachment/enclosure notation. If another document is attached to a letter, the word *Attachment* is keyed at the left margin. If the additional document is not attached, the word *Enclosure* is used. If more than one document is attached or enclosed, make the notation plural.

Copy notation. A copy notation indicates that a copy of the letter is being sent to someone other than the addressee. Key **c** and then tab to 0.5" to begin the name(s) of the person(s) to receive a copy. If there is more than one name, list names vertically as shown below (tap *Shift + Enter* between the names).

c   Hector Ramirez
        Ursula O'Donohue

Envelopes

Most word processing software includes an **Envelopes** feature to create envelopes for the letters you have keyed. This feature allows you to choose the size of the envelope, include a return address and delivery address, and print the envelope. The Size 10 (No. 10) envelope is the most frequently used envelope size for letters printed on 8.5" x 11" paper.

TIP You may need to Undo Automatic Capitalization to key the first letter in the reference initials or the copy notation in lowercase if AutoCorrect options are not changed.

Find and Replace

Home tab > Editing >
Find or Replace

TIP You can also use shortcut keys for Find (Ctrl + F) and Replace (Ctrl + H).

TIP The word you want to find can appear as part of other words. For example, *pay* may appear in *payment*. To prevent this, click the *More* button and select *Find whole words only*.

The **Find and Replace** dialog box (see Figure 5-2) can be used to quickly search for a keystroke, word, or phrase in a document and then replace that text with the desired keystroke, word, or phrase. All occurrences of the text in the document can be replaced at one time, or replacements can be made individually (selectively). You can refine this feature by using the More button to display various search and find and replace options. To access the Find and Replace dialog box, choose Replace from the Editing group (see Figure 5-3).

Figure 5-2 Find and Replace dialog box

Figure 5-3 Editing group

WP Applications 7

Activity 1

Font Group

For each feature, read and learn the feature described; then complete the activity as directed.

The Font group contains many features that can be used to change the appearance of text in a document. For example, the font, font size, and font color can be changed. Text can be highlighted, underlined, or have an effect applied to it. Numbers can be formatted in superscript or subscript formats. These features as well as others are contained in the Font group on the Home tab illustrated below in Figure 5-4.

1. Within the Font group, hover your mouse pointer over each of the 15 features to identify each feature and read the short description of it.

Figure 5-4 The Font group

Home tab > Font

2. Open a new document and read each sentence below; then key each sentence, applying the font commands as directed in the sentence.

   Bold, italicize, and underline this text in a red, 11-pt., Arial font.

   Apply a subscript number and superscript as shown: H_2O.[1]

   Highlight this text in yellow and apply a text effect of your choice.

   KEY AS SHOWN; USE CHANGE CASE TO MAKE IT SENTENCE CASE.

   Use Strikethrough on this text and then grow it to 16-pt. Calibri.

3. Make a copy of the first sentence and paste it after the last sentence. Use the Clear Formatting feature to erase the font features applied to the text.
4. **Save as:** *wp7 activity 1*.

<table>
<tr><td>

Activity 2

Hyphenation

Layout tab > Page Setup > Hyphenation

</td><td>

The **Hyphenation** feature automatically divides (hyphenates) words that would normally wrap to the next line. This makes the right margin more even, making the text more attractive.

1. Open a new document, and change the right and left margins to 2.5".
2. Key the text below in Courier New 12 pt. with hyphenation off.
3. Use the Hyphenation feature (Automatic option) to hyphenate the document.

> Use the Hyphenation feature to give text a professional appearance. When the Hyphenation feature is activated, the software divides long words between syllables at the end of lines. Using hyphenation makes the right margin less ragged. This feature is particularly helpful when keying in narrow columns.

4. **Save as:** *wp7 activity 2*.

</td></tr>
</table>

<table>
<tr><td>

Activity 3

Spelling & Grammar

Review tab > Proofing > Spelling & Grammar

NOTE The Grammar Check may or may not catch incorrect word usage *too* for *to* or *two*. If it does, a blue wavy underline appears. Even when using these features, it is important to proofread your documents.

</td><td>

Use the **Spelling & Grammar Check** to check for misspellings and grammar errors. The Spelling Check feature compares each word in the document to words in its dictionary (or dictionaries). If a word in a document is not identical to one in its dictionary, the word is flagged by a wavy red underline. Usually the Spelling Check lists words it *thinks* are likely corrections (replacements). The Grammar Check feature flags potential grammar errors with a wavy green underline. The Grammar Check also lists words it thinks will correct the grammar error.

1. Open a new document and key the paragraph below *exactly* as it is shown. Note how some errors are automatically corrected.
2. Use the Spelling & Grammar Check to identify errors. Correct all errors by editing or selecting a replacement.
3. Proofread after the Spelling & Grammar Check, and correct any errors Spelling & Grammar did not detect.

> Dr. Smith met with the students on Friday to reviiw for for there test. He told the students that their would be three sections to the test. The first secction would be multiplee choice, the second sction would be true/fals, and the last section would be shoot answer. He also said, "If you have spelling errors on you paper, you will have pionts deducted.

4. **Save as:** *wp7 activity 3*.

</td></tr>
</table>

Activity 4

Thesaurus

Review tab > Proofing >
Thesaurus

A **thesaurus** in your word processing software can be quickly accessed to help you find synonyms that will convey an appropriate meaning of the message you are writing. To find synonyms for a specific word, select that word and then use the path at the left to access the thesaurus. Or right-click the selected word and click *Synonyms* to display a list of synonyms from which you can select the word you want.

1. Open *df wp7 activity 4*. Find appropriate synonyms for the four words in blue font, and insert them into the text.
2. **Save as:** *wp7 activity 4*.

Activity 5

Insert Date & Time

Insert/Text/Date & Time

The **Insert Date & Time** feature is used to enter the date into a document automatically. Choose the appropriate format of the date to be inserted from the list of available formats as shown in Figure 5-5. If desired, you can choose to have the date updated automatically each time the document is opened or printed. The date on your computer must be current to insert the correct date in a document.

Some software provides an Automatic Completion (AutoComplete) feature, which also inserts the date automatically. When you start keying a month, AutoComplete recognizes the word and shows it in a tip box above the insertion point. By tapping the *Enter* key, you enter the remainder of the month automatically, without keying the remaining letters. When you tap the Space Bar after the month has been inserted, the tip box shows the complete date. Tapping the *Enter* key enters the complete date.

1. Open a new document and key the information below using 1.0 line spacing, Insert Date & Time as directed, and AutoComplete when applicable.
2. **Save as:** *wp7 activity 5*.

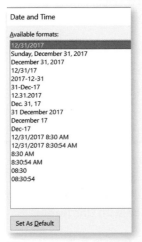

Figure 5-5 Date and Time formats

   1. Insert date by using <Insert Date & Time; do not select Update automatically>.
   2. Insert date by using <Insert Date & Time; select Update automatically>.
   3. Today is <Use Insert Date & Time; do not Update automatically>.
   4. Your balance as of <Use Insert Date & Time; select Update automatically> is $42.83.
   5. I received your check today, <Use Insert Date & Time; select Update automatically>.
   6. You will need to make sure to record today's date, <Use Insert Date & Time; do not select Update automatically>, on the form.

TIP The easiest way to remove space after a paragraph is to use the shortcut keys Shift + Enter.

The default settings leave 8 points of white space between lines each time Enter is tapped. The space can be removed by using the **Remove Space After Paragraph** feature. This feature can be accessed by following the path at the left. Alternatively, the space can be removed by using the **Text Wrapping Break** feature. To use this feature, tap and hold down the *Shift* key and tap the *Enter* key. In this unit, you will be instructed to use the **Shift + Enter** method when the space after a paragraph is to be removed.

1. Open a new document and key the text in the left column below, tapping *Enter* at the end of each line.
2. Tap *Enter* twice and key the text in the right column, holding down the *Shift* key and tapping *Enter* as instructed.
3. Compare the difference.
4. Select the first two lines of the text keyed from the left column, and use the *Remove Space After Paragraph* feature to remove the space after these two lines.
5. Compare the spacing of this text to the text where Shift + Enter was used to remove the space after the paragraphs—the spacing should be the same.
6. **Save as: *wp7 activity 6*.**

Mr. Ricardo Seanez (Tap *Enter*)

1538 Village Square (Tap *Enter*)

Altoona, WI 54720 (Tap *Enter*)

Dear Ricardo (Tap *Enter*)

I will be arriving in Altoona on July 15 for the next meeting.

Mr. Ricardo Seanez (Hold *Shift*; tap *Enter*)
1538 Village Square (Hold *Shift*; tap *Enter*)
Altoona, WI 54720 (Tap *Enter*)

Dear Ricardo (Tap *Enter*)

I will be arriving in Altoona on July 15 for the next meeting.

Activity 7

Envelopes

Mailings tab > Create > Envelopes

Use the Envelopes feature to create envelopes for your letters. This feature allows you to select the size of the envelope, key the return address and the delivery address, and print the envelope (see Figure 5-6). The delivery address can be keyed, inserted automatically from the letter file, or inserted from your Address Book. Electronic postage software can be used with this feature.

1. Open a new document, and use the Envelopes feature to format a small envelope (No. 6 3/4) using this information:

Figure 5-6
The Envelopes and Labels dialog box

Return address:
Ms. Carson Sanchez
270 Rancho Bauer Drive
Houston, TX 77079-3703

Mailing address:
Ms. Susan Keane
872 Mayflower Drive
Terre Haute, IN 47803-1199

2. **Save as:** *wp7 activity 7a*.

3. Open a new document and use the Envelopes feature to format a Size 10 using this information for the mailing address. A return address need not be keyed as it is assumed the business envelope has a preprinted return address on it.

Mr. Jacob Saunders
396 Hickory Hill Lane
Kalamazoo, MI 49009-0012

4. **Save as:** *wp7 activity 7b*.

Activity 8

Bullets and Numbering

Home tab > Paragraph > Bullets

Home tab > Paragraph > Numbering

Bullets (special characters) are used to enhance the appearance of text. Bullets are often used to add visual interest or emphasis. Examples of bullets are illustrated in Figure 5-7.

Numbering is used to show the proper order of a series of steps. Use numbers instead of bullets whenever the order of items is important. Examples of number format are illustrated in Figure 5-8.

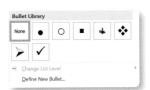

Figure 5-7 Bullet Library   **Figure 5-8** Numbering Library

1. Open a new document and key Activity A below using the ✓ Bullet style; tap *Enter* twice after keying the last bulleted item to end the bulleted list.
2. Key Activity B using the Numbering feature. Tap *Enter* twice after the last numbered item.
3. **Save as:** *wp7 activity 8*.

Activity A
Please be sure to bring the following:

✓ Paper
✓ Pencil
✓ Data files
✓ Keyboarding book

Activity B
The final 2017 standings in the American League East were:

1. Boston Red Sox
2. New York Yankees
3. Tampa Bay Rays
4. Toronto Blue Jays
5. Baltimore Orioles

Left Tab

Right Tab

Center Tab

Decimal Tab

Tabs are set locations at which text can be placed. By default, a Left tab is set every one-half inch on the Ruler and text appears to the right of it as you key if one or more manual tabs have not been set. Other tabs include Right tabs, Center tabs, and Decimal tabs (see tab symbols at left). A Right tab sets the start position so that text appears to the left of it as you type. Text that is keyed at a Center tab appears to the left and right of it. A Decimal tab aligns numbers on a decimal point, and text runs to the left or right depending on its position relative to the decimal point. In this activity, you will use the Ruler to set manual tabs (see Figure 5-9). Tabs also can be set or formatted using the Tabs dialog box that is accessed from the Paragraph dialog box launched from the Home tab.

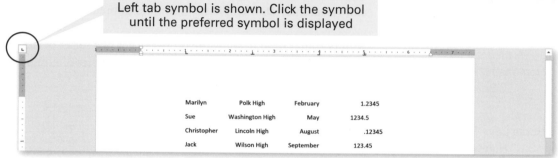

Left tab symbol is shown. Click the symbol until the preferred symbol is displayed

Marilyn	Polk High	February	1.2345
Sue	Washington High	May	1234.5
Christopher	Lincoln High	August	.12345
Jack	Wilson High	September	123.45

Figure 5-9 Ruler with tabs

★TIP If you don't see the Ruler at the top of your document, click *View*, then check the *Ruler* box. To change the type of tab, click the tab symbol on the left end of the Ruler until you see the type of tab you want.

1. Open a new, blank document.
2. Verify that the Ruler is displayed. If not, select *Ruler* in the Show group on the View tab to display it.
3. Set the following tabs on the Ruler: a Left tab at the 1" mark, a Center tab at the 2.5" mark, a Right tab at 4", and a Decimal tab at 5".
4. Key the following text from left to right, using the *Tab* key to move from one column to the next. Begin the first column at the Left tab, second column at the Center tab, third column at the Right tab, and fourth column at the Decimal tab. Tap *Enter* at the end of each line. Your copy should look like the copy in Figure 5-9.

★TIP You can move a tab on the Ruler by clicking and dragging it to the point you choose. You can delete a tab on the Ruler by clicking and dragging it off the Ruler.

Marilyn	Polk High	February	1.2345
Sue	Washington High	May	1234.5
Christopher	Lincoln High	August	.12345
Jack	Wilson High	September	123.45

5. Save the document as **wp7 activity 9** and close it.

Home tab > Paragraph >
Show/Hide

Word processing documents contain invisible formatting marks that can be displayed. Commonly used marks (see Figure 5-10) are

¶ to show the end of a paragraph,

→ to show a tab,

• to show a space between words.

Being able to see the formatting marks is helpful when editing a document or solving formatting problems. The formatting marks do not print.

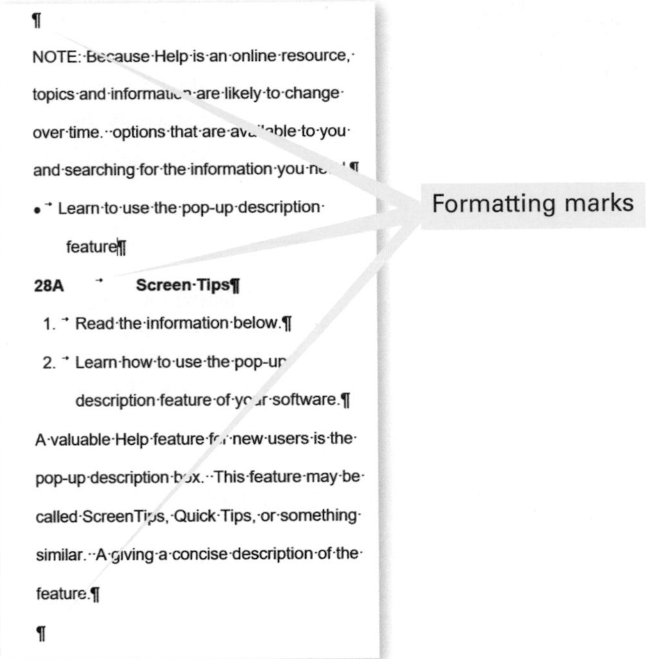

1. Open a new document and key the following text with Show/Hide ¶ activated. Tap *Enter* twice after the last bulleted item.

You can incorporate fitness into your daily routine by doing these three activities:

• Walk up stairs for one minute each day instead of taking the elevator. Within a year you should be a pound lighter without changing any other habits.
• Walk the dog, don't just watch the dog walk. In a nutshell—get moving!
• Perform at least 30 minutes of moderate activity each day. If necessary, do the 30 minutes in 10-minute intervals.

2. Review the keyed text, and note the formatting marks that are displayed.
3. **Save as:** *wp7 activity 10*.

Figure 5-10 Formatting marks

LESSON 32 Personal-Business Letters

OUTCOMES
• Format a personal-business letter in block format with open punctuation
• Format a personal-business letter in block format with mixed punctuation
• Find and replace text
• Arrange letter parts in correct order

32–34A

Warmup

Key each line twice at the beginning of each lesson; first for control, then for speed.

alphabet 1 Jay asked four zany questions before each good example was given.

figures 2 My mutual fund fell 4.87 points to 65.92 on Friday, May 25, 2018.

speed 3 The men may pay for a big emblem of the chapel with their profit.

gwam 1' | 1 | 2 | 3 | 4 | 5 | 6 | 7 | 8 | 9 | 10 | 11 | 12 | 13 |

Personal-Business Letter

1. Review the sample letter in Figure 5-11 and the guidelines for keying letters in the Application Guide at the beginning of this chapter.
2. Start a new *Word* document and key the model letter in Figure 5-11 using the guidelines shown in the figure.
3. Save the document as *32b letter* and close it.

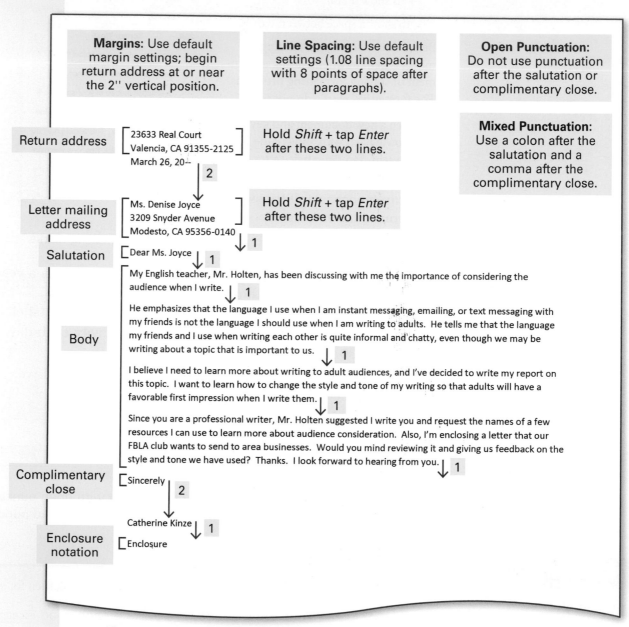

Figure 5-11 Personal-business letter in block format with open punctuation

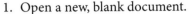

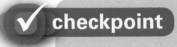

Personal-Business Letter

1. Open a new, blank document.
2. Key the letter shown below. Check the spelling and proofread the letter carefully. Correct all errors. Save the letter as *32c letter* and close it.

COLLABORATION

✔ checkpoint Check the format of a classmate's letter. Have that classmate check the format of your letter. Was mixed punctuation used? Discuss any errors that either of you found and correct them.

207 Brainard Road
Hartford, CT 06114-2207
May 15, 20--

Mr. Justin A. Alaron
Brighton Life Insurance Co.
I-84 & Route 322
Milldale, CT 06467-9371

Dear Mr. Alaron:

Your job in actuarial science is of great interest to me. I am a student at Milldale School and participate in the Shadow Experience Program (SEP). I learned about actuarial science while researching jobs related to mathematics. Math is my favorite subject, and I have done very well in all of my math classes. Math appears to be one of my strengths.

SEP encourages students to shadow a person who is working in a career field they are exploring. I would like to shadow you for one or two days so that I can learn more about what an actuary does. A brochure with more information about SEP is enclosed.

I can arrange to be with you at your office for one or two days during the coming month. Please send your written response to me so that I can present it to Ms. Michelle Kish, the SEP coordinator. Thank you.

Sincerely,

Ms. Valerie E. Lopez

Enclosure

How many times does *pay* appear in the document after the replacements have been made? Compare your answer with a classmate's answer.

checkpoint

Did you remove the periods after the abbreviations in the street addresses? Did you add the period to *Ms.*? Did you leave *Dr.* as the personal title? Did you add the comma between the city and state?

Activity 1

1. Open *df 32d replace1*. Make the following changes using Find and Replace.
   a. Replace *dairy* with *grocery store*.
   b. Replace all occurrences of *assessments* with *taxes*.
   c. Replace the second and fourth occurrences of *pay* with *earnings*.
   d. Replace *social security* with *Social Security*.
   e. Replace all occurrences of two spaces between sentences with one space.
2. Save the document as **32d replace1** and close it.

Activity 2

1. Open *df 32c replace2*. Make the following changes:
   a. Change *Rd.* to *Road*.
   b. Change *Str.* to *Street*.
   c. Change *Ave.* to *Avenue*.
   d. Change *Blvd.* to *Boulevard*.
   e. Change *Ln.* to *Lane*.
   f. Change *Dr.* to *Drive* in the street addresses but not the *Dr.* that appears as a personal title.
   g. Change *Miss* to *Ms*.
   h. Change *Ms. Stacey Bethel* to *Mrs. Stacey Bell*.
   i. Change *Ms. Ann Buck* to *Dr. Ann Buck*.
2. Use Find and Replace to insert a comma after the city name. Hint: In the Find what box, tap the *Space Bar* once and key **TX**. In the Replace with box, key a comma, tap *Space Bar* once, and key **TX**.
3. Save the document as **32c replace2** and close it.

Personal-Business Letter

1. Open *df 32e letter*. The letter parts are identified in red font. Arrange the letter in block format by using Cut and Paste to put the letter parts in the proper order. (Do not delete the text in red.) Use mixed punctuation.
2. Use Find and Replace to make these changes: *plane* to *airplane*, *scattered* to *soft*, and *positive* to *meaningful*.
3. Save the document as **32e letter**, print it, and close it. Exchange letters with a classmate and verify that the letter parts are in the correct order, mixed punctuation has been used, and the format is correct. Make any needed changes.

COLLABORATION

Digital Citizenship and Ethics Through texting and instant messaging, users of digital technologies have developed their own form of shorthand or texting slang. For example, most of us are familiar with HRU for "how are you?" and the popular LOL for "laughing out loud." This type of exchange is acceptable between friends and in casual, nonbusiness communications. But more and more, it is finding its way into the professional world.

According to a recent survey of human resource managers, strong written communication skills are essential not only to getting hired but also to advancing. Employers expect workers at every level to be able to string together clear, coherent thoughts in all forms of written communication. In a competitive job environment, successful digital citizens must be able to distinguish between appropriate writing for personal and professional purposes. They must pay close attention to the quality of their writing and how to use it effectively to reflect their best selves.

COLLABORATION

As a class, discuss the following:
1. How might the use of texting slang and shorthand in a business situation reflect negatively on an individual's communication skills?
2. What measures can you take now in your daily digital activities to strengthen your written communication skills?

LESSON 33   Business Letters, Additional Letter Parts, and Envelopes

OUTCOMES
- Learn to format business letters with additional letter parts
- Prepare envelopes
- Create a letter and envelope

33B

Business Letter from Model Copy

1. Review the Application Guide at the beginning of this chapter, paying particular attention to return address, date, and name of writer sections to learn differences between personal-business letters and business letters. Study the information on mixed punctuation and additional letter parts and preview the model business letter in Figure 5-12. Note the placement of letter parts, and spacing between them.
2. Format/key the model in Figure 5-12. Proofread and correct errors. Hyphenate the document.
3. Save as: *33b letter.*

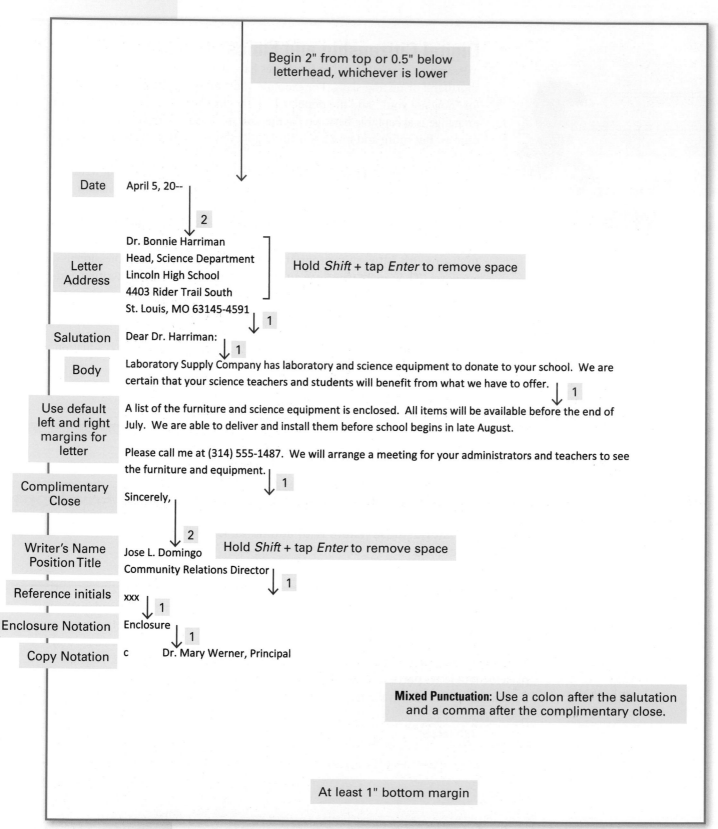

Begin 2" from top or 0.5" below letterhead, whichever is lower

Date April 5, 20--

2

Letter Address
Dr. Bonnie Harriman
Head, Science Department
Lincoln High School
4403 Rider Trail South
St. Louis, MO 63145-4591

Hold *Shift* + tap *Enter* to remove space

1

Salutation Dear Dr. Harriman:

1

Body Laboratory Supply Company has laboratory and science equipment to donate to your school. We are certain that your science teachers and students will benefit from what we have to offer.

1

Use default left and right margins for letter
A list of the furniture and science equipment is enclosed. All items will be available before the end of July. We are able to deliver and install them before school begins in late August.

Please call me at (314) 555-1487. We will arrange a meeting for your administrators and teachers to see the furniture and equipment.

1

Complimentary Close Sincerely,

2

Writer's Name Position Title
Jose L. Domingo
Community Relations Director

Hold *Shift* + tap *Enter* to remove space

1

Reference initials xxx

1

Enclosure Notation Enclosure

1

Copy Notation c   Dr. Mary Werner, Principal

Mixed Punctuation: Use a colon after the salutation and a comma after the complimentary close.

At least 1" bottom margin

Figure 5-12 Business letter in block format with mixed punctuation

Business Letter in Block Format with Open Punctuation

1. Format/key the letter below in block format with open punctuation using 14-pt. Times New Roman font.
2. Proofread and correct errors. Hyphenate the document. Revise as needed to avoid splitting the email address on two lines.
3. **Save as:** *33c letter.*

July 22, 20— | Financial Aid Office | Bethany College | P.O. Box 417 | Bethany, WV 26032-0417 | Ladies and Gentlemen

Cindy Stroka, who is entering Bethany College in the upcoming fall semester, was awarded the Donna Forde Keller Book Scholarship. The scholarship is valued at $500.

The scholarship is restricted to the purchase of textbooks; therefore, the $500 should be placed in a book fund for her use. Enclosed is a $500 check made payable to Bethany College for the scholarship.

This scholarship is administered by the Haverford High Alumni Association. If you need additional information, contact me at 412-555-1678 or harris.jim@fastmail.net. Thank you.

Sincerely | Jim Harris | HHAA Scholarship Chair | xxx | Enclosure | c Cindy Stroka

Envelopes

Mailings tab > Create > Envelopes

Review the *Envelopes* section of the Application Guide at the beginning of this chapter, then complete these activities.

Envelope 1

1. Open *df 33d letter*. Select the lines of the letter mailing address so the letter address will be used to create the delivery address.
2. Use the Envelopes feature to prepare a Size 10 envelope. Confirm that Laura Seerhoff's name and address appear in the Delivery address box.
3. If necessary, remove the check mark from the Return address Omit checkbox. Key the following in the Return address box.

Mrs. Karen Fernandez
4002 Concord Highway
Monroe, NC 28110-8233

4. Click the envelope in the Preview box to verify that a Size 10 envelope is being used. If there are specific instructions for your printer on where to feed the blank envelope for printing, follow them.
5. Print the envelope. Close the document without saving the changes.

Envelope 2

1. Open a new, blank document.
2. Use your instructor's name and school address as the delivery address and your name and home address as the return address to prepare a No. 10 envelope.
3. Print the envelope. When it has printed, close the file without saving.

33E

Personal-Business Letter with Envelope

1. Open a new, blank document. Key the personal-business letter below using block format and open punctuation style.
2. When you are finished, use the Print screen or Zoom to check the format. Save the letter as *33e letter*. Print it.
3. Create and print a Size 10 envelope using the letter mailing address for the delivery address and the writer's name and address for the return address.
4. Save the letter as *33f letter* and close it.

8503 Kirby Dr.
Houston, TX 77054-8220
May 5, 20--

Ms. Jenna St. John, Personnel Director
Regency Company
219 West Greene Road
Houston, TX 77067-4219

Dear Ms. St. John:

Ms. Anne D. Salgado, my teacher, told me about your company's Computer Learn Program. She speaks very highly of your company and the computer program. She thinks I would benefit greatly by taking this course. After learning more about the program, I agree that the course would help me.

I am in the seventh grade at Taft School. I have completed a computer applications course. I learned to use spreadsheets in word processing reports. I also have taken a programming course. It introduced me to Visual Basic and HTML. I developed and maintain a website for my baseball team. A copy of my last grade report is enclosed.

I would like to visit you to talk more about the summer program. Please telephone me at (713) 555-0121 or email me at <u>dougr@suresend.com</u> to suggest a meeting date. I can meet with you any day after school.

Thank you.

Sincerely,

Douglas H. Ruckert

Enclosure

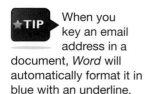

★TIP When you key an email address in a document, *Word* will automatically format it in blue with an underline.

LESSON 34   Modified Block Personal-Business Letters

OUTCOMES

- Set tabs and insert date and time
- Key a modified block personal-business letter with indented paragraphs
- Key a modified block personal-business letter with a list
- Compose a modified block personal-business letter

34B

Review: Setting Tabs and Inserting Date and Time

checkpoint

Compare your difference to that of a classmate. Who used the least amount of time?

1. Open a new, blank document. Use the Date & Time feature to insert the current date on the first line, using a format you choose. (Do not update automatically.) Tap *Enter* twice. Insert the time (including seconds) using a format you choose. (Do not update automatically.) Tap *Enter* twice.
2. Key the following text using a Left tab at 1", Center tab at 2.5", Decimal tab at 4", and Right tab at 5.5".

Mary	Hawthorn	8.046	Cincinnati
Kenneth	Jones	18.03	Orlando
Jan	Leffington	256	Philadelphia
Nancy	Montgomery	.98	Dayton

3. Tap *Enter* twice. Insert the time, using the same format you chose in step 1.
4. Subtract the time in step 1 from the time in step 3 to determine the difference. Key the difference two lines below the time.
5. Save the document as **34b practice** and close it.

34C

Modified Block Personal-Business Letter

You have learned to key personal-business letters using block format. In block format, all lines begin at the left margin. In modified block format, certain lines of the personal-business letter begin at or near the center of the page. The lines that begin at or near the center are the return address, date, complimentary close, typed signature, and typed title if it is included.

In addition, the first line of each paragraph may be indented 0.5" in a modified block letter. All other lines begin at the left margin. The spacing before and after the letter parts is the same as for block format.

Refer to the model copy in Figure 5-13 to view a personal-business letter arranged in modified block format. Notice the copy notation at the bottom left of the letter. If a copy notation is used, it is placed after the typed name, title, or enclosure notation, whichever is the last part of the letter.

1. Open a new, blank document. Set Left tabs at 0.5" and 3".
2. Key the model copy in Figure 5-13 as a personal-business letter in modified block format with indented paragraphs and open punctuation.
3. Use Find and Replace to change all occurrences of *Calc* to *Calculus*.
4. Use Print Preview to check the accuracy of the format. Proofread and correct all errors. Save the letter as **34c letter** and close it.

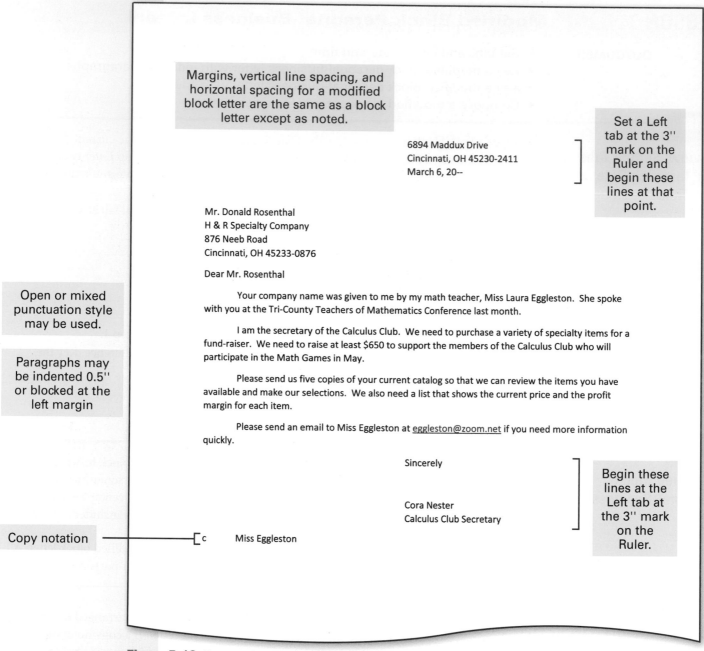

Figure 5-13 Personal-business letter in modified block format with indented paragraphs and open punctuation

The image contains the following labels and letter text:

Margins, vertical line spacing, and horizontal spacing for a modified block letter are the same as a block letter except as noted.

Set a Left tab at the 3'' mark on the Ruler and begin these lines at that point.

6894 Maddux Drive
Cincinnati, OH 45230-2411
March 6, 20--

Mr. Donald Rosenthal
H & R Specialty Company
876 Neeb Road
Cincinnati, OH 45233-0876

Dear Mr. Rosenthal

Open or mixed punctuation style may be used.

Your company name was given to me by my math teacher, Miss Laura Eggleston. She spoke with you at the Tri-County Teachers of Mathematics Conference last month.

Paragraphs may be indented 0.5'' or blocked at the left margin

I am the secretary of the Calculus Club. We need to purchase a variety of specialty items for a fund-raiser. We need to raise at least $650 to support the members of the Calculus Club who will participate in the Math Games in May.

Please send us five copies of your current catalog so that we can review the items you have available and make our selections. We also need a list that shows the current price and the profit margin for each item.

Please send an email to Miss Eggleston at eggleston@zoom.net if you need more information quickly.

Sincerely

Cora Nester
Calculus Club Secretary

Begin these lines at the Left tab at the 3'' mark on the Ruler.

Copy notation

c   Miss Eggleston

Modified Block Personal-Business Letter with List

1. Open a new, blank document. Key the letter on the next page in modified block format without indented paragraphs. Use mixed punctuation. Set a Left tab at 1.5" and a Right tab at 5" to key the list of plants. Insert the date so that it automatically updates.
2. Check spelling and grammar and proofread the letter carefully. Correct any errors. Save the document as *34d letter* and close the file.

207 Brainard Road
Hartford, CT 06114-2207
Insert date here

Mr. Glenn Rostello
3480 Martin Drive
North Olmsted, OH 44070-3000

Dear Mr. Rostello

Thank you for your inquiry about the best perennial plants to use along walkways. I have researched this topic and found several low-growing plants that will work well in our area.

Scientific Name	Common Name
Achillea ptarmica	Yarrow
Artemisia	Wormwood
Geranium	Geranium
Oenothera	Evening primrose
Sedum	Stonecrop
Trollius	Globeflower

Each of the above plants is available at our Ohio Street garden center. Anyone who buys plants this month will receive a 10 percent discount. If more than 15 plants are purchased, we will deliver and plant them for a small fee. When we do the planting, the plant has a one-year warranty.

Plcase say hello to me when you visit our store.

Sincerely

Harry Piper
Owner

Modified Block Personal-Business Letter

COLLABORATION

1. Open a new, blank document. Set tabs for a modified block letter with indented paragraphs.
2. Compose a letter to your teacher from you. Use your return address, insert the current date so that it does not update automatically, and address the letter to your teacher at your school's address. For the body of the letter, tell your teacher about a place you would like to visit for a class field trip. Give the name and the location or address. Describe the place. Explain why you think this would be a good place for your class to visit.
3. Check the spelling and proofread the letter carefully. Correct any errors. Use the Preview screen to check the format of the letter.
4. Save the letter as *34e letter*. Print the letter and close it.

 **checkpoint** Exchange papers with a classmate. Proofread and mark any errors you find in the letter. Make corrections to your letter if necessary.

Email and Letters

Warmup

Key each line twice. If time permits, key the lines again.

Alphabet

1 Javy quickly swam the dozen extra laps before Gus.

Figure/Symbol

2 Blake's cell number was changed to (835) 109-2647.

Speed

3 The six men may work down by the lake on the dock.

gwam 1' | 1 | 2 | 3 | 4 | 5 | 6 | 7 | 8 | 9 | 10 |

Activity 1
Assess Straight-Copy Skill

Key one or two 2' timed writings on both paragraphs combined. Print, proofread, circle errors, and determine *gwam*.

 all letters used

gwam 2'

    Money is more difficult to save than it is to   5
earn. Somebody is always willing to help you   9
spend what you make. If you confuse your needs   14
and wants, you can quickly spend much of it   18
yourself. Often, friends and relations can   22
become an additional significant drain if you   27
permit them to take advantage of you.   30

    And, of course, many politicians at all   34
levels think that they can spend your money for   39
you much better than you can do it yourself. It   44
is really amazing how ready some are to spend the   49
money of others. At times their motives may be   54
excellent; at other times, just selfish. Always   58
beware.   59

gwam 2' | 1 | 2 | 3 | 4 | 5 |

Activity 2
Email Message

1. Start *Outlook*. Create a new email message using your instructor's email address in the To box. Include the email address of a classmate in the Cc box.
2. Key **REPORT TOPIC** in the Subject box.
3. Key the email message below. If permitted, send the email. If not, ask your instructor to screen check the email and close it.

I have decided to do my report on Gettysburg. I went there last summer on a family vacation and have become very interested in this period of our country's history.

I know there are ample resources available because I have located several books in our school library and various resources on the Internet. Presently, I'm trying to define the topic I want to address. I plan to submit my preliminary outline to you by Friday.

Activity 3
Personal-Business Letter in Block Format

1. Start a new, blank *Word* document and key the letter below in block format with open punctuation.
2. Save the letter as *a1 activity3*, print, and close it.

206 Glenville Drive
Fort Mill, SC 29715-2647
Insert current date to update automatically

Mr. Connor Farrell
Longwell Technologies
7666 Charlotte Highway
Indian Land, SC 29707-4002

Dear Mr. Farrell

Ms. Rita Williams, my technology teacher at Indian Land Middle School, suggested I write to you because of my interest in information technology. She indicated that you serve on our school's technology advisory committee.

I am in the 8th grade and have completed a career exploration project relating to information technology. My next goal is to get advice from people in IT as to the high school courses I should complete.

Mr. Farrell, are there any specific math, science, and information technology courses that I should complete? Is there any advice you can give me about a specific major I should pursue when I'm in college? I have enclosed a list of the math, science, and IT courses I have taken in middle school and those that are available in our high school.

I appreciate any guidance you can give me. You can respond to me via email at j.hemingford@lscd.edu or text me at 803-555-0130. If you prefer, I could visit your office at a time that is convenient for you on the first Monday, Tuesday, or Wednesday of next month.

Sincerely

Joanne Hemingford

Enclosure

Activity 4
Personal-Business Letter in Modified Block Format

1. Open *df a1 activity4*. Format the letter in modified block format with indented paragraphs and mixed punctuation.
2. Save the letter as *a1 activity4*.
3. Create a Size 10 envelope with a letter address and a return address.
4. Print the envelope and letter and then close the document.

Skill Builder 4

A

Warmup

Key each line twice.

alphabet 1 Wusov amazed them by jumping quickly from the box.

spacing 2 am to|is an|by it|of us|an oak|is to pay|all of us

easy 3 The sorority may do the work for the city auditor.

gwam 1' | 1 | 2 | 3 | 4 | 5 | 6 | 7 | 8 | 9 | 10 |

B

Speed Check: Sentences

1. Key each line two times at the speed level (see box at the right).

2. Key two 30" timed writing on lines 7-10. If you finish the line, key it again. Try to increase your keying speed the second time you key the line.

★TIP
- After keying the last letter of a word, quickly tap the *Space Bar* and immediately begin keying the next word.
- After keying the period or question mark at the end of each line, quickly tap *Enter* and immediately begin keying the next line.

Speed Level of Practice

When the purpose of practice is to reach a new speed, use the speed level. Take the brakes off your fingers and experiment with new stroking patterns and new speeds. Do this by:

- reading two or three letters ahead of your keying to foresee stroking patterns
- getting the fingers ready for the combinations of letters to be keyed
- keeping your eyes on the copy in the book
- keying at the word level rather than letter by letter

1 What part did Edward get?

2 Reese liked to play ball.

3 She has three more games left.

4 When will he make the payment?

5 Felipe left for school an hour ago.

6 Mary has four more puppies to sell.

7 The girls won the game by eleven points.

8 Taisho finished the report on Wednesday.

9 Their runner fell with less than a lap to go.

10 Inez will finish the project by the deadline.

11 You can register for classes starting next Friday.

12 Jessica was elected president by just three votes.

gwam 30" | 2 | 4 | 6 | 8 | 10 | 12 | 14 | 16 | 18 | 20 |

Technique: Response Patterns

1. Key each line twice; DS between 2-line groups.

2. Key 1' timings on lines 10–12; determine *gwam* on each timing.

★TIP **Word response:** Key easy (balanced-hand) words as words.
Letter response: Key letters of one-hand words steadily and evenly, letter by letter.

Balanced-hand words

1 us so an by is or it do of go he if to me of ox am

2 an box air wig the and sir map pen men row fix jam

3 girl kept quay town auto busy firm dock held makes

One-hand words

4 be my up we on at no as oh as ax in at my up be we

5 no cat act red tax was you pin oil hip ear fat few

6 milk fast oily hymn base card safe draw pink gates

Balanced-hand phrases

7 to go|it is due|to the end|if it is|to do so|he is

8 pay the|for us|may do the|did he|make a|paid for a

9 he may|when did they|so do they|make a turn|to the

Balanced-hand sentences

10 I am to pay the six men if they do the work right.

11 Title to all of the lake land is held by the city.

12 The small ornament on their door is an ivory duck.

gwam 1' | 1 | 2 | 3 | 4 | 5 | 6 | 7 | 8 | 9 | 10 |

Timed Writing

1. Key a 1' timing on each ¶; determine *gwam*.

2. Key two 2' timings on ¶s 1–2 combined; determine *gwam*.

E all letters used

gwam 2'

```
              •    2    •    4    •    6    •    8    •
      To risk your own life for the good of others         5
    10    •    12    •    14    •    16    •    18    •
has always been seen as an admirable thing to do.          9
    20    •    22    •    24    •    26    •    28    •
Harriet Tubman was a slave in the South. She became       15
    30    •    32    •    34    •    36    •    38    •
a free woman when she was able to run away to the         19
    40    •    42    •    44    •    46    •    48    •
North. This freedom just did not mean much to her         24
    50    •    52    •    54    •    56    •
while so many others were still slaves.                   28

              •    2    •    4    •    6    •    8    •
      She quickly put her own life at risk by going       33
    10    •    12    •    14    •    16    •    18    •
back to the South. She did this to help others get        38
    20    •    22    •    24    •    26    •    28    •    30
free. She was able to help several hundred. This is       43
         •    32    •    34    •    36    •    38    •    40
a large number. During the Civil War she continued        48
         •    42    •    44    •    46    •    48    •    50
to exhibit the traits of an amazing hero. She served      53
         •    52    •    54    •    56    •
the Union as a spy and as a scout.                        57
```

gwam 2' | 1 | 2 | 3 | 4 | 5 |

Advanced Technology Skills 1

Keeping Resources Secure

OUTCOMES

- Safeguard files
- Maintain system security
- Recover from disasters
- Explore online and workplace safety issues

Safeguarding Files

Some strategies you learned in the *Basics of Good Digital Citizenship module* in Chapter 4 for maintaining your computer can also be used to safeguard its resources. When you back up files to an external drive or the cloud, for example, you have the option of copying files away from your system to a safe storage location. Any disaster that might affect your computer, such as fire, flood, tornado, or the like, will not completely wipe out your files if you have backups stored elsewhere.

You have some other options for safeguarding individual files to protect them from unauthorized access or to prevent users from changing content without permission. Password protection, editing restrictions, and permissions can be applied from within an application. You can also apply a digital signature as a way to authenticate the author of the document and indicate to other readers that any changes made to the document after the signature was applied may be unauthorized.

Password-Protecting a File

You are no doubt familiar with the value of using a password to prove your identity when you sign in to your computer or the Internet. You may also need to use a password when you set up online accounts that allow you to make secure transactions online.

Use a password to protect files or other resources

You can apply a password to files you create in application programs to protect them from unauthorized access. Password protection can prevent someone from opening the file without providing the correct password. In an application such as Microsoft *Word*, you can apply password protection from the File tab on the Ribbon, which is where you manage information about your Microsoft documents (see Figure AT1-1).

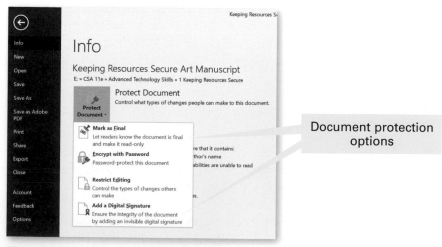

Figure AT1-1 Encrypt with password

File tab > Info > Protect Document > Encrypt with Password

1. Start Microsoft *Word.* In a new, blank document, key the following text:

   Protecting your files is a way of protecting scarce resources such as the time required to research, write, and edit a report.

2. Click the *File* tab, if necessary click *Info*, and then click *Protect Document*.

3. Click *Encrypt with Password* to open the Encrypt Document dialog box (see Figure AT1-2).

Figure AT1-2 Key a password in the Password box

4. Key your name as the password in the following format: First_Last. Click *OK*.

5. Rekey the password to confirm, and click *OK*.

6. Save the file in the location designated by your instructor as *at1 password*.

7. Click *File* and then click *Close*.

8. Open *File Explorer*, find the file, and open *at1 password*. When the Password dialog box appears, key your password and click *OK* to open the file.

9. Close the file, but leave *Word* open.

Maintaining System Security

Keeping your system secure is every bit as important as the routine maintenance you perform on your computer. Recovery from a determined cyberattack is almost always expensive in one way or another. If the only way to eliminate a virus or worm is to reformat your system, you could lose all your files.

As an individual computer user or in your role as a responsible business professional, you have an obligation to keep your system safe and secure. You have already read about some ways to keep your system secure, in the module *Basics of Good Digital Citizenship* in Chapter 4. The following sections cover the most important steps you can take to prevent or minimize the damage from a security breach.

Critical Defensive Measures

The best defense against security attacks is a good offense, in the form of good-quality antivirus and spyware applications. These applications are designed to scan your system continuously as you work, to check emails for problems, and even to recommend against opening some websites that may threaten your system.

Even the best security program, however, can fail to prevent access if it is not kept current with regular updates. Make sure that your antivirus program is always on and always up to date, and run a full system scan at least once a week.

Safeguarding your system is as important as maintaining it

It is equally important to keep other programs updated, especially browsers and your operating system. Many of the patches and fixes that are installed with updates to these programs address security issues, such as programming issues that can allow unauthorized access to your system.

Another important defensive application is a **firewall**. While antivirus and spyware programs can detect malware that has been downloaded to your computer, a firewall can prevent such malware from getting into your computer at all. A firewall works by checking incoming data against specific rules and then either allows the data to pass or blocks it. Because many computers today maintain a constant connection to the Internet whenever they are on, having a firewall in place to control the data stream is essential.

In a large organization, the IT department determines what kinds of data can pass through the firewall and monitors firewalls constantly for evidence of cyberattack. Home users rely on the firewalls that accompany their antivirus software or on the *Windows Defender Firewall*. Figure AT1-3 shows the *Windows Defender Firewall* is connected and is protecting access to the PC and network.

Figure AT1-3 *Windows Defender Firewall* settings

Permissions and Passwords

Whenever possible, limit access to your system or its files by restricting permissions and requiring passwords. You can control who has permission to make changes to your system by creating only one administrator account and making sure it is used only to perform routine system maintenance tasks.

You may be surprised to know that some routine tasks, such as browsing the Internet, can be more dangerous if you are using an administrator account. If you pick up a virus or a Trojan, your systems are at far greater risk when you are logged on as an administrator. This is the reason Microsoft suggests that you use a standard account for everyday tasks and use your administrator account only to adjust system settings.

When creating new user accounts, make a practice of creating standard accounts. The fewer people have permission to change system settings, the more secure your computer will be.

Get the most out of your password protection by using unique, strong passwords for every instance when you need a password. Using the same password over and over may make it easy for you to remember, but it will also make it easy for anyone who gains unauthorized access to your computer to get into sensitive files and important accounts. Likewise, make a practice of not sharing your password with anyone.

A strong password is at least 14 characters long, with a mixture of capital and lowercase letters, numbers, and symbols. Try to avoid obvious options such as your birthday, your address, or the names of friends or family members. Microsoft offers a simple method for converting a meaningful sentence into a strong password.

★TIP If you have a number of passwords to organize for access to sensitive information such as bank accounts, you may want to use a password manager such as LastPass, KeePass, or Dashlane, which allow you to store your account names and passwords in an encrypted database.

1. Start with a sentence:
    Wait and see what I bought for you
2. Remove spaces from the sentence:
    WaitandseewhatIboughtforyou
3. Replace words with numbers, symbols, or shorthand:
    W8&CwatIbot4U
4. Add length to the string with numbers that mean something to you:
    W8&CwatIbot4U91

If you doubt that you can remember your strong passwords, you can write them down and keep them in a safe place. Do not store your passwords on your computer or near your computer.

Commonsense Security Practices

Use common sense to avoid putting your computer and its resources at risk:

- Access only safe websites, and be careful what you download from the Internet.
- Don't run programs if you are not sure where they came from or that they are safe.
- Don't open attachments to email if you don't know the sender, and even then use caution. Some malware can use the email contact lists from legitimate users to send dangerous attachments. If you are not certain about an attachment, save it to your hard drive, and then use your antivirus software to scan the file.
- Turn off your computer when you are not using it. If you share a computer and cannot turn it off, log out of your account to protect your files.
- Keep your computer physically safe by making sure it cannot be reached from an open window. You can also attach a lock to secure your computer to an immovable object.

1. Review security procedures that you currently follow for your computer. For example, what kind of user account do you have? How often do you run a virus scan? What kind of firewall do you use?
2. Make a list of your current security procedures. Add to your list any procedures you are not doing that you should be doing.
3. Make a list of the passwords you currently use for various programs and accounts. Do you use some passwords more than once?
4. Review your passwords for strength. How could you modify some of your passwords to make them stronger?

Recovering from Disaster

An IT technician can help you recover from a virus attack

All computer users should have a plan of action in case of a virus or other malware infection. If you work for a company, you may be able to appeal to an IT department for aid, but if you are working in a small company or on your own, you should know the basic steps that will help you eliminate the threat.

Experts suggest you take the following steps when you discover your system has been infected.

1. First, disconnect the computer from any network it may be connected to, to avoid spreading the virus to other systems on the network. You may also need to disconnect the computer from the Internet, especially if you suspect your computer is being used to attack other systems.
2. Clean your system using your antivirus software. You may need to use special software tools to eliminate the virus infecting your computer. Your antivirus program's manufacturer can often offer free or pay-per-incident help to clean up your computer.
3. Reinstall any programs that have been damaged by the virus. This can mean reinstalling applications as well as your operating system. Make sure you have your original software (or activation codes) available to reinstall programs.
4. Scan your restored system to make sure all traces of the virus have been removed, making sure to use the most recent updates of your antivirus program.
5. Restore any files that have been lost or damaged, using your most recent uninfected backup.
6. Change all your passwords immediately. Some malware can capture your passwords, which can then be used by hackers to gain access to your programs and accounts.
7. Review your current security procedures to make sure you are doing everything you can to prevent another attack, and change procedures if you think they may have contributed to the attack.

Safeguarding your resources by following regular maintenance and standard security procedures can take time and effort. But the time, the effort, and the cost of repairing a system that has been damaged by outside attack can be far greater.

 **checkpoint** Create a chart that lists and illustrates the steps given in the previous section for recovering from a virus attack. Post the chart near your personal computer or in your notebook for quick reference in case of an emergency.

Exploring Online and Workplace Safety Issues

Online Safety

You have a responsibility to keep yourself safe when working or playing online. Careless behavior online can put not only your system but your own personal safety at risk.

- Beware of emails that seem to come from reputable sources but ask for sensitive information such as your account numbers.
- Never give your full name, personal address, phone number, school address, or other private information to individuals you do not know personally, and never agree to a face-to-face meeting alone with a person you have met online.
- If you are using a social network, follow their safety procedures to keep your account safe and control who sees your information.

**Practice workplace
safety first**

Workplace Safety

Setting up your computer and workspace correctly to avoid stress and strain on muscles, tendons, and bones is one aspect of workplace safety. To ensure that you are working comfortably and efficiently, follow these guidelines:

- Arrange your desk to minimize glare from overhead lights, desk lamps, and windows to avoid eyestrain.
- Keep hands, wrists, and forearms straight, in line, and parallel to the floor.
- Your head should be level or bent slightly forward; you should not have to look up at your monitor.
- Your shoulders and upper arms should be relaxed, and your elbows should be close to your body, bent between 90 and 120 degrees.
- Your feet should be fully supported on the floor or a footrest.
- Your back should be fully supported by your chair, and you should be sitting up straight or leaning back slightly.
- Your thighs and hips should be parallel to the floor, with knees about the same height as the hips and feet slightly forward.

To further reduce stress, change your working position frequently by stretching fingers, hands, and arms and by standing up and walking around occasionally. Some office desks are adjustable, allowing you to adjust the desk height or stand while working.

Maintaining a safe office environment is another important aspect of workplace safety. Some of the responsibility for office safety falls on your employer, who should ensure that the workplace has well-marked emergency exits, proper ventilation, no hazardous materials, adequate lighting, and secure doors and windows. You are responsible for reporting any problems such as light outages or locks that don't work properly. You are also responsible for using the office resources properly—don't, for example, overload outlets with multiple plugs that could result in electrical outages or fires, and don't operate office equipment in ways that might damage it.

Your employer should also have a safety policy in place that explains what to do in the event of a fire, explosion, natural disaster, or other catastrophe. Fire extinguishers and first-aid kits should be provided at convenient locations, and training should be provided in how to use extinguishers. You can contribute to your safety by keeping emergency supplies such as a flashlight, water bottle, and nonperishable food in your desk.

Before You Move On

Answer these questions to review what you have learned in Chapter 5.

1. When block format is used in a letter, all lines begin at the _____.
    LO 32A

2. When a letter is keyed, the line spacing should be set at _____.
    LO 32A

3. Identify the seven parts that should be included in a personal-business letter.
    LO 32A & 33B

4. Instead of keying a date in a letter, you can use the _____ feature to place the date in the letter. LO 34B

5. When modified block letter format is used, the return address, date, complimentary close, and typed signature begin at the _____ mark on the Ruler. LO 34C

6. Use the _____ feature to locate words in a document and change them to other words. LO 32D

7. A business letter is typically printed on _____ stationery.
    LO 33B & 33C

8. Name the three additional letter parts discussed in this chapter.
    LO 33B, 33C, & 33E

9. Describe the difference between mixed and open punctuation. LO 33C, 33E, & 34C

10. Name the most frequently used envelope size. LO 33D

11. _____ are used to set locations at which text can be placed.
    LO 34B, 34C, & 34D

Apply What You Have Learned

Business Letter from Arranged Copy

1. Format/key the letter on the next page in block format with mixed punctuation. Proofread and correct errors. Hyphenate the document. Change the font to 12 pt Arial.

2. Save as: *c5 letter 1*.

August 15, 20—

Ms. Amy McKenery
2128 Magill Drive
Odessa, TX 79764-0700

Dear Ms. McKenery:

Thank you for expressing an interest in establishing a scholarship to be awarded to a student who will be graduated at the end of this school year. As we discussed briefly on the telephone, the deadlines we need to meet are listed below:

1. Prepare the scholarship application by September 30.
2. Post scholarships on the school district website by October 10.
3. Receive scholarship dollars by November 1.
4. Receive scholarship applications by March 1.
5. Select and notify recipients by May 1.

Please complete the enclosed form and return it to me by September 1 so I can have a draft of the application prepared for you to review. If you have any questions, please call me at (943) 555-4612.

Again, thanks for giving back to your community to assist a worthy student.

Sincerely,

Alex Neu, Principal

xxx

Enclosure

Personal-Business Letter in Modified Block Format

1. Open *c5 letter1* and format it as a modified block letter with open punctuation and indented paragraphs.
2. Save the letter as *c5 letter2* and close it.

Personal-Business Letter in Block Format

1. Open *df c5 letter3*. Format the letter in block format with mixed punctuation. Use a 12-point Times New Roman font. Use your address as the return address. Insert the current date so that it updates automatically.
2. Use Find and Replace to make changes in the letter. Change *Doe* to *Ford*, *June* to *July*, *team* to *squad*, and *games* to *matches*.
3. Correct all spelling and grammar errors. Save the letter as *c5 letter3*.
4. Create a Size 10 envelope. Print the envelope. Close the letter.

CHAPTER 6

Creating Effective Reports

Lesson 35   MLA Reports

Lesson 36   Outlines and MLA Reports with Citations

Lesson 37   Reports in Standard, Unbound Format

Lesson 38   Multicolumn Documents with Text Boxes and Pictures

LESSONS 35–38

Reports, reports, reports! Everybody wants one—your science teacher, your math teacher, your English teacher. A **report** is a document that gives facts, ideas, or opinions about one or more topics. A review of a library book you have read is an example of a report. A summary of a science project you created is another example of a report. In this chapter, you will learn to use word processing software to format reports. **Format** means to place text on a page so that it looks good and is easy to read.

The reports will be arranged in standard format or the MLA format. *MLA* stands for *Modern Language Association*. School reports are often prepared using this format.

When you write reports, you may quote information from other sources. For example, you might include a quote from a magazine article. You will learn the in-text method of citing sources for quoted material. You also will learn how to format a page that lists all of the works cited in a report. An outline of a report is another report part that you will learn to format.

Solphoto/Shutterstock.com

Paragraph Alignment Commands

Home tab > Paragraph

Paragraph alignment refers to how text is placed on a page. In word processing terms, a **paragraph** is any amount of text that is keyed before the Enter key is tapped. A paragraph can be one word or several words or lines. Paragraphs can be aligned before or after text is keyed.

Figure 6-1 shows the toolbar buttons used to set alignment. Each button also shows how text will be placed on the page. **Align Left** starts all lines of the paragraph at the left margin. Align Left is the default paragraph alignment. **Align Right** ends all lines at the right margin. **Center** places an equal (or nearly equal) space between the text and each side margin. **Justify** starts all lines at the left margin and ends all full lines at the right margin.

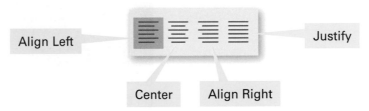

Figure 6-1 Alignment buttons

MLA Style Report

Your teachers may have you use a certain format when you write a report. In this lesson, you will learn to use a format suggested by the MLA. The MLA format is used in many schools. A sample report is here and in Figure 6-19.

For MLA report format, all margins are 1". The writer's last name and the page number appear in a header. The name and page number are right-aligned in the header area. Line spacing of 2.0 with 0 points after paragraphs is used for all lines (except the header). Report heading lines appear at the top of the report on separate lines and are aligned at the left margin. The headings are the writer's name, teacher's name, subject name, and date (day/month/year style). The report title comes after the headings and is centered. The first lines of paragraphs are indented 0.5".

MLA report format

Using the Numbering Feature for Outlines

Home tab > Paragraph > Numbering

Home tab > Paragraph > Decrease Indent or Increase Indent

An **outline** is a document that gives the main points of a subject. Outlines are helpful in planning and organizing reports. Frequently, they are prepared using the Numbering or Multilevel List feature. The Multilevel List button is to the right of the Numbering button. In this lesson, you will use the Numbering feature to prepare an outline that has multiple levels.

To move from one level to another within your outline, you can use the Decrease Indent or Increase Indent feature (see Figure 6-2). You also can move to different levels by using the Tab key or the Shift + Tab keys. Tapping the *Tab* key moves you to a lower level. Tapping the *Tab* key while pressing the *Shift* key moves you to a higher level in your outline.

Figure 6-2 Decrease Indent and Increase Indent

Different First Page

Insert tab > Header &
Footer > Header >
Edit Header > Different
First Page

When you format a report in MLA style, page numbers are right-aligned in a header and included on each page. In other report styles, the page number is not shown on the first page and page numbers may appear at the top or bottom of the page aligned at the left, at the right, or centered.

When the page number (or header or footer) is not to appear on the first page, double-click in the header or footer area to display the Header & Footer Tools Design tab, and select *Different First Page* in the Options group (shown in Figure 6-3).

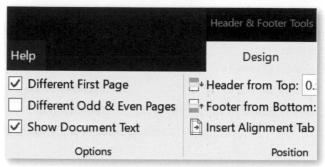

Figure 6-3 Different First Page option

Standard, Unbound Reports

Short reports are often prepared without covers and binders. If they are more than one page, a paper clip or staple in the upper-left corner usually holds them together. These reports are called **unbound reports** and are frequently formatted using a **standard format**.

The standard format for your reports will use the following:

Margins: Use the default margin settings on all pages and begin page 1 and the reference page at or near the 2" vertical position.

Page numbering: Do not number the first page; insert a centered page number in a footer or a right-aligned page number in a header for the second and subsequent pages.

Line spacing: Use the defaults (1.08 line spacing and 8 points of blank space after each paragraph).

Styles: Use Title style for the report title and Heading 1 style for the side headings in the default (*Word*) style set.

Textual citations: Key textual citations in parentheses in the body of the report at the point where the credit for paraphrased or quoted material is given. Quotations that are fewer than four keyed lines are enclosed in quotation marks. Long quotations that occupy four or more keyed lines are indented 0.5" from the left margin.

Reference list: Key and format *References* in Title style near the 2" vertical position. Key each reference using a 0.5" hanging indent style. Use the same line spacing that is used for the report body. Number the reference list page in the same manner that page 2 and subsequent pages are numbered.

A model of the standard, unbound format is shown in Figure 6-4.

1.08 line spacing with 8 points of space after paragraphs

Default 1" margins

Title style; title is keyed at or near the 2" vertical position

Internet Etiquette

What kind of Internet user are you? Are you the same kind of person on the Internet as you are when you meet face-to-face with a friend? Do you have respect for other people's time? Do you respect their privacy? Do you abuse the power the Internet gives you?

Rules of the Road

Heading 1 style

Several informal "rules of the road" are being created as more and more people communicate with one another on the Internet. The rules are called "netiquette." Netiquette covers the dos and don'ts of online communication. It includes the guidelines everyone should follow to be courteous to others. By using the rules, you will help yourself look good and avoid wasting other people's time and energy (Netiquette Basics, 2014).

Don't Use Capital Letters

When corresponding on the Internet, do not use all caps. Use all caps only to draw the reader's attention to one or a few words. Those who use proper netiquette are likely to interpret an internet message that is keyed in ALL CAPS as "shouting" and rude. Those interpretations can affect how your message is received (NetworkEtiquette.net, 2014).

Don't Be Offensive

A good question to ask yourself when you are communicating on the Internet is, "Would I say this to the person if we were communicating face to face?" If you answer "No", then you need to revise the message and proofread it as often as needed until you can answer "Yes" to the question (Netiquette, 2014).

***References* is keyed at or near the 2" vertical position**

References

Title style

Hanging indent

Netiquette. "The Core Rules of Netiquette." http://www.albion.com/netiquette/rule1.html (5 January 2014).

"Netiquette Basics." http://www.livinginternet.com/i/ia_nq_basics.htm (5 January 2014).

NetworkEtiquette.net. "The Rules of Netiquette." http://www.networketiquette.net/netiquette.htm (5 January 2014).

Figure 6-4 Standard unbound report format

Preformatted Text Boxes

Insert tab > Text >
Text Box > Simple Text Box

A **text box** is a container for text or graphics. Text boxes are used to call the reader's attention to specific text or graphics. They also are used to position several blocks of text on a page. You can choose a preformatted text box or draw your own.

The text box shown in Figure 6-5 was created by selecting *Simple Text Box* from the Built-in text box gallery. It has a border and contains placeholder text that will be replaced with text you key.

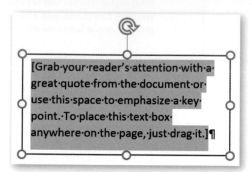

Figure 6-5 Built-in Simple Text Box

Draw and Size a Text Box

Insert tab > Text >
Text Box > Draw Text Box

If you choose, you can use the Draw Text Box option to create a text box from scratch instead of using a built-in one. Once it is drawn, the size of a text box can be changed to fit the text and space, and it can be moved to the desired position. A text box may have **borders** and/or **shading**— the default settings are a single-line border and no shading (fill) as shown in Figure 6-6.

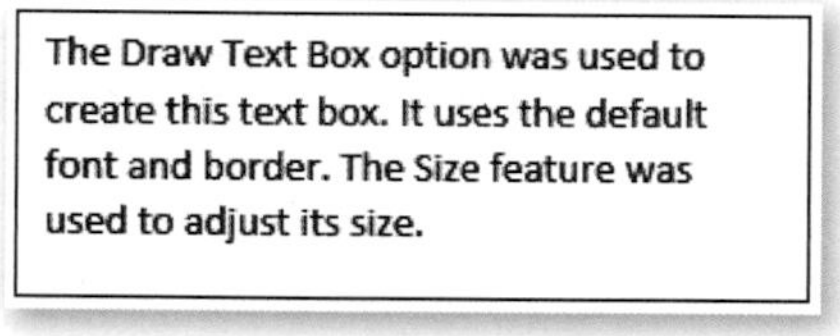

The Draw Text Box option was used to create this text box. It uses the default font and border. The Size feature was used to adjust its size.

Figure 6-6 Draw Text Box

Format a Text Box

Drawing Tools Format tab >
Shape Styles

Once a text box is inserted into your document, you can format it using the features available on the Drawing Tools Format tab that displays when a text box is selected. You can use features in the Shape Styles group shown in Figure 6-7 to select a preformatted style (Shape Styles gallery), change or add shading to the text box (Shape Fill), change or delete the border (Shape Outline), and add effects to the text box (Shape Effects).

Figure 6-7 Shape Styles group

Insert and Format Pictures

Insert tab > Illustrations > Pictures or Online Pictures

Pictures, including **clip art**, can be inserted or copied into a document. Clip art is ready-made drawings and photography. You can get pictures from files stored on your computer or from online sources. If you use pictures from the online sources, you must be careful not to violate copyright laws. *Word*'s Pictures and Online Pictures features can help you locate pictures for your documents.

When you select a picture, the Picture Tools Format tab opens (see Figure 6-8), and you can use the features on it to format, position, and size your picture.

Figure 6-8 Picture Styles, Arrange, and Size groups

Many of the features on the Picture Tools Format tab operate the same as or similar to those on the Drawing Tools Format tab that you use with text boxes. One difference is that when you size a picture, you need only change the width or height. When the width or height is changed, the other dimension automatically is changed to maintain the proper ratio of height to width.

To insert a picture that is stored on your computer or one that you are connected to, select *Pictures* from the Illustrations group to open the Insert Picture dialog box and navigate to the location of the picture file. To find and insert a picture from an online source, select *Online Pictures*. In the Insert Pictures dialog box, you can select and use an online source to search.

> ★**TIP** The ratio of width to height for a picture is called *aspect ratio*. By default, *Word* locks aspect ratio so that changing one dimension of the picture automatically changes the other a corresponding amount.

Multi-Column Document

Documents such as brochures and newsletters often have text in two or more columns on a page. The columns may be equal or unequal in width and length. A page may have a different number of columns. For example, a heading may be one column, and two or more columns of text may be below it. The text within the multiple columns often uses Justify alignment and is hyphenated.

WP Applications 8

Activity 1

Page Break

Insert tab > Pages > Page Break

Word processing software has two types of page breaks: **soft** and **hard**. Both kinds signal the ending of a page and the beginning of a new page. The software inserts a **soft page break** automatically when the current page is full (when the bottom margin is reached). You insert **hard page breaks** manually when you want a new page to begin before the current one is full (see Figure 6-9). When a hard page break is inserted, the word processing software adjusts any following soft page breaks so that those pages will be full before a new one is started. Hard page breaks do not move unless you move them. To move a hard page break, you can delete it and (1) let the software insert soft page breaks or (2) insert a new hard page break where you want it.

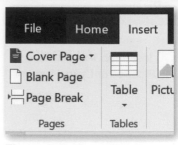

Figure 6-9 Page Break

1. Open a new document.
2. Key the roster sign-up sheet for the Red Sox shown below. Leave a 2" top margin on each page. Use 14-pt. Comic Sans for the font; 1.15" line spacing below the title and between the numbers; 12 players will be signing up for the team.
3. Insert a hard page break at the end of the Red Sox Roster page. Create sign-up sheets for the Mets, the Dodgers, and the Cubs, beginning each on a new page.
4. **Save as:** *wp8 activity 1*.

RED SOX ROSTER

1.

2.

11.

12.

Activity 2

Line and Page Breaks

Layout tab > Paragraph > Paragraph dialog box launcher > Line and Page Breaks

In multiple-page documents, the first line of a paragraph should not appear at the bottom of a page by itself (**orphan line**), and the last line of a paragraph should not appear by itself at the top of a page (**widow line**). The **Widow/Orphan control** feature prevents paragraphs from splitting incorrectly.

The **Keep with next** feature prevents a page break from occurring between two paragraphs. (See Figure 6-10.) Select this feature when a side heading appears as the last line at the bottom of a page and the text that relates to it begins on the next page.

Figure 6-10 Line and Page Breaks

1. Open *df wp8 activity 2*. An orphan line appears at the top of page 2.
2. Select all the text in the document, and turn on the Widow/Orphan control feature. The paragraph is automatically reformatted to prevent an orphan line.
3. **Save as:** *wp8 activity 2a*.
4. Tap *Enter* twice on page 1 before the title. Verify that a side heading appears as the last line on page 1, separated from the text to which it relates.
5. Place your insertion point on the side heading, and select the *Keep with next* feature to move the side heading to the top of page 2. Verify that the side heading moved to page 2.
6. **Save as:** *wp8 activity 3b*.

Activity 3

Page Numbers

Insert tab > Header & Footer > Page Number

Use the **Page Number** feature (see Figure 6-11) to place page numbers in specific locations on the printed page. Most software allows you to select the style of number (Arabic numerals—1, 2, 3; lowercase Roman numerals—i, ii, iii; uppercase Roman numerals—I, II, III). You can place numbers at the top or bottom of the page, aligned at the left margin, center, or right margin. Check the *Different First Page* box (Headers & Footers Tools/Design/Options) to keep the page number from appearing on the first page.

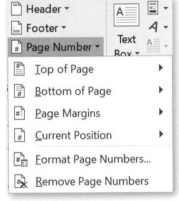

Figure 6-11 Page Numbers

1. Open *df wp8 activity 3*.
2. Number all five pages with the page number at the bottom center of the page. Hide the number on page 1.
3. Use *Print Preview* to verify that the page numbers have been added (pp. 2–5) or hidden (page 1).
4. **Save as:** *wp8 activity 3a*. Close the file.
5. Open *df wp8 activity 3* again. This time, number all five pages with the page number at the top right of the page. Key your name followed by a space before the page number. Do not hide your name and page number on page 1.
6. **Save as:** *wp8 activity 3b*.

Activity 4

Indentations

Home tab > Paragraph > Paragraph dialog box launcher > Indents and Spacing

Use the **Indent** feature to move text away from the margin. A **left indent** (**paragraph indent**) moves the text one tab stop to the right, away from the left margin, as shown below. A **hanging indent**, also shown below, moves all but the first line of a paragraph one tab stop to the right. Refer to Figure 6-12. Set the left indent under General/Alignment and the hanging indent under Indentation/Special in the Paragraph dialog box.

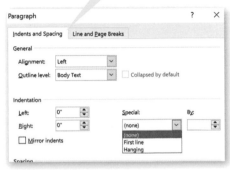

Indents and Spacing tab

Figure 6-12 Indents

Left (paragraph) indent 0.5"

This example shows text that is indented from the left margin. Notice that each line begins at the indentation point.

Hanging indent 0.5"

This example shows a hanging indent. Notice that the first line begins at the left margin, but the remaining lines begin at the indentation point.

1. Open a new document. Set margins at Wide and use Century Gothic 14-pt. font.
2. Key the two paragraphs shown above, indenting them as indicated. Tap *Enter* once between paragraphs. Clear the indent that was inserted in the first paragraph before keying the second one.
3. **Save as:** *wp8 activity 4*.

Activity 5

Styles

Home tab > Styles > Select style

A **style** is a collection of format settings for font, font size, color, paragraph spacing, alignment, and so on that are named and stored together in a style set (see Figure 6-13). The default style is named *Normal*. The Normal style uses Calibri 11-pt. black font, 1.08 line spacing, 8-pt. spacing after paragraphs, and left alignment.

Figure 6-13 Styles

As shown in Figure 6-13, each style set contains styles for titles, subtitles, and various headings that can be quickly applied to text to make it attractive and easy to read. To format text using the Styles feature, select the style set of your choice. Then select the text to be formatted, and click on the style with the desired formatting. The text will be automatically formatted, as shown in Figure 6-14.

Before Styles Applied	After Styles Applied
Title Subtitle Heading 1 Heading 2 Intense Quotation Intense Reference	Title Subtitle Heading 1 Heading 2 *Intense Quotation* INTENSE REFERENCE

Figure 6-14 Text before and after applying styles

1. Open *df wp8 activity 5*.
2. Select the text for the first line (Title).
3. Click the *Title* style button.
4. Select the next line of text, and click the corresponding style (*Subtitle*).
5. Repeat for each of the remaining lines of text.
6. **Save as:** *wp8 activity 5*.

Activity 6

Insert Footnote

References tab >
Footnotes > Insert
Footnote

One way to identify sources cited in your text is to add footnotes. The **Insert Footnote** feature (see Figure 6-15) can be used to automatically insert the footnote at the bottom of the same page as its reference. As you edit, add, or delete footnotes, changes in numbering and formatting are automatically made. Note: The **Insert Endnote** feature works in a similar way, except that endnotes appear at the end of the document. In this unit, you will use footnotes as a method to document sources.

Figure 6-15 Insert Footnote

1. Open file **df wp8 activity 6**. Insert the three footnotes shown below where indicated in the file. Tap *Enter* between footnotes. Delete (*Insert footnote No. x*) from the copy.

[1] Joan S. Ryan and Christie Ryan, *Managing Your Personal Finances 7e,* (Boston: South-Western Cengage Learning, 2016), p. 58.

[2] U.S. House of Representatives, Committee on Ways and Means, "The Tax Cuts and Jobs Act: What Our Historic Tax Reform Means for You and Your Family" https://waysandmeans.house.gov/wp-content/uploads/2017/11/WM_TCJA_TP.pdf (accessed March 26, 2018).

[3] Tax Policy Center, "Analysis of the Tax Cut and Jobs Act (Conference Agreement)," www.taxpolicycenter.org/publications/distributional-analysis-conference-agreement-tax-cuts-and-jobs-act (accessed March 26, 2018).

2. **Save as: wp8 activity 6**.

Activity 7

Insert Text from File

Insert tab > Text > Object >
Text from File > Browse to
file > Insert

To insert text from an existing file into a file that is open, use the **Text from File** feature shown in Figure 6-16.

1. Open a new document.
2. Leaving a 2" top margin, key the copy below (except the words printed in color). Use the Title style for the heading.

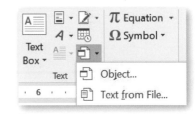

Figure 6-16 Text from File

Table Exams

Here is a list of the software features you will need to know for the first exam on tables.
<Insert **df wp8 activity 7a** file.>
For the second exam on tables, you will need to know the following table formatting software features.
<Insert **df wp8 activity 7b** file.>

3. Insert the **df wp8 activity 7a** and **df wp8 activity 7b** files where indicated in the text. Add space above paragraph 2.
4. **Save as: wp8 activity 7**.

Activity 8

Cover Page

Insert tab > Pages >
Cover Page

The **Cover Page** feature (see Figure 6-17) inserts a fully formatted cover page. The file contains placeholders for keying the title, author, date, etc. In this unit, you will create cover pages as new documents and delete the blank page that is automatically inserted following the cover page. To delete the blank page, use the *Show/Hide ¶ feature*, and delete the page break if it is visible. If it is not, go to the beginning of the blank page, and tap *Backspace* until the blank page is deleted.

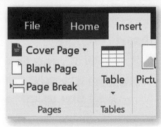

Figure 6-17 Cover Page

1. Open a new document.
2. Use the Cover Page feature to create a cover page using the **Sideline** style. Key the following information in the appropriate placeholders.

   Title Placeholder: Plains Indians
   Subtitle Placeholder: A Brief History
   Author Placeholder: Your Name
   Date Placeholder: Current Date

3. Apply a different style to the cover page you created.
4. Change the style back to *Sideline* style, and delete the blank page.
5. **Save as:** *wp8 activity 8*.

LESSON 35   MLA Reports

OUTCOMES

- Practice applying line spacing and selecting text
- Use paragraph alignment commands
- Apply font settings from the Home tab
- Insert page numbers in headers and footers
- Compose an MLA report

35–38A

Warmup

Key each line twice at the beginning of each lesson; first for content and then for speed.

alphabet   1   Frank questioned Tim over the jazz saxophone at my new nightclub.

fig/sym   2   The #5346 item will cost Ford & Sons $921.87 (less 10% for cash).

speed   3   If Jen signs the form, I may pay to dismantle the ancient chapel.

gwam 1' | 1 | 2 | 3 | 4 | 5 | 6 | 7 | 8 | 9 | 10 | 11 | 12 | 13 |

35B

Practice Line Spacing and Selecting Text

Home tab > Paragraph >
Line and Paragraph Spacing

1. Start *Word*. Open the document **df 35b report**.
2. Select the title and the paragraphs of the report and change line spacing to 2.0. (Recall that line spacing of 1.0 is called single spacing and line spacing of 2.0 is called double spacing.) Notice that there is more blank space between the paragraphs than between the lines within a paragraph in the document.
3. Delete the extra space between the paragraphs by using the *Remove Space After Paragraph* feature. The report should now be double-spaced with no extra blank space after the paragraphs.

★TIP To learn other ways to select text, open **df 35b select**. Practice the ways to select text described in the document.

★TIP If the Vertical Page Position indicator is not displayed on your status bar, right-click the status bar and select *Vertical Page Position*.

4. Select **School** in the title and change it to all capitals.
5. Begin the document at or near 2" from the top of the page. If the word *At* is not displayed on the bottom status bar as shown in Figure 6-18, follow the instructions in the Tip at the left.
6. Save the document as **35b report** and close it.

Page 1 of 1   At: 1"   192 words

Figure 6-18 Status bar

Vertical page position

35C

Paragraph Alignment

Home tab > Paragraph

1. Open **df 35c report**.
2. Center the title.
3. Use Align Left to format the first two paragraphs of the body.
4. Justify the third and fourth paragraphs.
5. Save the document as **35c report** and close it.

35D

Font Settings

Home tab > Font

1. Open **df 35d font** and move your pointer over each feature in the Font group on the Home tab to display and read the name and description of each feature.
2. Follow the directions in the file to use the font features in the Font group on the Home tab.
3. Save the document as **35d font** and close it.

★TIP Use Format Painter to copy formats to another place or multiple places in a document. On the Home tab, Clipboard group, click the *Format Painter* button once to copy the format to another place; double-click it to copy the format to multiple places.

Page Numbers in Headers and Footers

Insert tab > Header & Footer > Page Number

★TIP To exit a header or footer, double-click outside the header or footer area. To edit a header or footer, double-click in the header or footer area.

1. Open *df 35e report*. Format the text with Line Spacing 2.0 and remove any extra space after the paragraphs.

2. Access the *Page Number* options shown in the path to the left in this section and select *Plain Number 3* from the *Top of Page* options. Key your last name beginning at the blinking cursor that is to the left of the page number, and then tap the *Space Bar* once to insert a space between your last name and the page number. Double-click outside the header to exit it.

3. Insert a page number at the bottom of the page that uses the *Plain Number 2* style. Exit the footer area.

4. Save the document as *35e report* and close it.

✓ checkpoint Review your document. Both pages should have your last name and page number right-aligned as a header and a number centered as a footer.

Key an MLA Style Unbound Report

COLLABORATION

1. In a new, blank document, key the report in Figure 6-19 in MLA format as shown. Replace *20--* with the current year. Insert the writer's last name and page number right-aligned in a header.

2. Proofread the report and correct any errors. Save the document as *35f report* and close it.

✓ checkpoint Exchange reports with a classmate. Check each other's report to see if MLA-style guidelines were followed.

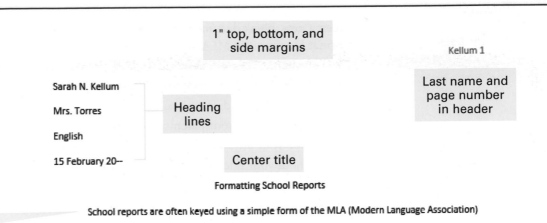

1" top, bottom, and side margins

Last name and page number in header

Sarah N. Kellum

Mrs. Torres

English

15 February 20--

Heading lines

Center title

Formatting School Reports

Line spacing 2.0 with 0 point space after for all lines and 0.5" indent on first lines of paragraphs

School reports are often keyed using a simple form of the MLA (Modern Language Association) style.

The top, bottom, left, and right margins on all pages are 1 inch. Right-align a page number in a header on each page. The writer's last name should come before the page number.

Double-space the entire report. The report heading lines begin 1 inch from the top of the page. Left-align and double-space the report heading lines. They include the writer's name, teacher's name, subject name, and date (day/month/year style) on separate lines.

Center the report title below the date. The title is keyed using rules for capitalizing and punctuating titles. The report title may be keyed in a slightly larger font size to make it stand out. However, it should not be underlined or placed in quotation marks.

Figure 6-19 MLA unbound report format

Compose an MLA Report

1. Open a new, blank document. Compose a short report (one to two pages) about yourself. Format the report in MLA style.

2. Use your name, your teacher's name, your class name, and the current date for the headings. Key your name and the word **Autobiography** for the title. For the body:

   - Tell about when and where you were born
   - Talk briefly about your parents, brothers and sisters, or other family members
   - Describe your physical appearance and your personality
   - Talk about your interests or hobbies
   - Name one or two jobs that you might like to have in the future

3. Save the document as *35g report* and close it.

LESSON 36   Outlines and MLA Reports with Citations

OUTCOMES

- Insert a bulleted list in an MLA report
- Create an outline using the Numbered List feature
- Apply paragraph indents
- Format an MLA report with citations
- Research a topic and prepare a report in MLA format

36B

MLA Report with Bulleted List

1. Open *df 36b report*. Format the document in correct MLA style. Use your name as the person writing the report. Create an appropriate header. Change *20--* to the current year in the report heading.

2. Change the numbered list to a bulleted list.

3. Check the format. Proofread carefully. Make corrections as needed. Save the document as *36b report* and close it.

★TIP To apply bullets or number to text that has already been keyed, click the *Bullets* or *Numbering* button in the Paragraph group on the Home tab.

36C

Outline Using the Numbering Feature

Home tab > Paragraph > Numbering

Activity 1

1. In a new, blank document, key the text on the next page as an outline. Use default margin settings. Center the outline title. Use a numbered list with Roman numerals for the outline topics and Decrease and Increase Indents to move from one level to another.

2. Proofread your outline and correct any misspelled words and formatting errors. Save the document as *36c outline1* and close it.

Computer Graphics

I. Introduction

II. Computer charts

    a. Bar charts

        i. Vertical bar

        ii. Horizontal bar

    b. Circle charts

        i. Whole circle

        ii. Exploded circle

    c. Line charts

        i. Without shaded areas

        ii. With shaded areas

Activity 2

1. Open **df 36c outline**. Select all the text in the document. Choose a numbering style from the Numbering Library to format the text as an outline.

2. Use *Decrease Indent* and *Increase Indent* as needed to show that *Breakfast* and *Lunch* are at the first level; *cereal, toast, orange juice, sandwich, chicken soup,* and *apple* are at the second level; and the remaining items are at the third level.

3. Check the format of the outline and make any necessary changes. Save the document as **36c outline2** and close it.

stockelements/Shutterstock.com

21st Century Skills: Media Literacy Think about the various ways you receive information. In addition to classroom lectures and studies, you might watch a television show, listen to a radio broadcast, browse the web, or read a magazine. As you process the information you receive daily, you form impressions and make interpretations and judgments. Consciously—or subconsciously—the many messages you process every day influence the decisions you make and have a significant impact on the way you live your life.

Think Critically

1. Think of an advertisement you have recently seen or heard. Where did you see or hear the ad? What was being advertised? How did the ad influence your opinion of the advertiser? Would you make a purchase based on the ad?

2. Write a short report about one of your favorite products (e.g., a brand of clothing or shoes or a favorite food or drink). Include at least three paragraphs that identify the product, who makes it, the target market, the format in which you saw it advertised (print, broadcast, web, etc.), and the key features of the product that convinced you to buy it. Save the document as directed by your instructor.

COLLABORATION

3. Share the report with your class. As a class, discuss the appeal of the product and why consumers with different demographic characteristics (such as age, gender, race, income level, etc.) would or would not buy it.

36D

Paragraph Indents

Home tab > Paragraph > Paragraph dialog box launcher

Paragraph dialog box launcher

In an MLA report, long quotes (four or more keyed lines) are indented 1" from the left margin to make them stand out from the rest of the report body. You can indent the paragraph by using the Increase Indent feature or by setting the left indentation in the Indents and Spacing options in the Paragraph dialog box. You can see an example of an indented quote on page 6-18.

In an MLA report, the list of references used is titled Works Cited. In other report styles, it may be titled References or Bibliography. The list of works cited is formatted using the **hanging indent** feature. The hanging indent format moves all lines except the first line away from the left margin. You can see an example of a hanging indent on page 6-18. With this indent style, the authors' names stand out and are easier to find.

1. Open *df 36d indents*.
2. This document contains part of a report. Select the second paragraph of the report, which is a long quote. Indent this paragraph by setting the Left indentation to 1" on the Indents and Spacing tab of the Paragraph dialog box.
3. Move to the next page of the document. This is a Works Cited page. Select all of the entries after the title and use a 0.5" hanging indent for the entries.
4. Save the document as *36d indents* and close it.

Works Cited Page Using Indents and Manual Page Breaks

In an MLA report, notes are placed in the body to mark material taken from other sources. These notes are called **citations**. For example, in a report that you write, you might quote from a magazine article. You should cite (give information about) where this material came from.

Citations are placed in parentheses in the report body. The following model shows an example of an in-text citation. Citations include the name(s) of the author(s) and page number(s) of the material.

Quotes of up to three keyed lines are placed in quotation marks. Long quotes (four or more keyed lines) are left-indented 1", as shown in the model. Summarized material is not put in quotation marks.

Lillian Jackson Braun is a popular mystery writer. Many people enjoy reading her books about an amateur detective and his cats. The cats, Koko and Yum Yum, know how to make themselves at home anywhere.

Indent long quotes 1"
It was their first night in the cabin by the creek. Qwilleran placed the cats' blue cushion on one bunk. They settled down contentedly, while he retired to the other bunk. Sometime during the night, the arrangement changed; in the morning Qwilleran was sharing his pillow with Yum Yum, and Koko was snuggled in the crook of his knee. (Braun 123) **In-text citation**

All references cited in a report in MLA style are listed on a separate page. This page is the last page of the report. It is called the Works Cited page. An example of a Works Cited page is shown in the following model.

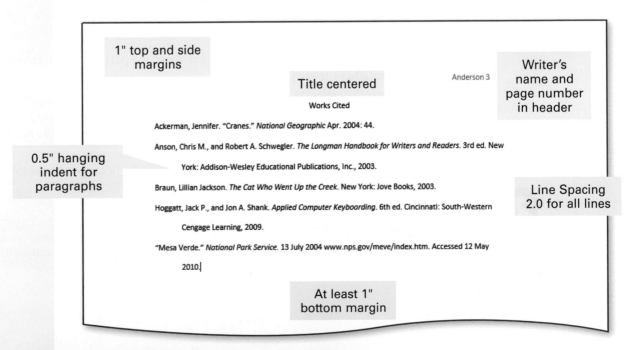

1" top and side margins

Title centered

Anderson 3

Writer's name and page number in header

Works Cited

Ackerman, Jennifer. "Cranes." *National Geographic* Apr. 2004: 44.

Anson, Chris M., and Robert A. Schwegler. *The Longman Handbook for Writers and Readers*. 3rd ed. New York: Addison-Wesley Educational Publications, Inc., 2003.

0.5" hanging indent for paragraphs

Braun, Lillian Jackson. *The Cat Who Went Up the Creek*. New York: Jove Books, 2003.

Hoggatt, Jack P., and Jon A. Shank. *Applied Computer Keyboarding*. 6th ed. Cincinnati: South-Western Cengage Learning, 2009.

Line Spacing 2.0 for all lines

"Mesa Verde." *National Park Service*. 13 July 2004 www.nps.gov/meve/index.htm. Accessed 12 May 2010.

At least 1" bottom margin

This page should have the same margins and header as the report body. The title, Works Cited, is centered at the top of the page. Line Spacing 2.0 is used for all lines on the Works Cited page. The works are placed in alphabetical order by author's last names, if known. If the author is not known, use the title of the work. A hanging indent is applied to the paragraphs.

1. Open **df 36e sources**. Add a header for the writer's last name and the page number.
2. Insert **(Anson and Schwegler 619)** as a citation at the end of the third sentence between the end quotation mark and the period.
3. Insert **(Hoggatt and Shank 169)** as a citation between the last word in the final sentence and the period.
4. Review the format of a Works Cited page on the previous page and then create a Works Cited page using the following two sources and the MLA style.

   Anson, Chris M., and Robert A. Schwegler. *The Longman Handbook for Writers and Readers*, 3rd ed. New York: Addison-Wesley Educational Publications, Inc., 2003.

   Hoggatt, Jack P., and Jon A. Shank. *Applied Computer Keyboarding*, 6th ed. Cincinnati: South-Western Cengage Learning, 2009.

5. Your Works Cited page should look similar to the model on page 6-18 (but with only two Works Cited entries). Save the document as **36e sources** and close it.

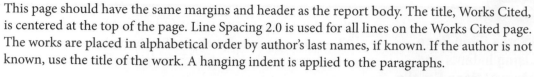

MLA Report with Works Cited

1. Do research and write a report about a U.S. national park. Find information about national parks in your local library or on the Internet. Then choose a park. In your report, you should include information such as:

   - The park location
   - A general description
   - Primary attractions
   - Other interesting information

2. Use at least two sources of information about the park. Note the reference information for each source.
3. Format the report in MLA style. Use an appropriate header, an appropriate title, and appropriate report headings. Write at least three paragraphs for the body. Include at least two in-text citations. Create a Works Cited page as the last page of the report. List all of the sources you used.
4. Proofread carefully and correct any errors or make necessary revisions to your text. Save the document as **36f report** and close it.

COLLABORATION

 Trade papers with a classmate. Ask your classmate to proofread your paper and mark errors you may have missed. Make corrections if necessary.

checkpoint

Did you place the period after the in-text citations? Is your Works Cited page on a separate page? Does page 2 have a header with the page number? Is Line Spacing 2.0 used for all lines?

36F

LESSON 37   Reports in Standard, Unbound Format

OUTCOMES

- Use the Different First Page feature
- Apply different styles to text
- Format a standard, unbound report with references
- Learn and use proofreaders' marks
- Format a standard, unbound report with proofreaders' marks

37B

Different First Page

Insert tab > Header & Footer >
Header > Edit Header >
Different First Page
or
Double-click existing header
or footer to open Header &
Footer Tools Design tab >
Different First Page

1. Open *df 37b page*.
2. Insert a page number centered at the bottom of each page.
3. Do not display the page number on page 1.
4. Verify that the page number does not appear on page 1 but that it does appear on page 2. Save the document as *37b page* and close it.

37C

Styles

Home tab > Styles

1. Open *37b page*.
2. Format the report title in *Title* style.
3. Format the side headings in *Heading 1* style. (You can use the Format Painter to quickly copy the format of the first side heading to each of the other side headings.)
4. Save the document as *37c styles* and close it.

Monkey Business Images/Shutterstock.com

Digital Citizenship and Ethics You've probably used the Internet to gather information for a school project, or maybe you visit websites as part of your classroom learning, or perhaps you've accessed an online tutorial to learn about effective study habits or how to write better essays. E-learning, or online education, has become a popular and accessible way for learners at all levels to take classes and further their academic pursuits. Many colleges and universities now offer online degree programs, and businesses often use online and computer-based training for employees.

E-learning offers many advantages, including:

- Flexible scheduling, which enables learners to complete coursework when it's convenient for them
- Self-paced learning, which allows participants to learn at their own pace as long as coursework is turned in by the due date
- No transportation costs or hassles, as you typically work from your home computer

As a class, discuss the following.

1. How have you used e-learning at home or in school within the last six months?

COLLABORATION

2. What are some drawbacks of taking online courses?

Format a Standard, Unbound Report

NOTE See *WP Applications 7* in Chapter 5 to review using Spelling & Grammar features.

1. Open *df 37d report*. Format all text in Calibri 11-pt. font. Verify that line spacing is set to 1.08 and that spacing after paragraph is set at 8 point.
2. Begin the report title near the 2" vertical position. Format the report title in *Title* style.
3. Format the four side headings in *Heading 1* style.
4. Insert a page break after the last paragraph of the report. Format *References* in *Title* style near the 2" vertical position on the new page.
5. Format the references in 0.5" hanging indent style.
6. Insert a centered page number in the footer. Do not display the number on the first page.
7. Use *Spelling & Grammar* to check for and correct errors. Proofread to find additional errors, if any. Save the document as *37d report* and close it.

37E

Proofreaders' Marks

Every document you create should be checked carefully. You should make sure it does not have spelling, punctuation, or format errors. **Proofreaders' marks** are letters and symbols used to show the errors or revisions in a document. These marks make it easy for you or someone else to make the changes noted in the copy. Study the following frequently used marks. Other marks are shown in the resource section of the textbook.

Mark	Action Required	Mark	Action Required
¶	Begin a new paragraph	≡	Capitalize
◡	Close up	ℒ	Delete
∧	Insert	*stet*	Let it stand
lc	Make lowercase	⌐	Move left
⌐	Move right	∿	Transpose

1. In a new, blank document, key the following text. Make corrections as indicated by the proofreaders' marks. Proofread to find one error that is not marked.
2. Save the document as *37e proof* and close it.

> *big*
> just⌐ how well do you adjust to ∧changes in your life?? You
> should recog◡nize that change is ⟨as⟩ certain as ~~life and~~
> *not*
> death and taxes. You can ∧avoid cha∿ne, but your can adjust
> *good*
> *lc* to it. How ⟨q⟩uickly◡you can do this is a ∧index of the
> success you are lik∿ley to have in the future◡~~years~~ ¶Can
> *stet*
> you think of ~~changes~~ that have affected you⌐ in the past
> year? Were you able to adjust to℘ them?

1. In a new, blank document, key the report on the next two pages in standard, unbound format. Make corrections as indicated by the proofreaders' marks.
2. Save the document as *37f report* and close it.

Hillsdale High School Update

During the past month, Hillsdale *High* School hired three new teachers. The new teachers, Ms. Anne Hartman, Mr. Terry Nolan, and Ms. Mary Knowles, officially ~~begin~~ *start* when school opens this year, but they have been at the high school on a regular basis to prepare their classrooms and courses for the new school year and to meet with the principal and other staff members.

About the New Teachers

Ms. Hartman has a B.S. degree from Clark College, *where* she majored in biology. Anne taught for three years at ~~at~~ Reynolds High before coming to Hillsdale. She has been very active in her church and community. She resides in Morningside with her husband, Dale, and two daughters, Ashlee and Melanie.

¶ Mr. Nolan has a B.A. degree with a major in English. He also has an M.S. degree from Garrett University. Terry taught for six years at Worthington High School before entering the business world, where he worked the last five years for Environmental Services, Inc. ~~Company~~. He and his wife, Sandy, are in the process of moving into the school district.

Ms. Knowles just completed her B.S. degree in Business Education. She returned to Clark College to earn her teaching certification after working at Integrated Computer Systems for the past four years. Mary is a graduate of Hillsdale High, and some may recall that she was a member of the softball team that won a state championship. Ms. Knowies lives with her husband, Ken, and young daughter, Martha, in Millerstown.

Grant Awarded

Mr. Gary Johnson, head of the Science department, will serve as the project director for the $75,000 grant Hillsdale High received from the Morris Foundation, The money will be used to purchase new software for the science laboratories. In addition, the grant supports a series of professional development workshops for the elementary, middle, and high school science teachers. This grant is the second one Hillsdale has received from this foundation during the past six years.

Professional Development

Early in the new school year, Dr. James Jenson, President, Center for the Improvement of Schools, will speak to all of the district's teachers. His presentation will focus on what changes schools need to make to prepare students for a world where business is carried out internationally, communications are instantaneous, and people from various societies must be able to live and work together.

LESSON 38   Multicolumn Documents with Text Boxes and Pictures

OUTCOMES

- Use a built-in text box
- Draw and size a text box
- Format a text box
- Insert and format pictures
- Create a document using Columns, Justify alignment, and First-line Indent
- Create a three-column document using Line between and Hyphenation
- Prepare a newsletter using pictures and text wrap

38B

Preformatted Text Boxes

Insert tab > Text > Text Box

1. Open a new, blank document.
2. Display the Text Box gallery using the path at the left. Select the *Simple Text Box* from the Built-in section of the gallery. A horizontally centered, preformatted text box appears, the text box is selected, and the placeholder text is highlighted.
3. Begin keying the following text in the text box—the placeholder text will be deleted, the text box will be resized, and text will wrap automatically to the next line. Do not tap Enter after the paragraph is keyed.

   This text box has a single-line border and no shading. When I begin keying, the placeholder text is removed and the text box is resized automatically to fit the amount of text I key in the text box.

4. Position the text box at the top left within the margins.
5. Save the document as **38b text box** and close it.

38C

Draw and Size a Text Box

Draw
Insert tab > Text > Text Box > Draw Text Box

 **TIP** A selected text box has **sizing handles** (small circles). To increase or decrease width or height, move the pointer over a sizing handle at the top, bottom, or side of the text box. When the pointer changes to a two-sided arrow, click and drag to adjust the box size. To increase or decrease height and width at the same time, drag a corner sizing handle.

1. Open a new, blank document. Center your name on line 1, key the text **Draw Text Box** on line 2, and then tap *Enter*.
2. Follow the **Draw** path at the left to select *Draw Text Box*. The insertion point changes to a cross. Move the cross about 1" or 2" to the left of and below the centered text. Click and drag to the right and then down until the text box you are drawing is about 3" wide and 2" tall to accommodate the text to be keyed in it. Release the mouse button. A text box appears, and the blinking insertion point inside the text box indicates where text will be inserted when you begin keying.
3. Key the following text in the text box. The text will wrap automatically to the next line. Do not tap Enter after the paragraph is keyed.

   This text box has a single-line border and no shading, which are the default settings. I keyed text into the text box, changed the size of the text box, and horizontally centered it. In the next activity, I will learn to change the format of a text box.

4. The text box should still be selected. To resize the text box so its height and/or width are appropriate to its contents and the space it will occupy, increase or decrease the Shape Height and Shape Width settings (see the *Size* path at the left) in the Size group as needed (see Figure 6-20). For this activity, the text box is to be **3"** wide; the height should be enough to accommodate the text (**1.5"**).

Size

Drawing Tools Format tab >
Size > Shape Height and/or
Shape Width

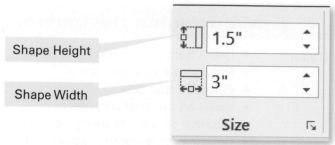

Figure 6-20 Shape Height and Shape Width

Align

Drawing Tools Format tab >
Arrange > Align > Choose
alignment

5. If needed, move the text box so it is horizontally centered below the second line of text. (Hint: Use the Align commands on the Format tab, not the Paragraph align commands on the Home tab.)

6. Save the document as *38c text box* and close it.

38D

Format a Text Box

Drawing Tools Format tab >
Format > Shape Styles

NOTE **See the Application Guide and Figure 6-7 for a review of Shape Styles.**

1. Open *df 38d text box* and select the first text box.

2. Use the path at the left to display the Shape Styles gallery in the Shape Styles group. Select a style from the gallery.

3. Adjust the text box width to **2.5"** and then adjust its height to accommodate the text. Center the text box horizontally.

4. Format the bottom text box by selecting a:
   a. Desired text box shade from the Shape Fill options.
   b. 3-point border in a desired color from the Shape Outline options. (Hint: Use the *Weight* option.)
   c. Desired shape effect from the Shape Effects options.

5. Change the width to 2.5" and adjust the height as needed to accommodate the text.

6. Save the document as *38d text box* and close it.

38E

Insert and Format Pictures

Online Pictures

Insert tab > Illustrations >
Online Pictures

Pictures

Insert tab > Illustrations >
Pictures

Activity 1

1. Open a new, blank document and insert a picture by doing one of the following:
   - If you are permitted to search the Internet for pictures, follow the **Online Pictures** path at the left, and then use an online service to find a picture of a penguin. Insert the desired picture.
   - To find a picture of penguins on your computer, follow the **Pictures** path at the left, and then look in the folder where your data files are stored for *df 38e penguins* (a picture file). Select the picture and then click *Insert*.

2. Select the picture to display the *Picture Tools Format* tab. Click the tab if necessary to display commands.

3. Change the *Shape Width* setting in the Size group to 3". Notice that the Shape Height setting changed automatically to maintain the proper aspect ratio.

★TIP Clip art and pictures you find on the Internet may be copyrighted. Read and follow the acceptable-use guidelines for clip art and pictures you find online.

4. Change the picture's position to top center using the *Position* feature in the Arrange group.
5. Move the picture down about 1" by dragging or nudging it with the arrow keys.
6. Scroll through the built-in picture styles in the Picture Styles group and select a style that you like.
7. Save the document as **38e penguins** and close it.

Activity 2

1. Open **df 38e laptops**. It contains three pictures that are left-aligned at the top, middle, and bottom.
2. Select the top left picture and do the following:
   a. Change its height to 2".
   b. Format it using a built-in style that does not have a border.
   c. Position it at the top right.
3. Select the left center picture.
   a. Change its width to 2".
   b. Format it using your choice of Picture Border and Picture Effects options.
   c. Position it at the bottom right.
4. Select the bottom left picture and format and size it as you choose. Position it in the middle center.
5. Save the document as **38e laptops** and close it.

38F

Multicolumn Document

First Line Indent
Home tab > Paragraph > Dialog box launcher > Indentation

1. Open a new, blank document. Key **Career Fair** in bold on the first line and center the text. Tap *Enter*.
2. Set the alignment to *Justify* (Home tab > Paragraph > Justify).
3. To automatically indent the first line of each paragraph 0.25", follow the **First-Line Indent** path at the left. Choose *First line* from the Special list and, if necessary, key **0.25"** in the By box as shown in Figure 6-21.

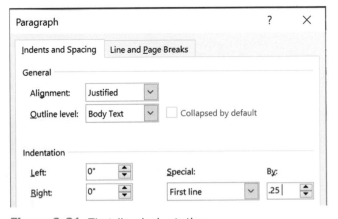

Figure 6-21 First-line indentation

Columns
Layout tab > Page Setup > Columns

4. Format the document for two columns of equal width by following the **Columns** path at the left to open the Columns gallery (see Figure 6-22). Select *Two* columns.

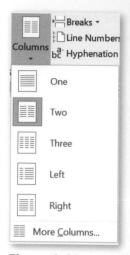

Figure 6-22 Columns gallery

5. Key the following text. The text will appear only in the first column.

Career Fair

The Career Fair will be held May 15 from 9 a.m. to 12:30 p.m. It will be in Room 214. Next week you will get a list of the employers who are coming. Each employer represents a different career. Therefore, there will be a variety of careers for you to explore.

You are urged to speak to as many of the employers as possible. Be sure to take notes about the education needed for each career. Also, ask them what they like and dislike about the career they represent. You will need to get the signature of each employer on the notes you take. Give the notes and signatures to your instructor.

Remember to act appropriately during the Career Fair. Use good grammar and speak clearly without using slang to make a favorable first impression. You should have an up-to-date resume to show the employers. This will quickly tell them your interests and the subjects you are taking.

Continuous Break

Layout tab > Page Setup > Breaks

6. To balance the text in two columns, click at the end of the last sentence. Follow the **Continuous Break** path at the left. In the Section Breaks list, click *Continuous*, as shown in Figure 6-23. The text should now be in two nearly equal columns.

7. Save the document as ***38f career fair*** and close it.

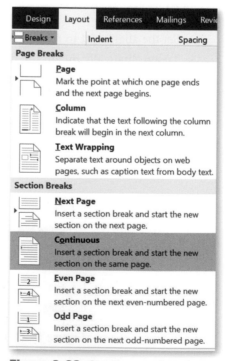

Figure 6-23 Continuous break

Three-Column Document

Line between
Layout tab > Page Setup >
Columns > More Columns >
Line between

Hyphenation
Layout tab > Page Setup >
Hyphenation

In this activity, you will change the number of columns in a document from two to three and insert a vertical line between the columns.

1. Open **38f career fair** that you created earlier. Follow the **Line between** path at the left. Select *Three* columns from the Presets as shown in Figure 6-24.

2. To insert a vertical line between the columns, click the *Line between* checkbox as shown in Figure 6-24.

3. Hyphenate the text by using the **Hyphenation** path at the left. Select the *Automatic* option as shown in Figure 6-25.

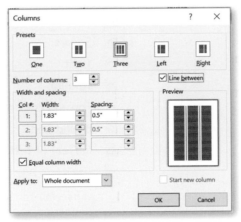

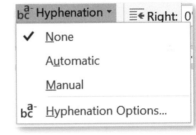

Figure 6-24 Insert Line between   **Figure 6-25** Automatic hyphenation

4. Save the document as **38g career fair**; print and close it.

COLLABORATION

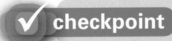 **checkpoint** Compare your printed document with a classmate's document. If they are different, determine why. Make corrections if necessary.

Newsletter with Pictures and Text Wrapping

Picture Tools Format tab >
Arrange > Wrap Text

1. Open **df 38h conference**. Change the page orientation to Landscape.

2. Insert a Continuous section break at the beginning of the paragraph after the title.

3. Format the text below the title in two columns with a vertical line between them. Adjust spacing so both columns begin at the same vertical position.

4. Click between words that are near the center of the *Special Events* paragraph. Insert the picture file **df 38h golfer**. Resize it so its height is 1".

5. To wrap the text tightly around the picture, select the picture and follow the path at left to open the Wrap Text options. Select the *Tight* option shown in Figure 6-26.

6. Nudge or drag the picture as needed so it is in the center of the text below the first line of text.
7. Click in the *Program* paragraph in the first column about 1" inch to right of center and on line 1. Insert the picture **df 38h speaker**. Resize it to **1"** high.

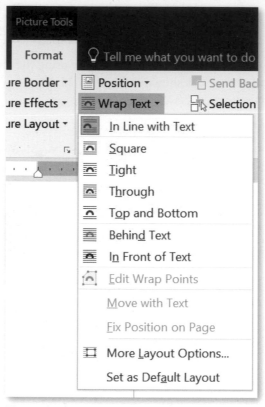

Figure 6-26 Wrap Text options

8. To position the picture in the upper-right portion of the *Program* paragraph, select *Square* from the Wrap Text options. Drag and nudge the picture so it is aligned at the right margin with its top aligned with the top of the text in line 1.
9. Spell-check, proofread, and correct errors. Save the document as **38h conference**; print and close it.

Skill Builder 5

Warmup

Key each line twice; then key a 1' timing on line 3. Determine *gwam*.

alphabet	1	Levi Lentz packed my bag with six quarts of juice.
CAPS LOCK	2	KANSAS is KS; TEXAS is TX; IDAHO is ID; IOWA is IA
easy	3	Jan may name a tutor to work with the eight girls.

gwam 1' | 1 | 2 | 3 | 4 | 5 | 6 | 7 | 8 | 9 | 10 |

B

Technique: Response Patterns

1. Key each line twice SS; DS between 2-line groups.
2. Key a 1' timing on lines 3, 6, 9, and 12.

letter response	1	pink safe tree face hill look only fact date start
	2	red dress|extra milk|union awards|pink car|you are
	3	Jim Carter started a car in my garage in Honolulu.
word response	4	with work dock half coal hair both busy city civic
	5	when they|fix their|pay the|did she|cut down|to it
	6	Diana and Jan may go to the island to do the work.
combination response	7	big cat air act did fat due joy got pin rug was us
	8	pink bowl|city street|their jump|extra chair|is at
	9	Ed Burns was with Steve when we started the feast.
letter	10	Jim saw a fat cat in a cab as we sat in my garage.
combination	11	Jay was the man you saw up at the lake in the bus.
word	12	I may go to the lake with the men to fix the door.

gwam 1' | 1 | 2 | 3 | 4 | 5 | 6 | 7 | 8 | 9 | 10 |

C

Speed Check: Sentences

Key two 30'' timings on each line. Try to increase your keying speed the second time you key the line. Determine *gwam* for the faster timing of each line.

1 Ben will be ready before noon.
2 Sam will bring his dog to the lake.
3 Jack did not fill the two cars with gas.
4 Jon will take the next test when he is ready.
5 Susan is to bring two or three copies of the play.
6 This may be the last time you will have to take a test.

gwam 30'' | 2 | 4 | 6 | 8 | 10 | 12 | 14 | 16 | 18 | 20 | 22 |

Quarter-Minute Checkpoints				
gwam	1/4'	1/2'	3/4'	Time
16	4	8	12	16
20	5	10	15	20
24	6	12	18	24
28	7	14	21	28
32	8	16	24	32
36	9	18	27	36
40	10	20	30	40

Guided (Paced) Timing Procedure

Establish a goal rate

1. Key a 1' timing on ¶ 1 of a set of ¶s that contain superior figures for guided timings, as in D below.

2. Using the *gwam* as a base, add 4 *gwam* to set your goal rate.

3. From column 1 of the table at the left, choose the speed nearest your goal rate. In the quarter-minute columns beside that speed, note the points in the copy you must reach to attain your goal rate.

4. Determine the checkpoint for each quarter minute from the word count above the lines in ¶ 1. (Example: Checkpoints for 24 *gwam* are 6, 12, 18, and 24.)

Practice procedure

1. Key two 1' timings on ¶ 1 at your goal rate guided by the quarter-minute calls (1/4, 1/2, 3/4, time). Try to reach each checkpoint before the guide is called.

2. Key two 1' timings on ¶ 2 of a set of ¶s in the same way.

3. If time permits, key a 2' writing on the set of ¶s combined, without the guides.

D

Speed Check: Paragraphs

1. Key a 1' timing on each ¶; determine *gwam* on each timing.

2. Using your better *gwam* as a base rate, set a goal rate and key two 1' guided timings on each ¶ as directed above.

3. Key two 2' unguided timings on ¶s 1–2 combined; determine *gwam*.

LA all letters used

gwam 2'

```
         •    2    •    4    •    6    •    8    •   10
    Is it possible for a mouse to make an individual     5
       •   12    •   14    •   16    •   18    •   20
quite wealthy? Yes, of course it is. If you do not      10
       •   22    •   24    •   26    •   28    •   30
believe it, consider Walt Disney. This individual      15
       •   32    •   34    •   36    •   38    •   40
came from a very humble beginning. But in the end,     20
       •   42    •   44    •   46    •   48    •   50
he was quite a wealthy person whose work brought       25
       •   52    •   54    •   56    •   58
great thrills to many children and adults.             29
         •    2    •    4    •    6    •    8    •
    A mouse, duck, and dog are just a few of the       33
    10    •   12    •   14    •   16    •   18    •
exquisite personalities he brought to life. After      38
    20    •   22    •   24    •   26    •   28    •
all these years, his work is still a part of many      43
    30    •   32    •   34    •   36    •   38    •
lives. People from all over the world travel many     48
    40    •   42    •   44    •   46    •   48    •
miles to visit this very amazing world of Disney.      53
    50    •   52    •   54    •   56    •   58    •
It would be impossible to picture this wonderful       58
    60    •   62    •
world without his work.                                61
```

gwam 2' | 1 | 2 | 3 | 4 | 5 |

OUTCOMES

- Explain the importance of research skills in a digital age
- Review strategies to improve Internet searches
- Evaluate website and other information resources
- Utilize fact-checking sites to verify research findings

Understanding the Need for Research Skills in a Digital Age

People in all walks of life now use the Internet as their primary research option. The adage, "You can find anything on the Internet" reflects the shift toward Internet searching as the quickest way to find information on any subject, from the lyrics of a song to symptoms of medical conditions to pictures of the Martian surface.

Whenever you do research, you must evaluate the information you find before you rely on it. Although it is important to evaluate information published in any format, evaluation is particularly important for information found on the Internet. Anyone can publish something on the Internet subject to very few restrictions or limitations.

Internet research skills are important in the digital age

We use the information we find on the Internet for a variety of purposes. We use it for entertainment, recreation, to make informed decisions, or to inform casual conversation. When we use information for research, we must be sure the information is reliable and authoritative. That puts us in the position of having to verify information and make judgments about whether it is appropriate. We need to think critically, as opposed to using information just because it is available to us or published on an Internet site. Developing your research skills is crucial to both academic and professional success.

In this module, you will review some Internet research strategies and learn other ways you can become a better researcher. More importantly, you will learn how to evaluate and fact-check your research results. Improving your Internet research skills will help you become a more productive and well-informed lifelong learner and citizen.

Improving Your Internet Search Results

If you have done any amount of searching on the Internet, you know that you often end up with lots of material to wade through to find exactly what you want. In this section, you will review some strategies learned in the Basic Technology module "Browsers and Search Features" in Chapter 3. In addition, you will learn tips and strategies that can help you improve your search results and how you organize the results when you get them.

Use your web browser properly. Modern web browsers have evolved over time and have become more sophisticated in their ability to perform research. Different search engines function differently. Google, Bing, and Yahoo! are among the leading and most well-known search engines. However, Duck Duck Go, Dogpile, and Yippy have features that make them valuable research tools as well. The type of research you are conducting will dictate the best search engine to use. Therefore, explore your search engine options.

Learn to use advanced search techniques. Effective Internet research depends heavily on how you search. What search engine(s) are you using? What keywords are you using? Are your search phrases worded as well as they could be? Do you use quotation marks for exact phrase searches? Are you using advanced search operators to expand or narrow the results? Using research strategies like these can improve the quality of your results.

Figure AT2-1 Strategically researching for results

Organize your bookmarks. It might sound obvious, but many people do not take the time to manage the bookmarks in their browser. If you are sorting through a lot of information, it is a lot easier if you make good use of bookmarks. The simplest method is using your browser's built-in bookmark manager. Create folders for specific things you are looking for, and store related sites and links in them.

Today, there are apps for bookmarking and annotating websites. For example, the *Diigo* app lets you bookmark and tag webpages. Tagging makes finding data easier because you only need to type in the tag to find anything tagged with those keywords. This type of app lets you highlight text directly on the webpage, add sticky notes for comments and reminders, among other features. However, if you are using Microsoft *Edge* as your Internet browser, these features are all available for you as part of the browser. Having a well-organized bookmarking system is a must for effective research.

Follow the web. Follow the web, surf the wave of information, and follow your intuition. Every link you click and page you read will take you closer to your research goal. Sometimes you may stumble onto a page that contains a bit more information than a previous one. Try searching for the names and places you find; stringing information together like this can often yield much better results. The more you use the web for research, the more expertise you will develop.

Evaluating Search Results

One important aspect of improving your Internet searching skills is learning how to evaluate the results you receive from a search. It is never wise to believe everything you read on the Internet. Outdated or downright wrong information is as easy to find as up-to-date reputable sources.

The criteria in Table AT2-1 are often used to evaluate any kind of information source, including those you may identify with an Internet search.

Accuracy	Are there typographical errors or obvious factual errors that lead you to question the accuracy of the information? Are there links to other sites that provide additional information that supports the information on the main site? Is there a bibliography that gives sources for the website's information?
Authority	Who created the website or wrote the specific article you are reviewing? If an article has an author, what are his or her credentials? Does he or she have the relevant education or experience to write with authority on the topic?
Objectivity	Websites created by some organizations may have a slant or a bias toward the opinions of that organization and consequently may not supply objective information. What can you determine about the agenda, hidden or obvious, of the organization behind the website?
Currency	When was the site created, and how recently has it been updated? Do links from the site work correctly? If not, the site may not be regularly maintained.
Coverage	Is the website appropriate for your search? If you are conducting research for a scholarly article, for example, you need to identify sites with an academic approach. Does the content include citations that indicate reputable sources?

Table AT2-1 Criteria for evaluating search results

Remember as you are evaluating your search results that the first website listed may not be the best or most reliable source—it may just be the site visited most often. Popular websites such as Wikipedia often show up at the top of the list, and you may indeed find plenty of good information in its pages. But keep in mind that **wikis** can be modified at any time by users anywhere in the world. Make sure you verify information you find in a source such as Wikipedia.

1. With the Google website open in your browser, key the search phrase **oil and gas drilling in national parks**. If necessary, select the *All* tab above the results.
2. In the search results that display, locate:
   a. An article that is obviously not current. What is the URL, what is the title, and what year was the article published?
   b. An article that comes from an obviously biased source. What organization authored the website, and what is its point of view?
   c. An article that attempts to give both sides of the story on drilling in national parks. What is the URL, and what is the title of the article?
3. Click the *News* tab at the top of the search results to see news stories about oil and gas drilling. What is the most recent news story filed on this subject? What is the URL, the title, and the point of view of the article?
4. Explore the other tabs at the top of the search results (Images, Videos, Maps, More). What other types of resources are available on the topic?
5. Close your browser.

Tips for Validating and Fact-Checking Research Results

It is easy to find just about any information you want on the Internet. The problem is that it is not always entirely accurate. In an age when claims of "fake news" are so prevalent, how do you verify the information you consume? Here are some questions you can ask to begin validating the results you find on the Internet.

- *What should you do if the results seem questionable?* Use Google, or some other search engine, to search for the exact same headline. If it is untrue, you should see links debunking the story.

- *What else can you do to assess the legitimacy of an Internet source?* Go to the site's About tab to learn more about the site and its potential bias. Also, a reputable source includes hyperlinks to research to support its claims.

- *Does it matter who wrote the article?* Search the author's name to verify their occupation and view other articles this person may have written. Check social media accounts and look for a blue check mark near the author's name on *Facebook* or *Twitter*. This means their occupation has been verified and they are who they say.

- *Can some information found on the Internet or social media start out true, but later be false?* Breaking news stories are good examples of this type of information. Sometimes news reporters speculate on events or identify the wrong person as a news story is unfolding. Other phrases such as "we are getting reports that" and "we are trying to confirm" should be red flags that the article's facts could be questionable.

- *How much misinformation is there on the Internet?* Unfortunately, more than we would like. In addition to unfolding truths mentioned above, there are people (and even governments) intentionally **trolling** the Internet and social media sites planting stories and making misstatements to push a particular ideology or provoke extreme emotions on a topic. Once a lie is told online, it is difficult to retrieve and correct.

Verify the facts of your research

ileezhun/Shutterstock.com

In general, it is good to read multiple sources to extract all the facts. Additionally, there are websites dedicated to verifying the truth behind the things we read or hear. The following list includes some of the most trusted fact-checking websites. A good fact-checking service writes with neutral wording and provides unbiased sources to support its claims. Bookmark these sites for your future fact-checking efforts.

- **PolitiFact** (*politifact.com*) is a fact-checking website that rates the accuracy of claims by elected officials and others who speak up in American politics.

- **Fact Check** (*factcheck.org*) is a nonpartisan, nonprofit "consumer advocate" for voters that aims to reduce the level of deception and confusion in U.S. politics.

- **Snopes** (*snopes.com*) has been the definitive Internet reference source for urban legends, folklore, myths, rumors, and misinformation for a long time.

- **Hoax Slayer** (*hoax-slayer.net*) is another service that debunks or validates Internet rumors and hoaxes.

- **The Poynter Institute** (*poynter.org*) is not a true fact-checking service, but it is a leader in distinguished journalism and produces credible and evidence-based content.

COLLABORATION

Also, several news organization such as NPR, CNN, and the POTUS XM Radio are recognized for their fair, unbiased coverage of news, politics, and current events. Add these to your list of sources to verify the information found on the Internet.

1. Using Microsoft *Edge* (or another browser), open the website *snopes.com*.

2. With a partner, explore the site. Discuss the kinds of topics you can find on this site. What is the most interesting story you find?

3. Open *politifact.com*. Discuss with your partner the top trending story on the site. What makes this article interesting or controversial?

4. Discuss how the *Snopes* and *PolitiFact* sites are alike and how they are different.

5. Open *hoax-slayer.net* and compare it to *Snopes*. How are they alike and different?

6. If time permits, share your findings with others in your class.

Communication Skills 3

ACTIVITY 1: Pronoun Agreement

1. Study each of the four rules.
   a. Key the *Learn* lines beneath each rule, noting how the rule is applied.
   b. Key the *Apply* lines, choosing correct pronouns.

Rule 1: A personal pronoun (*I, we, you, he, she, it, their, etc.*) agrees in **person** (first, second, or third) with the noun or other pronoun it represents.

Learn 1   If we finish our project by Monday, we can take Friday off. (1st person)

Learn 2   You may go to the game after you finish your assignment. (2nd person)

Learn 3   Alexander Joseph said he will be absent on Thursday. (3rd person)

Apply 4   Those who attended the play said (he, she, they) were impressed.

Apply 5   After you finish the last exam, (my, your) grade will be posted.

Apply 6   After we have lunch, (we, she, he,) should all go to a movie.

Rule 2: A personal pronoun agrees in **gender** (feminine, masculine, or neuter) with the noun or other pronoun it represents.

Learn 7   Ms. Kimble will leave her car at the airport on Friday. (feminine)

Learn 8   The car lost its shine from the rain and dirt storm. (neuter)

Apply 9   Each player will get a medal as he is introduced by (his, its) coach.

Apply 10 The car hit the black ice just before (he, it) landed in the ditch.

Rule 3: A personal pronoun agrees in **number** (singular or plural) with the noun or other pronoun it represents.

Learn 11 Justin likes his new cell phone he purchased last week. (singular)

Learn 12 The senators presented their bill before Congress. (plural)

Apply 13 The girls bought (her, their) coach a gift to thank (her, their).

Apply 14 The math teacher lost (his, its, their) grade book.

Rule 4: A personal pronoun that represents a collective noun (*team, committee, family,* etc.) may be singular or plural, depending on the meaning of the collective noun.

Learn 15 The USA men's swim team had its first meeting today. (acting as a unit)

Learn 16 Each family member kept their own schedule. (acting individually)

Apply 17 Each team member will meet individually with (its, their) coach.

Apply 18 The Budget Committee had presented (its, their) formal budget.

(continued on next page)

2. Key Proofread & Correct, using correct pronouns.
   a. Check answers.
   b. Using the rule number at the left of each line, study the rule relating to each error you made.
   c. Rekey each incorrect line, using correct pronouns.

Save as: CS3 ACTIVITY1

Proofread & Correct

Rules

2 1 Jose knew that (he, she, they) should practice more.

3 2 Individuals who enrolled say (he, she, they) enjoyed the class.

3 3 As soon as the game is over, I will do (our, my) homework.

2, 3 4 Manuel passed the exam (he, her, their) took on Friday.

2 5 The house had (her, his, its) well and septic tank.

1 6 As you improve, (his, your) playing time will increase.

1 7 I played the video game on (my, their, your) laptop.

3 8 The children got along very well with (her, his, their) teacher.

4 9 The student council had (its, their) meeting last Friday.

4 10 The team had to have (its, their) parents sign the form.

ACTIVITY 2: Word Choice

1. Study the definitions of the words.
2. Key the *Learn* line, noting the correct usage of each word.
3. Key the *Apply* lines, inserting the correct word(s).

Save as: CS3 ACTIVITY2

to (prep/adj) used to indicate action, relation, distance, direction	**cents** (n) specified portion of a dollar
too (adv) besides; also; to excessive degree	**sense** (n/vb) meaning intended or conveyed; perceive by sense organs; ability to judge
two (pron/adj) one plus one in number	**since** (adv/conj) after a definite time in the past; in view of the fact; because

Learn 1 I plan on going **to** at least **two** of the games if you go **too**.

Apply 2 (To, Too, Two) of the history students are going (to, too, two) take the exam early.

Apply 3 You will need (to, too, two) bring (to, too, two) boxes (to, too, two).

Learn 1 **Since** I changed the dollars and **cents** columns, the figures make **sense**.

Apply 2 (Cents, Sense, Since) you gave me a dollar, you will get 77 (cents, sense, since) back.

Apply 3 (Cents, Sense, Since) he doesn't have common (cents, sense, since), be careful.

ACTIVITY 3: Writing

Save as: CS3 ACTIVITY3

A job interviewer will often start the interview by saying, "Tell me about yourself."
Write a paragraph with your response to this request.

ACTIVITY 4: Speaking

Famous people come from all walks of life. Those who leave a lasting mark on society have one thing in common—the desire to make a difference in the world we live in. Listed below are 12 individuals who have made the world we live in a better place. Select one or two individuals from the list who you feel have made the greatest difference in our world. Prepare a few brief comments explaining why you choose them.

Susan B. Anthony	Walt Disney	Abraham Lincoln
Ludwig van Beethoven	Helen Keller	Nelson Mandela
Marie Curie	John F. Kennedy	Mother Teresa
Princess Diana	Martin Luther King	Oprah Winfrey

Before You Move On

Answer these questions to review what you have learned in Chapter 6.

1. A document that gives facts, ideas, or opinions about one or more topics is called a(n) _____ . LO 35A

2. What line spacing is used for an MLA report? LO 35F

3. What line spacing is used for an unbound report in standard format? LO 37D

4. The style of the letters, figures, symbols, and so on in a document is called the _____ . LO 35D

5. A collection of settings for font, font size, color, and so on is called a(n) _____ . LO 37C

6. A(n) _____ contains information that appears at the top of pages in a document. LO 35E

7. A(n) _____ contains information that is displayed at the bottom of the page. LO 35E

8. A(n) _____ shows an ordered list of topics to be included in a report. LO 36C

9. Where should the page number appear on an MLA report? LO 35F

10. What is the name of the page on which sources used in an MLA report are listed? LO 36D

11. _____ are letters and symbols used to show the errors in a document. LO 37E

12. A drawing object that is a container for text or graphics is a(n) _____ . LO 38B

13. One of the small squares that appears on the border of a selected graphic can be used to change its size is called a(n) _____ . LO 38C

14. The Pictures command is used to find pictures located on your _____ . LO 38E

15. Describe what *Word's* Columns feature does. LO 38F

16. To balance text in two or more columns, insert a(n) _____ section break at the end of the last column. LO 38F

Report in Standard, Unbound Format

1. Open **df c6 report1**.
2. Format the report in standard, unbound style. Do not number page 1.
3. Add the following text to the end of the report. Make the changes indicated by the proofreaders' marks.
4. Use Spelling & Grammar to check the document, and proofread the document carefully. Correct all errors.
5. Save the document as **c6 report 1** and close it.

Unfortunately, far too many tires are *abandoned* ~~thrown away~~ rather
than recycled. Abandoned tires often litter the sides of
our rivers and creeks. Many are *found* ~~hidden~~ in our forests.
Too often, worn-out tires are stacked in piles that are
ugly and provide breeding grounds for pests. These tire
piles are fire hazards. If they catch fire, they can
burn for weeks, ruining the air. The *heat of the* fire can cause the
rubber to decompose into oil. This oil is likely to
stet *dirty* ~~pollute~~ nearby ground and surface water, causing damage to
the environment.

The next time you change ~~your~~ tires, even on your bicycle,
make sure you dispose *of* them properly. If you can, leave
lc them at the ~~S~~tore where you buy the replac*e*ment tires. The
old tires can be recycled into useful products such as
buckets, shoes, mouse pads for computers, and dust pans.

Report in MLA Format

1. Open *df c6 report2*. Format the report in MLA style. Note: If a side heading appears at the bottom of a page without at least two lines of text below the heading, insert a page break to move the heading (and the line following it, if applicable) to the next page.
2. Create a Works Cited page with the following sources.
3. Use Spelling & Grammar and proofread the document carefully. Correct all errors. Save the document as *c6 report2* and close it.

Works Cited

Fulton-Calkins, Patsy, and Karin M. Stulz. *Procedures & Theory for Administrative Professionals*, 6th ed. Cincinnati: South-Western, 2009.

Law Dictionary. "What is Occupational Outlook Handbook?" 7 January 2014. thelawdictionary.org/occupational-outlook-handbook/#ixzz2oPofpoLF. Accessed 5 May 2018.

University of Waterloo. *Career Development eManual.* "Self-Assessment." 7 January 2014 www.cdm.uwaterloo.ca. Accessed 12 May 2018.

TIP When you key a URL in a reference, *Word* will automatically format it in blue with an underline.

Outline for Report

1. In a new, blank document, key the following outline using the Numbering feature and default margin settings.
2. Use Spelling & Grammar, proofread the document carefully, and correct all errors.
3. Save the document as *c6 outline* and close it.

The Ear

   I. Parts of the ear

      a. Outer ear

      b. Middle ear

      c. Inner ear

  II. How we hear

      a. How sounds reach the inner ear

      b. How the inner ear sends sounds to the brain

 III. Care of the ear

      a. Preventing ear infections

         i. Keeping fluids out of the ear

        ii. Cleaning the ear

      b. Preventing ear injury

Newsletter

1. Open *df c6 newsletter*.
2. Set top, bottom, and side margins to 0.75". Use Landscape orientation.
3. Tap *Enter* two or three times to insert space at the top of the document. Position the WordArt **Strategies for Success** as the main title at the top of the page and center it horizontally. Format it using Times New Roman font.
4. Place the pointer to the left of the *R* in *Reputation* in the first section heading and insert a Continuous section break after the title.
5. Arrange the text below the WordArt in three columns.
6. Format all text in 12-pt. Times New Roman font. Format the section headings in 14-pt. bold and left-align them.
7. Insert a text box between the first and second paragraphs. Set the height of the text box to 0.5" and the width to 2.5". Format it using a 1½-pt. border and a blue fill. Use the Top and Bottom text wrap option.
8. Key the following text in the text box. Change the font to bold, 10-pt. Times New Roman and center the text in the text box.

   A bad reputation can result from one mistake.

9. Place a copy (Copy/Paste) of the text box after the last line of the *Reputation and Choice* section. Delete the existing text and key the following text in the text box, formatting it the same as the other text box.

   Choices you make destroy or enhance your reputation.

10. Place another copy of the text box after the last line of the first paragraph of the *Learning about People* section. Delete the existing text and key the following text in the box, formatting it the same as the previous text boxes.

    Relating well to others is a major challenge.

11. Create another text box after the last paragraph of the *Learning about People* section. Delete the existing text and key the following text in the box, formatting the text the same as the other text boxes. Change the height of this text box to 0.3".

    Learn from experienced workers.

12. Hyphenate the text.
13. Insert a Continuous section break after the last paragraph to balance the columns.
14. Make needed formatting adjustments, spell-check the document, and proofread carefully. Correct all errors.
15. Save the document as *c6 newsletter*. Print the document and then close it.

 ★TIP Review the line endings. If a word in a text box is hyphenated, tap *Shift + Enter* before the hyphenated word to make the whole word appear on the next line.

CHAPTER 7

Organizing Information in Tables

Lesson 39   Basic Tables
Lesson 40   Tables: Merging and Splitting Cells
Lesson 41   Tables: Changing Row Height,
            Borders, and Shading

Lesson 42   Sort and Convert Tables
Assessment 2   Reports and Tables

LESSONS 39–42

A **table** is information arranged in rows and columns so that readers can easily understand it. Your textbooks use tables to show information that supports what you are learning. A table may contain dates and events. It may show states and their capital cities. Newspapers often use tables. Tables show the rankings of sports teams and players. Television programs and daily temperatures are usually reported in tables.

Think about how you use tables. Do you have a schedule of classes that shows your subjects, days and times, room numbers, and teacher names? Do you have a to-do list that shows what you plan to do each day? Do you have a list of frequently called phone numbers? In this chapter, you will learn to create tables to show information in a format that is easy to understand.

Robert Kneschke/Shutterstock.com

Application Guide

Convert Text to a Table

Insert > Tables > Table > Convert Text to Table

In addition to the Insert Table commands covered in WP Applications 9 later in this chapter, another way to create a table is to convert text that is separated by a tab, a comma, or another separator character into a table. For example, if you have a list of first names, last names, and birth dates separated by tabs and want to convert the list into a table, you can use the **Convert Text to Table** feature (see Figure 7-1). In this case, *Word* recognizes the tab as the separator and will divide the text into columns. The new paragraph mark at the end of each line will be used to begin a new row.

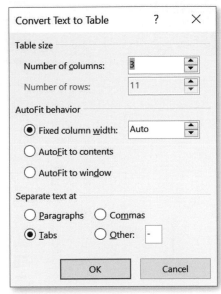

Figure 7-1 Convert Text to Table dialog box

Convert a Table to Text

Table Tools Layout tab > Data > Convert Table to Text

You can convert a table into text that is separated by tabs, commas, or other separators by using the **Convert Table to Text** feature shown in Figure 7-2.

Figure 7-2 Convert Table to Text dialog box

WP Applications 9

Activity 1

Insert Table

For each activity, read and learn the feature described; then complete the activity as directed.

There are several options for creating various kinds of tables. In this module, you will use two options within the Table feature to create tables—the table grid and the Insert Table command illustrated in Figure 7-3.

When the **table grid** is used, drag on the grid to select the number of columns and rows needed for the table. The illustration in Figure 7-4 shows the selection for a table with three columns and four rows (a 3 × 4 table).

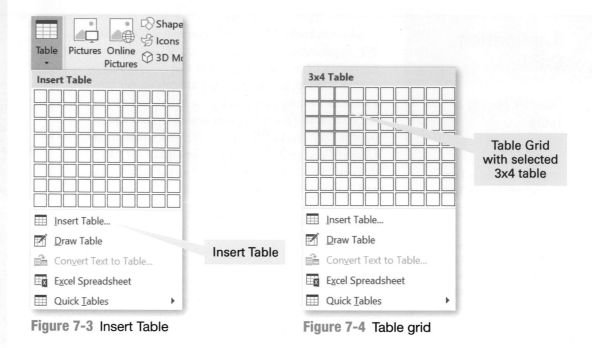

Figure 7-3 Insert Table   **Figure 7-4** Table grid

The dialog box shown in Figure 7-5 opens when Insert Table is clicked in the list of options. Key the desired number of columns and rows in the appropriate spaces and click *OK* to create the table.

Keying and Moving Around in a Table

When text is keyed in a cell, it wraps around in that cell instead of wrapping around to the next row. A line space is added to the cell each time the text wraps around.

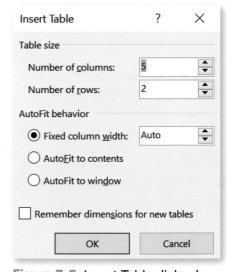

Figure 7-5 Insert Table dialog box

To fill in cells, use the *Tab* key or right arrow key to move from cell to cell (left to right) in a row and from row to row. To move back a cell, tap *Shift + Tab*. To move around in a filled-in table, use the arrow keys, *Tab*, or the mouse (click the desired cell). Tapping *Enter* after keying text in a cell will simply insert a blank line space in the cell.

1. Open a new document. Position your insertion point to have a 2" top margin.
2. Use the table grid to create a table with three columns and four rows (3 × 4 table).
3. Key the information in the following table into the table grid. Use the default alignment and column widths. Tap *Tab* to move from cell to cell and row to row.

Student	High School Class	Position
Jimmie Warner	Junior	Third Base
Harry Killingsworth	Senior	Second Base
Jiminez Sanchez	Sophomore	Center Field

4. Click at the left on the line below the table. Tap *Enter* twice and use the *Insert Table* command to create a table with four columns and five rows (4 × 5 table). Select the *AutoFit Contents* option in the AutoFit options.

5. Key the information in the following table into the table grid. Use the default alignment. Tap *Tab* to move from cell to cell and row to row.

> **NOTE** By selecting AutoFit Contents, the column widths will adjust automatically to be slightly larger than the longest entry in the column as you key.

Student	Home Room Teacher	Bus Route	Parking Pass
Mary Tillitson	Ms. Henrietta Jones	18	Yes
Janet Thompson	Mr. Jack Holliday	6	No
Joseph Larrimore	Dr. Kate Newsome	15	Yes
Maurice Quinnone	Mrs. Anne Guidos	9	No

6. **Save as:** *wp9 activity 1*.

Activity 2

Selecting and Formatting Cell Content

Table Tools Layout tab >
Table > Select

The formatting changes (bold, italic, alignment, etc.) that you have learned to make to text can also be made to the text within a table. You can do this prior to keying the text into the table, or it can be done after the text has been keyed. Make formatting changes by selecting the portion of the table (cell, row, column, or table) that is to be changed.

One option is to use the Select command to select the portion you want. Click in the table, use the path shown in the margin, and then select the desired portion (cell, column, row, or table) from the list as shown in Figure 7-6.

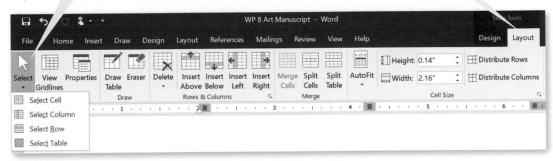

Figure 7-6 Using Select

Another option is to use the mouse to make your selection.

- To select a cell, double-click the cell; to select adjacent cells, click the first desired cell, drag through the desired cells, and release the mouse button. Apply the desired format changes(s).
- To select a row, move the insertion point just outside the left area of the table, and when the pointer turns into an open diagonal arrow, click the left mouse button to select the row, and then apply the desired format change(s).
- To select a column, move the insertion point to the top border of the table, and when the pointer turns to a solid down arrow, click the left mouse button to select the column, and then apply the desired format change(s).
- To select a table, move the insertion point over the table and click the Table Move handle at the upper-left corner of the table; then apply the desired format change(s).

1. Open **wp9 activity 1** you created in Activity 1.
2. Select the whole table at the top, and change the font in all cells to 12-pt. Arial.
3. Select row 1 and change it to bold, 14-pt. Arial, aligned at the center.
4. Center-align the cells in columns B and C.
5. Select the first row in the bottom table, and change the format to bold, 12-pt. Verdana, aligned at the center.
6. Select the cells C2 through C5 (C2:C5), and apply Right alignment.
7. Select the cells B2:B5 and D2:D5, and apply Center alignment.
8. Select the cells A2:A5, change the font to a dark red, and apply bold to the text.
9. **Save as:** **wp9 activity 2**.

Activity 3

Format Painter

Home tab > Clipboard > Format Painter

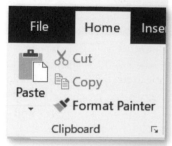

Figure 7-7 Format Painter

Use the **Format Painter** to quickly copy formatting from one place to another (see Figure 7-7). In tables, this feature is particularly useful when formatting cells that are not adjacent. Click the paintbrush icon (as shown in Figure 7-7) once to apply the formatting to one place in the table or document; double-click it to apply it to multiple places. When the Format Painter feature is activated, a paintbrush appears to the left of the insertion point. Click *Format Painter* again or tap *Esc* to turn off the Format Painter.

1. Open **df wp9 activity 3**.
2. Use the *Format Painter* to copy the formatting used for the name in column A to the other cells in columns B to E that have the same name.

   Suggestion: Preview the entries in the table. If a name in column A appears only once in columns B to E, click the *Format Painter* once to copy the formatting to the cell with the same name. If a name in column A appears more than once in columns B to E, click the *Format Painter* twice to copy the formatting to multiple locations. When all occurrences of a name have been formatted, click the *Format Painter* or *Esc* to deactivate it and repeat the process for the next name.

3. **Save as:** **wp9 activity 3**.

Use the **Table Properties** dialog box (shown in Figure 7-8) to center a table horizontally on a page. This will make the side margins (right and left margins) equal. Another method of centering a table horizontally is to select the table and click the *Center* button in the Paragraph group on the Home tab.

Use the Page *Vertical alignment* in the Page Setup dialog box (shown in Figure 7-9) to center a table vertically on the page. This will make the top and bottom margins equal.

Horizontal
Table Tools Layout tab >
Table > Properties

Vertical
Layout tab > Page Setup
dialog box launcher >
Layout tab in dialog box >
Page > Vertical alignment >
Center

Page Setup dialog box launcher

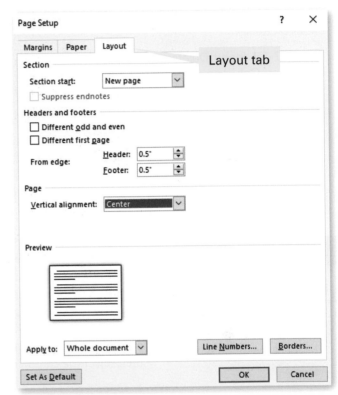

Figure 7-9 Page Setup dialog box

Figure 7-8 Table Properties dialog box

1. Open *wp9 activity 3* that you created in Activity 3, and center the table horizontally and vertically.
2. Save as: *wp9 activity 4*.

The **Table Tools Layout** tab can be used to edit or modify the layout of existing tables. The commands found in the **Rows & Columns** group (see Figure 7-10) are used to insert and delete rows and columns in an existing table. A cell, row, column, or entire table can be deleted using the *Delete* command. Use the *Insert* commands to place rows above or below existing rows and columns to the right or left of existing columns.

Table Tools Layout tab >
Rows & Columns

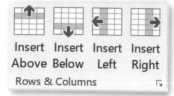

Figure 7-10 Insert/Delete Rows and Columns

1. Open *df wp9 activity 5*.
2. Delete the 2003 to 2009 award winners.
3. Insert the following information for the 2011 to 2017 award winners in the appropriate cells.

2017	Jose Altuve	Astros
2016	Mike Trout	Angels
2015	Josh Donaldson	Blue Jays
2014	Mike Trout	Angels
2013	Miguel Cabrera	Tigers
2012	Miguel Cabrera	Tigers
2011	Justin Verlander	Astros
2010	Josh Hamilton	Rangers

4. Delete the column showing the team for which the award winner played.
5. Undo the last change made to restore the deleted column.
6. Save as: *wp9 activity 5*.

Activity 6

Merge and Split Cells

Table Tools Layout tab >
Merge > Merge Cells or
Split Cells

Use the **Merge Cells** feature (see Figure 7-11) to join two or more adjacent cells in the same row or column into one cell. This feature is useful when information in the table spans more than one column or row. The main heading, for example, spans all columns. Use the **Split Cells** feature (also shown in Figure 7-11) to divide adjacent cells into multiple cells and columns. Select the cell(s) to be merged or split, and then select the command.

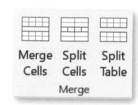

Figure 7-11 Merge and split cells

1. Open a new document, and create a table with four columns and five rows.
2. Use the *Merge Cells* and *Split Cells* features to make your table grid look like the one shown below. Then key the data in the table as shown, using Center alignment and 8-pt. Calibri font in all cells.
3. Save as: *wp9 activity 6*.

All cells in row 1 were merged into one cell that spans all five columns.				
Cells A2:A5 were merged into one cell.	Cell B2 was split into two cells and cells B3:B5 were merged.		Cells C2:C3 were merged; C4:C5 were merged and then split into four cells.	Cells D2:D3 were merged.
				Cells D4:D5 were merged.

Activity 7

Adjusting Column Width & Row Height

Table Tools Layout tab >
Cell Size

Figure 7-12 Adjusting column width and row height

The **Cell Size** group contains several features that can be used to change column widths and row heights (see Figure 7-12). Options within **AutoFit** can be used to format the width of columns. The **AutoFit Contents** feature automatically resizes the column widths based on the text in each column. The **AutoFit Window** feature automatically resizes the table so it begins and ends evenly at the left and right margins. If you want to specify an exact height of a row or a width for a column, key or select the desired size (in inches) in the **Height** or **Width** boxes.

1. Open *wp9 activity 3* that you created in Activity 3. Apply *AutoFit Contents* and then center the table horizontally.
2. **Save as:** *wp9 activity 7a*.
3. Open *wp9 activity 5* that you created in Activity 5, and set column A width at 0.57", column B at 1.15", and column C at 0.71". Set row 1 to be 0.5" high, and change the font of the text in row 1 to 16 pt. Center table horizontally on the page. Center the column heads.
4. **Save as:** *wp9 activity 7b*.

Activity 8

Portrait/Landscape Orientation

Layout tab > Page Setup >
Orientation

Portrait orientation. The way text is printed on a page determines what type of orientation is used. **Portrait orientation**, sometimes referred to as vertical—8½" × 11", has the short edge of the paper at the top of the page, as shown at the top right (see Figure 7-13).

Landscape orientation. **Landscape orientation**, sometimes referred to as horizontal—11" × 8½", has the wider edge of the paper at the top of the page, as shown at the bottom right. When a table is too wide to fit on the page in portrait orientation, switching to landscape orientation gives 2½ more inches to fit the table.

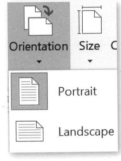

Figure 7-13 Page orientation

1. Open *df wp9 activity 8*.
2. Change the orientation to landscape.
3. Apply the AutoFit to Window command; center the table vertically.
4. **Save as:** *wp9 activity 8*.

Activity 9

Vertical Alignment

Table Tools Layout tab >
Alignment

Use the commands shown in the path at the left to change the vertical alignment of the text in cells. The text within a cell can be aligned in any one of the nine positions shown in Figure 7-14.

1. Open *df wp9 activity 9*.
2. Change row height as follows: row 1—0.6"; row 2—0.5"; rows 3–12—0.4".
3. Change vertical alignment as follows: cells A3:A12, bottom left; cells B3:B12, bottom center; and cells C3:C12, D3:D12, and E3:E12, bottom right. Center-align rows 1 and 2.
4. **Save as:** *wp9 activity 9*.

Top Left, Top Center, Top Right

Center Left, Center, Center Right

Bottom Left, Bottom Center, Bottom Right

Figure 7-14 Alignment options

Preformatted table styles that are available in the **Tables Styles** group (shown in Figure 7-15) can be used to improve the appearance of your table. As you move the mouse over each of the styles, your table will be formatted in that style. The style name is also displayed. When you find a style you prefer, click its style box. The selected table style can be modified by selecting or deselecting features in the Table Style Options group (shown in Figure 7-15) to further improve its appearance.

Click the More button to access additional styles

Figure 7-15 Table Style Options and Table Styles

1. Open *wp9 activity 7b* that you created in Activity 7.
2. Use a plain, grid, or list style table, no gridlines, and the color blue.
3. Deselect Header Row in the Table Style Options group.
4. Center the table horizontally.
5. Save as: *wp9 activity 10*.

Activity 11

Shading and Borders

Table Tools Design tab > Table Styles > Shading or Borders

Use the **Shading** and **Borders** features to enhance the appearance of tables when you are not using one of the preformatted table styles. The Shading feature allows you to fill in areas of the table with varying shades of color, as shown in Figure 7-16. Shading covers the selected area. It may be the entire table or a single cell, column, or row within a table.

By default, each cell in a table has thin, single-line borders around it. Features within the Borders group allow you to change the line thickness,

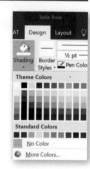

Figure 7-16 Shading colors

color, and style. The Borders drop-down list (illustrated in Figure 7-17) shows many of the options available for changing the default borders.

1. Open a new document and create a 5 × 6 table.
2. Shade cell B2 in a light blue color; cell C3 in a light black color; and column D in a light purple shade.
3. Remove the shading from cell D6, and shade row 6 in a light orange.
4. Remove all borders from cell A1; format cell E1 without a top or right border.
5. Format cell C2 with a 6-pt. dark red border on all sides.
6. Delete the borders from row 6 and column D.
7. **Save as: *wp9 activity 11*.**

Figure 7-17 Borders options

> ★TIP If you select the No Borders option before keying the text in your table, displaying gridlines that will not print may make it easier for you to move from cell to cell, merge cells, or split cells. Select the *View Gridlines* button in Table Tools Layout/Tables shown below.

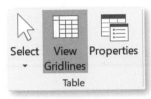

Activity 12

Sort

Table Tools Layout tab >
Data > Sort

Use the **Sort** feature to arrange text in alphabetical order and numbers in numerical order. Ascending order is from A to Z and 0 to 9. Entire tables or lists can be sorted, or parts of a table or list can be selected and sorted. If the table has a header row, select that option in the Sort dialog box shown in Figure 7-18 to exclude it from the sort.

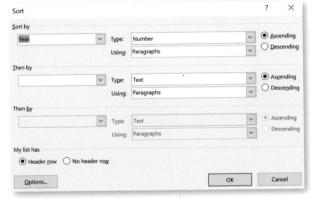

Figure 7-18 Sort options

1. Open *wp9 activity 7b* that you created in Activity 7.
2. Sort the listings in the table (exclude the column headings) in ascending order by year. Your selections should be the same as shown in the above illustration.
3. **Save as: *wp9 activity 12a*.**
4. Using *wp9 activity 12a* that you just created, sort the listings in the table in descending order by team name.
5. **Save as: *wp9 activity 12b*.**
6. Using *wp9 activity 12b* that you just created, sort the listings in the table in ascending order by player name.
7. **Save as: *wp9 activity 12c*.**

LESSON 39   Basic Tables

OUTCOMES
- Create tables
- Change widths of columns in tables
- Change table styles and heading styles
- Design a basic table

39–42A

Warmup

Key each line twice. If time permits, key the lines again.

Alphabet	1	Wesley Van Jantz quickly proofed the biology exam.
Figure/Symbol	2	On 08/13/18 Jorge paid invoice #291 for $2,358.64.
Speed	3	Pamela may hand signal to the big tug by the dock.

gwam   1' | 1 | 2 | 3 | 4 | 5 | 6 | 7 | 8 | 9 | 10 |

39B

Create a Table

Insert tab > Tables > Insert Table grid

Table 1

1. Start *Word* and open a new, blank document. Complete the following steps to create the table shown after step 5.
2. Beginning at or near the 2" vertical position, key the main heading **FUND-RAISING RESULTS FOR ROOM 202** using bold and center alignment. Tap *Enter* once.
3. Click the *Insert* tab, the *Table* drop-down list in the Tables group, and then use your mouse to create a table of four columns and five rows from the Insert Table grid as shown in Figure 7-19. A 4 × 5 table grid is inserted below the main heading.

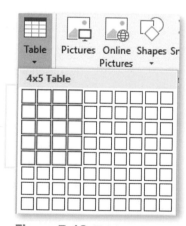

Squares selected to create 4 x 5 table

Figure 7-19 Table grid

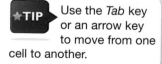
★TIP Use the *Tab* key or an arrow key to move from one cell to another.

4. Key the column headings in row 1, using bold and center alignment. Tap the *Tab* key one time to move to the next cell in row 1.
5. Key the data in the cells in rows 2–5 as shown in the table. Use the default alignment.

FUND-RAISING RESULTS FOR ROOM 202

Name	Amount	Name	Amount
Harry Xidas	$128.23	Mary Henry	$93.66
Julio Clemente	$114.56	Vinnie Werner	$91.42
Kerri Gorski	$106.09	Naomi Quinnones	$89.77
Lawrence Miller	$99.25	Betty Upton	$82.50

6. Select the cells under the column heading in column B, and change the alignment to Align Right.
7. Right-align the cells under the column head in column D.
8. Save the document as **39b table1** and close it.

Table 2

1. Open a new, blank document. Key the table's main heading, shown below, beginning at or near the 2" vertical position.
2. Insert a table grid that is four columns by six rows. Key the data shown below in the cells.

SPRING VALLEY MIDDLE SCHOOL FBLA OFFICERS

Name	Office	Room	Telephone
Jo Longo	President	218	330-555-0110
Bobbi Kite	Vice President	119	330-555-0134
Brent Diaz	Secretary	214	330-555-0159
Katie Verez	Treasurer	101	330-555-0162
Jerry Wilson	Parliamentarian	116	330-555-0177

3. Apply bold and center alignment to the main heading and column headings.
4. Use left alignment for words and right alignment for numbers for the cells in the rows under the column headings.
5. Save the document as **39b table2** and close it.

39C

Change Column Widths

Table Tools Layout tab >
Cell Size > AutoFit >
AutoFit Contents

Table 1

1. Open **39b table2** that you created in 39B.
2. Click inside a cell of the table to display the Table Tools Layout tab. In the Cell Size group, click *AutoFit* and choose *AutoFit Contents* as shown in Figure 7-20.
3. Note that the table is not centered horizontally after the change in column widths. You will learn to center a table horizontally in a later lesson. Save the document as **39c table1** and close it.

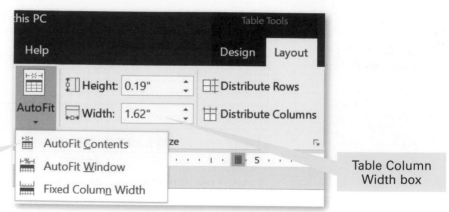

AutoFit Contents option

Table Column Width box

Figure 7-20 Use AutoFit to adjust column widths

Table 2

1. Open **39b table1** that you created in 39B.
2. Click a cell in column A and change its width to 1.5" by keying **1.5** in the Table Column Width box.
3. Click in a cell in column B and change its width to 1".
4. Use the same procedure to change the width of column C to 1.5" and column D to 1".
5. This table also will not be centered horizontally. Save the document as **39c table2** and close it.

Tables 3 and 4

1. Open the document **df 39c table**. Use the *AutoFit Content* option to change the column widths. Save the document as **39c table3** and then close it.
2. Open **df 39c table** again. Set the width for columns A and C to 1.6". Set the widths for columns B and D to 0.6". Save the document as **39c table4** and close it.

39D

Table Styles

Table Tools Design tab >
Table Styles

1. Open **39c table4** that you completed in 39C.
2. Click in a cell in the table to display the Table Tools Design tab. Click the *Plain Table 4* style (the fifth one in the first row) in the Table Styles group to format your table.
3. Remove the check from the *Banded Columns* box in the Table Style Options group to shade every other row in your table.
4. To remove the remaining shading in the table, choose the *Table Grid Light* style—the left one in row 1 of the Table Styles gallery.
5. Use options from the Table Styles group and the Table Style Options group to apply formatting that you believe is appropriate for this table.
6. Select the main heading of the table and apply the *Heading 1* style from the Styles group on the Home tab to format the main heading.
7. Use the *Heading 2* style to format the column headings.
8. Save your document as **39d table** and close it.

39E

Change Table Styles and Heading Styles

1. Open **39c table1** that you completed in 39C.
2. Using features in the Styles, Table Styles, and Table Style Options groups, format the table in an attractive, easy-to-read manner.
3. Save the document as **39e table** and close it.

39F

Design a Basic Table

1. Open a new, blank document. Beginning at or near the 2" vertical position, create the following table. Use AutoFit Contents to set column widths.
2. Using features in the Styles, Table Styles, and Table Style Options groups, format the table in an attractive, easy-to-read manner.
3. Proofread the table and correct all errors. Save the document as **39f table**. Print the table and then close it.

MONTHS OF THE YEAR IN ENGLISH AND SPANISH

English	Spanish	English	Spanish
January	enero	July	julio
February	febrero	August	agosto
March	marzo	September	septiembre
April	abril	October	octubre
May	mayo	November	noviembre
June	junio	December	diciembre

LESSON 40   Tables: Merging and Splitting Cells

OUTCOMES
- Center tables vertically and horizontally
- Select, merge, and split cells in tables
- Add and delete rows and columns in tables
- Insert a table in a letter

40B

Table Alignment

Tables are usually centered horizontally on a page. However, they can be aligned at the left or right margin. Tables, like letters and other documents, can be centered vertically on a page. When a table is used in the body of a report or letter, center it between the left and right margins.

Table 1

1. Open **39e table** that you created in Lesson 39. In the steps that follow, you will center the table vertically and horizontally.
2. Center-align the main heading.
3. Change the vertical position of the heading to 1.1". To center the table vertically, use the path at the left to display the Layout tab of the Page Setup dialog box. Select *Center* from the Vertical alignment list in the Page section as shown in Figure 7-21. The table should be centered vertically after you click *OK*.

Layout tab > Page Setup dialog box launcher > Layout tab

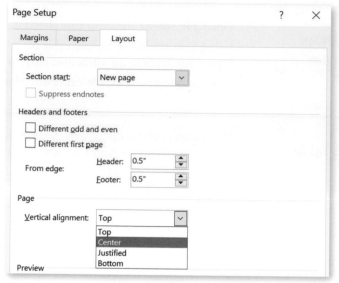

Figure 7-21 Vertical alignment

Table Tools Layout tab >
Table > Properties

4. To center the table horizontally, click in the table and then follow the path at the left to open the Table Properties dialog box. Click *Center* in the Alignment section as shown in Figure 7-22. After you click *OK*, the table should be centered horizontally between the left and right margins.

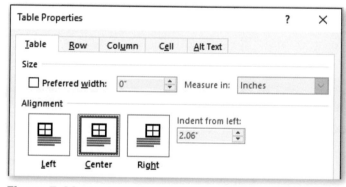

Figure 7-22 Center alignment

5. Save the document as **40b table1**. Complete the following CheckPoint and then close the document.

 **checkpoint** Is your table centered vertically and horizontally? Use the Print Preview screen to check the layout of the document.

Table 2

1. Open **39f table** that you created in Lesson 39.
2. Center-align the main heading. Change the top margin to about 1". Center the table vertically. Center the table horizontally. Use the Preview screen to check the placement.
3. Save the document as **40b table2** and close it.

Home tab > Paragraph >
Show/Hide

Use the Show/Hide ¶ button (see icon at left) to display table markers as shown in Figure 7-23. These markers are helpful when moving a table or selecting parts of a table.

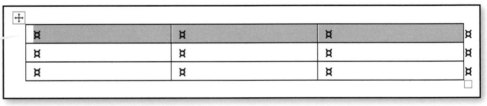

Figure 7-23 Table markers

Table 1

1. Open a new, blank document. Insert a table grid with three columns and three rows. Use the Show/Hide ¶ button to display table markers.
2. Using the mouse, point outside the gridlines and to the left of row 1. Click to select the row as shown in Figure 7-24.

Selected row

Figure 7-24 Selected row of cells

Merge Cells
Table Tools Layout tab >
Merge > Merge Cells

3. To merge the three cells in row 1, click *Merge Cells* in the Merge group on the Table Tools Layout tab. Row 1 should now have only one cell.
4. To split each cell in row 3 into two cells, select row 3. Click *Split Cells* in the Merge group on the Table Tools Layout tab to display the Split Cells dialog box shown in Figure 7-25.

Split Cells
Table Tools Layout tab >
Merge > Split Cells

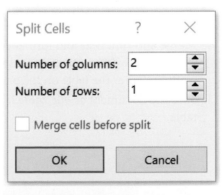

Figure 7-25 Split Cells dialog box

5. Key **2** in the Number of columns text box. Key **1** in the Number of rows text box. Remove the check mark from the *Merge cells before split* box. Click *OK*. Row 3 should now have six cells.

6. Key the following data in your table grid. Your grid should match the grid shown here. Format text in the cells as shown.

ELECTED CO-CAPTAINS					
Team Red		Team White		Team Blue	
Mary	Mark	Jose	Prajakar	Mario	Lynora

7. Use the *AutoFit Contents* command to change the column widths. Center the table horizontally and vertically on the page.

8. Save the document as **40c table1** and close it.

Table 2

1. Open a new, blank document. Create a table grid with four columns and five rows.

2. Use the *Merge Cells* and *Split Cells* commands to make your table grid look like the one shown here. Then key the data in the table as shown. Use center alignment in all cells.

All cells in row 1 were merged into one cell that spans all of the columns.			
These four cells were merged into one cell.		The cell below was split into four cells.	These two cells were merged.
	The cell above was split into two cells.		
			These two cells were merged.

3. Center the page vertically. Save the document as **40c table2** and close it.

Table 3

1. Open a new, blank document. Create a table grid with four columns and eight rows.

2. Merge and split cells and format cell entries as shown in the table that follows step 3. Then key the data in the table shown below. Use *AutoFit Contents* to change column widths. Center the table on the page horizontally. Center the page vertically.

3. Save the document as **40c table3**. Proofread and correct errors. Print and then close the table.

REFRESHMENT STAND STAFFING					
Saturday	8 a.m.-10 a.m.		10 a.m.-11 a.m.	11 a.m.-1 p.m.	
September 5	J. Triponey		M. McKeever	B. Hohn	
September 12	D. Ford	M. Lu	G. Bauer	A. Carr	V. Dee
September 19	C. Rickenbach			D. Mars	Z. Sia
September 26	A. Kopolovich			B. Gordon	
October 1	S. Creely	D. Sanchez		M. Nash	R. Janson
October 8	I. Che	A. Jaso	R. Dolphi	A. Berger	

40D

Add and Delete Rows and Columns

Table Tools Layout tab > Rows & Columns > Choose Insert or Delete option

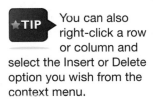

★TIP You can also right-click a row or column and select the Insert or Delete option you wish from the context menu.

Table 1

1. Open *df 40d table1*.
2. Select row 2 and delete it by following the path at the left to the Delete drop-down list options. Click *Delete Rows*.
3. To add a row below the last row, click in the last cell in the last row. Tap *Tab* to add a new row to the bottom of the table.
4. Key the following data in the last row:

2014	Germany	Argentina

5. To add a column between the first and second columns, click in column 1 and then follow the path at the left to the Insert options. Click *Insert Right*.
6. Key the following data in the cells in the new column that was inserted:

Site
Italy
United States
France
Japan/South Korea
Germany
South Africa
Brazil

7. To delete the last column, click in the last column. Select *Delete Columns* from the Delete drop-down list.
8. Save the document as *40d table1* and close it.

Table 2

1. Open *df 40d table2*. Insert a new column between the Birth Date and Email Address columns. Key the following data in the new column:

Phone Number
614-555-0133
614-555-0179
614-555-0144
614-555-0156
614-555-0184
614-555-0172
614-555-0141
614-555-0166
614-555-0111
614-555-0199
614-555-0139

2. Delete the Email Address column.

3. Delete row 10 (*Yarborough, Pam*) and row 4 (*Guitterez, Maria*). Add a row after row 2 (*Aceto, Jill*). (To add the row, click in row 2 and choose the *Table Tools Layout* tab. In the Rows & Columns group, click *Insert Below*.) Key the following data:

Bauer, Brianne	Left Back	10/14/97	614-555-0163

4. Add a row after row 5 (*Lei, Su*) and key the following data in the new row:

McCoy, Kim	Right Mid	03/01/98	614-555-0118

5. Add a row at the top of the table. Merge the cells in row 1. Using a bold font, key the following main heading in the new row:

TREESDALE ROSTER FOR SOCCER TOURNAMENT

6. Center the page vertically. Save the document as *40d table2* and close it.

40E

Letter with Table

1. Open *df 40e table*.
2. Add a column to the right of column 3 (Room). Key **% Gain** for the column heading.
3. Start the *Calculator* program. Find the percent of gain for each student by dividing the number in the Gain column by the number in the Beginning Amount column. Key the answers in the appropriate cells in the % Gain column. (Round numbers to one decimal place.)
4. Delete the last three columns (Beginning Amount, Ending Amount, and Gain).
5. Add a row at the top of the table. Merge the cells in row 1. Key the following title in row 1:

STOCK CLUB TOP PERFORMERS

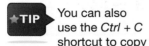
★TIP You can also use the *Ctrl + C* shortcut to copy and the *Ctrl + V* shortcut to paste the table.

6. Center-align the text in all cells and apply an appropriate table style.

7. Save the document as ***40e table*** and keep it open. Open ***df 40e letter***.

8. Make ***40e table*** the active window. Click the Table Move handle to select the entire table. Click the *Copy* button in the Clipboard group on the Home tab.

9. Make ***df 40e letter*** the active window. Click in the letter at the beginning of the second paragraph. Click *Paste* in the Clipboard group. The table should now appear in the letter.

10. Center the table horizontally. Save the letter as ***40e letter*** and print it. Close ***40e letter*** and ***40e table***.

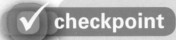
checkpoint Is the table centered between the margins? Compare your % Gain answers with those of a classmate and correct any answers that are wrong.

21st Century Skills: Leadership

Read about the characteristics of leadership in Appendix B, then complete Leadership Activity 1 in Appendix B. Consider these attributes of a successful leader, and key your responses to the Think Critically questions in the form of a paragraph.

- A successful leader accepts responsibility and accountability for results
- A successful leader has self-discipline, good character, and is committed to personal development
- A successful leader is a great communicator
- A successful leader has great people skills

Think Critically

1. What attributes of a successful leader apply to ethical and appropriate computer use?

2. How does use of netiquette demonstrate leadership qualities?

3. Describe ways in which you have demonstrated leadership abilities when using the computer, the Internet, or a mobile device such as a cell phone.

4. Key your responses in paragraph form. Submit your responses to your instructor.

sirtravelalot/Shutterstock.com

LESSON 41 Tables: Changing Row Height, Borders, and Shading

OUTCOMES

- Change row height and vertical alignment of cell data
- Format tables using borders and shading

Change Row Height and Vertical Alignment

Table 1

1. Open **df 41b table1**. You will change this table to look like the table in Figure 7-26.

MEN'S SOCCER WORLD CUP WINNERS

Year	Winner	Final Opponent
1998	France	Brazil
2002	Brazil	Germany
2006	Italy	France
2010	Spain	Netherlands
2014	Germany	Argentina

Figure 7-26 This table has changed row height and vertically centered cells

Row Height
Table Tools Layout tab >
Cell Size > Table Row Height

2. To change the row 1 height, click in row 1 and follow the **Row Height** path at the left. Key **0.5** in the Height box as shown in Figure 7-27.

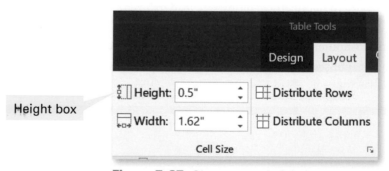

Figure 7-27 Change row height

Alignment
Table Tools Layout tab >
Alignment

3. To change the text alignment, select the cells in row 1. Follow the **Alignment** path at the left to display the Alignment options. Click the *Align Center* button shown in Figure 7-28.

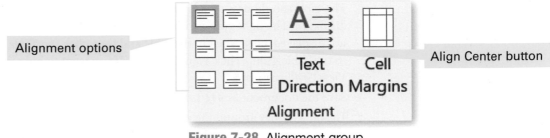

Alignment options

Text Direction

Cell Margins

Align Center button

Alignment

Figure 7-28 Alignment group

4. Using the process you used in step 2, set the height for rows 2–6 to **0.3"**. Set the vertical alignment for the cells to *Align Center Left*.
5. Save the document as **41b table1** and close it.

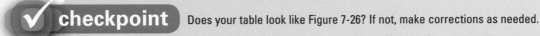

checkpoint Does your table look like Figure 7-26? If not, make corrections as needed.

Table 2

1. Open **df 41b table2**.
2. Change the height of row 1 to **0.7"**. Change the height of row 2 to **0.5"**. Change the height of the remaining rows to **0.3"**.
3. Change the alignment for all rows to *Align Center*.
4. Save the document as **41b table2**. Print and close the document.

41C

Borders and Shading

Table Tools Design tab >
Borders > Borders

1. Open **41b table2** that you saved earlier in this lesson.
2. Select the table. To format the table without borders, use the path at the left to access the Borders drop-down list. Select *No Border* from the list as shown in Figure 7-29.

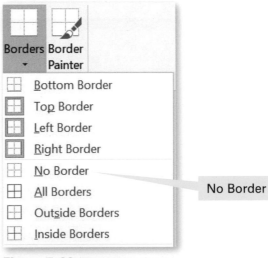

Figure 7-29 Border options

3. The table should now appear with no border lines. However, the table gridlines may be displayed. The light gray gridlines that appear on the screen will not print. If the gridlines are not displayed, click a cell in the table and then click the *Table Tools Layout* tab if necessary. In the Table group, click *View Gridlines*. If you want to hide the gridlines on the screen, click *View Gridlines* again.

4. Save the document as **41c table1** and do not close it.

5. To add a border around the main heading, select row 1 of the table. Choose the *Outside Borders* option from the Borders drop-down list. Row 1 should have a border.

Table Tools Design tab >
Table Styles > Shading

6. To add shading to row 1, follow the path at the left to open the shading options from the Shading drop-down list. Select a light color from the Theme Colors or Standard Colors that you like. Row 1 should be shaded.

7. Save the document as **41c table2**. Print it but do not close it.

8. Experiment with applying borders and shading to other cells, rows, and columns in the table. Close the table without saving changes.

Digital Citizenship and Ethics

Whether it's buying music and movies or shoes and shirts, the Internet has become a popular and convenient way to shop. However, shopping online comes with its own set of risks and responsibilities. For example:

Blend Images/Shutterstock.com

- You must pay attention to the purchases you charge on a credit card, including taxes and shipping and handling charges, and be aware of how much debt you are accumulating. The inability to pay off debt can severely damage your credit rating, which will prohibit you from taking out a loan or even renting an apartment.

- You must be able to discern credible and legitimate websites; otherwise, you may become the victim of a scam. As a class, discuss the following:

COLLABORATION

1. Share a recent example of when you used the Internet to research a product or service. What type of information did you find? How did it influence your purchasing decision?

2. How would you determine if a website is hosted by a reputable company?

LESSON 42 — Sort and Convert Tables

OUTCOMES

- Sort data in a table
- Convert text to a table
- Convert a table to text
- Research data and design a table

42B

Sort in Tables

Table Tools Layout tab >
Data > Sort

Table Sorts 1 and 2

1. Open *df 42b table1*. Save the document as **42b sort1**.
2. Click a cell in the table. Follow the path at the left to the Sort button. Click the *Sort* button to open the Sort dialog box shown in Figure 7-30.

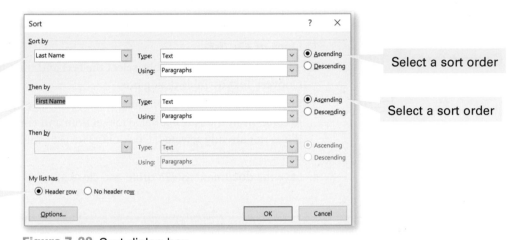

Select a column to sort by

Select a column for secondary sort

Select a sort order

Select a sort order

Select to use a header row

Figure 7-30 Sort dialog box

3. If necessary, select *Last Name* from the Sort by drop-down list. This will cause the data to be sorted first by the person's last name. The Type should be Text. Select *Ascending* for the sort order if it is not already selected.
4. Select *First Name* in the first Then by box. This will cause the data to be sorted next by the person's first name. The Type should be Text. Select *Ascending* for the sort order if it is not already selected.
5. Click the radio button by *Header row* if it is not already selected. This option means that the first row in your table contains column headings that will not be included in the sort. Click *OK*.

 **checkpoint** In the sorted table in step 5, Susan Abels should be listed first and Mary Venturino should be listed last. Jane O'Brien should be listed before June O'Brien.

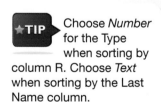 **★TIP** Choose *Number* for the Type when sorting by column R. Choose *Text* when sorting by the Last Name column.

6. Save the document and keep it open.
7. Sort the data by column R (runs) in descending order and then by the Last Name column in ascending order.

COLLABORATION

8. Save the document as **42b sort2**. Print and close the document.

 checkpoint Compare your *42b sort2* with that of a classmate. If the data is not sorted correctly, identify what is wrong and sort the table again.

Table Sorts 3 and 4

1. Open **df 42b table2**.
2. Sort the data by School in ascending order and then by Last in ascending order.
3. Save the document as **42b sort3** and leave it open.
4. Sort the data by School in ascending order and then by Points in descending order.
5. Save the document as **42b sort4** and close it.

42C

Convert Text to a Table

Insert tab > Tables > Table >
Convert Text to Table

1. Open **df 42c list**.
2. To convert the text to a table, select the text and then follow the path at the left to open the Convert Text to Table dialog box.
3. If necessary, key **3** in the Number of columns box in the Table size section; choose *AutoFit to contents* in the AutoFit behavior section; and choose *Tabs* in the Separate text at section if it is not already selected. Click *OK*. The list should appear as a three-column table with 11 rows.
4. Save the document as **42c table** and close it.

42D

Convert a Table to Text

Table Tools Layout tab >
Data > Convert to Text

1. Open **df 42b table2**.
2. To convert the table to text, click a cell in the table. Follow the path at the left to the *Convert to Text* button and click it to open the Convert Table to Text dialog box.
3. Click the radio button for *Tabs* if necessary. Click *OK*; the list should appear as a four-column list with 16 rows.
4. Save the document as **42d text** and close it.

42E

Key and Convert Text to Table

Insert tab > Tables > Table >
Convert Text to Table

1. Open a new, blank document. Set Left tabs at 3", 4.5", and 6".
2. Key the following list, using the *Tab* key to move across each row.

Last	First	School	Time
Belardus	Colleen	York	100.13
Davis	Kylie	Harris	100.72
Flogg	Martha	Jamestown	103.83
McLaughlin	Sarah	York	104.12
Toth	Jessica	Harris	103.45
Vernon	Andrea	Jamestown	102.69

3. Convert the text to a four-column table. AutoFit the table to its contents.

4. Sort the table by School in ascending order and then by Time in descending order.

5. Insert a row at the top of the grid, merge the cells, and key the following as a main heading:

GIRLS 100-YARD BUTTERFLY RESULTS

6. Format the table using an appropriate table style. Apply *Heading 1* style to the main heading and *Heading 2* style to the column headings. Center-align the main and column headings. Center the table horizontally and vertically.

7. Insert the following information at an appropriate place in the table.

```
Flogg      Martha    Harding    102.13
Sanchez    Corina    Harding    101.14
```

8. Change the height of rows 3–10 to **0.3"**.

9. Save the document as *42e table*. Print and close it.

COLLABORATION

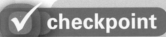 **checkpoint** Compare your table to a classmate's table. Is the sort correct? Were the rows inserted at the proper point? Is the table attractive and easy to read? Are there any errors?

42F

Research and Design a Table

COLLABORATION

1. Working with another student, choose ten first names for people. Do research in your local library or on the Internet to find the meaning of each name. Enter **first name meanings** or similar search terms in a search engine to find information on the Internet. Try to find similar information about each name so that you can report your findings in a table.

2. Design a table to report your research findings. The table should have a title, column headings, and cell entries to show each name and the information you learned about the name.

3. Key the information in the table and format the table to make it attractive and easy to read.

4. Sort the table by first name in alphabetical order.

5. Save the document as *42f table*. Print and then close the document.

Assessment 2 — Reports and Tables

Warmup

Key each line twice. If time permits, key the lines again.

Alphabet	1	Javy quickly swam the dozen extra laps before Gus.
Figure/Symbol	2	Blake's cell number was changed to (835) 109-2647.
Speed	3	The six men may work down by the lake on the dock.

gwam 1' | 1 | 2 | 3 | 4 | 5 | 6 | 7 | 8 | 9 | 10 |

Activity 1
Assess Straight-Copy Skill

Key one or two 2' timed writings on both paragraphs combined. Print, proofread, circle errors, and determine *gwam*.

LA **all letters used**   gwam 2'

Ask students and they will quickly tell   4
you they like to talk about money. However,   8
students often focus on how much extra money   13
they need to purchase new technology or   17
clothing for a special event, such as a Prom   21
or concert. It is amazing that the need to   25
save money frequently is not a part of their   30
conversation.   31

The best way to have enough money to pay   35
the expenses for things that you enjoy is to plan 40
ahead. A budget is an excellent financial tool   45
used to manage money. Make a list of your income, 50
expenses, and savings. Then use the information   54
to make wise decisions.   57

gwam 2' | 1 | 2 | 3 | 4 | 5 |

Activity 2
MLA Report

1. Start *Word* and open a new, blank document. Key the report below and on the next page in MLA format. Key your last name and page number as a header. Use your name, your teacher's name, your course name, and the current date for the header.
2. Save the report as *a2 activity2*, print, and then close it.

Female Nobel Laureates in Physics and Chemistry

The Nobel Foundation was established in 1901 when Alfred B. Nobel (1883–96), inventor of dynamite, bequeathed $9 million so that the interest earned could be distributed to individuals judged to have most benefited humankind in physics, chemistry, physiology or medicine, literature, and promotion of peace (The World Almanac and Book of Facts, 2011, p. 266).

The first woman to receive a Nobel Prize was Marie Curie in 1903. Including her 1903 award, 44 women have received a Nobel Prize 45 times. Between 1901 and 2013, the Nobel Prize in Physics has been awarded 107 times to 195 different individuals, including two women. During the same time period, the Nobel Prize in Chemistry has been awarded 105 times to 165 different individuals, including four women (Nobel Prize Awarded Women).

Female Nobel Laureates in Physics

Marie Curie received the Nobel Prize in Physics in 1903. She shared this award with Pierre Curie, her husband, and Henri Becquerel. These individuals were honored "in recognition of the extraordinary services they have rendered by their joint researches on the radiation phenomena" (Nobel Prize Awarded Women).

Maria Goeppert Mayer and J. Hans D. Jensen shared part of the Nobel Prize in Physics in 1963 "for their discoveries concerning nuclear shell structure" (Nobel Prize Awarded Women).

Female Nobel Laureates in Chemistry

Marie Curie was the first woman to receive the Nobel Prize for Chemistry and the only woman between 1903 and 2013 to receive two Nobel Prizes. She received her award for chemistry in 1911 "in recognition of her service to the advancement of chemistry by the discovery of the elements radium and polonium, by the isolation of radium and the study of the nature and compounds of this remarkable element" (Nobel Prize Awarded Women).

In 1935, Irene Joliot-Curie, the daughter of Pierre and Marie Curie, shared the Nobel Prize in Chemistry with her husband, Frederic Joliot, "in recognition of their synthesis of new radioactive elements" (Nobel Prize Awarded Women).

In 1964, Dorothy Crowfoot Hodgkin received the chemistry award "for her determination by X-ray techniques of the structures of important biochemical substances" (Nobel Prize Awarded Women).

The most recent woman to be awarded the Nobel Prize in Chemistry was Ada E. Yonath for "studies of the structure and function of the ribosome" in 2009 (Nobel Prize Awarded Women).

Works Cited

"Nobel Prize Awarded Women." *Nobelprize.org*. Nobel Media AB 2018. Accessed 2 Apr 2018.

The World Almanac and Book of Facts, 2017, New York, NY: World Almanac Books, 2017, p. 276.

Activity 3
Standard, Unbound Report

1. Open *df a2 activity3*. Format the text in standard, unbound report format.
2. Format the last paragraph as a long quotation.
3. Key the following text below the long quotation.
4. Save the report as *a2 activity3*, print, and close it.

Dual-Enrollment Courses

Many high schools have partnered with local two- and four-year colleges to provide college-level courses to high school students. While dual-enrollment programs vary widely, they typically involve the student taking a college-level course at the high school or at the college campus. If the course is taken at the student's high school, it is frequently taught by the high school faculty. If the course is taken at the college campus, the high school student is typically enrolled in a regular class with college students. Other variations may include the college professor teaching the course at the high school or high school students enrolling in summer classes at the college (Getting College Credit in High School: Worth It?).

Because of the variety of and differences among the dual-enrollment programs, colleges may or may not accept the college-level course for AP or AS.

Other Advantages

In addition to the possibility of shortening the time and lessening the costs to earn a college degree, there are other advantages to taking college-level courses in high school. One is that these programs prepare students for the academic rigor of college courses. With this preparation, students are likely to have a better transition to the college classroom, resulting in a more positive experience.

Another advantage is that having AP, IB, and/or dual-enrollment courses noted on your high school transcript or college application shows the college admission personnel that you are willing to challenge yourself academically by taking the most demanding courses.

References

Fox Business. "Getting College Credit in High School: Worth It?" www.foxbusiness.com/personal-finance/2012/01/20/getting-college-credit-in-high-school-worth-it/ (15 March 2018).

The Princeton Review. "An Intro to Getting College Credit in High School." 02/09/2011. in.princetonreview.com/in/2011/02/an-intro-to-getting-college-credit-in-high-school.html (15 March 2018).

National Association for College Admission Counseling. "Earning College Credit in High School." www.nacacnet.org/studentinfo/articles/Pages/EarningCollegeCredit.aspx (15 March 2018).

Activity 4
Table

1. Open a new, blank document. Create the table shown below using the following information.
   a. Insert a 5 × 9 table grid. Set the width for column 1 to 1.5"; columns 2, 3, and 4 to 0.8"; and column 5 to 1".
   b. Bold the main heading and column headings; use Align Center for the main heading and column headings.
   c. Use left alignment for entries in column 1; center alignment for entries in columns 2 and 3; and right alignment for entries in columns 4 and 5.

SCCL Investment Club First Quarter Portfolio Report				
Stock		**Shares Owned**	**Current Share Price**	**Current Stock Value**
Company	**Symbol**			
Hershey Company	HSY	210	$104.25	$21,892.50
McDonald's	MCD	178	103.39	18,403.42
Nike	NKE	265	75.40	19,981.00
Range Resources	RRC	130	87.23	11,339.90
3D Systems	DDD	90	68.57	6,171.30
Coca-Cola	KO	164	38.32	6,284.48

2. Add a row at the bottom of the table and key the information in it as shown below:

Current Portfolio Value	$84,072.60

3. Center the table horizontally and vertically and add a 3-point outside border around the table. Shade the first and last row of the table using a light color.
4. Save the table as *a2 activity4*; print and close it.

Activity 5
Table

1. Open *df a2 activity5* and make the following changes:
   a. Delete the Derek Stanton row and add this row at the bottom:

Fred Gaskin	6	208	724	95	819

   b. Change row heights to 0.4".
   c. Delete columns 4 and 5.
   d. Sort the table by Total Sales in descending order.
   e. Insert a row at the top and key this as a main heading: **Top Sellers by Grade and Room**.
   f. Center the table vertically and horizontally; apply an appropriate style and then apply Align Center to all cells.
2. Save the table as *a2 activity5*; print and close it.

Activity 6
Convert Text to Table

1. Open *df a2 activity6* and convert it to a table.
2. Apply AutoFit Contents to set column widths.
3. Center-align the main heading, column headings, and columns 3 and 4.
4. Apply an appropriate style; center the table horizontally and vertically.
5. Save the table as *a2 activity6*; print and close it.

Skill Builder 6

A

Warmup

Key each line twice;
then a 1' timing on line 3;
determine *gwam*.

alphabet 1 J. Fox made five quick plays to win the big prize.

? 2 Where is Madison? Did she call? Is she to go, too?

easy 3 Pam owns the big dock, but they own the lake land.

| gwam | 1' | 1 | 2 | 3 | 4 | 5 | 6 | 7 | 8 | 9 | 10 | |

B

Speed Building

Key each line twice SS with
a DS between 2-line groups.

TIP
- Reach up without moving hands away from your body.
- Reach down without moving hands toward your body.

za/az 1 zap lazy lizard pizza hazard bazaar frazzle dazzle
       2 Zack and Hazel zapped the lazy lizard in the maze.

ol/lo 3 old load olive look fold lost bold loan allow told
       4 Olympia told the lonely man to load the long logs.

ws/sw 5 swing cows sweet glows swept mows sword knows swap
       6 He swung the sword over the sweaty cows and swine.

ju/ft 7 often jury draft judge left just hefty juice after
       8 Jud, the fifth juror on my left, just wants juice.

       9 deal need debit edit deed edge deli used dent desk
ed/de 10 Jed needed to edit the deed made by the defendant.

C

**Rough Draft
(Edited Copy)**

1. Study the proofreaders' marks shown below.

2. Key each sentence twice SS; DS between 2-line groups. Make all editing (handwritten) changes.

∧ = insert
= add space
∿ = transpose
𝒆 = delete
⌒ = close up
≡ = capitalize

1 A first draft is a preliminary or tentative one.

2 It is where the creator gets his/thoughts on paper.

3 After the draft is created, it will be looked over.

4 Reviewing is the step where a persone refines copy.

5 Proof readers' marks are used edit the original copy.

6 The edting changes will be then be made to the copy.

7 After the change have been made, read the copy agian.

8 more changes still may need to be made to the copy.

9 Edting proof reading does take a lot time and effort.

10 error free copy is worth the trouble, however.

Speed Check: Straight Copy

1. Key two 1' timings on ¶ 1 and then on ¶ 2.

2. Key two 2' timings on ¶s 1–2 combined; determine *gwam*.

LA all letters used

gwam 2'

His mother signed her name with an X. His   4
father had no schooling. Could a President come   9
from such a humble background? President Lincoln   14
did. Lincoln was not just a President, he is often   19
recognized as one of the best to ever hold the office.   24

Honest Abe, as he was often called, always gave   29
the extra effort needed to be a success. Whether the   34
job was splitting logs, being a lawyer, or being   39
President, he always gave it his best. Dealing with   44
the Civil War required a man who gave his best effort.   50

gwam 2' | 1 | 2 | 3 | 4 | 5 |

Skill Transfer: Straight Copy and Rough Draft

1. Key each ¶ once SS; DS between ¶s.

2. Key two 1' timings on each ¶; determine *gwam* on each timing.

Straight copy

gwam 1'

Documents free of errors make a good impression.   10

When a document has no errors, readers can focus on   20

the content. Errors distract readers and can cause   30

them to think less of the message.   37

Therefore, it is important to proofread the   9

final copy of a document several times to make sure   19

it contains no errors before it leaves your desk.   29

Readers of error-free documents form a positive image   39

of the person who wrote the message.   47

Rough draft

When a ~~negative~~ positive image of the person who wrote the ~~the~~   10

messge is formed a the message is ~~less~~ more likely to succeed.   21

remember, you never get a ~~another~~ second chance to # make a good first   33

impression.   36

Advanced Technology Skills 3

Maintaining a System

OUTCOMES

- Discuss the importance of regular system maintenance
- Learn software maintenance tasks
- Learn hardware maintenance tasks
- Set up a maintenance schedule

Understanding the Importance of Routine Maintenance

Maintaining a computer system is not merely a good idea; it is essential to safeguarding your investment in hardware and software. If you intend to continue to work efficiently, you need to schedule maintenance on a routine basis. Regular maintenance is an important responsibility not only for an organization's IT department but also for the individual user.

A number of problems can occur if a system's hardware and software are not maintained. For instance:

- Your computer may start slowly or take an unusual amount of time to perform routine tasks
- Applications may stop working temporarily, or the entire system may lock up
- Your Internet connection may be slow

Maintaining your system can prevent catastrophes

You can eliminate some common problems that affect computer performance by performing regular maintenance on your software and hardware. *Windows* provides system tools specifically designed to help you keep your system in tune. Even if you are not a computer expert, you can also do some physical maintenance on your system that will help to prevent hardware problems. Setting up and following a checklist of regular maintenance procedures is the best way to ensure that you and your system can work at optimum efficiency.

The following sections discuss maintenance tasks that any computer user can perform. More advanced maintenance tasks should be undertaken only by professionals. Tasks that should be performed only by a computer specialist include any chore requiring a computer's case to be opened, such as cleaning inside the case, upgrading RAM, or replacing a hard drive.

Performing Software Maintenance

A slow computer that freezes up or fails to process data efficiently is likely to have some or all of the following problems:

- Unnecessary files such as temporary files or files that download when you view some webpages
- Too many programs or processes running at the same time, particularly at start-up
- Fragmented files
- Computer viruses or spyware
- Inadequate hardware for the programs running

The issue of inadequate hardware—not enough RAM, or a processor that is not fast enough for the programs you want to run—is one that should be addressed when you are buying the system or software, and thus it is not really part of a routine maintenance program.

The issue of what programs start with the computer is one that should be handled by an expert. Other issues on this list can, however, be handled by regular use of standard maintenance utilities and a reasonable approach to what you install on your system.

Checking for Viruses and Spyware

A problem that frequently causes your system to run slowly is an undetected collection of spyware or malware. A problem that can prevent your computer from running at all is infection by one or more of the many hundreds of viruses that are constantly circulating around the Internet (see Figure AT3-1).

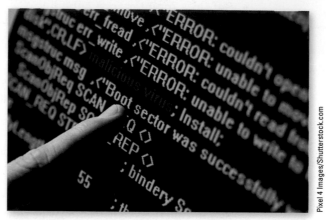

Figure AT3-1 Computer viruses can lead to serious system problems

Every system needs a program for detecting malware, and every user needs a plan for running that program on a regular basis. Malware such as viruses and spyware are all too easy to pick up during web browsing sessions and from plausible-seeming email messages. It is essential to detect dangerous programs before they can infect your system. You can configure detection programs to scan on a regular schedule to locate potential threats.

You may have separate programs for detecting viruses and controlling spyware, or you may use one program that detects all kinds of malware. Many malware detection programs are available for free download, although you may not receive automatic updates to them unless you pay for the programs.

More than any other program, antivirus and spyware programs must be kept up to date because new threats are always arising. Antivirus and spyware programs generally configure themselves to search for updates automatically every day so you do not have to remember to do so, but it is your responsibility to make sure the automatic updates are turned on and working correctly. If you do not have automatic updates on, you need to schedule updates on a frequent basis.

It is also important to view settings to see what the program is checking during regular scans. You should confirm that it is checking all files on all drives in your system, as well as email and instant messaging attachments. You usually also have some control over checking of other threats, such as tracking cookies and unwanted scripts.

1. Open your antivirus program by keying its name in the *Type here to search* box. Ask your teacher for the name of the program your lab or school is using.
2. Check the current schedule for scanning your system. How often is the scan scheduled, and when does the scan begin? (continued on next page)

 Antivirus software should always be configured to start with the operating system. This is especially important if the computer has a live Internet connection when it is running.

 If your antivirus software starts with the operating system, you can also open it by clicking the *Show hidden icons* button (small up arrow on the right side of the taskbar next to the People icon) and clicking the icon for your antivirus app.

★TIP If you are not using an administrator account, the settings will be grayed out, but you will still be able to see them.

3. Check the update schedule to make sure automatic updates are on.

4. View settings to see what kinds of files the program is checking and what other kinds of threats the program is looking for.

5. Close the antivirus program without making any changes.

Keeping Other Programs Updated

As with antivirus and spyware programs, you should make sure that programs such as the operating system, browser, and other important applications are configured to receive and install regular updates. Keeping software up to date is part of any good maintenance program. Updates address issues such as security problems and operational improvements; by updating regularly, you ensure that your programs are working as efficiently as they can.

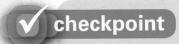 You dislike seeing prompts to update your operating system, and you especially dislike the way your operating system installs them after you turn off your computer. You decide to turn off automatic updates and instead make a note to yourself to update your operating system once a month. Will your decision help you work more efficiently?

Performing Hardware Maintenance

Most serious inside-the-case hardware maintenance should be done by IT professionals, but you can perform a number of chores outside the box that will improve system performance and help you avoid having to call in the pros. Turn off the computer before doing these tasks.

 TIP Never spray any kind of liquid near any computer component. Always spray on the cleaning cloth.

- Wipe the monitor with a soft, damp cloth to remove dust, fingerprints, and other spots that interfere with your view of the screen. The dampening agent depends on the type of monitor; check maintenance information from the monitor's manufacturer to determine the best cleaning agent for your monitor.

- Vacuum around the computer case to remove dust and hair. Dust that has been sucked into a computer case by the system fan can collect on hardware inside the case and ultimately cause it to fail.

 TIP Keyboards that are shared by a number of individuals can spread infectious diseases such as colds and the flu. Keep your keyboard clean!

- An amazing amount of dust and dirt can collect around the keys of the keyboard, causing keys to stick. On a laptop, material that sifts in around the keys may end up inside the computer, where it can affect the motherboard and other sensitive components. Use a can of compressed air to blow away dirt. Then dampen a cloth with alcohol or a disinfectant to wipe each key.

- Wipe the mouse and each of its buttons or wheels with a damp cloth to clean. You can also improve mouse operations by cleaning the mouse pad with a damp cloth (or just replace the mouse pad periodically).

In addition to performing these types of routine maintenance, you can head off trouble by adhering to some common computer safety rules.

- Keep air vents unobstructed to prevent the computer from overheating.

- Keep food and liquids away from your computer. Spilled liquids may damage your keyboard or, in a laptop, may ultimately corrode the motherboard.

- Keep wiring under control to prevent people from tripping over cords and knocking computer components to the ground.

Avoid computer problems by taking safety precautions

- Avoid electrical discharge anywhere near the inside of your computer. Electrical vacuum cleaners, which are prone to static electricity, are usually not used when cleaning the inside of a computer for this reason.
- Keep your computer in a room-temperature environment; avoid locations with excessive heat or cold.

Setting Up a Maintenance Schedule

Knowing what you can do to maintain your computer system is half the battle; your next step is to set up a schedule for performing those tasks. If you work in a company, it is likely that your IT department has such a schedule in place already. If you are an individual user, you are responsible for creating and following your own schedule.

Experts suggest that you schedule tasks on a daily, weekly, or monthly basis according to how important the tasks are for your system's operational well-being. Table AT3-1 shows suggested frequency of maintenance tasks. It is recommended that some tasks, such as operating system and important software updates, be performed automatically. You may want to perform some, such as backups, more often.

Daily	Check for antivirus updates
	Check for spyware updates
Weekly	Update *Windows* and other applications
	Delete temporary files
	Do a full backup of important files
	Run a complete virus/spyware scan
Monthly or as needed	Defragment the hard drive (if this is not automatic)
	Uninstall programs not being used regularly
	Clean computer components

Table AT3-1 Suggested maintenance schedule

checkpoint

1. Following the guidelines on maintenance you have read about in this module, create a table or chart for the next month and assign regular maintenance tasks by day, week, or month.
2. Create a checklist to post beside your computer that shows maintenance tasks so you can check them off as you complete them.

Before You Move On

Answer **True** or **False** to each question to review what you have learned in Chapter 7.

1. Table rows run horizontally, and columns run vertically. LO 39B

2. The place where a row and a column cross each other is called a subrow. LO 39B

3. To select an entire table, click the Table Move handle. LO 40C

4. When AutoFit Contents is used, the table grid may have varying column widths, but none will be narrower than 1 inch. LO 39C

5. Center tables vertically by selecting Center in the Layout tab of the Page Setup dialog box. LO 40B

6. Cells in adjacent rows and cells in adjacent columns can be merged. LO 40C

7. Rows can be added above or below existing rows. LO 40D

8. All row heights in a table must be the same size. LO 41B

9. The default placement for data in a cell is left and top alignment. LO 41B

10. Only table columns with numbers can be sorted. LO 42B

Apply What You Have Learned

Revise and Format a Table

1. Open *df c7 table1*.
2. Add a column at the right and key the following information in that column.

April
504
605
589
1698

3. Add a row after Helen Goins and key the following information. Then correct the totals in row 6.

Jim Jones	582	631	768	604

4. Make the width of column A 1.3" and columns B–E 1".
5. Insert a row at the top, merge the cells, and key the following main heading:

SUPER GIANT CORPORATION UNITS SOLD

6. Change the height of row 1 to 0.5" and the height of rows 2–7 to 0.3".
7. Apply a table style to make the table attractive and easy to read.
8. Right-align all numbers and center-align main and column headings. Vertically center all cell entries. Center the table horizontally and vertically on the page.
9. Save the document as *c7 table1* and close it.

Create and Format a Table

1. Open *df c7 list*.
2. Convert the list to a table using the tabs as the separators and AutoFit Contents.
3. Sort the list by last name and then first name, both in ascending order.
4. Insert a row at the top and key **BATTING AVERAGES** as a centered main heading.
5. Apply an appropriate table style and make formatting changes so that the table is attractive and easy to read. Center the table horizontally.
6. Save the document as *c7 table2* but do not close it.
7. Sort *c7 table2* by Average in descending order.
8. Save the document as *c7 table3* and close it.

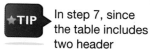 **★TIP** In step 7, since the table includes two header rows (a main heading and column heading), select only the rows you want sorted (rows 3–9); then perform the sort. Otherwise, the software recognizes the main heading as the header row and includes the column headings in the sort.

Lesson 43 Slide Layout and Design Themes

Lesson 44 Add Graphics to Slides

Lesson 45 Tables, Graphs, and Charts

Lesson 46 Use PowerPoint Designer to Enhance Slides

Lessons 47–48 Create and Deliver a Presentation

Assessment 3 Presentations

Application Guide

What Is an Electronic Presentation?

Electronic presentations are computer-generated visual aids (usually slide shows) that help to communicate information. Presentations can combine text, graphics, audio, video, and animation to deliver and support key points. With the powerful features of presentation software such as Microsoft *PowerPoint*, you can create attractive and engaging presentations with ease.

Presentations are an important part of communication in business. Presentations are given to inform, to persuade, and/or to entertain. Visual aids generally make a speaker more effective in delivering his or her message. That is because the speaker is using two senses (hearing and sight) rather than just one. The probability of a person understanding and retaining something seen as well as heard is much greater than if it is just heard. For example, if you had never heard of a giraffe before, you would have a better idea of what a giraffe was if the speaker talked about a giraffe and showed pictures of one than if the speaker only talked about what a giraffe was.

Echo/Cultura/Getty Images

With presentation software, visuals (slides) can be created that can be projected on a large screen for a large audience to view or shown on a computer for a smaller audience. Webpages, audience handouts, and speaker notes can also be created using presentation software.

What Are the Key Features of Presentation Software?

PowerPoint shares many features with *Word* and other *Office* applications. *PowerPoint* uses the Ribbon interface that organizes commands in groups. It has a title bar, window control buttons, zoom controls, and a status bar similar to those you have seen in *Word*.

Features that help you to work with slides are shown in Figure 8-1. These features are described after the figure.

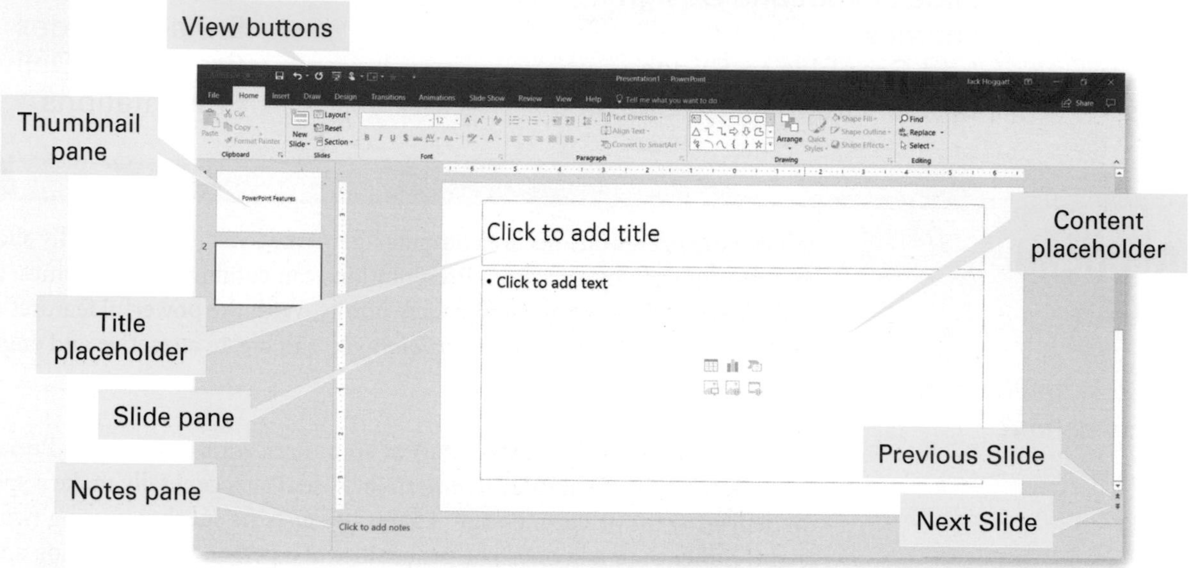

Figure 8-1 *PowerPoint* window in Normal View

- The **Thumbnail pane** displays small images of the slides that have been created. You can click a thumbnail to select a slide.

- The **Slide pane** displays the current slide.

- **Placeholders** are boxes with dotted borders that are part of most slide layouts. These boxes hold title and body text or objects such as charts, tables, and pictures.

- The **Notes pane** allows you to key notes about the slide.

- The **Previous Slide** and **Next Slide** buttons display the previous or next slide in the Slide pane.

- The **view buttons** allow you to view the slides in several different ways depending on what you are doing.

What Is a Design Theme?

PowerPoint comes with files containing design themes (see examples in Figures 8-2 and 8-3). A **design theme** provides a consistent, attractive look. All the person creating the presentation has to do is select the slide layout, key the information, and insert appropriate graphics. The fonts and font sizes, places for keying information, background design, and color schemes are preset for each design theme. Even though these themes are preset, they can be changed to better fit the needs of the user. Using design themes gives your presentations a professional appearance. Design themes are also known as templates.

Figure 8-2 Vapor Trail design theme (Title Slide)

Figure 8-3 Atlas design theme (Title Slide)

What Are Variants?

Each design theme comes in a variety of colors. Once the design theme is selected, the color schemes associated with the selected design theme are shown in the Variants group on the Design tab to the right of the Themes group. In the Variants group, you can also change fonts, effects, and background styles. Figures 8-4 and 8-5 show two variants of the Atlas design theme.

Figure 8-4 Atlas design theme with variant color and font change

Figure 8-5 Atlas design theme with color, font, and background change

Open *df variants pp* to view additional variant changes.

What Is a Slide Layout?

Layout refers to the way text and graphics are arranged on the slide. Presentation software allows the user to select a slide layout for each slide from a menu, as shown in Figure 8-6. Some of the more common layouts include:

- Title Slide
- Title and Content
- Section Header
- Two Content
- Comparison

- Title Only
- Blank
- Content with Caption
- Picture with Caption

Note in Figures 8-7 through 8-12 how different the same slide layout appears when shown in a different design theme.

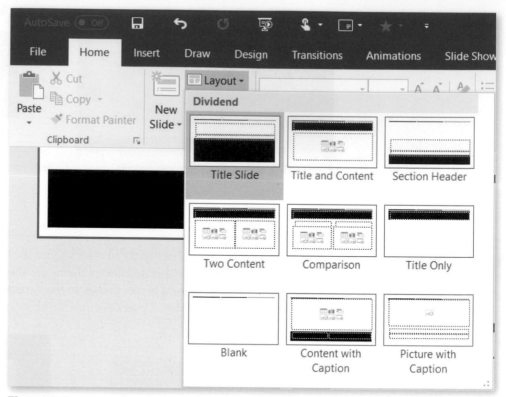

Figure 8-6 Slide layouts

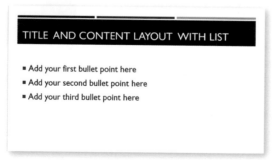

Figure 8-7 Title and Content layout— Dividend design theme

Figure 8-8 Title and Content layout— Frame design theme

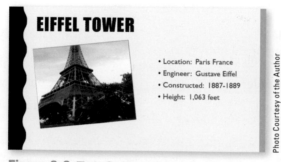

Figure 8-9 Two Content layout—Badge design theme

Figure 8-10 Two Content layout—Gallery design theme

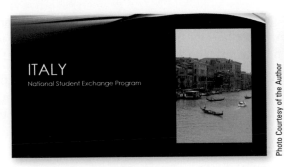

Figure 8-11 Picture with Caption layout—Vapor Trail design theme

Figure 8-12 Picture with Caption layout—Retrospect design theme

What Is Designer?

After selecting a design theme and entering content into your slides, such as text, pictures, or charts, if you have an *Office 365* subscription and an Internet connection you can use the *PowerPoint* **Designer** feature located on the Design tab. Designer automatically generates ideas for slide layout and design in the Design Ideas pane on the right-hand side of the screen as shown in Figure 8-13. Select a Design Idea by clicking it, and that idea will be previewed in the center pane. If you don't like it, click another Design Idea or change back to the original design by clicking the *Undo* button or by pressing *Ctrl + Z*. You can also use color variants with Designer, as shown in Figure 8-14.

★TIP To use Designer, you must have an *Office 365* subscription and have access to the Internet. The first time you use Designer you may also have to turn on intelligent services (enabling Microsoft Office applications to collect document content and search terms).

Figure 8-13 Title Slide layout—Atlas design theme with Design Ideas

Figure 8-14 Title Slide layout—Atlas design theme modified with Design Idea and color variant

Open **df designer pp** to view examples of other slide layout and design changes you can make using Designer.

What Options Are Available to View Slides?

View tab > Presentation Views > Select desired view

As you are working in presentation software, there are different view options available. Each view serves a distinct purpose for creating, editing, and viewing slides:

- **Normal View.** Normal View is used for creating and editing individual slides, viewing miniatures of slides that have already been created, and creating notes.

- **Outline View.** Outline View is used for creating and editing individual slides, outlining, and creating notes. This view shows the text on your slides in outline form.

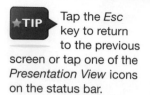
- **Notes Page View.** Notes Page View can be used to create and edit speaker notes. Use Notes Page View to see how the notes will look prior to printing to avoid unnecessary printing if changes need to be made.

- **Reading View.** Reading View presents each slide one at a time, filling up most of the screen. In Reading View, the status bar stays active, allowing you to see which slide number you are viewing and to view the previous slide or the next slide by clicking the arrows on the status bar.

- **Slide Sorter View.** Slide Sorter View shows all the slides in miniature. This is helpful for rearranging slides and for applying features to several slides at a time.

- **Slide Show.** You can click the *Slide Show* icon in the status bar to see how the slides will look during a presentation. This is helpful for rehearsing and presenting your slide show.

These views can be accessed through the View tab as shown in Figure 8-15 or by clicking the icons at the bottom of the screen on the status bar as shown in Figure 8-16. Each of the views are shown in Figures 8-17 through 8-21.

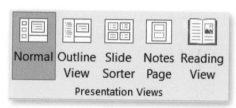

Figure 8-15 View tab—Presentation Views

Figure 8-16 View icons

Normal

Outline View

Figure 8-17 Normal View with Notes

Photo Courtesy of the Author

Figure 8-18 Outline View

Photo Courtesy of the Author

Reading
View

Switzerland

Figure 8-19 Reading View

Switzerland

Figure 8-20 Slide Show View

Slide
Sorter

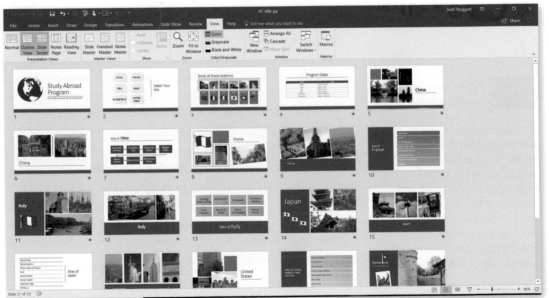

Figure 8-21 Slide Sorter View

LESSON 43 Slide Layout and Design Themes

- Navigate through an existing presentation
- Create a title slide
- Change the design theme
- Create a bulleted list slide

43A–48A

Warmup

Key each line twice.

alphabet 1 Jake Lopez may give a few more racquetball exhibitions in Dallas.

figures 2 Ray quickly found the total of 8.16, 9.43, and 10.25 to be 27.84.

speed 3 Bob's neighbor may dismantle the ancient shanty in the big field.

gwam 1' | 1 | 2 | 3 | 4 | 5 | 6 | 7 | 8 | 9 | 10 | 11 | 12 |

43B

View Presentation

1. Open *df 43b pp* in your presentation software program. The file opens in Normal View showing slide 1.
2. Click the *Slide Show* icon at the bottom of the screen (see Figure 8-22) and view the slide show, noting the different design themes and layout options. Tap the *Enter* key or the down arrow key, or click the mouse, to advance to the next slide.
3. When the black End of slide show screen appears, tap the *down arrow*, tap *Esc*, or click to return to Normal View. Then click the *Slide Sorter View* icon on the status bar. Next, click and hold on *slide 4* until an orange border appears on the slide and drag it to the space between slides 2 and 3. Notice how slide 4 becomes slide 3 and slide 3 becomes slide 4.
4. Click *Slide Sorter View* again. Notice how it returns you to Normal View.
5. Click the *Normal View* icon a couple of times. Note how it goes from Normal View to Outline View and then back to Normal View.
6. Click the *Slide Sorter View* icon. Switch the order of slides 20 and 21. Return to Normal View.
7. Scroll to the top of the Thumbnail pane and click *slide 1*. Notice the notes beneath each slide. Click the *Notes* icon on the status bar to show or hide the notes beneath the slide. Read each note and then use the down arrow key to go to the next slide.
8. Close the presentation without saving.

★TIP When running a slide show, you may see a small toolbar in the lower-left corner of the slide. This toolbar allows you to navigate to the next or previous slide and perform other actions on the current slide. If you do not see the toolbar, hover the mouse near the lower-left corner of the screen.

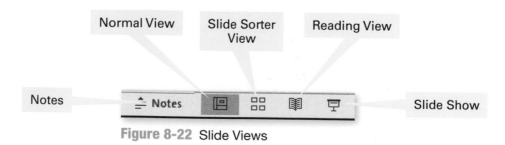

Figure 8-22 Slide Views

Create Title Slide

Design tab > Themes

★TIP If the AutoSave feature of *Office* is turned on, you will see Save a Copy instead of Save As on the File tab.

Title slide. A presentation should begin with a title slide. Include the presentation title, presenter name, and other relevant information.

1. Start a new presentation.
2. Select the *Quotable* design theme. The Title Slide layout appears on your screen. If you do not have the Quotable theme, open *df 43c quotable pp*.
3. Create the title slide as shown in Figure 8-23 by clicking in the *Click to add title* box and keying **Professional Presentations**, then clicking in the *Click to add subtitle* box and keying **Caden Parker - Multimedia Design Services**.
4. Increase the font size of the title of the presentation to 66 pt. and the name of the presenter and the company name to 28 pt.
5. Save as: *43c pp*.

Figure 8-23 Slide 1—Title slide

Create Title and Content Slide

Home tab > Slides > New Slide > Title and Content

Title and Content (bulleted lists). Use the Title and Content layout for lists to guide discussion and help the audience follow a speaker's ideas (see Figure 8-24). If too much information is placed on a single slide, the text becomes difficult to read. Keep the information on the slide brief—do not write complete sentences. Be concise.

When creating lists, be sure to:

- Focus on one main idea
- Add several supporting items
- Limit the number of lines on one slide to six
- Limit long wraparound lines of text

1. Continue with or open **43c pp** and insert three new slides with the Title and Content (bulleted list) layout after the slide you created in 43C.
2. Create the slides shown in Figures 8-25 through 8-27.
3. Save as: *43d pp*.

Title

Bulleted list

Figure 8-24 Title and Content layout

Figure 8-25 Slide 2—Bulleted list 1

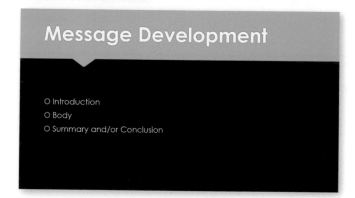

Figure 8-26 Slide 3—Bulleted list 2

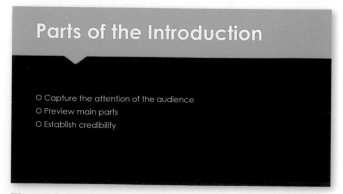

Figure 8-27 Slide 4—Bulleted list 3

Change Design Theme

Design tab > Themes >
Select desired theme

1. Continue with or open *43d pp*. On the *Design* tab, click the *More* button in the Themes group to display the Themes gallery. Hover the mouse over several designs (such as those shown in Figures 8-28 through 8-30), and see how the appearance of the different layouts changes with each template. Compose a brief paragraph explaining which of the designs you prefer and why.

2. Choose the *Crop* design theme.

3. **Save as:** *43e pp*.

Figure 8-28 Vapor Trail design theme

Figure 8-29 Wisp design theme

Figure 8-30 Crop design theme

LESSON 44 Add Graphics to Slides

- Describe how to use appropriate graphic images, lines, and shapes
- Insert, position, and size graphic images, photos, lines, and shapes
- Create and enhance slides with graphics

44B

Insert Graphics

Insert tab > Pictures [or Online Pictures] > [Browse to picture file] > Insert

Graphics. **Graphics** can enhance a message and help convey ideas. Graphic images might include Online Pictures available with *PowerPoint* or other sources such as the Internet (see Figure 8-31). Graphic images could also include photos or even original artwork scanned and converted to a digitized image. Internet content such as photography, clip art, video, and music is protected by copyright law, and you may need permission from the owner or author of the content.

Use graphics only when they are relevant to your topic and contribute to your presentation. Choose graphics that will not distract the audience. Images can often be used to add humor. Be creative, but use images in good taste. An image isn't necessary on every slide in a presentation.

1. Open *df 44b pp*. Insert an appropriate graphic from Online Pictures or from *df 44b graphic inserts* on slide 1 (see Figure 8-32) and slide 2 (see Figure 8-33). Size and position the graphic attractively.
2. Save as: *44b pp*.

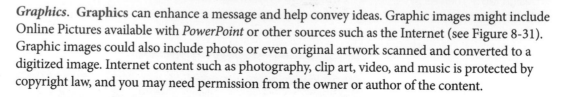

Figure 8-31 Sample graphics

Figure 8-32 Slide 1—Title slide with inserted graphic

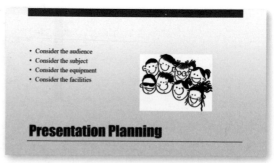

Figure 8-33 Slide 2—Bulleted list with picture

Photos. It has been said that a picture is worth a thousand words. Pictures help a speaker convey a clear message with fewer words. Photos can bring a slide to life and make the presentation more interesting. See Figure 8-34.

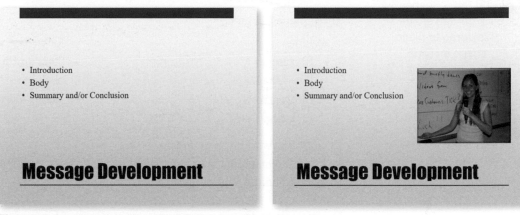

Figure 8-34 Slide 3 without photo and with photo

Complete these steps to copy, insert, size, and position a photo:

1. Continue with or open **44b pp**. Click *slide 3*, Message Development, in the Thumbnail pane.
2. Open **df 44c pp**.
3. Click to select *Photo 1* from **df 44c pp** and copy it (*Ctrl + C*).
4. Click *slide 3* of **44b pp** and paste the photo you copied (*Ctrl + V*).
5. Position Photo 1 as shown in Figure 8-34 by clicking the photo and dragging it to the desired location.
6. Size Photo 1 by using the sizing handles (sizing handles are illustrated in Figure 8-35). Click a sizing handle and drag inward to decrease the size or drag away from the center to increase the size.
7. Go back to **df 44c pp**, click *Photo 2*, and copy it.
8. Click *slide 4* in the Thumbnail pane of **44b pp** and insert the photo you copied.
9. Position and size Photo 2 attractively on slide 4.
10. Close **df 44c pp**.
11. **Save as:** **44c pp**.

★TIP To keep the proportions of an image the same as the original, press and hold Shift as you drag a sizing handle.

sizing handle

Click and drag handle in to make smaller

Click and drag handle out to make larger

Figure 8-35 Sizing handles

Insert tab > Shapes >
Click desired shape >
Click/drag to place
shape on slide

Shapes. Ready-made shapes can be inserted into your presentation. Some examples are shown in Figure 8-36. Arrow shapes can be used to focus an audience's attention on key points. Lines can be used to separate sections of a visual, to emphasize key words, or to connect elements. Boxes, too, can separate elements and provide a distinctive background for text.

These shapes include:

- Lines
- Rectangles
- Basic shapes
- Block arrows
- Equation shapes

- Flowchart shapes
- Stars and banners
- Callouts
- Action buttons

Insert tab > Shapes >
Rectangles: Rounded
Corners

1. Continue with or open *44c pp*.
2. Insert a rectangular shape with rounded corners big enough to cover the clip art image inserted on the title slide (see Figure 8-37).

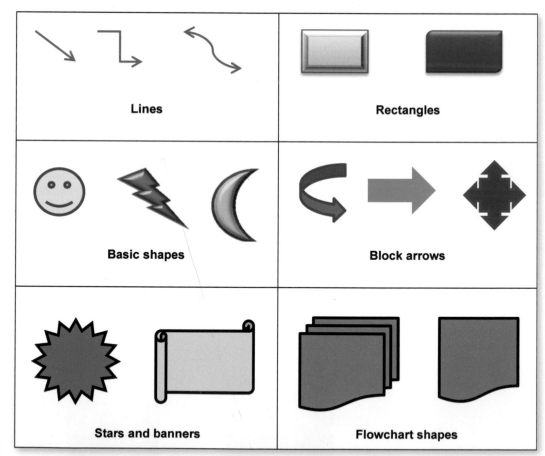

Figure 8-36 Sample shapes

Figure 8-37 Insert Shape

3. On the *Format* tab in the Shape Styles group, click the white icon with the red outline to change the red rectangle to a white rectangle (see Figure 8-38).

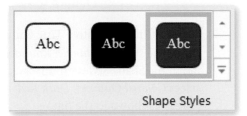

Figure 8-38 Change Shape color

4. If necessary, click the white rectangle to select it.
5. On the Format tab, in the Arrange group, click the drop-down arrow of *Send Backward* and then click *Send Backward.* The image should now appear on top of the white rectangle (see Figure 8-39).

Figure 8-39 Send Backward format feature

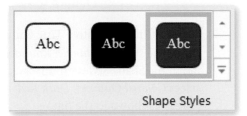

★TIP When you move a graphic on a slide, you may notice dotted guide lines that appear to show you when the image is centered vertically and/or horizontally.

6. Click and drag the sizing handles to resize the rectangle and image if needed.
7. If the Ruler isn't showing above the slide, click the *View* tab and click the square box before *Ruler* in the Show group to activate it.
8. Using the Ruler as a guide, center the white rectangle horizontally in the red square a little above vertical center. Then center the graphic image in the white rectangle by clicking and dragging it to the approximate center.
9. Save as: *44d pp*.

Create Slides with Shapes

1. Continue with or open **44d pp**. Study Figure 8-40 before completing the steps to create the slide.

Figure 8-40 Slide 5

2. Insert a fifth slide with a Title Only layout and key the title as shown in Figure 8-40.
3. Insert the shape *Rectangle: Rounded Corners*. Click the shape; on the Drawing Tools Format tab in the Shape Styles group, click the *More* button to display the Shape Styles gallery and select *Colored Outline - Dark Red, Accent 6* (end of the first row). Position the shape approximately as shown in the figure.
4. Right-click the rectangle and select *Size and Position* from the bottom of the context menu. In the pane at the right, set the Height at 2" and the Width at 3" (see Figure 8-41).

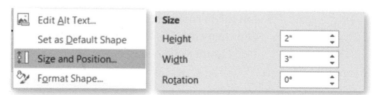

Figure 8-41 Sizing a shape

5. Create the second rectangle by copying and pasting the rectangle you just created. Position the new rectangle as shown in Figure 8-40. Change the Shape Style to *Subtle Effect – Dark Red, Accent 1*.
6. Insert a *Star: 5 Points* shape. Set the Height and Width of the star at .75". Change the Shape Style to *Light 1 Outline, Colored Fill - Dark Red, Accent 1*. Position the star as shown in the figure.
7. Copy, paste, and position a second star as shown. Change the Shape Style to *Light 1 Outline, Colored Fill - Black, Dark 1*.
8. Click the white rectangle. Use Arial font, 18 pt. bold for the text and key **Vary type sizes to show level of importance**. Click the red rectangle, change the font size to 14 pt. bold, and key the same text.
9. Save as: **44e pp**.

1. Continue with or open **44e pp**.
2. Insert two slides with Two Content layout after slide 5.
3. Create the slides as shown in Figures 8-42 and 8-43. Insert an appropriate image from Online Pictures or another appropriate source. Size and position the images appropriately.
4. Save as: **44f pp**.

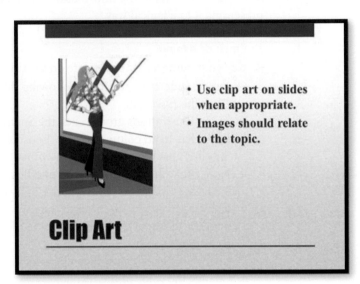

Figure 8-42 Slide 6

Figure 8-43 Slide 7

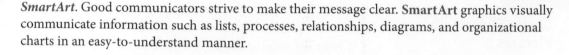

44G

Create Slides with SmartArt

Insert tab > Illustrations > SmartArt

SmartArt. Good communicators strive to make their message clear. **SmartArt** graphics visually communicate information such as lists, processes, relationships, diagrams, and organizational charts in an easy-to-understand manner.

Text can be made more interesting and appealing by using SmartArt graphics, which not only draw attention to the information but make it easier to understand by simplifying it and presenting it in a logical way.

1. Open *df 44g pp*.
2. Key your name and current date on the title slide.
3. Complete slide 2 (Figure 8-44) following these steps:
   a. Click the *Insert* tab.
   b. In the Illustrations group, click the *SmartArt* button.
   c. In the left-hand column of the Choose a SmartArt Graphic dialog, click *List* to display SmartArt list formats. Notice the other types of SmartArt formats that are available.
   d. Notice that the first icon in the middle column is selected, and that the name of the SmartArt Graphic is shown in the right-hand column (Basic Block List).
   e. Use the arrow keys to move to the icon that looks like the one shown on slide 2. The name of the SmartArt you are looking for is Vertical Box List (the second icon in the second row).
   f. Click *Vertical Box List*, then click *OK* to insert the graphic into slide 2.
   g. Change the color of the text boxes by clicking the *Change Colors* button on the Design tab.
   h. Under the Colorful heading, click the first set of colors (*Colorful – Accent Colors*).
   i. Key the three names of the Architectural Styles in the text boxes as shown in Figure 8-44 and in the left margin of this activity.
4. For slide 4 (Figure 8-45), use the *Basic Block List* SmartArt. Delete the fifth text box, and add the text to the remaining four boxes as shown. If necessary, resize by clicking one of the four corner handles on the SmartArt and dragging inward or outward. Move the SmartArt as needed by clicking the *SmartArt*, then clicking any border line and dragging the SmartArt to desired location.
5. For slide 9 (Figure 8-46), use *Vertical Box List*. For slide 11 (Figure 8-47), use *Vertical Chevron List*. Change the color of the SmartArt inserts to *Colorful – Accent Colors*, and add text as shown.
6. Use Slide Show View to view the presentation.
7. Save as: *44g pp*.

Slide 2

Queen Anne

Tudor Revival

Georgian Revival

Slide 4

Steep Gables

Multiple Stories

Intricate Woodwork

Many Porches

Slide 9

Steep Gable Roofs

Bargeboards in Gables

Tudor-Arched Openings

Slide 11

Double-Hung Windows

Dormers

Classical Cornice

Figure 8-44 Slide 2

Photo Courtesy of the Author

Figure 8-45 Slide 4

Photo Courtesy of the Author

Figure 8-46 Slide 9

Photo Courtesy of the Author

Figure 8-47 Slide 11

LESSON 45 Tables, Graphs, and Charts

- Create tables, graphics, and charts to convey information in a presentation
- Recognize which graph or chart to use for particular situations
- Describe the key elements of graphs and charts

45B

Create a Table

Home tab > Slides > New
Slide > Title and Content >
Click Insert Table icon

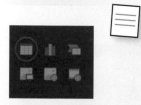

Figure 8-48 Slide 1

Tables. Tables can be used to organize information in presentations to compare and contrast facts or figures and to list data. Tables can be created in *PowerPoint*, or they can be created in *Word* or *Excel* and inserted into *PowerPoint*.

1. Open **df 45b Madison pp**.
2. Create a title slide using **FBLA Membership** for the main heading and **Committee Report for 2013–2017** for the secondary heading, as shown in Figure 8-48.
3. Create a second slide titled **FBLA Membership by Year** using the Title and Content layout. Click the *Insert Table* icon in the center of the slide. Create a table with 3 columns and 6 rows. Include the information shown in Figure 8-49, centering all columns.
4. Save as: **45b pp**.

Figure 8-49 Slide 2

45C

Learn Graph Elements

Graph Elements. Numeric information can be easier to understand when shown as a graph or chart rather than in text. The relationship between data sets or trends can be compared using bar graphs, line graphs, area graphs, or pie charts. Each type of graph or chart is best suited for a particular situation.

- **Bar and Column graph**—comparison of item quantities
- **Line graph**—quantity changes over time or distance
- **Pie chart**—parts of a whole

Elements common to most graphs are identified on the bar graph shown in Figure 8-50. They include:

- **X-axis**—the horizontal axis; usually for categories
- **Y-axis**—the vertical axis; usually for values
- **Scale**—numbers on the Y- or X-axis representing quantities
- **Tick marks**—coordinate marks on the graph to help guide the reader

- **Grids**—lines that extend from tick marks to make it easier to see data values
- **Labels**—names used to identity parts of the graph
- **Legend**—the key that identifies the shading, coloring, or patterns used for the information shown in the graph

To change the design of the graph, click on the graph to select it. This activates the Chart Tools context tab in the Ribbon. The Chart Styles under the Design tab allow you to select from a variety of preset designs. Notice the difference between the appearances of the two graphs shown in Figure 8-50 when different designs are applied.

Same slide with
Chart Style 4

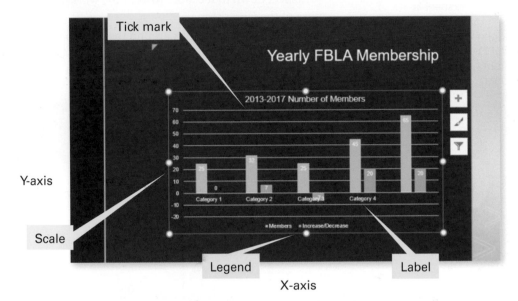

Figure 8-50 Slide 3—Graphic elements, Chart Style 1

45D

Create Bar and Column Graphs

Chart Tools > Design tab >
Chart Styles > Style 4

Bar and Column Graphs. Bar and Column graphs compare one or more sets of data that are plotted on the horizontal X-axis and the vertical Y-axis. One axis usually contains category information (such as years or months); the other axis usually contains measured quantity values (numbers).

Vertical bars (columns) and horizontal bars (bars) are easy to interpret; the baseline scale should begin at zero for consistent comparisons when several graphs are used. Special effects can be added, but a simple graph is effective for showing relationships.

1. Open **45b pp** and insert a new slide with *Title and Content* layout for slide 3. Create the column graph as shown earlier in Figure 8-50 Slide 3 with the instructions that follow.
2. In the center of the slide, click the *Insert Chart* icon to display the Insert Chart dialog box. The left-hand column of dialog box lists the types of charts that you can create—Column, Line, Pie, etc.

3. Select *Column* from the left-hand column if not already selected. At the top of the right-hand column, icons show the various types of column charts that can be created. An illustration of the type selected is shown beneath the selected icon.

4. Click several of the icons to see the different kinds of column styles available. Move the mouse pointer over the illustration to enlarge it.

5. Double-click *Clustered Column* (the first icon) to insert the chart on the slide and to bring up a worksheet where you can enter your data. Enter the data and headings as shown in Figure 8-51. The worksheet can be expanded by hovering the pointer on the bottom edge of the worksheet to bring up the double-headed arrow, then dragging the bottom edge of the worksheet down to see more rows of the worksheet. You can also use the scroll bars to see more of the worksheet.

6. Click and drag the blue box around the data so that only the data in columns B and C is included, as shown in Figure 8-51. The data in column D can be deleted or left in as only the data in the blue box is included in the chart.

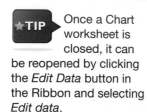 **★TIP** Once a Chart worksheet is closed, it can be reopened by clicking the *Edit Data* button in the Ribbon and selecting *Edit data*.

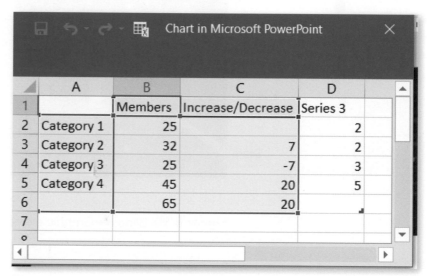

	A	B	C	D
1		Members	Increase/Decrease	Series 3
2	Category 1	25		2
3	Category 2	32	7	2
4	Category 3	25	-7	3
5	Category 4	45	20	5
6		65	20	
7				

Figure 8-51 Chart data and headings

7. Close the worksheet.

8. On slide 3, enter the Title **Yearly FBLA Membership** and Chart Title **2013–2017 Number of Members**.

9. With the chart selected, change the Chart Style to Style 4 by clicking the *Design* tab on the Ribbon and selecting *Style 4* in the Chart Styles group.

10. **Save as:** *45d pp*.

Create Line Graph

Home tab > New Slide >
Title and Content > Insert
Chart icon > Line

Line graphs. Line graphs display changes in quantities over time or distance. Usually the X-axis shows a particular period of time or distance. The Y-axis shows measurements of quantity at different times or distances. The baseline of the Y-axis should be zero to provide a consistent reference point when several graphs are used in a presentation.

When the numbers for the X-axis are keyed, lines appear connecting the values on the graph to reflect the changes in amounts. A grid with vertical lines helps the viewer interpret quantities. Several sets of data can be displayed by using lines in different colors. Various options are available for placing titles, legends, and labels on line graphs.

1. Open *45d pp* and create the line graph shown in Figure 8-52 for slide 4, using Title and Content layout. Review the instructions for creating the column graph in 45D if needed.

   - 2013   25
   - 2014   32
   - 2015   25
   - 2016   45
   - 2017   65

2. Change the Design Chart Style to Style 8.
3. Save as: *45e pp*.

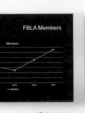

Same slide with Chart
Style 8

Figure 8-52 Slide 4—Line graph with Chart Style 8

Create Pie Chart

To create pie chart:

Home tab > New Slide >
Title and Content > Insert
Chart icon > Pie

To change chart style:

Chart Tools > Design tab >
Chart Styles > Choose style

Pie Charts. Pie charts are best used to display parts of a whole. They show clearly the proportional relationship of only one set of values. The set of values cannot include negative numbers. Without any numbers displayed, the chart shows only general relationships. In the examples shown below, the different colors used for the pie slices are identified in a legend. Colors used on the pie chart should provide adequate contrast between the slices. Consider also the color scheme of your entire presentation so that the pie chart will coordinate with other visuals.

Pie Chart 1

1. Open *45e pp*.
2. Create the pie chart shown in Figure 8-53 as slide 5. Use Design Chart Style 8 and Centered Data Labels using the path shown at the left.

Figure 8-53 Slide 5—Pie Chart, Style 8

To include numbers on pie slices:

Chart Tools > Design tab > Chart Layouts > Add Chart Element > Data Labels > Center

To change to Doughnut Pie:

Chart Tools > Design tab > Type > Change Chart Type > Pie > Doughnut

To change chart style:

Chart Tools > Design tab > Chart Styles > Choose style number

★TIP To display the Design and Format tabs for charts, be sure that the chart is selected.

Pie Chart 2

1. In Normal View, copy slide 5 in the Thumbnail pane and paste it beneath slide 5.
2. With slide 6 active, click the pie chart and change the chart to *Doughnut Pie* format with Chart *Style 8* (see Figure 8-54). Use the commands shown at the left.
3. Save as: *45f pp*.

Figure 8-54 Slide 6—Doughnut Pie chart

Use Designer to Enhance Slides

- Create picture slides with Designer
- Create text slides with Designer
- Create a slide show independently using Designer

46B

Enhance Slides with Designer

Designer is a powerful feature of *PowerPoint* that allows you to generate professional looking slides in seconds. It is as simple as selecting a design theme, selecting a slide layout, deciding on slide content, and choosing from the ideas created by Designer. When using Designer, options are automatically generated in the Design Ideas pane that you can select and use for your slides.

Complete the following steps to learn how to create professional-looking slides using Designer.

★TIP To use Designer, you must have an *Office 365* subscription and have access to the Internet. The first time you use Designer you may also have to turn on intelligent services (enabling Microsoft Office applications to collect document content and search terms).

1. Open a new file and select the *Atlas* design theme; if you don't have the Atlas theme, open **df 46b Atlas pp**.
2. Select *Title Only* slide layout.
3. Decide on slide content. For this slide the content will be the three pictures stored in **df 46b photos pp**. Open the file and copy the three photos by holding down the Shift key, clicking on each photo, and pressing *Ctrl + C*. Then paste the photos to the Title Only slide layout selected in step 2.
4. View the design ideas displayed in the Design Ideas pane as shown in Figure 8-55.

Design tab > Designer > Design Ideas

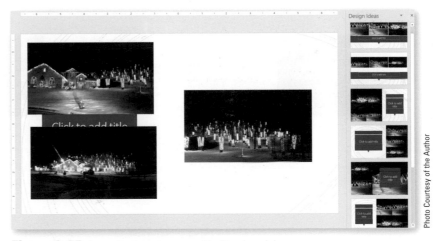

Figure 8-55 Inserted pictures with Design Ideas

5. Select one of the design ideas by clicking it to see it in the slide pane. If this isn't the image you want, click another design idea until you find the one you want to use. To return to the original slide, press *Ctrl + Z*.
6. When you decide on an option, finish the slide by keying **Happy Holidays** for the title. Increase the font size to 60 pt. and bold the text. Click and drag the text box to center it vertically in the red area of the slide (see Figure 8-56).

Figure 8-56 Design option

7. Create the slide shown in Figure 8-57 using the Title and Content layout.
8. Display Design Ideas for your slide and select the design idea you like best. Figure 8-58 shows one option.
9. **Save as:** *46b pp*.

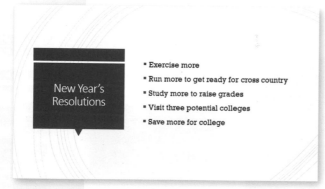

Figure 8-57 Atlas Title and Content layout

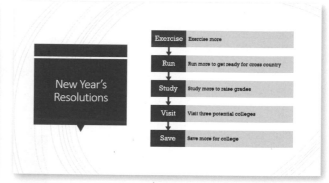

Figure 8-58 Design option

Practice Generating Slides with Designer

C More Travel Agency is promoting Steamboat Springs as a summer travel destination. They contacted your instructor and requested her to invite five students to create electronic slide presentations to be submitted to them. They will use one of those submitted to play during the day on one of their large office monitors to entice clients to consider Steamboat Springs for their summer vacation plans. They have provided a file of photos to be used in the presentation—*df 46c travel agency photos*.

Because your class just learned to use *PowerPoint* Designer, your instructor decided to have each student in the class create a presentation. She will select the five best to submit to the agency.

The only directions the agency provided were to keep the presentation to 15 slides or less, group like photos together, and be creative with your slide titles. Use your best judgment in all other aspects of creating the slide show.

Your instructor created an example of what the first and last slides of the presentation could look like to start you thinking about the presentation (see Figures 8-59 and 8-60).

Save as: *46c C More Travel Agency.*

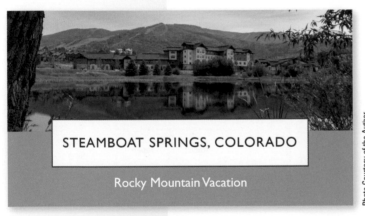

Figure 8-59 Title slide

Figure 8-60 Final slide

Lessons 47–48   Create and Deliver a Presentation

OUTCOMES
- Create a presentation
- Deliver a presentation

47–48B

Create a Presentation

Your teacher coordinates the Study Abroad Program. Over the summer she had Janet Logan, a student who participated in the program last year, develop a slide presentation for the next meeting of students interested in the program. Before leaving for college, Janet left a hard copy of the slides (see Figure 8-61) along with the electronic files containing the presentation *(df 47-48b pp)* and the photo file *(df 47-48b photos pp)*.

When your teacher reviewed the file yesterday, she found that the electronic file Janet gave her included only part of the presentation slides shown on the hard copy. Because she has no way of contacting the student, she would like you to recreate the slide presentation using the hard copy as your model.

If you have access to the Designer feature, you can select from the Design Ideas offered. However, the slides should include the same photos and text as the ones shown in Figure 8-61. (Note: You only have to create the odd-numbered slides. The smaller, even-numbered slides in the figure have been completed.) Save as *47-48b pp*.

Slide 1—Title Slide with graphic

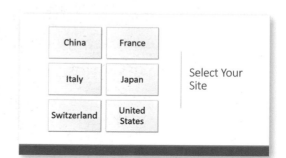

Slide 2

Slide 3—Title and Content

Slide 4

Slide 5—Title Only

Slide 6

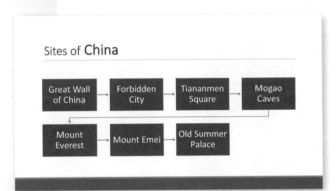

Slide 7—Title and Content

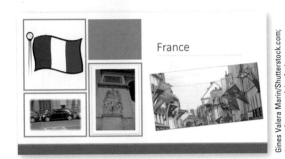

Slide 8

Slide 9—Title Only

Slide 10

Slide 11—Two Content

Slide 12

| Leaning Tower of Pisa | Grand Canal | Colosseum | St. Peter's Basilica |
| Trevi Fountain | Statue of David | Ponte Saint'Angelo | Roman Forum |

Sites of Italy

Slide 13—Title and Content

Japan

Slide 14

Gines Valera Marin/Shutterstock.com; Photos Courtesy of the Author

Japan

Slide 15—Title and Content

Photos Courtesy of the Author

Mount Fuji
Tokyo Skytree
Tokyo Imperial Palace
To-ji
Osaka Castel
Himeji Castle
Japanese Alps
Kofuku-ji

Sites of Japan

Slide 16

United States

Slide 17—Picture with Caption

Gines Valera Marin/Shutterstock.com; Photos Courtesy of the Author

United States

Slide 18

Photos Courtesy of the Author

Sites of United States in New York City

Statue of Liberty
Central Park
Times Square
Empire State Building
One World Trade Center
Ellis Island
Wall Street
Headquarters of the United Nations

Slide 19—Title and Content

Switzerland
STUDY ABROAD PROGRAM

Slide 20

Gines Valera Marin/Shutterstock.com; Photos Courtesy of the Author

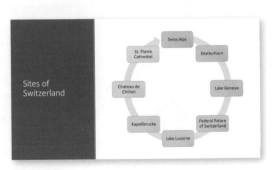

Slide 21—Title Only

Slide 22

Slide 23—Final slide, copy of slide 1

Figure 8-61 Slides for Lesson 47–48B presentation

47–48C

Create a Presentation

COLLABORATION

Because you did such a good job creating the slides for the travel agency in 47–48B, you and two of your classmates have been invited to give the presentation to students who are interested in participating in the Study Abroad Program next year.

Each of you will gather information about two of the countries that were included in the slide presentation:

- China
- Italy
- Switzerland
- France
- Japan
- United States (New York)

Use the Internet and/or reference books to learn more about the places listed in the presentation. Because students who attend the presentation could be living in one of these countries next year, be sure to include cultural differences among the countries in the presentation. You may need to create a few additional slides to cover these differences in your presentation. Add speaker notes to the presentation after finishing the slides by clicking beneath each slide in the *Click to add notes* box.

Divide the presentation among the group members so that each member has an equal part of the presentation. Then read the information on the next page about presentation delivery and study the evaluation form.

Deliver a Presentation

iStock.com/GlobalStock

Planning and preparing a presentation is only half the task of giving a good presentation. The other half is the delivery. Positive thinking is a must for a good presenter. Prepare and practice before the presentation. This will help you be confident that you can do a good job. Don't worry that the presentation will not be perfect. Set a goal of being a better speaker each time you present, not of being a perfect speaker each time. Practice these tips to improve your presentation skills.

- **Know your message**. Knowing the message well allows you to talk with the audience rather than read to them.
- **Look at the audience**. Make eye contact with one person briefly (for 2 to 3 seconds). Then move on to another person.
- **Look confident**. Stand erect and show that you want to communicate with the audience. Avoid unnecessary movement.
- **Let your personality come through**. Be natural; let the audience know who you are. Show your enthusiasm for the topic you are presenting.
- **Vary the volume and rate at which you speak**. Slow down to emphasize points. Speed up on points that you are sure your audience is familiar with. Don't be afraid to pause. It gives greater impact to your message and allows your audience time to think about what you have said.
- **Use gestures and facial expressions**. A smile, frown, or puzzled look, when appropriate, can help communicate your message. Make sure your gestures are natural.
- **Know how to use the visuals**. Practice using the visual aids you have chosen for the presentation. Glance briefly at each visual as you display it; then focus back on the audience.

Practice your presentation with your group members. After the first person presents his or her part, the other two members should offer suggestions on how the first presenter can improve. Suggestions should include comments based on the evaluation form (shown in Figure 8-62 and also provided in the file **df 47-48d eval form**). After providing feedback to the first presenter, the other group members should present their parts and receive feedback. Your instructor may ask you to present to the class.

	Excellent	Good	Need(s) Improvement	Comments
The introduction to the topic is				
The body of the presentation is				
The visual aids are				
The speaker's ability to use the visual aids is				
The speaker's enthusiasm is				
The speaker's eye contact is				
The speaker's gestures are				
The speaker's confidence is				
The speaker's vocal variation is				
The speaker's facial expressions are				
The closing is				

Figure 8-62 Presentation evaluation form

Assessment 3 — Presentations

**Slide Show
Assessment**

1. Start a new presentation.
2. Select the *Dividend* design theme. If the Dividend design theme isn't available, open **df a3 dividend**.
3. Create the slides shown in Figure 8-63.
4. Open **df a3 images** for the images to include on the slides.
5. **Save as:** *assessment3 pp*.

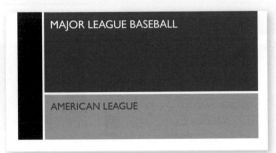

Slide 1—Title Slide

David W. Leindecker/Shutterstock.com

Slide 2—Blank

Aleks Melnik/Shutterstock.com

Slide 3—Title and Content

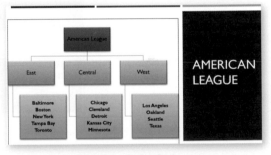

Slide 4—Title Only

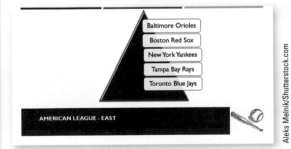

Aleks Melnik/Shutterstock.com

Slide 5—Content with Caption

Slide 6—Title and Content

Slide 7—Title and Content (Use data from slide 6 for graph worksheet.)

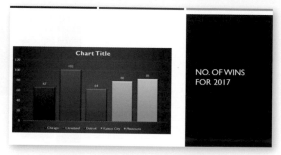

Slide 8—Title and Content

Slide 9—Title and Content

Slide 10—Title and Content

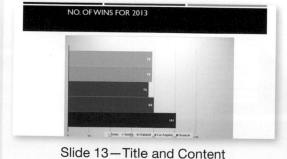

Slide 11—Title Only

Slide 12—Title and Content

Slide 13—Title and Content

Slide 14—Blank

Figure 8-63 Slides for Assessment 3 - Presentations

Skill Builder 7

A

Warmup

Key each line twice SS; then key a 1' timing on line 3. Determine *gwam*.

alphabet

1 Kevin can fix the unique jade owl as my big prize.

spacing

2 She will be able to see the dogs in a week or two.

easy

3 A box with the form is on the chair by the mantle.

gwam 1' | 1 | 2 | 3 | 4 | 5 | 6 | 7 | 8 | 9 | 10 |

B

Difficult-Reach Mastery

Key each line twice SS; DS between 2-line groups.

Adjacent keys

1 Her posh party on their new patio was a real bash.
2 Robert knew that we had to pool our points to win.
3 Juan will try to stop a fast break down the court.
4 Bart saw her buy a red suit at a new shop in town.

Long direct reaches

5 Betty is expected to excel in this next long race.
6 My fervor for gym events was once my unique trait.
7 Music as a unique force is no myth in any country.
8 Lynda has since found many facts we must now face.

Reaches with 3rd and 4th fingers

9 Nick said the cash price for gas was up last week.
10 My squad set a quarter quota to equal our request.
11 Zane played a zany tune that amazed the jazz band.
12 The poet will opt for a top spot in our port town.

C

Speed Check: Sentences

Key two 30'' timings on each line. Try to increase your keying speed the second time you key the line. Determine *gwam* for the faster timing of each line.

1 Yizel will take the test soon.
2 Nick will take his turn on Tuesday.
3 Felipe will apply for a job at the bank.
4 Marsha took both computers in to be repaired.
5 Their next ballgame will be in two or three weeks.
6 The repairs ended up costing much more than he thought.

gwam 30'' | 2 | 4 | 6 | 8 | 10 | 12 | 14 | 16 | 18 | 20 | 21 |

Technique: Response Patterns

1. Key each line twice SS; DS between 2-line groups.

2. Key a 1' timing on lines 10–12; determine *gwam* on each line.

One-hand words (Think and key by letter response.)

1 bear aware data gave edge states race great street

2 ink pin you hook milk moon only join union million

3 were you|up on|are in fact|my taxes are|star gazed

Balanced-hand words (Think and key by word response.)

4 oak box land sign make busy kept foal handle gowns

5 chair disown mantle right world theme towns theory

6 go to the|it may work|did he make|she is|he may go

One-hand sentences (Think and key by letter response.)

7 Jim gazed at a radar gadget we gave him in a case.

8 Dave saved a dazed polo pony as we sat on a knoll.

9 Carter gave him a minimum rate on state oil taxes.

Balanced-hand sentences (Think and key by word response.)

10 Rick may make them turn by the lake by their sign.

11 Jane may go to the city to work for the six firms.

12 Ken may make the girl pay for the keys to the bus.

gwam 1' | 1 | 2 | 3 | 4 | 5 | 6 | 7 | 8 | 9 | 10 |

Speed Building: Guided Writing

1. Key one 1' unguided and two 1' guided timings on each ¶.

2. Key two 2' unguided timings on ¶s 1–2 combined; determine *gwam*.

Quarter-Minute Checkpoints

gwam	1/4'	1/2'	3/4'	1'
20	5	10	15	20
24	6	12	18	24
28	7	14	21	28
32	8	16	24	32
36	9	18	27	36
40	10	20	30	40
44	11	22	33	44
48	12	24	36	48
52	13	26	39	52
56	14	28	42	56

LA all letters used

gwam 2'

	•	2	•	4	•	6	•	8	•	10	•	

```
        •     2     •     4     •     6     •     8     •     10    •
     Laura Ingalls Wilder is a beloved writer of books for        5
     12    •     14    •     16    •     18    •     20    •     22    •
children. Most of her books are based on her own experiences      11
     24    •     26    •     28    •     30    •     32    •     34    •
as a youth. Her first book was about her life in Wisconsin.       17
     36    •     38    •     40    •     42    •     44    •     46    •
From just reading such a book, children fantasize about what      23
     48    •     50    •     52    •     54    •     56    •     58
it would have been like to live during this interesting           29
        •     60    •     62    •
time period of our nation.                                        31

        •     2     •     4     •     6     •     8     •     10    •
     Besides writing about her own life and the lives of her      37
     12    •     14    •     16    •     18    •     20    •     22    •
family members, she also wrote about the life of her husband,     43
24    •     26    •     28    •     30    •     32    •     34    •     36
Almanzo, and his family. Her second book was about the early      49
        •     38    •     40    •     42    •     44    •     46    •     48
years of his life growing up on a farm near the Canadian bor-     55
        •     50    •     52    •     54    •     56    •     58    •     60
der in the state of New York. Through these exquisite books,      62
        •     62    •     64    •     66    •     68    •
this period of time in our history is preserved.                  66
```

gwam 2' | 1 | 2 | 3 | 4 | 5 | 6 |

Advanced Technology Skills 4 — Working in the Cloud

OUTCOMES

- Describe cloud computing
- Understand how to use online applications
- Discuss the importance of sharing documents online

Understanding Cloud Computing

Cloud computing is applications and services that are delivered to clients over the Internet. Some of these services are free, such as the web email services available from providers like Microsoft and Google. Other services are provided by producers who want to deliver a specific product to customers who will pay for the right to use the product, as shown in Figure AT4-1.

Figure AT4-1 Producers make services available through the cloud to clients

TierneyMJ/Shutterstock.com

Suppose, for example, a software designer has developed a new database program aimed specifically at managing and manipulating health records. The designer could distribute the program using physical means—copying to DVDs that are packaged in boxes and then shipped to various retail outlets—or the designer could save time and money by making the program available via the cloud to clients who want to use the program in their own companies. Clearly, there are advantages to distributing the service by Internet.

Cloud computing is sometimes discussed in terms of **private clouds** and the **public cloud**. Services offered to everyone over the Internet are said to use the public cloud. If the services are offered only within one large company or organization, using the company network and behind the company firewall, they are in a private cloud.

Cloud computing has advantages for both producers and clients.

- Costs are often reduced for the producer. The producer needs a server to connect to the cloud and storage to contain the data generated by the program, electricity to keep everything running, and premises for the hardware. This can be far more cost-effective than running a software replicating and distribution business.

- Programs can be easily updated. The producer updates on the server, and every client is automatically updated at the same time.

- Costs can also be reduced for clients. Rather than having to buy or license numerous copies of an application, clients often pay a subscription fee to use the cloud application, or even pay according to how much time they spend using it. Companies may also save because they do not have to develop specialized software themselves; they can instead purchase it from a service that bears all the costs of development.

- Cloud computing can be far more flexible than traditional approaches to providing hardware and software to employees. If a business upturn leads to hiring of new employees who need applications immediately, providing applications through the cloud can be faster than having to buy new copies of software and then get that software installed.

- Companies that are using cloud computing no longer have to have space for their own servers. Instead, storage is provided off-site on the servers of the provider that is offering the specific application.

- Employees of client companies can have access to their applications even if they are not on company premises, a great convenience for employees who travel or telecommute.

- Organizations may no longer need the same amount of IT support they require when they have all their network and storage onsite.

In an organization that follows the principles of information systems, cloud computing can be an important way to control costs while keeping communications technology at a high level.

Cloud computing can have some drawbacks, however.

Cloud computing services store client data in multiple redundant servers

- When a program is in the public cloud, data is stored by the service provider, and the client has no control over the storage. Clients may not even know where the data is being stored. The client may risk losing data if something happens to the service provider's hardware. For this reason, a public cloud service provider often builds in a number of **redundant** systems, so that all client data can be copied to one or more backup systems.

- Clients that are using cloud services may find that their operations are tied to the health of the service provider. If that company has financial woes or fails, what happens to the client data being stored? It is sometimes not easy to move data from one cloud service provider to another.

- Clients have no way to oversee the policies of the service provider, such as how often data is backed up and what disaster recovery procedures are in place.

- Depending on the type of Internet connection, applications may run more slowly than they do on a local computer. And if the Internet connection is lost, users have no access to online resources.

- Security can also be an issue, especially for companies that generate sensitive information. Many companies will not want to use services that result in their data being stored somewhere else.

- Another aspect to the security issue is the possibility of an unauthorized user gaining access to secure data, which may be especially easy because users can log in from anywhere. As you have already learned in this unit, there are ways to control access using passwords and other forms of authentication, and these methods need to be rigorously enforced to keep resources secure.

A savvy computer user will consider both the risks and rewards of working in the cloud before choosing this kind of information technology.

1. What do you think is the chief advantage of working with cloud services?
2. If you were a cloud service provider, why would it be critical to have redundant data storage systems?

Working with Online Applications

Online applications (or online apps) provide a way to accomplish specific tasks on the Internet, such as finding directions, browsing multimedia content, and sending email. Online versions of office applications allow you to create office documents such as presentations and spreadsheets and handle tasks and appointments.

Online apps are viewed from within your web browser. The software for the application is stored on the host server rather than on your local computer, and the data you input to the online app is also sent to the server for processing and storage.

Some online apps are available through subscription, such as the Microsoft *Office 365* applications that include free storage in the cloud on Microsoft *OneDrive*. Microsoft also offers a free *Office Online* app that allows you to open *Office* files in your web browser. Other online apps, such as Google Apps, are designed to be installed on a corporate domain, allowing all company employees to access apps such as Google Docs, Google Calendar, and other communications apps.

Microsoft *OneDrive* gives easy access to your *Word, Excel, PowerPoint,* and *OneNote* files. You can organize, manipulate, and search for files on *OneDrive* using *File Explorer* (see Figure AT4-2). Google Drive is another online option that offers access to online word processing (*Docs*), spreadsheet (*Sheets*), and presentation (*Slides*) apps.

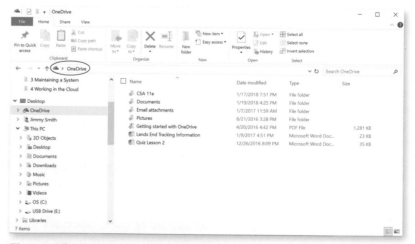

Figure AT4-2 Access Microsoft *OneDrive* files through *File Explorer*

The *Office Online* versions of *Word, Excel, PowerPoint,* and *OneNote* resemble their *Office 365* versions, with the familiar Ribbon interface, as shown in Figure AT4-3. Each app has only a few tabs, in comparison with the *Office 365* version, but the commands available on these tabs allow users to perform tasks such as formatting and styling text, inserting pictures and clip art (and SmartArt, in *PowerPoint*), performing calculations and creating charts in *Excel*, and changing views in all applications.

Figure AT4-3 *Office Online* version of Microsoft *Word*

You have the option to open an *Office Online* document on your local computer in the *Office 365* version of the application. Opening an online file in your local *Office* application allows you to work on it at times you do not have an Internet connection, such as when you are traveling. Changes that you save update the online version so that it is always the most recent version.

NOTE In *Office 365*, if AutoSave is enabled, your files are automatically and continuously saved to *OneDrive*.

If you do not want to create a document in *OneDrive* but want an existing document to be stored in *OneDrive*, you can click *Save As* in the *File* tab, then select *OneDrive* as the location to store your file (see Figure AT4-4). Once you upload the file, you can view it and work with it in *OneDrive* just as if you were editing it on your local computer.

Save As-select *OneDrive*

File information is entered as with *File Explorer*

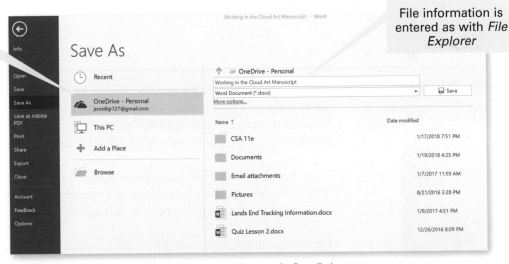

Figure AT4-4 Saving a document on Microsoft *OneDrive*

As for working in the cloud in general, working with online applications has both advantages and disadvantages. On the plus side:

- You can access your files from anywhere, on any computer, at any time. All you require is a computer with an Internet connection.

- Applications such as the *Office* suite no longer have to be bought and stored on every computer, a savings in software costs.

- Updates are handled by the service provider, so users can be assured they are always working with the most up-to-date version.

On the minus side:

- Experienced users may be more likely to prefer the desktop versions of familiar applications, which can have more features and options.

- Online applications require an Internet connection. Using online apps may be a problem in regions where online access is not available or not dependable.

- Even when a good Internet connection is available, applications may run more slowly over the Internet than they do on a local desktop.

- Users cannot be completely certain that their data, stored by the online application service, is completely secure.

1. When you create and save a document in an online application, where is that document stored?

2. Why do you think a sales representative might choose to use online applications rather than desktop applications?

3. What do you think is the most important drawback to using online applications exclusively, rather than desktop applications?

Sharing Information Online

Evgeniya Uvarova/Shutterstock.com

Sharing information online allows team members to work anywhere

One of the most important reasons to work with a cloud platform such as the Microsoft *One-Drive* is the ease with which you can share files with others. Today, it is not unusual for members of a team to be working in different offices, different cities, or even different countries. Online applications allow team members to access documents anytime and anywhere.

Team members can create documents online or easily upload existing files for others to review. When all team members have access to a shared folder accessed by browser, the process of working together on a project can be fast and efficient.

Other advantages to sharing information online include the following:

- Multiple users can work on a single document at the same time, and as changes are made to the document, everyone's version of it updates.

- Working with the most up-to-date version of a document allows team members to identify and correct mistakes in a timely fashion. Mistakes often cost money, and minimizing them can help to keep a project not only on schedule but on budget.

- Sharing information online can be a green alternative. Rather than printing multiple drafts of a report for all team members to view and edit, the document can be edited online, with the input of all team members resolved to create the final report.

Sharing a document online usually requires the user to change the permission status for a file or folder. You may have the option of sharing with selected persons or with everyone to make the file or folder public. A good example of a folder you might want to make public in this way would be a photo album you want to share widely. If you are sharing a folder that may contain sensitive information, you would limit access to the fewest number of people possible. You may also have the option of specifying whether a sharer can simply view a file or can edit files and add or delete files from a folder.

Once you have selected the people to share files or folders, you can, if desired, send them a notification to let them know they have access to the folder. Once you have designated users to share your folder, they can see documents you are sharing with them and are able to open those documents and view or edit them.

1. What factors do you need to consider when building a team for a project that might use online applications and shared files?
2. Who do you think should decide which team members get access to which documents online?
3. What disadvantages do you see to sharing information online with coworkers or project team members?

Before You Move On

Use the following words to complete the sentences:

bar and column graphs	design theme	Designer
dress	electronic presentations	graphics
inform	layout	Normal
sizing handles	Slide Show	SmartArt
speak	Thumbnail pane	title slide

1. _____ are computer-generated visual aids (usually slide shows) used to help communicate information. Application Guide

2. Presentations are given to _____, to persuade, and/or to entertain. Application Guide

3. The _____ displays small images of the slides that have been created. Application Guide

4. A _____ provides a consistent, attractive look. Application Guide

5. _____ refers to the way text and graphics are arranged on the slide. Application Guide

6. _____ View is used for creating and editing individual slides, viewing miniatures of slides that have already been created, and creating notes. Application Guide

7. _____ View is used to see how the slides will look during a presentation. Application Guide

8. A presentation should begin with a _____. LO 43C

9. _____ can enhance a message and help convey ideas. LO 44B

10. _____ graphics visually communicate information such as lists, processes, relationships, diagrams, and organizational charts. LO 44G

11. _____ compare one or more sets of data that are plotted on the horizontal X-axis and the vertical Y-axis. LO 45D

12. _____ is a powerful feature of *PowerPoint* that allows you to generate professional-looking slides in seconds. LO 46B

13. Use the _____ to make images smaller or large. LO 44C

14. A speaker should _____ professionally. LO 44F

15. A speaker should _____ clearly. LO 44F

Lesson 49   Workbook and Worksheet Basics
Lesson 50   Format and Print Worksheets
Lesson 51   Using Formulas and Functions
Lesson 52   Editing Worksheets

Lesson 53   Enhancing Worksheet Skills
Lesson 54   Worksheets with Charts
Assessment 4   Worksheets

Application Guide

What Is Spreadsheet Software?

Spreadsheet software is a computer program used to record, report, and analyze information, especially information that relates to numbers. Many different types of employees in business, education, and government use spreadsheet software in a variety of ways. Spreadsheet software is especially useful when you need to make repetitive calculations accurately, quickly, and easily. It works equally well with simple and complex calculations.

Numbers can be added, subtracted, multiplied, and divided in a worksheet, and formulas are used to perform calculations quickly and accurately. Additionally, charts can be constructed to present the worksheet information graphically.

One big advantage of spreadsheet software is that when a number is changed, all related "answers" are automatically recalculated. For example, you can use spreadsheet software to quickly calculate how money saved today will grow at various interest rates over various periods of time by changing the values for the rate and time.

Microsoft *Excel* is a popular spreadsheet application that is part of the Microsoft *Office* suite of programs. Using *Excel* is fun once you master how to use rows, columns, and cells. In this chapter you will learn how to:

- Work with worksheets
- Edit worksheets
- Format worksheets
- Use formulas and functions
- Create charts

iStock.com/Jacob Wackerhausen

What Are Worksheets and Workbooks?

Worksheet. A **worksheet** is one spreadsheet. Worksheets contain information organized in rows and columns.

Workbook. A **workbook** is a file that contains one or more worksheets, usually related. For example, the workbook shown in Figure 9-1 is a file containing the monthly payroll. Notice the file name (*Monthly Payroll*) and the sheet tabs (*January, February, March, and April*). The worksheet for the month of March is opened and partially displayed in the figure. When spreadsheet software is opened, a worksheet will appear on the screen. Other worksheets in the workbook appear as **sheet tabs** at the bottom of the screen (see Figure 9-1). Additional worksheets can be inserted into the workbook as needed.

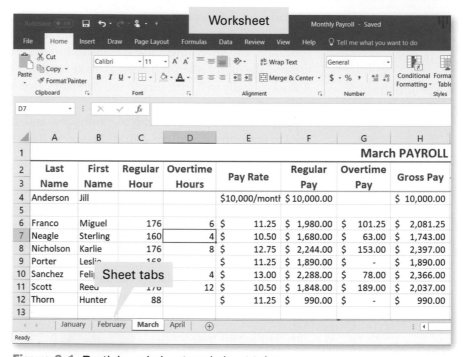

Figure 9-1 Partial worksheet and sheet tabs

What Are the Basic Parts of a Worksheet?

Cells. A worksheet contains **cells** where information is keyed. The cells are arranged in rows and columns (see Figure 9-2).

Columns. **Columns** run vertically in a worksheet. Each column has a heading (letters from A to Z, AA to AZ, etc.) running left to right across the worksheet (see Figure 9-2).

Rows. **Rows** run horizontally in a worksheet. Each row has a heading (a number) running up and down the left side of the worksheet (see Figure 9-2).

The Excel Worksheet Window

The *Excel* worksheet window has many features that you have used in *Word* and *PowerPoint* windows. These include:

- **Title bar**—Displays the worksheet file name
- **Quick Access toolbar**—Used to access frequently used commands
- **File tab**—Used to access *Office* file commands
- **Ribbon**—Displays tools and commands grouped by category
- **Ribbon tabs**—Used to access various ribbons
- **Zoom**—Controls used to zoom in and out
- **View buttons**—Used to switch between views
- **Status bar**—Displays information about the active document
- **Scroll bars**—Used to move the screen up and down or left and right

The *Excel* worksheet window also has features that are used only with spreadsheet software. They are illustrated in Figure 9-2. Notice that the file is for Monthly Sales. The active worksheet is for the month of January. Worksheets for each month of the year have been set up and can be activated by clicking on the worksheet tab of the month you want to activate.

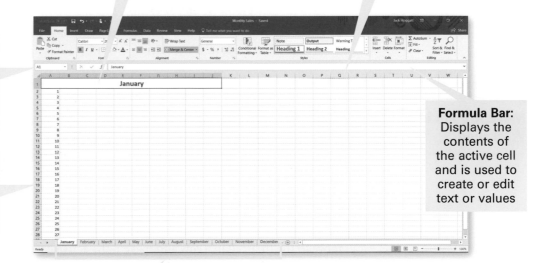

Active cell: Highlighted with a thick border, stores information that is keyed while it is active

Columns: Identified by **letters** that run horizontally

Name Box: Identifies the active cell(s) by a letter(s) and number(s)

Formula Bar: Displays the contents of the active cell and is used to create or edit text or values

Rows: Identified by **numbers** that run vertically

Worksheet tabs: Identify the active worksheet and the number or names of the worksheets in the workbook

Figure 9-2 Worksheet elements

LESSON 49   Workbook and Worksheet Basics

OUTCOMES

- Learn about workbooks, worksheets, and worksheet parts
- Open and close *Excel*; open, save, and close a workbook
- Move around in a worksheet
- Enter and align labels and values
- View and print gridlines and headings

49A

Workbooks, Worksheets, and Worksheet Parts

The Application Guide at the beginning of this chapter provides information on workbooks, worksheets, and worksheet parts. Review the Guide and then complete the following activity.

1. Start *Word*. Open the document **df 49a worksheet**. Answer the questions and complete the activity as directed, referring to Figure 9-2 as needed.

2. Save the document as **49a worksheet** and close *Word*.

49B

Open and Close Excel and Open and Save a Workbook

Excel spreadsheet software is opened and closed in the same manner that you opened and closed *Word* and *PowerPoint* software in preceding chapters. Likewise, new and existing workbooks are opened, saved, and closed in the same way as word processing documents and presentation slide shows.

1. Start *Excel*. Click *Blank workbook*. A new workbook opens with cell A1 (the cell address) active in the Sheet1 worksheet. Key your first name in cell A1.

2. Save the workbook as **49b first** and close it.

3. Open the workbook **df 49b last** and key your last name in cell A1. Save the worksheet as **49b last** and close it. Close *Excel*.

49C

Move Around in a Worksheet

When you enter information in a worksheet, it is placed in the active cell. The **active cell** is the current location of the insertion point. Thus, the active cell changes when you move the insertion point from cell to cell. You can identify the active cell by looking at its border. The active cell is the cell with the thick border around it. (See Figure 9-3)

To activate (select) a cell with the mouse, move the pointer to the desired cell and click. You also can use the arrow keys and the Tab and Enter keys to activate a different cell.

To move from one cell to another quickly, you can use keyboard shortcuts. For example, to move to the first cell in a row and make it the active cell, tap *Home*. To move to cell A1, press *Ctrl + Home*. To move the active cell down one page, tap *Page Down* (Pg Dn).

In this activity, you will practice moving around a worksheet using the mouse and the keyboard and changing column width by dragging.

1. Open a new workbook. Click cell *C4* to select it. Cell C4 is now the active cell; key your first name in the cell. Note that the active cell address appears in the Name Box as shown in Figure 9-3.

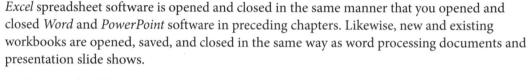

Figure 9-3 The active cell is shown in the Name Box

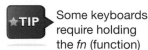
2. Use the mouse to make cell *A12* active and key your first name. Use the mouse to make cell *B24* active and key your first name. You may need to use the scroll bars to display the area you want.

3. Use the arrow keys to make cell *D11* active and key your first name. Use the arrow keys to make cell *F30* active and key your first name. Use the arrow keys to make cell *P30* active and key your first name.

4. Use *Page Down* and arrow keys to make *J100* active; key your last name. Use *Page Up* and arrow keys to make *L40* active and key your last name.

5. Tap the *F5* key (found in the row of function keys at the top of the keyboard) to open the Go To dialog box. Key **H100** in the Reference box. Click *OK*. H100 should be the active cell; key your last name.

6. Tap *Ctrl + Home* to make cell *A1* active and key your last name. Tap the *Tab* key once to make cell *B1* active; key your last name. Tap the *Enter* key to make cell *A2* active; key your last name.

7. Increase the width of column A by moving the cursor over the line between column A and column B. Once the cursor is placed over the line, it will change to a line with arrows pointing right and left (see Figure 9-4).

   Click and drag to the right until the Width box shows 10.00 as in Figure 9-4. If your entire last name isn't showing, click and drag until it does. Repeat to increase the width of column B to 10.00 or to show your last name.

8. Save the worksheet as *49c cells* and close it.

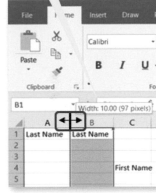

Figure 9-4 Column width

49D

Enter and Align Labels and Values

Data keyed into a cell is automatically assigned a label or value status. When only numbers are keyed into a cell, the value status is assigned and the data is right-aligned (see Figure 9-5). When letters and/or symbols (with or without numbers) are keyed into a cell, the label status is assigned and the data is left-aligned.

To record entered data, tap *Tab* to move the active cell to the right or *Enter* to move the active cell to the cell beneath the one where you just entered the data. You also can move the active cell to another cell with the arrow keys, click the *Enter* icon on the Formula Bar, or move the active cell to another cell with the arrow keys to record the data. The Enter icon is shown in Figure 9-5. If you want to change the alignment that was automatically assigned to labels and values, use the desired alignment option in the Alignment group on the Home tab.

If you make a mistake when entering data, use the *Delete* or *Backspace* key to remove text or numbers. If you find an error after you have left a cell, select the *cell* that has the error. Key the correct data and tap *Tab* or *Enter*. The new data you key will replace the error.

You might begin keying data and then want to stop, perhaps because you realize you are in the wrong cell. To cancel data entry, tap the *Esc* key before tapping *Tab* or *Enter*. You also can click the *Cancel* icon on the Formula Bar to cancel data entry. The Cancel icon also is shown in Figure 9-5.

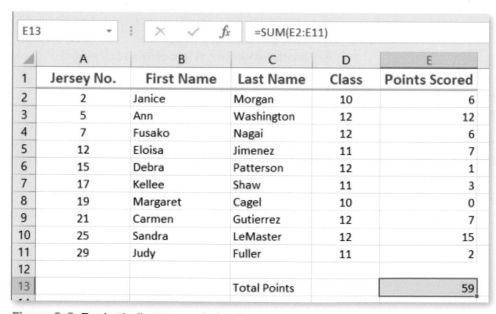

Figure 9-5 Label and value alignment

1. Study Figure 9-6.

Figure 9-6 Basketball stats worksheet

2. Open **df 49d stats**.

3. The headings for the worksheet shown in Figure 9-6 have been entered. The E13 cell has been shaded a light green and has a formula entered in it that will calculate the Total Points scored. You will learn in future lessons how to enter formulas.

4. Key **6** for Janice Morgan's points scored in E2; notice that the Total Points still shows 0 even though you have keyed Janice's points. Tap *Enter*, press the down arrow, or click in cell *E3* to move the active cell to *E3*; notice the Total Points cell now displays 6, or the total points

entered in the column. Key the remainder of the Points Scored column, observing how the Total Points amount changes each time you tap the *Enter* key or the down arrow key or move to another cell. If you entered the points correctly, you should have 59 total points.

5. Next, change the heading style to *Heading 2*. Press *Ctrl + Home* to position the active cell in A1. Hold down the *Shift* key and use the right arrow key to highlight the five column headings. Then click the *Cell Styles* button and click *Heading 2* as shown in Figure 9-7. The headings change to that style.

Home tab > Styles > Cell Styles > Heading 2

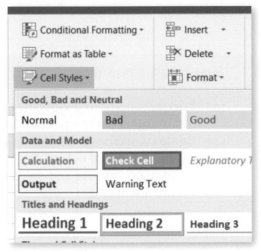

Figure 9-7 Worksheet heading cell styles

6. Key the jersey numbers shown in Figure 9-6 in the Jersey No. column (column A). Change to center alignment by selecting cells *A1* through *A11* and then clicking the *Center* button in the Alignment group on the Home tab as shown in Figure 9-8.

Figure 9-8 Alignment group

7. Enter the remaining data shown in Figure 9-6 into the table. Center the Class column.

8. **Save as:** *49d stats*.

★TIP To center an entire column, hover over the column letter to display a down arrow pointer and then click to select the whole column. Then click the *Center* button in the Alignment group of the Home tab.

NOTE **In addition to the horizontal alignment commands (Left, Center, and Right), there are vertical alignment commands (Top Align, Middle Align, and Bottom Align) that you will use in a later activity.**

49E

View and Print Gridlines and Row and Column Headings

Gridlines (cell borders) and headings (row numbers and column letters) may or may not be viewed on the monitor or printed on a worksheet. The default settings are to display (view) the headings on the monitor but not print them. Therefore, if you want to print the gridlines or headings, you will need to check the appropriate Print checkboxes shown in Figure 9-9. If you do not want to view the gridlines or headings on the monitor, you will need to deselect the appropriate View checkbox shown in Figure 9-9.

1. If needed, open **49d stats** from the previous activity.
2. Follow the path at the left to access the Sheet Options group. Set the sheet options to view and print the gridlines, but do not view or print the headings.
3. Save the workbook as **49e stats** and close it.

Figure 9-9 Gridlines and headings

LESSON 50   Format and Print Worksheets

OUTCOMES

- Preview and print a worksheet
- Set margins and page orientation
- Center worksheets horizontally and vertically
- Select a range of cells
- Format worksheets and cell content
- Create a worksheet

50A

Preview and Print a Worksheet

Worksheets can be previewed so you can see how the worksheet will look when printed. As shown in Figure 9-10, you can display a page of a worksheet by using the Print Preview feature that displays when the Print screen is accessed via the Print Preview path at the left. If you want to enlarge the worksheet, click the *Zoom to Page* icon at the lower-right corner. If you want to display the margins, click the *Show Margins* icon at the lower-right corner. After previewing the worksheet, you can return to it to make additional changes, or, if no changes are needed, you can print it using the Print path at the left.

Print Preview
File tab > Print

Print
File tab > Print > Print

⭐**TIP** You can also use the shortcut keys *Ctrl + P* to access Print Preview and Print.

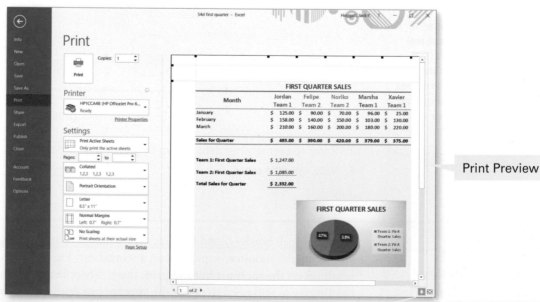

Figure 9-10 Print Preview with Show Margins and Zoom to Page activated

1. Open the workbook *df 50a worksheet*.
2. Click the *File* tab and then *Print* in the left column to preview it.
3. An error was made in recording the quiz scores. Sue had a 70 on Quiz 1. Return to the worksheet and change cell B7 to **70** to correct this error. Notice how the total points for Sue automatically changes from 580 to 550 and the MIN changes from 89 to 70.
4. Print the worksheet.
5. Save the workbook as *50a worksheet* and close it.

50B

Margins and Page Orientation

Margins
Page Layout tab > Page Setup > Margins

Page Orientation
Page Layout tab > Page Setup > Orientation

The Margins feature can be used to change the amount of white space between the top, bottom, left, and right edges of the worksheet. The default setting is typically 0.7" for the left and right margins and 0.75" for the top and bottom margins. Other frequently used margins can be selected, or custom margins can be set. See Figure 9-11 for the Page Setup dialog box for margins that displays when Custom Margins is selected. The path at the left can be used to change margins.

As in *Word*, the default page orientation for *Excel* is Portrait, which prints vertically on 8.5" × 11" paper. Landscape orientation can be selected and will print vertically on 11" × 8.5" paper. The path at the left is used to set page orientation. See Figure 9-12.

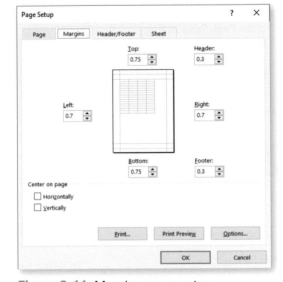

Figure 9-11 Margins page setup

1. Open the workbook *df 50a worksheet*.
2. Change page orientation to *Landscape*.
3. Change the margins to 2" by selecting *Custom Margins* from the Margins menu to open the Page Setup dialog box. Click *Margins* if it has not already been selected. Key **2** in the top, bottom, left, and right margin boxes.
4. Preview the worksheet and then print it without making additional changes.
5. Save the workbook as *50b worksheet*, but do not close it.

Figure 9-12 Change page orientation

Center Worksheets

Page Layout tab > Page
Setup > Margins >
Custom Margins

> **NOTE** You can click
> the *Print*
> *Preview* button at the bottom
> of the Page Setup dialog
> box to go directly to the
> same print preview that is
> displayed when you select
> *Print* on the File tab.

Worksheets, like tables in *Word*, can be centered horizontally and/or vertically to make them more attractive when printed.

1. If needed, open **50b worksheet**.
2. Change margins to *Normal* and page orientation to *Portrait*.
3. Follow the path at the left to access the Page Setup dialog box and then check *Horizontally* (if necessary) and *Vertically* under Center on page (see Figure 9-11) and click *OK*.
4. Preview the worksheet.
5. Save the workbook as **50c worksheet** and close it.

Select a Range of Cells

A range of cells may be selected to perform an operation (move, cut, copy, clear, format, print, etc.) on more than one cell at a time. A **range** is identified by the cell in the upper-left corner and the cell in the lower-right corner, usually separated by a colon. For example, B4:C10 is the range of cells from cell B4 through C10.

To select a range of cells, highlight the cell in the upper-left corner of the range. Hold down the left mouse button, and drag to the cell at the lower-right corner of the range. Once the range has been selected, release the mouse button and perform the desired operation(s) to format cell content in much the same way as text is formatted in a word processing document. To deselect a range of cells, click a cell outside the range.

1. Open the workbook **df 50d range**. Use features from the Font group to make the following changes:
   a. Select the range of cells *A1:D1* and apply bold.
   b. Select the range of cells *A2:D5* and change the font color to red.
   c. Select the range of cells *A6:D7* and change the font style to italic.
   d. Select the range of cells *A8:D9* and use a yellow fill.
2. Save the workbook as **50d range** and close it.

Format Worksheets
and Cell Content

Home tab > Alignment or
Number

Worksheets that you create for your own use can be very informal. You may enter data quickly and think little about the format. However, worksheets that will be attached to reports or letters or shared with others should be formatted carefully. The worksheet should present data in a format that is easy to read. Follow these general guidelines for worksheet appearance:

A **worksheet title** describes the content of a worksheet. Unless otherwise directed, key the title in all capital letters. Apply bold and center-align the title across the columns that have data.

A **column heading** appears at the top of a column and describes the data in the column. Unless directed otherwise, key column heads in bold, capital and lowercase letters, and use center alignment.

Key data in cells using the default font unless otherwise directed. Data in cells can be aligned left, aligned right, or centered. Usually, numbers are aligned right and words are aligned left or centered.

Set a 2" top margin or center the worksheet data vertically on a page. Center worksheet data horizontally on the page.

In 49D you formatted and aligned column headings. You can use features on the various Ribbon tabs (Home, Page Layout, etc.) to format worksheets as you have done with word processing documents. Some of the Alignment and Number group features that will be used in this activity are shown in Figure 9-13. In Lesson 51, you will learn to use more features in the Number group.

Figure 9-13 Home tab Alignment and Number groups

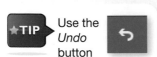
Use the *Undo* button on the Quick Access toolbar to undo your last command.

1. Open the workbook *df 50e format*.
2. Position your pointer over each of the features in the Alignment and Number groups, and read the description of each feature that is displayed.
3. Key the following data in the cell range *A9:C12*. After keying the second number in each row, tap *Enter* to complete the formulas in column D.

Rhonda	74	68
Sandy	64	68
Tom	54	58
Vera	61	70

4. Select the cell range *A2:D2* and use *Wrap Text, Middle Align,* and *Center* in the Alignment group and *Bold* in the Font group to format the column headings.
5. Select the cell range *B3:C12*. Click the *Accounting Number Format* button and then click the *Decrease Decimal* button twice so no decimals are displayed.

6. Select the cell range *D3:D12*. Click the *Percent Style* button, and then use the *Increase Decimal* feature to display one decimal place.

7. Key **COOKIE SALES REPORT** in cell A1. Select the cell range *A1:D1*. Click *Merge & Center*, then *Bold*, and then increase the font size to *14*.

8. Center the worksheet horizontally and vertically on the page and preview it.

9. Save the workbook as **50e format** and close it.

1. Open a new workbook and key the worksheet data below. Wrap the text in the cell range *A2:E2*.

2. Format the worksheet title in 14-point bold and center it across the columns.

3. Format the column headings in 12-point bold and center them vertically and horizontally.

4. Format the numbers using Accounting Number Format with no decimals. Notice how it rounds numbers five or above up when you decrease the decimal amount.

5. Center the worksheet horizontally and vertically on the page in Portrait orientation and change the setting to print gridlines.

6. Preview the worksheet, make any necessary changes, and then print it.

7. Save the workbook as **50f worksheet** and close it.

SIX MONTH SALES				
Month	Gregg Abels	Luiz Callia	Maria Forde	Sandra Sharpe
January	55.67	66.23	73.59	69.02
February	24.57	76.54	35.69	64.32
March	69.30	30.96	57.92	79.08
April	47.83	62.12	43.90	54.02
May	50.42	50.92	45.00	53.21
June	54.30	60.98	57.81	60.23

LESSON 51   Using Formulas and Functions

OUTCOMES
- Format numbers
- Use formulas
- Use functions
- Create a worksheet with functions and formulas

When numbers are keyed into a worksheet, the software formats them as General, the default format. As you learned in the previous lesson, you can use features in the Number group to change the format to a more appropriate format. In this activity, you will use the formats you have learned as well as others that are available.

You can select predefined number formats from the Number Format list (see Figure 9-14). If the predefined format doesn't provide the desired format, click *More Number Formats* at the bottom of the list to open the Format Cells dialog box with the Number tab displayed. You can select the desired number format in the Category list, and then select additional formatting choices from any options that are shown to the right of the Category list.

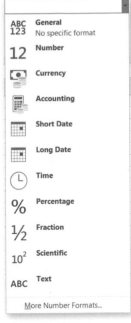

Figure 9-14 Number Format list

Worksheet 1

1. Open the workbook *df 51a numbers1* and use the Number Format drop-down list and other Number commands to format the numbers as directed.
2. Save the workbook as *51a numbers1* and close it.

Worksheet 2

1. Open the workbook *df 51a numbers2*.
2. Format cells in A1:A7 using Number format, three decimal places, and comma separators.
3. Format cells in B1:B7 using Currency format.
4. Format cells in C1:C7 using Accounting format with no decimal places.
5. Format cells in D1:D7 using Percentage format with two decimal places.
6. Format cells in A9:D9 using Special, Type: Phone Number.
7. Format cells in A10:D10 using Special, Type: Social Security Number.
8. Format cells in A11:D11 using Short Date format.
9. Format cells in A12:D12 using Long Date format.
10. Format cells in A13:D13 using Date, Type: March 14, 2012.
11. Save the workbook as *51a numbers2* and close it.

> ★TIP You will find the Special number format on the Number tab of the Format Cells dialog box.

51B

Formulas

Formulas are equations that perform calculations on values in a worksheet. You can key formulas to add, subtract, multiply, and divide numbers. To enter a formula to solve math problems, select the cell in which the answer is to appear. Key an equals (=) sign to indicate that the following text and numbers will be a formula. Enter the formula and tap *Enter* or click the *Enter* icon (the check mark) on the Formula Bar. The formula will appear in the Formula Bar, and the results will appear in the cell as shown in Figure 9-15.

Formulas are solved in this order:

1. Calculations inside parentheses are done before those outside parentheses.
2. Multiplication and division are done in the order they occur.
3. Addition and subtraction are done in the order they occur.

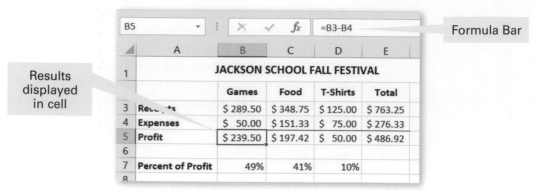

Figure 9-15 Formulas appear in the Formula Bar

In this activity, you will use formulas to calculate dollar amounts and percentages related to games, food, and T-shirt sales at a school festival.

1. Open the workbook **df 51b festival**.

2. At the festival, 25 T-shirts were sold at $5.00 each. To calculate the Receipts for the T-shirts, key **=5*25** in cell D3. As you key the formula, it will appear in both the cell and the Formula Bar. Tap *Enter* or click the *Enter* icon on the Formula Bar. The answer (125) should appear in the cell (see Figure 9-16).

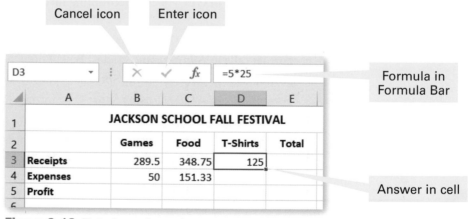

Figure 9-16 Entering a formula

3. The expense for the T-shirts is $3.00 each. In cell D4, key **=3*25** and tap *Enter*. The answer (75) should appear in the cell.

4. In cell E3, calculate the total receipts from games, food, and T-shirts by keying **=B3+C3+D3** as the formula. The answer (763.25) should appear in the cell.

5. In cell E4, enter a formula to find the total expenses for games, food, and T-shirts. (Hint: The answer should be 276.33.)

6. Profit is the amount of money from receipts that is left after expenses are paid. To find the profit for games, key **=B3–B4** in cell B5. The answer should be 239.50.

7. In cell C5, enter a formula to find the profit for food. In cell D5, enter a formula to find the profit for T-shirts. In cell E5, enter a formula to find the total profit. (Hint: The total profit should be 486.92.)

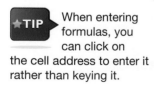

★TIP When entering formulas, you can click on the cell address to enter it rather than keying it.

8. Click in cell *A7* and key **Percent of Profit**.

9. The percent of the total profit that came from game sales is equal to the profit from games ($239.50) divided by the total profit ($486.92) or B5/E5. In cell B7, key **=B5/E5** as the formula. The answer (0.4918672) should appear in the cell. Enter formulas to calculate the Percent of Profit for Food in C7 and for T-Shirts in D7.

10. Format cells B3:E5 using Accounting Number Format with 2 decimals, and format cells B7:D7 in Percent Style with no decimals.

Home tab > Font > Borders

11. Select cells *B4:E4*. On the Home tab in the Font group, click the drop-down arrow on the *Borders* button and select *Bottom Border*.

12. Change the top margin to **3"**. Center the table horizontally. Print the worksheet without the gridlines showing.

13. Save the workbook as *51b festival* and close it.

51C

Functions

Spreadsheet software has built-in functions. A **function** is a predefined formula that can be used to perform calculations. For example, the SUM function is used to add numbers. Other commonly used functions include the following.

- The **Average** function finds the average of the numbers in a range of cells.
- The **Count** function counts how many entries there are in a range of cells.
- The **Min** function finds the smallest number in a range of cells.
- The **Max** function finds the largest number in a range of cells.

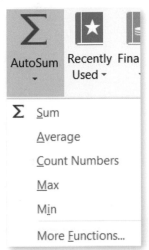

Instead of keying the function's name (Sum, Average, Min, or Max) and the cell range in the Formula Bar, you can click the cell in which you want the answer to appear, click the *AutoSum* button (see Figure 9-17), and select the desired option from the menu. *Excel* will automatically select the cell range next to the active cell and identify the range selected with a moving border. If the range selected by *Excel* is not correct, key the correct range or use the mouse to select the correct range. Click the *Enter* icon to calculate the answer. The AutoSum button can be accessed by following one of the paths given at the left.

Formulas tab > Function Library > AutoSum
or
Home tab > Editing > AutoSum

Figure 9-17 AutoSum options

1. Open a new workbook and key the following data. Center the title across columns A through G. Apply 12-point bold to the title. Apply center alignment and bold to the column heads in row 2.

	A	B	C	D	E	F	G
1	COMPUTER CLASS QUIZ SCORES						
2	Name	Quiz 1	Quiz 2	Quiz 3	Quiz 4	Quiz 5	Quiz 6
3	Joe	90	90	90	100	90	90
4	Mary	89	90	90	79	90	90
5	Paul	100	100	100	100	100	100
6	Carl	100	80	90	100	90	90
7	Sue	90	100	100	100	100	80
8	Twila	90	90	90	80	80	80

2. Go to cell H2 and key **Total**. Apply bold and center alignment if necessary.
3. Go to cell H3, click the *AutoSum* drop-down arrow, and select *Sum*. Verify the range of cells in the formula is correct. If not, edit the cell range. Tap *Enter* or click the *Enter* icon to calculate the answer, which should be 550.
4. You can copy and paste formulas to one or more other cells by using the Copy and Paste commands. The formula will adjust to contain cell addresses for the new cells. To copy the formula in cell H3 to H4:H8, select cell *H3* and click *Copy* (note that the selected cell is indicated by a dashed cell border). Select cells *H4:H8*. Click the *Paste* button. Tap *Esc* on the keyboard to remove the dashed border of the cell that was copied.
5. Go to cell I2 and key **Average**. Apply bold and center alignment if necessary.
6. Go to cell I3 and use the *Average* function to find the average of the numbers in cells B3:G3. Do not include the Total (H3) in the average. The correct answer is 91.66667.
7. Copy and paste the formula in I3 to cells I4:I8.
8. Go to cell A9 and key **MIN**. Select cell *B9* and use the Min function to find the smallest number in cells B3:B8. The correct answer is 89. Copy and paste the formula in cell B9 to C9:G9.
9. In cell A10, key **MAX**. In cell B10, use the Max function to find the highest score in cells B3:B8. The correct answer is 100.
10. Copy and paste the formula in cell B10 to cells C10:G10.
11. Select cells *A8:G8* and apply a bottom border.
12. Center the worksheet title over cells A1:I1.
13. Change the top margin to **2"**. Select the option to center the table horizontally on the page. Print the worksheet without gridlines.

COLLABORATION

14. Save the workbook as *51c quiz*. Complete the CheckPoint.

checkpoint   Ask a classmate to check your worksheet. Make corrections and print the worksheet again if errors are found. Then close the workbook.

51D

Formulas and Functions

1. Open the workbook *df 51d stats*.
2. Enter a formula in cell F3 to calculate the individual batting averages (Hits/At Bats) using three decimal places. Copy and paste this formula to cells F4:F10.
3. In cell B11, use the AutoSum function to calculate the total for cells B3:B10. Copy and paste this formula to cells C11:E11.
4. In cell F12, enter a formula using the Min function to display the lowest average. Adjust the format for three decimal places if necessary.
5. In cell F13, enter a formula using the Max function to display the highest average. Adjust the format for three decimal places if necessary.
6. Change the top margin to **2"** and center the worksheet horizontally. Print the worksheet without gridlines.
7. Save the workbook as *51d stats* and close it.

LESSON 52   Editing Worksheets

OUTCOMES
- Edit cell contents
- Change column widths and row heights
- Clear and delete cell contents and formats
- Modify a worksheet

52A

Edit Cell Contents

Data entered in a cell can be edited (changed or corrected). To edit all the data in the cell, click the cell and key the new data (see Figure 9-18); the old data is automatically deleted.

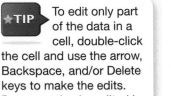
★TIP To edit only part of the data in a cell, double-click the cell and use the arrow, Backspace, and/or Delete keys to make the edits. Data can also be edited in the Formula Bar. Click the cell to be edited and then click the Formula Bar and make your edits there.

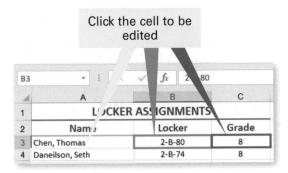

Figure 9-18 Edit data

1. Open the workbook *df 52a lockers* and make the following edits.
2. Seth's name is spelled **Danielson**; make the correction.
3. Change Rebecca Jones to **Jones, Rebecca**.
4. Felipe's last name is **Sanchez**; he is in the 8th grade.
5. Thomas Chen is in the 7th grade; his locker is **3-A-80**.
6. Add **Joyce Williams** to the list. She is in the 8th grade; her locker is **2-B-10**.
7. Change the alignment to **Center** for the Locker and Grade entries.

52B

Change Column Width and Row Height

You can use several methods to change the column width and row height in a worksheet. You can specify a column width or row height. You can change the column width and row height by using the mouse. You can use the AutoFit Column Width or AutoFit Row Height features. By default, row height changes automatically to fit the largest font used in a row.

Home tab > Cells > Format

1. Open the workbook *df 52b players*.
2. To set the width of column A to 10 characters, select any cell in column A. Follow the path at the left and click *Column Width* in the Cell Size section of the Format drop-down menu. Key **10** in the Column Width dialog box as shown in Figure 9-19. Click *OK*.
3. To resize column B using your mouse, move your pointer to the right border of the column B heading area. The pointer changes to a two-sided arrow as

Figure 9-19 Column Width dialog box

shown in Figure 9-20. Double-click. The column width adjusts to display the longest item in the column.

Figure 9-20 AutoFit column width using mouse

4. You also can change a column width by using the AutoFit Column Width feature. Click the *column C* heading to select the column. Click the *Format* button on the Home tab. Select *AutoFit Column Width* in the Cell Size section. (See Figure 9-21.) The width will become wide enough to accommodate the longest item in the column.

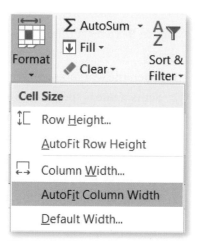

Figure 9-21 AutoFit Column Width feature

5. Another way to change the column width using the mouse is to move your pointer to the right border of the column heading area. When the pointer changes to a two-sided arrow, click and drag the right column border so it is slightly wider than the longest item in the column. Release the mouse button, and the column width will change. Use this procedure to increase the width of column D to fit *Sophomore* in the cell.

6. Select the row 1 content. Increase the font size from 11 to 14. Notice that the row height increases automatically to fit the larger font size.

7. Select cell *C2*. Key **Requested** before *Position*. Wrap the text in cell C2.

Home tab > Alignment > Wrap Text

8. To make rows 3 through 8 taller, select cells *A3* through *A8*. Click the *Format* button on the Home tab in the Cells group and then click *Row Height* to open the Row Height dialog box. Key **20** in the Row Height dialog box. Click *OK*.

9. Save the workbook as **52b players** and close it.

Clear and Delete Cell Contents and/or Formats

Home tab > Editing > Clear

COLLABORATION

checkpoint

Compare your printed copy with that of a classmate to see if the contents and formats have been deleted or cleared correctly.

When you select one or more cells to edit the cell contents, only the text or numbers are changed. If the cell has been formatted, any new text you key will have the same format. As shown in Figure 9-22, you can use the Clear button to clear the contents of a cell (Clear Contents), the format of a cell (Clear Formats), or both (Clear All).

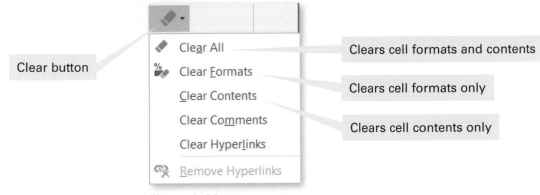

Figure 9-22 Clear options

1. Open the workbook **df 52c schedule**.
2. Select cell *F2*. Tap the *Delete* key. This clears (deletes) the cell contents only; the cell format remains. In cell F2, key **Friday** and tap *Enter*. Notice that the text appears in bold because the format was not deleted.
3. Select cell *B5*. Press the *Ctrl* key and click cell *B7*. Both cells should be selected. Still pressing the *Ctrl* key, click cell *D5*. All of these cells should be selected (highlighted). Release the *Ctrl* key.
4. Click the *Clear* button in the Editing group on the Home tab. Choose *Clear Formats* as shown in Figure 9-22. The data will remain, but the bold format will be removed from these cells.
5. Select cells *A10:F11*. Click the *Clear* button and choose *Clear All* to clear the contents and formats in these cells.
6. Select the remaining names that have bold or italic format. Clear the cell formats.
7. Center the worksheet horizontally and vertically and print it with gridlines.
8. Save the workbook as **52c schedule** and close it.

Modify a Worksheet

1. Open the workbook **df 52d budget**.
2. Change cell A1 to **BUDGET AND MONTHLY EXPENSES**. Apply 14-point bold formatting. Center the title over columns A through F.
3. Apply center alignment and bold to the column heads in row 2.
4. Use Cut and Paste to move the data in cells A18:B18 to cells A3:B3.
5. Clear the contents of cells A16:E17.
6. Change the value in cell E15 to **95**.
7. Copy cell B3 to cells C3:E3. Copy cell B4 to cells C4:E4.
8. Clear the contents in cells A10:B10.
9. Move cells A15:E15 to A10:E10.

10. Apply a bottom border to cells B14:E14.

11. Enter formulas in cells B15:E15 to calculate the sum of the numbers in columns B, C, D, and E.

12. Select cells *B3:E15* and apply the Accounting number format with no decimal places.

13. Go to cell F2 and key **March %**. Apply bold and center alignment if it is not applied automatically.

14. In cell F3, enter a formula to calculate the percent the March Savings amount is of the Budget Savings amount. Format cell F3 for Percent Style with no decimal places. Copy the formula to cells F4:F14.

15. AutoFit the column widths and set the top margin to 2". Select the option to center the data horizontally on the page. Print the worksheet with no gridlines.

16. Save the workbook as *52d budget*, print it, and close it.

Digital Citizenship and Ethics

Through the Internet, people are now able to conduct many of their banking and financial transactions without ever having to leave their homes. Using electronic fund transfers (EFTs), you can move money from one account to another, make deposits, and pay bills quickly and easily from your home computer or mobile phone. EFTs require that you have electronic access to your bank account and have the authority to conduct transactions. Most people find EFTs to be convenient and effective, but there are some concerns:

Cheryl Savan/Shutterstock.com

- Errors can occur even in an automated system. You should check your account statements diligently.

- Funds are usually released quicker from your accounts than when using a paper system, so you must be sure there is enough money in the account to cover the transaction.

- When paying bills, there is often a two- to four-day processing period, so you must initiate the payment early enough to avoid a late payment and a late fee.

COLLABORATION

As a class, discuss the following:

1. Provide examples of how you already use EFTs or could use them to manage your personal finances.

2. What security risks should you consider when using EFTs?

LESSON 53   Enhancing Worksheet Skills

OUTCOMES

- Insert and delete rows and columns
- Sort worksheet data
- Modify a worksheet
- Create a worksheet in a word processing document

53A

Insert and Delete Rows and Columns

When you create or edit worksheets, you may find that you need to insert or delete a row or column of data. One or more rows or columns can be inserted at a time. Columns may be added at the left edge or within a worksheet. Rows may be added at the top edge or within a worksheet.

1. Open the workbook *df 53a vehicles*.
2. To insert a column between columns B and C, click a cell in *column C*. Follow the **Insert Columns** path at the left to insert a new column C. Key the following data in the cells C2 through C5:

   Cell C2: Trailers

   Cell C3: 13

   Cell C4: 17

   Cell C5: 21

Insert Columns
Home tab > Cells > Insert >
Insert Sheet Columns

3. To insert two rows between rows 3 (Holt) and 4 (Nedro), point to the row 4 heading area. When the pointer changes to a right arrow, click and drag down to select two rows (rows 4 and 5). Release the mouse button. Selected rows are shown in Figure 9-23.

	A	B	C	D
1	**VEHICLE RECORDS**			
2	Name	Cars	Trailers	Vans
3	Holt	225	13	115
4	Nedro	243	17	97
5	Peters	212	21	87
6				

Figure 9-23 Selected rows

Insert Rows
Home tab > Cells > Insert >
Insert Sheet Rows

4. Use the **Insert Rows** path at the left to insert two new rows. (*Excel* inserts the number of rows that are selected when you click the Insert feature.)
5. Key the following information in the rows:

   Row 4: James | 211 | 11 | 83

   Row 5: Long | 197 | 7 | 71

Delete Columns
Home tab > Cells > Delete >
Delete Sheet Columns

6. To delete column B, click a cell in *column B* and then use the **Delete Columns** path at the left to select *Delete Sheet Columns*. Column B (Cars) is deleted and all columns to its right move to the left. Click the *Undo* button in the Quick Access toolbar or press *Ctrl + Z* to restore the column.

Delete Rows
Home tab > Cells > Delete >
Delete Sheet Rows

7. To delete row 6 (Nedro), point to the row heading, click to select the row, and then use the **Delete Rows** path at the left. Row 7 becomes row 6. Click the *Undo* button or press *Ctrl + Z* to restore the row.
8. Save the workbook as *53a vehicles* and close it.

Sort Worksheet Data

Sorting means arranging or grouping items in a particular order. You can sort data in a worksheet the same way you sort data in a table. Use *ascending* order to arrange text from A to Z or numbers from lowest to highest. Use *descending* order to arrange text from Z to A or numbers from highest to lowest.

It is good practice to rename and save a workbook before doing a sort. This lets you keep a copy of the information in its original order.

Home tab > Editing >
Sort & Filter

1. Open the workbook *df 53b art*. Save the workbook as **53b art by name**.
2. To sort the data by names in columns A and B in ascending order, click cell *A3*.
3. Follow the path at the left and select *Custom Sort* from the Sort & Filter drop-down list. The Sort dialog box opens.
4. Select *Last Name* in the Sort by box list if necessary. Click the *Add Level* button in the upper-left corner. Click the arrow at the right of the Then by box and choose *First Name*. Verify that the Sort On text boxes display Cell Values and that the Order text boxes display A to Z. The My data has headers checkbox in the upper-right corner of the dialog box should be selected. Your Sort dialog box should match the selections shown in Figure 9-24. Click *OK*.

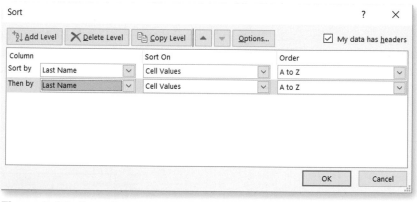

Figure 9-24 Sort dialog box

5. Verify that the names are sorted in alphabetical order. Verify that the first names also are in alphabetical order when the last names are the same.
6. Set the top margin to 2". Select the option to center the worksheet horizontally on the page. Print the worksheet. Save the workbook, using the same name. Close the workbook.

Smallest to Largest
Home tab > Editing > Sort &
Filter > Sort Smallest to
Largest

7. Open the original data file *df 53b art* again. To quickly sort the list by the Period column so the reader can easily see a list of students for each class, select cell *C3*. Follow the **Smallest to Largest** path at the left. Check the sorted data. The information should be sorted by period. The first six names should be the same as those shown in Figure 9-25. Save the workbook as **53b art by period** and close it.

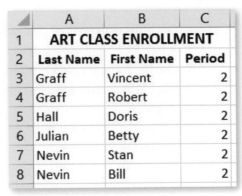

Figure 9-25 Sort by period

8. Open the original data file **df 53b art** again. This time you will sort the list by period from smallest to largest and then alphabetically by first and last name within each period.

9. Click cell *A3*. Access and select *Custom Sort*. In the first-level Sort by box, choose *Period*. Click *Add Level* and select *Last Name* in the Then by box. Click *Add Level* and select *First Name* in the second Then by box. Click *OK*.

10. Verify that your list is sorted by period with period 2 listed first and then alphabetically by last name and then first name within each period. The first seven names in your list should be the same as those shown in Figure 9-26.

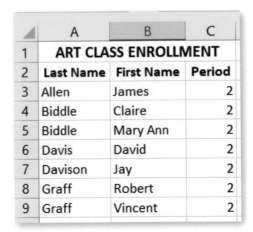

Figure 9-26 Sort by period and name

11. Save the workbook as **53b art by period and name** and close it.

Modify a Worksheet

1. Open the workbook *df 53c dinner*. Save the workbook as **53c dinner by ticket**.
2. Select *A2:F2* and use the *Wrap Text* feature to display the column headings on two lines.
3. Use the *AutoFit Column* Width feature to adjust the column widths.
4. Click cell *C3*. Sort the data below the column heads by ticket number from smallest to largest.
5. Center the worksheet horizontally and vertically on the page.
6. Access the Print Preview screen. Notice that the preview displays page 1 of a two-page worksheet. You can print it on one page by changing the scaling option. Click the *No Scaling* drop-down arrow in the Settings list. Choose the *Fit Sheet on One Page* option. *Excel* scales down the size of the columns and rows so the worksheet appears on one page.
7. Save the workbook again, but do not close it.
8. Save the **53c dinner by ticket** workbook as **53c dinner by name**.
9. Sort the data below the column heads in ascending order by last name and then by first name. Check to see that the sorted list has the names in alphabetical order.
10. Save the workbook again. Print the worksheet with gridlines. Complete the CheckPoint below and then close the workbook.

COLLABORATION

 **checkpoint** Compare your printed worksheet with that of a classmate. Make corrections if necessary.

Create a Worksheet in a Word Processing Document

In this activity, you will create an Excel worksheet in a *Word* document.

1. Start *Word*. Open the document **df 53d memo**.
2. Position the insertion point at the end of the first paragraph and tap *Enter* to insert a line. Position the insertion point at the center of the line (Home tab > Paragraph > Center).
3. Follow the path at the left to insert an *Excel* worksheet in the word processing document.
4. When the *Excel* ribbon and worksheet appear, key the information shown below.

Insert tab > Tables > Table > Excel Spreadsheet

MILLIONS OF U.S. CHILDREN UNDER AGE 18						
Ages	**1970**	**1980**	**1990**	**2000**	**2010**	**2020**
0 to 5	20.9	19.6	22.5	23.1	24.3	26.1
6 to 11	24.6	20.8	21.6	25.0	24.6	25.1
12 to 17	24.3	23.3	20.1	24.2	25.3	24.9

5. In cell A6, key **Totals**. In cells B6:G6, find the sum of the children from age 0 to 17.
6. Center-align all cell contents; use one decimal place for numbers in cells B3:G6; bold the entries in rows 1, 2, and 6.
7. When the worksheet is completed, use the bottom sizing handle to hide all rows below row 6. (Only rows 1 through 6 should be visible, as shown in Figure 9-27.)

⊿	A	B	C	D	E	F	G
1	MILLIONS OF U.S. CHILDREN UNDER AGE 18						
2	Ages	1970	1980	1990	2000	2010	2020
3	0 to 5	20.9	19.6	22.5	23.1	24.3	26.1
4	6 to 11	24.6	20.8	21.6	25.0	24.6	25.1
5	12 to 17	24.3	23.3	20.1	24.2	25.3	24.9
6	Totals	69.8	63.7	64.2	72.3	74.2	76.1

Sheet1

Sizing handles

Figure 9-27 Resize the worksheet to hide unused rows

8. Click outside the worksheet to view the worksheet object in the *Word* document. If necessary, insert/delete space above and below the worksheet to balance the white space around the worksheet.

9. Save the document as **53d memo**. Print the memo. Close *Word*.

LESSON 54   **Worksheets with Charts**

OUTCOMES

- Create column, bar, and pie charts in a worksheet
- Change the chart type
- Change chart layouts and styles
- Create a worksheet and chart

54A

Column, Bar, and Pie Charts

Charts are important because they show information graphically. This allows the audience to better understand the data. You can create many different kinds of charts with spreadsheet software, including column, bar, and pie charts. **Column charts** and **bar charts** compare values across categories of data. **Pie charts** show what percentage each value is of a total value. If you need help deciding which chart type to use, you can use *Excel*'s Recommended Charts feature.

In this activity, you will prepare a column, bar, and pie chart using the default chart style and default chart elements. Default chart elements include a **chart title** that identifies the chart contents and a **legend** that identifies the chart's data categories. The charts you will create are shown in Figures 9-28 through 9-30.

Figure 9-28 Clustered Column chart - Style 8

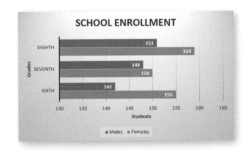

Figure 9-29 Bar chart - Style 1

Figure 9-30 Pie chart - Style 3

Insert tab > Charts > Insert Column or Bar Chart

Design tab > Chart Styles gallery > Style 8

Insert tab > Charts > Insert Column or Bar Chart

Insert tab > Charts > Insert Pie or Doughnut Chart

1. Open the workbook *df 54a sales*.
2. Begin a column chart by selecting cells *A2:C5* as the range of cells to be charted.
3. Follow the path at the left to display column chart types. Click *Clustered Column* in the 2-D Column section to insert the chart into the worksheet.
4. Click the *Chart Title* text box and key **SALES REPORT** as the chart title. Click outside the text box to enter the text. Notice that the chart has a legend as well as the chart contents.
5. With the chart still active, follow the path at the left to change the Chart Style to Style 8.
6. To print just the chart, select the chart and then print it as you would print other worksheets. To print both the chart and the data on the worksheet, select the chart, move it to the left below the data, click outside the chart area, and then print. In this activity, print just the chart.
7. Save the workbook as *54a sales* and close it.
8. Open *df 54a school*.
9. Begin a bar chart by selecting cells *A2:C5* as the range of cells to be charted.
10. Follow the path at the left to display bar chart types. Click *Clustered Bar* in the 2-D Bar section.
11. Key **SCHOOL ENROLLMENT** as the chart title.
12. Print the chart and the data on one worksheet (refer to step 6 above, if needed).
13. Save the workbook as *54a school* and close it.
14. Open the workbook *df 54a expenses*.
15. Begin a pie chart by selecting cells *A2:B7* as the range of cells to be charted.
16. Follow the path at the left to display pie chart types. Click *3-D Pie* in the 3-D Pie section.
17. Key **MONTHLY EXPENSES** as the chart title.
18. Change the Chart Style to *Style 3* to show what percent each item makes up of the total monthly expenses (click the pie chart to activate the Design tab, then click *Style 3* in the Chart Styles gallery).
19. Print the chart on the page without the data.
20. Save the workbook as *54a expenses* and close it.

54B

Change Chart Type

The chart you initially select to display your data can be changed to other chart types to help you decide which type best displays your data. In addition to column, bar, and pie charts, you can select line, area, and doughnut charts.

In this activity, you will change a column chart to a line chart (see Figure 9-31), a bar chart to an area chart (see Figure 9-32), and a pie chart to a doughnut chart (see Figure 9-33).

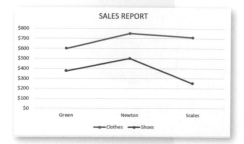

Figure 9-31 Line chart

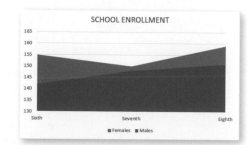

Figure 9-32 Area chart

Figure 9-33 Doughnut chart

Insert tab > Charts > Insert Line or Area Chart

Insert tab > Charts > Insert Line or Area Chart

Insert tab > Charts > Insert Pie or Doughnut Chart

1. Open **54a sales** and click the chart to activate it.
2. Follow the path at the left and select the *Line with Markers* chart type to change the column chart to a line chart.
3. Save the workbook as **54b sales** and close it.
4. Open **54a school** and click the chart to activate it.
5. Follow the path at the left and select the *Area* chart type in the 2-D Area section to change the bar chart to an area chart.
6. Save the workbook as **54b school** and close it.
7. Open **54a expenses** and click the chart to activate it.
8. Follow the path at the left and select the *Doughnut* chart type to change the pie chart to a doughnut chart.
9. Save the workbook as **54b expenses** and close it.

54C

Change Chart Layout and Styles

Once you have created a chart, you can change the chart layout to display chart parts such as axis titles, data labels, gridlines, etc., that are not displayed in the default layout. Also, you can choose not to display chart parts such as the chart title and legend that are displayed in the default chart layout.

The three buttons shown in Figure 9-34 appear at the right of a selected chart. The Chart Elements button (the plus sign icon) shows the list of major chart elements you can display or not display in your chart. Those with a checkmark display, and those not checked do not display. You can change what is displayed by adding or removing checks. The middle button is the Chart Styles button that can be used to change the overall appearance of your chart, including the color of bars, columns, lines, pie slices, etc. The bottom button, Chart Filters, can be used to choose the data points and names to display on the chart.

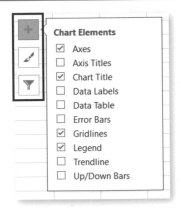

Figure 9-34 Chart Elements, Chart Styles, and Chart Filters buttons

★TIP If you cannot see the axis title box clearly, resize the chart by selecting a corner sizing handle and dragging it outward until the axis title box is clearly visible.

NOTE Axis titles display in the style that goes with the selected Chart Style, so even if you type in lower or mixed case, it may appear in all caps.

In this activity, you will change the layout and styles of two charts.

1. Open **54a sales** and click the chart to select it. Click the *Chart Elements* button.
2. To display data labels in the chart, click to check the *Data Labels* box. Notice that values for each column have been inserted above that column.
3. To display axis titles in the chart, check the *Axis Titles* box. Notice that AXIS TITLE boxes have been inserted to the left of the vertical axis and below the horizontal axis. Click the vertical axis box, select the *AXIS TITLE* text, key **Sales**, and then click outside the box. *SALES* displays as the axis title. Click the horizontal axis box, key **Salesperson**, and then click outside the box to display *SALESPERSON* as the axis title.
4. To change the chart style, click the *Chart Styles* button (the middle button) and scroll through the options. Select *Style 8* from the options.
5. Save the workbook as **54c sales** and close it.
6. Open **54a school**.
7. Display the chart with axis titles and data labels, and without gridlines.

8. Key **Grade** as the horizontal axis title and **Students** for the vertical axis title.
9. Choose a chart style that you prefer.
10. Save the workbook as **54c school**, print the chart and the data on the same worksheet, and close the workbook.

54D

Format a Worksheet and Add a Chart

★TIP Refer to earlier worksheet lessons as needed.

1. Open **df 54D first quarter**, study Figure 9-35, and then follow these steps to complete the worksheet.

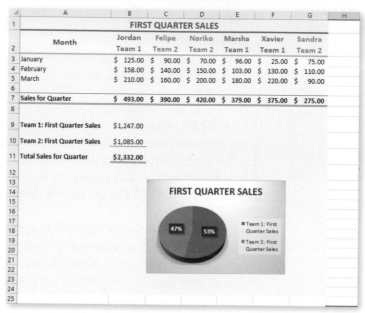

Figure 9-35 First Quarter Sales

Home tab > Styles > Cell Styles > Heading 1

2. *Merge & Center* the worksheet title *FIRST QUARTER SALES* in A1:G1
3. Format the worksheet title with *Heading 1* format using the path at the left.
4. Change the width of column A to *26*.
5. Change the width of columns B-G to *10*.
6. Change the height of rows 9-12 to *25*.
7. Enter the following information for row 2 and apply *Wrap Text*.

Month	Jordan Team 1	Felipe Team 2	Noriko Team 2	Marsha Team 1	Xavier Team 1	Sandra Team 2

Home tab > Styles > Cell Styles > Heading 2

8. For Alignment select *Middle Align* and *Center* for row 2.
9. Format the column headings in row 2 with *Heading 2* format using the path at the left.
10. Enter formulas in 7B:7G to calculate Sales for Quarter for each team member.

Home tab > Styles > Cell Styles > Total

11. Format row 7 with the *Total* heading format using the path at the left.
12. Change the font color headings for Team 1 members to *Blue, Accent 1*. Change the font color for Team 2 members to *Orange, Accent 2*.
13. Change the number format to *Accounting* for B3:G11.

14. Enter a formula to calculate the Team 1 First Quarter Sales in B9, the Team 2 First Quarter Sales in B10, and the Total Sales for Quarter in B11. Apply the *Total* Heading format to cell B11.

15. Select cells *A9:B10*. Insert a *3-D Pie Chart - Style 3* chart showing percentage of the sales each team had for the first quarter. Using the path at the left, size the chart 2" high by 3" wide. Enter **FIRST QUARTER SALES** as the Chart Title. Position the top-left corner of the chart in the top-left corner of cell C13.

Format tab > Size >
2'' Height x 3'' Width

16. Select cells *A1* through *G24*. Follow the path at the left to apply the *Gold, Accent 4, Lighter, 80%* Fill Color.

Home tab > Font >
Fill Color

17. **Save as:** *54d first quarter*.

sirtravelalot/Shutterstock.com

21st Century Skills: Productivity and Accountability

Spreadsheets are a powerful tool for calculating, managing, and analyzing numerical data. Businesses use spreadsheets to record market research, measure performance, and create financial documents. Another valuable use of spreadsheets is creating charts and graphs to help illustrate complex numerical information and identify trends.

Assume you are the production manager for a manufacturing company. You want to analyze the productivity of workers on first shift (6 a.m.–2 p.m.), second shift (2 p.m.–10 p.m.), and third shift (10 p.m.–6 a.m.). To do this, you have collected the following information on the number of units produced per shift.

	Shift 1	Shift 2	Shift 3
Monday	145	120	109
Tuesday	147	119	112
Wednesday	144	123	112
Thursday	147	125	111
Friday	140	124	110

Think Critically

1. Open a new workbook and enter the data shown above.
2. Create a column chart to illustrate the number of units produced per shift. Save the workbook as directed by your teacher.
3. Evaluate the chart. What might account for the lower outputs for shifts 2 and 3?

Assessment 4 — Worksheets

Warmup

Key each line twice. If time permits, key the lines again.

Alphabet

1 Gus Javon quickly baked extra pizza for the women.

Figures/Symbol

2 Janet paid Jon $1,347.75; John paid Ken $2,690.85.

Speed

3 Kamela may work with the city auditor on the form.

gwam 1' | 1 | 2 | 3 | 4 | 5 | 6 | 7 | 8 | 9 | 10 |

Activity 1
Assess Straight-Copy Skill

Key one or two 2' or 3' timed writings on all paragraphs combined. Print, proofread, circle errors, and determine *gwam*.

A all letters used

	gwam 2'	3'

Liz, who is nearing the end of her third year of ... 5 / 3
high school, is a quality young person. She is an ... 10 / 7
above-average student who always makes high grades. ... 15 / 10
Liz is taking challenging English, mathematics, and ... 20 / 13
computer application courses and an advanced science ... 25 / 17
class for which she can earn college credit. She has ... 31 / 20
played soccer and softball for three years and was ... 36 / 24
one of the top soccer players in the county last year. ... 41 / 27
She holds offices in several student organizations and ... 47 / 31
is an officer of the honor society at her high school. ... 52 / 35

Liz, like many other young adults, is trying to ... 57 / 38
make career plans. She is very good with computers, ... 62 / 41
math, and science and enjoys these classes. She ... 67 / 44
thinks she would like to be a physics teacher. She ... 72 / 48
has, however, received signals from many friends and ... 77 / 51
family members that she should not aspire to a career ... 82 / 55
in science, especially physics, because it is a field ... 87 / 58
dominated by men. She does not want such discouraging ... 93 / 62
comments to shake her desire. ... 96 / 64

A teacher who supports her career goal suggested ... 100 / 67
she research roles for women in science. An Internet ... 106 / 70
search quickly led her to organizations that help women ... 111 / 74
in science network with each other. Also, many of ... 116 / 77
these groups provide opportunities for young women to be ... 122 / 81
mentored by women in their field of interest. Liz is ... 127 / 85
encouraged by her research. She plans to enroll in ... 132 / 88
the next mentoring program of the chapter of women ... 137 / 91
scientists in her city. ... 139 / 93

gwam 2' | 1 | 2 | 3 | 4 | 5 |
3' | 1 | 2 | 3 |

1. Open a new *Excel* workbook. Key the worksheet shown here.

	A	B	C	D	E	F	G	H
1	Last Name	First Name	Week 1	Week 2	Week 3	Week 4	Week 5	Total
2	James	Brett	1	0	3	0	2	
3	Tobin	Tryell	0	0	0	2	1	
4	Sutton	Kyle	0	1	1	0	0	
5	Saag	Noah	2	3	1	3	2	
6	Franklin	Ryan	0	1	0	0	1	
7	Doyle	Connor	0	0	0	1	0	
8	Hart	Derek	1	1	0	0	0	

2. Wrap the text in cells A1 and B1 and AutoFit column widths.
3. Calculate the total for each row in column H.
4. Sort the worksheet by column H in descending order.
5. Merge & Center **Weekly Total** in cells A9:B9. Format row 9 with the *Total* Cell Style format.
6. Calculate the total for columns C–H in row 9.
7. Insert a row at the top and Merge & Center **TOUCHDOWN SCORERS FOR THE BEARCATS** across the columns. Format the title as a *Heading 1* Cell Style.
8. Format row 2 with *Heading 2* Cell Style; Select *Middle Align* and *Center Alignment* for row 2.
9. Set row height at 20 for row 1 and rows 3–10.
10. Center the worksheet horizontally with a 2" top margin. Preview the worksheet and print it without gridlines.
11. Save the workbook as *a4 activity2* and close it.

1. Open *df a4 activity3*.
2. In cell H3, use the *Min* function to find the low share price for Company A. Copy the formula to cells H4:H10.
3. In cell I3, use the *Max* function to identify the high share price for Company A. Copy this to cells I4:I10.
4. In cell J3, enter a formula to subtract cell H3 from cell I3. Copy this formula to cells J4:J10.
5. Insert a column between columns G and H.
6. Merge & Center cells H1 and H2.

7. Key **YTD % Change** in the merged cell and wrap the text.
8. In cell H3, calculate the YTD % Change by entering this formula: **=(G3–B3)/B3**. Copy the formula to cells H4:H10.
9. Format numbers in columns B–G and I–K as *Currency* with two decimal places.
10. Format numbers in column H as *Percentage* with two decimal places.
11. Merge cells A1 and A2.
12. In cell A11, key **Average**.
13. In cell B11, calculate the average share price in column B. Copy the formula to cells C11:G11
14. Format entries in row A11:G11 with the *Total* Cell Style.
15. Format rows 1 and 2 with the *Heading 2* Cell Style.
16. Use center align in cells A3:A11.
17. Use center align in rows 1 and 2.
18. Set column widths to 11.
19. Insert a row at the top of the worksheet and center **YEAR-TO-DATE STOCK PORTFOLIO ANALYSIS** as a title across columns A–K using *Heading 1* Cell Style.
20. Change orientation to Landscape, center the worksheet horizontally and vertically on the page, and select to print gridlines. Fit the sheet on one page.
21. Preview and print the worksheet.
22. Save the workbook as *a4 activity3* and close it.

**Activity 4
Column Chart**

1. Open the workbook *df a4 activity4*.
2. Insert a *3-D Clustered Column* chart using the default layout and chart elements.
3. Use the worksheet title for the chart title and add data labels to the chart.
4. Select *Style 3* Chart Style.
5. Print the chart and the worksheet together.
6. Save the workbook as *a4 activity4* and close it.

**Activity 5
Change Chart Type
and Style**

1. Open the workbook *df a4 activity5*.
2. Change the pie chart to a *Doughnut* chart. Change the chart style to *Style 3*.
3. Print the chart only.
4. Save the workbook as *a4 activity5* and close it.

Skill Builder 8

alphabet 1 The exquisite prize, a framed clock, was to be given to Jay.

spacing 2 it has|it will be|to your|by then|in our|it may be|to do the

easy 3 The maid was with the dog and six girls by the field of hay.

gwam 1' | 1 | 2 | 3 | 4 | 5 | 6 | 7 | 8 | 9 | 10 | 11 | 12 |

B

Technique: Response Patterns

Key each line twice SS.

★TIP Keep keystroking movement limited to the fingers.

Emphasize continuity and rhythm with curved, upright fingers.

A Katrina Karrigan ate the meal of apples, bananas, and pears.

B Bobby bought a beach ball and big balloons for the big bash.

C Cody can serve cake and coffee to the cold campers at lunch.

D David did all he could to dazzle the crowd with wild dances.

E Elaine left her new sled in an old shed near the gray house.

F Frank found a file folder his father had left in the office.

G Gloria got the giggles when the juggler gave Glen his glove.

H Hugh helped his big brother haul in the fishing net for her.

I Inez sings in a trio that is part of a big choir at college.

J Jason just joined the jury to judge the major jazz festival.

K Nikki McKay kept the black kayaks at the dock for Kay Kintz.

L Lola left her doll collection for a village gallery to sell.

M Mona asked her mom to make more malted milk for the mission.

gwam 1' | 1 | 2 | 3 | 4 | 5 | 6 | 7 | 8 | 9 | 10 | 11 | 12 |

C

Speed Check

Key three 30" timings on each line. Try to go faster on each timing.

1 The firm kept half of us busy.

2 The girls work for the island firm.

3 Diane may blame the girls for the fight.

4 Pay the man for the work he did on the autos.

5 The social for the maid is to be held in the city.

6 Jake may sign the form if they do an audit of the firm.

gwam 30" | 2 | 4 | 6 | 8 | 10 | 12 | 14 | 16 | 18 | 20 | 22 |

Technique: Tab Key

Key each line twice SS;
DS between 2-line groups

Tab→ Jay	Tab→ Dan	Tab→ Sue	Tab→ Ann
Lea	Don	Sam	Pat
Stan	Juan	Jack	Seth
Sara	Judy	Vera	Ruth
Maria	Cally	Alexa	Lydia
Amien	Andre	Elgin	Blake

E

Speed Building

1. Key one 1' unguided
   and two 1' guided
   timings on each ¶.

2. Key two 2' unguided
   timings on ¶s 1–2
   combined; determine
   gwam.

A all letters used

gwam 2'

•   2   •   4   •   6   •   8   •   10
Austria is a rather small country, about three times   5
•   12   •   14   •   16   •   18   •   20   •   22
the size of Vermont, located between Germany and Italy. The   11
•   24   •   26   •   28   •   30   •   32   •   34   •
best known of the cities in this country is Vienna. Over the 17
36   •   38   •   40   •   42   •   44   •   46   •
years this city has been known for its contributions to the   23
48   •   50   •   52   •   54   •   56   •   58   •
culture in the region, particularly in the area of performing 29
60   •   62   •   64   •   66   •   68   •   70   •
arts. Another place that has played an important part in the 35
72   •   74   •   76   •   78   •   80   •   82   •   84
exquisite culture of the area is the beautiful city of Salzburg. 42
•   2   •   4   •   6   •   8   •   10   •
Salzburg is recognized as a great city for the performing   47
12   •   14   •   16   •   18   •   20   •   22   •   24
arts, particularly music. Just as important, however, is that 53
•   26   •   28   •   30   •   32   •   34   •   36
the city is the birthplace of Wolfgang Amadeus Mozart, one of 60
•   38   •   40   •   42   •   44   •   46   •   48   •
the greatest composers of all time. Perhaps no other composer 65
50   •   52   •   54   •   56   •   58   •   60   •
had an earlier start at his professional endeavors than did   71
62   •   64   •   66   •   68   •   70   •   72
Mozart. It is thought that he began playing at the age of   77
•   74   •   76   •   78   •   80   •   82   •
four and began his composing at the early age of five.   82

gwam 2' | 1 | 2 | 3 | 4 | 5 | 6 |

Quarter-Minute Checkpoints

gwam	1/4'	1/2'	3/4'	1'
20	5	10	15	20
24	6	12	18	24
28	7	14	21	28
32	8	16	24	32
36	9	18	27	36
40	10	20	30	40
44	11	22	33	44
48	12	24	36	48
52	13	26	39	52
56	14	28	42	56

Advanced Technology Skills 5

Digital Communication and Collaboration Tools

OUTCOMES
- Define digital communication
- Define digital collaboration tools
- Describe digital communication and collaboration tools
- Explain the uses for digital communication and collaboration tools in school and business

Defining Digital Communication

Most of us use digital communication and collaboration tools on a daily basis. We use our cell phones to make calls or send text messages. We use instant messaging to exchange electronic messages in real time on social networking or other websites. We transfer electronic files via email. We connect to the Internet with our computers and smartphones.

Digital communication is the electronic exchange of information. **Digital collaboration tools** allow individuals to have conversations and share ideas with others from anywhere. They provide users with quick—often instantaneous—access to each other as well as to enormous electronic databases that store volumes of information. Digital collaboration technology goes beyond just simple communication by providing tools needed to share, modify, plan, and create with others in a different city, state, or around the globe. Doctors retrieve a patient's medical records, issue prescriptions, and evaluate test results at the click of a *button*. Companies can use videoconferencing to communicate "face-to-face" with employees in remote locations, thus saving travel costs and boosting worker productivity.

Digital technology tools have transformed the way we communicate and collaborate. New and faster tools come on the market regularly. As a successful digital citizen, you should understand the various technologies and devices that are becoming mainstream for communication.

Alone or with a partner, respond to these questions:

1. What digital communication technologies do you use at school? At home?
2. Assume you do not have access to the digital technologies that you listed for question 1 above. How would you accomplish the same things?
3. How might a company use digital communication and collaboration tools in their business?

Digital technologies help us communicate better

violetkaipa/Shutterstock.com

COLLABORATION

Basic Digital Communication Tools: Cell/Smartphone

A **cell phone**, or mobile phone, is used for communication over a cellular network. There are numerous plans and carriers. Many carriers have plans tailored for small and larger users including options that bundle popular features and usage patterns, making them very cost-effective. Today, the majority of the U.S. population is connected via mobile technology.

Growth in demand for advanced mobile devices boasting powerful memory and larger screens has outpaced the rest of the mobile phone market. A **smartphone** is a cell phone offering advanced capabilities with computer-like functionality. A smartphone incorporates advanced features like email, texting, Internet access, and ebook readers. Most smartphones include a camera and video recorder, web browsing, and the ability to view and edit documents. Many models have global positioning system (GPS) capability and can access thousands of other applications.

Digital Communication and Collaboration Tools

Videoconferencing creates a "face-to-face" environment from remote locations

Social networking sites are used by individuals and businesses

Blogs provide forums for us to share our interests with others

Video and web conferencing transmit and receive images and voice in real time. With web conferencing, you can share documents and applications and communicate as if you were face-to-face with individuals anywhere in the world. Time and money that would be spent on traveling can be used to conduct meetings. You can share documents, make presentations, and conduct meetings on short notice.

Social networking sites provide a venue for individuals or organizations with common interests, like an online community. Internet-based social networking sites allow users to share content and interact with those who have similar interests. Social networking has expanded to include a company's customers, a celebrity's fans, and a politician's constituents. This has created a great opportunity for businesses to generate interaction with present and potential customers. With an ongoing commitment of effort, you can create a niche market through sites such as LinkedIn, Facebook, and Twitter.

Chat tools provide communication over the Internet using software or apps such as an instant messenger. Chat is commonly used in place of email when there is a need to communicate live in real time. Chat tools can be used for both internal and external organizational communication. They can be placed on a website to allow customers and customer service representatives to correspond in real time. Utilizing chat tools may require a free software download. There are many options available, including Google Talk and Skype. Features can vary from simple one-on-one messaging to highly developed tools for group chat, file transfer, video, and document collaboration.

A **blog** is a website, similar to an online journal, that includes entries made by individuals. Blogs typically focus on a specific subject and provide users with forums to talk about various topics like sports, music, politics, cooking, or travel.

There are many other types of blogs, differing not only in the type of content, but also in the way that content is delivered or written. There are personal blogs, collaborative or group blogs, corporate and organizational blogs, and blogs that aggregate feeds from selected information outlets to provide a combined view for their readers. Blogs can be organized around various types of media like videos, photos, and sketches where members post using these formats rather than the written word. When established correctly, a blog can be a great way to connect people to share ideas and foster innovation.

Podcasting is a form of audio broadcasting on the Internet. Podcasts can be created by anyone who has a microphone or digital video camera and a computer with recording software. Podcasts are often distributed in "episodes," meaning new podcasts are made available on a regular basis. People can browse through the categories or subscribe to specific podcast feeds, which will download to their audio players automatically. Although podcasts are generally audio files created for digital music players, the same technology can be used to prepare and transmit images, text, and video to any capable device. Podcasts can be an effective way to communicate with audiences around the world or to deliver professional development information to employees.

1. Study the information in the following table.

Teens and Digital Communications Usage*
Methods of Communication Daily with Friends

Communication Method	2006	2015
Face-to-face	31%	25%
Text messages	27%	55%
Talk via cell phone	55%	19%
Instant messaging	30%	27%
Social media	--	23%
Email	15%	6%
Video chat	--	7%
Video games	--	13%
Messaging apps (*Kik* and *WhatsApp*)	--	14%

*Pew Internet & American Life Project http://www.pewinternet.org/
-- Method did not exist or response was insignificant

COLLABORATION

2. With a partner or in a small group, respond to the following questions. Record your group's responses to share with the class later.

   - In the 10 years represented in the table, what are the most surprising changes you find in the data?

   - Do the percentages in 2015 fairly represent how you communicate daily with your friends today? How are they similar? What are the differences?

   - Are there methods of communicating with your friends not mentioned in the table?

   - Based on the table and projecting out another 10 years, how would you predict teens will be communicating with their friends on a daily basis?

3. Report your group's responses to your class. As a class, discuss the similarities and differences the various small groups found in their analysis.

Communication Skills 4

ACTIVITY 1: Subject/Verb Agreement

1. Study each of the six rules.
   a. Key the *Learn* line(s) beneath each rule, noting how the rule is applied.
   b. Key the *Apply* line(s), choosing correct verbs.

Rule 1: Use a singular verb with a singular subject (noun or pronoun); use a plural verb with a plural subject and with a compound subject (two nouns or pronouns joined by *and*).

Learn	1	Senator Vermillion was delayed by heavy traffic.
Learn	2	The markets are at all-time highs.
Learn	3	The Democratic and Republican candidates have arrived.
Apply	4	Mr. Tanaka (was, were) assigned to Dr. Grimaldi.
Apply	5	The dancers (is, are) ready for their next performance.
Apply	6	Carman Gonzalez and Jay Hefner (was, were) elected.

Rule 2: Use the plural verb *do not* or *don't* with pronoun subjects *I, we, you,* and *they* as well as with plural nouns; use the singular verb *does not* or *doesn't* with pronouns *he, she,* and *it* as well as with singular nouns.

Learn	7	I do not like this color of fabric; you don't either.
Learn	8	He does not have to forfeit if he doesn't have five players.
Apply	9	They (doesn't, don't) advertise online, so I (doesn't, don't) know.
Apply	10	Jim and Sara (doesn't, don't) swim; they (doesn't, don't) plan to go.

Rule 3: Use singular verbs with indefinite pronouns (*each, every, any, either, neither, one,* etc.) and with *all* and *some* used as subjects if their modifiers are singular (but use plural verbs with *all* and *some* if their modifiers are plural).

Learn	11	Each of these students has performed a solo at a concert.
Learn	12	Some members have not paid next year's fees.
Learn	13	All the men are to be paid overtime for the holiday hours.
Apply	14	Neither of them (was, were) in class on Thursday.
Apply	15	Some of the boxes (was, were) completely empty.
Apply	16	Every one of the girls on the team (is, are) supposed to play.

Rule 4: Use a singular verb with a singular subject that is separated from the verb by the phrase *as well as* or *in addition to*; use a plural verb with a plural subject so separated.

Learn	17	The door, in addition to the windows, has to be replaced.
Learn	18	The three cars, as well as the truck, have to be sold.
Apply	19	The president, as well as the treasurer, (was, were) let go.
Apply	20	Three students, in addition to their teacher, (was, were) invited.

Rule 5: Use a singular verb if *number* is used as the subject and is preceded by *the*; use a plural verb if *number* is the subject and is preceded by *a*.

Learn	21	The number of jobs available is very low.
Learn	22	A number of the cars were damaged in the hailstorm.
Apply	23	The number of applicants for the job (is, are) unusually low.
Apply	24	A number of the students (has, have) already voted.

(continued on next page)

> Rule 6: Use a singular verb with singular subjects linked by *or* or *nor*, but if one subject is singular and the other is plural, the verb agrees with the nearer subject.

Learn 25 Neither the President nor Vice President was able to attend.

Learn 26 Either the owner or his coaches are to participate.

Apply 27 If neither Tom nor his parents (go, goes), there will be room.

Apply 28 Either Jon or Kay (was, were) nominated for the award.

2. Key Proofread & Correct, using correct verbs.
   a. Check answers.
   b. Using the rule number at the left of each line, study the rule relating to each error you made.
   c. Rekey each incorrect line, using correct verbs.

Save as: CS4 ACTIVITY1

Proofread & Correct

Rules

1 1 Dr. Fields and Dr. Fuentes (is, are) speaking at the conference.

1 2 They (has, have) been accepted to both Harvard and Stanford.

2 3 You (doesn't, don't) have the spreadsheet test until Friday.

2 4 Why (doesn't, don't) he wait until Monday to bring treats?

3 5 Neither of the children (was, were) allowed to have a phone.

3 6 One of the program team members (is, are) likely to be promoted.

5 7 The number of people who voted on Monday (is, are) quite small.

4 8 The teacher, as well as her student teacher, (is, are) authorized.

6 9 Neither the principal nor her assistant (was, were) available.

5 10 A number of the athletes (is, are) ineligible because of grades.

ACTIVITY 2: Word Choice

1. Study the definitions of the words.
2. Key the *Learn* line noting the correct usage of each word.
3. Key the *Apply* lines, inserting the correct word(s).

Save as: CS4 ACTIVITY2

some (n/adv) unknown or unspecified unit or thing; to a degree or extent	**hour** (n) the 24th part of a day; a particular time
sum (n/vb) the whole amount; the total; to find a total; summary of points	**our** (adj) of or relating to ourselves as possessors

Learn 1 The total **sum** awarded did not satisfy **some** of the people.

Apply 2 The first grader said, "The (some, sum) of five and two is seven."

Apply 3 (Some, sum) of the students were able to find the correct (some, sum) for the problem.

Learn 1 The first **hour** of **our** class will be used for going over the next assignment.

Apply 2 What (hour, our) of the day would you like to have (hour, our) group perform?

Apply 3 Minutes turned into (hours, ours) as we waited for (hour, our) turn to perform.

ACTIVITY 3: Writing

1. Study the quotations.
2. Compose a ¶ to show your understanding of honesty and truth.
3. Compose a 2nd ¶ to describe an incident in which honesty and truth *should* prevail but don't.
4. Proofread and correct.

Save as: **CS4 ACTIVITY3**

Honesty's the best policy.
—Cervantes

To be honest . . . here is a task for all that a man has of fortitude.
—Robert Louis Stevenson

Piety requires us to honor truth above our friends.
—Aristotle

The dignity of truth is lost with protesting.
—Ben Jonson

ACTIVITY 4: Speaking

Student clubs and organizations provide an opportunity to develop skills that you will use throughout your personal and professional life. These skills include leadership skills, interpersonal skills, oral and written communication skills, time management skills, and unique skills related to the focus of the organization. Select a club at your school or one that you would like to start and prepare a speech to inform your classmates about the benefits derived from involvement in the organization you selected.

Before You Move On

Answer **True** or **False** to each question to review what you have learned in Chapter 9.

1. Each workbook can contain only one worksheet. LO 49A

2. A worksheet has rows that run vertically and columns that run horizontally. LO 49A

3. Letters are used to identify worksheet columns. LO 49A

4. Cells can be merged in a word processing table but not in a worksheet. LO 50E

5. By default, numbers are automatically right-aligned when they are entered. LO 49D

6. A worksheet can be printed with or without gridlines. LO 49E

7. The contents of one cell cannot be copied to more than one other cell. LO 51C

8. More than one row or column can be inserted or deleted at the same time. LO 53A

9. A function is a predefined formula. LO 51C

10. The contents of a cell can be cleared, but the format cannot be cleared. LO 52C

11. Words in a worksheet can be sorted only in ascending order. LO 53B

12. An *Excel* worksheet can be prepared in a *Word* document. LO 53D

13. Charts that have a title should not have a legend. LO 54A

14. Bar charts present information in vertical columns. LO 54A

15. Chart titles and legends are included in the default chart elements. LO 54A

Lesson 55 Create a Database
Lesson 56 Create a Database Form
Lesson 57 Add Fields, Delete Fields, and Edit Records
Lesson 58 Work with Database Queries, Filters, and Sorts
Lesson 59 Work with Database Reports
Assessment 5 Database Basics

Application Guide

What Is Database Software?

A **database** is an organized collection of facts and figures (information). A phone book, which includes names, addresses, and phone numbers, is an example of an old-fashioned database in printed form.

Today, most databases are stored in electronic form. Names and addresses, inventories, sales records, and client information are just a few examples of information that is stored in a database. Having information in a database makes it easy to compile and arrange data to answer questions and make well-informed decisions. Databases also work behind the scenes to make it possible for you to use social media, shop online, store contacts on your phone, and perform many other activities we now take for granted.

This chapter introduces you to the basics of databases and database software and shows you how to create simple databases. Learning how to use database software such as Microsoft *Access* is challenging, yet fun. Once you master how to define and sequence fields for recording information, you will be able to sort, filter, and run queries to access (gather) information for making sound decisions. In this chapter, you will learn to:

- Work with a database
- Create a database
- Add records
- Edit records, add fields, and delete records
- Perform sorts, filters, and queries

iStock.com/EdStock

What Are the Components of a Database?

A database includes tables for entering and storing information, **forms** for entering and displaying information, **reports** for summarizing and presenting information, and **queries** for drawing information from one or more tables. Figure 10-1 shows the components that can be created in a database. These components are accessed by clicking the *Create* tab in *Access*.

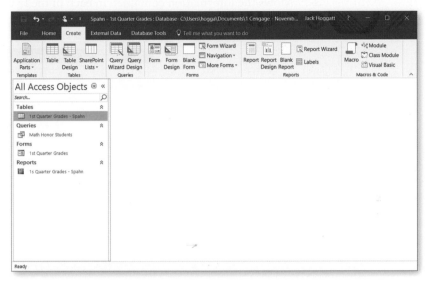

Figure 10-1 *Access* window with Create tab on the Ribbon

The left pane in the figure displays Access Objects that have been created in this file. In Figure 10-1, *Tables* contains the data for 1st Quarter Grades; *Queries* contains a query that produces a list of all students who achieved a 3.5 average during first quarter; *Forms* contains a form that displays the first quarter grades of only one student at a time (to be used during parent conferences); and *Reports* contains a report on 1st Quarter Grades that will be forwarded to the school administrative offices where student records are maintained.

What Is a Database Table?

Create tab > Tables > Table

Database tables are created by the user in software programs such as *Access* for inputting, organizing, and storing information. The tables are set up to contain columns and rows of information. In a database table, the columns are called **fields** and the rows are called **records**. The insertion point in Figure 10-2 is in Field 3 of Record 3.

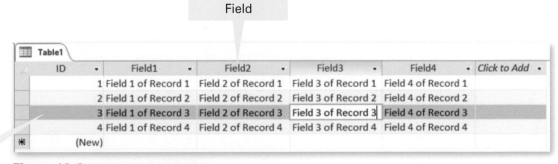

Figure 10-2 Fields and records

The table illustrated in Figure 10-3 has five of the fields showing—*ID, Last Name, First Name, Courtesy Title,* and *Address.* Fourteen of the 36 records in the database are visible in the illustration.

Record 12, the registration record for Trey Pavlikcova, is highlighted in the illustration and shows the information contained in each of the five fields. The database table is the foundation from which forms, queries, and reports are created.

Figure 10-3 Database table

What Is Defining and Sequencing Fields of Database Tables?

Fields can be defined and sequenced in either **Datasheet View** (Figure 10-4) or **Design View** (Figure 10-5 on the next page). In Datasheet View, a field can be defined and sequenced by clicking *Click to Add,* selecting a data type, and keying the field name.

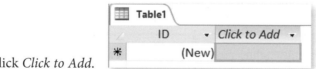

1. Click *Click to Add.*

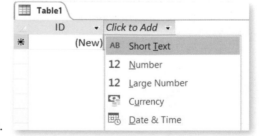

2. Select a data type.

3. Key a field name.

Figure 10-4 Datasheet View

The **data type** determines the kinds of values that can be displayed in the field. The most common data types are **AutoNumber** (automatic sequential or random numbering of records), **Text** (text or a combination of text and numbers), **Number** (used in mathematical calculations), **Currency** (used in mathematical calculations), and **Date & Time** (date and time values).

When defining and sequencing fields in Design View, the fields in the table are defined before entering data. The *Description* field is used to describe the content of each field. At the bottom of the Design View screen, Field Properties for each field can be set. The Field Properties available change depending on the data type selected. Figure 10-5 shows the properties that can be set when you select *Currency* for the data type.

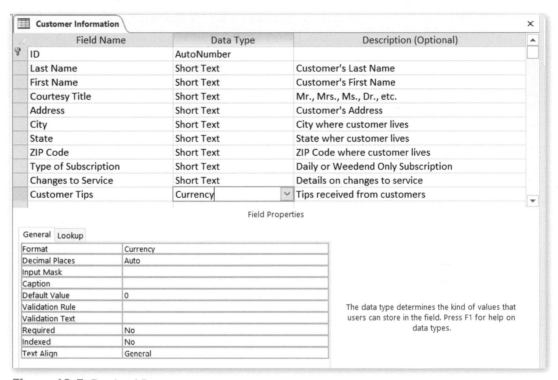

Figure 10-5 Design View

When feasible, fields should be arranged in the same order as the data in the **source document** (paper form from which data is keyed). Doing so reduces the time needed to enter the field contents and maintain the records. Figure 10-5 shows the field names (and sequence of the fields), data type, and description of the fields for the database table illustrated earlier in Figure 10-3. The **primary key** shown before the first field name is used to identify each record in the table with a number. In this case, a unique ID number would automatically be assigned to each member's record.

What Is a Database Form?

Create tab > Forms > Form

Database forms are created from database tables and queries. Forms are used for keying, viewing, and editing data.

Database forms are computerized versions of paper forms such as a job application or a credit card application. On a printed form, you fill in the blanks with the information that is requested, such as your name and address. In a database form, the blanks in which information is entered are called *fields*. In the example above, *Last Name, First Name, Address, City, State,* etc. are field names. When the blanks are filled in, the form becomes a *record*. The form illustrated in Figure 10-6 is a record for student ID 22871, showing the student's schedule.

Depending on the software used, a variety of different form formats are available. The form may show only one record (as shown in Figure 10-6), or it may show multiple records in the database. Forms can be created manually or by using a software wizard.

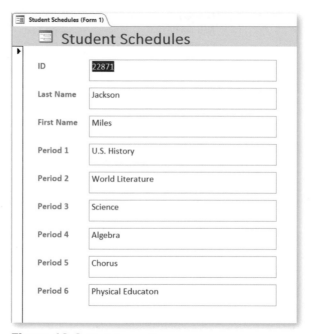

Figure 10-6 Database form

What Is a Database Query?

Create tab > Queries > Query Design

Queries are questions. The Query feature of a database software program allows you to ask for specific information to be retrieved from tables that have been created. For example, the query shown in Figure 10-7 is based on a newspaper customer database. The query pulls information from the Customer Information table to answer the question, "Who are the *Weekend Only* customers?" with the results shown in Figure 10-8.

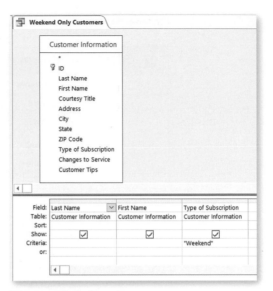

Figure 10-7 Database query

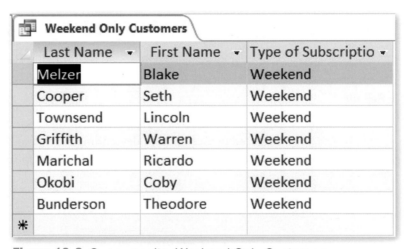

Figure 10-8 Query results: Weekend Only Customers

What Is a Database Report?

Create tab > Reports > Report

Report

Database reports are created from database tables and queries. *Reports* are used for organizing, summarizing, and printing information. The easiest way to generate a report is by simply clicking *Report* in the Reports group. This gives you a report of all the fields in the table. See Figure 10-9. Note that not all the fields are shown in the illustration.

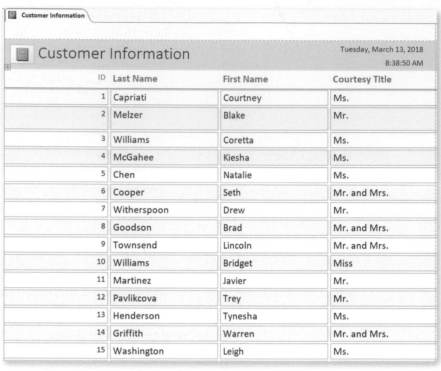

Figure 10-9 Database report using *Report*

Create tab > Reports >
Report Wizard

Report Wizard

Use the Report Wizard to customize the design of the report. Using the Report Wizard, specific fields can be selected to be included in the report, desired groupings can be specified, fields can be sorted in ascending or descending order, and layouts can be selected. Note in Figure 10-10 that the records have been grouped by subscription type (Daily/Weekend).

Customer Service Type

Type of Subscription	Address	Last Name	First Name
Daily	13400 Hyacinth Court	Capriati	Courtney
	13407 Hyacinth Court	Sharpe	Jamal
	13413 Hyacinth Court	Washington	Leigh
	13416 Hyacinth Court	Jackson	Javon
	13419 Jonquil Place	Fairchild	Alonzo
	13420 Hyacinth Court	Henderson	Tynesha
	13427 Jonquil Place	Newberg	Micah
	13429 Hyacinth Court	Williams	Bridget
	13433 Hyacinth Court	Goodson	Brad
	13433 Jonquil Place	Hawthorne	William
	13436 Jonquil Place	Williams	Coretta
	13441 Hyacinth Court	McGahee	Kiesha
	13445 Jonquil Place	Martinez	Javier
Weekend	13407 Jonquil Place	Melzer	Blake
	13414 Jonquil Place	Bunderson	Theodore
	13425 Jonquil Place	Griffith	Warren
	13445 Hyacinth Court	Marichal	Ricardo
	13447 Jonquil Place	Townsend	Lincoln
	13451 Jonquil Place	Cooper	Seth

Figure 10-10 Database report using the *Report Wizard*

What Is a Modified Table/Form?

A modified table or form is one that has been changed after it was created. Rather than creating a new database table or form each time information needs to be changed, database software allows changes to be made to existing tables and forms. Some of the most common changes that can be made include changing field properties, changing field names, adding new fields, and deleting fields no longer needed.

New fields often need to be added to accommodate additional information. Once the field is added, the new information can be keyed for each record. Sometimes the information in an existing field becomes outdated or is simply no longer needed. When this happens, the field can be deleted and all the information in that field is deleted. Before deleting a field, careful consideration should be given to make sure that the information will not be needed in the future. It is simple to delete the information, but time consuming to rekey information once deleted.

What Is a Sort?

Home tab > Sort & Filter > Ascending or Descending

The **Sort** feature can be used to sequence (order) records and forms. This feature allows sorts in ascending or descending order of words (alphabetically) or numbers (numerically). Ascending order is from A to Z and 0 to 9; descending order is from Z to A and 9 to 0.

A sort can be done on one field or on multiple fields. Figure 10-11 shows a sort by *Last Name* in ascending order.

ID Number	Last Name	First Name	Grade	Class Period 1
80356	Barneson	Joanne	7	Keyboarding Apps
72914	Bjorkman	Lance	8	English
73381	Blake	Jan	7	U.S. History
83247	Castillo	Juan	8	Math
66783	Chang	Taylor	8	History
11583	Chu	Chou	7	U.S. History
83564	Crandall	Rebecca	8	History

Student Schedules

Figure 10-11 Sort by Last Name

What Is a Multiple Sort?

When a multiple sort is created, the first sort is called the **primary sort** and the second is called the **secondary sort**.

What Is a Filter?

Home tab > Sort & Filter > Filter

The **filter** feature is used to display specific records in a table instead of all the records. In the example in Figure 10-12, the filter was used to show only students in the Keyboarding Apps class. This is done by clicking the field name (*Class Period 1*) and then clicking the *Filter* icon in the Ribbon (shown at the left). This brings up the Filter dialog box. Next, click *Select All* to remove the check marks. Then click on the items that you want to remain after the filter, in this case *Keyboarding Apps*. Finally, click *OK*. Figure 10-13 shows the filtered results.

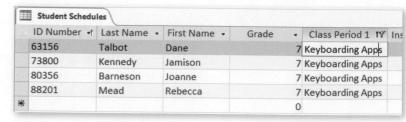

Figure 10-13 Filter results

Figure 10-12 Filter dialog box

Dean Drobot/Shutterstock.com

Digital Citizenship and Ethics

A **cyber predator** is someone who uses the Internet to hunt for victims whom they take advantage of in many ways—sexually, emotionally, psychologically, or financially. Cyber predators know how to manipulate kids. They create trust and friendship where none should exist.

Cyber predators are the dark side of social networking and other forms of online communication. They frequently log on to chat groups or game sites and pose as other kids. They try to gradually gain your trust and encourage you to talk about your problems. Even if you don't chat with strangers, personal information you post on sites such as *Facebook* can make you a target.

As a class, discuss the following.

1. Give examples of how to identify a cyber predator.
2. How can you avoid being the victim of a cyber predator?
3. What should you do if you receive a message that is suggestive, obscene, aggressive, or threatening?

COLLABORATION

LESSON 55   Create a Database

OUTCOMES

- Create a database
- Create and save a table
- Add records to a table
- Preview and print a table

55A

Create a Database

> **NOTE** **Review the Application Guide at the beginning of this chapter before starting this activity.**

> ★**TIP** Based on installation options or software preferences selected by you or other users on your computer, your screens may differ from those shown in this chapter.

The first step in creating a database is to create and save a new database file. In this lesson, you will create a database and design a table to store data for a student's school schedule. Creating a database using *Access* is similar to creating a document using *Word*.

1. Start *Access* and click *Blank database* as shown in Figure 10-14.

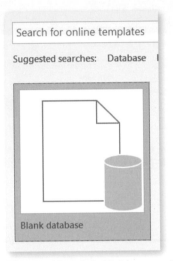

Figure 10-14 Initial screen in *Access*

2. Click in the box under File Name and key **55 schedule** for the file name as shown in Figure 10-15.

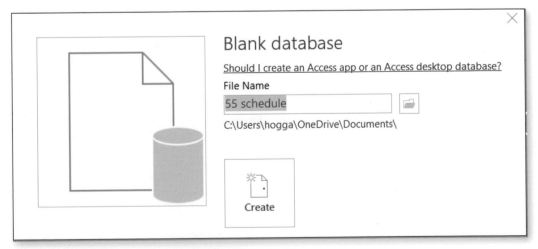

Figure 10-15 Name the new database

3. Click the folder icon next to the file name and navigate to the location where you are saving files for this chapter.

4. Open the folder where you are saving the work you do in this chapter and click *OK* to save *55 schedule*.

5. Click *Create* to create the blank database.

6. *Access* opens the new database with Table1 displayed, as shown in Figure 10-16. Click the table's *Close* button to close the table.

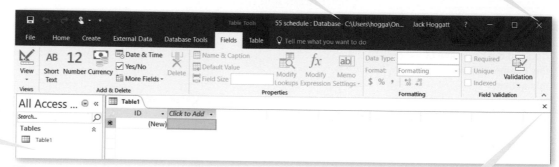

Figure 10-16 New database with table

55B

Create and Save a Table

Once you create a database file, you can create tables within that file to store data. Recall that a table is made up of records and fields. A record is a row of information (data) in a table (Figure 10-17). A field is a column of information (data) in a table (Figure 10-18).

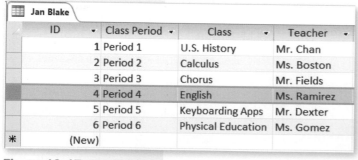

Figure 10-17 Record (row)

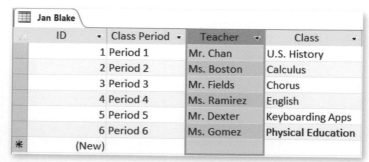

Figure 10-18 Field (column)

Table Design

Before creating a table, you should take time to plan the design of the table. Planning the design will save you the time and frustration of having to modify it later. You should consider the types of data (names, amounts, descriptions) that will be stored in the table. You also should consider how the data will be used. For example, sorting data by state will be easy if you include a State field in the table, rather than storing state data along with other information in an Address field.

Data Types

Choosing the data type for each field is an important step in designing a table. The **data type** determines the kind of data a field can hold. You can use several types of data, some of which are shown in Table 10-1.

Data Type	Description
Short Text	For letters or numbers that do not require calculations
Number	For numeric values to be used in calculations
Date/Time	For dates and times
Currency	For dollar values
AutoNumber	Numbers assigned in order by *Access*
Yes/No	For data that can only be Yes or No
Calculated Field	Shows the result of a calculation of other fields in the same table

Table 10-1 Data types

Primary Key

When you create an *Access* table, you can select one field in the table to be the primary key. A *primary key* is a field chosen to identify each record in a table. *Access* does not allow duplicate data to be entered in the primary key field. The value in the primary key must be unique for every record.

For example, in a table containing data for students at a school, each student would have a student ID number. Each student's ID number would be different from all other ID numbers. The field that holds the student's ID number can be set as the primary key. This would prevent a user from accidentally entering the same ID number for two different students.

You can choose a field to set as the primary key. You also can let *Access* create a primary key field for you.

The *55 schedule* database that you created will store data about class schedules in a simple table. The table will have four fields: ID, Class Period, Class, and Teacher. The data type for the ID field will be AutoNumber, and the other fields will use the default Short Text data type.

Create tab > Tables >
Table Design

1. In the *55 schedule* database, click the *Create* tab. In the Tables group, click *Table Design* (Figure 10-19).

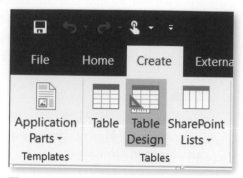

Figure 10-19 Create a new table using Table Design

★TIP The fields can be defined directly in a new table by using the *Click to Add* feature or by using Design View. Design View includes a *Description* option.

2. The new table opens in DesignView with the insertion point blinking under *Field Name*. Key **Class Period**. Tap *Tab* to move to the Data Type field; then tap *Tab* to accept the default data type (Short Text) and move to the Description field. Key the information shown in Figure 10-20. Use *Tab* to move from field to field or use the mouse to click where you want to key.

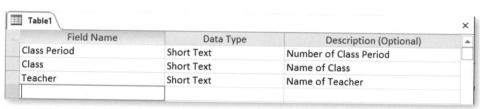

Figure 10-20 Table in Design View

3. Click the table's *Close* button. Click *Yes* to save changes to the table design. Key **Jan Blake** for the Table Name and click *OK* (Figure 10-21).

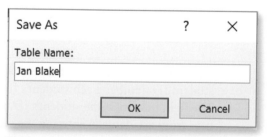

Figure 10-21 Save the table design

★TIP You can also click the *Primary Key* button to set the primary key for a table.

4. A prompt appears asking whether you want to create a primary key. Click *Yes*. *Access* creates a field named ID to be the primary key. This prevents any duplicate values from being entered in the primary key field.

You are now ready to add records to the table.

Add Records to a Table

As you work in an *Access* database, you will use a number of different views. You create a table in Design View, for example, but you must switch to Datasheet View to enter records in the table. You use the *View* command in the Views group on the Home or Design tab to switch between different *Access* views.

Activity 1

You have now created a database file (*55 schedule*) and a database table (*Jan Blake*). In this activity, you add records to the table.

1. Open the *Jan Blake* table in Datasheet View if necessary by double-clicking the object in the Navigation pane.

2. Click to place the insertion point beneath Class Period and key **Period 1**. Tap *Tab* once to move the insertion point to the Class field. Key **U.S. History**, which is Jan Blake's first class. Tap *Tab* to move the insertion point to the Teacher field. Key **Mr. Chan**, the name of Jan Blake's history teacher. (See Figure 10-22.)

> **★TIP** Move from column to column by tapping *Tab*, by clicking a cell, or by using the arrow keys.

Figure 10-22 Jan Blake database table

3. Enter the remaining classes shown in the following table.

ID	Class Period	Class	Teacher
1	Period 1	U.S. History	Mr. Chan
2	Period 2	Algebra	Ms. Boston
3	Period 3	Chorus	Mr. Fields
4	Period 4	English	Ms. Ramirez
5	Period 5	Keyboarding Apps	Mr. Dexter
6	Period 6	Physical Education	Ms. Gomez

> **NOTE** The ID field in the table was created automatically when you chose to create a primary key. The field type is AutoNumber. This means that you do not enter data in this field. *Access* automatically assigns a number in this field to each record you create.

4. Look at Record 5 that contains *Keyboarding Apps*. The column is not wide enough to show all of the information. You can adjust column widths to fit the data.

5. Place the pointer on the column border (vertical line) to the right of the word *Class* (the column head). The pointer will appear as a double-headed arrow with a vertical line. Double-click the column border. The column width adjusts to fit the longest item in the column.

6. Close the table. When you are asked whether you want to save changes to the layout of the table, click *Yes*.

7. Complete the following CheckPoint.

> **★TIP** When you tap *Tab* in the last field of a record, a new blank record is created.

> **★TIP** The data is automatically saved when a table is closed.

COLLABORATION

✓ checkpoint Switch seats with one of your classmates. Open your classmate's *Jan Blake* table to see if it is set up correctly. Make sure all classes are included. Check for keying and spelling errors.

Activity 2

You now know how to create a table and enter data. Practice what you have learned by creating a table for Miles Jackson's schedule like the one you created for Jan Blake.

Use Table Design to create the table. Use Datasheet View to enter the information displayed below. Review Lesson 55B as needed for creating the table design. The design is the same as the one created for Jan Blake. Remember to adjust the column width to fit the information.

ID	Class Period	Class	Teacher
1	Period 1	U.S. History	Mr. Chan
2	Period 2	World Literature	Ms. Jepson
3	Period 3	Science	Mr. Sanchez
4	Period 4	Algebra	Ms. Schultz
5	Period 5	Chorus	Mr. Fields
6	Period 6	Physical Education	Mr. Gerig

Activity 3

When the design of a new table is to be the same as a table previously created, you can copy the existing table rather than repeating all the steps to create the design of the table. Create a table for Rebecca Mead's schedule and enter the information for the table by completing these steps.

1. Click Jan Blake's table in the Navigation pane and copy (*Ctrl + C*) and paste (*Ctrl + V*).
2. In the Paste Table As dialog box (Figure 10-23), select *Structure Only*; otherwise, all the data in Jan Blake's table will be copied in the new table.
3. Select the table name *Copy Of Jan Blake* and key **Rebecca Mead**. Click *OK*.

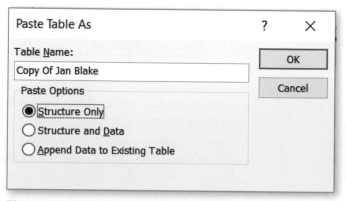

Figure 10-23 Copy and name a table

4. The new table for Rebecca Mead appears in the Navigation pane beneath the tables that have already been created. Double-click the table to open it.

5. Enter Rebecca Mead's schedule into the table from the information shown below.

ID	Class Period	Class	Teacher
1	Period 1	Keyboarding Apps	Mr. Dexter
2	Period 2	Civics	Ms. Blakely
3	Period 3	Biology	Mr. Weston
4	Period 4	Algebra	Mr. Carver
5	Period 5	World Literature	Mr. Dexter
6	Period 6	Physical Education	Ms. Gomez

6. Close the tables.

Activity 4

1. Create a table with Jamison Kennedy's schedule by copying and pasting Jan Blake's schedule. However, this time select *Structure and Data* and key **Jamison Kennedy**. Click *OK*.
2. Open the table. Notice Jan Blake's schedule now appears as the schedule for Jamison Kennedy because you copied and pasted using *Structure and Data*.
3. Click the Period 1 cell. Since you want Period 1 left in this cell, tap the *Tab* key (or the *Enter* key) to move to the next cell. Enter **Keyboarding Apps** for his first period class and then tap *Tab* to move to the next cell and enter **Mr. Dexter** for the teacher.
4. Because Jamison's second-, third-, and fourth-period classes are the same as Jan Blake's, click and highlight *Keyboarding Apps* in the fifth-period class cell and enter **U.S. History**. Tab to the next cell and enter **Mr. Chan**.
5. Jamison has Physical Education for sixth period, but the instructor is **Mr. Gerig**. Use the down arrow key to move to make this change.
6. Verify the changes to make sure they are correct. Notice that by using *Structure and Data*, you only had to enter information in 5 cells rather than 18 cells. When only a few changes need to be made, using *Structure and Data* rather than *Structure Only* can save time.
7. Close the tables.

55D

Preview and Print a Table

File tab > Print > Print Preview

When in Print Preview, you can use the features in the Page Size and the Page Layout groups to change the paper size, orientation, and margins, as shown in Figure 10-24. If the document is currently set for Portrait orientation and you want Landscape orientation, simply click the *Landscape* button. Margins can be changed by using the *Margins* button for preset margins or *Page Setup* to specify custom margins.

1. Open the table for Miles Jackson.
2. Follow the path at the left to see how the table looks using Print Preview.
3. Click the table a couple of times to switch between a full-page and a close-up view of the table. Notice that the table name (*Miles Jackson*) and the current date appear at the top of the page. *Page 1* appears at the bottom of the page.

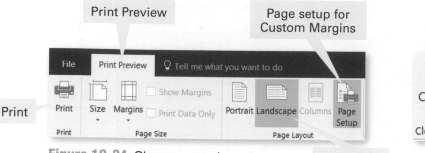

Print Preview

Page setup for Custom Margins

Close Print Preview

Close Preview

Print

Landscape

Figure 10-24 Change page layout

4. Change the orientation to *Landscape*.

5. Click the *Page Setup* button to change the top margin to 2".

6. Print the table by clicking *Print* on the Print Preview tab.

7. Click *Close Print Preview*.

8. Close the table and then click the *Close* button to exit *Access*. Click *Yes* if you are asked if it's ok to empty the Clipboard.

checkpoint Check your printed table. Have you completed all instructions? Are names spelled correctly? Great job! You now know how to create a database table and enter records.

LESSON 56

Create a Database Form

OUTCOMES

• Create a database, create a table, and enter records
• Create a database form
• Create a form using a wizard

56A

Plan and Create a Database

When you design a database, it is important to make it easy to use the data. You need to consider whether you can have all the data in one table or if you need several tables.

The database you created in Lesson 55 is not designed for storing and using large amounts of data. If there are 600 students at Lincoln Junior High, it would be very cumbersome, and users would become very frustrated trying to find a specific student's table out of the 600 tables created to accommodate each student's information individually. Schedules would have to be viewed one at a time. Searching or sorting the data would be difficult.

TIP To review creating a database, see Lesson 55A. To review creating a table, see Lesson 55B.

A database with one table that includes all students would be more useful. It would allow users to search and sort the data much more efficiently. In this activity, you will create a database with one table to store schedule data for students at Lincoln Junior High.

1. Start *Access* and create a new database. Use *56 lincoln* for the file name.

2. Click the *Views* icon in the View group on the Table Tools Design tab and select *Design View* to create a table. Save the table as **Student Schedules**. Enter the field names, data types, and descriptions shown in the following table. You can use the drop-down arrow to select the data type or start keying the data type and it will display in the Data Type box. As soon as it appears, tap *Tab* or *Enter* to quickly move to the next cell and enter the description.

Field Name	Data Type	Description
ID Number	Short Text	Student's ID Number
Last Name	Short Text	Student's Last Name
First Name	Short Text	Student's First Name
Period 1	Short Text	Class Period 1
Period 2	Short Text	Class Period 2
Period 3	Short Text	Class Period 3
Period 4	Short Text	Class Period 4
Period 5	Short Text	Class Period 5
Period 6	Short Text	Class Period 6

3. Note the ID Number field name was automatically selected as the Primary Key field. If you wanted to select a different field for the Primary Key field, you would select the desired row and click *Primary Key*.

4. Use the path at the left to display Datasheet View. Save the table.

5. Three student records are shown below. Enter the records into the *Student Schedules* table. After you enter the data, adjust the column widths to fit the longest entry in each column.

ID Number	35981	48263	52596
Last Name	Hansen	Martinez	Castello
First Name	Brittany	Rico	Mary
Period 1	English	U.S. History	Biology
Period 2	U.S. History	Algebra	Chorus
Period 3	Keyboarding Apps	Physical Ed	World History
Period 4	Algebra	Chorus	Physical Ed
Period 5	Chorus	World Literature	English
Period 6	Biology	Biology	Algebra

6. Enter the schedules for Jan Blake (ID Number 73381), Miles Jackson (ID Number 22871), Rebecca Mead (ID Number 88201), and Jamison Kennedy (ID Number 73800). Refer to 78C for their schedules.

7. Leave the table open to complete 56B.

You have already learned how to enter data into the database table using Datasheet View. Data can also be entered using a database form. A *form* is an object used to enter or display data. The Form command automatically creates a form based on an open table and includes all of the fields from the table.

A new form you create using the Form command displays in Layout View. This view can be used to adjust the appearance of the form. To enter records using a form, you must use Form View.

You are now ready to create a form from the *Student Schedules* table in the *56 lincoln* database.

Create tab > Forms > Form

1. With the *Student Schedules* table open, follow the path at the left and click *Form*. A form with all of the fields in the *Student Schedules* table is created. The new form displays in Layout View. Miles Jackson's record is shown in Figure 10-25.

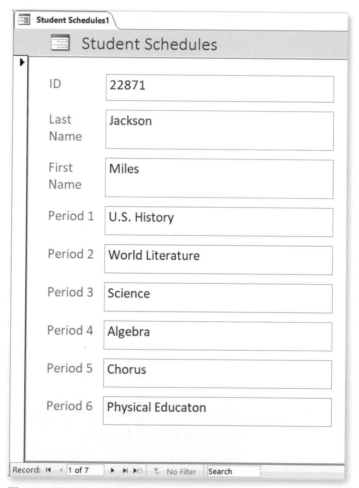

Figure 10-25 Student Schedules form

2. The arrows at the bottom of the screen can be used to move from record to record, as shown on the next page. Click each of the arrows in turn. As you click each arrow, notice the record that is displayed before and after clicking the arrow.

★TIP When you tap *Tab* in the last field of a record, a new blank record is created.

Click	To Go
◄	To the first record
►	Forward one record
◄	Back one record
►|	To the last record
►*	To a new blank record

3. Click the tab for the *Student Schedules* table. Click the table's *Close* button. Click the form's *Close* button. Click *Yes* to save changes to the design of the *Student Schedules* form. Save the form as **Student Schedules (Form 1)**.

4. Open *Student Schedules (Form 1)*. Go to a new blank record. Enter the data for three students as follows.

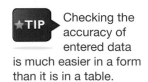

★TIP Checking the accuracy of entered data is much easier in a form than it is in a table.

ID Number	11583	25781	22854
Last Name	Chu	Santos	Hefner
First Name	Chou	Felipe	Amanda
Period 1	U.S. History	English	Algebra
Period 2	English	Algebra	U.S. History
Period 3	Keyboarding Apps	Keyboarding Apps	Physical Ed
Period 4	Biology	Biology	Biology
Period 5	Algebra	Art	English
Period 6	Art	World History	Chorus

5. When you finish entering the data, close the form by clicking its *Close* button.

6. Open the *Student Schedules* table. (If it is already open, you must close and reopen it in order to see the records that were just added.)

7. Notice that the new records are in the table. The records were automatically arranged in ascending order by ID Number. Read the following CheckPoint and then close the table.

 **checkpoint** You should now have ten records in the *Student Schedules* table.

Create a Form Using a Wizard

Using the Form command is a quick way to create a form. Forms can also be created using the Form Wizard. The Form Wizard asks a series of questions and creates the form based on the answers. The Form Wizard gives you more choices about how the form will look and what fields you want to include.

1. Open the database **56 lincoln** that you created in 56A if necessary.

2. Click the *Create* tab on the Ribbon. In the Forms group, click *Form Wizard*. The Form Wizard opens as shown in Figure 10-26.

3. Notice that your *Student Schedules* table is identified in the Tables/ Queries box and its fields are listed in Available Fields. Because you have only one table, the name of that table (*Student Schedules*) appears in the Tables/Queries box. If you had several tables, you could select the table from which you wanted to prepare the form. (To select a table, click the down arrow and choose the desired table.)

Figure 10-26 Form Wizard

★TIP The > button moves only the highlighted field over to the Selected Fields window.

4. Click the double-arrow (>>) button to select all of the fields and include them in the form. Click *Next*.

5. The next Wizard screen lets you select the form layout. Select *Tabular* and then click *Next*.

6. Finally, you will be prompted to give the form a title. Key **Student Schedules Form 2**. Select the option *Open the form to view or enter information*. (See Figure 10-27.) Click *Finish*.

7. The form appears on your screen in Form View, displaying the ten records that you entered earlier.

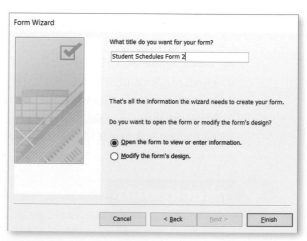

Figure 10-27 Enter a title for the form in the Form Wizard

8. Move to a new blank record at the bottom of the form. Enter data for the three following records.

ID Number	52798	63156	23927
Last Name	Schuricht	Talbot	Davenport
First Name	Jessica	Dane	Mitchell
Period 1	Algebra	Keyboarding Apps	Biology
Period 2	U.S. History	U.S. History	U.S. History
Period 3	Physical Ed	English	English
Period 4	Chorus	Algebra	Algebra
Period 5	English	Chorus	Chorus
Period 6	Biology	Biology	Keyboarding Apps

★TIP Before opening Print Preview, double-click the right border line of each column heading to adjust the width of the columns.

9. Close the form and open the *Student Schedules* table. Notice that the records you added using the form are now included in the table. Notice that the records have again been arranged by ID Number.

File tab > Print > Print Preview

10. Open Print Preview. In the Page Layout group, change the Orientation to *Landscape*. Refer to 55D, if needed.

11. While in Print Preview, determine whether the *Student Schedules* table will print on one page. If it doesn't fit on one page, what suggestions would you have for making it fit on one page?

12. Complete the CheckPoint, and then close the database.

 **checkpoint** Check each record for spelling and keying errors. Make the necessary corrections, adjust the width of any fields if necessary, and close the table. Save any layout changes if necessary.

LESSON 57 Add Fields, Delete Fields, and Edit Records

OUTCOMES
- Add and delete table fields
- Edit database records
- Modify a database table

57A

Add and Delete Table Fields

After creating a database table, you might want to add or delete fields. For example, in the *Student Schedules* table, including the name of the instructor for each class period would be helpful. If Lincoln High School changed to a five-period day, Period 6 would need to be deleted from the table.

To add fields to a table, you begin by opening the table in Design View. You insert a new row in the table where you want the field to appear. Then you enter a field name, data type, and description. After you save the table, you are ready to enter data in the new field for the existing records or for new records.

To delete fields from a table, you begin by opening the table in Design View. Then you select and delete the field. You will learn to add and delete fields in the activities that follow.

Access has a Save As command like the one you have used in other *Office* applications to save files using a new name. This feature is useful when you want to make changes to a database and still keep a copy of the original database.

File tab > Save As > Access Database (default)

Home tab > Views > Design View

Activity 1

In this activity, you will add fields to a database table.

1. Open the **df 57 lincoln** database.
2. Use the *Save As* command to save the database as **57 lincoln** in the folder in which you save your work for this class.
3. In the **57 lincoln** database, open the *Student Schedules* table in Design View.
4. Right-click anywhere in the row with the field name Class Period 2. Choose *Insert Rows* from the pop-up menu. (See Figure 10-28.)
5. A new row is inserted above the selected row. In the new row, key **Instructor 1** for the field name. Choose *Short Text* for the data type. For the description, key **Name of Instructor for Class Period 1**.
6. Repeat the procedure to insert a row for the name of the instructor for each class period. For the last class (Period 6), enter the data in the blank row under *Class Period 6*. (See Figure 10-29.)

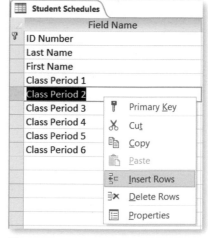

Figure 10-28 Insert a new row

> **★TIP** Virus protection software can disable some database content. If the message "Security Warning Some active content in the database has been disabled" is displayed when you open a database, click the *Enable Content* button. Depending on your virus protection software, you might have to enable content every time you open a database.

> **★TIP** If you insert the row in the wrong place, click the *Undo* button or press *Ctrl + Z*.

Field Name	Data Type	
ID Number	Short Text	Student's ID number
Last Name	Short Text	Student's last name
First Name	Short Text	Student's first name
Class Period 1	Short Text	Name of period 1 class
Instructor 1	Short Text	Name of Instructor for Class Period 1
Class Period 2	Short Text	Name of period 2 class
Instructor 2	Short Text	Name of Instructor for Class Period 2
Class Period 3	Short Text	Name of period 3 class
Instructor 3	Short Text	Name of Instructor for Class Period 3
Class Period 4	Short Text	Name of period 4 class
Instructor 4	Short Text	Name of Instructor for Class Period 4
Class Period 5	Short Text	Name of period 5 class
Instructor 5	Short Text	Name of Instructor for Class Period 5
Class Period 6	Short Text	Name of period 6 class
Instructor 6	Short Text	Name of Instructor for Class Period 6

Figure 10-29 Table with fields added

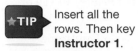

TIP Insert all the rows. Then key **Instructor 1**. Copy *Instructor* and then paste it and key **2**. You will only need to key the number. Using this procedure for the Description column will save having to key *Name of Instructor for Class Period* each time.

Find

7. Switch to Datasheet View. Click *Yes* to the prompt *Do you want to save the table now?* to save the changes to the table design.

8. Create a form automatically (*Create* > *Forms* > *Form*). Once the form is created, close it. Click *Yes* to the prompt *Do you want to save the changes to the design of the form?* Key **Student Schedules** (**Form 3**) for the name of the form. Click *OK*.

9. Open *Student Schedules* (*Form 3*) and enter the names of the instructors for each class for the students shown below. Use the *Tab* or *Enter* key to move from field to field. To quickly find the next person, click the *Last Name* box of the form. Then click the *Find* feature (shown at the left), key the next name (**Santos**) in the Find What box, and then click *Find Next*.

	Chu	Santos	Hansen	Martinez	Castello
Instructor 1	Johnson	Fenn	Ramos	Johnson	Baker
Instructor 2	Fenn	Hintze	Johnson	Hintze	Strauss
Instructor 3	Hamilton	Hamilton	Hamilton	Vasquez	McDowell
Instructor 4	Boyer	Baker	Wallace	D'Angelo	Vasquez
Instructor 5	Hintze	Burdette	Strauss	Ramos	Fenn
Instructor 6	Burdette	McDowell	Boyer	Baker	Wallace

10. Close the form. Close the *57 lincoln* database.

Activity 2

In this activity, you will add and delete fields in an existing database.

TIP Enter the composer's name in a search engine or an online encyclopedia to find data about him.

1. Open ***df 57 composers*** and save it as ***57 composers*** in the folder in which you save your work for this class.

2. Open the *Composers* (*1600–1799*) table in Design View.

3. Insert a new field after the Life field. Key **Birthplace** for the field name. Select *Short Text* for the data type. For the description, key **Composer's Birthplace**.

4. Switch to Datasheet View and save the changes to the table. Print the table in Landscape orientation. Close the database.

5. Work with another student to find the country where each composer was born. For example, Bach was born in Germany. Access the Internet and find the birth country for three of the remaining composers. Your classmate should find data for the other three composers. Share your data with each other.

COLLABORATION

6. Open ***57 composers***. Open the *Composers* (*1600–1799*) table. Update the table with the birthplaces you found in your research.

The table has data in the Teachers field for only one record. You have decided that this data is not needed.

 checkpoint

Exchange tables with a class-mate and check each other's work. Make corrections to your table if necessary.

7. Switch to Design View. Right-click the row that has *Teachers* for the field name. Choose *Delete Rows* from the pop-up menu.

8. You will be asked whether you want to permanently delete the selected field(s) and all of the data in the field(s). Click *Yes*. The field will be deleted.

9. Switch to Datasheet View and click *Yes* to save the table. Print the table in Landscape orientation. Close the database.

Congratulations! You now know how to update records as well as add and delete fields in an existing database table.

57B

Edit Records

Reasons for Editing Records

Information changes over time. Errors are sometimes made in entering data. As a result of these errors and changes, the data in a database may need to be corrected or updated. **Edits** (changes and corrections) may be needed for a variety of reasons. For example, if a person moves to a new house, his or her address data would need to be updated. A student may change classes. An incorrect address may be entered. All of those situations require that edits be made to the database.

Methods for Editing Records

Editing database records is similar to editing word processing documents. You begin by moving to the location where the change is to be made. You can use the Delete or Backspace keys to delete data. You also can delete entire records.

In a small table, you can locate records easily by scrolling through the rows. However, many databases are large, and scrolling to find a certain record to edit is not so easy. You can use the Find feature to locate a record quickly. You can use the Replace feature to change several occurrences of data in a table. You can make edits to records in Datasheet View or using a form.

In this activity, you will edit records in the database you used earlier in this lesson.

1. Open the **57 lincoln** database you worked with in 57A, Activity 1.

2. Open the *Student Schedules* table. You need to edit the record for the student with ID 48263. If necessary, click the first record that appears in the ID Number field. To search by ID Number, a number in the ID Number field must be active or you can change the Look In: box from *Current field* to *Current document*.

3. On the Home tab, click *Find* in the Find group. In the Find What box, key **48263**. (See Figure 10-30.) Click *Find Next*. The record for the student with this ID, Rico Martinez, will be displayed in *Student Schedules*.

★TIP Use the *Ctrl + F* keyboard shortcut to quickly access the Find and Replace dialog box.

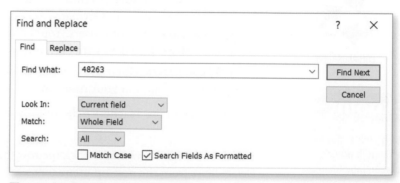

Figure 10-30 Find tab in the Find and Replace dialog box

4. Click *Cancel* to close the Find box. Use the mouse or the *Tab* key to move to the First Name field. Change the name from Rico to **Ricardo**.

5. Use Find to move to the record for Felipe Santos, ID Number 25781. Remember that the ID Number field has to be active when searching for an ID Number. Felipe has changed Biology instructors. He has switched from Baker to **Boyer**. The class still meets during the fourth class period. Update his record.

6. Brittany Hansen, ID Number 35981, has **U.S. History** during the first class period and **English** during the second class period. Her English teacher is **Fenn**. Her history teacher is **Johnson**. Update her record.

7. Mary Castello moved last week. You need to delete her record from the table. Since you do not know Mary's ID Number, use the *Find* feature to locate her last name. Once you find Mary's record, click any field of the record. From the Records group of the Home tab, click the down arrow on the *Delete* button. Click *Delete Record*. Note that the next record is now displayed. Choose *Yes* when asked if you are sure you want to delete the record.

8. Miss Hintze, who teaches math, was recently married. Her new last name is Hintze-Braun. You will use the Replace feature to update the table with her new name. Click *Replace* from the Find group of the Home tab. The Find and Replace dialog box displays the Replace tab as shown in Figure 10-31.

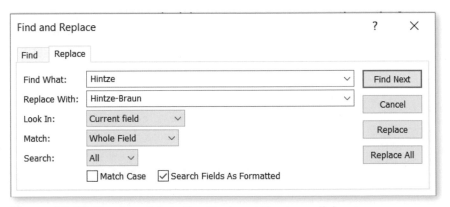

Figure 10-31 Replace tab in the Find and Replace dialog box

9. In the Find What box, key **Hintze**. In the Replace With box, key **Hintze-Braun**. In the Look In box, select *Current document* so that the search will include the entire table rather than just the field that is currently selected.

10. Click *Replace All*. A dialog box displays telling you that you will not be able to undo this operation. Click *Yes* to continue. Click *Cancel* to close the Find and Replace box.

11. Using the Replace feature, edit all records in the table to change *Education* to **Ed** (no period in the abbreviations). Click the *Match* down arrow and select *Any Part of Field*.

12. Widen or shorten the columns in the table as needed to display the complete field title and the complete information in the field. Close the table. Save layout changes.

Modify a Database Table

The principal of Lincoln Junior High would like the *Student Schedules* table in the **57 lincoln** database modified to include a field for the grade level of the students. The field should be placed after the First Name field. Use **Grade** for the field name. Use **Number** as the data type and **Grade Level of Student** for the description.

After you add the field to the table, enter the grade level for all students. Ferrero, Chang, Bjorkman, Guillermo, Thomson, J. Hefner, LaRoche, Hansen, Sisson, Castillo, Crandall, McMillian, and Painter are all in grade 8; the rest of the students are in grade 7. Close the table and exit *Access*.

LESSON 58   Work with Database Queries, Filters, and Sorts

OUTCOMES

- Create a query in Design View
- Filter data by selection
- Sort records

58A

Create a Query in Design View

Generally, databases contain large amounts of data. Queries and filters are used to display only certain records from the database. For example, you may want to know how many seventh-grade students are enrolled in Algebra I this semester. A query would allow you to extract from the database all the students who are enrolled in Algebra I this semester who are seventh graders. In this lesson, you learn to use queries and filters to find (mine) data to answer questions.

A query is a database object that displays certain data that you describe. You describe the data by entering criteria. The criteria might be the field name, data in a certain field, or data that is not in a field. For example, the database for Lincoln Junior High has records for students in grades 7 and 8. You can create a query that will display only records for students in grade 8. A query allows you to include all of the fields included in a table or only selected ones. When you create the query to show only records for eighth-grade students, for example, you may want only their first name, last name, and grade included.

In this activity, you create a query to show the Last Name, First Name, and Grade fields for eighth-grade students.

1. Open **df 58 lincoln**. Save the database as **58 lincoln** in the folder where you are storing files for this lesson.
2. In the **58 lincoln** database file, follow the path at the left and click *Query Design*. The query design grid opens as shown in Figure 10-32. The Show Table dialog box is open.
3. The table *Student Schedules* is selected in the Show Table dialog box. Click *Add*. The *Student Schedules* fields list box appears in the query window. Click *Close* on the Show Table dialog box.
4. Click the down arrow in the query design grid in the first column by *Field*. The list of field names will appear. Select *ID Number*.
5. Tab to the next column. Click the down arrow in the second column and select *Last Name*.

Create tab > Queries > Query Design

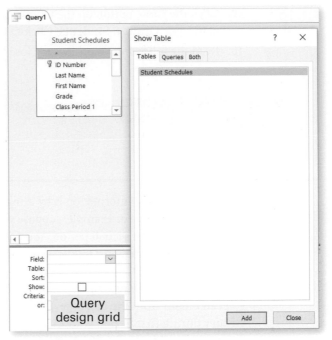

Figure 10-32 Show Table dialog box and query design grid

6. Tab to the next column. Click the down arrow in the third column and select *First Name*.

7. Tab to the next column. Click the down arrow in the fourth column and select *Grade*. In the Criteria row for this column, key **8**. Your design grid should look like the one in Figure 10-33.

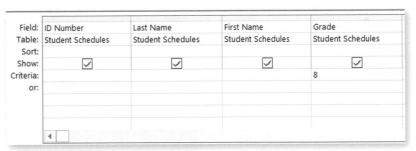

Field:	ID Number	Last Name	First Name	Grade
Table:	Student Schedules	Student Schedules	Student Schedules	Student Schedules
Sort:				
Show:	☑	☑	☑	☑
Criteria:				8
or:				

Figure 10-33 Query design grid

8. On the Query Tools *Design* tab in the Results group, click the *Run* button (Figure 10-34). The query results display in a table.

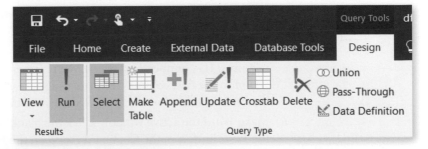

Figure 10-34 Run button

9. Click the *Close* button on the Query1 tab and click *Yes* to save the query. For the query name, key **Grade 8 Students**. Click *OK*.

10. Read the following CheckPoint. Close the query window. Continue with the next activity.

 **checkpoint** Did the query results table show 13 records? All records should be for students in grade 8.

Filter by Selection

Another way to find information is by using a filter. A filter hides records in a table that do not match your criteria. For example, suppose you want to find all of the records for students who are taking English in second period. You can apply a filter that will hide all other records. Filtered records are not deleted, just hidden. They will be displayed again when the filter is removed.

Ms. Tonia Cross, the principal at Lincoln Junior High, has requested some information that you can obtain from the database. She wants to know which seventh-grade students have U.S. History during first period with Mr. Johnson. In this activity, you will use the Filter by Selection feature to provide the information the principal wants.

1. Open the *Student Schedules* table.

2. Click in a cell in the Class Period 1 column that contains the entry *U.S. History*. On the Home tab in the Sort & Filter group, click the *Selection* button. Select *Equals "U.S. History"*. (See Figure 10-35.) Only records with *U.S. History* in the Class Period 1 field display.

Figure 10-35 Selection button

3. Click a cell in the Instructor 1 column that contains *Johnson*. Click the *Selection* button again. Select *Equals "Johnson"*. Only records for seventh-graders with *U.S. History* in the first class period who have *Johnson* for an instructor will display.

4. Leave *Access* open. Start *Word*. Open **df 58 memo** from your data files. Save the file as **58 memo** in the location where you store files for this class.

5. Make *Access* the active window. In the *Student Schedules* filtered table, select the following columns: ID Number, Last Name, First Name, Grade, Class Period 1, and Instructor 1. (Point to the first column head and drag across to select the columns.) Click the *Copy* button in the Clipboard group on the Home tab.

6. Make *Word* the active window. Click the blank line below the paragraph of the memo. Click the *Paste* button in the Clipboard group on the Home tab. The table appears in your memo. Center the table horizontally.

7. Change *Student Name* to your name in the memo heading. Add the current date in the heading. Save the memo again, using the same name. Print and close the memo. Close *Word*.

8. Make *Access* the active window if necessary. The Toggle Filter button can be used to remove the filter or to apply the filter. Click the *Toggle Filter* button in the Sort & Filter group to remove the filter. (See Figure 10-36.)

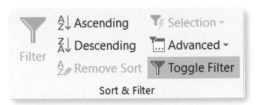

Figure 10-36 Toggle Filter button

9. All records should now be displayed in the table. Click *Toggle Filter* again to apply the filter. The six records for the seventh-graders with *U.S. History* in the first class period taught by *Johnson* will again be displayed. Click *Toggle Filter* to remove the filter. Leave the *Student Schedules* table open.

58C

Sort Records

The Sort feature allows you to arrange the information in a table or query in a certain order. The information can be sorted in ascending order (0 to 100 or A to Z) or descending order (100 to 0 or Z to A).

In this activity, you will use the Sort feature to arrange records in the *Student Schedules* table in various ways.

1. Click any cell in the Last Name field. Click the *Ascending* button in the Sort & Filter group on the Home tab. The buttons used to sort data are shown in Figure 10-37. The Last Name field should be alphabetized starting with *Barneson*.

Figure 10-37 Sort buttons

2. Now you will use the Sort feature to arrange the records by the Grade field in ascending order. Click any cell in the Grade field. Click the *Ascending* button. The data is shown with all seventh-graders first and then all eighth-graders.

3. Now you will arrange the records by the Grade field in descending order. Click any cell in the Grade field if necessary. Click the *Descending* button. The data is shown with all eighth-graders first.

4. Close the *Student Schedules* table. Choose *No* if asked if you want to save design changes to the table. Close the database.

Query, Filter, and Sort Records

In this activity, you will create a query in a database that contains information for a newspaper delivery route.

1. Open *df 58 newspaper* and save it as *58 newspaper* in the folder where you save your work for this class.
2. Create a query in Query Design View. Base the query on the *Customer Information* table. Include the First Name, Last Name, and Address fields in the query.
3. Run the query.
4. Select (highlight) *only* the word *Hyacinth* in the Address field in the first record in the results table. Click the *Selection* button on the Home tab. Click *Contains "Hyacinth"*. Only records that have the word *Hyacinth* in the street address should be displayed.
5. If necessary, click a cell in the Address field. Click the *Ascending* sort button to arrange the customers by their street address in ascending order.
6. Print the query results table that has been filtered and sorted. Use Portrait orientation.
7. Close the query results table without saving changes. Close *Access*.

✓ checkpoint

Does your query results table have 11 records? The address of the first record should be 13400 Hyacinth Court, and the address of the last record should be 13452 Hyacinth Court.

LESSON 59   Work with Database Reports

OUTCOMES
- Create a report
- Create a query and report

59A

Create a Report

A *report* is a database object used to display data. Reports can be formatted to show data in a format that is easy to read. The top part of a report is shown in Figure 10-38. Reports can contain data from tables or queries. You can create an AutoReport from an open table or query. You can use the Report Wizard to create a report or mailing labels. In this lesson, you will create a report using the Report Wizard.

Johnson's Period 1 Class

Class Period 1	Last Name	First Name	Instructor 1
U.S. History	Chu	Chou	Johnson
	Foster	Erika	Johnson
	Garner	Shelby	Johnson
	Hansen	Brittany	Johnson
	Hennessy	Mathew	Johnson
	Martinez	Ricardo	Johnson

Figure 10-38 Database report

The Report Wizard

The Report Wizard allows you to create a report by making a series of choices. You can choose the:

- Table or query on which the report is based
- Fields to include in the report
- Way fields will be grouped in the report
- Way records will be sorted in the report
- Layout of the report

If you do not like the results of your choices, you can delete the report and create a new one using different choices. You also can make changes to a report in Layout or Design View.

1. Open **df 59 lincoln**. Save the database as **59 lincoln**.
2. You will create a report to show data from the *Student Schedules* table. On the Create tab in the Reports group, click *Report Wizard*.
3. Use the down arrow on the box beneath Tables/Queries to view the options.
4. Select *Table: Student Schedules*.
5. Click the *First Name* field in the list under Available Fields. Click the single right arrow (>) button to move the field to the Selected Fields box. Do the same for the other fields to be included in the report: Last Name and Grade. Your screen should look like Figure 10-39. Click *Next*.

TIP If you move the wrong field to the Selected Fields column, highlight the field name and click the left arrow (<) to move the field back to the Available Fields column.

Figure 10-39 Report Wizard opening screen

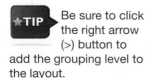
TIP Be sure to click the right arrow (>) button to add the grouping level to the layout.

6. The next prompt asks if you want to add any grouping levels. Select *Grade* and click the right arrow (>) button to move the field name to the next column. Click *Next* to continue.
7. The next prompt asks for the sort order you want for your records. Click the down arrow in the first box and select *Last Name* (Figure 10-40). You would like the report in *Ascending* order. Click *Next* to continue.

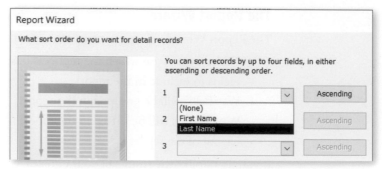

Figure 10-40 Report Wizard sort order screen

8. The next screen allows you to select a report layout. Select *Stepped* for the layout and *Portrait* for the orientation, if not already selected. Click *Next* to continue.

9. On the last screen, key **Lincoln Junior High Students** for the report title. If necessary, select *Preview the report*. Click *Finish*.

10. The report is saved and opens in Print Preview. Compare your report with the top portion of the report shown in Figure 10-41.

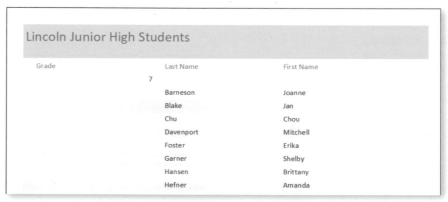

Figure 10-41 Lincoln Junior High Students report

11. Print the report and then close it.

59B

Create a Query and a Report

For this activity, you will create a report showing the first name, last name, class, and instructor for all students taking a class from Mr. Johnson during first period. Before creating the report, you will need to create a query to get the data for the report.

1. In the *59 lincoln* database, create a query in Design View. Base the query on the *Student Schedules* table. Include these fields in the query: First Name, Last Name, Class Period 1, Instructor 1. In the Instructor 1 column on the Criteria row, key **Johnson**. The query design grid should look like Figure 10-42.

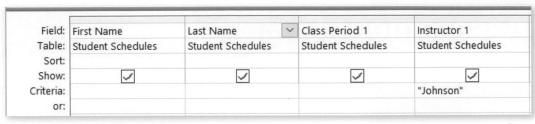

Field:	First Name	Last Name	Class Period 1	Instructor 1
Table:	Student Schedules	Student Schedules	Student Schedules	Student Schedules
Sort:				
Show:	☑	☑	☑	☑
Criteria:				"Johnson"
or:				

Figure 10-42 Query design grid

Compare your printed report with the one shown in Figure 10-38 on page 10-31.

2. Run the query. Look over the query results. You should see six records. Save and close the query results table using the name **Period 1 Johnson**.

3. Create a report using the Report Wizard. Base the report on the *Period 1 Johnson* query. Include all of the fields in the report.

4. Group the report by the Class Period 1 field. Sort the report by the Last Name field in ascending order. Choose *Block* for the layout and *Portrait* for the orientation.

5. Key **Johnson's Period 1 Class** as the report title.

6. Preview and print the report. Then close the database and exit *Access*.

Assessment 5 — Database Basics

Warmup

Key each line twice. If time permits, key the lines again.

Alphabet 1 Vick Lentz packed my bag with six quarts of juice.

Space Bar 2 Did she go to the bus depot to try to get the job?

Speed 3 She may blame Janel for the problem with the auto.

gwam 1' | 1 | 2 | 3 | 4 | 5 | 6 | 7 | 8 | 9 | 10 |

Activity 1
Timed Writings

1. Key two 1' timings on each ¶; determine *gwam*.

2. Key three 2' timings on ¶s 1–2 combined; determine *gwam*.

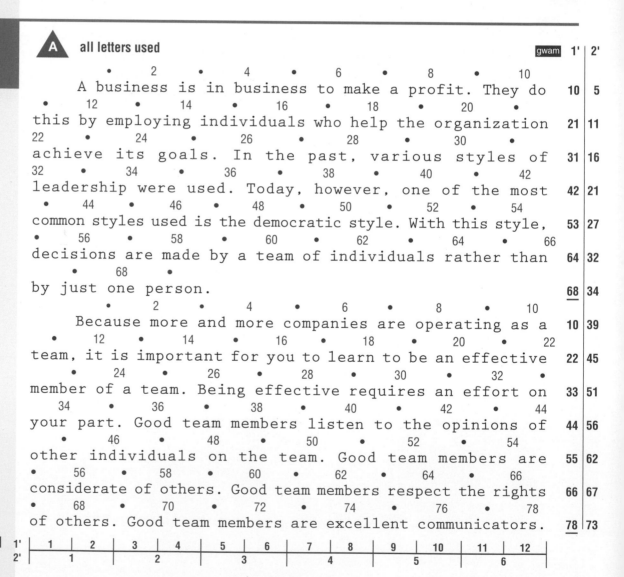

A all letters used

gwam 1' | 2'

A business is in business to make a profit. They do — 10 | 5

this by employing individuals who help the organization — 21 | 11

achieve its goals. In the past, various styles of — 31 | 16

leadership were used. Today, however, one of the most — 42 | 21

common styles used is the democratic style. With this style, — 53 | 27

decisions are made by a team of individuals rather than — 64 | 32

by just one person. — 68 | 34

Because more and more companies are operating as a — 10 | 39

team, it is important for you to learn to be an effective — 22 | 45

member of a team. Being effective requires an effort on — 33 | 51

your part. Good team members listen to the opinions of — 44 | 56

other individuals on the team. Good team members are — 55 | 62

considerate of others. Good team members respect the rights — 66 | 67

of others. Good team members are excellent communicators. — 78 | 73

gwam 1' | 1 | 2 | 3 | 4 | 5 | 6 | 7 | 8 | 9 | 10 | 11 | 12 |
     2' | 1 | 2 | 3 | 4 | 5 | 6 |

Activity 2
Create a Database and a Table

1. Create a new database using *a5 activity2* for the file name.
2. Create and save a table using **First Six Weeks** for the table name; use the following field names.
   - Default ID field
   - Student Name
   - Homework 1
   - Quiz 1
   - Homework 2
   - Quiz 2
   - Homework 3
   - Quiz 3
   - Exam
3. Enter the records given in the following table.

Student Name	Homework 1	Quiz 1	Homework 2	Quiz 2	Homework 3	Quiz 3	Exam
Abbott, J	10	9	10	8	10	8	98
Anderson, J	9	8	8	7	9	6	76
Brooks, H	10	8	10	9	9	8	88
Chen, S	9	8	10	9	8	6	56
Cook, I	8	8	9	9	10	6	95
Denver, G	8	7	9	7	10	6	83
Etheridge, M	8	7	9	8	8	7	50
Fernandez, M	5	8	7	9	8	8	77

4. Adjust each column width to fit the longest item in the column.
5. Sort the records in descending order by Exam.
6. Print the table and then close it.
7. Close the database.

1. Open the database **df a5 activity3**; save the database as **a5 activity 3**.
2. Make the changes shown below to the *First Six Weeks* table.

   - Jimanez should be spelled Jimenez
   - Brooks had a 98 on the exam
   - Van Horn had an 8 on Quiz 1
   - Thompson had a 64 on the exam
   - Suzuki had a 6 on Quiz 3

3. The scores on Quiz 3 were not very good. The instructor decided not to use those grades in calculating the grades for the first six weeks. Delete the column for Quiz 3 from the table.
4. Create a form using **First Six Weeks** for the form name. Use the form to enter the information shown below for the last two students.

Student Name	Homework 1	Quiz 1	Homework 2	Quiz 2	Homework 3	Exam
Young, C	10	6	9	6	10	67
Zelmer, W	5	10	7	10	8	88

5. Use Query Design to create a query showing students with exam scores of 90 or above. Include the student name and the exam score. Sort the exam scores in Descending order. Print the query. Save the query as **Exam Scores of 90 or Above**.
6. Use the Report Wizard to create a report with the following fields and specifications:

   - Student Name
   - Homework 1
   - Homework 2
   - Homework 3

   Grouping: none
   Sort: none
   Layout: Tabular
   Orientation: Portrait
   Title of report: **Homework**

7. View the report in Print Preview, print the report, and then close the report.
8. Close the database.

Skill Builder 9

A

Warmup

Key each line twice.

alphabet 1 Zelda might fix the job growth plans very quickly on Monday.

spacing 2 did go|to the|you can go|has been able|if you can|to see the

easy 3 The six men with the problems may wish to visit the tax man.

gwam 1' | 1 | 2 | 3 | 4 | 5 | 6 | 7 | 8 | 9 | 10 | 11 | 12 |

B

Technique: Response Patterns

Key each line twice.

 TIP Keep keystroking movement limited to the fingers.

Emphasize continuity and rhythm with curved, upright fingers.

N Nadine knew her aunt made lemonade and sun tea this morning.
O Owen took the book from the shelf to copy his favorite poem.
P Pamela added a pinch of pepper and paprika to a pot of soup.
Q Quent posed quick quiz questions to his quiet croquet squad.
R Risa used a rubber raft to rescue four girls from the river.

S Silas said his sister has won six medals in just four meets.
T Trisha told a tall tale about three little kittens in a tub.
U Ursula asked the usual questions about four issues you face.
V Vinny voted for five very vital issues of value to everyone.
W Wilt wants to walk in the walkathon next week and show well.

X Xania next expects them to fix the extra fax machine by six.
Y Yuri said your yellow yacht was the envy of every yachtsman.
Z Zoella and a zany friend ate a sizzling pizza in the piazza.

gwam 1' | 1 | 2 | 3 | 4 | 5 | 6 | 7 | 8 | 9 | 10 | 11 | 12 |

C

Skill Building

Key each line twice.

Space Bar

1 and the see was you she can run ask took turn they were next
2 I will be able to fix the desk and chair for you next month.

Word response

3 the pay and pen make city rush lake both did dock half field
4 I may make a big sign to hang by the door of the civic hall.

Double letters

5 book grass arrow jelly little dollar illness vaccine collect
6 Kelly Pizzaro was a little foolish at the football assembly.

gwam 1' | 1 | 2 | 3 | 4 | 5 | 6 | 7 | 8 | 9 | 10 | 11 | 12 |

Skill Building

1. Key three 1' timings on the paragraph; determine *gwam*.

2. Key two 2' timings on the paragraph; determine *gwam*.

A all letters used

gwam 2'

```
       •    2    •    4    •    6    •    8    •    10   •
     Many, if not most, people thought that Thomas Jefferson        6
  12   •   14   •   16   •   18   •   20   •   22   •
was one of the very best writers in our country. Perhaps his       12
  24   •   26   •   28   •   30   •   32   •   34   •   36
best as well as his most influential example of writing was the    18
       •   38   •   40   •   42   •   44   •   46   •   48
Declaration of Independence. He was asked to work with both        24
       •   50   •   52   •   54   •   56   •   58   •   60
John Adams and Benjamin Franklin to justify why it was so          30
       •   62   •   64   •   66   •   68   •   70   •   72
important for all people to be independent. Many people believe    36
       •   74   •   76   •   78   •   80   •   82   •   84
that, at the very least, we all should be able to recognize        42
       •   86   •   88   •   90   •   92   •   94   •   96   •
some of the important parts of this well-known document. For       48
       98   •  100   •  102   •  104   •  106   •  108   •
example, "We hold these truths to be self-evident, that all        54
      110   •  112   •  114   •  116   •  118   •  120   •
men are created equal, that they are endowed by their Creator      60
      122   •  124   •  126   •  128   •  130   •  132   •
with certain unalienable Rights, that among those are Life,        66
      134   •  136   •  138   •  140   •
Liberty, and the pursuit of Happiness."                            70
```

gwam 2' | 1 | 2 | 3 | 4 | 5 | 6 |

Skill Building

1. Key one 1' unguided and two 1' guided timings on each ¶; determine *gwam*.

2. Key two 2' unguided timings on ¶s 1–2 combined; determine *gwam*.

Quarter-Minute Checkpoints			
gwam	1/4'	1/2'	3/4'	1'
20	5	10	15	20
24	6	12	18	24
28	7	14	21	28
32	8	16	24	32
36	9	18	27	36
40	10	20	30	40
44	11	22	33	44
48	12	24	36	48
52	13	26	39	52
56	14	28	42	56

A all letters used

gwam 2'

```
       •    2    •    4    •    6    •    8    •    10   •
     Who was Shakespeare? Few would question that he was the        6
  12   •   14   •   16   •   18   •   20   •   22   •
greatest individual, or one of the greatest individuals, ever      12
  24   •   26   •   28   •   30   •   32   •   34   •
to write a play. His works have endured the test of time.          17
  36   •   38   •   40   •   42   •   44   •   46   •
Productions of his plays continue to take place on the stages      23
  48   •   50   •   52   •   54   •   56   •   58   •
of theatres all over the world. Shakespeare was an expert          29
  60   •   62   •   64   •   66   •   68   •   70   •
at creating comedies and tragedies, both of which would often      35
  72   •   74   •   76   •
leave the audience in tears.                                       38

       •    2    •    4    •    6    •    8    •    10   •
     Few of those who put pen to paper have been as successful      44
  12   •   14   •   16   •   18   •   20   •   22   •
at creating prized images for their readers as Shakespeare.        50
  24   •   26   •   28   •   30   •   32   •   34   •   36   •
Every character he created has a life of its own. More middle and  56
       38   •   40   •   42   •   44   •   46   •   48   •
high school students are likely to know about the tragedy that     63
  50   •   52   •   54   •   56   •   58   •   60   •   62
Romeo and Juliet experienced than middle and high school students  69
       •   64   •   66   •   68   •   70   •   72   •
know  about  the  one  that  took  place  at  Pearl  Harbor.       74
```

gwam 2' | 1 | 2 | 3 | 4 | 5 | 6 |

Advanced Technology Skills 6 — Digital Well-Being and Safety

OUTCOMES
- Describe responsible digital behavior
- Understand cyberbullying and flaming
- Explain physical and mental health issues related to digital technologies
- Understand personal digital safety

Responsible Digital Behavior

Be courteous when using digital technology

Have you ever been in the middle of a face-to-face conversation when the person you are talking to abruptly interrupts you to reply to a text message? Or maybe you've been annoyed by another passenger on the bus or train speaking loudly on his cell phone, or by someone walking through a store carrying on a conversation as if no one else was around.

Digital technologies have provided us with quicker and sometimes easier ways to communicate, but they have also led to a decline in face-to-face interaction. In turn, communication has become highly impersonal, making it easy to forget the good manners and etiquette we practice in face-to-face contact.

Digital etiquette is an informal set of rules governing the proper and courteous behaviors expected of digital technology users. Successful digital citizens are honest, respectful of others, and capable of adjusting their use of digital technologies to adapt to the situation. For example, when you walk into a library, you should know to turn off your cell phone; when you participate in a chat room, you should know the rules and expectations; when you are in a classroom, you should not be texting your friends. In general, you should think of digital etiquette as an extension of the manners you practice every day in your personal, academic, and business relationships. When you are using your digital devices, be courteous to those around you.

Cyberbullying and Flaming

Cyberbullying is a serious concern and an irresponsible use of digital technologies

We're all familiar with the schoolyard bully—the kid who teases others or steals their lunch or pushes and punches in order to intimidate. Bullies have been around a long time, but today's digital technologies have given them a new platform from which they can threaten, harass, or torment others. This is known as **cyberbullying**.

Cyberbullying takes many forms; for example, groups of people can decide to pick on or ignore certain individuals on social networking sites; email is used to forward harassing messages or computer viruses to unpopular kids; and threatening messages can be sent via text messaging, chat rooms, and message boards.

Another form of cyberbullying is **flaming**, or bashing, which is hostile and overly harsh arguments made via Internet forums, chat rooms, video-sharing websites, and even game servers. These arguments typically focus on heated or sensitive real-world issues, but they can also target less important, even mundane issues. They are intended to cause trouble rather than actually discuss the issue at hand.

Cyberbullying is a serious concern in the digital community, and, more and more, authorities are taking action against those who bully others online. As a responsible digital citizen, you can do your part to help stop cyberbullying. The first rule is to respect others. Always watch what you say online, and be careful about the images you send or post. You may think only a few people will see, but whatever you share online could be made public within minutes. If you are the victim of cyberbullying or see it going on, keep records of offending content, and report it to an adult you trust.

1. Open a new word processing document, and save it as *at6 bullying flyer*.
2. Use the following text to create a flyer on cyberbullying. You can create the flyer from scratch or use a template. Insert photos and graphics as desired.

Stop the Cyberbully!

The Internet may be the world's greatest playground, but just because you don't interact face-to-face with others, you still need to play nice. Those who don't play nice are often engaged in cyberbullying, or using online communications technology to harass or upset someone.

Examples of cyberbullying include:

- Posting inappropriate content or photos on a website.
- Sending a threatening or malicious text or email message.
- Forwarding computer viruses.
- Flaming, or bashing the views and opinions of others on websites, forums, chat rooms, and game servers.

Don't be a bystander. If you are the victim of cyberbullying or see it happening, take action.

- Keep records of the offending messages, photos, or online chats.
- Tell an adult you trust about the cyberbullying.
- Learn how to block the cyberbully.
- Support and stand up for the victim.

3. With your instructor's permission, print the flyer and post it at your school (see Figure AT6-1).

Figure AT6-1 Sample flyer on cyberbullying

Physical and Mental Health Issues

Working on a laptop while lying on your bed or the floor can result in poor posture

You might find it hard to imagine that digital technologies can be dangerous to your physical and mental health. But to be a successful digital citizen, you must learn how to recognize these risks and protect your health. Some of the most common dangers include the following:

- Carpal tunnel syndrome (CTS), which is a condition of pain and weakness in the hand or wrist caused by repetitive motions, such as keyboarding and using a mouse. You can minimize the risk of developing CTS by arranging your space so that you can sit in a comfortable position while you do your work or digital activities.

- Eyestrain, also called computer vision syndrome, which results from staring at a digital screen for hours at a time without a break. Doctors recommend stopping every 20 minutes and looking at something 20 feet away for 20 seconds.

- Poor posture, as a result of using digital technologies on inappropriate surfaces, such as a bed or the floor, or bending the neck to look down at a mobile device. You should use a computer on a hard surface, such as a table or desk, and avoid use for extended periods of time in one position.

- Phoning and texting while driving or biking, which is a leading cause of accidents.

- Addiction, or psychological dependence on the online experience. This can lead to a variety of other problems including a decline in social interaction, sleep disorders, obesity due to decreased physical activity, and poor performance in school and on the job.

The key to minimizing or eliminating both physical and mental health risks is to find a balance between the use of digital technologies and your time away from the screen. Limit your time in front of a screen or on your cell phone so that it does not interfere with other activities, such as doing homework, interacting with family and friends, and engaging in physical activity.

1. Open a blank presentation, and save it as *at6 digital health*.
2. Create a presentation consisting of at least six slides on the health risks associated with digital technologies. You may use information presented in this lesson or do further research using the Internet and other resources. Use appropriate slide layouts and insert images and graphics as necessary.
3. Share your presentation with the class.

Understanding Personal Digital Safety

You should avoid sharing the address of your employer with a stranger you have communicated with online

You've probably seen stories like this on the news: a girl exchanges messages with someone online, thinking it's just another kid interested in the latest movies or the hottest band. However, the "friend" turns out to be an adult, who showed up one day at the girl's after-school job, followed her to the parking lot, forced her into his car, and assaulted her.

It's scary, and it's not something anyone likes to think about, but you have to know: there are bad adults out there waiting to take advantage of vulnerable kids. Law enforcement officials estimate that more than 5,000 kids every year become victims as a result of their online activity.

How can you avoid becoming a statistic? Here are some guidelines:

- Do not share your address or phone numbers or those of your employer, friends, and relatives.
- Do not become "friends" or chat with people you do not know.
- Never agree to a face-to-face meeting with a stranger you have met online.

Even the content you share online with friends and acquaintances can play a role in your personal safety and welfare. Every string of text you write and photo or video you post, referred to as your **digital footprint**, leaves a trail of information about you for millions of other digital users to read and view. Even applying privacy settings on social networking accounts does not ensure that personal information will stay private. That's why it is important to always keep private information *private*.

- Do not discuss personal issues or social plans online, even with your close friends. Make a phone call or talk face-to-face.
- Avoid gossip and contributing to the rumor mill. This is a form of cyberbullying and can have serious consequences for all parties involved.
- Respect the privacy of others. Sharing information about friends and acquaintances or tagging photos can be an unwelcome intrusion in their lives.
- Refrain from sharing personal photos and videos.

When in doubt about what is or is not appropriate for sharing online, consider the fact that anything you transmit digitally becomes a permanent part of cyberspace and will be around for the long term. So you have to ask yourself, "Do I want a college admissions officer or a prospective employer or even my current friends and family to see or read this about me?"

Creating a Safety Survey

1. Open the data file **df at6 safety**. Save as: **at6 safety**. The document contains a list of questions on online safety with point values assigned so participants can assess their safety level.

2. Reformat the questions in table format with subtotal rows and a row at the bottom for the total score (see Figure AT6-2). Apply other formatting that will enhance the survey's appearance and make it "user-friendly."

3. With your instructor's permission, print the survey and complete it. How did your score rank? What things could you change to make you safer in the online world?

Online Safety Survey

DIRECTIONS: For each item, circle the corresponding value to indicate **Yes** or **No**. Calculate the subtotal for each section and then total your section scores. Compare your score to the safety scale provided.

	Yes	No
1. Profile—what kind of information is in your profile?		
Your street address	10	0
The town/city where you live	3	0
Your school name	3	0
Your phone/cell number	10	0
After school activities or sport teams	4	0
Subtotal		
2. Pictures—what kind of pictures do you share?		
Have you posted your picture publicly online?	4	0
Have you posted pictures of you or your friends online with identifying information about them?	8	0
Have you ever sent a picture you would be embarrassed for your family to see?	8	0
Have you ever sent a picture to someone who you met for the first time online?	10	0
Subtotal		
3. Screen name—how do you identify yourself?		
Does your screen name explicitly refer to you as a boy, girl, male, female?	3	0
Could your screen name reveal your city/address?	4	0
Does your screen name contain your age?	4	0
Does your screen name indicate your school name?	4	0
Subtotal		
4. Accessing information—passwords and connections		
Does your password contain a combination of letters and numbers?	-2	10
Is your password your pet's name or your birthdate?	3	0
Is your password the same as your username?	5	0
Is your password one that your friends may be able to guess?	5	0
Do you use the same password for all your accounts?	5	0
Do you change your password regularly?	-5	3
When away, do you access the Internet via a secure/trusted Wi-Fi network?	-5	10
When away, are you always aware of the source of your online connection?	0	10
Subtotal		
5. Social networking sites (MySpace, Facebook, YouTube, chat rooms, etc.)		
Do you participate on a social networking site?	2	0*
*If No, enter your subtotal below and skip to the next section.		
Do you participate on more than one social networking site?	5	0

	Yes	No
Is your profile listed as private?	-5	5
Do you know how to make your profile private, but choose not to?	10	0
Have you ever added someone as a "friend" who is not your friend in person?	5	0
Have you ever allowed someone to add you as a "friend" that you don't know in person	5	0
Subtotal		
6. Online conversations—communicating with friends, family, and others		
Have you had an online conversation that could be embarrassing if it was made public?	10	0
Do you realize that online conversations can be captured, saved, and/or printed?	0	5
Have you ever had a conversation with someone online who made you feel uncomfortable?	5	0*
*If No, calculate your subtotal below and skip to the next section.		
Have you had more than one conversation with the same person who made you feel uncomfortable?	10	0
Did you tell a friend about the person who made you feel uncomfortable?	-3	5
Did you tell a trusted adult about the person who made you feel uncomfortable?	-5	5
Did you tell a parent or guardian about the person who made you uncomfortable?	-5	10
Subtotal		
7. Meeting offline		
Have you ever met someone in person who you met first online?	10	0*
*If No, enter your subtotal below.		
Did you meet in a public/crowded place?	2	10
Did you go alone?	10	0
Did you take a friend along with you?	-5	10
Did you keep the meeting a secret?	10	-3
Did you tell a friend or friends where you were going?	-3	10
Did you tell a parent or guardian where you were going?	-3	10
Subtotal		
TOTAL SCORE		

Rate Yourself

0 to 30	Very safe
31 to 70	Pretty safe
71 to 111	Be more careful out there!
112 to 152	Taking too much risk!
153 to 183	You could be in serious danger!
Over 183	You could be a victim!

Figure AT6-2 Sample safety survey

Karramba Production/Shutterstock.com

Communication Skills 5

ACTIVITY 1: Terminal Punctuation

1. Study each of the five rules.
   a. Key the *Learn* line(s) beneath each rule, noting how the rule is applied.
   b. Key the *Apply* line(s), using correct terminal punctuation

Terminal Punctuation: Period

Rule 1: Use a period at the end of a declarative sentence (a sentence that is not regarded as a question or exclamation).

Learn 1 Will Ferrell is one of the actors in *Daddy's Home 2*.

Apply 2 Taylor Swift had two songs on the "Top 100" chart

Rule 2: Use a period at the end of a polite request stated in the form of a question but not intended as one.

Learn 3 Simon, will you please make the corrections to the document.

Apply 4 Samantha, will you let me know if Dr. Watt returns my call

Terminal Punctuation: Question Mark

Rule 3: Use a question mark at the end of a sentence intended as a question.

Learn 5 How many years have the Houston Astros won the World Series?

Apply 6 Mary, have you and Jason set a date for the wedding

Rule 4: For emphasis, a question mark may be used after each item in a series of interrogative expressions.

Learn 7 Can we count on wins from Sandra? from Jay? from Jo?

Apply 8 What did you plan for breakfast for lunch for dinner

Terminal Punctuation: Exclamation Point

Rule 5: Use an exclamation point after emphatic (forceful) exclamations and after phrases and sentences that are clearly exclamatory.

Learn 9 The coach screamed, "Stay with your man!"

Learn 10 "Fantastic!" the director yelled at the end of the performance.

Apply 11 "Incredible" was how the announcer described the perfect game.

Apply 12 Hans yelled, "Watch out, you almost ran over that girl"

2. Key Proofread & Correct, using correct terminal punctuation.
   a. Check answers.
   b. Using the rule number(s) at the left of each line, study the rule relating to each error you made.
   c. Rekey each incorrect line, using correct terminal punctuation.

   Save as: CS5 ACTIVITY1

Proofread & Correct

Rules

5 1 The boy's mother screamed, "My son is still in the house"

1 2 The manager is going to take us to lunch on Thursday

3 3 Do you know the date of Julie and Mark's anniversary

4 4 Did you collect the dues from Fernando from Judy from Nick

2 5 The teacher said, "Jon, will you please pick up your mess"

(continued on next page)

ACTIVITY 2: Word Choice

1. Study the definitions of the words.
2. Key the *Learn* line(s) noting the correct usage of each word.
3. Key the *Apply* line(s), inserting the correct word(s).

Save as: CS5 ACTIVITY2

do (vb) to bring about; to carry out	**for** (prep/conj) used to indicate purpose; on behalf of; because; because of
due (adj) owed or owing as a debt; having reached the date for payment	**four** (n) the fourth in a set or series

Learn 1 **Do** you know when the three library books are **due**?

Apply 2 The next payment will be (do, due) on Tuesday, March 24.

Apply 3 I (do, due) not know when I will be available to meet again.

Learn 1 The **four** men asked **for** a salary increase **for** the next **four** years.

Apply 2 The manager left (for, four) and hour just before (for, four) o'clock.

Apply 3 The (for, four) coached were mad after waiting (for, four) an hour.

ACTIVITY 3: Writing

Complete as directed.

Save as: CS5 ACTIVITY3

Write a paragraph or two explaining how you would respond during a job interview to the following question:

What are your strengths? Give specific example(s) of how you have used those strengths to excel in your classes or extracurricular activities.

ACTIVITY 4: Speaking

A job is often viewed as something you do to earn money. A career, on the other hand, is viewed as doing what you love to do and getting paid for doing it. For the next class period come prepared to share with your classmates information about the career you would like to pursue after you graduate from school. Your remarks should include what the career is, what employment opportunities are available, what the education requirements for employment in this field are, and what the employment outlook is for this type of career.

Tips for Interviewing
• Learn about the company
• Anticipate interview questions and be ready to respond
• Dress to make a good first impression
• Practice interviewing
• Work on your nonverbal expression:
• Smile
• Good eye contact
• Posture

Before You Move On

Answer these questions to review what you have learned in Chapter 10.

1. A database is a collection of information that is stored in database objects. Name four database objects that you used in this chapter. LO 55A

2. A database _____ contains all of the information about one person or item. LO 55B

3. A database _____ holds one piece of information from a database record. LO 55B

4. The _____ determines the kind of data a field can hold. LO 55B

5. Data can be entered into a database table in Datasheet view or using a database _____. LO 56B

6. The data type used for letters or numbers that do not require calculations is _____. LO 55B

7. You create a form automatically based on a table that has 12 fields in each record. Which of those fields will be included in the form? LO 56B

8. When you create a form using the Form Wizard, which fields can you include in the form? LO 56C

9. Explain the difference between Landscape and Portrait orientation. LO 56C

10. To add a field to an existing table, open the table in _____ View. LO 57A

11. What is the purpose of a query? LO 58A

12. What is the purpose of a filter? LO 58A

13. What software feature can be used to arrange the data in a column in a database table in ascending order? LO 58C

14. What is a database report? How does it differ from a database table? LO 59A

15. A field chosen to uniquely identify each record in an *Access* database table is called the _____. *Access* will not allow duplicate data to be entered in this field. LO 55A

Newhouse Realty

Work Assignment

Photo Courtesy of the Author

Newhouse Realty hires students to work during seasonal peak periods. You have been hired as an office assistant to help Janet Marshall, office manager, prepare documents for the annual *Parade of Homes*, which is sponsored by Newhouse Realty. The owner of Newhouse Realty, Blake Newhouse, has several projects that he needs completed as well.

The *Parade of Homes* is a showing open to the general public of newly constructed homes that feature the latest innovations in the housing industry. This year, Newhouse Realty agents (Steve Chen, Justin McIntyre, Justin O'Dell, Maria Perez, and Cynthia Stone) will be inviting former clients to attend a private showing prior to the *Parade of Homes*.

In your position you will be required to use:

- **Word** to process letters, tables, and a flyer
- **Outlook** to process emails
- **Access** to create and update databases
- **Excel** to construct a worksheet to calculate commissions
- **PowerPoint** to design a slide presentation for the open house

Processing Instructions

★TIP You can find formatting examples for emails, letters, and other documents in Appendix C, Reference Guide, available on the student companion website.

Janet Marshall will attach general processing instructions to each task you are given. If a date is not provided on the document, use the date included with the instructions.

You are expected to produce error-free documents; proofread and correct your work carefully before presenting it for approval. Print each project when completed unless otherwise directed by your instructor.

As with a real job, you will be expected to work independently and learn on your own how to do some things that you haven't previously been taught using resources that are available to you. You will also be expected to use your decision-making skills to format documents attractively whenever specific instructions are not provided. Since Newhouse Realty has based its word processing manual on the *Century 21* textbook, you can refer to this text in making formatting decisions. In addition, you can use the Help feature of your software to review a feature you may have forgotten or to learn new features you may need.

File Names

In order to quickly assess information, Newhouse Realty has established a file-naming system that is used by company employees. It is very simple. All files you create should be named with *newhouse*, followed by the project number (*newhouse project 1, newhouse project 2*, etc.).

Data Files

Some of the projects you will be working on have already been started or require information from previously created documents. You will need to access the company data files to complete these projects.

Company Email

Company email addresses are available in the *Company Email Addresses* table of the *df newhouse realty* database.

When an email is sent to more than one individual, put email addresses in alphabetical order by last name.

Emails for Mr. Newhouse

Mr. Newhouse often creates email messages on his tablet while commuting on the train. When Janet Marshall keys the messages for him, she uses the following subject line: *Message from Blake Newhouse*. You should use the same subject line for messages you key for him.

Mr. Newhouse would like a copy of all emails sent on his behalf. Bcc Ms. Marshall on all correspondence.

Client Information

A table with client information has been included in the *df newhouse realty* database. The *Clients* table includes client names, addresses, and phone numbers.

Newhouse Letter Format

Letters are to be keyed in block format with mixed punctuation. Use 12-pt. Arial. Include your reference initials on all letters.

When something is enclosed with a letter, key **Enclosure** at the left margin one line beneath reference initials.

Copy notations are keyed at the left margin one line beneath reference initials (or one line beneath the enclosure notation, if an enclosure is included). Leave one space after the c before keying the name of the person receiving the copy. (This is different from what you previously learned. Many companies have their own variation of what you learned in the textbook. Of course, you will always adhere to their guidelines.)

Newhouse Realty

315 Parkview Terrace
Minneapolis, MN 55416-3430

May 16, 20--

Mr. and Mrs. Jackson Higgins
825 W. Oak Street
Stillwater, MN 55082-4122

Dear Mr. and Mrs. Higgins:

We are pleased to have you take part in our private showing of the homes that will be in this year's Parade of Homes. The eight homes you will see combine quality construction, professional decorating, and exclusive landscaping to make this year's show the best ever.

I have made arrangements with Maria Perez to show you the homes. Please meet her at our office at 10 a.m. on Friday, June 5. It will take approximately two hours to visit the homes.

I am looking forward to hearing your comments about the homes after the showing. If you have any questions prior to the showing, please telephone me.

Sincerely,

Janet Marshall
Office Manager

jm

c Maria Perez

From
Janet Marshall

Mr. Newhouse prepared these emails on the train on the way to work today. The first one goes to our five agents. The second one goes to Rebecca St. John. Please get their email addresses from the company database (*df newhouse realty*).

Remember to copy Mr. Newhouse and Bcc me.

JM   **5/12**

The response from former home buyers who are interested in the private showing of this year's Parade of Homes has been excellent. Meeting with past customers to determine if we can be of further assistance to them with their housing requirements is a real opportunity for us. All of the individuals invited have been in their present homes for over five years and may be ready to consider the purchase of a new home.

Janet will be coordinating schedules for the two days of the private showing. We should have your schedule ready within the next two or three days. A meeting will be held on May 20 at 8:30 a.m. to discuss specific details for the Parade of Homes.

Rebecca, last month when we were discussing some of the details for the Parade of Homes private showing, you indicated that you would be willing to handle the arrangements for refreshments. I would like to take you up on that offer if it still stands.

Please stop by my office sometime this week so that we can discuss a few of the specifics.

From
Janet Marshall

Prepare a table from the information shown on the attached. Use **Featured Homes** for the main heading and **Week of June 14 – 21** for the secondary heading. Use *df home photo1*, *df home photo2*, *df home photo3*, *df home photo4*, and *df home photo5* for the inserts.

JM   5/13

Insert *df home photo1*	$998,900 678 Centennial Place Minneapolis, MN 55404 5 Beds 4,780 Sq. Ft. 3 Full Baths 1 Half Bath
Insert *df home photo2*	$989,500 8400 Cottagewood Terrace NE Minneapolis, MN 55432 5 Beds 4,600 Sq. Ft. 3 Full Baths 2 Half Baths
Insert *df home photo3*	$650,000 6300 Stauder Circle Edina, MN 55436 4 Beds 3,970 Sq. Ft. 2 Full Baths 2 Half Baths
Insert *df home photo4*	$499,900 10308 52nd Avenue N Plymouth, MN 55446 4 Beds 3,300 Sq. Ft. 2 Full Baths 1 Half Bath
Insert *df home photo5*	$425,000 3513 Sheridan Avenue S Minneapolis, MN 55410 3 Beds 3,150 Sq. Ft. 2 Full Baths 1 Half Bath

Project 3

**From
Janet Marshall**

Justin McIntyre would like us to invite Mr. and Mrs. Jacob Nivins to the home showing. I've attached a hard copy of the letter template we are using since my computer isn't letting me access the electronic file.

After you rekey the letter, save it because our sales agents may have others they want invited. The address information is in our client db.

JM   5/13

May 1, 20--

(Title) (First Name) (Last Name)
(Address)
(City), (State) (Zip)

Dear (Courtesy Title) (Last Name):

The 20-- Parade of Homes will be held June 7 – 21. This year we are planning something new. A limited number of our previous home buyers from Newhouse Realty are being invited to participate in a private showing prior to the public opening of the Parade of Homes.

The private showing will give Newhouse Realty agents the time needed to point out the many fine features of the quality homes being shown this year and to answer any questions you may have. With so many people taking part in the Parade of Homes, it is difficult to give our preferred customers the attention they deserve during the days the homes are shown to the public.

If you are interested in this free showing, sign and return the enclosed card. We look forward to showing you the outstanding homes built for this year's home show.

Sincerely,

Janet M. Marshall
Office Manager

Project 4

**From
Janet Marshall**

Rekey the listing of homes that will be in this year's Parade of Homes with the additions I have made. Use **PARADE OF HOMES** for the main heading and **June 7-21, 20--**, as the secondary heading. After you key the table, sort the builders in ascending alphabetical order. Apply one of the *Grid Tables* styles from Table Styles and then center column headings.

JM   5/14

Address	Builder	Price
360 Brookdale Lane	Greenway Construction	$375,000
608 Candlewood Court	Newhouse Realty	$579,000
625 Candlewood Court	Newhouse Realty	$429,000
900 Hawthorne Avenue	Gill & Sons Construction	$639,000
3809 Glacier Place	Kasota Contractors	$329,000
608 Hillswick Trail	Anderson Builders	$475,000
712 Kirkwood Circle	Lancaster & Sons	$599,000
376 Brookdale Lane	Knox Home Builders	$409,000

Project 5

From Janet Marshall

Design a flyer for the Parade of Homes. Be sure to include all the information shown on the attached sheet. The seven builders are listed with some of the other documents I've given you to key. Make sure to list them in alphabetical order. Include another *df home with driveway* or online picture of a home at the bottom of the flyer above *Sponsored by Newhouse Realty Company.*

JM   **5/14**

20-- Parade of Homes

June 7 – 21

Monday – Friday 5 p.m. to 9 p.m.

Saturday & Sunday 10 a.m. to 6 p.m.

Featuring homes built by

[List the seven homebuilders in alphabetical order]

Sponsored by Newhouse Realty Company

Project 6

From Janet Marshall

Create a worksheet titled **Sales Commissions Since May 1**. The company commission is 6% of the sales price; the agent's commission is 2.5%. Try to get the information to fit on one page. I've attached the information for the 11 homes that have sold along with the columns I would like on the worksheet.

After entering the information, sort by sales agent.

JM   **5/15**

Columns on worksheet:

- **A.** Address of Homes Sold
- **B.** City
- **C.** State
- **D.** Sales Agent
- **E.** Sales Price
- **F.** Company Commission (0.06)
- **G.** Sales Agent Commission (0.025)

Homes sold:

1. 705 Shenandoah Lane N. | Minneapolis | MN | McIntyre | $365,000
2. 719 Comstock Lane | Minneapolis | MN | Perez | $399,000
3. 875 St. Albans Street | Roseville | MN | Stone | $265,900
4. 535 Birch Lake Avenue | White Bear Lake | MN | McIntyre | $330,000
5. 1729 Hawthorne Drive | Hopkins | MN | McIntyre | $285,000
6. 88 North William Street | Stillwater | MN | Perez | $279,000
7. 338 Betty Crocker Drive | St. Louis Park | MN | McIntyre | $268,900
8. 873 St. Croix Heights | Hudson | WI | Stone | $275,000

9. 872 Oak Terrace | White Bear Lake | MN | Chen | $329,900

10. 1218 Jessamine Avenue | St. Paul | MN | Perez | $255,500

11. 108 Franklin Terrace | Minneapolis | MN | O'Dell | $525,900

Mr. Newhouse would like some additional information on the worksheet. Add a totals row for the Sales Price, Company Commission, and Sales Agent Commission. Beneath the Totals row of the Sales Agent Commission column, display and label the Lowest (MIN), Highest (MAX), and Average (AVERAGE) sales agent commission as shown below.

875 St. Albans Street	Roseville	MN	Stone	$265,900.00	$15,954.00	$6,647.50
873 St. Croix Heights	Hudson	WI	Stone	$275,000.00	$16,500.00	$6,875.00
	Totals			Total	Total	Total
	Lowest					MIN
	Highest					MAX
	Average					AVERAGE

Project 7

From Janet Marshall

Please make a copy of *df newhouse realty* and save it as *newhouse project 7*. Open the Clients table in the database and sort it by Last Name in *Ascending* order. Make the edits to the *Clients* table shown on the attached. After making the edits, create the client report described on the attached.

JM   5/15

1. The spelling for Malarie McNally should be **Mallory McNally**.

2. Felipe Garcia got married; his wife's name is **Jessica**. Also change the title for this record to **Mr. and Mrs**.

3. Tyler Bunnell's address is **670** Myrtle Street rather than 671.

4. Tarin Chan's phone number should be **612-555-0188**.

Using the *Report Wizard*, create a report using all of the fields except Title. Group the report by State and then by City. Sort by Last Name in ascending order. Use Stepped Layout and Landscape orientation. Use Clients Report for the title.

From Janet Marshall

Three more clients accepted invitations to the showing. Send the attached letter, *df acceptance letter*. You will need to replace the information in red with the appropriate information. The letters go to:

Ms. Stacy Rice
Mr. and Mrs. Travis McDowell
Mr. Theodore Farrell

Their addresses are in the *Clients* table of the database you updated for Project 7.

Justin O'Dell will show Ms. Rice and Mr. Farrell the homes on Saturday, June 6, at 7 p.m. Maria Perez will show Mr. and Mrs. McDowell the homes on Friday, June 5, at 1 p.m.

JM   **5/16**

Newhouse Realty

315 Parkview Terrace
Minneapolis, MN 55416-3430

May 16, 20--

Mr. and Mrs. Jackson Higgins
825 W. Oak Street
Stillwater, MN 55082-4122

Dear Mr. and Mrs. Higgins:

We are pleased to have you take part in our private showing of the homes that will be in this year's Parade of Homes. The eight homes you will see combine quality construction, professional decorating, and exclusive landscaping to make this year's show the best ever.

I have made arrangements with (Agent's Name) to show you the homes. Please meet (him/her) at our office at (time) on (Friday/Saturday), June (5/6). It will take approximately two hours to visit the homes.

I am looking forward to hearing your comments about the homes after the showing. If you have any questions prior to the showing, please telephone me.

Sincerely,

Janet Marshall
Office Manager

xx

c (Agent's Name)

From
Janet Marshall

Create a *PowerPoint* presentation featuring the Heber House built by Newhouse Realty for our private showing during the Parade of Homes. I've outlined the text and layout for each slide on the attached. Use *df project 9* for the photos.

JM   **5/19**

Photo Courtesy of the Author

NOTE Use the *PowerPoint* help feature or Chapter 15 of the text to review how to apply transitions between slides.

Slide No.	Slide Layout	Caption	Photo No.	Content
1	Title Slide	The Heber House Parade of Homes June 7–21	1	
2	Picture with Caption	Stylish Contemporary	2–3	
3	Title and Content	About the Home		• Two Story • 4,025 Sq. Ft. • 3 Bedrooms • 2½ Baths • Professionally Decorated
4	Two Content	The Great Room	4	• Two-Story Ceiling • Large Wall of Windows • Elegant Fireplace
5	Title Only	The Great Room	5–7	
6	Two Content	Spacious Kitchen	8	• Island • Corner Pantry • Gas Double Ovens • Gas Cooktop
7	Title Only	Kitchen & Dining Area	9	
8	Two Content	Master Bedroom Suite	10–11	• Walk-In Closet • European Glass Shower • Double Sinks • Garden Tub • Cathedral Ceiling
9	Title and Content	Additional Rooms		• Two Bedrooms • Play Area for Kids • Family Room with Wet Bar and Fireplace • Balcony Ready Room • First-Floor Laundry
10	Title and Content	Property Information		• **Architecture:** Contemporary • **Basement type:** Full, poured • **Heating:** Gas forced air • **Lot size:** 75 x 145 • **Taxes:** $8,900 • **Sewer, water:** Public • **Schools:** Park Elementary Brooklyn Junior High Champlin Park Senior High
11	Title and Content	Parade of Homes Sponsored by Newton Realty June 7–21		Insert an online picture of a house.

I've attached a copy of the Parade of Homes schedule I sent to Justin O'Dell for June 5. Please use the *df newhouse memo* template and create his schedule for June 6. Use a different color for the table to distinguish it from the June 5 schedule. Use the Clients table in the updated database for the phone numbers.

Send a copy of the memo to Blake Newhouse and me.

JM   **5/19**

Newhouse Realty

Memo

To:	Justin O'Dell
From:	Janet Marshall
cc:	Blake Newhouse
Date:	May 19, 20--
Re:	Schedule for June 5

Justin, the table below shows your schedule for showings on June 5. Please let me know if you have any questions.

Client	Phone	Time
Mr. and Mrs. Warren Sabbatini	651-555-0179	10 a.m.
Miss Candace Wilcox	651-555-0115	
Dr. and Mrs. Michael Vaughn	608-555-0144	1 p.m.
Mr. Timothy Giani	651-555-0120	
Ms. Alison Koosman	651-555-0147	4 p.m.
Mr. and Mrs. Felipe Garcia	612-555-0164	
Mr. and Mrs. Chase McNally	715-555-0122	7 p.m.
Mr. Scott Sackett	612-555-0184	

Schedule for Justin O'Dell
June 6

Mrs. Jayne Boyer	10 a.m.
Mr. Brandon Vanderbilt	
Dr. Javier Tallmadge	1 p.m.
Dr. and Mrs. Evan Ross	
Ms. Tasha Lang	4 p.m.
Mr. Loren Rizzo	
Ms. Stacy Rice	7 p.m.
Mr. Theodore Farrell	

Project 11

From Janet Marshall

Please format the attached as a letter for my signature. Address the letter to:

Mr. and Mrs. Parker Anderson
1320 Lorl Lane #3
Ogden, UT 84404-4396

JM   5/19

Dear Mr. and Mrs. Taylor:

Judith Johnson, personnel manager of Owen & Caden Production Company, informed me that you have accepted a position with them and will be moving to Minnesota the first part of July. I know you will enjoy living in this area.

A copy of the "Mover's Guide" published by our real estate company is enclosed. It is designed to give helpful hints on making the move as painless as possible. We hope you will find it useful as you organize for the move to Minnesota.

If we can be of assistance to you in locating a place to rent or a home to purchase, please telephone our office (612-555-0101).

Sincerely,

Project 12

From Janet Marshall

Create a new database (*newhouse project 12*) with a table to store the information taken from the *Sales Commission* worksheet. Use the column headings from the worksheet for the database fields. Save the table as *Agent Sales Commissions*.

JM   5/20

Sales Commissions Since May 1					
Address of Homes Sold	City	State	Sales Agent	Sales Price	Sales Agent Commission (0.025)
872 Oak Terrace	White Bear Lake	MN	Chen	$329,900.00	$8,247.50
705 Shenandoah Lane N.	Minneapolis	MN	McIntyre	$365,000.00	$9,125.00
535 Birch Lake Avenue	White Bear Lake	MN	McIntyre	$330,000.00	$8,250.00
1729 Hawthorne Drive	Hopkins	MN	McIntyre	$285,000.00	$7,125.00
338 Betty Crocker Drive	St. Louis Park	MN	McIntyre	$268,900.00	$6,722.50
108 Franklin Terrace	Minneapolis	MN	O'Dell	$525,900.00	$13,147.50
719 Comstock Lane	Minneapolis	MN	Perez	$399,000.00	$9,975.00
88 North William Street	Stillwater	MN	Perez	$279,000.00	$6,975.00
1218 Jessamine Avenue	St. Paul	MN	Perez	$255,500.00	$6,387.50
875 St. Albans Street	Roseville	MN	Stone	$265,900.00	$6,647.50
873 St. Croix Heights	Hudson	WI	Stone	$275,000.00	$6,875.00

After you complete the database, please create a query that shows the sales agent, the sales price, and sales agent commission. Use McIntyre as the criteria for the sales agent field. Save as McIntyre Sales Commission.

Project 13

From Janet Marshall

Mr. Newhouse thought you did a great job with the *Sales Commission* worksheet. He would like you to add a worksheet to the workbook with the information shown on the attached, grouping the sales for each agent. The heading for Sheet 2 should be **May 1-7 Sales Commissions** Change the main heading on Sheet 1 to **Sales Commissions**.

JM   5/21

May 1-7 Sales Commissions

Address of Homes Sold	City	State	Sales Agent	Sales Price
872 Oak Terrace	White Bear Lake	MN	Chen	$289,900
Agent Total			Chen	$289,900
705 Shenandoah Lane N.	Minneapolis	MN	McIntyre	$365,000
535 Birch Lake Avenue	White Bear Lake	MN	McIntyre	$330,000
1729 Hawthorne Drive	Hopkins	MN	McIntyre	$285,000
338 Betty Crocker Drive	St. Louis Park	MN	McIntyre	$268,900
Agent Total			McIntyre	$1,248,900

Include an "Agent Total" for each agent as shown above and below and a "Total Company Sales" at the bottom as shown below.

875 St. Albans Street	Roseville	MN	Stone	$265,900
873 St. Croix Heights	Hudson	WI	Stone	$275,000
Agent Total			Stone	$540,900
Total Company Sales				$3,309,100

Project 14

From Janet Marshall

One more improvement for the workbook: Can you add a chart to the Sheet 2 worksheet? See my suggestions, attached.

JM   5/21

Let's create a chart that compares the total sales of each sales agent. You can select the agent's name in column D and the total sales for each agent in column E and then create a column chart.

Insert an appropriate chart title, and then apply a chart style of your choice.

Mr. Newhouse would like a hard copy of this information, so please position the chart so that you can print both the data and the chart on one sheet.

Project 15

From Janet Marshall

Here are the sales for the week of May 8-14. Open **newhouse project 14** and save it as **newhouse project 15**. Update Sheet 1 with the information shown on the attached. After you enter the new information, sort it by sales agent. Add Sheet 3 with the May 8-14 sales information as you did with Sheet 2 for May 1-7. Give the sheet tabs names by double-clicking the tab and keying the following names.

Sheet 1: **Sales Commissions**

Sheet 2: **May 1-7 Sales**

Sheet 3: **May 8-14 Sales**

Please use a different color for the Sheet 3 chart than the Sheet 2 chart.

JM   **5/22**

Address	City	State	Agent	Price
358 James Road	Bloomington	MN	O'Dell	$355,900
1358 Heritage Lane	Lakeville	MN	Chen	$489,500
689 Phoenix Street	Golden Valley	MN	O'Dell	$549,000
38 Vinewood Lane	Maple Grove	MN	Stone	$388,900
207 Douglas Avenue	Minneapolis	MN	McIntrye	$244,000
1129 Brookside Circle	Bloomington	MN	Perez	$348,900
810 Chestnut Drive	Eden Prairie	MN	O'Dell	$445,000
2982 Walnut Street	Hudson	WI	Stone	$398,000
3188 University Avenue	St. Paul	MN	McIntrye	$349,000
2201 Emerald Lane	Woodbury	MN	McIntrye	$395,000
509 Headley Avenue N.	Oakdale	MN	O'Dell	$456,000
1588 Oak Terrace	White Bear Lake	MN	Chen	$329,900

Enhance and Master Your Skills

In Cycle 2 (Chapters 11 through 17), enhance your abilities by reinforcing and mastering your skills.

CHAPTER 11

Managing Communications and Schedules

Lesson 60	Create and Edit Contact Groups
Lesson 61	Organize and Manage Emails
Lesson 62	Schedule Meetings and Print Calendars

Application Guide

Managing Messages, Contacts, and Calendars

To keep track of your personal friends and business associates, you can use your email contact list to create Contact Groups. For example, you can have study groups, sports teams, church groups, and other associations. You can add or remove members of these groups as necessary. These groups allow you to send email messages to the group rather than having to send messages individually.

Smartphones, tablets, and other mobile devices have made email and messaging more accessible than ever. The vast amounts of email being sent and received have made managing and classifying messages more difficult. How do you separate the "junk" from the "good stuff"? How do you set up a system to help you organize your messages so you can find them later? Junk filters help you automatically sort through your email messages and more efficiently address those of importance.

Managing your time is difficult. Whether you are a student or a business professional, it is sometimes hard to keep track of all the responsibilities and tasks you need to remember. You can use your calendar program to keep track of your class schedule and appointments, schedule meetings, and share your schedule with others. Managing your schedule using a calendar can increase productivity while maximizing the time you spend with friends and family. Software such as Microsoft *Outlook* (Figure 11-1) combines these functions in one location.

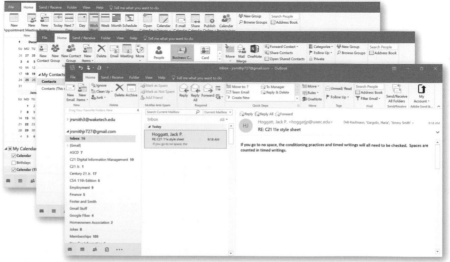

Figure 11-1 Microsoft *Outlook* manages messages, contacts, and schedules

Editing Contacts

People > Double-click contact

When you create a business or personal contact, you store information about that person such as address, phone number, and job title. You can also record notes such as the name of a project you worked on together. It is important to keep your contact information current and accurate. You can edit existing contact information quickly and easily.

Creating Contact Groups

People > Home tab > New > New Contact Group

When you frequently email several contacts as a group for personal or work purposes, you can create a **Contact Group** and name it. A Contact Group allows you to work more efficiently when emailing because you can send a message to the group rather than to each contact individually. For example, you could create a group named Friends and add your friends to the group. Whenever you want to send the same email message to all your friends, you enter the Contact Group, Friends, as the recipient, and every group member will receive the email message.

Adding/Removing Contact Group Members

People > My Contacts (in Navigation pane) > Double-click group > Add Members or Remove Member

As the group changes, you can add or remove members. When you add a member, you can choose the source of the contact information you want to add to your Contact Group. Removing a contact from a Contact Group does not delete the contact from your contact list or address book.

Creating New Email Folders

Mail > Folder tab > New > New Folder

A cluttered and unorganized mailbox can make it difficult to find the email you need. By creating new mail folders, you can group messages related to each other. For example, you can group messages by project, topic, contact, or other categories that make sense to you. You can even create a folder for all the messages from your friends or family.

iStock.com/Squaredpixels

Junk Email Folder

Mail > Navigation pane > Junk Email folder

A message suspected of being junk is moved to the Junk Email folder. You should periodically check messages in the Junk Email folder to verify that legitimate messages were not classified as junk. See Figure 11-2.

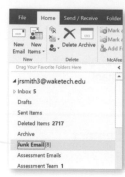

Junk Email folder

Figure 11-2 Junk Email folder

Junk Email Filter

Mail > Home tab > Delete > Junk > Junk Email Options

The Junk Email filter helps reduce unwanted messages in your Inbox. Junk mail, also known as **spam**, is moved by the filter to the Junk Email folder. The filter evaluates each incoming message to assess whether or not it might be spam, based on several factors such as the message content, the time the message was sent, and so on. By default, there is no automatic filtering. You can make the Junk Email filter more aggressive by changing the level of protection. See Figure 11-3.

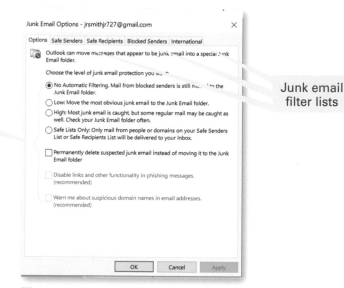

Levels of junk email protection

Junk email filter lists

Figure 11-3 Junk Email Options

Junk Email Filter Lists

Mail > Home tab > Delete > Junk > Junk Email Options

While the Junk Email filter checks all incoming messages automatically, the Junk Email filter lists give you more control over what is considered spam. You can add names, email addresses, and domains to these lists to allow messages from sources you trust or block messages from specific email addresses and domains that you do not know or trust. See the tabs at the top of Figure 11-3 for the filter lists available to you. Each filter tab focuses on a characteristic of the message:

Safe Senders—Email from addresses or domain names on your Safe Senders List will never be treated as junk email

Safe Recipients—Email sent to addresses or domain names on your Safe Recipients List will never be treated as junk email

Blocked Senders—Email from addresses or domain names on your Block Senders List will always be treated as junk email

International—Block messages that come from another country/region or that appear in another character or alphabet

Creating Meetings

Calendar > Home tab >
New > New Meeting

In a business, you will likely have to schedule meetings with colleagues or reply to a meeting invitation. A **meeting** is an appointment that includes others to whom you send an invitation. The person who creates the meeting and sends the invitation is the **meeting organizer**. The meeting organizer schedules a meeting by creating an email meeting request or invitation to a meeting that is sent to each attendee.

Replying to a Meeting Request

In many cases, the meeting organizer would like attendees to respond whether or not they can attend the meeting. If the meeting organizer requests a response and the attendee's software supports this feature, the attendee can choose from four response options: Accept, Tentative, Decline, or Propose New Time.

If the attendee accepts or tentatively accepts a meeting request, the invitation is deleted from the Inbox, and the meeting is added to his or her calendar. A meeting response is sent to the meeting organizer. The meeting response can be found in the Sent Items folder near the bottom of the Navigation pane.

If the attendee declines the meeting request, it is deleted from his or her Inbox and the meeting is not added to the calendar. A response is sent to the meeting organizer and can be found in the Sent Items folder.

Proposing a New Meeting Time

If the attendee has a conflict with the meeting request, he or she can propose a new time for the meeting. A proposal is sent to the meeting organizer via email indicating that the attendee tentatively accepts the request but proposes the meeting be held at a different time or date.

Creating Additional Calendars

Calendar > Folder tab >
New > New Calendar

In addition to your main calendar, you can create other calendars. For example, you can create a calendar for personal appointments.

Printing Calendars

Calendar > File tab >
Print > Settings

You can print a daily, weekly, or monthly view of your calendar for posting or sharing with friends or colleagues. Table 11-1 lists the print styles available for printing your calendar.

Table 11-1 Print Styles for Calendars

Daily	Prints a daily appointment schedule for a specific date including one day per page, a daily task list, an area for notes, and a two-month calendar.
Weekly Agenda	Prints a seven-day calendar with one week per page and a two-month calendar.
Weekly Calendar	Prints a seven-day calendar with one week per page, an hourly schedule, and a two-month calendar.
Monthly	Prints five weeks per page of a particular month or date range and a two-month calendar.
Tri-fold	Prints each day, including a daily task list and a weekly schedule.
Calendar Details	Prints calendar items and supporting details.

iStock.com/Johnnyscriv

LESSON 60　Create and Edit Contact Groups

OUTCOMES

- Create a Contact Group
- Add/remove contacts from the group
- Modify a Contact Group

alphabet　1　Jewel had Zeb quickly give him five or six points on the test.

fig/sym　2　I did receive checks #456 & #869, which total $12,790, on 03/18/18.

speed　3　He paid the man eight bucks for the big antique ornament and map.

gwam 1' | 1 | 2 | 3 | 4 | 5 | 6 | 7 | 8 | 9 | 10 | 11 | 12 | 13 |

60B

Edit Contacts

People > Double-click contact

1. Open *df 60b contacts*.
2. Key the six contacts into your contact list.
3. Select five friends or family members, and add them to your contact list. For their Job title, key **Friend** or **Family**.

After contacts have been keyed into your contact list, they can be easily edited.

- Double-click the contact file.
- Key the new or additional information.
- Click *Save & Close*. See Figure 11-4.

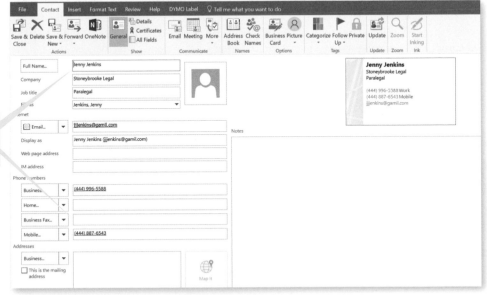

Add missing data or key updated contact information

Figure 11-4 Editing Contact information

4. For Mike Sweety, add the phone number **919-449-8767** and change his title to **Owner**.
5. For Kathryn Zinna, add the email address **kzina@fullertown.net**.
6. For Mark Cummings, add the webpage address **www.FullertownBakerySupply.com**.
7. For Misty Walker, add the fax number **919-888-4949**.
8. For Pat Smith, change the Job title to **CFO**.

60C

Create Contact Groups

People > Home tab >
New > New Contact Group

Often, you will want to send the same information to several contacts in your contact list. Creating a Contact Group allows you to send emails more efficiently. An email message addressed to a Contact Group is sent to every member of the group. Rather than sending multiple individual messages, you send only one message. For example, you can send a message to the 25 members of the drama club by placing the members in a Contact Group and sending a single message to the group.

- When you click New Contact Group, an Untitled—Contact Group window is displayed. See Figure 11-5.

- Key the name of the new group; then click *Save & Close*.

New Contact Group

Add name of Contact Group

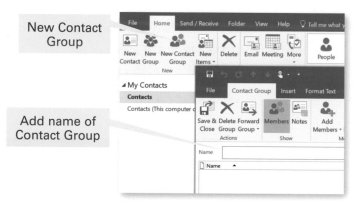

Figure 11-5 New Contact Group

1. Create a Contact Group and name it **Bakery Businesses**. Click *Save & Close*.

60D

Add Members to a Contact Group

People > Double-click the
Contact Group > Contact
Group tab > Members >
Add Members

A Contact Group is not useful until you add members to it. You will add members immediately after creating the Contact Group, and you may add members later if the group grows. It is important to keep your contact list, including your Contact Groups, up to date.

- Double-click the *Contact Group*.

- Click *Add Members*. A drop-down menu appears for you to select the source of the new group member.

- Select the source. If the source is your Address Book, double-click the contact. The selected contact appears in the Members box at the bottom of the dialog box. If there are other contacts from the Address Book you want to add, keep double-clicking until all members are selected.

- Click *OK* and the members are added to your Contact Group. See Figure 11-6.

Figure 11-6 Add a member to a Contact Group

1. Double-click the *Bakery Businesses* group.
2. From your Address Book, add all the contacts related to bakery businesses. You should have six contacts in the group.
3. Click *Save & Close*.

60E

Remove Members from a Contact Group

People > Double-click
Contact Group > Contact
Group tab > Select member
> Remove Member

Over time, groups change—for example, when an employee leaves a business or a company's sales representative has changed. When members leave a group, they should be removed from the Contact Group as well.

- Double-click the *Contact Group*.
- Select the member you wish to remove.
- Click *Remove Member*; then click *Save & Close*. See Figure 11-7.

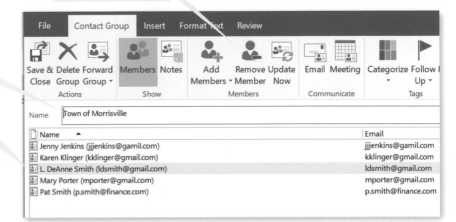

Figure 11-7 Remove a member from a Contact Group

1. In the *Bakery Business* group, remove Misty Walker from the group.
2. Click *Save & Close*.

1. Create another Contact Group, and name it **Friends and Family**. Click *Save & Close*.
2. Double-click the *Friends and Family* group.
3. From your Address Book, add all of the friends and family contacts to this group. You should have five contacts in the group.
4. Remove a member from the Contact Group. Add the member to the group again, or add a different member to the group.
5. Click *Save & Close*.

Digital Citizenship and Ethics

According to recent research, 60 percent of students aged 10–14 own a cell phone, as do close to 85 percent of teens between the ages of 15 and 18. While cell phones and smartphones provide a convenient and quick way to communicate and can be invaluable in emergency situations, they are also frequently misused or used irresponsibly in social and public situations. Following are some cell phone etiquette tips:

- Turn your phone off in schools, theaters, libraries, and doctor's offices
- Do not use your cell phone while you are doing something else, such as driving, riding a bike, or simply having a conversation with others
- Do not shout or speak loudly to compensate for a bad connection

As a class, discuss the following:

COLLABORATION

1. How is a cell phone useful for school?
2. What are some of the health risks associated with extensive cell phone usage?

LESSON 61   Organize and Manage Emails

OUTCOMES

- Create folders to organize/manage emails
- Learn about the Junk Email folder
- Use the Junk filter to remove unwanted emails

61B

Create a New Email Folder

Mail > Folder tab >
New > New Folder

 TIP If you want to see your most used or favorite folders at the top of the Navigation pane, you can right-click a folder and then click *Show in Favorites*.

A cluttered and unorganized mailbox can make it difficult to find the email you need. Creating new mail folders can be used to reduce the clutter.

- In the Navigation pane, right-click the folder you want to organize.
- Click *New Folder* and key the name for the new folder in the dialog box (see Figure 11-8). Click *OK*.
- Your new folder appears beneath the original folder in the Navigation pane.
- To further organize your files, you can create folders within folders. For example, within a folder named School Activities, you may have other folders to separate school projects, sports teams, and FBLA activities.

Key the name of new folder

Figure 11-8 Create New Folder dialog box

1. Create the following email folders: **Friends, Family, School Activities,** and **Act Now**.

61C

Junk Email Folder

Mail > Home tab >
Delete > Junk

A message suspected of being junk is automatically moved to the Junk Email folder in the Navigation pane. You should periodically check messages in the Junk Email folder to ensure that legitimate messages were not classified as junk. Reclassifying messages that are erroneously moved into the Junk Email folder can improve the accuracy of automated classification.

- From the Junk pull-down menu, you can reclassify messages sent to the Junk Email folder in error.
- If a message is not junk, select the message and click Not Junk. This sends the message back to your Inbox.
- From this menu, you can Block Sender, Never Block Sender, Never Block Sender's Domain, and Never Block this Group or Mailing List. These options tell the software how to handle emails from the identified sources. See Figure 11-9.

Figure 11-9 Junk Email reclassification options

1. Check your Junk Email folder. Use one of the reclassification options to move any messages that are not junk back to your Inbox.

2. For other messages, consider using the other reclassification options from the Junk pull-down menu.

61D

Junk Email Filters

Mail > Home tab > Delete > Junk > Junk Email Options

From the Junk pull-down menu, you selected settings that automatically move messages that appear to be junk into a special Junk Email folder. See Figure 11-9. You can use Junk Email Options at the bottom of the pull-down menu to choose the level of junk email protection you want, specify safe senders and recipients, block senders, and block email from international email addresses or in foreign languages.

1. Select *Junk E-mail Options* from the Junk pull-down menu. The Junk Email Options dialog box displays.

2. Under the Options tab, increase your level of junk email protection to either *Low* or *High*. Verify that the "Disable Links" and "Warn me" boxes are checked. These options protect you from phishing messages (scams that ask you for personal or confidential information) and warn you about suspicious domain names. Click *Apply* after making changes.

3. Explore the other tabs to see how you can increase your level of protection from junk email.

michaeljung/Shutterstock.com

21st Century Skills: Productivity and Accountability

Email has become one of the most common ways for computer users to communicate, both personally and for business purposes. Although email is considered less formal than other business communications, it is still important to articulate your thoughts and ideas effectively in an email message. You should:

- Write in complete, active sentences
- Organize using paragraphs and bulleted or numbered lists
- Proofread and check your spelling

Most importantly, you should always know your audience and understand that your message could be shared either intentionally or by mistake with someone else.

With a partner, respond to these questions. Ask your instructor if you will need to turn in this activity for grading.

COLLABORATION

1. What perception might you form of a person who sends an email that has spelling and grammatical errors?

2. When might email not be the best form of communication?

LESSON 62　Schedule Meetings and Print Calendars

OUTCOMES

- Schedule a meeting
- Reply to a meeting request
- Propose a new meeting time
- Create additional calendars
- Print calendars in various styles

62B

Create Meetings

Calendar > Home tab >
New > New Meeting

In business or at school, you will have to schedule meetings with colleagues or classmates or reply to a meeting invitation. Your calendar allows you to create meetings with members of your contact list or Contact Groups.

- Click *New Meeting* in the Home tab of the Calendar window. A Meeting window appears for you to fill in the details of the meeting. See Figure 11-10.
- Select contacts to invite to the meeting. The email addresses will appear in the To text box.
- Key the title or purpose of your meeting in the Subject text box
- Key the location of the meeting in the Location text box
- Use the drop-down boxes to select the Start time and End time of your meeting
- Click the *Response Options* drop-down arrow in the Attendees group. You will notice both Request Response and Allow New Time Proposals boxes are checked. These options request the attendee to respond to the invitation or to offer a new time for the meeting. See Figure 11-11.
- Click *Send* and your meeting invitation will be sent to the selected contacts' Inbox

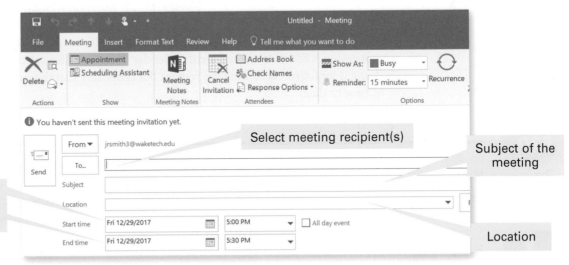

Figure 11-10 Meeting request window

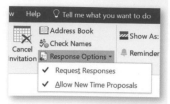

Figure 11-11 Response Options

1. Choose four classmates to invite to a meeting. If their contact information is not in your contact list, add them now.
2. In the Meeting window, invite the four classmates to a **Project Team Meeting** one week from today from 4:00 to 5:00 p.m. The location is the school library. Request a response, and allow invitees to propose a new time for the meeting.
3. Send your meeting request.

62C

Reply to a Meeting Request/Invitation

When you open a meeting request, you will notice a *Please respond* icon. This means the meeting organizer wants you to indicate if you will be at the meeting. You will also notice the choices for your response across the top of the email request. See Figure 11-12.

Figure 11-12 Meeting request responses

If the attendee selects Accept or Tentative, the invitation is deleted from the Inbox and the meeting is added to the recipient's calendar. If the attendee selects Propose New Time, he or she is tentatively accepting the request but proposing that the meeting be held at a different time or date.

62D

Propose a New Meeting Time

If you are unable to attend the meeting or want to attend but not at the date/time proposed, you have an option to suggest a new meeting time. In Figure 11-13, you see the Propose New Time option for responding to meeting requests. This option allows you either to tentatively accept but propose a new meeting time, or decline but propose a new meeting time. Rather than just declining the meeting request, you can let the meeting organizer know you are interested in meeting but cannot attend at the time proposed in the request.

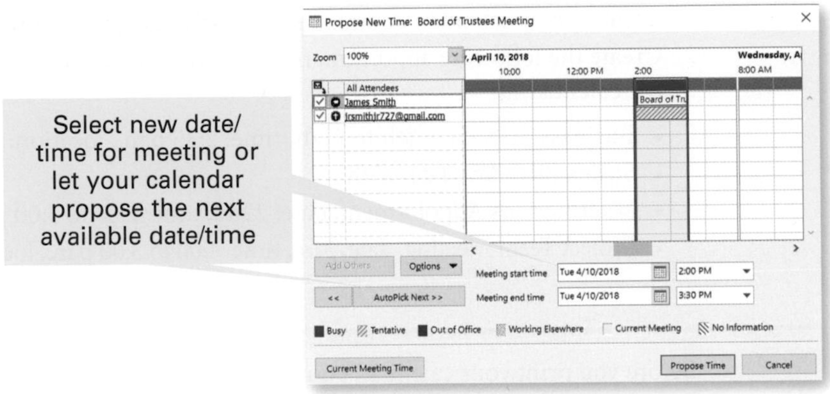

Select new date/
time for meeting or
let your calendar
propose the next
available date/time

Figure 11-13 Proposing a new meeting time

1. Open the meeting request sent by a classmate.
2. Select *Propose New Time*, and tentatively accept and propose that the meeting be changed to 5:00 p.m. on the same date.
3. If you received more than one meeting request, decline all other requests.

62E

Create Additional Calendars

Calendar > Folder tab >
New > New Calendar

In addition to your main calendar that you use to schedule important items for work or school, you can create additional calendars. For example, you can create a sporting event calendar to record your practice schedule, games, and tournaments.

- Display the Create New Folder dialog box. Key the name of your new calendar. See Figure 11-14.
- Click *OK*. The new calendar appears in the Calendar Navigation pane.
- To view the new calendar, select the checkbox for the calendar.

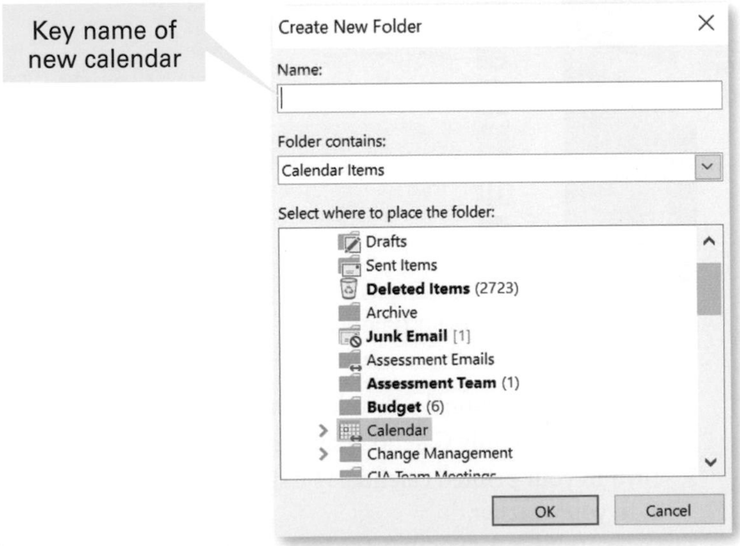

Key name of
new calendar

Figure 11-14 Create New Calendar folder

1. Create a new calendar, and name it **Jackie's Personal Calendar**.
2. Create the following appointments in Jackie's Personal Calendar. Use the current month for the calendar.

- Business Trip, date: 8th to 12th, time: 2:35 p.m., location: Boston Marriott
- Susie's Birthday, date: 15th
- Veterinarian's Appointment, date: 22nd, time: 2:00 to 3:00 p.m., location: 1124 Walker Street
- Project Team Meeting, date: 31st, time: 1:00 to 3:00 p.m., location: 5th Floor Conference Room

62F

Print Calendars

Calendar > File tab >
Print

Before you print your calendar, you need to specify how you want it to appear (the Print style). You can choose from Daily, Weekly Agenda, Weekly, Monthly, Tri-fold, and Calendar Details styles. See Table 11-1 earlier in the chapter for an explanation of the Print styles.

- Select the Print style.
- Specify Start and End dates. See Figure 11-15.
- Click *Print*.

Figure 11-15 Printing a calendar

1. Print Jackie's Personal Calendar, which you created in the previous activity.
2. Select the Monthly Calendar setting. Use the current month for the Start and End dates.
3. Turn in your printed calendar. Be sure to write your name on the calendar before turning it in to your teacher.
4. Delete Jackie's Personal Calendar by right-clicking *Jackie's Personal Calendar* in the Calendar Navigation pane. Select *Delete Calendar*. Confirm that you wish to delete the calendar when prompted.

Skill Builder 10

A

Warmup

Key each line twice.

alphabet

1 Jack liked reviewing the problems on the tax quiz on Friday.

home/1st

2 Hans and Jason had a small van all fall. Max has a sad mask.

easy

3 The auditor may work with vigor to form the bus audit panel.

gwam 1' | 1 | 2 | 3 | 4 | 5 | 6 | 7 | 8 | 9 | 10 | 11 | 12 |

B

Technique Mastery: Individual Letters

Key each line twice.

- Curved, upright fingers
- Quick keystrokes

Emphasize continuity and rhythm with curved, upright fingers.

A After Nariaki ate the pancake, he had an apple and a banana.

B Ben Buhl became a better batter by batting big rubber balls.

C Chi Chang from Creek Circle caught a raccoon for Cara Locke.

D Did David and Dick Adams decide to delay the departure date?

E Ed and Eileen were selected to chaperone the evening events.

F Jeff Flores officially failed four of five finals on Friday.

G Garth and Gregg glanced at the gaggle of geese on the grass.

H His haphazard shots helped through half of the hockey match.

I Ida insisted on living in Illinois, Indiana, or Mississippi.

J Jackie objected to taking Jay's jeans and jersey on the jet.

K Ken kept Kay's snack in a knapsack in the back of the kayak.

L Lillian and Layne will fill the two small holes in the lane.

M The minimum amount may make the mission impossible for many.

gwam 1' | 1 | 2 | 3 | 4 | 5 | 6 | 7 | 8 | 9 | 10 | 11 | 12 |

C

Speed Check: Sentences

1. Key a 20" writing on lines 1–5.

2. Key two 30" writings on lines 6–10. Try to increase your keying speed the second time you key each line.

1 Dr. Cox is running late today.

2 Ichiro baked Sandy a birthday cake.

3 Kellee will meet us here after the game.

4 Gordon will be leaving for college on Friday.

5 Juan and Jay finished the project late last night.

6 This is the first time that I have been to Los Angeles.

7 Juan informed Dave the price for gas went up last week.

8 Yuki decreased her electric bill by almost ten percent.

9 Orlando may go with us to the city and work for Pamela.

10 The eight busy men may go to the lake and fix the sign.

gwam 30" | 2 | 4 | 6 | 8 | 10 | 12 | 14 | 16 | 18 | 20 | 22 |

D

Speed Building: Guided Writing

1. Key one 1' unguided and two 1' guided timings on each ¶; determine *gwam*.

2. Key two 2' unguided timings on ¶s 1–2 combined; determine *gwam*.

3. Key one 3' unguided timing on ¶s 1–2 combined; determine *gwam*.

Quarter-Minute Checkpoints				
gwam	1/4'	1/2'	3/4'	Time
16	4	8	12	16
20	5	10	15	20
24	6	12	18	24
28	7	14	21	28
32	8	16	24	32
36	9	18	27	36
40	10	20	30	40

A all letters used

gwam 2' | 3'

You must be an extra-special individual if you — 5 | 3

are recognized throughout the world. Eleanor Roosevelt — 10 | 7

was such a unique individual. All through her life she — 16 | 10

supported the cause of the less fortunate. Quite often — 21 | 14

you could find her trying to help people find — 25 | 17

meaningful work. — 27 | 18

Women's, racial, and youth issues were other — 31 | 21

causes that she spent an amazing amount of time — 36 | 24

working on. Being the first lady gave her a platform — 41 | 28

to further these causes. Serving on the United — 46 | 31

Nations gave her the opportunity to continue to — 51 | 34

support these just causes on the world level. — 55 | 37

gwam 2' | 1 | 2 | 3 | 4 | 5 | 6 |
3' | 1 | 2 | 3 | 4 |

Planning for Your Career 1 — Preparing a Career Portfolio and Reference List

OUTCOMES

- Identify appropriate contents for a career portfolio
- Prepare a reference list

Employment Documents

When searching for a job, employment documents provide job applicants with opportunities to present their best qualities to prospective employers. These qualities are represented by the content of the documents as well as by their accuracy, format, and neatness. It is essential that you learn how to prepare the employment documents presented in the Preparing for Your Career modules to create favorable impressions throughout the various stages of the employment process.

fizkes/Shutterstock.com

Career Portfolio

Pop Paul-Catalin/Shutterstock.com

Early in your job search, you should build a **career portfolio** that contains information about you and samples of items that show how your previous activities and achievements relate to the job you are pursuing. You should consider compiling a printed version and a digital version of your portfolio. A printed version should be taken to the personal interview so its contents can be conveniently and quickly shared with the interviewers at appropriate times. A copy of your digital version can be given to the interviewers for them to refer to as they make their decisions as to which applicant will be hired for the position. The contents of the career portfolio can include such things as:

- Industry certifications, letters, awards, newspaper articles, programs, brochures, etc. that document your accomplishments
- Samples of your writing and projects you have completed
- Course names and descriptions that are important for the job you are seeking
- Your personal resume and list of references
- Letters of reference

1. Open a new *Word* document and briefly describe the career you are presently planning to pursue upon graduation from high school or college.
2. Key a list that identifies the items you would include in your career portfolio and indicate why you would include them.
3. Save as: *pc1 portfolio*.

Reference Lists

Figure PC1-1 Reference list

You should choose your references carefully, as employers use them to confirm what they have learned about you from your employment documents and the personal interview and to learn more about the kind of employee you are likely to be. Teachers, clergy, and current or previous employers usually make good references.

Choose references who can speak positively about your accomplishments and abilities to work effectively and efficiently to accomplish team and personal goals as well as your personal attributes. After you have selected your references, you must ask them if they are willing to serve as your reference. If they agree, confirm that you have correct information to include on your reference list. Verify that you have the correct spelling of their names; company name and position title, if applicable; and mailing address, email address, and telephone number(s).

It is a good practice to keep your references informed about your progress in searching for a job. You can do this by telephoning or emailing them as needed. When you accept a position, write a note to your references thanking them and letting them know what position you have accepted.

Reference lists (as shown in Figure PC1-1) should contain your name and contact information centered at the top of the page and the contact information for each reference. Format the information attractively on a page. The reference list shown below was arranged in table format, started 2" from the top of the page, centered horizontally, and printed without gridlines.

References for

Gretchen Klettner
151 Meeting Street
Charleston, SC 29401
843-555-6450
gretchenk.66@mxn.com

References

Mrs. Paulette Wylie	Mr. James D. Ekaitis	Rev. David Donnelly
143 Tradd Street	Internship Coordinator	Associate Pastor
Charleston, SC 29401	Williams & Beatty, Inc.	Victory Church
843-555-1792	210 Wentworth Street	66 Dunneman Street
wyliep143e@quiktime.net	Charleston, SC 29401	Charleston, SC 29403
	843-555-7813	843-555-3342
	jekaitis@wb.com	pastor.david@victory.org

An alternate design could use a 2" top margin and default side margins. A title, such as *References for*, could be centered in a slightly larger font size. Center your name and contact information as shown above with the space removed between the lines within this section. Key each reference as a blocked paragraph using default vertical spacing.

1. Open a new *Word* document and key the information above as a reference list. You decide all formatting features.
2. Save as: *pc1 references*.

Personal Reference List

1. Identify at least three people you want to serve as your references during your job search.
2. Open a new *Word* document and insert a 3-column table with at least 3 rows.
   - In column 1, key the names of the persons you have identified
   - In column 2, briefly describe why you have chosen each person
   - In column 3, identify the information you need to get from each person to complete your reference list
   - Insert an appropriate title and column headings for your table and format it so it is attractive and easy to read
3. Save as: *pc1 my references*.

Before You Move On

1. What allows you to work more efficiently by sending the same email message to several related personal or business associates? LO 60C

2. You can file messages by project, topic, contact, or other categories by creating _____. LO 61B

3. What is the purpose of the Junk Email folder? LO 61C

4. Name the four filters you can use to screen your email messages. LO 61D

5. Junk email is also known as _____. LO 61C

6. What are the four responses you can give to reply to a meeting request? LO 62C

7. How can managing your email help you to be more efficient and effective at school or work? LO 61D

8. Name three of the six styles for which you can print your *Outlook* calendar. LO 62F

9. What is another name for the person sending a meeting request? LO 62B

10. What is the purpose of the "Propose a New Time" response for a meeting request? LO 62D

11. Why is it a good idea to check your Junk Email folder periodically? LO 61C

Apply What You Have Learned

Create a Contact Group

1. Enter the following list of new business contacts:

Grant Shillings Vice President New Street Investment Banks 2433 Westbrook Parkway Greenville, NC 27834 252-639-5555 (Business) 252-539-8866 (Cell)	Rebecca Berry Senior Loan Officer First Colonial Bank 1776 Bicentennial Street Swansboro, NC 28584 910-229-4963 (Business)
Joan Dewar Investor Bethel Savings and Loan 3356 Swift Creek Way Bethel, NC 27812 252-778-8582 (Business) 252-539-0253 (Cell)	Hillary Banks Mortgage Officer Second Street Bank 1313 Mockingbird Lane Ayden, NC 28513 252-664-2535 (Business)

West Smith	Benjamin Martin
Chief Financial Officer	Investment Strategist
First Citizens Bank	New Street Investment Banks
1369 Doolittle Mill Road	2433 Westbrook Parkway
Greenville, NC 27534	Greenville, NC 27834
252-798-4654 (Business)	252-639-5555 (Business)
	252-753-5566 (Cell)

2. Select four of the new contacts and create a group named "Charity Donors."

3. Select two of the new contacts and create a group named "Stakeholders."

4. Select two classmates and enter the contact information. For their job title use "Principal Investor."

5. Delete two members of the Charity Donors.

6. Add one classmate to the Stakeholders group.

7. When you have completed each item, raise your hand and ask your instructor to screen check that you have performed each item correctly.

8. Check with your instructor to see if you should remove these items from your *Outlook* account.

Calendar

- Pair with a classmate or use your instructor's contact information. If your classmate's contact information is not in your Contacts list, enter it now.

- Send a meeting request to your classmate (or instructor) inviting him/her to a Stakeholder's Meeting from 10:30 a.m. to Noon at the Indian Lake Towers to discuss the upcoming Board of Trustees' Meeting.

- When you receive your meeting request, propose a new meeting time for 11:30 a.m. to 1:30 p.m. Accept the meeting request when it returns.

- When you have completed each item, raise your hand and ask your instructor to screen check that you have performed each item correctly.

- Once your instructor has verified your work is correct, delete or remove these items from *Outlook*.

CHAPTER 12

Managing Written Communication

Lesson 63   Business and Personal-Business Letters Review

Lesson 64   Mail Merge and Data Source Files

Lesson 65   Main Document Files and Mail Merge Management

Lesson 66   Mail Merge Labels and Directories

Assessment 6   Enhanced Email and Letters

Application Guide

Understanding Mail Merge

Many businesses and other types of organizations communicate with their existing or prospective customers, clients, or members by means of letters, newsletters, promotional pieces, etc. For example, banks send out credit card offers, cable and other utility companies send out special offers, corporations must send out privacy notices on a regular basis, and restaurants send out advertisements, etc. One effective way to manage documents that are the same for everyone except for things like name, address, and account balance is to use the Mail Merge feature.

When using **Mail Merge**, you combine one file that has the information that is the same for all recipients with a second file that contains the information that is different for each recipient. When combined, a personalized document for each recipient is prepared.

The file that contains the text and graphics that are the same for each version of the merged document is called the main document. A file that contains the information to be merged into the main document is called the data source. For example, the names and addresses of the recipients of a letter are contained in a data source file. When combined, a **merged file** is generated.

Frequently, main document and data source files are used repeatedly after they have been updated. The capability to reuse these files with the Mail Merge feature increases the effectiveness of managing written communications.

Beginning with Lesson 64 in this chapter, you will prepare main document files and data source files and then merge them using the **Mail Merge Wizard**. The merged files you will create are letters, labels, and directories.

Pablo Calvog/Shutterstock.com

LESSON 63 — Business and Personal-Business Letters Review

OUTCOMES

- Review personal-business and business letters in block format and modified block format
- Use word processing features for font, hyphenation, spelling and grammar check, and removing space after paragraphs

63–66A

Warmup

Key each line twice at the beginning of each lesson; first for control; then for speed.

alphabet 1 We realize expert judges may check the value of the unique books.

figures 2 A teacher will have 75 test items from pages 289-306 for Unit 41.

speed 3 The dorm officials may name six sorority girls to go to a social.

gwam 1' | 1 | 2 | 3 | 4 | 5 | 6 | 7 | 8 | 9 | 10 | 11 | 12 | 13 |

63B

Letters

Letter 1 (Personal-Business Letter)

1. Format the text below as a modified block style personal-business letter with mixed punctuation, using Arial 14 pt. font and hyphenation.
2. **Save as:** *63b letter1.*

1331 Penn Ridge Court | Coraopolis, PA 15108-6001 | May 20, 20-- | Mrs. Helena Lopez| Community Healthcare | 911 Center Avenue | Sewickley, PA 15143-0900 | Dear Mrs. Lopez

My father will be retiring from full-time employment at the end of this coming July. He and my mother will lose their health insurance that is provided by their employer as of July 31.

I am trying to assist them in securing insurance to supplement the coverage provided by Medicare. Will you please send me information explaining the plans available through Community Healthcare. At the moment, they seem to be primarily interested in electing the traditional Medicare coverage and want to purchase a Part B supplemental policy and Part D for prescription drug coverage.

Once we have had time to review the information, we will contact you to set up an appointment. Thank you.

Sincerely | Richard Courtney

Letter 2 (Business Letter)

1. Format the letter below as a block style business letter with open punctuation, using Calibri 12-point font and hyphenation.
2. **Save as:** *63b letter2.*

March 5, 20-- | Attention Human Resources Department | Central Life Assurance, Inc. | 1520 W. Ohio Street | Indianapolis, IN 46222-1578 |Ladies and Gentlemen

The Action Fitness Center is offering an introductory membership to employees of area corporations. This membership is for 90 days and costs only $50, the regular monthly membership fee.

During this 90-day trial period, your employees can use the indoor running track, weight-lifting stations, and exercise equipment (including treadmills, stair climbers, and rowing machines).

Your employees can also enroll in any of the aerobics, weight-control, and healthy-eating classes that are offered on a regular basis.

To take advantage of this offer, distribute the enclosed cards to interested employees. These cards can be presented on the first visit.

Sincerely | Ned V. Mowry | President | xx | Enclosures | c Mary Parker, Club Membership Coordinator

 ★TIP When a company name is used in the closing lines, tap *Enter* once after the complimentary close and key the name in ALL CAPS; then tap *Enter* twice and key the writer's name.

Letter 3 (Business Letter)

1. If needed, open **63b letter2** and format it using modified block with no paragraph indentations, mixed punctuation, and Times New Roman 12 point.
2. Add the subject line: **EMPLOYEE TRIAL MEMBERSHIP**.
3. Bold the name of the fitness center in the body of the letter.
4. Add the center's name as a company name in the closing lines (see Tip at the left).
5. **Save as: 63b letter3**.

LESSON 64   Mail Merge and Data Source Files

OUTCOMES
- Perform a mail merge
- Create and edit data source files

64B

Mail Merge

Mailings tab > Start Mail Merge > Start Mail Merge > Step-by-Step Mail Merge Wizard

The Mail Merge feature is often used to merge a letter file (main document) with a name and address file (data source) to create a personalized letter (merged file) to each person in the data source file.

Data sources can be word processing, spreadsheet, database, or email files. In this chapter, you use data sources created in *Word*.

You can use the Mail Merge Wizard task pane to lead you through the process of setting up and performing a mail merge, or you can use the commands on the Mailings tab. In this lesson, you use the Mail Merge Wizard to set up and perform mail merges. As Figure 12-1 shows, the Select document type options in Step 1 of 6 in the Mail Merge Wizard can be used to create letters, email messages, envelopes, labels, and a directory.

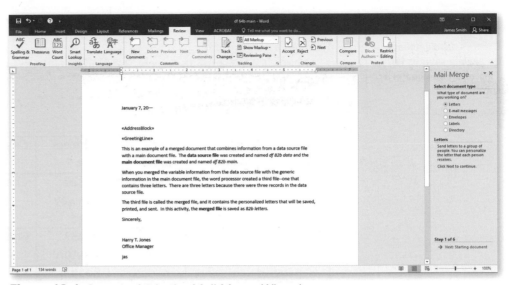

Figure 12-1 Step 1 of 6 in the Mail Merge Wizard

1. Open the main document file (**df 64b main**) and the Mail Merge Wizard.
2. In Step 1, if necessary choose *Letters* as the type of document and click *Next: Starting document* at the bottom of the pane to continue.
3. In Step 2, if necessary choose *Use the current document* as the starting document and click *Next*.
4. In Step 3, if necessary choose *Use an existing list* and then click *Browse* and browse to **df 64b data**, the data file that contains the recipient's information. Click *Open* to bring up the Mail Merge Recipients dialog box. Click *OK* to accept the recipients. Click *Next* to go to step 4 of the Wizard.
5. In Step 4, the letter is keyed and the merge fields are inserted. Because the letter is already keyed and contains the needed merge fields, Step 4 is complete; click *Next* to proceed to Step 5.
6. In Step 5, preview the three letters by using the forward (>>) or backward (<<) double chevrons in the task pane. Click *Next*.
7. In Step 6, select the *Print* option in the task pane and choose to print the *Current record*. Make sure the appropriate printer is selected and click *OK* to print the letter or *Cancel* to cancel printing.
8. **Save as:** **64b letters** and close the file.

★TIP To save a copy of all the letters, click *Edit Individual Letters* in the task pane in Step 6 of the Mail Merge Wizard. Choose *All* in the Merge New Document dialog box. Click *OK* and then save the letters.

64C

Create Data Sources

Insert tab > Tables > Table

The data source file contains unique information for each individual or item. Each individual or item is called a **record**, and each record contains **fields**. Fields are the information about the item or individual, such as her or his title, first name, last name, street address, city, state, and zipcode. The column headings in the data source table are the names of the fields.

When you create a main document, you will insert the fields (called **placeholders** or **merge fields**) into the document at the desired locations.

Once you have created your data source and inserted the merge fields into the main document, you can perform the merge.

NOTE You also can use database tables as data sources for mail merges. See Chapter 17, Lesson 85.

Data Source 1

1. Open a new *Word* file.
2. Use the Table feature to create a data source with three records, each with seven fields, as shown below.
3. Save as: *64c data1*.

Title	First Name	Last Name	Address Line 1	City	State	Zipcode
Mr.	Harold	Dominicus	14820 Conway Road	Chesterfield	MO	63025-1003
Mrs.	Noreen	Mueller	15037 Clayton Road	Chesterfield	MO	63017-8734
Ms.	Elizabeth	Theilet	1843 Ross Avenue	St. Louis	MO	63146-5577

StockLite/Shutterstock.com

COLLABORATION

Digital Citizenship and Ethics

Blogs are a common way for web users to share their opinions, ideas, products, and services. The word *blog* is derived from the words *web log*, an online personal journal typically written and maintained by an individual (referred to as a *blogger*). A blog consists of regular commentary on issues that are important to the blogger.

Blogs are easy to set up and enable just about anyone to bring their opinions to the forefront for all to read. A feature of many blogs is the ability for readers to respond with their own comments, thus providing a forum that promotes dialogue among people with a common interest. All blogs allow postings to be linked to other blogs, creating a network of blogs called the *blogosphere*. As a class, discuss the following:

1. What opportunities do blogs provide for education and collaboration?
2. What are some drawbacks of blogs?

Data Source 2

1. Create a data source using the 15 records shown below.
2. Use the column headings as field names.
3. **Save as: *64c data2*.**

Title	First Name	Last Name	Address Line 1	City	State	Zipcode
Mr.	Daniel	Raible	13811 Seagoville Road	Dallas	TX	75253-1380
Ms.	Sally	Lysle	3707 S. Peachtree Road	Mesquite	TX	75180-3707
Mrs.	Luz	Ruiz	13105 Timothy Lane	Mesquite	TX	75180-1310
Mrs.	Jane	Alam	1414 Alstadt Street	Hutchins	TX	75141-3792
Ms.	Stacey	Bethel	1717 Castle Drive	Garland	TX	75040-1717
Dr.	Jash	Sharik	2021 E. Park Boulevard	Plano	TX	75074-2021
Mr.	Jack	Dunn	4007 Latham Drive	Plano	TX	75023-4000
Mrs.	Helen	Wever	1001 Cuero Drive	Garland	TX	75040-1001
Ms.	Ann	Buck	1919 Senter Road	Irving	TX	75060-1919
Mr.	Peter	Como	701 W. State Street	Garland	TX	75040-0701
Ms.	Karen	Rolle	1026 F Avenue	Plano	TX	75074-3591
Mr.	Dale	Zeman	4412 Legacy Drive	Plano	TX	75024-4412
Mr.	Yu	Wei	12726 Audelia Road	Dallas	TX	75243-7789
Ms.	Anne	Sige	532 N. Story Road	Irving	TX	75061-0506
Mr.	David	White	3700 Chaha Road	Rowlett	TX	75088-3700

Edit Data Sources

Layout tab > Page
Setup > Orientation >
Landscape

You can edit both records and fields in a data source. For example, you can add records to, delete records from, revise records in, or sort records in an existing data source file.

Also, you can add, delete, or revise fields in an existing data source file. Data source files can be word processing, spreadsheet, database, or email files.

Data Source 1

1. Open **64c data1** and make the following changes:
   a. In Record 3, change Elizabeth's title to **Mrs.** and last name to **Popelas**.
   b. Delete the record for Harold Dominicus, and add these two records:

   Dr. Eugene Whitman, 531 Kiefer Road, Ballwin, MO 63025-0531
   Ms. Joyce Royal, 417 Weidman Road, Ballwin, MO 63011-0321

   c. Change the orientation of the file to Landscape.
   d. Add two fields (**Company** and **Email**), and then insert the company name and email address in each record as indicated below:

   Mueller—**Allmor Corporation;** mueller@AC.com
   Popelas—**Kurtz Consumer Discount;** epopelas@kurtz.com
   Whitman—**Whitman Family Practice;** whitman@wfc.com
   Royal—**Better Delivery, Inc.;** jroyal2@betdel.com

2. **Save as:** **64d data1** and compare your data source file to the one shown below.

Title	First Name	Last Name	Address Line 1	City	State	Zipcode	Company	Email
Mrs.	Noreen	Mueller	15037 Clayton Road	Chesterfield	MO	63017-8734	Allmor Corporation	mueller@AC.com
Mrs.	Elizabeth	Popelas	1843 Ross Avenue	St. Louis	MO	63146-5577	Kurtz Consumer Discount	epopelas@kurtz.com
Dr.	Eugene	Whitman	531 Kiefer Road	Ballwin	MO	63205-0531	Whitman Family Practice	whitman@wfc.com
Ms.	Joyce	Royal	417 Weidman Road	Ballwin	MO	63011-0321	Better Delivery, Inc.	jroyal@betdel.com

Data Source 2

1. Open *df 64d data2*.
2. Add the records in the table below to *df 64d data2*.

Field Name	Record 1	Record 2	Record 3
Title	Mrs.	Dr.	Ms.
First name	LaJunta	Vjay	Rita
Last name	Greene	Awan	Martz
Address Line 1	8606 Wiley Post Avenue	1148 Hyde Park Boulevard	601 Centinela Avenue
City	Los Angeles	Inglewood	Inglewood
State	CA	CA	CA
Zipcode	90045-8600	90302-2640	90302-5519

3. Add a **Company** field and a **Plan** field to *df 64d data2*, the data source table.

Records 1–4			Records 5–8		
Last Name	Company	Plan	Last Name	Company	Plan
Perez	P & B Auto Trim	Family	Barichal	Ace Auto Parts	Husband/Wife
Brletich	Security Auto Service	Family	Greene	Greene Auction House	Husband/Wife
Kamerer	Bank and Trust	Individual	Awan	Inglewood Orthopedics	Individual
Neumann	Lawndale Bakery	Individual	Martz	Hercules.com	Parent/Child

4. Key the additional information for the 8 records above into *df 64d data2*.
5. **Save as:** *64d data2*.

OUTCOMES

- Create main document files
- Merge main document files and data source files
- Edit mail merge documents
- Select recipients for a mail merge

65B

Create a Main Document Setup and Perform a Mail Merge

The main document file contains the generic text and format of the document that remains constant in each letter, plus the merge fields. After the data source has been selected, the merge fields are inserted into the main document file where the variable information from the data source is to appear. For example, the *Address block* and *Greeting line* in Figure 12-2 are examples of merge fields inserted into a main document as it is written. The letter address lines will replace the <<AddressBlock>> merge field and a salutation will replace the <<GreetingLine>> merge field when the data source file and main file are merged.

The merge process creates the merged file, which consists of a document for each record included in the merge. Each document contains the personalized information for one individual in the data source.

1. Open a new *Word* document, and then open the Mail Merge Wizard.
2. In Step 1, select *Letters*.
3. In Step 2, select *Use the current document*.
4. In Step 3, browse for the data source file **64d data1** and accept the list of recipients.
5. In Step 4, key the letter shown on the next page in block format with open punctuation, using the Wizard to insert the *Address block* and *Greeting line* merge fields. Save the letter as **65b main**.
6. In Step 5, preview your letters. If necessary, remove the space between the lines of the letter address and make any other formatting changes.
7. In Step 6, print the Popelas letter and save the merged file as **65b merge**.

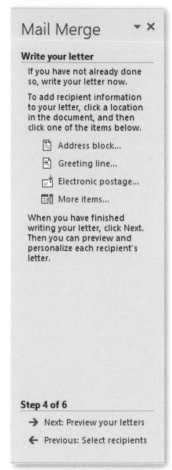

Figure 12-2 Mail Merge Wizard Step 4

January 15, 20—

<<AddressBlock>>

<<GreetingLine>>

It was a pleasure to meet you last week to discuss your long-term health-care needs. As you requested, I have charted the various policy features from three leading insurance providers.

The chart shows the various options each provider extends and the cost for each option. You can select those that meet your needs the best.

I will call you in a week to arrange an appointment so we can discuss this matter thoroughly.

Sincerely

Katherine Porter
Agent

xx

Enclosure

65C

Mail Merge Application

1. Open a new *Word* document, and then open the Mail Merge Wizard.
2. Use the information below to create the main document in block letter format with mixed punctuation. The data source file is the updated *64c data2* from Lesson 63D.
3. Save the main document as *65c main*, and then merge the main document and data source files using the Mail Merge Wizard. Make sure the third paragraph has the *Title* and *Last Name* fields merged. Adjust spacing as needed.
4. Print the Raible and White letters. Save merged letters as *65c merge*.

October 5, 20—

<<AddressBlock>>

<<GreetingLine>>

Thank you for attending the recent open house reception sponsored by the Dallas Area Environmental Health Association. We hope that you enjoyed meeting our expert staff of scientists, physicians, nutritionists, technicians, and others who work on your behalf to improve your quality of life.

Headaches, sinusitis, fatigue, joint aches, and asthma are some of the common ailments that are often caused by our environment. The Dallas Area Environmental Health Association is dedicated to conducting the research that documents the link between the common ailments and the environment so effective treatments can be offered.

<<Title>> <<Last Name>>, now that you know more about the Association, we ask you to schedule a 20-minute consultation with one of our staff members to discuss your health concerns. This consultation is free and carries no obligation to use our services. Just call me at 972-555-0119 to schedule a mutually convenient time.

Sincerely, | Margarita L. Jiminez | Director of Services | xx

65D

Mail Merge: Letters to Selected Recipients

Mailings tab > Start Mail Merge > Start Mail Merge > Step-by-Step Mail Merge Wizard

When linking the data source file to the main document, you can edit the recipient list in a variety of ways. One frequent edit is to specify those in the data source who are not to receive the merged document. When the merge is performed, a letter will not be created for the records not selected. The checks to the left of the names in Figure 12-3 indicate the individuals who will receive the document. Those with no check will not receive the document.

You can also refine your recipient list by sorting the records on one or more of the fields in the record and by filtering your list to include only the records you want to include in the merge by using the options in the lower part of the Mail Merge Recipients dialog box.

1. Open a new *Word* document, and then open the Mail Merge Wizard.
2. Using **65c main** and **64c data2**, use the Mail Merge Wizard to refine your recipient list and create a letter for each record with Plano in the City field.
3. Print the letters.
4. **Save as:** **65d plano**.

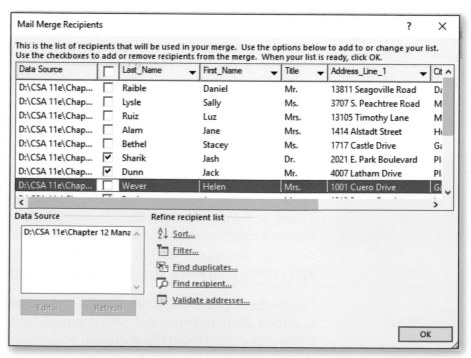

Figure 12-3 Selecting recipients in the Mail Merge Recipients dialog box

1. Open a new *Word* document, and then open the Mail Merge Wizard.
2. Create a main document file using modified block letter format with paragraph indentations and mixed punctuation that will be linked to the data source file **64d data2**. Center the letter vertically on the page. Save the main document file as **65e main**.
3. Edit the recipient list so letters are sent to all except those with Inglewood in the *City* field. Complete the merge and save the merged file as **65e merge**.
4. Print the Barichal letter.

May 25, 20—

<<AddressBlock>>

<<GreetingLine>>

 We know what a burden it is for small businesses like <<Company>> to offer excellent health insurance benefits to employees. That is why First Health is holding an informational session at the Hartley Hotel on Wednesday, June 10, from 4:30 p.m. to 6 p.m.

 <<Title>> <<Last Name>>, we invite you and another representative from <<Company>> to join us. You will learn about the major features of our medical, dental, and long-term disability coverage so that you can compare them to your present plan's features. We are convinced that you will be pleasantly surprised by what we can offer at affordable premiums.

 Please use the enclosed card to reserve your places at the informational session. Refreshments will be served, and you will have ample time to discuss your specific needs with one of our staff members who will be attending.

Sincerely, | Robyn L. Young-Masters | Regional Marketing Manager |

xx | Enclosure | <<First Name>>, Tom Durkin has told me a great deal about the success of <<Company>>, and I am looking forward to meeting you to find what you are doing to be so successful in such a competitive field.

LESSON 66   Mail Merge Labels and Directories

OUTCOME

- Use mail merge to prepare labels (address labels and name badges) and directories

66B

Mail Merge: Labels, Badges, and Directory

Mailings tab > Start Mail Merge > Start Mail Merge > Step-by-Step Mail Merge Wizard

★TIP Be sure to click the *Update all labels* button in Step 4 of the Wizard; otherwise only the first label will be filled in.

Mail Merge can be used for many other tasks. Frequently, labels (address labels, name badges, etc.), directories, and envelopes are prepared by using the Mail Merge Wizard to create these types of documents in the same manner it was used to create personalized letters. In this lesson, you create address labels, name badges, and a directory.

Address Labels

1. Open a new *Word* document and the Mail Merge Wizard.
2. In Step 1, select *Labels*.
3. In Step 2, select *Change document layout* and then click *Label options* and select your address labels. Unless directed otherwise, select 5160 Address Labels from the *Avery US Letter* vendor list and click *OK*.
4. In Step 3, browse to find **df 66b data** that will be used as the data source, click *Open*, and then click *OK* to select all recipients.
5. In Step 4, select Address Block to insert the merge fields, click *OK*, and then click *Update all labels* (see Figure 12-4).
6. In Step 5, preview the labels and make any necessary changes.
7. In Step 6, save the merged file as **66b labels** and then print the labels. Compare your labels to those shown in Figure 12-5 on the next page.
8. Close the file.

> **Mail Merge** ▾ ✕
>
> **Arrange your labels**
>
> If you have not already done so, lay out your label using the first label on the sheet.
>
> To add recipient information to your label, click a location in the first label, and then click one of the items below.
>
> 📄 Address block...
>
> 📄 Greeting line...
>
> ✍ Electronic postage...
>
> ▦ More items...
>
> When you have finished arranging your label, click Next. Then you can preview each recipient's label and make any individual changes.
>
> **Replicate labels**
>
> You can copy the layout of the first label to the other labels on the page by clicking the button below.
>
> [Update all labels]
>
> **Step 4 of 6**
>
> → Next: Preview your labels
>
> ← Previous: Select recipients

Figure 12-4 Insert merge fields and update all labels in Step 4

Name Badges

1. Open a new *Word* document and the Mail Merge Wizard.
2. In Step 1, select *Labels*.
3. In Step 2, select *Change document layout* and then click *Label options* and select your address labels. Unless directed otherwise, select 5095 Self Adhesive Name Badges from the *Avery US Letter* vendor list.
4. In Step 3, browse to find **df 66b data** that will be used as the data source.
5. In Step 4, Using the *More items* option, insert the *First_Name* field, tap *Space Bar*, then insert the *Last_Name* field on line 1 of the name badge and the *City* field on line 2. Format all three fields in Calibri 18-point font and center-align them. Update all labels.
6. In Step 5, preview the labels and make any necessary changes.
7. In Step 6, save the merged file as **66b badges** and then print the first page of badges. Compare your name badges to those shown in Figure 12-5.
8. Close the file.

Directory

1. Open a new *Word* document and the Mail Merge Wizard.
2. In Step 1, select *Directory.*
3. In Step 2, select *Use the current document.*
4. In Step 3, browse to find ***df 66b data*** that will be used as the data source.
5. In Step 4, Using the *More items* option, insert the *Last_Name* field, *First_Name* field, and *Email* field. Insert a comma and space between the *Last_Name* and *First_Name* fields; align the names at the left margin. Align the email addresses at the right margin using a right dot leader tab set at 6.5". Tap *Enter* once after the *Email* field.
6. In Step 5, preview the directory entry and make any necessary changes.
7. In Step 6, select *To new document.* Insert the words **Email Directory** center-aligned above the first directory entry, print the directory, and save the merged file as ***66b directory***. Compare your directory to the one shown in Figure 12-5.
8. Close the file.

Home tab > Paragraph > More button > Tabs button > Tab stop position 6.5'', Alignment Right, Leader type 2, OK

Your completed address labels, name badges, and directory should look like Figure 12-5.

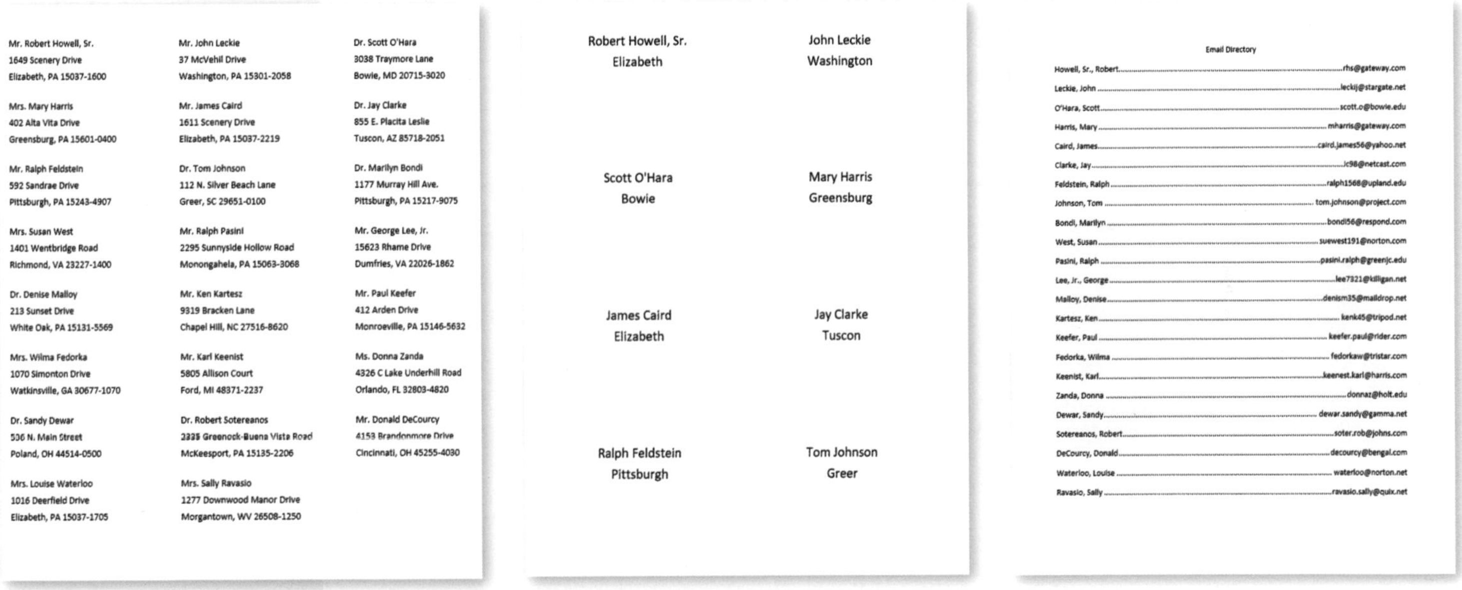

Mr. Robert Howell, Sr. 1649 Scenery Drive Elizabeth, PA 15037-1600	Mr. John Leckie 37 McVehil Drive Washington, PA 15301-2058	Dr. Scott O'Hara 3038 Traymore Lane Bowie, MD 20715-3020
Mrs. Mary Harris 402 Alta Vita Drive Greensburg, PA 15601-0400	Mr. James Caird 1611 Scenery Drive Elizabeth, PA 15037-2219	Dr. Jay Clarke 855 E. Placita Leslie Tuscon, AZ 85718-2051
Mr. Ralph Feldstein 592 Sandrae Drive Pittsburgh, PA 15243-4907	Dr. Tom Johnson 112 N. Silver Beach Lane Greer, SC 29651-0100	Dr. Marilyn Bondi 1177 Murray Hill Ave. Pittsburgh, PA 15217-9075
Mrs. Susan West 1401 Wentbridge Road Richmond, VA 23227-1400	Mr. Ralph Pasini 2295 Sunnyside Hollow Road Monongahela, PA 15063-3068	Mr. George Lee, Jr. 15623 Rhame Drive Dumfries, VA 22026-1862
Dr. Denise Malloy 213 Sunset Drive White Oak, PA 15131-5569	Mr. Ken Kartesz 9319 Bracken Lane Chapel Hill, NC 27516-8620	Mr. Paul Keefer 412 Arden Drive Monroeville, PA 15146-5632
Mrs. Wilma Fedorka 1070 Simonton Drive Watkinsville, GA 30677-1070	Mr. Karl Keenist 5805 Allison Court Ford, MI 48371-2237	Ms. Donna Zanda 4326 C Lake Underhill Road Orlando, FL 32803-4820
Dr. Sandy Dewar 536 N. Main Street Poland, OH 44514-0500	Dr. Robert Sotereanos 2335 Greenock-Buena Vista Road McKeesport, PA 15135-2206	Mr. Donald DeCourcy 4153 Brandonmore Drive Cincinnati, OH 45255-4030
Mrs. Louise Waterloo 1016 Deerfield Drive Elizabeth, PA 15037-1705	Mrs. Sally Ravasio 1277 Downwood Manor Drive Morgantown, WV 26508-1250	

Robert Howell, Sr. Elizabeth	John Leckie Washington
Scott O'Hara Bowie	Mary Harris Greensburg
James Caird Elizabeth	Jay Clarke Tuscon
Ralph Feldstein Pittsburgh	Tom Johnson Greer

Email Directory

Howell, Sr., Robert.......rhs@gateway.com
Leckie, John.......leckij@stargate.net
O'Hara, Scott.......scott.o@bowie.edu
Harris, Mary.......mharris@gateway.com
Caird, James.......caird.james56@yahoo.net
Clarke, Jay.......jc98@netcast.com
Feldstein, Ralph.......ralph1568@upland.edu
Johnson, Tom.......tom.johnson@project.com
Bondi, Marilyn.......bondi56@respond.com
West, Susan.......suewest191@norton.com
Pasini, Ralph.......pasini.ralph@greenjc.edu
Lee, Jr., George.......lee7321@killigan.net
Malloy, Denise.......denism35@maildrop.net
Kartesz, Ken.......kenk45@tripod.net
Keefer, Paul.......keefer.paul@rider.com
Fedorka, Wilma.......fedorkaw@tristar.com
Keenist, Karl.......keenest.karl@harris.com
Zanda, Donna.......donnaz@holt.edu
Dewar, Sandy.......dewar.sandy@gamma.net
Sotereanos, Robert.......soter.rob@johns.com
DeCourcy, Donald.......decourcy@bengal.com
Waterloo, Louise.......waterloo@norton.net
Ravasio, Sally.......ravasio.sally@quix.net

Figure 12-5 Address labels, name badges, and email directory

Mail Merge: Selecting Records for Labels, Badges, and Directory

Use data source **64c data2** to prepare the address labels, name badges, and directory as directed below. Unless directed otherwise, use the same address label and name badge that were used in 66B.

Address Labels

Prepare a standard mailing label for each record that has *Garland* or *Mesquite* in the *City* field. Save the merged file as **66c labels**. Print the labels.

Name Badges

Prepare a name badge for each record that has *Plano* or *Irving* in the *City* field. Horizontally center the *First Name* and *Last Name* fields on one line. Center the *City* field on the next line. Use an appropriate-sized font. Save the name badges as **66c badges**. Print the badges.

Directory

Prepare a directory listing all records in alphabetical order by City and then by Last Name within City. Left-align last and first names (insert a comma and space between the last and first names) and set a dot leader right tab at the 6.5" position for the city. Include a heading **CITY DIRECTORY**, center-aligned before the directory entries. Save the directory as **66c directory**. Print the directory.

iStock.com/philsajonesen

21st Century Skills: Collaborate with Others

The ability to work well with others is one of the most important skills an employer looks for in job candidates. When you work with others to achieve a common goal, you demonstrate your willingness to share ideas and produce results that will benefit you, your team, and your company. Technology has facilitated teamwork in the workplace.

- Through videoconferencing, employees at virtually any location around the world can see and speak to each other
- Collaborative software enables multiple users in different locations to work on an electronic file at the same time
- Blogs allow web users to post commentary on selected topics and issues and respond to those comments posted by others
- Wikis are websites that allow multiple users to add and edit content in real time

Think Critically

1. In teams of three or four, brainstorm ideas for a wiki on a current school topic. Some possibilities include school recycling programs, bullying, and Internet acceptable-use policies.
2. Create a list of tasks to be completed to create the wiki, such as writing articles and gathering photos or artwork. Assign at least one task to each team member.
3. In a *Word* document, prepare the wiki content. **Save as: c12 21century**.

COLLABORATION

Assessment 6 — Enhanced Email and Letters

Key each line twice at the beginning of each lesson; first for control, then speed.

alphabet 1 Wixie plans to study my notes just before taking the civics quiz.

figures 2 Our soccer league had 4,129 boys and 3,687 girls playing in 2005.

speed 3 The busy fieldhand kept the fox in a big pen to keep it in sight.

gwam 1' | 1 | 2 | 3 | 4 | 5 | 6 | 7 | 8 | 9 | 10 | 11 | 12 | 13 |

Timed Writing

Key 2 5' writings on all paragraphs combined. Print, proofread, circle errors, and determine *gwam*.

A all letters used

	gwam	3'	5'

Many people support the notion that a worker — 3 | 2 | 42

with a healthy body and mind is a valued worker. — 6 | 4 | 44

Healthy employees often have a greater chance for — 9 | 6 | 46

professional growth, produce more on the job, are — 13 | 8 | 48

happier with their lives, and are likely to be more — 16 | 10 | 50

successful than employees who are in poor physical — 20 | 12 | 52

health or are not mentally alert. — 22 | 13 | 54

If you want to have a healthy body, you should — 25 | 15 | 55

try to complete appropriate activities during your — 28 | 17 | 57

leisure time or try to find ways to enhance the — 31 | 19 | 59

level of your physical activity during your regular — 35 | 21 | 61

school day or workday. Brisk walking is a great way — 38 | 23 | 63

to bring exercise into daily activities with amazing — 42 | 25 | 66

ease and quick results. — 43 | 26 | 67

Fast walks from your residence to the bus stop, — 46 | 28 | 68

from the bus stop to your class, or from one class to — 50 | 30 | 70

another are very good ways to reap the benefits — 53 | 32 | 72

of exercise while you carry out your daily activities. — 57 | 34 | 75

Doing isometric exercises as you study, read, or — 60 | 36 | 76

watch television will produce excellent results. — 63 | 38 | 78

You should, of course, do only exercises that — 66 | 40 | 80

will not disrupt others. — 68 | 41 | 81

gwam 3' | 1 | 2 | 3 | 4 |
5' | 1 | 2 | 3 |

Activity 1
Email

1. Format and key the text below as an email to your instructor. Be sure to proofread and correct all errors before sending. Use **PROFESSIONAL DEVELOPMENT OPPORTUNITIES** for the subject line. Send a copy of the email to yourself.

As you are aware, our company has implemented a new program for professional development this year. Every employee will be given time off with pay to participate in an approved seminar. Executive Development Seminars will be presenting four seminars in San Francisco August 13–17 that have been approved. These seminars include:

- Speak Like a Pro
- Write Like a Pro
- Dress Like a Pro
- Dine Like a Pro

I have placed brochures in the break room. If you are interested in attending one of the seminars, let me know, and I'll complete your registration forms.

2. Print a copy of the email.

Activity 2
Contacts

1. Open *Outlook*. Create a new contact folder called **My Contacts**. Enter the information from the three business cards below into the contacts file. Print a copy of the file in Business Card view.

Erik N. Howard

Technology Specialists

310 Garrison St.
Portland, ME 04102
207.512.2846 ph
207.512.2800 fax
www.howarden@g-mail.com

Activity 3
Appointments

1. Record the appointments shown below.
2. Change the Calendar view to Work Week.
3. Print a copy of the calendar for the week.

- Board Meeting on June 18, *<current year>*, from 8 to 11:30 a.m. in the Lincoln Conference Room.
- Board Luncheon on June 18, *<current year>*, from 12:00 to 1:30 p.m. at Bartorolli's.
- Jamison Russell, Vice President of Riley Manufacturing, on June 17, *<current year>*, from 1:30 to 3:00 p.m.
- Vivian Bloomfield, Manager of Garnett Enterprises, on June 19, *<current year>*, from 8:30 to 9:30 a.m.
- Chamber of Commerce meeting on June 17, *<current year>*, from 5:30 to 7:30 p.m. at Carter's Restaurant.

Activity 4
Notes

1. Input the notes shown below using the Notes feature.

- Get the agenda ready for the June 23 opening meeting with branch managers.
- Call Brookstone Travel Agency to discuss discounts for volume travel.
- Check with Paul to discuss his role at the branch managers meeting.
- Schedule meeting with Ms. St. Claire to finalize board luncheon.
- Call Jamal Carter to get report on the Gender Communication seminar.

Activity 5
Create a Data Source File

1. Using the Table feature in *Word*, key the following data source. Make the rows 0.2" high and use AutoFit Contents to set column widths.
2. Save as: **a6 data1**.

Title	First Name	Last Name	Address 1	City	State	Zipcode
Ms.	Gaynell	Boucher	88 Strophmore Road	Haines City	FL	33844
Mr.	Kenneth	Chomas	2912 John Morris Street	Sebring	FL	33872
Mr.	Roy	Crawford	9180 Springfield Drive	Jacksonville	FL	32256
Mrs.	Teresa	George	962 SW 114th Way	Ft Lauderdale	FL	33325
Mr.	Fred	Graham	1634 SE 28th Street	Cape Coral	FL	33904
Mrs.	Lorraine	Hommell	603 Shorewood Drive	Cape Canaveral	FL	32920
Mrs.	Alberta	Lasch	102 Pinehurst Lane	Boca Raton	FL	33431
Ms.	Kay	Matthews	3606 Landings Way, Apt 103	Tampa	FL	33624
Ms.	Barbara	McKeever	14961 Egan Lane	Miami Lakes	FL	33014
Mrs.	Sandra	Preuss	5814 Silver Moon Avenue	Tampa	FL	33625
Mr.	Kenneth	Provins	10019 Colonade Drive	Tampa	FL	33667
Mr.	Robert	Stevenson	331 Garfield Avenue	Lake Placid	FL	33852
Mrs.	Betty	Wawrin	8950 Park Boulevard	Seminole	FL	33777
Mr.	James	Westwood	6207 Riverwalk Lane	Juniper	FL	33458
Mr.	Robert	Young	12526 Terrence Road	Summerfield	FL	34491

Activity 6
Edit a Data Source File

1. If needed, open **a6 data1**. Change the orientation to Landscape.
2. Change Ms. Kay Matthews to **Mrs. Kay Collins**.
3. Add a column at the right, key **Career Field** as the column heading, and insert the following in that column for the persons named below:

Last Name	Career Field
Chomas	Education
George	Accounting
Collins	Engineering
Preuss	Marketing
Provins	Political Science
Wawrin	Psychology
Young	Finance

4. Sort the table by Zip code in ascending order.
5. Save as: **a6 data2**.

1. Open a new *Word* document and then open the Mail Merge Wizard.
2. Using the data source file *a6 data2* and the information below, create a main document in block letter format with mixed punctuation for every alumnus who has an entry in the *Career Field* column in the data source file. Adjust spacing as needed. Save the main document as *a6 main* and the merged letters as *a6 merge*.
3. Print the first two letters.

September 15, 20—

<<AddressBlock>>

<<GreetingLine>>

Thank you for agreeing to participate in the Hamilton College Career Fair on October 7 at the Charles Center for Leadership. It is important that current students have an opportunity to meet and discuss career objectives with Hamilton College alumni who have expertise in the students' chosen fields of study.

Plan to arrive at the CCL by 9:30 a.m. and report to the registration area in the lobby area inside the main entrance. From 10:15 a.m. to 12 noon, students pursuing a career in <<Career Field>> will be able to meet with you in one of the conference rooms.

<<First Name>>, I look forward to having you on campus for this popular event. I hope you will be able to join the faculty, academic administrators, student leaders, and me for lunch. The lunch should end by 1:30 p.m.

If you need any other information, don't hesitate to call me at 800-555-9470 or email me at fjburns@hamilton.edu.

Sincerely

Fred J. Burns, Director
Career Planning and Placement

Enclosure

xx

<<FirstName>>, I've enclosed a parking pass that permits you to park in any campus parking lot.

Activity 8
Mail Merge: Labels and Badges

1. Open a new *Word* document and then open the Mail Merge Wizard.
2. Using *a6 data2*, create a mailing label for every alumnus who has an entry in the Career Field column. Unless directed otherwise, select 5160 Address Labels from the Avery US Letter vendor list. Save the labels as *a6 labels*. Print the labels.
3. Using the Mail Merge Wizard and *a6 data2*, create an attractive name badge for every alumnus who has an entry in the Career Field column. The badges should show each person's name and city. Unless directed otherwise, select 5095 Adhesive Name Badges from the Avery US Letter vendor list. Save the labels as *a6 badges*. Print the name badges.

Skill Builder 11

A

Warmup

Key each line twice.

alphabet 1 Wayne gave Zelda exact requirements for taking the pulp job.

az/za 2 Zelda and Zane played a zany tune that amazed the jazz band.

easy 3 Rick may bicycle to the ancient city chapel by the big lake.

gwam 1' | 1 | 2 | 3 | 4 | 5 | 6 | 7 | 8 | 9 | 10 | 11 | 12 |

B

Technique Mastery: Individual Letters

Key each line twice.

 ★TIP Limit keystroking movement to fingers; keep hands and arms motionless.

Emphasize continuity and rhythm with curved, upright fingers.

N A new nanny can tend Hanna's nephew on Monday and Wednesday.

O Two of the seven women opposed showing more shows on Monday.

P Phil's playful puppy pulled the paper wrapping off the pear.

Q Quincy quickly questioned the adequacy of the quirky quotes.

R Our receiver tried to recover after arm surgery on Thursday.

S Russ said it seems senseless to suggest this to his sisters.

T Ty took title to two cottages the last time he went to town.

U Uko usually rushes uptown to see us unload the sugar trucks.

V Vivian voted to review the vivid videos when she visits Val.

W Will waved wildly when a swimmer went wading into the water.

X Six tax experts explained that Mary was exempt from the tax.

Y Your younger boy yearns to see the Yankees play in New York.

Z Zelda quizzed Zack on the zoology quiz in the sizzling heat.

gwam 1' | 1 | 2 | 3 | 4 | 5 | 6 | 7 | 8 | 9 | 10 | 11 | 12 |

C

Skill Building

Key each line twice.

Space Bar

1 day son new map cop let kite just the quit year bay vote not
2 She may see me next week to talk about a party for the team.

Word response

3 me dye may bit pen pan cow sir doe form lamb lake busy their
4 The doorman kept the big bushel of corn for the eight girls.

Double letters

5 Neillsville berry dollar trees wheels sheep tomorrow village
6 All three of the village cottonwood trees had green ribbons.

gwam 1' | 1 | 2 | 3 | 4 | 5 | 6 | 7 | 8 | 9 | 10 | 11 | 12 |

D

Speed Check: Sentences

1. Key a 30" writing on each line.

2. If time allows, key an additional 30" on selected lines.

1 Tomas left just before supper.
2 When will you be able to return it?
3 He has two more final exams to complete.
4 Their next concert will be held in September.
5 Jacob and Sarah left for San Francisco on Tuesday.
6 Orlando wanted to see the last home game of the season.

gwam 30" | 2 | 4 | 6 | 8 | 10 | 12 | 14 | 16 | 18 | 20 | 22 |

E

Speed Building

1. Key a 1' timing on each ¶; determine *gwam*.

2. Key a 2' timing on ¶s 1–2 combined; determine *gwam*.

3. Key a 3' timing on ¶s 1–2 combined; determine *gwam* and number of errors.

Quarter-Minute Checkpoints			
gwam	1/4'	1/2'	3/4'	1'
24	6	12	18	24
28	7	14	21	28
32	8	16	24	32
36	9	18	27	36
40	10	20	30	40
44	11	22	33	44
48	12	24	36	48
52	13	26	39	52
56	14	28	42	56
60	15	30	45	60

A all letters used
gwam 2' | 3'

"I left my heart in San Francisco." This expression 5 | 3
becomes much easier to understand after an individual has 11 | 7
visited the city near the bay. San Francisco is one of 16 | 11
the most interesting areas to visit throughout the entire 22 | 15
world. The history of this city is unique. Even though 28 | 18
people inhabited the area long before the gold rush, it was 33 | 22
the prospect of getting rich that brought about the fast 39 | 26
growth of the city. 41 | 27

It is difficult to write about just one thing that this 47 | 31
exquisite city is known for. Spectacular views, cable cars, 53 | 35
the Golden Gate Bridge, and Fisherman's Wharf are only a 58 | 39
few of the many things that are associated with this amazing 64 | 43
city. The city is also known for the diversity of its people. 70 | 47
In fact, there are three separate cities within the city, 76 | 51
Chinatown being the best known. 79 | 53

gwam 2' | 1 | 2 | 3 | 4 | 5 | 6
3' | 1 | 2 | 3 | 4

Planning for Your Career 2 — Developing a Resume

OUTCOMES

- Format a print resume
- Prepare a digital resume

Print Resumes

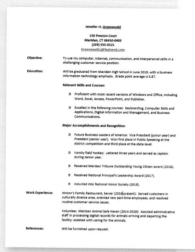

Figure PC2-1 Print resume

A **resume** is an honest summary of your experiences and qualifications for the position you are seeking (see Figure PC2-1). For most job seekers, the resume (print or digital) is one of the first employment documents that can demonstrate your suitability for the position. Prospective employers typically scan each resume very quickly to determine which applicants deserve a personal interview. If your resume does not clearly show how your abilities and activities relate to the position you are seeking or if your resume contains language errors or keyboarding errors, you will not likely be given further consideration.

Print resumes are those printed on paper. They are usually submitted to a prospective employer as an enclosure with your letter of application, included in your print portfolio, and distributed to those interviewing you. In most cases, a print resume for a recent high school graduate should be limited to one page. The information presented usually covers six major areas:

- *Personal information* (your name, home address, email address, and telephone number[s])
- *Position objective* (clear definition of position desired)
- *Education* (courses and/or program taken, skills acquired, grade point average [and grades earned in courses directly related to job competence], and graduation date)
- *School and/or community activities or accomplishments* (organizations, leadership positions, and honors and awards)
- *Work experience* (position name, name and location of employer, and brief description of responsibilities)
- *References* (names of people familiar with your character, personality, and work habits) that will be provided upon request

In general, the most important information is presented first, which means that most people who have recently graduated from high school will list educational background before work experience, unless their work experience is directly related to the desired position. The information in each section is listed in chronological order with the most recent first. The reference section is usually last on the page.

1. Study the printed resume model in Figure PC2-2.
2. Open a new *Word* document. Use default settings for margins and font.
3. Using the table feature, insert a 2 by 5 table. Set the width of column 1 at 1.5" and column 2 at 5". Merge the cells in row 1 and key the name and contact information as shown in the resume model.
4. Key the remaining text in the four rows, formatting it as shown in the model resume.
5. Remove all table borders. If desired, make adjustments to the white space between paragraphs to enhance appearance.
6. Save as: *pc2 print resume*.

Jennifer H. Greenawald

150 Preston Court
Meriden, CT 06450-0403
(203) 555-0121
Greenawald.j@fastsend.com

Objective: To use my computer, Internet, communication, and interpersonal skills in a challenging customer service position.

Education: Will be graduated from Meriden High School in June 2019, with a business information technology emphasis. Grade point average is 3.87.

Relevant Skills and Courses:

□ Proficient with most recent versions of Windows and Office, including Word, Excel, Access, PowerPoint, and Publisher.

□ Excelled in the following courses: Keyboarding, Computer Skills and Applications, Digital Information and Management, and Business Communications.

Major Accomplishments and Recognition:

□ Future Business Leaders of America: Vice President (junior year) and President (senior year). Won first place in Public Speaking at the district competition and third place at the state level.

□ Varsity field hockey: Lettered three years and served as captain during senior year.

□ Received Meriden Tribune Outstanding Young Citizen award (2018).

□ Received National Principal's Leadership Award (2017).

□ Inducted into National Honor Society (2016).

Work Experience: Hinton's Family Restaurant, Server (2016-present): Served customers in culturally diverse area, oriented new part-time employees, and resolved routine customer service issues.

Volunteer, Meriden Animal Safe Haven (2014-2016): Assisted administrative staff in processing digital records for animals arriving and departing the facility; assisted with caring for the animals.

References: Will be furnished upon request.

Figure PC2-2 Print resume model

Personal Print Resume

Use the following guidelines when creating your print resume.

- Use a simple design. Default top, bottom, and side margins are acceptable but may vary slightly depending on the amount of information presented. Use an appropriate amount of white space between lines and between resume sections.
- Key your name at the top of the page on a line by itself. Key your address below your name, and list each telephone number on a separate line. Include a business-appropriate email address below the last line. If needed, obtain and use an email address that does not use nicknames or "cute" names that convey a message that you are not mature.
- Arrange the resume parts attractively on the page. The arrangement may vary with personal preference and the purpose of the resume.
- Use boldface and plain bullets to attract attention; avoid using italic and ALL CAPS because they are more difficult to read, especially when used with large blocks of text
- Use a basic font, such as 11-point Calibri or 12-point Times New Roman
- Use white, ivory, or light-colored (gray or tan) paper, standard size (8.5" x 11") for a print resume
- Don't insert your photograph in the resume

1. Open a new *Word* document.
2. Prepare a first draft of your print resume. Be concerned primarily with keying the major sections and the information you want to include in your resume. You will format and edit your resume later in this module.
3. Save as: ***pc2 my draft resume***.

Digital Resumes

Figure PC2-3 Digital resume

Many companies convert the information on a resume into a database file that is stored on a computer, and then software is used to search the files for specific information to select applicants for further consideration. Employers may search for education level, work experience, or keywords that are closely related to the position being filled.

Use a digital version of your resume when you are requested to submit a resume that will be scanned, send your resume as an email message or attachment, or submit your resume as part of an online application process. If you are asked to send your resume as an email attachment but not told which version to send, consider sending the print and digital versions. That way, the employer will have a copy that is likely to be accurately converted to a database file and a more attractive version that can be printed and distributed to those involved in the hiring decision. See Figure PC2-3.

Your digital resume should use a standard font and size such as 11-point Calibri or 12-point Times New Roman. Do not use word processing features such as indentations, columns, borders, and shading; and text enhancements, such as bold, bullets, text effects, underlines, etc. These features can cause errors or disappear entirely or partially when a resume is processed for storage in a computer database.

To increase the likelihood that your resume will be selected in a database search, consider replacing the Objective section with a Summary section (see Figure PC2-4). The summary contains keywords describing your education, positions held, and skills that relate to the position being sought.

Adam Tyrell
15550 Burnt Store Road
Punta Gorda, FL 33955-1500
941-555-6367
tyrell.adam@speedconnect.net

SUMMARY

Strong communication and telephone skills, excellent keyboarding, computer, and Internet skills, and good organizational and personal skills.

EDUCATION

Will be graduated from Garrison High School in June 2019 with a strong background in academic and business information technology. Grade point average of 3.64.

RELEVANT COURSES

AP English (11-12), Computer Skills and Applications I and II (10), Digital Communications Information (11), Computer Assisted Design (11), Sport Marketing (12).

MAJOR AWARDS AND RECOGNITION

National Principal's Leadership Award (2018), 1st Place in Regional Computer Fair (2013), Punta Gorda Rotary Club Student of the Month (2017), National Honor Society (2017-present).

EXTRA-CURRICULAR ACTIVITIES

PGHS Golf Team (9-12), PGHS Interact Club (member 10-12; Historian 12), PGHS Class Treasurer (12), PGHS Musicals (9-12), PGHS Future Business Leaders of America (10-12),

COMMUNITY SERVICE

Punta Gorda Methodist Church Vacation Bible School teacher assistant (2015-2018), Race for the Cure publicity committee (2018), Fallen Timber Animal Shelter student helper (2017), PGHS Senior Citizens Breakfast server (2016-2017), United Youth Camp student helper (2018).

WORK EXPERIENCE

DeCesare Brothers Restaurant (2017 to present): Take and serve customer orders, balance receipts for restaurant, ensure customer satisfaction, assisted in redesign of menu distributed to customers.

Certified soccer official (2017 to present): Officiate boys and girls (ages 8 to 18) indoor soccer matches at Family Sports Complex.

REFERENCES

Will be furnished upon request.

Figure PC2-4 Digital resume model

1. Study the digital resume model in Figure PC2-4.
2. Open a new *Word* document.
3. Using the defaults margins and font settings, key the digital resume.
4. Save as: **pc2 digital resume**.

Personal Digital Resume

1. Open **pc2 my draft resume**.
2. Review the information and make any desired changes, additions, or deletions to the information you want to include in your resume.
3. Using the information above, prepare a digital version of your resume.
4. Save as: **pc2 my digital resume**.

Resume Tools

Review tab > Resume > Resume Assistant

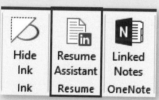

Figure PC2-5 Resume Assistant

Microsoft *Word* in *Office 365* and *Office 2019* includes two tools to help you in developing your resume: Resume Assistant and resume templates. Resume Assistant (see Figure PC2-5) provides suggestions from LinkedIn to help you create or update your resume. *Word* also provides dozens of online templates for resumes that you can use to format a professional looking resume. When you create a resume from a template file, the Resume Assistant pane automatically opens, as shown in Figure PC2-6. To find a template, click the *File* tab, click *New*, select a resume template from the Featured templates, or enter **resume** in the Search for online templates box.

1. Click the *Resume Assistant* button on the Review tab in the Resume group.
2. Enter a job role and industry that you'd like to explore.
3. Notice the work experience examples from LinkedIn.
4. Scroll down the Resume Assistant pane to the list of Top skills for the job role you've chosen.
5. Create a Word document that lists the Role, Industry, and four or five top skills for this job.
6. Save as: **pc2 top skills**.

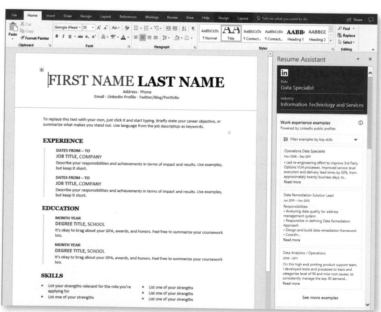

Figure PC2-6 Using a resume template

Communication Skills 6: Comma Usage

1. Study each of the 6 rules.
   a. Key the *Learn* line(s) beneath each rule, noting how the rule is applied.
   b. Key the *Apply* lines, inserting commas correctly.

Rule 1: Use a comma after (a) introductory phrases or clauses and (b) words in a series.

Learn	1	When you receive the statistics, please give me a copy.
Learn	2	Our next three meetings are on May 1, June 5, and July 6.
Apply	3	If you go to the game Robert and I would like to go with you.
Apply	4	Roberto's grocery list included milk eggs and bread.

Rule 2: Do not use a comma to separate two items treated as a single unit within a series.

Learn	5	Maria likes ham and eggs, toast, and milk for breakfast.
Apply	6	We have cookies and cream chocolate and strawberry ice cream.
Apply	7	I decided on trays of fruit vegetables and cheese and crackers.

Rule 3: Use a comma before short direct quotations.

Learn	8	The client said, "Is Mr. Fitzgerald or Ms. Ruiz available?"
Apply	9	Alexander asked "Have you seen *Gone with the Wind*?"
Apply	10	Dr. Suzuki said "Your final exam will be next Friday."

Rule 4: Use a comma before and after a word or words in apposition (words that come together and refer to the same person or thing).

Learn	11	Mr. Kennedy, the assistant principal, will address the issue.
Apply	12	Babe Ruth a baseball legend was a fan favorite for many years.
Apply	13	The director Mark Hill wanted all scenes completed this week.

Rule 5: Use a comma to set off words of direct address (the name of a person spoken to).

Learn	14	Please let me know, Joseph, when the package arrives.
Apply	15	Juan how much more time do you need to complete the job?
Apply	16	The completion date Elizabeth is yet to be determined.

Rule 6: Use a comma to set off nonrestrictive clauses (not necessary to the meaning of the sentence); however, do not use commas to set off restrictive clauses (necessary to the meaning of the sentence).

Learn	17	The report, which Mr. Jones approved, needs to be distributed.
Learn	18	The section that outlines the budget is being revised.
Apply	19	The book which won top honors dealt with women's issues.
Apply	20	The player with the highest batting average was given a plaque.

(continued on next page)

2. Key Proofread & Correct, inserting commas correctly.
   a. Check answers.
   b. Using the rule number(s) at the left of each line, study the rule relating to each error you made.
   c. Rekey each incorrect line, inserting commas correctly.

Save as: CS6 ACTIVITY1

Proofread & Correct

Rules		
1	1	Casandra's preferred colors are blue yellow and purple.
1	2	When he finished his piano lesson he went to a movie.
1,2	3	I snacked on cheese and crackers fruit and potato chips.
3	4	Ms. Finn ask "Who was the main character in *The Fountainhead*?"
4	5	Mrs. Sanchez the English teacher will direct the school play
5	6	Why do you keep asking Karen to turn your work in late?
6	7	The play which Judy directed was very well received.
6	8	Only students who have excellent grades are invited to join.
3	9	Mr. Fenton said "We will meet on Tuesday rather than Monday."
6	10	Justin who is from Moorcroft played for the University of Utah.

ACTIVITY 2: Word Choice

1. Study the definitions of the words.
2. Key the *Learn* line, noting the correct usage of each word.
3. Key the *Apply* lines, inserting the correct word(s).

Save as: CS6 ACTIVITY2

farther (adv) greater distance	**whose** (adj) of or to whom something belongs
further (adv) in greater depth, extent, or importance; additional	**who's** (cont)) who is

Learn 1 The **farther** I drive, the **further** my mind wanders.

Apply 2 With (farther, further) effort, I ran (farther, further) ahead of the group.

Apply 3 Tom could see (farther, further) into the distance than Jane.

Apply 4 With (farther, further) practice, he threw the javelin (farther, further).

Learn 1 **Who's** to say **whose** fault it is that we scored only one touchdown?

Apply 2 (Whose, Who's) kite is it, and (whose, who's) going to fly it?

Apply 3 (Whose, Who's) going to accompany Mr. Smith to the store?

Apply 4 (Whose, Who's) knit sweater is hanging in the closet?

ACTIVITY 3: Writing

Save as: CS6 ACTIVITY3

Write a paragraph or two explaining how you would respond during a job interview to the following question: Why are you interested in this position and why should I hire you for the position?

According to the statistics included in the National Center for Education Statistics *Condition of Education 2017** report, approximately 47 percent of the population 25 to 34 years old in the United States had attained a postsecondary degree. The reasons students go on to institutions of higher learning vary. Some of the reasons include: (1) increase employment options, (2) meet new friends with common interests, (3) gain knowledge and learn new skills, (4) job security, and (5) higher income potential.

2017 Annual Earning of Young Adults*:

Who completed high school as highest level	$30,500
Who attained an associate's degree	$36,900
Who attained a bachelor's degree	$50,000

Study educational and employment opportunities that you would like to pursue. Be prepared to discuss your plans after you graduate with a small group of your classmates. Your remarks should include what employment opportunities you plan to pursue and what education requirements need to be met in order to be considered for positions in this area of employment.

*Condition of Education 2017, https://nces.ed.gov/pubsearch/pubsinfo.asp?pubid=2017144.

Before You Move On

1. Explain the concept of mail merge. LO 64B

2. The mail merge file containing the information that is the same for everyone is called the _____. LO 64B

3. The mail merge file containing the information that is different for everyone is called the _____. LO 64C

4. The _____ is used to merge the main document and data source file. LO 65B, 65C, 65D, 65E, 66B

5. What are four types of documents that can be created by using mail merge? LO 66B, 66C

6. A _____ is the information about the item or individual, such as last name, first name, or street address. LO 64C, 64D

7. In the main document, what is placed in the document to insert fields at the desired location? LO 64C

8. In a mail merge data source file, each individual or item is called a _____. LO 64C

9. When the main document and data source are combined, it is called a _____. LO 65B, 65C, 65D, 65E

Apply What You Have Learned

Personal-Business Letter with Mixed Punctuation from Unarranged Copy

1. Format/key the letter below using block format and mixed punctuation. Use the Insert Date & Time function or AutoCorrect to insert the date—do not select Update automatically.
2. Change the font to 12-pt. Arial. Hyphenate the document. Proofread and correct errors.
3. Save as: *c12 letter1*.

6920 Dalzell Place | Pittsburgh, PA 15217-6000 | <Insert Date> | Mr. Phillip Hendon | 119 Cornwalis Drive | McKeesport, PA 15135-1000 | Dear Mr. Hendon:

I want to thank you for helping me with funds to attend Camp Kennedy Space Camp from August 11 through August 15.

My learning experience began with the flight from Pittsburgh to Orlando. It was my very first airplane ride. I was very nervous before taking off, but once we started to climb into the sky, I was thoroughly enjoying the view of Pittsburgh and the wonderful feeling that comes from the thrust of the engines taking us up through the soft clouds. The landing in Orlando was equally as exciting.

The five days at camp were just great. I learned so much! I experienced the thrill of spaceflight through an actual motion-based simulator. We got to work in teams to investigate space travel and to design space exploration vehicles and habitats. I really enjoyed meeting and talking with an astronaut who is training for an upcoming flight. She was so informative and knew exactly what to say to us. Furthermore, I got to enjoy the company of other youngsters who are as interested in space as I am.

Again, thanks for supporting me in achieving this important goal. Your generosity is greatly appreciated, and it has impacted my education in a very meaningful way.

Sincerely, | Josh Satterfield

Business Letter from Unarranged Copy

1. Format/key the letter below in block format with open punctuation. Change the font to 10-pt. Calibri.
2. Proofread and correct errors. Hyphenate the document.
3. Save as: *c12 letter2*.

November 1, 20-- | Mr. Max R. Rice | Foster Plaza Seven | 23 Oak Street | Schiller Park, IL 60176-6932 | Dear Mr. Rice

If the dental plan you chose last year has not delivered everything you thought it would, we have some good news for you. Dental Benefits Plus is now available to all Barclay, Inc. employees during this open enrollment period.

Dental Benefits Plus is part of the All-American family of healthcare products. Members of Dental Benefits Plus enjoy many advantages, including:

- Convenience: a nationwide network of over 50,000 dentists
- Affordability: low copays for high-quality services
- Support: a qualified support staff you can contact 24 hours a day, 7 days a week
- Availability: offered in 50 states and the District of Columbia
- Honesty: no hidden costs or surprise fees

These advantages as well as others are described in greater detail in the enclosed booklet. You can enroll any time before December 31. Mr. James Rothie, the customer service representative in your area is available to assist you with any questions you may have. You can contact him at (866) 555-1258.

Thank you for considering Dental Benefits Plus.

Sincerely | Janet Kingston | Regional Enrollment Manager | xxx | Enclosure |

c James Rothie

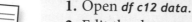

Mail Merge: Editing a Data Source

1. Open *df c12 data*.

2. Edit the data source by adding records for these three individuals:

Mr.	Daniel	Raible	13811 Seagonville Road	Dallas	TX	75253-1380
Mrs.	Luz	Ruiz	13105 Timothy Lane	Mesquite	TX	75180-1310
Dr.	Jash	Sharik	2021 E. Park Boulevard	Plano	TX	75074-2021

3. Change Mrs. Alma Nolfi's address to **1919 Senter Road, Irving, TX 75060-1919**.

4. Save the file as *c12 data*.

Mail Merge: Create a Main Document and Merge Files

1. Open a new *Word* document and access the Mail Merge Wizard.

2. Create a letter using the current document and the existing list *c12 data* as the data source.

3. Format the main document as a block letter with open punctuation. Key the current date and insert the Address block field for the address and the Greeting line field where appropriate (select *Greeting line* from the task pane, click *OK* and tap *Enter* once). Then key the letter body and closing lines as shown here:

What a pleasant surprise it was to find your $100 donation to your alma mater's FBLA Chapter in my mail today. I think it is great that you think highly enough of FBLA and your high school to help fund our activities.

Your contribution will be used to pay the travel and lodging expenses for one of our members who will be competing at the upcoming state conference.

If you are ever in our area and would like to visit the school or speak to the FBLA members about your education, activities, or career; let me know. I would be happy to see what we can arrange.

Sincerely

Ms. Gretchen Tullis
FBLA Sponsor
xx

4. Preview your letters and make any necessary revisions.

5. Print the first two letters and save the letters as *c12 merged*.

CHAPTER 13

Reporting with Style

Lesson 67	Unbound and MLA Report Review	Lesson 69	Collaborative Report with Footnotes
Lesson 68	Bound Reports	Lesson 70	Two-Column Reports with Pictures

Application Guide

Bound Reports

Reports are written to provide the reader with information. Reports may be formatted as unbound reports or as bound reports. Unbound reports are formatted with a 1" left margin for all pages, while bound reports are formatted with a 1.5" left margin on all pages to accommodate the binding. The other margins are the same for bound and unbound reports.

Standard Margins— Bound Report

	First Page	Second Page and Subsequent Pages
Left Margin (LM)	1.5"	1.5"
Right Margin (RM)	1"	1"
Top Margin (TM)	2"	1"
Bottom Margin (BM)	Approximately 1"	Approximately 1"
Page Number	Optional, bottom at center if used	Top; right-aligned

Internal Spacing

All parts of the report are SS using the 1.08 default line spacing.

Long quotes. Quoted material of four or more lines should be indented 0.5" from the left margin.

Enumerated items. To format numbers and bullets, the default 0.25" indentation should be used.

Titles and Headings

Title. The title of the report is formatted using the *Title* style, 28-pt. Calibri Light font (Headings). Add a hard return after the title.

Side headings. Side headings are keyed at the left margin and formatted using *Heading 1* style, 16-pt. Calibri font. Capitalize the first letters of all words except prepositions in titles and side headings.

Paragraph headings. Paragraph headings are keyed at the left margin using *Heading 3* style. Capitalize only the first letter of the first word and any proper nouns. Place a period after the heading.

Pressmaster/Shutterstock.com

Page Numbering

Insert tab > Header & Footer > Page Number

The first page of a report is usually not numbered. However, if a page number is used on the first page, center it at the bottom of the page. On the second and subsequent pages, position the page number at the top of the page using right alignment.

Documentation

Textual citations and footnotes for bound reports are formatted in the same manner as you learned for unbound and MLA reports in Chapter 6. However, the left margin is adjusted to allow for binding of the report. Review the following guidelines to refresh your memory.

Textual citation. The textual citation method of documentation includes the name(s) of the author(s), the date of the referenced publication, and the page numbers(s) of the material cited. For example, (**McWilliams, 2009, 138**) would be inserted in the text following the citation.

When a textual citation appears at the end of a sentence, the end-of-sentence punctuation follows the textual citation. However, if a textual citation follows a long quote that is indented from the margin, the end-of-sentence punctuation precedes the textual citation.

When the author's name is used in the text introducing the quotation, only the year of publication and the page number(s) appear in parentheses. For example, *McWilliams (2009, 138) said that . . .* would be keyed for the citation. For electronic references, include the author's name and the year. When there are two articles by the same author, the title of the article will also be included.

Footnotes. The footnotes method of documentation identifies the reference cited by a superscript number . . . .[1] The complete documentation for the reference is placed at the bottom of the same page and is identified with the same superscript number. Footnotes should be numbered consecutively throughout the report. Each footnote is indented 0.5" and SS, with a DS between footnotes. Following is an example of a footnote for a journal article.

[1]**Richard G. Harris, "Globalization, Trade, and Income,"** *Canadian Journal of Economics,* **November 1993, p. 755.**

> **★TIP** If software is used to create the footnotes, minor reformatting may need to be done in order to have the footnote indented 0.5" and SS with a DS between footnotes.

Ellipsis

An ellipsis (. . .) is used to indicate material omitted from a quotation. An ellipsis is three periods, each preceded and followed by a space. If the omitted material occurs at the end of a sentence, include the period or other punctuation before the ellipsis, as shown in the following example.

> In ancient Greece, plays were performed only a few times a year. . . . The festivals were held to honor Dionysius in the hope that he would bless the Greeks. . . . (Prince and Jackson, 1997, 35)

References, Bibliography, or Works Cited Page

Home tab > Paragraph >
Line and Paragraph Spacing

★TIP Move the hanging indent to 0.5", and verify that the Line and Paragraph Spacing defaults are set correctly before keying the references page.

References, Bibliography, or Works Cited pages are formatted for bound reports in the same manner as you learned for unbound and MLA reports in Chapter 6. However, the left margin is adjusted to allow for binding of the report. Review the following guidelines to refresh your memory.

All references used in a report are listed alphabetically by author's last name at the end of the report on a separate page using the title *References* (or *Bibliography* or *Works Cited*). Use the same margins as for the first page of the report and include a page number. SS each reference. Use the default line (1.08) and paragraph spacing settings. Begin the first line of each reference at the left margin; use the Hanging Indent feature to indent other lines 0.5".

The title of the page (*References*, *Bibliography*, or *Works Cited*) is formatted with the same style that was used for the report title.

Table of Contents

A table of contents lists the headings of a report and the page numbers where those headings can be found in the report. A table of contents makes it easy for a reader to see what is included in the report and to locate a specific section of the report. The table of contents, as shown in Figure 13-1, can be created manually or electronically using the Table of Contents feature of the software.

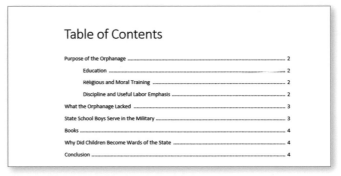

Figure 13-1 Sample table of contents

Manual Table of Contents

The side and top margins for the table of contents are the same as those used for the first page of the report. Key **Table of Contents** (using the Title style, 2" from top). Then list side and paragraph headings (if included). Side headings are started at left margin; paragraph headings are indented 0.5". Page numbers for each entry are keyed at the right margin; use a right dot leader tab to insert page numbers. Space once before and once after inserting the dot leader to leave a space after the heading and before the page number.

References tab >
Table of Contents >
Table of Contents >
Automatic Table 2

Page layout tab >
Page Setup > Breaks >
Section Breaks

Electronic Table of Contents

After keying and formatting a report, creating a table of contents is a relatively easy task when using the software features. Place the cursor where you want the table of contents to appear. Next, click the *Table of Contents* button, located in the Table of Contents group on the References tab. Then select the table of contents style you would like to use. Insert a **section break** to place the table of contents on a separate page and to allow you to use the Roman numeral format (i, ii, iii, and iv) on the table of contents page and then change to Arabic numbers (1, 2, 3, and 4) on the report pages.

Cover Page

Insert tab > Pages >
Cover Page

TIP The cover page template (Whisp) shown in Figure 13-3 called for a document subtitle. That placeholder was deleted because the report had no subtitle.

A cover or title page is prepared for most bound reports (see Figure 13-2). To format a cover page, center the title (Title, 28 point) in ALL CAPS (for a manual cover page) approximately 2" from the top. Center the student's name in capital and lowercase letters (Heading 1, 16 point) approximately 5" from the top. The date (Heading 2, 13 point) should be centered approximately 9" from the top. The font color should be the same for all text, normally black or blue. To further emphasize the title page, the text on the page may be bolded. Margin settings are the same as the report body.

A template from the Cover Page feature of Microsoft *Word* can also be used (see Figure 13-3) to format professional-looking cover pages. A **template** is a master copy of a set of predefined styles for a particular type of document. A template may contain text and formatting for margins, line spacing, colors, borders, styles, and themes. A template contains placeholder text you can replace with your own text. In addition to the Cover Page feature, other cover page templates are available online.

Figure 13-2 Manually formatted cover page

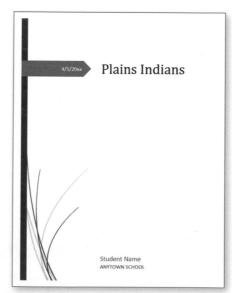

Figure 13-3 Template-formatted cover page

LESSON 67

Unbound and MLA Report Review

OUTCOMES

- Format unbound reports with cover page
- Format MLA reports with footnotes and textual citations and Works Cited pages
- Use previously learned word processing features to process reports

67–70A

Warmup

Key each line twice at the beginning of each lesson, first for control and then for speed.

alphabet 1 We moved quickly to pack an extra dozen lanyards Bif just bought.

fig/sym 2 I sold 22 at $45 less 13%, 8 at $69 less 5%, & 16 at $70 less 8%.

speed 3 Both of the men risk a big penalty if they dismantle their autos.

gwam 1' | 1 | 2 | 3 | 4 | 5 | 6 | 7 | 8 | 9 | 10 | 11 | 12 | 13 |

67B

Two-Page Unbound Report

1. Open a new document, and key the report below as shown.
2. Insert the text from *df 67b text* after the last line of the report.
3. Adjust the width of the table so it extends to the left and right margins; center the column headings.
4. Change formatting as needed to create an unbound report.
5. Insert page numbers that are right-aligned at the top; hide the page number on page 1.
6. Proofread and correct any errors.
7. **Save as:** *67b report*.

The Importance of Saving Money

Most professional planners advise school-aged children to open a savings account and then make regular deposits whenever they receive money for doing chores or as gifts on birthdays and holidays. The primary advantage of doing this is to get into the habit of saving and having your money grow by earning interest. When you are in your teens, you may also choose to make higher-yielding and higher-risk investments in stocks and bonds to help you save for your future education; however, opening a savings account and making regular deposits is a critical first step to a secure financial future.

Financial Plan

A good financial plan is one that makes you feel good now in anticipation of what you will be able to do with your savings in the future. How much do you need to save now and in the near future to attend the college or technical school of your choice, to purchase your first automobile, or to purchase furniture when you decide to move into your own apartment? Experts agree that saving is simpler when you set financial goals that are important to you.

67C

Cover Page

1. Using a cover page template of your choice, create a cover page for the report you keyed in 67B. Use your name as the writer and the current date. Delete all placeholders not used as well as the blank page following the cover sheet.
2. **Save as:** **67c cover page**.

67D

MLA Report with Footnotes

1. Open a new document, and key the text below in MLA format. Include your last name in the page number and your name, teacher's name, your course name, and today's date in the report identification lines. Make the necessary revisions as you key. Do not insert the footnote at this time.

Leadership Seminar Progress Report

Development of the leadership seminars for supervisors *and first-line managers* is progressing on schedule. One seminar will be conducted at *each of the four* our Indiana plants. The primary objectives of the seminars *is* are to have the participants understand the following points:

change to bulleted list

1. The importance of having leaders at all levels of the corporation.
2. The definition of *effective* leadership.
3. How leadership traits are developed for use within the corporation *and the community*.
4. That various styles of leadership exist and that there is no one best leadership style.

Seminar Presenter

Three *of our* staff members observed training sessions conducted by five *professional* prominent training and development companies before selecting the firm to conduct these leadership seminars. Derme & Associates, Inc., a *local* consulting firm specializing in career enhancement seminars, has been selected to develop and conduct the seminars.

One *primary* reason for selecting Derme & Associates is that they will develop the content of the seminars around Odgers' definition of leadership,[1] which we want to emphasize with employees.

2. Insert the text from file *df 67d text* below the last line. Change the text from the Normal style to the appropriate line and paragraph spacing for an MLA report.
3. If needed, format the bulleted lists so they both have the same bullet symbol and the symbol is aligned with the indent of the first line of each paragraph.
4. Format the last paragraph as a long quotation.

5. Key the following footnotes where indicated in the text; then delete the text in red.

   [1] Pattie Odgers, *Administrative Office Management*, 13 edition (Cincinnati: South-Western Cengage Learning, 2005) 74.

   [2] Robert F. Russell and A. Gregory Stone, "A Review of Servant Leadership Attributes: Developing a Practical Model," *Leadership & Organizational Development Journal*, 23.3-4 (2015) 145–158.

   [3] Patsy Fulton-Calkins and Karin M. Stulz, *Procedures & Theory for Administrative Professionals*, 7 edition (Cincinnati: South-Western Cengage Learning, 2013) 454.

6. Key a Works Cited page using the following sources.

   Fulton-Calkins, Patsy, and Karin M. Stulz. *Procedures & Theory for Administrative Professionals*. 7 edition. Cincinnati: South-Western Cengage Learning, 2013.

   Odgers, Pattie. *Administrative Office Management*. 13 edition. Cincinnati: South-Western Cengage Learning, 2005.

   Russell, Robert F., and A. Gregory Stone. "A Review of Servant Leadership Attributes: Developing a Practical Model." *Leadership & Organizational Development Journal*, 23.3-4 (2015).

7. Proofread the document carefully to find the five embedded errors. Correct errors detected.
8. Save as: *67d report*.

67E

MLA Report with Textual Citations

1. Open *df 67e text* and format it as an MLA report with a Works Cited page, using your name for the student, your teacher's name, your course name, and today's date. Use 11-pt. Times New Roman font, and make all formatting decisions according to the guides presented in this unit.

2. Insert the following sources on a Works Cited page.

   ### Works Cited

   Railton, Stephen. "Your Mark Twain." etext.lib.virginia.edu/railton /sc_as_mt/yourmt13.html (accessed January 25, 2011).

   Railton, Stephen. "Sam Clemens as Mark Twain." etext.virginia.edu/ railton/sc_as_mt/cathompg.html (accessed January 25, 2011).

   Waisman, Michael. "About Mark Twain." www.geocities.com/swaisman /huckfinn.htm (accessed January 25, 2011).

3. Proofread and correct errors.
4. Save as: *67e report*.

OUTCOME

• Format a bound report with footnotes

68B

Bound Report with Footnotes

Photo Courtesy of the Author

1. Review the Application Guide at the beginning of this chapter for bound reports; study the model report on p. 13-9. Note the format of the footnotes.
2. Key the first page of *The Faces of Mt. Rushmore* report from the model on p. 13-9; continue keying the report from the rough-draft copy that follows the model.
3. The information for footnotes 2–5 is provided in the left column of the rough-draft copy.
4. Proofread your copy and correct errors.
5. **Save as:** *68b report*.

21st Century Skills: Make Judgments and Decisions

Caroline is the manager of a customer service center for a large online retailer. She manages close to 30 service representatives whose primary responsibility is taking customer orders over the phone. She has just been told by upper management that starting the next week, the service representatives will also be responsible for selling additional products to customers who call to place orders. Caroline informs the reps of the change during a weekly department meeting. She immediately hears groans and complaints from several of the workers. Their primary complaint is that they don't want to sell anything. Sales, they claim, is not in their job description.

Caroline is concerned that morale in the department will be affected by those with negative attitudes about the change.

Digital Vision/Photodisc/Jupiter Images

Think Critically

1. Evaluate the manner in which Caroline announced the added responsibility to her department. Do you think her approach was appropriate?
2. With a partner, brainstorm ideas and strategies for how Caroline could have more successfully promoted this new responsibility to the service reps. Create a new word processing document, and write a report that summarizes your strategy. Save the document as *c13 21century*.

COLLABORATION

The Faces of Mt. Rushmore

Title

1.5" LM

1.0" RM

The Black Hills of South Dakota and Wyoming is the home to two national forests (Black Hills National Forest and Custer National Forest), three national grasslands (Buffalo Gap National Grassland, Grand River National Grassland, and Fort Pierre National Grassland), and several national treasures (Badlands, Devils Tower, Jewel Cave, Minuteman Missile National Historic Site, and Wind Cave National Park). This area of the United States was also home to many historical legendary figures. Among the more famous legends of the Black Hills were Native Americans Crazy Horse, Sitting Bull, and Red Cloud. General Custer, Wild Bill Hickok, Calamity Jane, and Jim Bridger are other legendary figures that are part of the colorful history of this region. The main attraction in the Black Hills, however, is Mt. Rushmore. Mt. Rushmore draws close to three million visitors to this part of the country each year.

Mt. Rushmore
Side Heading

Mt. Rushmore honors four presidents whose contributions to the United States of America during their lifetime are historic in nature. George Washington, Thomas Jefferson, Abraham Lincoln, and Theodore Roosevelt are the *Faces of Mt. Rushmore*. These four granite faces sculptured by Gutzon Borglum tower 5,500 feet above sea level and are scaled to men who would stand 465 feet tall. Each head is as tall as a six-story building.[1]

Footnote Superscript

Paragraph Heading

George Washington. George Washington is often referred to as the father of this country because of the central role he played in its formation. After serving in the French and Indian War, Washington became a lasting part of history from his service as the commander of the Continental Army and later as the first President of the United States of America. Some individuals seek such leadership positions for the recognition and fame. Others serve and continue to serve because of their civic responsibility.

Long Quote

> Several times in his life, George Washington set aside his hopes for a quiet life to serve his country. After winning the battle of Yorktown in 1781, Washington ached to return home. Still, he led the army until a peace treaty was signed two years later. In 1787, though ill, he yielded to friends who urged him to attend the Constitutional Convention.

Footnote

---

[1]Black Hills Badlands and Lake Association, http://blackhillsbadlands.com/home/thingstodo/parksmonuments/mtrushmore (December 29, 2011).

Bound Report with Footnotes (continue with rough draft on next page)

After his first term as president, Washington sought to retire. Once again,

Washington was persuaded to stay on to keep the young republic stable.[2]

Thomas Jefferson

A patriot, an author, a President, and a land purchaser are but a few of *the* things Thomas

Jefferson was known for *#* that landed his face on Mt. Rushmore *and his imprint* on the history of the United

States. As a patriot he was steadfast in his commit*ment* to this country. As the primary

author of the Declaration of Independence, he created a document that *was the beginning of moving* this country

from a colony of the English to an independent country. *During his presidency,* The United States almost doubled

in size with the Louisiana Purchase in 1803 for approximately $15 *million*.

Abraham Lincoln

The most controversial of the *four* Presidents of Mt. Rushmore was Abraham Lincoln. Even

before he was elected there were discussions in the South about leaving the the Union if

he should be elected. Within a few weeks of when he took the oath of office, Fort Sumter

was taken over by the Confederate troops. This marked the beginning of the civil war.[3]

Lincoln is remembered for many things; however, he may best be remembered for the

Gettysburg Address, *a speech* that is a profound statement *of American ideals*. The Gettysburg Address was only ten

sentences long and took about three minutes to deliver. [4]

Theodore Roosevelt

Of the *four* Presidents, Theodore Roosevelt was the most colorful. Active in New York Politics

at an early age, he arrived on the national *scene* stage with the notoriety achieved as a member

of the Rough Riders, a volunteer cavalry brigade noted for the battle *at San Juan Hill* in Cuba. While the

"other Roosevelt," Franklin, was noted for the New Deal (providing relief and reform during

Footnotes 2-5

[2]James W. Davidson and Michael B. Stoff, *The American Nation* (Upper Saddle River, NJ: Prentice Hall, 2003), p. 266.

[3]Davidson, pp. 478–481.

[4]Davidson, p. 508.

[5]Gerald A. Danzer, et al., *The Americans, Reconstruction to the 21st Century* (Evanston, IL: McDougal Littell Inc., 2003), pp. 318–319.

the Great Depression), Theodore was noted for the Square Deal—progressive reforms to protect the common people against big business.[5]

Summary

As one stands and gazes up at the faces of these four Presidents, it is easy to imagine how the face of our nation would be dramatically changed without the contributions of these four men. It is altogether fitting that their faces are chiseled into the granite of this nation.

68C

References Page

1. Review the Application Guide at the beginning of this chapter for preparing a references/works cited page.
2. Use the information from the footnotes to prepare a references page for the report. Proofread; correct errors.
3. Save as: **68c references page**.

68D

Cover Page

1. Review the Cover Page section of the Application Guide at the beginning of this chapter.
2. First, manually create a cover page for the *Faces of Mount Rushmore* report. Then open **df 68d cover page** to prepare a cover page based on a template for the report.
3. Save as: **68d cover page**.

68E

Table of Contents

1. Review the Application Guide at the beginning of this chapter for preparing a table of contents.
2. Prepare a table of contents for the report.
3. Save as: **68e table of contents**.

Your cover page and table of contents should look like this:

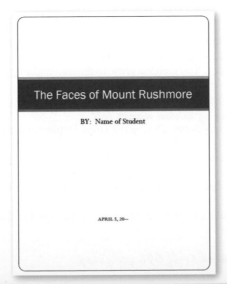

OUTCOMES
- Format a collaborative report
- Format footnotes provided by group members
- Insert text files that need reformatting to match the destination file

69B

Bound Report

You are working on a report project on the Minnesota State Public School for Dependent and Neglected Children with fellow students Rebecca Caden, Steven Fong, Maria Gonzalez, and Josh Parker. As part of your contribution to the project, you agreed to key and format the final report.

Some of the copy for the report was given to you as hard copy (see below). The rest of the report was given to you as electronic files. You will need to reformat some of the files so all parts of the report are in the same font and font size. For this report, all side headings should be in *Heading 2* style.

The guidelines for the report state that the report is to be keyed as a bound report with footnotes. When completed, the report should look like one report completed by five people, not five separate reports put into one report.

Save as: **69b report**.

Photo Courtesy of the Author

[1]"Minnesota State Public School for Dependent and Neglected Children," Museum Brochure, February 14, 2009.

Remember the Orphans

If you take exit 42B off of 135 south of Minneapolis/St. Paul you will soon find yourself in

Owatonna, Minnesota, driving past a large stately structure with an imposing turret

located
~~positioned~~ up on a hill. Stopping and looking at the structure, you can't help but feel that

to be told *and entering the main building,*
there is a story. By driving up to the parking lot you will learn that there are stories. Some

many *left*
have been told; more have been un~~told~~.

¶ In 1885 the Minnesota State Public School for dependent and neglected children was

dependent,
created by the state legislature. The doors of this structure were opened to orphaned and

starting in 1886
neglected children. The campus grew to thirteen buildings, and the school would become

third *10,635*
the 3rd largest orphanage in the U.S. in the 1920's with (get number for here) wards

, some of whom never left
passing through its doors. During the Great Depression, the orphanage was the home to as

many as 500 wards of the state. If you listen carefully as you read the signboards (signage)

and wander the halls, you can still hear the sounds of the children's voices that once

inhabited the halls even though the doors were closed to the orphanage for the last time in

1945.[1]

Insert 1: df 69b gonzalez

Purpose of the Orphanage

The primary purpose of the orphanage was to provide a place to live for children whose *on a short-term basis* ∧ parents were unable *or unwilling* ∧ to provide a home for them. In many instances, but not all, children were provided with resources and opportunities that they would not have had otherwise.

As you peruse the displays in the museum it quickly becomes evident that this orphanage was established to serve several purposes in addition to providing a roof over their head.

Education.

Insert 2a : df 69b Parker

Religious and Moral Training.

Insert 2b : df 69b parker

Discipline and Useful Labor Emphasis. There was a steadfast belief in the value of work at the school. Students either worked at the school or were signed to indentured contracts. "It is believed labor, no matter how dreary the task, or how paltry the remuneration, is good for the children. Each child, no matter the age, should be a part of some 'worth-while, demanding activity' each day."[1] Many of the children were required to be up doing chores by 5 a.m., others by 6 a.m. ∧ *Wards of the state were signed to indentured contracts with local farmers. Some of the outcomes were less than desirable. Erwin Varns, Ward of the State from 1932-1944, shares his experience with indenture contracts.*

Insert 3 : df 69b caden

What the Orphanage Lacked

Insert 4 : df 69b Fong

State School Boys Serve in the Military

Insert 5 : df 69b gonzalez2

[1] Minnesota State Public School for Dependent and Neglected Children, "History," www.orphanagemuseum.com/history.php (January 10, 2012).

Books

Other wards of the state (or their children) wrote books that provide additional insight into what it was like being a ward of the state and living at the State School during their childhood. Some of the publications include:

alphabetize

- ***Boy from C-11 Case #9164, A Memoir*** *(Harvey Ronglien)*

- ***While the Locust Slept*** (Peter Razor)

- ***My Light at the End of the Tunnel*** (Helen Bowers)

- ***Iris Blossom and Boxing Gloves*** (Iris Wright)

- ***No Tears Allowed*** (Eva Carlson Jensen)

- ***Patty's Journey*** (Donna Scott Norling)

- ***Crackers and Milk*** *(Arlene Nelson)*

Why Did Children Become Wards of the State

Insert 6 : df 69b caden2

Conclusion

Many of the orphanages that once dotted the landscape of the United States have closed their doors. they have been replaced by foster care and adoption programs. Hofwever, in many less developed nations, orphanages are still common place and continue to be the home to many of the world's children.

69C

Table of Contents

1. Prepare a table of contents for the report.
2. Save as: **69c table of contents**.

69D

References Page

1. Use the information from the footnotes to prepare a references page for the report. Proofread; correct errors.
2. Save as: **69d references page**.

69E

Cover Page

1. Prepare a cover page for the *Remember the Orphans* report. Use an appropriate template to create the cover page. Insert a picture of the orphanage (*df 69e picture*) on the cover page.
2. Save as: **69e cover page**.

LESSON 70 Two-Column Reports with Pictures

OUTCOMES

- Format a two-column report
- Set margins for a two-column report
- Insert pictures in a report
- Format pictures in a report
- Size and position pictures in a report

70B

Report with Two Columns

Page Layout tab > Page Setup > Columns > Two

Page Layout tab > Page Setup > Margins > Custom Margins

Your teacher thought your group report was excellent and would like you to submit it to the local magazine for possible publication. You need to reformat the report into two columns to follow the magazine's submission requirements, as shown in Figure 13-4.

This can be done by using the *Columns* feature of the Page Setup group found on the Page Layout tab.

The magazine wants the margins set at 0.5" for all margins. Change the font color for all headings in the report to *Orange, Accent 2, Darker 50%*. Remove the page numbers.

Open **69b report** and make the changes required for submitting the report for possible publication. Keep the report open to complete 70C.

Photos Courtesy of the Author

Figure 13-4 Two-column report

70C

Insert Pictures in the Report

The magazine also encourages that pictures be included with submissions. Your teacher provided you with a file of pictures (*df 70c pictures*) with captions to include and suggested that you use software features to make the pictures appear as though they were taken during the period the school was open. Change the picture style to soft edges, and change the pictures to sepia, as follows.

1. Open the file **df 70c pictures**.
2. Click the first picture.
3. Click the *Picture Tools Format* tab.
4. Click *Soft Edge Rectangle* in the Picture Styles gallery.
5. Click each picture and press *Ctrl + Y* to change the picture style to *Soft Edge Rectangle*.

Photo Courtesy of the Author

6. Right-click the first picture.
7. Click *Format Picture* to bring up Format Picture pane.
8. Click the *Picture* icon under Format Picture (see Figure 13-5).

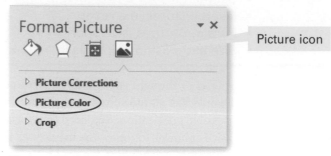

Figure 13-5 Format Picture

9. If the options are not showing under Picture Color, click *Picture Color*.
10. Click the Recolor icon under Picture Color (see Figure 13-6).

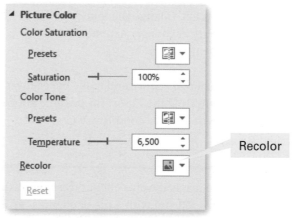

Figure 13-6 Picture Color dialog box

11. Click *Sepia* in the Recolor gallery, as shown in Figure 13-7.

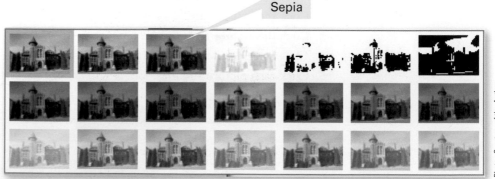

Photos Courtesy of the Author

Figure 13-7 Recolor choices

12. Close the Format Picture pane.

13. Click each picture and press *Ctrl + Y* to change the picture color to Sepia.

★TIP The Ctrl + Y shortcut can only apply one formatting change at a time.

Photo Courtesy of the Author

14. Insert the pictures and captions into the report at appropriate places; see Figure 13-4.

15. The size of some of the pictures may need adjustments to make the copy a better fit.

16. With the two-column format, the footnotes will look better on the page by changing the tab to 0.25" rather than 0.5". Make this change.

17. **Save as:** *70c report*.

✓ **checkpoint**   Compare the first page of your report to Figure 13-4.

Skill Builder 12

Warmup

Key each line twice.

alphabet 1 Extensive painting of the gazebo was quickly completed by Jerome.

one-hand 2 John Reese Edwards served poppy seed bread as a sweet noon treat.

speed 3 Keith and I may go to the island to dismantle the bicycle shanty.

gwam 1' | 1 | 2 | 3 | 4 | 5 | 6 | 7 | 8 | 9 | 10 | 11 | 12 | 13 |

B

Technique: Letter Keys

Key each line twice.

 ★TIP Limit keystroking action to the fingers; keep hands and arms motionless.

Emphasize continuity and rhythm with curved, upright fingers.

A Katrina baked Marsha a loaf of bread to take to the Alameda fair.
B Barbara and Bob Babbitt both saw the two blackbirds in the lobby.
C Carl, the eccentric character with a classic crew cut, may catch.
D David and Eddie dodged the duck as it waddled down the dark road.
E Ellen needed Steven to help her complete the spreadsheet on time.
F Before I left, Faye found forty to fifty feet of flowered fabric.
G George and Greg thought the good-looking neighbor was gregarious.
H John, Hank, and Sarah helped her haul the huge bush to the trash.

gwam 1' | 1 | 2 | 3 | 4 | 5 | 6 | 7 | 8 | 9 | 10 | 11 | 12 | 13 |

C

Technique: Tab

1. Set left tabs at 1.5", 3", 4.5", and 6.
2. Key each line twice (key word, tap *Tab*, key next word).

Concentrate on quick tab spacing; keep eyes on copy.

Monday	Tuesday	Wednesday	Thursday	Friday
January	February	March	April	May
New York	California	Texas	Florida	Illinois

Speed Forcing Drill

Key each line once at top speed; then try to complete each sentence on the 15", 12", or 10" call as directed by your instructor. Force speed to higher levels as you move from sentence to sentence.

Emphasis: high-frequency balanced-hand words

	gwam	15"	12"	10"
Hal paid the men for the work they did on the rig.		40	50	60
Orlando and I did the work for the eight busy men.		40	50	60
Helen and Rodney may do the handiwork for the neighbor.		44	55	66
When I visit the neighbor, Jan may go down to the dock.		44	55	66
Alan and I laid six of the eight signs by the antique chair.		48	60	72
Pamela and Vivian may sign the proxy if they audit the firm.		48	60	72
Chris may go with the widow to visit the city and see the chapel.		52	65	78
The maid may go with them when they go to the city for the gowns.		52	65	78

Skill Check

1. Key a 1' timing on ¶ 1; determine *gwam*.

2. Add 2–4 *gwam* to the rate attained in step 1; determine quarter-minute checkpoints from the chart below.

3. Key two 1' guided timings on ¶ 1 to increase speed.

4. Practice ¶ 2 in the same way.

5. Key two 3' timings on ¶s 1 and 2 combined; determine *gwam* and the number of errors.

Quarter-Minute Checkpoints

gwam	1/4'	1/2'	3/4'	Time
16	4	8	12	16
20	5	10	15	20
24	6	12	18	24
28	7	14	21	28
32	8	16	24	32
36	9	18	27	36
40	10	20	30	40

A all letters used   gwam 3'

	gwam 3'
Who lived a more colorful and interesting	3
existence than this President? He lived on a ranch in	6
the west and was a member of the Rough Riders. He was	10
a historian. His travel included an African safari.	13
He was quite involved in the development of the	16
Panama Canal. He was the youngest person who became	20
President of the United States; however, he was not	23
the youngest person ever elected as President of the	27
United States. And these activities were just a small	30
sample of his many accomplishments.	33
Theodore Roosevelt was an active and involved	36
man. He lived life to the fullest and tried to make	39
the world a better place for others. Today, we still	43
benefit from some of his many deeds. Some of the	46
national forests in the West came about as a result of	49
legislation enacted during the time he was President.	53
He worked with college leaders to organize the	56
National Collegiate Athletic Association.	59

gwam 3' | 1 | 2 | 3 | 4 |

Planning for Your Career 3 | Preparing Employment Application Letters

OUTCOMES

- Compose an employment application letter
- Prepare a personal print resume

Employment Application Letters

An **employment application letter** should always accompany a resume, whether print or digital. This personal-business letter should be limited to one page (Figure PC3-1). The application letter should include three topics—generally in three to five paragraphs. The first topic should specify the position you are applying for and may state how you learned of the opening and something positive about the company.

The second topic (one to three paragraphs) should include evidence that you qualify for the position. This is the place to interpret information presented in your resume and to show how your qualifications relate to the job you are applying for to create a favorable impression. The last paragraph should request an interview and give precise information for contacting you to arrange it.

1. Open a new *Word* document.
2. Key the employment application letter below and on the next page as a personal-business letter in block format with mixed punctuation.
3. Check the content of this application letter against the guidelines above.
4. Save as: *pc3 app letter 1*.

Figure PC3-1 Employment application letter

150 Preston Court | Meriden, CT 06450-0403 | May 10, 20— | Ms. Jenna St. John | Personnel Director | Harper Insurance Company |3 Colony Street | Meriden, CT 06450-4219 | Dear Ms. St. John

Ms. Anne D. Salgado, my business and information technology instructor, informed me of the customer service position within your company that will be available June 15. She speaks very highly of your organization. After learning more about the position, I am confident that I am qualified and would like to be considered for the position.

Currently I am completing my senior year at Meriden High School. All of my elective courses have been computer and business-related courses. I have completed the advanced digital information and management course where we integrated advanced word processing, spreadsheet, database, and presentation software features to prepare business documents. I have also taken the business communications course that enhanced my oral and written communication skills.

My work experience and school activities have given me the opportunity to work with people to achieve group goals. Participating in FBLA has given me an appreciation of the business world and the opportunity to develop my leadership and public speaking skills.

The opportunity to interview with you for this position will be greatly appreciated. You can call me at (203) 555-0121 or email me at Greenawald.j@fastsend.com to arrange an interview.

Sincerely | Jennifer H. Greenawald | Enclosure

Application Letters

1. Open *pc3 app letter 1*.
2. Revise the letter as necessary to apply for each position advertised.
3. **Save as:** *pc3 app letter 2*, *pc3 app letter 3*, and *pc3 app letter 4*.

CUSTOMER SERVICE	CUSTOMER SERVICE REPRESENTATIVE	CUSTOMER SERVICE OPPORTUNITY
Meriden College is seeking both full-time and part-time motivated individuals to provide customer service to the college community. Good analytical, mathematical, personal computer skills are required. Excellent communications and interpersonal skills are essential. We will provide training for our network-based systems. *Meriden College is an affirmative action, equal opportunity employer.* Please respond with letter and resume to: J. W. Salazar Meriden College 13 Broad Street Meriden, CT 06450-0100 or email: resume@exchange.hr.mc.edu	IHM, an international direct marketing company, is currently seeking candidates to work in our customer service center. IHM has openings for full- and part-time positions to handle customer inquiries for the U.S. and Canada. **We have openings for Spanish-speaking reps.** To qualify, you must have excellent telephone and communication skills, strong keyboarding and PC skills, the ability to work in a structured environment, and a desire to learn. Please mail or fax resume and letter to: Human Resources Department, IHM 1264 Main Street Meriden, CT 06450-1000 Fax: (203) 555-0153	**PTI** is seeking an outstanding individual for our expanding Customer Service team. Qualified candidates will demonstrate strong organizational skills, creativity, powerful problem-solving ability and a passion for delighting customers. Strong computer skills including knowledge of suite software is essential. If you are interested in an exceptional opportunity to be a part of a growing organization where you can have a real impact, submit your employment documents to: hr@pti.com Precision Therapeutics, Inc. Suite 30 637 Colony Street Meriden, CT 06450-5000

Personal Print Resume

1. Open *pc2 print resume* or *pc2 digital resume* (files you created in the Planning for Your Career 2 module in Chapter 12), whichever you prefer, to use to prepare a final draft of your personal print resume.
2. Review the information and make any desired changes, additions, or deletions to the information you want to include in your print resume. Also decide how your print resume will be formatted.
3. Using the information and desired format, prepare a print version of your resume.
4. **Save as:** *pc3 my resume*.

Before You Move On

1. Bound reports are formatted with a _____ left margin to allow for binding. LO 68 B

2. Which page of a report is usually not numbered? LO 68B

3. What is used to indicate material is omitted from a quotation? LO 69B

4. The _____ lists the headings of a report and the page number where those headings can be found in a report. LO 68E

5. A table of contents can be created either _____ or _____ . LO 68E, 69C

6. A _____ is prepared for most reports and can be created manually or using a template. LO 68D, 69E

7. Where can adjustments be made to a picture? LO 70C

8. What shortcut can be used to apply one formatting change to more than one picture? LO 70C

Apply What You Have Learned

Photo Courtesy of the Author

Bound Report

1. Format the following text as a bound report with footnotes.
2. Proofread your copy and correct any errors.
3. Save as: *c13 report*.

Seven Wonders of the World

Key **"Seven Wonders of the World"** into any Internet search engine, and you will be given numerous sites to visit. The original Seven Wonders of the World (also referred to as Seven Wonders of the Ancient World) included:[1]

- Great Pyramid of Giza
- Hanging Gardens of Babylon
- Temple of Artemis
- Statue of Zeus at Olympia
- Mausoleum of Maussollos at Halicarnassus
- Colossus of Rhodes
- Lighthouse of Alexandria

The only remaining one of these ancient structures is the Great Pyramid of Giza located near Cairo, Egypt. Today, many other lists exist proclaiming their "Wonders of the World." *USA Today's* list even includes the Internet as one of their seven. An interesting historical list is the "Seven Wonders of the Industrial World."

Seven Wonders of the Industrial World

Another list, Seven Wonders of the Industrial World,[2] includes wonders made by man that made the world a different place, improving the lives of those who inhabit it. Three of the wonders included on this list are engineering endeavors undertaken in the United States–the Brooklyn Bridge, the First Transcontinental Railroad, and Hoover Dam.

Brooklyn Bridge. Today, the Brooklyn Bridge is a landmark of New York. In early 1870, the year construction on the Brooklyn Bridge started, the East River separated Manhattan from Brooklyn. Thirteen years later, the almost 6,000-foot bridge connected the two cities, making it much easier for the horse-drawn carriages and pedestrians to reach their destinations. Over 140 years later, the legendary bridge has been modernized to accommodate six lanes of automobile traffic.

As with all great engineering feats, the cost of creating the structure (slightly over $15 million) was almost as breathtaking as the structure itself. "If you don't believe that, I have a bridge in Brooklyn to sell you."

First Transcontinental Railroad. "Making the world a smaller place" could be used in conjunction with several of the industrial world wonders. It is most true with the first transcontinental railroad. The railroad joined the nation with 1,776 miles of track, making it possible to travel from coast to coast in approximately a week. Today, we travel from coast to coast in a matter of hours, but in 1869 the primary means of travel were the stagecoach lines, a much slower and more dangerous means of travel.

The railroad system transported not only people but goods, making what was produced on one coast much more available to those living on the opposite coast or anywhere in between.

The railroad took approximately six years to complete, with the final spike being driven on May 10, 1869, at Promontory Summit in Utah.

Completing the 1,776 miles of track was a huge undertaking for the Union Pacific and the Central Pacific. Much of the track laid by the Union Pacific was done by a workforce comprised of Irish laborers and veterans of both the Union and Confederate armies, with much of the track laid in the Utah territory being done by Mormons. The portion of the track completed by Central Pacific was completed mainly by Chinese immigrants. The men were paid between one and three dollars a day, with the Chinese immigrants receiving less, which resulted in their going on strike.[3]

Footnotes

[1] "Seven Wonders of the World," www.newworldencyclopedia.org/entry/Seven_Wonders_of_the_World (May 1, 2018).

[2] Deborah Cadbury, "Seven Wonders of the Industrial World," www.bbc.co.uk/history/british/victorians/seven_wonders_01.shtml (May 1, 2018).

[3] "First Transcontinental Railroad," http://schools-wikipedia.org/wp/f/First_Transcontinental_Railroad.htm (May 1, 2018).

Footnotes (continued)

[4]James W. Davidson and Michael B. Stoff, *The American Nation* (Upper Saddle River, NJ: Prentice Hall, 2003), p. 6.

[5]"Hoover Dam," http://en.wikipedia.org/wiki/Hoover_Dam (May 1, 2018).

[6]"Hoover Dam Visitors Guide," www.arizona-leisure.com /hoover-dam.html (May 1, 2018).

Hoover Dam. Hoover Dam is a breathtaking structure well worth visiting. It is considered one of the greatest engineering projects ever undertaken by man. "The presence of the dam makes it possible for people to live in an area that is largely desert. Surrounding farmland is irrigated, and there is a ready supply of water and electric power."[4]

Hoover Dam, named after President Herbert Hoover, is located between the borders of Nevada and Arizona approximately 30 miles southeast of Las Vegas. Originally called Boulder Dam, the dam was not only the largest concrete structure in the world but also the largest hydroelectric power–generating station in the world when it was completed in 1936. Since that time, larger hydroelectric generating stations have been built as well as larger concrete structures.[5] Hoover Dam stands over 726 feet tall and is 1,244 feet wide. By comparison the Empire State Building is approximately 1,450 feet tall.

The engineering marvel, which was believed by many to be impossible to build, took the collaboration efforts of over 200 engineers and approximately 7,000 dam workers to build. The dam was completed in five years, almost two years ahead of schedule despite the harsh conditions and extreme dangers that the dam workers endured during the construction.[6]

The popularity of the dam is established by the seven million visitors from around the world who visit the site each year. By comparison Mt. Rushmore attracts about three million visitors annually.

Almost as impressive as Hoover Dam itself is the Hoover Dam bypass bridge that was completed in 2010. The cost of the bypass project is estimated at around $240 million; the cost of Hoover Dam is estimated at $50 million. The bridge arches majestically over the Colorado River, connecting Nevada and Arizona.

Conclusion

Even though these industrial wonders were constructed many years ago, they still have a huge impact on the lives of Americans. Whether it is connecting two cities, two states, or the entire United States, the social and economic impact of these wonders is as great today as it was when they were constructed years ago.

Reference Page

1. Use the information from the footnotes to prepare a references page for the report. Proofread; correct errors.
2. **Save as:** *c13 reference page*.

Table of Contents

1. Prepare a table of contents for the report.
2. **Save as:** *c13 table of contents*.

Cover Page

1. Prepare a cover page for the report. Use an appropriate template to create the cover page. Insert a picture of Hoover Dam *(df c13 pictures)* on the cover page.
2. **Save as:** *c13 cover page*.

| Lesson 71 | Table Tabs, Indentations, and Lists | Lesson 73 | Table Calculations and Analysis |
| Lesson 72 | Tables with Repeated Headings | Assessment 7 | Enhanced Reports and Tables |

LESSONS 71–73

Tables are frequently used in business to convey information in an attractive, easy-to-read format. The table may be a separate document or part of another document such as a letter, memo, report, newsletter, and so on. Tables organize information and make it easier to compare data. For example, tables typically provide information about where an aspect of business has been, is now, or is going.

In this chapter, you will process many tables that are routinely used in business. They include tables that report information relating to sales, inventories, distributors, customers, budgets, payroll matters, work schedules, forms of business ownership, and other information needed to carry out business-related functions.

Yuri Arcurs/Shutterstock.com

Hanging Indents and Decimal Tabs in Tables

> **★TIP** Select all the cells in the column in which the tab or indentation is to be used before setting the tab or indentation. Otherwise the change will only apply in the cell where the insertion point is positioned.

Decimal tabs and hanging indentation can be used to position numbers and text in columns to make the information in table cells easy to read. The horizontal Ruler can be used to set the tabs and indentation (see Figures 14-1 and 14-2).

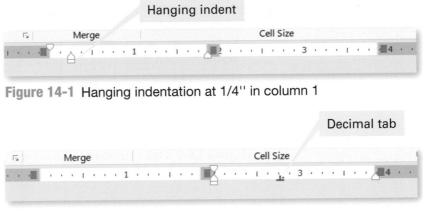

Figure 14-1 Hanging indentation at 1/4'' in column 1

Figure 14-2 Decimal tab at 2 3/4'' in column 2

Table with Bulleted and Numbered Lists

Home tab > Paragraph > Bullets or Numbering

The **Bullets** and **Numbering** features can be used in tables as they are used in paragraphs. In some instances, you may want to use the horizontal Ruler bar to decrease the indent on the bulleted or numbered items to make the list more attractive.

Change Text Direction

Table Tools Layout tab > Alignment > Text Direction

By default, text is arranged horizontally in tables. In some instances where the table has a number of narrow columns, the readability and appearance of the table may be improved if the column headings are displayed vertically with center alignment. To display the text vertically, use the **Text Direction** feature shown in Figure 14-3.

Figure 14-3 Text Direction

Repeat Table Headers

Table Tools layout tab > Data > Repeat Header Rows

When a table is longer than one page, you can use Repeat Header Rows (Figure 14-4) to repeat header lines on second and subsequent pages to make the additional pages easier to understand.

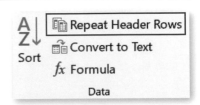

Figure 14-4 Repeat Header Rows

Cell Margins

Table Tools Layout tab > Alignment > Cell Margins

The Cell Margins feature (Figure 14-5) enables you to control how close text within a cell comes to the cell borders by changing the Top, Bottom, Left, and Right margins in the Table Options dialog box (Figure 14-6). You can also change the amount of space between cells in the Table Options dialog box. This feature can be used to enhance the appearance and readability of a table.

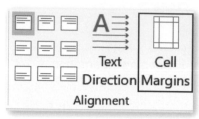

Figure 14-5 Cell Margins

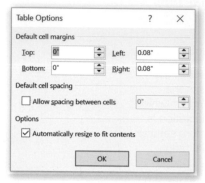

Figure 14-6 Table Options dialog box

Insert Space After Table

Home tab > Paragraph > Line and Paragraph Spacing > Add Space Before Paragraph

When you key a table in a document, the amount of space above and below the table should be the same. When the table is inserted into a *Word* document that uses the 1.08 default line spacing with 8 pt. of space after paragraphs, space should be added above the paragraph following the table, if needed. The space can be added by clicking the paragraph below the table, clicking the *Line and Paragraph Spacing* drop-down list, and selecting *Add Space Before Paragraph* (see Figure 14-7).

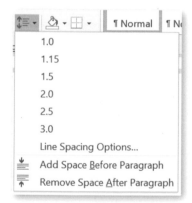

Figure 14-7 Add Space Before Paragraph

SUM Function in a Formula

Table Tools Layout tab > Data > Formula

The Formula feature (see Figure 14-8) in most word processing software can be used to calculate answers to basic math problems, such as addition (+), subtraction (−), multiplication (*), and division (/) when numbers are keyed in a table. Word processing software can also recalculate answers when numbers are changed in a table.

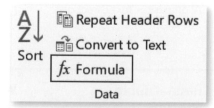

Figure 14-8 Formula

The built-in SUM function is the default formula that appears in the Formula box if you choose the Formula feature when the insertion point is below a column of numbers (see the default formula =SUM(ABOVE) in Figure 14-9) or in the cell to the right of a row of numbers (see the default formula =SUM(LEFT) in Figure 14-10).

While you can work with basic formulas in word processing software, spreadsheet software will perform the basic and more complex calculations in a more efficient manner.

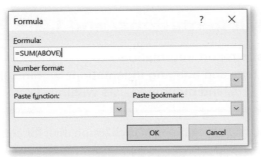

Figure 14-9 =SUM(ABOVE) formula

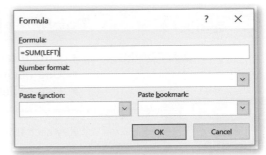

Figure 14-10 =SUM(LEFT) formula

AVERAGE, MAXIMUM, MINIMUM, and COUNT Functions

Table Tools Layout tab > Data > Formula

In addition to the SUM function, there are other mathematical functions you can access from the Formula feature. You can use the AVERAGE function to compute the average of a series of numbers, the MAX function to identify the largest number in a series of numbers, the MIN function to identify the smallest number in a series of numbers, and the COUNT function to count the number of numeric values in a series of numbers.

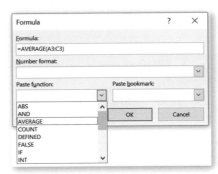

Figure 14-11 AVERAGE function

To change from the SUM function to another, click in the cell where the answer is to appear, display the Formula dialog box using the path at left, delete the existing formula but not the = sign, choose the desired function from the Paste function drop-down list, and key the desired direction (LEFT, RIGHT, ABOVE) or cell references (such as A3:C3) between the parentheses (see Figure 14-11).

Writing Formulas

Table Tools Layout tab > Data > Formula

In addition to using the built-in functions such as SUM and AVERAGE, formulas can be written in the Formula dialog box to add (+), subtract (−), multiply (*), and divide (/) numbers using the symbols shown in the parentheses.

To enter a formula, click in the cell where the answer is to appear, display the Formula dialog box, delete the existing formula but not the = sign, and write (key) the formula you desire—do not space between the parts of the formula.

Recalculate Formulas

Right-click formula cell > Update Field

Unlike spreadsheet software, word processing software does not update an answer immediately when a change is made to a number that was used in the calculation. However, the answer will be updated automatically when the document is reopened. If an immediate update is desired, select the answer (field) to be updated, and then right-click and select *Update Field* from the list (Figure 14-12). Alternatively, you can select the answer to be updated and tap *F9*.

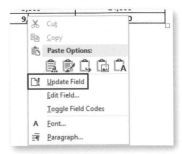

Figure 14-12 Update Field

LESSON 71   Table Tabs, Indentations, and Lists

OUTCOMES

- Create tables to report information
- Use decimal tabs and hanging indentations within cells
- Use bulleted lists, and numbered lists within cells

71A–73A

Warmup

Key each line twice at the beginning of each lesson; first for control, second for speed.

alphabet 1 Jaxie amazed the partial crowd by kicking five quick field goals.

figures 2 Call 555.375.4698 by May 27 to set the 10 a.m. meeting with Sara.

speed 3 Their visit may end the problems and make the firm a tidy profit.

71B

Review: Table

1. Open a new word processing document, and key the following table, using the alignments and merging cells as shown.

NOTE Review Chapter 7 for basic skills in creating and formatting tables.

INVENTORY OF DISCONTINUED APPLIANCES			
Appliance	**Model Number**	**Inventory Remaining**	
		Last Month	**This Month**
Microwave Oven	M-010-B	135	101
Dishwasher	D-320-A	25	20
Refrigerator	R-279-C	47	29
Garbage Disposal	G-345-G	74	68

2. Format the table to make it attractive and easy to read by applying an appropriate Table Style.
3. Center the table on the page.
4. Save as: **71b table**.

71C

Table with Decimal Tabs and Hanging Indentation

1. Open a new word processing document. Using a top margin of 2", create a 2 × 4 table with column widths of 2".
2. Set a hanging indent at 1/4" in column 1 and a decimal tab at 2 3/4" in column 2 to make it easier to compare and understand the numbers.

3. Key the following information in the table.

Hanging Indent at ¼"	Decimal Tab at 2 ¾"
As I key this text, it wraps to the next line with a hanging indent.	1.2345 12.345 123.45
The hanging indent can make text easier to read in cells.	0.98765 9876.5
As I key the numbers in column 2, they will line up at the decimal point	456.789 45.67 4.5

4. Save as: **71c table**.

71D

Table with Bulleted and Numbered Lists

Home tab > Paragraph > Bullets or Numbering

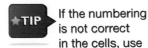 If the numbering is not correct in the cells, use the Auto Correct pop-up icon to change to the desired numbering—either *Restart Numbering* or *Continue Numbering*.

1. Open a new word processing document. Using a top margin of 2", create a 2 × 3 table.
2. Key the following information as shown. Decrease the bullet indent to about 1/8" in column 1. Use the default indent for the items in column 2.

Bulleted List with Decreased Indent	Numbered List with Default Indent
• Monday	1. Monday
• Tuesday	2. Tuesday
• Wednesday	3. Wednesday
• Thursday	1. Thursday
• Friday	2. Friday
• Saturday	3. Saturday
• Sunday	4. Sunday

3. Save as: **71d table**.

71E

Tables

Table 1

1. Open a new word processing document. Create a 3 × 7 table with column widths of 1.5".
2. Key the information on the next page as shown using Center Left alignment and hanging indentation in column 2 and a decimal tab at or near 3.5" in column 3.

Current Distributor by Product Number		
Item	**Distributor**	**Product Number**
Desktop Computer	Wells and Greene, Greenville, PA	1356.7946
LCD Monitor	Derkson Brothers, Newton Falls, OH	13.90569
Wireless Mouse	Wells and Greene, Greenville, PA	985.45
Wireless Keyboard	Malone Supplies Indian Land, SC	1035.0793
Wireless Printer	James Coleman, Inc., Chicago, IL	564.68

3. Format the table to make it attractive and easy to read. Center it on the page.
4. **Save as:** *71e table1*.

Table 2

1. Open a new word processing document. Create a 3 × 5 table.
2. Key the following information as shown using a bulleted list and numbered list, each with decreased indentation.

BUSINESS DOCUMENTS		
Category	**Document Type**	**Word Processing Features Frequently Used**
Correspondence	• Memorandums • Personal-Business Letter • Business Letters	1. Margins 2. Vertical Line spacing 3. Font Attributes
Reports	• Unbound Report • Unbound Report with Footnotes • Reference Page • Cover Page	1. Styles 2. Insert Footnote 3. Hard Page Break 4. Cover Page
Tables	• Basic Table using AutoFit • Table with Merged Cells • Table with Table Styles • Table with Reference	1. Insert Table/AutoFit to Contents 2. Merge Cells 3. Table Styles 4. Add Space After Table

3. Format the table appropriately. Center it on the page.
4. **Save as:** *71e table2*.

The Eastern Region Sales for the first quarter of the current year are: Jim Colson sold 175 units in January, 215 in February, and 195 in March. Libby Reed sold 193 in January, 217 in February, and 155 in March. Gwen Gassner sold 145 in January, 231 in February, and 203 in March.

1. Using the information above, key a 5 × 5 table. In row 1, merge the cells and key **First Quarter Eastern Region Sales**.

2. In row 2, starting in column A, key the following as column headings: **Sales Rep, January, February, March, Quarter**.

3. In rows 3–5, key the information for each sales rep, and then compute the quarterly sales for each rep in column E and the total for each month in row 6.

4. Format the table to make it easy to read and understand.

5. Using the information in your table or the paragraph in step 1, answer the following questions. Key your answers at the left margin below the table.
   a. Who had the highest quarterly sales?
   b. Who had the highest January sales?
   c. Who had the highest February sales?
   d. Who had the highest March sales?

6. Did you use the table to answer the questions because it organizes the information so it is easier to read and understand?

7. **Save as:** *71f table*.

wavebreakmedia/Shutterstock.com

LESSON 72

Tables with Repeated Headings

OUTCOMES

- Change the direction of text in tables
- Repeat header row in a long table
- Change cell margins
- Insert space after a table located between lines of text

Table Tools Layout tab > Alignment > Text Direction

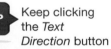
★TIP Keep clicking the *Text Direction* button to cycle through the available directions.

Table 1

1. Open *df 72b table*.

2. Display the text in row 2 vertically with text starting at the bottom of the cell, using Bottom Center align. If necessary, adjust row 2 so its height is high enough to fit the highest entry.

3. Adjust column widths to AutoFit contents.

4. Center the table on the page vertically and horizontally.

5. **Save as:** *72b table1*.

Table 2

1. Open a new word processing document, and key the following table, using Table Styles and Table Styles Options to format the table as shown on the next page.

Work Schedule for Coming Week							
Day	**Employee**						
	Melanie Delmar	Derek Evans	Kyle Landers	Brett Acheson	Melanie Dansick	Catherine Lash	Sandy Hixson
Monday	9-5	Off	9-5	Off	9-5	1-9	1-9
Tuesday	9-5	Off	1-9	1-9	Off	9-5	9-5
Wednesday	Off	9-5	1-9	9-5	Off	9-5	1-9
Thursday	Off	9-5	9-5	1-9	1-9	Off	9-5
Friday	1-9	1-9	Off	9-5	9-5	Off	9-5
Saturday	1-9	1-9	Off	9-5	9-5	9-5	Off
Sunday	9-5	9-5	9-5	Off	1-9	1-9	Off

2. Center the table at the top of the page.

3. **Save as:** *72b table2*.

Table 3

1. Open a new word processing document, and key the following table as shown.

WHAT THE UNITED STATES CONSTITUTION PROVIDES		
The Executive Branch	**The Legislative Branch**	**The Judicial Branch**
• President administers and enforces federal laws • President chosen by electors who have been chosen by the states	• A bicameral or two-house legislature • Each state has equal number of representatives in the Senate • Representation in the House determined by state population • Simple majority required to enact legislation	• National court system directed by the Supreme Court • Courts to hear cases related to national laws, treaties, the Constitution; cases between states, between citizens of different states, or between a state and citizens of another state

2. Set row 1 and 2 height at 0.5".

3. Format the table appropriately using Table Styles and Table Style Options.

4. Center the table on the page vertically and horizontally.

5. **Save as:** *72b table3*.

Table Tools Layout tab >
Data > Repeat Header
Rows

1. Open a new word processing document.
2. Create a 3 × 25 table using *AutoFit Window*.
3. Select all rows and change height to 0.5".
4. Key the following text in row 1:

Column Heading 1	Column Heading 2	Column Heading 3

5. Position the insertion point in row 1 and select the *Repeat Header Rows* feature.
6. Verify that the column headings appear in the first row on page 2.
7. Save as: **72c table1**.
8. Repeat steps 1–3.
9. Key the following text, and merge cells in row 1 and row 2 as shown.

Merged Cells (A1 and A2)	Merged Cells (B1 and C1)	
	Column Heading 1	Column Heading 2

10. Position the insertion point in row 1, and select *Repeat Header Rows*.
11. Verify that the column headings in rows 1 and 2 appear in the first two rows on page 2.
12. Save as: **72c table2**.

72D

Cell Margins

Table Tools Layout tab >
Alignment > Cell Margins

1. Open **df 72d table**.
2. Use the path at left to access the Table Options dialog box, and change the Top and Bottom margins to 0.05", the Left and Right margins to 0.12", and set spacing between cells to 0.03". Make sure the *Automatically resize to fit contents* option is checked, and click *OK*.
3. Click *Allow spacing between cells* and change the setting to 0.03".
4. Center the table at the top of the page.
5. Save as: **72d table**.

72E

Insert Space After Table

Home tab > Paragraph >
Line and Paragraph
Spacing > Add Space
Before Paragraph

1. Open a new word processing document.
2. Key the following line of text, and then tap *Enter*.
   The table will be keyed after this paragraph.
3. Insert a 4 × 5 table grid.
4. Position your insertion point on the line below the table.
5. Use the *Add Space Before Paragraph* command.
6. Key this line of text on the line below the table, and then tap *Enter*.
   Space has been added above this paragraph.
7. Verify that the space above and below the table appears to be the same.
8. Save as: **72e table**.

Table 1

1. Open a new word processing document.
2. Key the following table, formatting it as shown.

MONTHLY BUDGET						
Utility	**January**	**February**	**March**	**April**	**May**	**June**
Telephone		$73	$45	$45	$45	$45
Sewage	$75			$75		
Cable	$50	$50	$50	$57	$57	$57
Electricity	$111	$109	$66	$79	$113	$102
Natural Gas	$295	$300	$321	$214	$68	$63
Water	$45	$48	$45	$49	$45	$51
Garbage		$57			$57	
Internet	$60	$60	$60	$60	$51	$51

3. Improve the appearance of the table by changing the cell margins. Change the top and bottom margins to 0.05", the side margins to 0.15", and insert 0.02" space between cells.
4. Position it attractively on the page.
5. **Save as:** *72f table1*.

Table Tools Layout tab >
Data > Sort

Table 2

1. Open *df 72f table2*.
2. Sort the table to arrange column 1 in ascending order.
3. Align all cells center left.
4. Repeat the header rows on the second page.
5. **Save as:** *72f table2*.

LESSON 73   Table Calculations and Analysis

OUTCOMES

- Perform basic mathematical calculations in tables by using the SUM, AVERAGE, MINIMUM, MAXIMUM, and COUNT functions
- Write formulas to perform basic mathematical calculations in tables
- Update calculations in tables
- Analyze the contents of a table

73B

SUM Function in a Formula

Table Tools Layout tab >
Data > Formula

1. Open a new word processing document, and key the following 4 × 4 table.

10	20	30	
400	500	600	
7000	8000	9000	

2. In cell D1, calculate the sum of the numbers in cells A1:C1.
3. In cell D2, calculate the sum of the numbers in cells A2:C2.
4. In cell D3, calculate the sum of the numbers in cells A3:C3.
5. In cell A4, calculate the sum of the numbers in cells A1:A3.

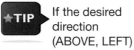

TIP If the desired direction (ABOVE, LEFT) is not displayed in the formula, replace it with the desired direction.

6. In cell B4, calculate the sum of the numbers in cells B1:B3.
7. In cell C4, calculate the sum of the numbers in cells C1:C3.
8. In cell D4, calculate the sum of the numbers in cells A1:C3.
9. **Save as: 73b sum.**

73C

AVERAGE, MAXIMUM, MINIMUM, and COUNT Functions

Table Tools Layout tab >
Data > Formula

1. Open a new word processing document, and key the following 4 × 5 table.

110	220	330	
2000	2100	2500	
3400	2400	1200	
5500	3590	2900	

2. In cell D1, calculate the average of the numbers in cells A1:C1.
3. In cell A5, calculate the average of the numbers in cells A1:A4. Change the number format to #,##0. (Hint: Change the number format in the Formula dialog box.)
4. In cell D2, identify the maximum number in cells A2:C2.
5. In cell B5, identify the maximum number in cells B1:B4.
6. In cell D3, identify the minimum number in cells A3:C3.
7. In cell C5, report how many numbers are in D1:D4.
8. In cell D5, report the average of the numbers in cells A1:C4. Change the number format to #,##0.
9. **Save as: 73c functions.**

Writing Formulas

Table Tools Layout tab >
Data > Formula

1. Open a new word processing document, and key the following 4 × 4 table.

11	22	33	
44	55	66	
77	88	99	

2. In cell D1, write a formula that adds cell A2 to B1 and then subtracts cell C2.

3. In cell D2, write a formula that divides cell B3 by cell B1 and then subtracts 4. Change the number format to 0.

4. In cell D3, write a formula that adds cells A3 and C3 and divides that total by cell B1.

5. In cell A4, write a formula that calculates the difference between cell C1 and B1 and divides that result by B1.

6. In cell B4, write a formula that calculates the percent that cell B1 is of B3.

7. In cell C4, write a formula that adds 1000 to cell C2 and B2 and then multiplies that result by 2.

8. Save as: **73d formulas**.

Recalculate Formulas

1. Open **73b sum**.
2. Change cell C1 to 130.
3. Update the answer in cell D1.
4. Update the answer in cell C4.
5. Update the answer in cell D4.
6. Save as: **73e change**.

Formulas

1. Open **df 73f table**.
2. Calculate the Total Cycling miles in column F for rows 4:10 and the Total Jogging miles in column G for the same rows.
3. In row 11, calculate the averages for each column B:E.
4. In row 12, identify the maximum number in each row 4:10 for each column B:E.
5. Right-align all numbers.
6. Format the table appropriately.
7. Shade cells F12 and G12 to indicate they have no calculations.
8. Compare the format of your table to that shown here.

★TIP In general, spreadsheets like *Excel* are easier to use for formulas and calculations.

HARRY LUKAS EXERCISE LOG						
Day	**Week 1**		**Week 2**		**Total Cycling**	**Total Jogging**
	Cycling	**Jogging**	**Cycling**	**Jogging**		
Monday	10	0	15	2	25	2
Tuesday	15	0	18	4	33	4
Wedensday	0	6	0	8	0	14
Thursday	20	3	12	4	32	7
Friday	10	5	6	6	16	11
Saturday	0	8	10	3	10	11
Sunday	24	0	22	0	46	0
Average	11.29	3.14	11.86	3.86	20.25	6.13
Maximum	24	8	22	8		

9. Save as: **73f table**.

1. Key the following table, formatting as shown.

Monthly Budget		
Income	**Typical Teenager**	**Mine**
• Wages/Paycheck	$185	
• Allowance	40	
• Interest from Savings	5	
• Gifts	20	
• Other	0	
Total Monthly Income		
Expenses		
• Cell Phone	25	
• Clothes	70	
• Donations to Charity	10	
• Eating Out/Snacks/Fun	60	
• Gas for Family Car	35	
• Gifts	15	
• Savings Account	15	
• School Expenses	20	
• Other	0	
Total Monthly Expenses		

2. Compute the monthly income in cell B8 and the Total Monthly Expenses in cell B19.

3. Analysis:
   a. Do the income and expenses balance?
   b. In cell C10, record the percent of the typical teenager's income that she spends for her cell phone.
   c. If the teenager suddenly finds that her income from her job is going to be $30 lower each month due to a reduction in the hours she works, what expense item(s) would you recommend she immediately reduce to retain a balanced budget? Shade the cell of the expense item(s) in column 2 that you would reduce.

4. In column C, key your estimate of your monthly income and expenses. For example, if you receive approximately $300 each year from others for gifts, divide the $300 by 12 to get a monthly figure.

5. Analysis:
   a. Do your income and expenses balance? If not, make the appropriate adjustments to get a balanced budget.
   b. Add a column to the right of the last column. Use Percent as the column heading and merge row 1 cells as needed.
   c. In the cell to the right of your highest expense item, calculate what percent it is of your total income.

d. If your monthly income is likely to be reduced by 10 percent for the next six months, identify the expense(s) you would reduce to maintain a balanced budget. Shade the cell of the expense item(s) in column 3 that you could reduce.

e. If you are certain that your income would increase by 10 percent during the next six months, identify the expense(s) you would increase to maintain a balanced budget. Bold and italicize the font of the text in the cells in column 3 that would be increased.

6. Save as: *73g analysis*.

Rawpixel.com/Shutterstock.com

21st Century Skills: Creativity and Innovation

Being a creative thinker and communicating ideas with others are important skills, whether you are in the classroom, on the job, or in a social situation. When you are willing to suggest and share ideas, you demonstrate your originality and inventiveness. When you are open and responsive to the ideas and perspectives of others, you show consideration and cooperation.

In teams of three to four, develop a class newsletter to be published on your school's website. The newsletter should include a minimum of three articles and at least two graphics. Article ideas include recent projects, field trips, guest speakers, upcoming tests or assignments, study tips, teacher profiles, or student achievements. Divide duties as necessary. Save the newsletter and exchange with other teams. When all teams have read your newsletter, submit to your instructor as directed.

Think Critically

COLLABORATION

1. Creativity can mean a lot of different things. How do you define creativity?
2. What idea creation techniques do you think work best for groups? What about for you individually?
3. What positive things can you learn from an idea that "flops"?

sixninepixels/Shutterstock.com

Digital Citizenship and Ethics

Samantha is a high school student who just got her own laptop computer. She uses it for schoolwork and also to chat with friends, watch videos, play games, and surf the web. She often takes it to school or to the library and works on it in different rooms of her home. After a few months, Samantha notices a dull ache in her hands and wrists and has also begun to experience headaches more frequently. In addition, her mother has noticed redness in her eyes. At a visit to the family doctor, Samantha learns that her health problems are caused by her extended use of the new laptop.

As we use digital technologies, it is important to recognize the dangers they pose to our physical health. Some of the most common dangers include the following:

- Carpal tunnel syndrome, which is a condition of pain and weakness in the hand or wrist caused by repetitive motions, such as keyboarding and using a mouse
- Eyestrain, also called computer vision syndrome, which results from staring at a digital screen for hours at a time without a break
- Poor posture, as a result of using digital technologies on inappropriate surfaces, such as a bed or the floor, or bending the neck to look down at mobile devices for extended periods

COLLABORATION

As a class, discuss the following:

1. In addition to the physical dangers discussed above, what other risks are involved with extended use of digital technologies?
2. What measures can you take to minimize or eliminate the physical risks associated with digital technologies?

Assessment 7

Enhanced Reports and Tables

Warmup

Key each line twice at the beginning of each lesson; first for control, then speed.

alphabet	1	Zev and Che saw pilots quickly taxi many big jets from the gates.
figures	2	She sold 105 shirts, 28 belts, 94 skirts, 36 suits, and 47 coats.
speed	3	Jen sat by the right aisle for the sorority ritual at the chapel.

gwam 1' | 1 | 2 | 3 | 4 | 5 | 6 | 7 | 8 | 9 | 10 | 11 | 12 | 13 |

Activity 1
Timed Writings

Key two 5' writings on all paragraphs combined; find *gwam* and errors.

A all letters used

gwam 3' | 5'

	3'	5'
Small businesses are the majority of United States	3	2
businesses. They are a critical part of the economy. As we	7	4
analyze the information, they provide jobs for more than	11	7
half of the workers in our country. Each year, most of the	15	9
new jobs developed come from small businesses. They generate	19	11
more than half of the income of our country. Small businesses	23	14
have been and will always be a powerful force in the economy.	27	16
Small businesses often create more innovations than do	31	18
larger corporations. Small companies often attract competent	35	21
and talented people who develop new products or new ways to	39	23
use current products. These small business owners have gone	43	26
on to gain immense fame and fortune. Some of the founders of	47	28
these great empires have gained a place in our own history.	50	30
Others have changed the way business is done today. At the end	55	33
of the day, we quote their great wisdom and we try to duplicate	59	35
their successes in hopes that one day our ideas will become a success.	63	38
Small businesses benefit us in other ways and offer	67	40
us the products and services we have grown to expect. Their	71	43
impact is felt at home and around the globe. They provide	75	45
revenue and are the engines that drive our local, state,	78	47
and national economies. Small businesses provide growth and	82	49
innovation to the areas in which they were founded.	86	51

gwam 3' | 1 | 2 | 3 | 4 | 5 |
gwam 5' | 1 | 2 | 3 |

1. Format and key the text below as an unbound report, using styles appropriately for the title and side headings. Do not key the text in red.

Career Planning

Career planning is an important, ongoing process. It is important because the career you choose will affect your quality of life.

One important step in career planning is to define your goals.

> Exploring career fields and job opportunities will be an important part of your work life not only for your first job, but for your entire career. Career paths are rarely straightforward. Instead, your career path will evolve as you and your situation evolve: your interests and passions, your skills and experience, the economy, and your situation in life. [Insert footnote 1 here.]

Another useful step in career planning is to develop a personal profile of your skills, interests, and values.

Skills

An analysis of your skills is likely to reveal that you have many different kinds: (1) functional skills that determine how well you manage time, communicate, and motivate people; (2) adaptive skills that determine your efficiency, flexibility, reliability, and enthusiasm; and (3) technical skills such as keyboarding, computer, and language skills that are required for many jobs.

Values

Values are "the social principles, goals, or standards held or accepted by individuals," [Insert footnote 2 here.] and you should identify them early so that you can pursue a career that will improve your chances to acquire them. Values include the importance you place on family, security, wealth, prestige, creativity, power, and independence.

Interests

Interests are best described as activities you like and enthusiastically pursue. By listing and analyzing your interests, you should be able to identify a desirable work environment. For example, your list is likely to reveal if you like to work with things or people, work alone or with others, lead or follow others, or be indoors or outdoors.

2. Insert the following footnotes where indicated in the text.

[1] Lauri Harwood, Lisa M. Owens, and Krystal Kadakia, *Your Career: How to Make it Happen*, 9th ed. (Boston, MA: Cengage, 2017) p. 10.

[2] Ann K. Jordan and Tena B. Crews, *Investigating Your Career*, 3rd ed. (Boston, MA: Cengage, 2017) p. 16–17.

3. Format and key the following as a separate reference page at the end.

References

Harwood, Lauri, Lisa M. Owens, and Krystal Kadakia, *Your Career: How to Make it Happen*, 9th ed. Boston, MA: Cengage, 2017.

Jordan, Ann K. and Tena B. Crews. *Investigating Your Career*. 3rd ed. Boston, MA: Cengage, 2017.

4. Number the pages at the top right, and hide the number on page 1.
5. Hyphenate the report, check spelling, proofread, and correct all errors. Adjust page endings as necessary.
6. **Save as:** *a7 activity2*.

Activity 3
Cover Page

1. Using the Wisp built-in style, create a cover page for the report you just keyed. Include the report title, your name, your school name, and the current date. Delete unused placeholders as well as the blank page following the cover page.
2. **Save as:** *a7 activity3*.

Activity 4
Report with Table of Contents

1. Open *df a7 report4* and format it as a report.
2. Key **Jones Memorial Hospital Update** as the first line of the report. Format it in Title style.
3. Format the side headings in Heading 1 style.
4. Insert a page number at the bottom center of the pages, but hide it on page 1.
5. Insert a table of contents before page 1. It should contain page numbers and dot leaders.
6. Key **Page** above the first page number.
7. Key **Table of Contents** in Title Style as the first line on the page.
8. **Save as:** *a7 activity4*.

Activity 5
Newsletter

1. Open *df a7 newsletter*.
2. Key the following information at the top of the newsletter:

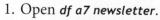

Healthscape
Published by Jones Memorial Hospital   February 20—

3. Format as a two-column newsletter, but have the heading information you inserted span the width of both columns.
4. Position the WordArt (Healthscape) as the title of the newsletter.

5. Use 1.0 line spacing, 10-pt. spacing after paragraphs, justification, and hyphenation for the report body.
6. Format the side headings in Heading 1 style.
7. Insert a vertical line between the columns.
8. Insert the text below in a shaded text box between the first and second articles on page 1.

Tip of the Week
Skiers may injure their thumbs when falling if they're using ski poles with molded plastic grips, which are not flexible. The American Physical Therapy Association recommends using ski poles with soft webbing or leather straps.

9. You decide all other formatting.
10. Save as: *a7 activity5*.

Activity 6
Table with Formulas

1. Open *Word* and create a 7 × 6 table grid.
2. Set column 1 width at 0.7"; set columns 2–7 width at 0.6"; set row 1 height at 1".
3. Bottom center-align cells in row 1.
4. Center-align cells A2:A6.
5. Set a decimal tab at or near the center of cells B2:G6.
6. Key the table below.

Zone	Time	Gal per Min	Monday	Wednesday	Friday	Sunday
1	6.7	15.8			0	
2	10	14	0		0	
3	8.15	12.25				
4	9.33	1.3	0	0		0
Totals						

7. Merge cells A6:C6 and right-align the cell contents.
8. Insert a row at the top. Set its height to 0.17". Merge cells A1:A2; merge cells B1:B2; merge cells C1:C2.
9. Merge cells D1:G1; key **Irrigation Days** in the merged cells; center-align the text.
10. Insert a row at the top; merge the cells; key **IRRIGATION SYSTEM WATER USAGE** in the merged cells; center-align the text.
11. Key a formula in each empty cell in range D2:G5 that calculates the gallons used each day to two decimal places.

12. Key a formula in cells D6:G6 that calculates the total for each day.
13. Center the table on the page.
14. Bold rows 1, 2, 3, and 8.
15. Increase top and bottom cell margins to 0.03".
16. Save as: *a7 activity6*.

Activity 7
Table with Formatting

1. Open a blank *Word* document.
2. Key the table below using the following formatting guides:
   a. Set row height so each row is at least 0.5".
   b. Set column A width to 1.25", columns B and D to 2.5", and column C to 1.5".
   c. Use Align Center in cells in rows 1 and 2; use Align Center Left in cells in rows 3–5.
   d. Center the table on the page in landscape orientation.
   e. Apply shading as shown.
3. Save as: *a7 activity7*.

Central Administration Support Services Staffing Chart			
Current Position Title	**Proposed Position Title**	**Immediate Supervisor**	**Administrators and Staff Supported**
Secretary	Confidential Senior Administrative Assistant, Superintendent	D. Griffiths, Superintendent	• D. Griffiths, Superintendent • C. Nezzo, Director of Student Achievement • B. Zestawniak, Public Relations Director
Clerk	Administrative Assistant, General and Business Operations	J. Zanone, Business Manager	• J. Zanone, Business Manager • C. Nezzo, Director of Student Achievement • B. Zestawniak, Public Relations Director
Payroll Officer	Administrative Assistant, Payroll and Personnel		• J. Zanone, Business Manager
Bookkeeper	Administrative Assistant, Financial Operations		• J. Zanone, Business Manager

Activity 8
Table with Calculations

1. Open *Word* and create a 7 × 6 table grid as shown below. Merge the cells in column A.
2. Key the main heading **MONTHLY DEDUCTIONS** in Times New Roman, 14-pt. caps, and bold. Change the text direction as shown, Align Center, and apply White, Background 1, Darker 15% shading. Change the width of column A to 0.5".
3. Change the height of row 1 to 1.1". Key the column headings in bold, 12-pt. font, then center them vertically and horizontally in the cells; change the text direction of the headings in columns C–F.
4. Key the table; adjust column widths and center the table horizontally.
5. Insert the totals in the last row and last column. Totals should contain a comma and two decimal places. Use a decimal tab to align all numbers. Change the height of rows 2–7 to 0.25"; center text vertically in the cells.
6. Change Courtney's Disability Insurance to **55.00** and Jonathan's 401 K Contribution to **550.00**. Update the totals to reflect the changes.
7. Proofread and correct any errors; save as: ***a7 activity8***.

MONTHLY DEDUCTIONS	**Employee**	**401 K Contribution**	**Health Insurance**	**Disability Insurance**	**Total Deduction**
	Julia Barnes	500.00	685.00	35.00	
	Charlie McDonnel	375.00	450.00	35.00	
	Courtney Posey	425.00	420.00	0.00	
	Jonathan Conner	600.00	375.00	55.00	
	Boris Kennedy	525.00	510.00	55.00	
	Total				

Skill Builder 13

A

Warmup

Key each line twice.

alphabet 1 Jack Dentinger will have a quiet nap before his big zoology exam.

one hand 2 You deferred my tax case after my union crew traced my wage card.

speed 3 The firms may make a profit if they handle their risk work right.

gwam 1' | 1 | 2 | 3 | 4 | 5 | 6 | 7 | 8 | 9 | 10 | 11 | 12 | 13 |

B

Technique: Letter Keys

Key each line twice.

 TIP Keep fingers curved and upright.

Emphasize continuity and rhythm with curved, upright fingers.

I 1 Michigan, Illinois, Indiana, and Missouri are all in the Midwest.

J 2 Jeff juggled jobs to join Jane for juice with the judge and jury.

K 3 Katie knocked the knickknacks off the kiosk with her knobby knee.

L 4 Please allow me to be a little late with all legal illustrations.

M 5 Mary is immensely immature; her mannerisms make me extremely mad.

N 6 Nancy knew she would win the nomination at their next convention.

O 7 Roberto opposed opening the store on Monday mornings before noon.

P 8 Pam wrapped the peppermints in purple paper for the photographer.

Q 9 Qwin quietly queried Quincy on the quantity and quality of quail.

gwam 1' | 1 | 2 | 3 | 4 | 5 | 6 | 7 | 8 | 9 | 10 | 11 | 12 | 13 |

C

Speed Building

1. Key a 1' timing on ¶ 1; key four more 1' timings on ¶ 1, trying to go faster each time.

2. Repeat the procedure for ¶ 2.

 LA all letters used

gwam 1'

Government is the structure by which public laws are	11
made for a group of people. It can take many forms. For	22
example, in one type of structure, the populace has the right	34
to elect citizens to govern for them and make the laws and	45
policies. This way of making the laws is called a	57
representative government.	61
Democracy or republic form of government are two names	11
that are quite often used to refer to this type of governance	23
by the people. This type of a structure is in direct contrast	35
to a dictatorship, in which all the decisions are made by just	48
one person.	50

gwam 1' | 1 | 2 | 3 | 4 | 5 | 6 | 7 | 8 | 9 | 10 | 11 | 12 |

Speed Forcing Drill

Key each line once at top speed; then try to complete each sentence on the 15'', 12'', or 10'' call as directed by your instructor. Force speed to higher levels as you move from sentence to sentence.

Emphasis: high-frequency balanced-hand words

	gwam	15"	12"	10"
Glen and I may key the forms for the city auditor.		40	50	60
He may make a sign to hang by the door of the bus.		40	50	60
They may make a profit if they do all of the busy work.		44	55	66
Six of the men may bid for good land on the big island.		44	55	66
If he pays for the bus to the social, the girls may also go.		48	60	72
The neighbor paid the maid for the work she did on the dock.		48	60	72
It is their civic duty to handle their problems with proficiency.		52	65	78
Helen is to pay the firm for all the work they do on the autobus.		52	65	78

Keying Technique

1. Key each line once.
2. Key two 30" writings on each even-numbered line.

alphabet

1 zebra extra vicious dozen happen just quick forgot way limp exact
2 Everyone except Meg and Joe passed the final weekly biology quiz.

speed

3 the and six work name make wish lake city eight formal auto firms
4 Dick and Jane may sign the forms to fix the problem for the firm.

bottom row

5 modern zebra extinct moving backbone moon vacate exam computerize
6 Zeno's vaccine injection for smallpox can be given in six months.

third row

7 you tip rip terror yet peer quit were pet tire terrier pepper out
8 Our two terrier puppies were too little to take to your pet show.

double letters

9 footnote scanner less process letters office cell suppress footer
10 Jill, my office assistant, will process the four letters by noon.

balanced hands

11 wish then turn us auto big eight down city busy end firm it goals
12 If the firm pays for the social, the eight officials may also go.

Shift keys

13 The New York Times|Gone with the Wind|Chicago Tribune|WordPerfect
14 Alan L. Mari finished writing "Planning for Changing Technology."

adjacent keys

15 were open top ask rest twenty point tree master merge option asks
16 The sort option was well received by all three new group members.

Space Bar

17 it is fix and fox go key do by box men pen six so the to when big
18 Did they use the right audit form to check the new city bus line?

gwam | 1' | 1 | 2 | 3 | 4 | 5 | 6 | 7 | 8 | 9 | 10 | 11 | 12 | 13 |

Planning for Your Career 4

Preparing for the Personal Interview

OUTCOME

• Prepare for a personal employment interview

Understanding the Personal Interview Process

The **personal interview** is a very important part of the employment process. While the interview may be conducted in a variety of ways and may involve one or more persons over one or more days, most interviews have common purposes. First, the interview provides the employer an opportunity to assess your personal attributes, demeanor, job qualifications, etc. in a formal setting to assist them in selecting the best person for the position. Second, the interview provides you with an opportunity to demonstrate that you are the best candidate and to gather information that will help you decide if you want the position.

You will likely approach the interview with some nervousness, but your nervousness can be tempered by knowing that the employer has selected you as one of the candidates they want to learn more about. If they were not interested in pursuing you, you would not get to the interview stage. You can also temper your nervousness by being very well prepared for the interview. In this module, you will focus on preparing yourself by researching the employer, preparing responses to anticipated interview questions, preparing questions that you want to ask the interviewer(s), and displaying appropriate conduct on the day of the interview.

Researching Employers

Prior to your scheduled interview, you should research the employer to learn about such things as the mission of the organization, the products and/or services it provides, the number of locations it has, how the area in which the position you are applying for fits within the organization, and the personnel within the area. Learning about the employer will help you provide appropriate responses and will demonstrate to the interviewers that you have initiative and a willingness to learn. If the employer has a website, use it as a resource. If you know someone who works for the employer, contact them to get the desired information.

1. Identify a business or organization in which you would like to complete a summer internship, and assume you have a personal interview scheduled. Use the Internet or another resource to gather information about its mission, primary products or services, and other information you believe will help you in your interview.

2. Open a new *Word* document and compose two paragraphs describing what you have learned about the employer.

3. **Save as:** *pc4 research*.

Developing Responses to Interview Questions

Although it is not possible to know in advance the specific questions you will be asked during the interview, it is still beneficial to develop responses to questions in areas that are typically pursued in an interview. Here is a sample of typical questions you may be asked in the interview for the internship position:

• How would your favorite teacher describe you?

• How will this internship position help you achieve your educational and/or career goals?

- Describe a recent conflict you had with another student and what you did to resolve it.
- What obstacle have you had to overcome in your life and what did you do to overcome it?
- What achievement are you most proud of and why?

1. Open a new *Word* document.
2. Using the same internship position used in the previous activity, compose your response to at least two of the bulleted questions that would prepare you for an interview for the position.
3. Save as: **pc4 responses**.

Asking Questions at the Interview

During the interview, it is likely that you will be given an opportunity to ask questions. Take advantage of these opportunities so you will be better able to decide if you want to accept the job if it is offered to you. Try to ask questions that relate to the requirements of the job, the people you will be working with, how performance is measured, information about working for the employer, etc. Do not ask questions about wages and benefits until a job offer has been made. Here is a sample of questions that would be appropriate for the internship position:

- What personal qualities do you want the intern to possess?
- Tell me about the people I will be working with.
- How will you assess my performance and will I have an opportunity to learn from the assessment?
- Why do you like working for this employer?
- Will I need training or an orientation period for this position?

1. Open a new *Word* document.
2. Access the Internet and identify and research a few resources you can use to develop questions you would ask interviewer(s). If desired, use *interviewee questions* as the search terms. Copy and paste into the *Word* document at least two resources that you found most helpful and include at least two questions you feel would be appropriate to ask during the interview.
3. Save as: **pc4 resources**.

Creating a Favorable Impression at the Interview

It is important that you create a favorable impression with everyone you meet on the day of the interview. By doing the following, you are more likely to accomplish that goal:

- Present a professional appearance by wearing clean, conservative clothing that fits properly. Choose a conservative hair style, remove any unusual jewelry or piercings, and cover tattoos. Do not wear perfume or cologne.
- Take your career portfolio, including multiple copies of your resume and reference list, to the interview.
- Plan your travel carefully so you arrive at least 10 minutes early at the specified meeting location.

- Greet all people with a smile, shake hands firmly, and make eye contact during your conversations. Show respect by using personal titles and last names if they are known.

- Listen intently and speak professionally at all times. Use a pleasant tone of voice and exhibit self-confidence when you speak or answer questions.
- Answer questions with concrete examples, show examples of your work, and use your knowledge of the company at appropriate times when answering interviewer questions.
- At the close of the interview, state your interest in the position and confidence that you can do the job. Ask the interviewer if there is anything else you should do and when they expect to notify you about the hiring decision.

1. Open a new *Word* document and develop, in a few paragraphs, a plan that you can implement to enhance the probability of success whenever a new interview has been scheduled.

2. **Save as:** *pc4 interview*.

Communication Skills 7

Karramba Production/Shutterstock.com

ACTIVITY 1: Internal Punctuation: Comma and Colon

1. Study each of the six rules.
   a. Key the *Learn* line(s) beneath each rule, noting how the rule is applied.
   b. Key the *Apply* lines, using commas and colons correctly.

Internal Punctuation: Comma

Rule 1: Use a comma to separate the day from the year and the city from the state.

Learn	1	Kennedy delivered his inaugural address on January 20, 1961.
Learn	2	Jack was born in Craig, Colorado; Sally in Casper, Wyoming.
Apply	3	The attack on Pearl Harbor took place on December 7 1941.
Apply	4	I attended the National FBLA conference in Denver Colorado?

Rule 2: Use a comma to separate two or more parallel adjectives (adjectives that could be separated by the word *and* instead of a comma).

Learn	5	The big, ornate mansion was put on the market in June.
Learn	6	Jasmine bought a small, fluffy dog for Jason for his birthday.
Apply	7	The big ugly desk had been around for many years.
Apply	8	The tall skinny player made the winning shot at the buzzer.

Rule 3: Use a comma to separate (a) unrelated groups of figures that occur together and (b) whole numbers into groups of three digits each. (Note: Policy, year, page, room, telephone, invoice, and most serial numbers are keyed without commas.)

Learn	9	By the year 2025, 1,350 fewer students will be enrolled.
Learn	10	Policy No. A375058 covers your 1965 Ford Mustang.
Apply	11	During 2023 1205 people moved to LaCrosse Wisconsin.
Apply	12	Invoice No. 7835A56 was for the 1200 new books.

Internal Punctuation: Colon

Rule 4: Use a colon to introduce an enumeration or a listing.

Learn	13	These are the candidates: Jay Chen, Chris Lee, and Cody Cox.
Apply	14	These are the ingredients flour, sugar, shortening, and eggs.
Apply	15	Everything fit in the box gloves, sweaters, coats, and socks.

Rule 5: Use a colon to introduce a question or a quotation.

Learn	16	Here's the real question: Who can improve our current situation?
Learn	17	Who said: "A bird in the hand is worth two in the bush"?
Apply	18	She quoted Ben Franklin "A penny saved is a penny earned."
Apply	19	His question was "How much is the down payment?"

Rule 6: Use a colon between hours and minutes expressed in figures.

Learn	20	The game starts at 5:00 p.m.; the other game starts at 7:30 p.m.
Apply	21	You can work the 800 a.m. shift or the 430 p.m. shift.
Apply	22	She told us to be here at 730 a.m. since the test starts at 800 a.m.

(continued on next page)

2. Key Proofread & Correct, inserting commas and colons correctly.
   a. Check answers.
   b. Using the rule number(s) at the left of each line, study the rule relating to each error you made.
   c. Rekey each incorrect line, inserting commas and colons correctly.

Save as: CS7 ACTIVITY1

Proofread & Correct

Rules

1	1	The game was held at Target Field in Minneapolis St. Paul.
1	2	FDR gave the speech to the U.S. Congress on December 8 1941.
1	3	The Jefferson Memorial was dedicated on April 13 1943.
2	4	The loud obnoxious fan was finally removed from the stadium.
2	5	The bright red dress she wore to the dance was very elegant.
3	6	The Yankees drew 45381 fans on Friday and 53800 on Sunday.
3	7	Invoice No. 1477 is for the furniture for Rooms 1033 and 1201.
1,3	8	Policy F8800BA6108 was paid through December 31 2021.
3	9	One of the townhouses on State Street was listed at $299000
4	10	These students were excused Mark Gee, May Chen and Rob Cox.
5	11	He quoted Shakespeare "This above all, to thine own self be true."
5	12	Here is the real question Who will pay for the proposed tax cuts?
6	13	Jordan is scheduled to present at 630 p.m. on February 25.
6	14	On Saturday you will work from 930 a.m. until 430 p.m.
2	15	The big powerful linebacker sacked the quarterback three times.

ACTIVITY 2: Word Choice

1. Study the definitions of the words.
2. Key the *Learn* line(s) noting the correct usage of each word.
3. Key the *Apply* lines, inserting the correct word(s).

Save as: CS7 ACTIVITY2

| **affect** (vb) to influence | **complement** (n) something that completes or makes up a whole |
| **effect** (n) result; consequence; (vb) to cause; to accomplish | **compliment** (n) an expression of praise or congratulation |

Learn 1 The **effect** of the recent change will **affect** our annual profit.

Apply 2 Will cutting the staff 25 percent (affect/effect) worker morale?

Apply 3 What (affect/effect) will new equipment have on productivity?

Learn 4 Jo's **compliment** to Dan was that his tie **complemented** his suit.

Apply 5 The laser printer is a (complement/compliment) to the system.

Apply 6 Gloria accepted Kevin's (complement/compliment) with a smile.

ACTIVITY 3: Speaking

Save as: CS7 ACTIVITY3

On any given night it is estimated that over a half million people in the United States are living on the streets, in shelters, in automobiles, in boxes, and in tents. Many of those who are homeless are children. Discuss the issue of homeless in the United States with several of your classmates and come up with a recommendation to present to the class on how your group would address this issue.

Before You Move On

Answer each question to review what you have learned in Chapter 14.

1. The horizontal Ruler can be used to set tabs and indentations. True or False? LO 71C

2. Bullets and numbering can be used in tables as they are in paragraphs. True or False? LO 71D

3. The _____ _____ feature can be used to display text vertically. LO 72B

4. Which feature is used to repeat header lines on second and subsequent pages of a table to make additional pages easier to understand? LO 72C

5. What does the Cell Margins feature allow in tables? LO 72D

6. When you key a table in a document, the amount of space above and below a table should be the same. True or False? LO 72E

7. Microsoft *Word* allows you to calculate answers to basic math problems in tables. True or False? LO 73B

8. What allows you to use mathematical functions other than SUM? LO 73C

9. How do you enter a formula in a *Word* table? LO 73D

10. What are the two ways *Word* updates a calculation when changes are made to table contents? LO 73E

Apply What You Have Learned

Table: Add/Delete Rows and Columns

1. Open *df c14 table1*.
2. Delete all rows with players who have played four years.
3. Delete *Years Played* column.
4. Insert a column before the email address, and key the telephone numbers below, starting in cell E3.

Telephone
555-678-1033
555-678-1709
555-348-0144
555-374-3056
555-678-2133
555-472-0337
555-678-1678
555-374-4585

5. Insert three rows at the bottom, and key the following information in the rows.

Bauer, Brianne	Left Back	11/04/04	555-374-6032	bauer.b@telstar.net
Haupt, Janet	Right Back	09/14/03	555-678-5502	rback.haupt@ford.net
Trianez, Dee	Left Wing	06/05/05	555-348-8173	trianez77@alt.com

6. Sort the data entries by last name.
7. Insert a row at the top, merge cells, and key **HURRICANES TENTATIVE STARTING LINEUP** as the heading for the table in bold 18-pt. font; format column headings in bold 16-pt. font; use 14-pt. font for all other rows.
8. Change orientation to landscape.
9. Center-align columns C and D; left-align all others.
10. Apply an appropriate table style.
11. Center table on the page.
12. Save as: *c14 table 1*.

Table with Borders and Shading

1. Open *df c14 table2*.
2. Use the information in the table below to finish keying any columns that are incomplete. Merge, split, and align cells as needed to complete the layout as shown below.
3. Format the main heading in bold, 16-pt. font and column headings in bold, 12-pt. font.
4. Apply a double-line border around all cells, and shade the cells so they are similar to what is shown below.
5. Center the table on the page in landscape orientation.
6. Save as: *c14 table2*.

ACCOUNTING MAJOR					
General Electives (40 credits)				Business Core (32 credits)	Accounting Requirements (28 credits)
Category I (9 Credits)	Category II (9 Credits)	Category III (11 credits)	Category IV (11 Credits)	Acct 201 Acct 202 Bcom 206 Bcom 207 MIS 240 Bsad 300 Bsad 305 Fin 320 Mktg 330 Mgmt 340 Mgmt 341 Mgmt 449	Acct 301 Acct 302 Acct 314 Acct 315 Acct 317 Acct 321 Acct 450 Acct 460 Fin 326 Fin 327
CJ 202 Math 111 Math 245	Biol 102 Chem 101 Geog 104	Econ 103 Econ 104 Psyc 100 Soc 101	No specific courses required.		
Category I – Communications and Analytical Skills Category II – Natural Sciences Category III – Social Sciences Category IV – Humanities					

Central Valley Education Foundation

Work Assignment

You are a student at Central Valley High School (CVHS) who is completing the first half of a 20-hour service learning requirement. You have been assigned to the Central Valley Education Foundation (CVEF), a group that strives to ensure that all children in Central Valley School District start school ready to learn and graduate from high school prepared for lifelong learning, careers, and citizenship.

CVEF is led by a director and several full-time staff members. You will be working as an administrative assistant to Marilyn Hardy, Assistant Director, who is responsible for administering a scholarship program and a student loan program for CVHS graduates.

In this position you will be required to use:

- *Word* to prepare tables, letters, reports, and data sources
- *Outlook* for email communication
- *Excel* to construct worksheets to calculate student loans
- *PowerPoint* to design a slide presentation on scholarship opportunities

You have met with the CVEF director and your supervisor, Ms. Hardy, to learn about CVEF's mission and activities as well as such things as your work hours, work station, access to the network and communication devices, and so on. To orient you further, your first assignments will be to review a few existing documents to learn more about the scholarship and student loan programs.

Spiroview Inc/Shutterstock.com

Monkey Business Images/Shutterstock.com

General

For the purposes of this simulation, assume you are completing your service learning during the Fall. This assumption is necessary because many of the documents and transactions are date specific, requiring the use of past, current, and future dates.

Additionally, Ms. Hardy has provided the following guidelines for you.

1. You are to follow all directions that are given.
2. If a formatting guide or direction is not given, use what you have learned in your digital information management course at CVHS to prepare the documents.
3. Always be alert to and correct errors in punctuation, capitalization, spelling, and word usage.
4. You should apply what you have learned and use your creativity to prepare other documents if specific instructions are not provided.

Correspondence

Prepare all letters in modified block format with mixed punctuation and no paragraph indentations. Supply an appropriate salutation and complimentary close and use your reference initials and other letter parts as needed.

Reports

Use the unbound report format with footnotes to prepare reports. Unless directed otherwise, apply an appropriate style set. Number all pages except page 1.

Tables and Charts

Unless directed otherwise, you can determine whether spreadsheet or word processing software should be used to prepare tables. Be sure to format and identify the various parts of these documents so the reader can easily read and interpret the data you present. Print the loan worksheets on one sheet of paper unless directed otherwise.

File Names

In order to quickly access information, CVEF has established a simple file-naming system. All files you create should be named with *cvef* followed by the job number and brief descriptive word (*cvef job2 loans*, for example). Specific instructions are included in the To Do List for each job.

Job 1

Table

To learn more about the scholarship program you will be working with, follow the directions that I have used for other new employees on the To Do List. It will also give me useful information about you.

mh

To Do List

1. Open *df cvef job1 scholarships*.
2. Review the criteria for all the scholarships and select three to five scholarships for which you could apply. Create a table that shows the name, amount, and criteria for each of them. You can copy this information from the scholarship matrix if you want.
3. Add a column at the right and include a few reasons why you believe you meet the criteria for the scholarships you selected.
4. Save the file as *cvef job1 scholarships*.

Job 2

Email

Prepare an email to thank the Ricks Family for their scholarship donation. See the To Do List for more information.

mh

To Do List

1. Create a new email message to Mr. Marcus Ricks for his scholarship donation in honor of his mother.
2. Enter Marcus' email address: **mrricks@tristar.com**.
3. Key **THANK YOU FOR YOUR DONATION** as the subject.
4. Key the following as the email message.

   On behalf of the Central Valley Education Foundation Board of Directors, please accept our appreciation of the generous donation you and your family made in honor of your mother, Mrs. Kathleen Ricks, a longtime faculty member at Central Valley High School.

   Mrs. Ricks was a dedicated teacher who loved to work with students. Her love of mathematics inspired all her students to give 100% in her classes. In addition to being respected by her students, the Central Valley High School faculty and administration appreciated her service to the student, school, and community.

   This generous donation gives Mrs. Ricks an ongoing way to touch the lives of students. Thank you again for your donation.

5. Proofread and correct errors.
6. Print one copy and submit to your instructor for grading.

Job 3

Worksheet

We have just received a list of new student loans. I need you to update the List of Loan Principals for Students Attending College. See the To Do List for more information.

mh

To Do List

1. Open *df cvef job3 loans*.
2. Update the *In College* worksheet with the following information. If the student record already exists, add a line and add the new loan under the student's previous loan(s). Student records should be alphabetical according to last name, and a solid grid line should separate each student in the list.

Last Name	First Name	Expected Grad Date	Date of Loan	Principal	Interest Rate
Bidwell	Karley	5-22	7-18	2500	4.0%
Gozdach	Justin	5-20	7-18	2500	4.0%
Collins	Kate	5-20	7-18	2500	4.0%
Forsythe	Kyle	5-19	7-18	2500	4.0%
Smart	Michael	5-22	10-18	2500	4.0%
Steffen	Terry	5-20	8-18	2500	4.0%
Sredy	Louis	5-20	10-18	2500	4.0%
Wilkins	Matthew	5-21	7-18	2500	4.0%
Staley	Brandon	5-21	7-18	2500	4.0%
Sutter	Harry	5-20	8-18	2500	4.0%

3. Add a line at the bottom of the table and merge the first four columns. Key **Total Outstanding Loan Principal** in the merged cells and right-align.

4. Insert the formula to total the Principal column.

5. Use Cell Styles to format the worksheet attractively; proofread and correct any errors.

6. Save the file as *cvef job3 loans*.

Job 4

Report

The CVEF Board of Directors is meeting in a few days. I need to prepare a proposal that money from the CVEF loan program be used to fund a scholarship. See the To Do List to find out what I need at this time.

mh

To Do List

Open *df cvef job4 bennett*, a draft I prepared. One of my colleagues proofed it and suggested changes. Please review her suggestions and then accept/reject them. Format the proposal as a report. I should have the Financial section done within a day or two and you can add it then. It will go at the end of the report. Save the file as *cvef job4 bennett*.

Job 5

Presentation

Can you rough out a presentation on scholarship opportunities available to CVHS students? I started the presentation but did not finish. See the To Do List for more information. Once approved, you can polish the presentation.

mh

To Do List

1. Open *df cvef job5 presentation*.

2. Insert an appropriate title slide. Note on the title slide that the CVEF has been supporting CVHS students for 50 years.

3. Use the *df cvef job1 scholarships* file and create a slide for each scholarship not already included in the presentation.

4. Add the scholarship amounts in parentheses by each scholarship award.

5. Save the file as *cvef job5 presentation*.

Job 6

Worksheet

I need a worksheet showing the amount and percent of net worth increase from 2003 through 2017 using the info on the To Do List. This worksheet will become part of the Financial section of the Bennett proposal that I'm drafting now.

mh

To Do List

Year	Net Worth		Year	Net Worth
2003	$152,339		2011	$196,208
2004	$154,306		2012	$201,021
2005	$157,512		2013	$204,107
2006	$162,060		2014	$205,782
2007	$163,409		2015	$214,219
2008	$169,818		2016	$219,827
2009	$182,261		2017	$224,141
2010	$192,773			

Year	Net Worth	Increase	% Inc

1. Display the data in four columns, using the column titles shown above.
2. Compute the Increase and % Inc.
3. Add a line chart displaying the data, titled **CVEF Loan Program Net Worth**.
4. Save the file as *cvef job6 net worth*.

Job 7

Report

We're now ready to finish the Bennett proposal. See the To Do List. Let me know when it is done so I can view it.

mh

To Do List

1. Access the Bennett proposal you worked on earlier (Job 4).
2. Insert the text from *df cvef job7 insert* at the end of the report.
3. Using *cvef job6 net worth*, copy/paste the line chart into the Bennett proposal where indicated so it links to the chart in the worksheet.
4. Copy/paste the worksheet in this same file into the Bennett proposal where indicated. Link it to the worksheet as well.
5. Check the formatting of the report.
6. Save the file as *cvef job7 bennett*.

Job 8

Email

Compose an email to Mr. Bailey Jones, President of the Central Valley Chamber of Commerce, accepting his invitation for the CVEF to present at the next Chamber of Commerce meeting. See the To Do List for more information.

mh

To Do List

1. Enter Bailey's email address: **bljones5@telnet.com**.
2. Key **CHAMBER OF COMMERCE PRESENTATION** as the subject.
3. In the body of the email message thank Mr. Jones for the invitation and confirm the next meeting date, time, and location: July 27, *<current year>* at 7:30 p.m. at the Chamber of Commerce building in downtown Central Valley. Inform him the presentation will last approximately 15–20 minutes followed by time for questions and answers.
4. Proofread and correct errors.
5. Print one copy and submit to your instructor for grading.

We are having an unusually high number of borrowers not making payments as required. The Board of Directors approved the policy at the right at its last meeting. Please format this as a table and print a copy for our next meeting when we review each borrower's record.

mh

To Do List

1   Key the table below, applying an attractive style.

2. Print a copy and save as ***cvef job9 policy***.

Policy for Handling CVEF Delinquent Loan Payments*

Step	Situation	Initial Action	Subsequent Action
1	At least 3 missed payments within most recent 6-month period	Send statement to borrower with note to make payments.	If not resolved, proceed to Step 2 when needed.
2	At least 6 missed payments within most recent 9-month period	Send letter to borrowers requesting they contact CVEF to seek resolution.	If not resolved, proceed to Step 3 when needed.
3	At least 10 missed payments within most recent 12-month period	Send certified letters to borrowers requesting full payment of delinquent amount to avoid legal proceedings.	If not resolved within 30 days, proceed to Step 4.
4	Satisfactory resolution at Step 3 not achieved	Send certified letter to borrowers notifying them that a legal complaint will be filed in 15 days if payment is not received within 10 days.	If not settled within 10 days, proceed to Step 5.
5	Satisfactory resolution at Step 4 not achieved	File legal complaint in appropriate court.	

*This revised policy was approved by the CVEF Board of Directors in October 2017.

The Finance Department has forwarded us the names of students graduating, with the amounts of their student loans. Please update our records. See the To Do List for specific information.

mh

To Do List

1. Open *df cvef job10 repay*.
2. Add to the worksheet the names of who will begin repaying their student loans six months after graduating. Their first payment will begin in November 2018. Fill in the information for all other columns where appropriate.

Last Name	First Name	Loan Amount
Dennard	Danielle	$2500
Karenoski	Jordan	$1500
Morris	Jerry	$1500
Parry	Larry	$5000
Pulman	John	$8000
Robinson	Denise	$1500
Targent	Caroline	$1000

3. Additionally, please note that Alexi Kenney and Angela Walsh have completed repaying their loans. Both students paid off their loans effective July 2018.
4. Add a line at the bottom of the table. In column B, key **Totals** and right-align.
5. Insert the formula to total the beginning principal column.
6. Insert the formula to total the remaining balance column.
7. Make sure all cells are formatted appropriately. Proofread and correct any errors.
8. Save the file as *cvef job10 repay*.

Your work on the Central Valley Chapter of Commerce presentation has been approved. See the To Do List.

mh

To Do List

1. Open *cvef job5 presentation*.
2. Apply an attractive design, appropriate transitions, clip art or online pictures (on a few slides) related to the slide topics. Use *PowerPoint Designer* Design Ideas if they are available to enhance your slides.
3. Add a closing slide thanking the Chamber for its support and involvement in Central Valley Schools.
4. Save the presentation as *cvef job11 presentation*.

Job 12

Letter

Here's a draft of the letter I want to send to Ms. Simmons, who is at Step 5. Date the letter November 5 of this year. You can get her address from her account statement in one of the CVEF Loans workbooks. Send a copy of the letter to her mother, Mrs. Hazel Simmons, and her father, Mr. John Simmons. Identify them by name in the copy notation. Supply all other needed letter parts. Use **CVEF Assistant Director** as my title.

mh

To Do List

You have not been making payments on your Central Valley Education Foundation (CVEF) loan for an extended period of time. Please see the enclosed payment record.

It is imperative that you contact me immediately to discuss this matter. If we do not get a satisfactory resolution, CVEF will file a legal complaint in the local district court 15 days from the date of this letter. The complaint will be filed against you and your parents since they also signed the promissory notes. We will request that the court order you to pay the entire loan balance, legal fees, and court costs.

Please call me at 412-555-0337 so we can attempt to resolve this issue without needing to take legal action.

Save the letter as *cvef job12 letter*.

Job 13

Promissory Note

Jim Howser is ready to sign for his loan. Prepare a promissory note that he and his parents can sign.

mh

To Do List

Amount and Rate: $2,000 at 5%

Date: November 7, 20--

Student's name: James H. Howser

Parents' names: John and Rita Howser

Expected graduation date: December 2020

1. Use *df cvef job13 note* (a template file) and info above to prepare the note.
2. Save the note as *cvef job13 note*.

Job 14

Presentation

I prepared slides for my presentation at the upcoming financial aid meeting with CVHS parents and students. I need you to make the presentation attractive and easy to read. See the To Do List for more info.

mh

To Do List

1. Open *df cvef job14 presentation* and insert this text on a new slide at the end:

   WHY SHOULD I TAKE A CVEF LOAN?
   - There is no interest charged while you are in college.
   - The interest rate is usually lower than student loans from other sources.

2. Apply an attractive design, appropriate transitions, and clip art (on a few slides) that is related to high school and/or loans. If available, apply appropriate Design Ideas.
3. Save the file as *cvef job14 presentation*.

Donation Form

The Board approved the Bennett scholarship, so we need to get it added to our website. We also need to post an updated form for those who want to establish a scholarship. See the To Do List for the copy and directions.

mh

To Do List

1. Insert the following copy into the *df cvef job15 scholarships* file. It should be listed first in the group that targets all students. Save the revised list as *cvef job15 scholarships*.

The Dr. Frank R. Bennett Scholarship	$2,000	Applicants should have a sustained record of academic excellence and participation in extra-curricular activities, community activities, and personal development and responsibility activities.

2. Here's the copy for the donation form. Use 1.0 line spacing and 6 pts. after paragraphs and format it appropriately and attractively.

Participating in the CVEF Scholarship Program

During the first four years of CVEF's scholarship program, 502 applications were received for the 54 scholarships CVEF has administered and over $50,000 have been awarded to the recipients. We believe the number of applicants evidence the need to continue the scholarship program and increase the dollars awarded.

You, too, can participate in this worthwhile program by choosing one of the following:

■ **I/we want to establish a named scholarship.** A named scholarship requires a minimum award of at least $1,000 for one or more years. Complete the form below and return this page to the address below. You will be contacted and given more information about establishing your scholarship.

■ **I/we want to contribute to the CVEF General Scholarship fund.** Those contributing $100 or more will be listed as funders on a Central Valley Alumni Association scholarship. Complete the form below and return this page and your check made payable to CVEF Scholarship Program to the address below.

Name(s) of Donors: _____

Mailing Address: _____

_____

Email Address: _____ Phone: _____

Thank you!!! Please return this page to:

Ms. Marilyn Hardy
CVEF Assistant Director
801 Round Hill Road
Elizabeth, PA 15037-8000

Since CVEF is a Section 501(c) organization, all contributions for scholarships are tax deductible to the extent allowed by law. Please consult with your tax attorney about your scholarship.

3. Save the donation form as **cvef job15 donation**.
4. Open **cvef job11 presentation** and add a slide for the new scholarship and update slide 2 to reflect the additional scholarship.
5. Save the updated presentation as **cvef job15 presentation**.

Job 16

Data Source

I need a data source file of the students with loans who are still in college so I can send them a progress form to complete nearer the end of the year. Please create a data source file using this information. Create the file with the following fields: FirstName, LastName, AddressLine1, City, State, PostalCode. After you have the data entered, sort alphabetically by last name, then first name.

mh

Karley Bidwell 530 Simpson Howell Road Elizabeth, PA 15037-1045	Cole Wehner 3393 Long Hollow Road Elizabeth, PA 15037-9823
Kelsey Bidwell 530 Simpson Howell Road Elizabeth, PA 15037-1045	Juan Vasquez 225 Oberdick Drive McKeesport, PA 15135-2956
Matthew Wilkins 229 Firden Drive Monongahela, PA 15063-4378	Kyle Forsythe 188 Donna Drive Elizabeth, PA 15037-3067
Kate Collins 5724 Meade Street Elizabeth, PA 15037-7601	Justin Gozdach 847-15 West Newton Road Elizabeth, PA 15037-4178
Derek DiPerno 1120 E. Smithfield Street McKeesport, PA 15135-8712	Lorie Tanselli 922 Grant Street Elizabeth, PA 15037-6390
Connor DiPerno 1120 E. Smithfield Street McKeesport, PA 15135-8712	Harry Sutter 43 River Road Buena Vista, PA 15018-4085
Terry Steffen 264 Oak Lane Monongahela, PA 15063-6543	Kara Quatrini 670 Fallen Timber Road Elizabeth, PA 15037-4680
Michael Smart 312 Rock Run Road Elizabeth, PA 15037-9876	Ronald Reddick 175 Holt Road Elizabeth, PA 15037-0246
Louis Sredy 210 Grouse Drive Elizabeth, PA 15037-3928	Brandon Staley 207 Schaffer Avenue Elizabeth, PA 15037-6713

Save the file as **cvef job16 data**.

CHAPTER 15

Communicating Effectively with Enhanced Presentations

Lesson 74	Enhance Slide Show Presentations with Screen Clippings	Lesson 76	Enhance Slide Show Presentations with Audio
Lesson 75	Enhance Slide Show Presentations with Graphics, Animations, and Transitions	Lesson 77	Deliver an Effective Presentation
		Assessment 8	Enhanced Presentations

Application Guide

Animations

Animations tab > Animation > select animation type

In Chapter 8, you learned the basics of using presentation software to create electronic presentations. In this chapter, you practice those skills and add new skills to enhance your presentations. Rather than have a slide appear in its entirety, animations can be used to make text, graphics, and other objects appear one at a time. After text, graphics, or an object appears, animations can be used to change the size and color of the item as well as to move the item on the slide. This allows control of how the information is presented as well as adding interest to the presentation.

A variety of animations are available. A few examples include *Fade*, *Spin*, *Float In*, *Swivel*, and *Bounce*. **Animation schemes** are options that are preset. They range from very subtle to very glitzy. The scheme chosen should add interest without taking away from the message. **Custom animation** allows several different animations to be included on each slide.

Use the Animations tab to access the Animation group to select an animation. Use the More drop-down arrow in the Animation group to see additional *Entrance*, *Emphasis*, and *Exit* animations. *Entrance* animations are added when the slide first displays, and *Exit* animations are added when the slide is done displaying. *Emphasis* animations enhance slide elements while the slide is displaying. See Figure 15-1.

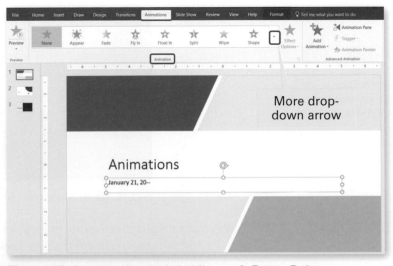

Figure 15-1 Animations tab in Microsoft *PowerPoint*

Design Tips

As you learned in Chapter 8, *PowerPoint* comes with a variety of design themes to provide a consistent, attractive look. Use design themes to give your presentations a professional appearance. As you create a slide show, also consider the following design Do's and Don'ts:

- Do use bulleted lists to present concepts one at a time (see Figure 15-2). If you have access to the Designer feature, try Design Ideas for bulleted lists and other elements (Figure 15-3).

- Do use keywords and phrases rather than complete sentences.

- Do use contrasting background colors that make text stand out. Use light text against a dark background or dark text against a light background.

- Do choose a font size that the audience can read—even in the back of the room.

- Do use sound and animation to make a point, but not to distract from your message.

- Don't overcrowd slides. Two slides might be better than one.

- Don't overuse clip art. Photos have more impact.

- Don't overuse animations and transitions.

Figure 15-2 Bulleted list

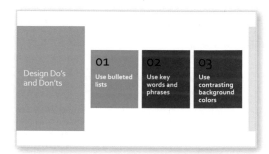

Figure 15-3 Designer bulleted list

Hyperlinks

Insert tab > Links > Link

★TIP An easy way to insert a hyperlink is to copy and paste (or key) the webpage address on the slide followed by a space; the address is converted to a hyperlink.

A **hyperlink** is text that is colored and underlined that you click to take you from the current location in the electronic file to another location in the file, in another file, or on the web. See the example in Figure 15-4. You can also add hyperlinks to images.

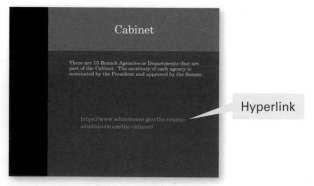

Figure 15-4 Slide with hyperlink

This means that a presenter can create hyperlinks to move from the current slide in a presentation to an Internet site that relates to the topic. You can also select any text or image in a slide, right-click, and click *Link* to create a hyperlink from that text or image.

Navigation Shortcuts

During a presentation, you can use the shortcut menu (illustrated in Figure 15-5) to display the next, previous, or last viewed slide. The shortcut menu is displayed by right clicking while in Slide Show View.

The first slide, the last slide, or any slide in a slide show can also be displayed by using the following keyboard shortcuts:

- Start a presentation from the beginning: *F5*
- Start a presentation from the current slide: *Shift + F5*
- Show Presenter View: *Alt + F5*

Knowing shortcuts is particularly helpful when your audience has a question relating to what has previously been discussed or when the presenter wants to show a slide that is placed after the one currently being shown to address a question from the audience or to make changes.

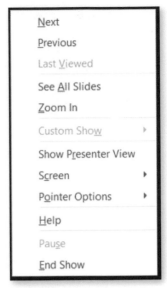

Figure 15-5 Shortcut menu available during a presentation

Presenter View

Slide Show tab > Monitors > Use Presenter View

The **Presenter View** feature projects the Slide Show View on a larger monitor while putting a "speaker view" with tools for the presenter on the laptop screen. Presenter View shows the current slide and previews the next slide, and includes a timer, a Tools feature, a Slide Navigator, and a Notes pane (see Figure 15-6). Presenter View makes giving a professional presentation easier and allows the presenter to focus on the audience.

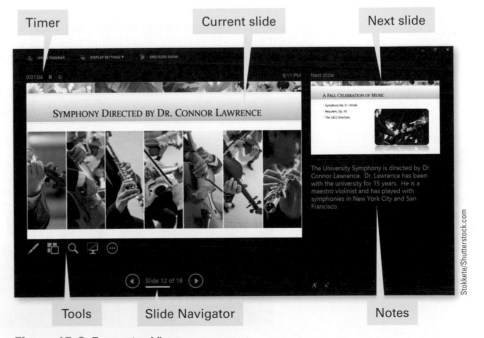

Figure 15-6 Presenter View

The Presenter View tools shown in Figure 15-7 include:

- *Pen and laser pointer tools*—Draws the attention of the audience to specific parts of a slide.
- *See all slides*—Shows all slides included in the slide show and allows the presenter to quickly access any slide without having to go forward or backward one slide at a time. This feature is particularly helpful when the audience has a question that you can answer with another slide that is included in the presentation.
- *Zoom into the slide*—Allows the speaker to zoom in on a portion of the slide. It increases the size of the portion being zoomed in on like a magnifying glass.
- *Black the screen*—Allows the speaker to draw the attention of the audience back to speaker by turning the slide black.
- *More slide show options*—Allows the speaker to do additional tasks while giving a presentation. This includes such things as making the taskbar visible and bringing up a Help feature that shows general shortcuts that can be used to run the slide show more efficiently.

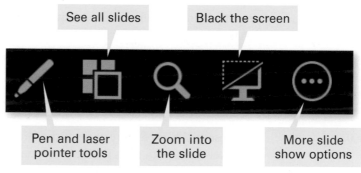

Figure 15-7 Presenter View tools

Pictures and Video

Insert tab > Images

Insert tab > Media > Video

TIP When inserting any type of picture or media, care must be taken not to violate copyright laws.

As you learned in Chapter 8, pictures can be inserted in an electronic presentation from a number of different sources such as scanners, cameras, files, and the Internet. Video can also be inserted into a presentation, from online sources or your own PC. Inserting pictures and video, as shown in Figure 15-8, enhances a slide show and captures and keeps the audience's attention.

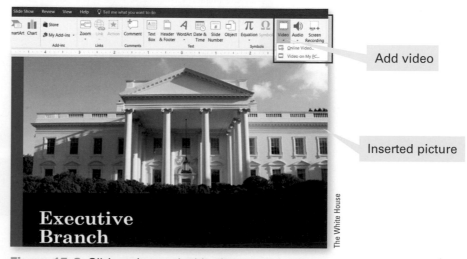

Figure 15-8 Slide enhanced with picture and video

Screen Clipping

Insert tab > Images > Screenshot

The **Screen Clipping** feature takes a snapshot of all or part of the screen. This feature can be used to enhance the slides in your presentation with relevant information and attention-grabbing photos and illustrations. You can take screen clippings of photos, computer application screens, documents, websites, etc.

The Screen Clipping feature allows you to emphasize what you want. For example, rather than placing the entire photo of the White House on the slide as shown in Figure 15-8, you could use the Screen Clipping feature to place only the entrance to the White House as shown in Figure 15-9. Once captured, the screen clipping can be sized and moved to create the desired impact.

Figure 15-9 Screen clipping

Audio

Insert tab > Media > Audio

Audio is another way to enhance a presentation. When people hear something as well as see it, they are much more likely to retain it.

Most electronic presentation software allows you to insert audio from your computer or record sound directly into the presentation.

The sound capability allows a presenter to bring variety and credibility to a presentation. Hearing John F. Kennedy say "Ask not what your country can do for you, ask what you can do for your country" has much greater impact than if the presenter reads the quote. Having background music play as you show pictures has more impact than just showing the pictures.

Timing

Slide Show tab > Set Up > Rehearse Timings

The Slide Timing feature controls the speed with which one slide replaces another. Setting times tells the software how long each slide will remain on the screen.

The amount of time allocated to each slide in the slide show can be specified. For example, you may want each slide to appear on the screen for 5 seconds. This type of timing would be appropriate for a year-end banquet slide show where you want to review the year's activities through pictures.

For some slide shows, you want to vary the amount of time given to each slide. If one slide is a simple picture and the next is a complicated table, 5 seconds may be more than enough for the simple picture, but wouldn't be enough time for the complicated table. The Rehearse Timings feature can be used to set varying amounts of time between slides.

Transitions

Transitions tab >
Transition to This Slide >
select transition type

Slide **transition** is the term used to describe how the display changes from one slide to the next. When no transition is applied, slides go from one directly to the next. Transition effects can make it appear as though the next slide dissolves in or appears through a circle, for example. When you select a transition, it is automatically previewed on your slide so you can see how it will look. There are a variety of transitions to choose from. Some are much more glitzy than others. Care should be taken that transitions enhance the presentation rather than detract from it.

Figure 15-10 shows an opening slide using the *Curtains* transition. The *Curtains* transition was selected to show the start of the slide show similar to the opening of curtains at the opening of a play. Figure 15-11 shows the transition between slide 1 and slide 2 using the *Ripple* transition. This transition was used to represent the changes of the four seasons.

Figure 15-10 Slide with *Curtains* transition

Figure 15-11 Slide with *Ripple* transition

LESSON 74

Enhance Slide Show Presentations with Screen Clippings

OUTCOMES

- Insert a screen clipping using the Screenshot feature
- Create a slide show with graphics
- Insert slides from other files

74A–77A

Warmup

Key each line twice daily.

alphabet	1	Zelda Jamestown backed up and forged down the exquisite driveway.
one hand	2	Better grades were agreed upon after I stated my adverse opinion.
speed	3	The neighbor may fix the problem with the turn signal on the bus.

gwam 1' | 1 | 2 | 3 | 4 | 5 | 6 | 7 | 8 | 9 | 10 | 11 | 12 | 13 |

74B

Insert a Screen Clipping

Insert tab > Images > Screenshot > Screen Clipping

Images enhance slide shows. Images can be pictures that you have taken, scanned pictures from books, pictures from files, or images from the Internet. As you use work created by others, you have to be mindful of copyright laws. The following image is a picture you would like to use in the slide show of Park City, Utah, that you are creating. This can be done by following these steps.

1. Open *df 74b*. This document includes two photos you'd like to use in your presentation.
2. Open a new Blank presentation in *PowerPoint*. Make sure both the *PowerPoint* window and the *Word* window are displayed on your screen.
3. Change the layout of the first slide to *Blank*.
4. Click the *Insert* tab and then click *Screenshot* as shown in Figure 15-12.
5. Click *Screen Clipping* at the bottom of the drop-down menu (Figure 15-13). Your screen shows all open items on your desktop grayed out, and the pointer changes to a "crosshairs" icon.

Figure 15-12 Screenshot feature

Figure 15-13 Screen Clipping feature

6. You don't want the power lines above the fence included in the photo. Position the cursor at the left-hand side of the first picture in the *Word* document a little beneath the power lines. Click and drag over the portion of the image that you want to capture to crop the photo as shown in Figure 15-14.

Figure 15-14 Screen clipping of photo

7. Release the click. The cropped picture appears on your *PowerPoint* slide.
8. If you have the Designer feature, it provides some Design Ideas for you. Complete the slide by selecting a Design Idea similar to the one shown in Figure 15-15. (If you do not have the Designer feature, select a similar Picture Style from the *Picture Tools Format* tab.)
9. Insert another blank slide.
10. Use the Screen Clipping feature and Designer or Picture Tools to create a slide using Picture 2 from **df 74b** similar to the one shown in Figure 15-16.
11. Close the *Word* document.
12. Save the *PowerPoint* file as **74b pp**.

Figure 15-15 Design Idea for picture 1

Figure 15-16 Design Idea for picture 2

74C

Create a Slide Show with Pictures and Screen Clippings

Insert tab > Images > Screenshot > Screen Clipping

1. After creating the slides of Park City, you have decided to enter an art show with pictures you have taken. You have narrowed down the choices to the ones shown in Figure 15-17. These pictures are available in the folder **df 74c photos**. The rules state that you must submit a slide show with 15 slides to include the title slide. However, you can have several pictures on one slide as shown in Figure 15-18.

Figure 15-17 Art show photos

2. Create a title slide with the information shown in Figure 15-19. You can select any design theme or use a blank one.

Figure 15-18 Design Idea for rock formation photos

Figure 15-19 Title slide

20-- Art Show Entry

Your Name

3. Use the Screen Clipping feature to crop the pictures to highlight the main feature of the photo. For example, if you decide to have the picture of the elk in the slide presentation, the elk should be as large as possible. This can be done by cropping out part of the forest. If you selected the lighthouse on Lake Superior, however, you don't want to crop much because the beauty of the picture is that the lighthouse is high on a cliff.

4. The rules state that slide 9 must include two photos and slide 15 must include three photos. Reuse the three photos shown in Figure 15-18 for slide 15 to end the slide presentation. To include more than one photo on the slide, simply insert the photos on the slide and let the Designer feature do the layout work for you. Choose the Design Idea that displays your photos most attractively. Alternatively, you can move and resize the photos in a pleasing arrangement. The slide in Figure 15-18 features rock formations from Colorado, Wyoming, and Minnesota.

5. **Save as:** *74c pp*.

74D

Create a Slide Show with Hyperlink

Insert tab > Links > Link > Key Internet Address in Address box > Click *OK*

Create a slide show about the government of the United States by following these steps.

1. Open *df 74d pp*; change the colors of the View design theme to *Blue Warm* by clicking the *Design* tab, then clicking the *More* drop-down arrow of the Variants group. Next, click *Colors* and then click *Blue Warm* as shown in Figure 15-20.

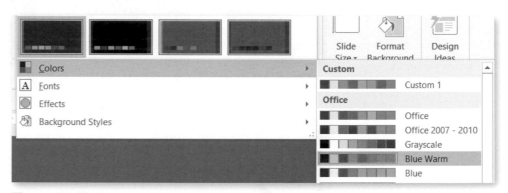

Figure 15-20 Design theme colors

2. Create the 11 slides shown in Figure 15-21. The slides will be used again in Lessons 75–77. If Designer doesn't offer you the exact same designs as shown here, choose ones that are similar. Slides 3, 7, and 9 should have the same design and slides 4, 5, and 6 should have the same design. You will need to decide on the appropriate slide layout. Many of the slides use the Title and Content layout with bulleted lists, enhanced by selecting one of the automatically generated Design Ideas.

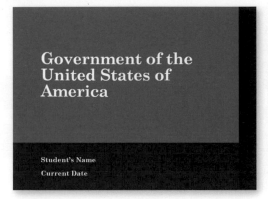

Slide 1

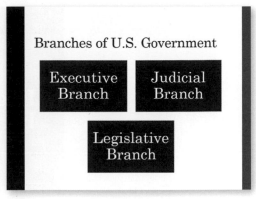

Slide 2

Slide 3

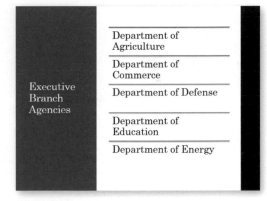

Slide 4

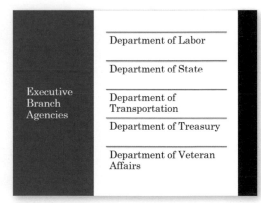

Slide 5

Slide 6

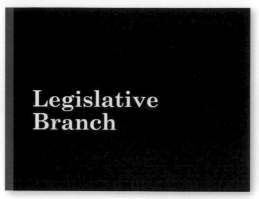

Slide 7

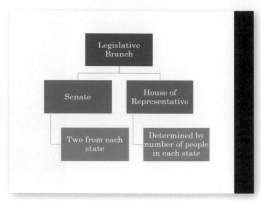

Slide 8

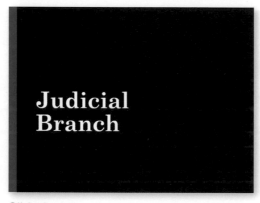

Slide 9

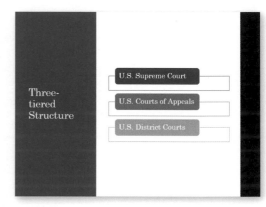

Slide 10

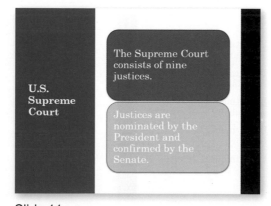

Slide 11

Figure 15-21 Slides for Lesson 74D

3. On slide 4, highlight *Executive Branch Agencies*. Add a hyperlink to this text by clicking the *Insert* tab, then clicking the *Link* button in the Links group to display the Insert Hyperlink dialog box. In the Address box, key the link www.whitehouse.gov/administration/cabinet (see Figure 15-22). Click *OK* to create the hyperlink. The hyperlinked text on the slide shows as blue and underlined.

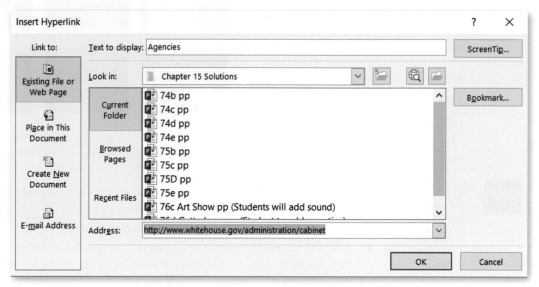

Figure 15-22 Insert hyperlink

4. Check the hyperlink by hovering the pointer over the text *Executive Branch Agencies*. Hold down the *Ctrl* key (the pointer changes to a hand icon) and click. The website should open in your browser. Close your browser.
5. **Save as: *74d pp*.**

74E

Insert Slides in a Slide Show

Slides from one presentation can be copied and pasted into another presentation. This feature is particularly helpful when putting together a group presentation or when using previously created slides in a new presentation.

Continue working on the presentation about the Government of the United States of America by inserting slides from another file into the file you started. Follow the procedure outlined here to copy and paste slides from one file to another file.

1. Open *df 74e pp*.
2. With the slides in Slide Sorter View, hold down the *Ctrl* key and click the first four slides to select them (see Figure 15-23).
3. On the Home tab in the Clipboard group, click the *Copy* button to copy the four slides to the Clipboard.

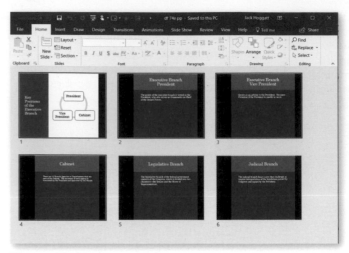

Figure 15-23 Copy slides

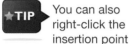

★TIP You can also right-click the insertion point and choose *Keep Source Formatting* from the Paste Options that display.

4. Open the file you created for **74d pp** if it is not already open.

5. Position the pointer between slides 3 and 4 and click. A line appears to indicate where you are going to insert the slide(s). Read all of step 6 before completing it.

6. On the Home tab in the Clipboard group, click the *Paste* drop-down arrow to show the Paste menu (Figure 15-24). Click the second icon, *Keep Source Formatting*. (If you use shortcut keys *Ctrl + V* or simply click the top of the *Paste* button to paste, you will lose the source formatting.)

Figure 15-24 Keep Source Formatting

7. Copy slide 5 from **df 74d pp** and paste the slide after the *Legislative Branch* slide using the same procedure.

8. Copy and paste slide 6 from **df 74d pp** after the *Judicial Branch* slide.

9. **Save as:** **74e pp**.

LESSON 75

Enhance Slide Show Presentations with Graphics, Animations, and Transitions

OUTCOMES
- Add animations to a slide show
- Add transitions to a slide show
- Add graphics to enhance a slide show
- Add notes to a slide show

75B

Add Animations to a Slide Show

Animations tab >
Animation > select
animation

Animations are special effects that can be included to enhance a presentation. For example, using animations, each item in a bulleted list can be made to appear one at a time. This allows the presenter to control not only what the audience sees but when they see it. The presenter can discuss the first point before the next point appears, thus keeping the audience focused on the point that is being discussed. When the speaker is ready to discuss the next point, the second point in the bulleted list can be made to appear.

In addition to the entrance animation effect, animation can be used for emphasis, to exit, and for motion paths. An example of the exit animation effect would be removing each of five possible answers from a slide at a time (exit), leaving only the correct answer. A motion path is the direction an object follows across the slide. Paths can be the standard paths available or customized by the person creating the presentation.

Add animations to a presentation by following these steps:

1. Open *df 75b pp*.
2. In Normal View bring up slide 2.
3. Click the placeholder containing the names as shown in Figure 15-25.

Figure 15-25 Bulleted items

4. On the *Animations* tab in the Animation group, click the *More* button as shown in Figure 15-26 to display the Animation gallery.

Figure 15-26 Animation options

5. Click the *Float In* animation as shown in Figure 15-27.

Figure 15-27 Select an animation

6. Click *Slide Show View*.
7. Tap *Enter* to make the members appear.
8. Tap *Esc* to return to Normal View. Note the animation/transition icon that now appears before slide 2 in the Thumbnail pane and the numbers that appears before the bulleted items in the placeholder box as shown in Figure 15-28.

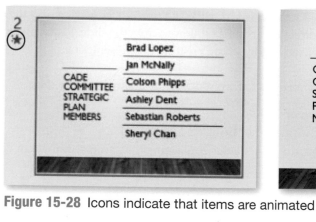

Figure 15-28 Icons indicate that items are animated

9. Include these entrance animations for the bulleted lists on the following slides.
   a. Slide 3: Shape
   b. Slide 4: Fade
   c. Slide 5: Split
   d. Slide 6: Wipe
   e. Slide 7: Split
10. On slides 5 and 7, to get the boxes to come in one by one, with the list selected, click the *Effect Options* button to the right of the Animation group. If necessary, select *Vertical In* for the *Direction*. Click *Effect Options* again and then click *One by One* for the sequence as shown in Figure 15-29. For slide 7 change the *Direction* to *Horizontal Out* and the Sequence to *One by One*.
11. Click *slide 1*; click *Slide Show View* to view the animation effects.
12. Save as: **75b pp.**

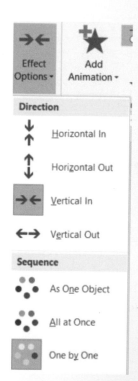

Figure 15-29 Effect Options

Add Transitions to a Slide Show

Transitions tab >
Transition to This Slide >
select transition

Animations are the special effects that occur with the graphics and text of each slide. Transitions are special effects placed between slides to enhance a slide show. A few of these special effects are illustrated in Figure 15-30.

Figure 15-30 Transitions are displayed between slides

Including transitions adds excitement to your visuals. Transitions also capture and help maintain your audience's attention. The process of adding transitions to a presentation is very similar to adding animations.

1. Open **75b pp**.
2. Click *slide 1*.
3. Click the *Transitions tab*.
4. Click the *More* button located on the Transition to This Slide group to display the Transitions gallery.
5. Click the *Fracture* transition icon in the Exciting group.
6. Include these transitions from the Exciting group to the following slides.
   a. Slide 2: Fall Over
   b. Slide 3: Honeycomb
   c. Slide 4: Shred
   d. Slide 5: Doors
   e. Slide 6: Vortex
   f. Slide 7: Box
7. View the slide show to see the effect of adding transitions to a slide show.
8. **Save as: 75c pp**.

★TIP The amount of glitz added to this presentation was just to illustrate the various animations and transitions that are available. If this were a real presentation, it would be too much. Don't overuse animations and transitions; it will make your audience focus on the slide show rather than on what is being presented.

Enhance the *Government of the United States of America* slide show that you created for 74e by adding photos. If Internet access is not available, use the folder *df 75d photos* for the photos.

1. Open *74e pp*.
2. On the *Executive Branch* slide (slide 3), include a photo of the White House. The photo in Figure 15-31 is a screen clipping from:

   https://obamawhitehouse.archives.gov/1600/executive-branch

Figure 15-31 White House

3. On the *Legislative Branch* slide (slide 11), include a photo of the U.S. Capitol Building (Figure 15-32).

   https://obamawhitehouse.archives.gov/1600/legislative-branch

Figure 15-32 U.S. Capitol Building

4. On the *Judicial Branch* slide (slide 14), include a photo of the Supreme Court Building (Figure 15-33).

   https://obamawhitehouse.archives.gov/1600/judicial-branch

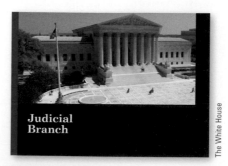

Figure 15-33 Supreme Court Building

5. Add the Transitions and Animations as shown in Table 15-1.
6. After completing the transitions and animations, **save as:** **_75d pp_**.

Table 15-1 Transitions and Animations for 75D

Slide	Transition	Animation	Effect Option	
Slide 1	Curtains			
Slide 2	Ripple	Float In	↓ ⦿	One by One
Slide 3	Honeycomb			
Slide 4	Ripple	Split	→← ⦿	One by One
Slide 5	Cube	Fly In	↑ From Bottom	
Slide 6	Cube	Fly In	↑ From Bottom	
Slide 7	Cube	Fly In	↑ From Bottom	
Slide 8	Switch			
Slide 9	Switch			
Slide 10	Switch			
Slide 11	Honeycomb			
Slide 12	Cube	Fly In	↑ From Bottom	
Slide13	Ripple	Wipe	→ ⦿	Level One by One

(Continued)

Slide	Transition	Animation	Effect Option
Slide14	Honeycomb		
Slide 15	Cube	Fly In	↑ From Bottom
Slide 16	Ripple	Fade	Level One by One
Slide 17	Ripple	Wheel	Level One by One

21st Century Skills: Information, Communications, and Technology (ICT) Literacy

Today's technology has drastically changed the way we present and exchange information. Through word processing and other types of software applications, we can quickly and easily prepare professional-looking correspondence, reports, tables, and other types of documents.

Being a proficient user of software applications, including word processing, spreadsheet, presentation, and database programs, is an important skill both in the classroom and on the job. Further, knowing how to use these tools to effectively communicate information and ideas will help you succeed in all areas of your life.

Think Critically

Open a new presentation file, and create slides for each of the following software applications. Key the information as shown for each application, and then list at least two types of files you could create with each type of application. Insert graphics and apply formats as desired to enhance the presentation.

wavebreakmedia/Shutterstock.com

- **Word Processing**: Use to create text documents.
- **Spreadsheet**: Use to create worksheets for recording and calculating data.
- **Presentation**: Use to create multimedia slide shows.
- **Database**: Use to organize and manage data.

Save the presentation as directed by your instructor.

Add Notes to a Slide Show

You will be giving the slide show you just created to foreign exchange students at your school. In Normal View, notes for each slide can be placed beneath the slide by clicking the *Notes* icon on the status bar and then clicking in the *Notes* pane and keying the note as shown in Figure 15-34.

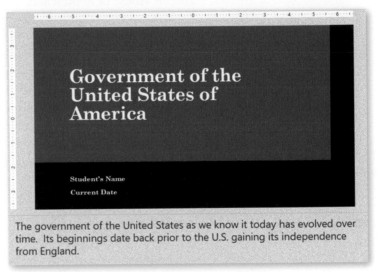

Figure 15-34 Notes pane below each slide

1. Open *75d pp*. Key the following notes for each slide.

   Slide 1: The government of the United States as we know it today has evolved over time. Its beginnings date back prior to the U.S. gaining its independence from England.

   Slide 2: Today we have three branches of government. They include:
   the Executive Branch,
   the Judicial Branch, and
   the Legislative Branch.

   Slide 3: Let's start by talking about the Executive Branch.

   Slide 4: There are three key positions in the Executive Branch. They are the President, the Vice President, and the Cabinet.

   Slide 5: As you can see, the President of the United States is in charge of the Executive Branch. He serves as Commander in Chief of the Armed Forces, appoints cabinet members, and oversees the executive departments that we will be discussing later on in the presentation.

   Slide 6: In addition to serving as an advisor to the president, the Vice President is the President of the Senate. If there is a tie, the Vice President casts the deciding vote.

   Slide 7: These 15 departments are also referred to as Executive Departments. In addition to these departments, there are also independent agencies, and other boards, commissions, and committees that are part of the Executive Branch.

   Slide 8: Let's take a look at the 15 agencies within the Cabinet. (Briefly explain the role of each department and tell them they will receive a handout at the end of your presentation that explains more fully the role of each department.)

   Slide 9: The next five departments are: (Highlight each department.)

Slide 10: And the final five departments are: (Highlight each department.)

Slide 11: Now that we know a little about the Executive Branch, let's talk briefly about the Legislative Branch of government.

Slide 12: The Legislative Branch consists of Congress. Congress has two parts—the Senate and the House of Representatives.

Slide 13: As shown on this slide, there are two senators elected from each state. They are elected for a term of six years. The terms of the senators are staggered so that one-third of the Senate seats are up for election every two years. With each state having two senators, each state is given equal representation regardless of size or population.

The House of Representatives, on the other hand, is based on the population of each state. As the population changes within states, the number of representatives allocated to that state may also change.

File tab > Print > Full Page Slides drop-down > Notes Pages > Print

2. Review slides 14–17. Create a note appropriate for each of these slides.
3. Print copies of your notes pages to have available for Lesson 77.
4. **Save as:** *75e pp*.

| LESSON 76 | **Enhance Slide Show Presentations with Audio** |

OUTCOMES

- Learn about various types of audio that can be inserted in a slide show
- Create a slide show with audio and automatic slide timing for playback

76B

Insert Audio in a Slide Show

Adding audio to a presentation is quite simple. You can add audio that has been downloaded to the computer, or you can record audio.

Follow these steps to add audio to the slide presentation that you are creating to enter in an art show.

Insert tab > Media > Audio

1. Open *74c pp*.
2. On the *Insert* tab in the Media group, click *Audio*, then click *Audio on My PC* (Figure 15-35). This should open to a folder with the music files you have downloaded to your PC, or you can navigate to this folder.

Figure 15-35 Audio

★TIP To have all slides use the same transition, click the first slide and then select the transition you want to use. After selecting the transition, click the *Apply To All* check box in the Timing group.

3. Click the downloaded audio you want to insert.
4. Click the *Insert* button in the Insert Audio dialog box. An audio speaker icon and playback controls are inserted in the slide, and the Audio Tools Playback tab is selected on the Ribbon. (If you don't see the Playback tab, double-click the speaker icon.)

5. Click the *Play* icon on the playback controls under the speaker icon to hear the beginning of your audio; then click *Pause* to stop the audio.
6. On the Playback tab in the Audio Options group, click the *Start* drop-down arrow and then click *Automatically* to have the recording start automatically when you start the slide show.
7. Click to check the box before *Play Across Slides* to have the audio play throughout the slide presentation.
8. Click to check the box before *Loop until Stopped* to have the audio play continuously throughout the slide presentation even if the audio finishes before the slide show has completed.
9. Click the box *Hide During Show* so that the speaker icon isn't showing on the slide when the slide show is presenting. See Figure 15-36.

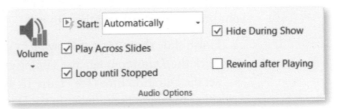

Figure 15-36 Audio Options

10. After trying several transitions, you have decided to go with the *Curtains* transition for all slides except the last one. The *Curtains* transition unveils each photo. Use *Vortex* for the last transition to give a dramatic ending. Apply these transitions.
11. Use the Animation feature to make the two photos on slide 9 come onto the screen one at a time using the *Wheel* animation and the *8 Spokes* Effect Option. To do this, click the first photo and select the *Wheel* animation. Then click *Effect Options* button and click *8 Spokes* (Figure 15-37). Repeat this procedure for the second photo.

Figure 15-37 Effect Options

TIP It is a good idea to periodically save your work in case of technology (computer or software) failure or even electrical outage. If such failures happen, you will need to recreate only what was lost since the last time the file was saved. For this activity, you will save the file here and then again in 76C using the same file name.

12. Use the Animation feature to make the three photos on slide 15 (or the last slide) come onto the screen one at a time using the *Wheel* animation and the *8 Spokes* Effect Option.
13. Preview the slide show to make sure audio, transitions, and animations are working correctly.
14. **Save as:** *76c Art Show pp* and continue with 76C to complete timing options and set up the slide show.

76C

Timing Options and Slide Show Setup

The rules for the art show state that the slide show must run automatically while the judges are completing their evaluations. You will need to set the amount of time you want each slide to remain on the screen and the duration of the transitions. You will also need to set the slide show up so that it automatically starts over when it advances to the last slide. Follow these steps to set your presentation up to do these things.

1. Finish slide show *76c Art Show pp* by completing the following steps.
2. Click the *Transitions* tab; the Timing group is on the right-hand side of the Ribbon.
3. Set the Duration time (see Figure 15-40) for the slide transition to 06.00. Notice you can either highlight the number in the Duration box and key **6**, or you can use the up or down arrows to advance it to 06.00.
4. Click *Apply To All* so that the duration is set for 06.00 on all slides.
5. Set the amount of time you want each slide to remain on the screen to 8 seconds (00:08.00) by using the up or down arrows following the word *After*.
6. Click *Apply To All* to set the time for 8 seconds for all slides to remain on the screen. Note that this also changed the transition for the last slide to *Curtains*. You will need to change it back to *Vortex*.
7. If there is a check mark in the box before *On Mouse Click*, click the mark to remove it. When you are done, the Timing group should look like the one in Figure 15-38.

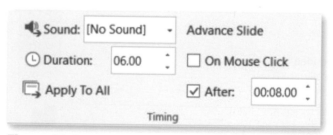

Figure 15-38 Timing group

8. Next set the slide show to repeat itself after advancing to the last slide. Click the *Slide Show tab*.
9. In the Set Up group, click *Set Up Slide Show*.
10. In the Set Up Show dialog box, click *Browsed by an individual (window)*.
11. Click the *Loop continuously until 'Esc'* box.
12. Under Advance slides, check that the *Using timings, if present* circle is selected. See Figure 15-39.

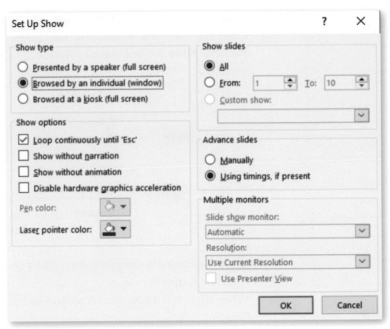

Figure 15-39 Set up slide show

13. Click *OK*.
14. Play the slide show to verify transitions, audio, and that the slide show loops continuously. Tap *Esc* to stop the slide show.
15. **Save as: *76c Art Show pp*.**

76D

Create Slide Show with Recorded Narrative and Automatic Slide Timing

Insert tab > Media > Audio > Record Audio

★TIP Audio is not recorded during transitions, so a second of silence needs to be included at the beginning and end of the recording to make sure the narration is not cut off when transitioning between slides.

Recorded audio can be inserted in a slide show to replace having an actual speaker present for parts or all of the slide show. If no speaker is physically present, the slide show will need to be set up to run automatically. Each slide can be set up to have its own recording. This makes it easy to make changes to the narrative on an individual slide rather than having to re-record the entire audio. If each slide has its own recording, it is also much easier to add additional slides at any time. It also makes it easy to update the slide show whenever needed.

A slide show on the Gettysburg Address has been started, but still needs Civil War pictures, narration, timing, and slide show set up. Complete the following steps to finalize the slide show.

1. Print a copy of the script (*df 76d script*). The script is also shown after these steps.
2. Open *df 76d Gettysburg pp*.
3. Search the Internet and use the Screenshot feature or use Online Pictures to add pictures of the Civil War to slides 6–9.
4. For all slides use the *Reveal* transition. (Click *Apply To All* in the Timing group after selecting the *Reveal* transition on the first slide to automatically put the *Reveal* transition between all slides.)
5. In the Timing group, click *On Mouse Click* to remove the check in the box.
6. In the Timing group, click the box before *After* to put a check in it. Then key **2.00** in the box or use the up arrow to put in 2.00 seconds. Click *Apply To All* so that slides will advance automatically after 2 seconds rather than On Mouse Click. (When there is a recording on the slide, the slide won't advance until the recording has finished playing.)

---

7. Click *slide 2* in the Thumbnail pane, the first slide to have a recorded narrative.
8. Open the Record Sound dialog box (Insert > Media > Audio > Record Audio). Change the Name to **Slide 2**. See Figure 15-40.

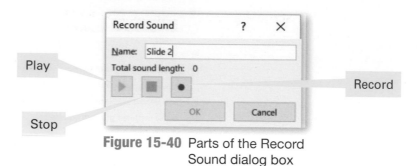

Figure 15-40 Parts of the Record Sound dialog box

9. Click the *Record* button (red dot), wait a second, and then record the narrative for slide 2 from the script.
10. When done recording, wait a second and stop recording by clicking the *Stop* button (square).
11. Preview the recording by clicking the *Play* button. If you are not satisfied, click the *Record* button and re-record the narrative for the slide.
12. Once you are satisfied with the recording, click *OK* to save the recording.
13. Complete the recordings for the remaining slides using the same procedure.
14. Click the *Slide Show* tab. In the Set Up group, click *Set Up Slide Show*.
15. For *Show type* select *Browsed by an individual (window)*.
16. For *Show Options* select *Loop continuously until 'Esc'*.
17. *Show slides* should be set for *All*, and *Advance slides* should be set for *Using timings, if present*. See Figure 15-41.

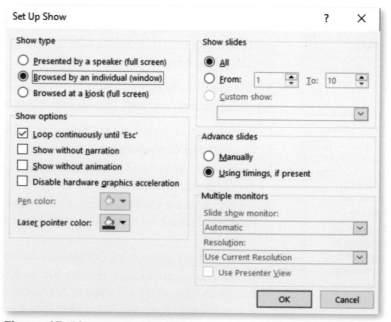

Figure 15-41 Set up slide show

18. Click *OK* to save your settings.
19. Preview the slide show to make sure it runs continuously and that all recordings are working.
20. **Save as:** *76d Gettysburg pp*.

Script for the Gettysburg Address by Abraham Lincoln slide presentation

Slide 2:   Abraham Lincoln is one of the best-known presidents of the United States. He was our sixteenth president and held office from 1861 until 1865, when he was assassinated.

Slide 3:   The Gettysburg Address is a speech delivered by President Lincoln at the dedication of the Gettysburg National Cemetery to honor those who died in the Battle of Gettysburg during the Civil War.

Slide 4:   Four score and seven years ago our fathers brought forth on this continent, a new nation, conceived in Liberty, and dedicated to the proposition that all men are created equal.

Slide 5:   Now we are engaged in a great civil war, testing whether that nation, or any nation so conceived and so dedicated, can long endure. We are met on a great battlefield of that war.

Slide 6:   We have come to dedicate a portion of that field, as a final resting place for those who here gave their lives that that nation might live. It is altogether fitting and proper that we should do this.

Slide 7:   But, in a larger sense, we cannot dedicate—we cannot consecrate—we cannot hallow—this ground. The brave men, living and dead, who struggled here, have consecrated it, far above our poor power to add or detract.

Slide 8:   The world will little note, nor long remember what we say here, but it can never forget what they did here. It is for us the living, rather, to be dedicated here to the unfinished work which they who fought here have thus far so nobly advanced.

Slide 9:   It is rather for us to be here dedicated to the great task remaining before us—that from these honored dead we take increased devotion to that cause for which they gave the last full measure of devotion—that we here highly resolve that these dead shall not have died in vain—that this nation, under God, shall have a new birth of freedom—and that government of the people, by the people, for the people, shall not perish from the earth.

LESSON 77   Deliver an Effective Presentation

OUTCOMES
- Learn the keys for delivering an effective presentation
- Practice the keys for delivering an effective presentation
- Deliver an effective presentation with a slide show

77B

Keys for Delivering an Effective Presentation

Speaker Notes

The notes that you created for the *Government of the United States of America* presentation (75E) should only be used as an aid when you are practicing your presentation. They should remind you of what you want to say during your practice sessions.

You will know when you have practiced the presentation enough, because you will be able to give the presentation by quickly looking at the slides (and then right back at the audience) as they appear on the screen. The words on the slides will act as an outline to remind you of the key points you want to make.

Don't be concerned about giving the presentation word for word as it appears in the notes. If you do, it sounds memorized. Memorized speeches come across as unnatural; the speaker is not able to develop a rapport with the audience.

However, there is one part of the speech that you should consider memorizing. Experts generally advise speakers to memorize the first sentence. This allows you to have a strong opening and come across as knowledgeable and confident. If you memorize the first sentence, practice it so that it seems natural. This can be done by pausing in appropriate places and using vocal variety—speed, volume.

Definitely don't make the mistake that is often made by beginning presenters—bringing the speaker notes to the podium and then reading to, rather than presenting to, the audience. Speakers who read to their audience are not as credible as those who speak to their audience.

By being well prepared and only glancing at the screen as the next slide comes up, you come across as natural. This also allows you to focus on the audience rather than on your notes.

Keys for Effective Delivery

Review the tips in Chapter 8, Lesson 47-48D on pages 8-28 to 8-32 for effectively delivering a presentation.

77C

Practice Giving a Presentation

Using the suggestions in the previous sections and in Chapter 8 for delivering a presentation, practice giving the *Government of the United States of America* presentation that you created in Lessons 74 and 75.

77D

Deliver an Effective Presentation

COLLABORATION

1. Open **df 77d eval form** and review the form that will be used to evaluate your presentations in this unit.
2. Break up into groups of three. Each student in your group will give the presentation that was developed in Lessons 74 and 75. While one student is giving the presentation, the other two will evaluate it using the evaluation form.

1. Open *df Music of the Four Seasons Performance*.
2. There are 18 slides in the presentation, of which eight are slides with the Blank layout. Create the eight slides shown in Figure 15-42. The number of the blank slide in the data file should match the slide number shown in the left-hand column when it is created. You will need to change the layout for the slides to correspond to the slides as shown in the figure. Use *df McIntyre Music Photo File* for the photos shown in the slides. The Design Ideas may be slightly different than those shown here but should include the same information and photos.
3. Add the transitions and animations that are indicated in the left-hand column for each slide. On slides where animation occurs, you will need to increase the time settings so that the text stays on the screen long enough for the audience to read the text.
4. Insert appropriate music that will *Play Across Slides, Loop until Stopped,* and *Hide During Show*.
5. Save as: *Assessment 8 - Student Name*

Slide 3 (Morph transition)	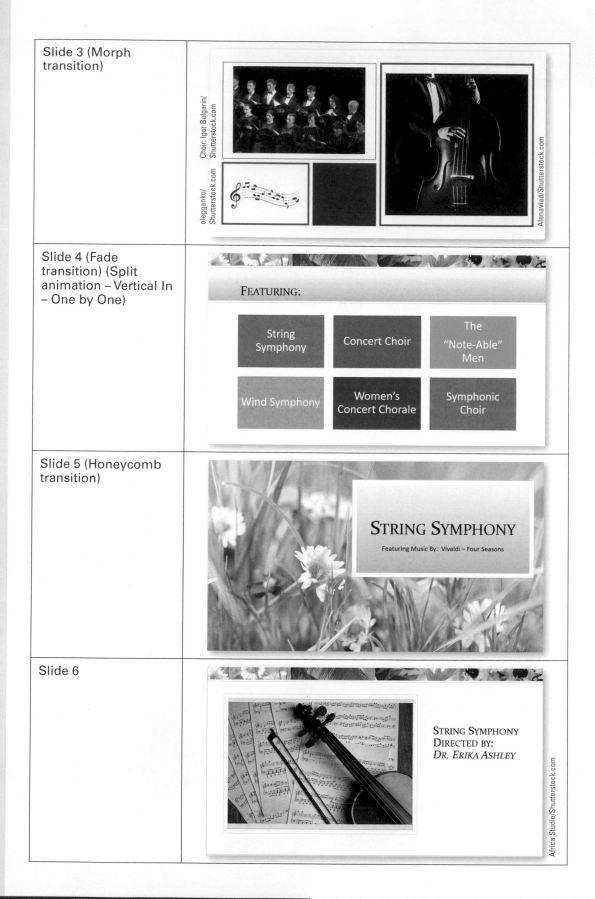
Slide 4 (Fade transition) (Split animation – Vertical In – One by One)	
Slide 5 (Honeycomb transition)	
Slide 6	

Slide 7 (Gallery transition) (Fly In animation – From Bottom – By Paragraph)	**AN ALL SEASONS CELEBRATION OF MUSIC**
	
	▪ Spring
	  ▪ Featuring Marguerite Larson, Maestro Violinist
	▪ Autumn
	  ▪ Featuring Colton Van Parks, Maestro Violinist
	▪ Summer
	  ▪ Featuring Camila Richert, Maestro Violinist
	▪ Winter
	  ▪ Featuring Jackson Ferge, Maestro Violinist
	
	Violoin
	
	Violoin: GraphicsRF/Shutterstock.com

Slide 8	**WOMEN'S CONCERT CHORALE**
Slide 9 (Gallery transition)	**WOMEN'S CONCERT CHORALE DIRECTED BY: DR. GAVIN MARAVICH** Double tap to add text Sunward Art/Shutterstock.com
Slide 10	**A SUMMER CELEBRATION OF MUSIC** ♫ Summertime ♫ A Summer Song ♫ I Will Remember You ♫ Stars and Stripes Forever Allies Interactive/Shutterstock.com

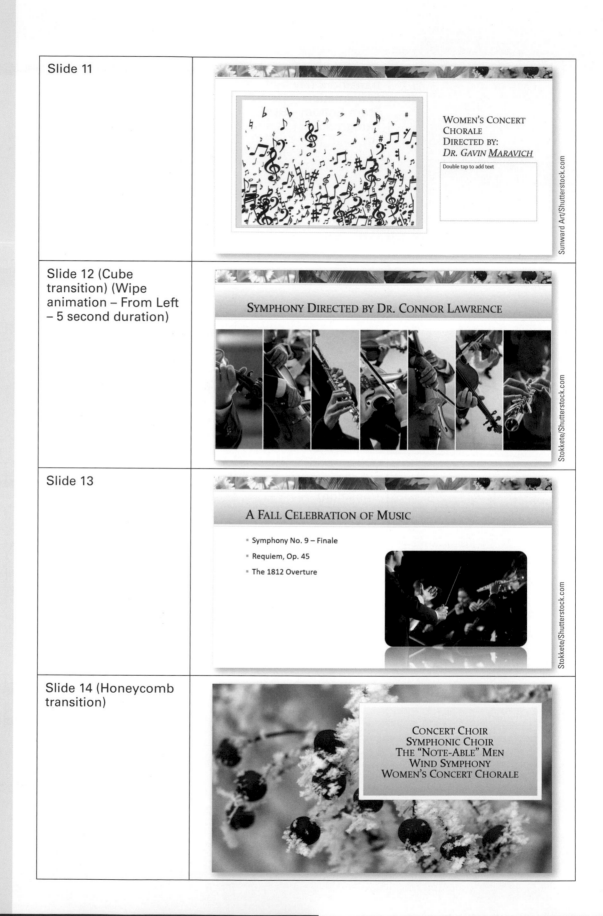

Slide 11	
Slide 12 (Cube transition) (Wipe animation – From Left – 5 second duration)	
Slide 13	
Slide 14 (Honeycomb transition)	

Slide 15 (Wind transition) (Use *Shapes* to create lines between photos. Use *Picture Border* on the *Format* tab to add box around the music notes. Use *Shape Fill* on the *Format* tab and change fill on text box to *black*. Change letter color to *white*.)	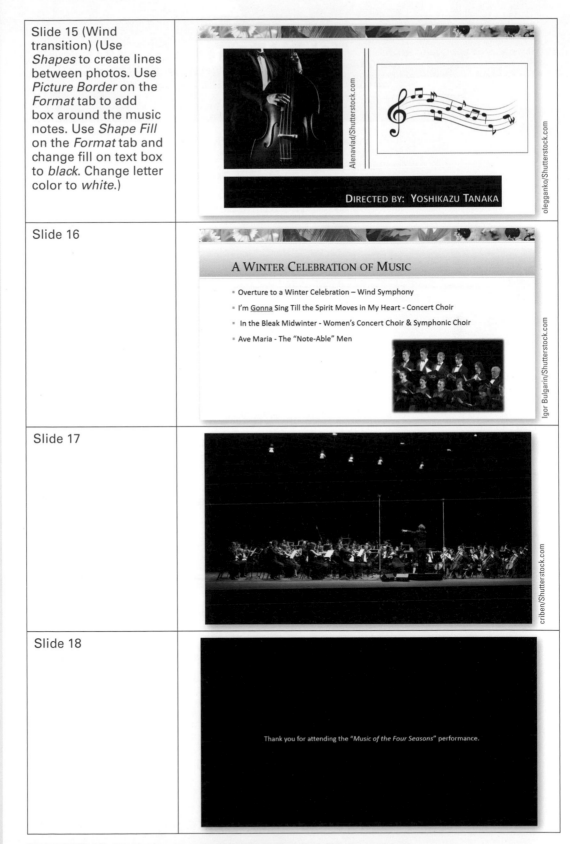
Slide 16	
Slide 17	
Slide 18	

Figure 15-42 Slides for Assessment 8: Enhanced Presentations

Skill Builder 14

Warmup

alphabet 1 Dave and Jackson may win the next big prize for our racquet club.

3rd/1st rows 2 Anna needs to use a little more effort to boost her keying skill.

speed 3 The eight men in the shanty paid for a big bus to go to the city.

gwam 1' | 1 | 2 | 3 | 4 | 5 | 6 | 7 | 8 | 9 | 10 | 11 | 12 | 13 |

B

Technique: Letter Keys

Key each line twice.

TIP Limit keystroking action to the fingers; keep hands and arms motionless.

Emphasize continuity and rhythm with curved, upright fingers.

R Raindrops bore down upon three robbers during the February storm.

S The Mets, Astros, Reds, Twins, Jays, and Cubs sold season passes.

T Trent bought the teal teakettle on the stove in downtown Seattle.

U Ursula usually rushes to the music museum on Tuesday, not Sunday.

V Vivacious Eve viewed seven vivid violets in the vases in the van.

W We swore we would work with the two wonderful kids for two weeks.

X Rex Baxter explained the extra excise tax to excited expatriates.

Y Yes, Ky is very busy trying to justify buying the yellow bicycle.

Z Dazed, Zelda zigzagged to a plaza by the zoo to see a lazy zebra.

gwam 1' | 1 | 2 | 3 | 4 | 5 | 6 | 7 | 8 | 9 | 10 | 11 | 12 | 13 |

C

Technique: Tabs

1. Set left tabs at 1.5", 3", and 4.5".
2. Key the copy at the right, using the *Tab* key to move from column to column.

				words
North Carolina	North Dakota	Ohio	Oklahoma	8
Raleigh	Bismarck	Columbus	Oklahoma City	16
Oregon	Pennsylvania	Rhode Island	South Carolina	26
Salem	Harrisburg	Providence	Columbia	33
South Dakota	Tennessee	Texas	Utah	40
Pierre	Nashville	Austin	Salt Lake City	48
Vermont	Virginia	Washington	West Virginia	56
Montpelier	Richmond	Tacoma	Charleston	64
Wisconsin	Wyoming			67
Madison	Cheyenne			71

D

Speed Forcing Drill
gwam

Key each line once at top speed; then try to complete each sentence on the 15", 12", or 10" call as directed by your instructor. Force speed to higher levels as you move from sentence to sentence.

Emphasis: high-frequency balanced-hand words

	gwam	15"	12"	10"
Janel may go to the dock to visit the eight girls.		40	50	60
She is to go with them to the city to see the dog.		40	50	60
The sorority girls paid for the auto to go to the city.		44	55	66
She is to go to the city with us to sign the six forms.		44	55	66
Dick may go to the big island to fix the auto for the widow.		48	60	72
Hank and the big dog slept by the antique chair on the dock.		48	60	72
Rick is to make a turn to the right at the big sign for downtown.		52	65	78
Vivian may go with us to the city to do the work for the auditor.		52	65	78

E

Skill Check

1. Key a 1' timing on ¶ 1; determine *gwam*.

2. Add 2–4 *gwam* to the rate attained in step 1; determine quarter-minute checkpoints from the chart below.

3. Key two 1' guided timings on ¶ 1 to increase speed.

4. Practice ¶ 2 in the same way.

5. Key two 3' timings on ¶s 1 and 2 combined; determine *gwam* and the number of errors.

Quarter-Minute Checkpoints

gwam	1/4'	1/2'	3/4'	Time
16	4	8	12	16
20	5	10	15	20
24	6	12	18	24
28	7	14	21	28
32	8	16	24	32
36	9	18	27	36
40	10	20	30	40

A all letters used

	gwam	3'	

Extraordinary would be an appropriate word to use to | 3 | 70

describe Michaelangelo. It would be a really good word to | 7 | 74

express how an individual might feel about the statue of David. | 11 | 78

It would also be an excellent choice of words for describing | 15 | 82

the exquisite works of art on the ceiling of the Sistine Chapel. | 20 | 87

It would be just as fine a word to use to describe the dome of | 24 | 91

Saint Peter's Basilica. Each of these outstanding works of art | 28 | 95

was completed by Michelangelo, quite an extraordinary person. | 32 | 99

The paintings, sculptures, and architecture of this man | 36 | 103

are recognized throughout the world. Michelangelo was born in | 40 | 107

Caprese, Italy, but spent much of his early life in the city | 44 | 111

of Florence. Here he spent a great deal of time in the | 47 | 114

workshops of artists. His father did not approve of his doing | 52 | 118

so, because artists were considered to be manual laborers. His | 56 | 122

father considered this to be beneath the dignity of his family | 60 | 127

members. This did not stop the young artist, who would | 63 | 130

eventually become one of the greatest of all times. | 67 | 134

Planning for Your Career 5

Application Forms and Post-interview Documents

OUTCOMES

- Prepare an employment application form
- Prepare an interview follow-up letter

Employment Application Forms

Many companies require an applicant to complete an **application form** even though a resume and application letter have been received. Applicants often fill in forms at the company, using a pen to write on a printed form or keying information into an **online employment application form** (see Figure PC5-1). You should strive to provide information that is accurate, complete, legible, and neat.

Much of the information required for the application form is likely to be on your resume and reference list; therefore, you should have copies of both available when you complete the employment application form. However, you should be prepared to provide information such as Social Security number, name and telephone number of your present supervisor, grade point averages, pay rates, etc. that is not on your resume or reference list.

Sometimes applicants may take an application form home, complete it, and return it by mail or in person. In this case, the information should be printed in blue or black ink on the form. To lessen the chance of error on a printed application, make a copy of the blank form to complete as a rough draft.

1. Study the sample employment application form in Figure PC5-1, paying particular attention to the information you would need to complete the form.
2. Open *df pc5 form*. Print one copy of the form.

Employment Application

Your application will be considered active for 30 days—to be considered for a job after that you must reapply.

PERSONAL INFORMATION

Name (Last, First)		Social Security Number	Current Date ___/___/___	Home Phone:
Address (Number, Street, City, State, Zip Code)			Date of Birth: ___/___/___	Cell Phone:

Are you a citizen of the U.S. or do you have a legal right to work in the U.S.? ☐ Yes ☐ No		Have you ever been convicted of a felony? ☐ Yes ☐ No If yes, explain
Are You Employed Now? ☐ Yes ☐ No	If yes, may we inquire of your present employer? ☐ Yes ☐ No	If yes, give name and number of person to call
Position Desired	☐ Full-Time ☐ Part-Time ☐ Summer ☐ Temporary ☐ Anytime	Available start date: ___/___/___ Total hours available each week: _____ Hours available each day: ___ M ___ T ___ W ___ R ___ F ___ S ___ S

Education

	Name and Location of Schools Attended	Years	Program	GPA	Graduated?
College					☐ Yes ☐ No
High School					☐ Yes ☐ No
Other					☐ Yes ☐ No

Subjects/research, special training, activities, honors, &/or skills directly related to position desired

Employment History (list last position first & you may include volunteer work)

From - To (Mo. & Yr.)	Name and Address	Position	Rate of Pay

References (list three persons not related to you, whom you have known at least one year)

Name	Address	Phone Number

I certify that the information given in this application is true and complete o the best of my knowledge. I understand that I shall not become an employee until I have signed an employment agreement with the final approval of the employer and that such employment will be subject to verification of previous employment data provided in this application, any related documents, or data sheet. I know that a report may be made that will include information concerning any factor the employer might find relevant to the position for which I am applying, and that I can make a written request for additional information as to the nature and scope of the report if one is made.

Applicant's Signature _____   Date _____

Figure PC5-1 Application forms can be printed or filled out online

3. Assume you have been interviewed for the customer service position at Meriden College (see job posting in Planning for Your Career 3, Chapter 13, page 13-XX) and have been asked to fill out an employment application form after the interview. You may use your reference list and resume to complete the form.

4. If you could not provide applicable requested information, make a list of the needed information and describe where you might find it and how you will make sure that information is available if needed in the future. Save your list as *pc5 list*.

5. Submit your completed employment application form and list to your instructor.

Interview Follow-up Letter

An **interview follow-up letter** is sent to the person(s) interviewing you to thank them for the time given and courtesies extended to you during the job interview. The purpose of this letter is to let each interviewer know that you are still interested in the job, and it reminds him or her of your application and qualifications. This letter should be sent as an email attachment within 24 hours after the interview to increase the likelihood that it is received before an applicant is selected for the job. Because many people do not send a follow-up letter, doing so may give you a competitive advantage when you are one of the top finalists for a position.

1. Key the follow-up letter with the text shown below as a personal-business letter in block style with mixed punctuation.

2. **Save as:** *pc5 follow-up letter*.

150 Preston Court | Meriden, CT 06450-0403 | May 25, 20-- | Ms. Jenna St. John | Personnel Director | Harper Insurance Company | 3 Colony Street | Meriden, CT 06450-4127 | Dear Ms. St. John

Thank you for discussing the customer service opening at Regency Insurance Company. I have a much better understanding of the position after meeting with you and Mr. Meade.

Mr. Meade was extremely helpful in explaining the specific job responsibilities. My previous jobs and my business technology classes required me to complete many of the tasks that he mentioned. With minimal training, I believe I could be an asset to your company.

Even though I realize it will be a real challenge to replace a person like Mr. Meade, it is a challenge that I will welcome. If there is further information that would be helpful as you consider my application, please let me know.

Sincerely, | Jennifer H. Greenawald

Figure PC5-2 Interview follow-up letter

Compose Interview Follow-up Letter

1. Assume you have been interviewed for the Meriden College customer support position (see page 13-XX).

2. Using the follow-up letter you just keyed as an example, compose a follow-up letter.

3. **Save as:** *pc5 follow-up letter 2*.

Communication Skills 8:
Semicolon and Italics Usage

ACTIVITY 1: Internal Punctuation: Semicolon and Italics

1. Study each of the six rules.
   a. Key the *Learn* line beneath each rule, noting how the rule is applied.
   b. Key the *Apply* lines, using semicolons and italics correctly.

Internal Punctuation: Semicolon

Rule 1: Use a semicolon to separate two or more independent clauses in a compound sentence when the conjunction is omitted.

Learn   1   Parker enjoys tennis; he takes lessons and practices every day.

Apply   2   Ed likes biology he is especially interested in human genetics.

Apply   3   Ashley Nicole is a junior in college she is studying economics.

Rule 2: Use a semicolon to separate independent clauses when they are joined by a conjunctive adverb (*however, therefore, consequently,* etc.).

Learn   4   Vi is allergic to chocolate; however, she likes how it tastes.

Apply   5   I like problem solving consequently I stay calm under pressure.

Apply   6   Lee builds beautiful furniture therefore many want to hire him.

Rule 3: Use a semicolon to separate a series of phrases or clauses (especially if they contain commas) that are introduced by a colon).

Learn   7   I work in these cities: Tampa, FL; Athens, GA; and Napa, CA.

Apply   8   The overcharges include: May, $175 June, $250 and July $273.

Apply   9   The top earners are: Vine, $2,470 Gray, $3,881 and Lark, $4,000.

Rule 4: Place the semicolon outside the closing quotation mark. (A period and a comma are placed inside the closing quotation mark.)

Learn   10   Ms. Carlin talked about "needs"; Mr. Carlin explained "wants."

Apply   11   He said, "I can do this" she said, "Together we can do this"

Apply   12   Jack's mom said, "be honest and work hard" Jack said, "I will"

Internal Punctuation: *Italics*

Rule 5: Use italics to indicate titles/names of books, movies, magazines, and newspapers. (Titles and names may also be keyed in ALL CAPS or underlined.)

Learn   13   He cited articles from *The New York Post* and *The Boston Globe.*

Apply   14   Be sure to read the book Thomas Jefferson: The Art of Power.

Apply   15   If you love nature, you will probably enjoy Natural Geographic.

Rule 6: Use italics to call attention to words or phrases (or use quotation marks or underline).

Learn   16   Some students incorrectly use <u>their</u>, <u>there</u>, and <u>they're</u>.

Apply   17   *The New York Times* is often referred to casually as The Times.

Apply   18   The United States flag was nicknamed Old Glory.

> **NOTE**   **Use a continuous underline unless each word is to be considered separately as shown below. Do not underline punctuation marks (commas, for example) between separately underlined words.**

(continued on next page)

2. Key Proofread & Correct, using semicolons and italics correctly.
   a. Check answers.
   b. Using the rule number(s) at the left of each line, study the rule relating to each error you made.
   c. Rekey each incorrect line, using semicolons and italics correctly.

Save as: CS8 ACTIVITY1

Proofread & Correct

Rules

1	1	Owen enjoys playing the piano he practices every day.
1	2	Maria Gonzalez Gomez had the highest grade Cooper Sands had the next highest.
2	3	Justin works 30 hours a week however, he still has a 3.75 grade point average.
3	4	The top scorers were: Jackson, 36 Buxton, 27 and Washington, 22.
2	5	The concert starts at 7:30 p.m. however you should be in your seat by 7:45. p.m.
3	6	They are considering these locations Denver, CO Seattle, WA and Dallas, TX.
1, 4	7	Erika said, "I won the race" Jamison said, "Congratulation, that is great"
1, 4	8	Robert Frost authored "The Road Not Taken" Edgar Allen Poe authored "The Raven"
5	9	Jane want to see "Start Wars: The Last Jedi" Jay wanted to see "Pitch Perfect 3"
6	10	California is called "The Golden State" Texas is called "The Lone Star State"

ACTIVITY 2: Word Choice

Study the definitions of the words.
2. Key the *Learn* line noting the correct usage of each word.
3. Key the *Apply* lines, inserting the correct word(s).

Save as: CS8 ACTIVITY2

| **principal** (n/adj) a person in authority; a capital sum; main, primary | **stationary** (adj) fixed in position, course, or mode; unchanging in condition |
| **principle** (n) a rule | **stationery** (n) paper and envelopes used for processing personal and business documents |

Learn 1 The new **principal** is guided by the **principle** of fairness.

Apply 2 The (principal/principle) reason I'm here is to record the talk.

Apply 3 What (principal/principle) of law was applied in the case?

Learn 1 We store **stationery** on **stationary** shelves in the supply room.

Apply 2 Desks remain (stationary/stationery), but we'll shift the files.

Apply 3 Were you able to get a good discount on (stationary/stationery)?

ACTIVITY 3: Write to Learn

Complete as directed.

Save as: CS8 ACTIVITY3

Write a paragraph or two explaining how you would respond during a job interview to the following question:

What are your plans for the next five years?

ACTIVITY 4: Speaking

COLLABORATION

The number of people in the United States over the age of 65 is increasing. The quality of life for many elderly people is dependent upon volunteers. With several of your class members, discuss what you could do to help improve the quality of life for elderly individuals in your area who could use your assistance. Once you have discussed ways to improve the quality of life for senior citizens, prepare a few comments to share with the rest of the class.

Before You Move On

1. Rather than have a slide appear in its entirety, _____ can be used to make text, graphics, and other objects appear one at a time. LO 75B

2. A _____ is used to take you from the current location in the electronic file to another location in the file, in another file, or on the web. Application Guide

3. Slide _____ is the term used to describe how the display changes from one slide to the next. LO 75C

4. Presenter View includes six features. Name four of them. Application Guide

5. As you create a slide show, you should consider design tip Do's and Don'ts. List three of the Do's and Don'ts that were presented in this chapter. Application Guide

Answer **True** or **False** to questions 6–15.

6. Use complete sentences on all slides rather than keywords and phrases. Application Guide

7. It is better to use two slides than to overcrowd one slide. Application Guide

8. Pictures are too distracting; they should only be used in a presentation when absolutely necessary. Application Guide

9. Audio should be used in every presentation. Application Guide

10. You should key everything you are going to say during a presentation in the Notes section of the slide so you can read it to the audience when you give the presentation. LO 77B

11. It is easy to update a slide that contains audio because each slide can have its own recording. LO 76D

12. Slides from one file can be copied and pasted with slides in another file. LO 74E

13. The design theme colors can be changed by using the Shapes feature. LO 74D

14. You can use the Screen Clipping feature to include only part of what is on a photo. LO 74C

15. One of the animations is called *Curtains*. LO 75C

CHAPTER 16

Preparing and Analyzing Financial Worksheets

Lesson 78 Formatting and Worksheet Skills
Lesson 79 Cell References
Lesson 80 "What If," IF Function, and Formatting

Lesson 81 Integrating Worksheet and Word Processing Documents
Lesson 82 Spreadsheet Applications
Assessment 9 Enhanced Worksheets

Application Guide

Change Worksheet Views

View tab > Workbook Views
or
Status bar icons

When a new worksheet is opened, it is displayed in **Normal View** with the formula bar, gridlines, and row and column headings displayed. Normal View is used mostly when entering and formatting data. Other views are available: **Page Layout View** lets you focus on how your worksheet will look when it is printed and is used to see headers and footers; **Page Break Preview** lets you see how data appears on pages and is used to insert page breaks. These three views can be accessed from the **status bar** (shown in Figure 16-1) or from the **View tab** (shown in Figure 16-2).

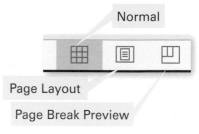

Figure 16-1 Status bar views

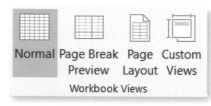

Figure 16-2 View tab views

Freeze/Unfreeze Columns and Rows

View tab > Window > Freeze Panes

Often an entire worksheet cannot be seen on the screen because when you scroll through the worksheet, the information in the column and row headings disappears from the screen. You can **freeze** the column and row headings so they remain visible as you scroll to other parts of the worksheet. Figure 16-3 describes three choices that can be selected.

Rows and columns can be unfrozen when the feature is no longer needed.

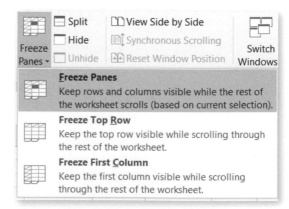

Figure 16-3 Freeze panes, top row, or first column

Increase or Decrease Cell Indents

Home tab > Alignment > Increase Indent or Decrease Indent

Use the **Increase Indent** and **Decrease Indent** features shown in Figure 16-4 to help distinguish categories or set text apart within cells. The amount of the indent can be increased or decreased by clicking the proper Indent button or changing the indent setting in the Format Cells dialog box.

Figure 16-4 Decrease & Increase Indents

Figure 16-5 shows text that has had indents increased and decreased.

	A
1	This text is not indented from the left.
2	This text is indented once from the left.
3	This text is indented three from the left.
4	This text was indented three times and then the indent was decreased once.
5	This text was indented four times and then the indent was decreased once.

Figure 16-5 Increase or decrease cell indent examples

Insert Headers and Footers

Insert tab > Text > Header & Footer

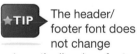

The header/footer font does not change automatically when font changes are made in the worksheet.

Worksheets can contain headers and footers in much the same way as word processing documents can (see Figure 16-6). You can select predefined headers/footers from the spreadsheet software, or you can create custom headers/footers. The font, font style, and font size can also be specified. In addition, the header/footer may be left-, center-, or right-aligned.

Figure 16-6 Header & Footer

Special elements, identified in Figure 16-7, can be entered in the header/footer to print the date, time, page number, filename, etc.

Figure 16-7 Header & Footer Elements

Features in the Options group (see Figure 16-8) can be selected so the footer does not appear on the first page of a worksheet or is different on odd and even pages.

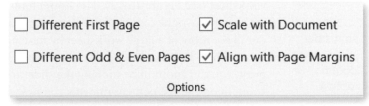

Figure 16-8 Header & Footer Options

Set Print Area

Page Layout tab >
Page Setup > Print Area >
Set Print Area

File tab > Print > Settings >
Make selection

By default, most spreadsheet software prints all the information displayed in a worksheet. If you need to print only a portion, select the range of cells you want to print, select the *Set Print Area* command (see Figure 16-9). When the Print command is selected, only that portion of the worksheet you selected will print. Use the *Clear Print Area* to remove the selection.

The Print Active Sheets options (Print Active Sheets, Print Entire Workbook, and Print Selection) in the Settings section of the Print screen (see Figure 16-10) can be used to set what is to be printed.

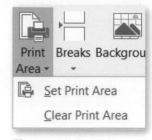

Figure 16-9 Set Print Area/Clear Print Area

Figure 16-10 Print Active Sheets options on the Print screen

Vertical Cell Alignment

Home tab > Alignment >
Top Align, Middle Align,
or Bottom Align

In addition to aligning text horizontally within a cell by using the Align Left, Center, and Align Right buttons in the Home tab Alignment group, you can specify vertical alignment with the Top Align, Middle Align, or Bottom Align buttons in the same group. Figure 16-11 shows that Middle Align has been selected for vertical alignment and Center has been selected for horizontal alignment.

Figure 16-11 Alignment options

Zooming the View

Zoom slider on status bar
or
View tab > Zoom >
Select Zoom option

The Zoom feature lets you control what you see in a worksheet (see Figure 16-12). The Zoom tools are located at the bottom-right corner of the status bar. You can zoom out to see more of a large worksheet by moving the slider toward the – icon or clicking the – icon. To enlarge the print, you can zoom in by moving the slider toward the + icon or clicking the + icon. As you zoom in or out, the percent informs you how much the magnification deviates from 100%, which is the normal magnification.

Figure 16-12 Zoom slider on the status bar

You can also use the Zoom features on the View tab to set a specific Zoom level, return the Zoom to 100%, or Zoom in to a selection.

LESSON 78 — Formatting and Worksheet Skills

OUTCOMES

- Use AutoFill
- Change text orientation
- Organize worksheets by renaming and repositioning them
- Insert and delete worksheets
- Convert text to columns

78A–82A

Warmup

Key each line twice at the beginning of each lesson; first for control, then speed.

alphabet 1 Zebb likely will be top judge for the exclusive quarter-mile run.

figures 2 This association has 16,873 members in 290 chapters in 45 states.

speed 3 Jamel is proficient when he roams right field with vigor and pep.

gwam 1' | 1 | 2 | 3 | 4 | 5 | 6 | 7 | 8 | 9 | 10 | 11 | 12 | 13 |

78B

AutoFill

Information can be quickly copied to adjacent cells by using the *AutoFill* feature. By using the Fill Handle, data can be entered in a series or copied to adjacent cells. The Fill Handle is the black plus sign that appears when the pointer is positioned on the lower-right corner of the selected cell. AutoFill is frequently used to enter a series of numbers, days, months, etc. and to copy text, values, or formulas to adjacent cells.

Activity 1

1. Open *df 78b calendar*.
2. In cell A2, key **Sunday**.
3. Move the pointer over the lower right-hand corner of the cell to bring up the Fill Handle, which is the black plus sign as shown in Figure 16-13. Click and drag the Fill Handle to cell G2. The days of the week automatically fill in.

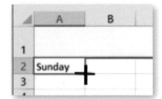

Figure 16-13 Fill Handle

4. Select *Heading 2* Cell Style for A2:G2 and select middle and center.
5. Set the row height at **25**; set the column width at **14**.
6. Select a light blue fill color for row 2.
7. In cell D3, key the number **1**. Drag the Fill Handle from D3 to G3. To make the numbers fill in consecutively, click the *Auto Fill Options* button and select *Fill Series* as shown in Figure 16-14.
8. In cell A4, key **5**. Drag the Fill Handle from A4 to G4 and select *Fill Series* in the Auto Fill Options. Repeat the procedure to complete the 31 days in January.
9. Highlight A3:G7 and change the font size to *14*; set the row height at *50*.
10. On the Page Layout tab in the Sheet Options group, select *Print* under Gridlines.
11. In the Page Setup group, change to *Landscape* orientation.
12. In the Page Setup group, use *Custom Margins* to center the worksheet horizontally and vertically on the page.

★TIP If the software inserts a series when you want a copy or a copy when you want a series, select the desired action in the AutoFill Options button that appears after the cells in the fill range have been selected.

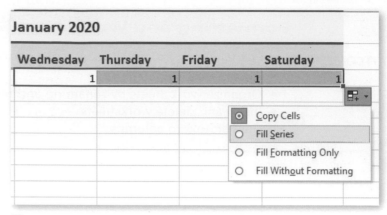

Figure 16-14 AutoFill options

13. Highlight *A1:G7*. Set this as the print area by clicking the *Print Area* button in the Page Setup group and selecting *Set Print Area*.
14. Print the calendar.
15. **Save as:** *78b calendar*.

Activity 2

1. Open a new blank worksheet.
2. In cell A1, key **5**; key **10** in A2.
3. Highlight A1:A2 and drag the Fill Handle to A12. Notice that each number increased by 5, the pattern that you established in cells A1 and A2.
4. Key **10** in B1 and **20** in B2. Highlight B1:B2 and drag the Fill Handle to B6.
5. In D1, key your name and tap *Enter*. Click in *D1* and copy (Ctrl + C) your name and paste (Ctrl + V) it in F1. Click in *H1* and paste. Tap *Esc*.
6. Key **5** in D8, **7** in E8, **3** in F8, **10** in D9, **2** in E9, and **10** in F9.
7. In G8, enter the formula **=D8+E8+F8**.
8. Copy the formula to D9. Notice that it adds D9 + E9 + F9.
9. Paste the formula in G10. Notice that a 0 comes up. Key **10** in D10, **5** in E10, and **20** in F10. Notice how it adds the amount in G10 each time a number is entered.
10. **Save as:** *78b auto fill*.

★TIP An easy way to add numbers in a row or column is to click the *AutoSum* button in the Editing group of the Home tab and tap *Enter*.

78C

Change Text Orientation

Home tab > Alignment > Orientation

Text can be rotated to various diagonal or vertical angles to change the orientation. The Text Orientation feature (see Figure 16-15) is used when column headings are longer than the information in the columns as shown in Figure 16-16. Rotated text is helpful when horizontal spacing needs to be reduced because it often takes less horizontal space but more vertical space.

Figure 16-15 Text orientation

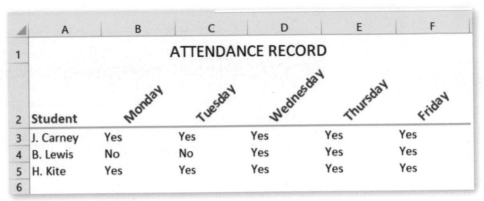

Figure 16-16 Rotated text

Activity 1

1. Open a new worksheet, and key the worksheet shown in Figure 16-16. Change the Text Orientation of the column headings to *Angle Counterclockwise*. Merge and center the heading and change it to 16 point. Adjust column widths to fit the contents and hide the gridlines.

2. **Save as:** *78c orientation1*.

Activity 2

1. Open *df 78c orientation2*.

2. AutoFill the remainder of column A as shown in the figure below using the Fill Handle.

3. Enter the numbers shown in the figure in columns C, D, and F using the Fill Handle. You will need to change one number in column C and maybe one number in column F depending on whether or not you AutoFilled F7.

4. Complete the columns B and E entries.

	A	B	C	D	E	F
1	Month	Albert	Mary Ann	Roberto	Yin Chi	Zeb
2	September	1	0	0	0	1
3	October	0	0	0	2	1
4	November	1	1	0	1	1
5	December	1	0	0	0	1
6	January	1	0	0	0	1
7	February	0	0	0	0	0

5. Center the column headings.

6. Use *Rotate Text Up* to rotate the column heading text for columns B through F.

7. Change the column headings from Rotate Text Up to *Angle Counterclockwise*, and left-align the headings.

8. **Save as:** *78c orientation2*.

Organize Sheets

Home tab > Cells >
Format > Select desired
Organize Sheets option
or
Right-click sheet tab and
select option

 **TIP** The quickest way to move a worksheet tab is by clicking it and dragging it to the desired position.

When a new Excel workbook is opened, it contains one worksheet by default. The worksheet has a **sheet tab** at the bottom left and it is named **Sheet1**. If you want to add one or more worksheets to the workbook, click the + (plus sign) to the right of the sheet tab once for each worksheet you want to add. Each sheet tab is given a name (Sheet2, Sheet3, etc.). You can access any of the worksheets by clicking its sheet tab.

Organize Sheets

Rename Sheet

Move or Copy Sheet...

Tab Color ▶

Figure 16-17 Organize Sheets options

Worksheet tabs can be renamed and/or colored using the Organize Sheets options (see Figure 16-17). The Organize Sheets features can also be used to move or copy worksheets. Access these features by clicking the *Format* button in the Cells group on the Home tab.

1. Open a new worksheet.
2. Add four additional worksheets to the workbook.
3. Rename Sheet1 **2022**, Sheet2 **2020**, Sheet3 **2021**, Sheet4 **2019**, and Sheet5 **2018**.
4. Reposition the worksheets so they are numbered consecutively starting with 2018 at the left.
5. Apply a different color to each worksheet tab.
6. **Save as: *78d sheet tabs*.**

Insert and Delete Sheets

Home tab > Cells >
Insert or Delete > Insert
Sheet or Delete Sheet

 TIP Sheets can be inserted or deleted by right-clicking on the sheet tab and then making the desired selection.

Additional worksheets can be inserted into a workbook by using the Insert Sheet feature, or existing sheets can be deleted from a workbook by using the Delete Sheet feature. The Insert Sheet feature enables you to keep related worksheets together in one workbook. For example, you might want to keep track of your savings on an annual basis over several years by having one worksheet for each year within the same workbook instead of creating a different file for each year. The Insert Sheet and the Delete Sheet features can be selected from the respective Insert or Delete drop-down lists in the Cells group of the Home tab (see Figure 16-18).

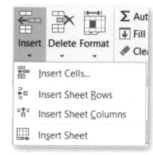

Figure 16-18 Insert sheet

1. Open *df 78e sheets*.
2. Delete the worksheet named *Loans*.
3. Insert a new worksheet, and name it **Contacts**.
4. Arrange the worksheets in alphabetical order from left to right.
5. Apply a color to each tab.
6. **Save as: *78e sheets*.**

78F

Convert Text to Columns

Data tab > Data Tools >
Text to Columns

The Convert Text to Columns feature helps you separate information entered in cells in one column into cells in multiple columns. For example, if the cells in a column contain first and last names, you can separate them so the first name appears in one column and the last name appears in a second column without rekeying the names. The *Convert Text to Columns Wizard* (see Figure 16-19) is used to make this change. The Wizard uses commas, tabs, spaces, etc. to separate the information.

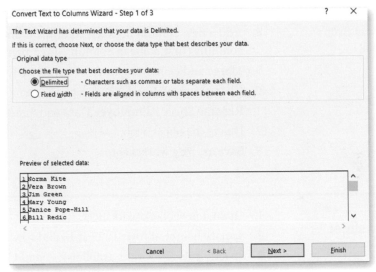

Figure 16-19 Convert Text to Columns Wizard

 **TIP** If there is not an empty column to the right of the column you are dividing, data in that column will be replaced, so make sure you add a column or ensure that the column to the right is empty before converting one text column to two columns.

TIP To remove the space before the state in the new column, use both comma and space as delimiters.

1. Open *df 78f convert*.
2. Insert a new column between columns A and B.
3. Complete steps 4–8 to convert the text in cells A1:A10 to two columns (A and B) by using the space between the names as the delimiter.
4. Highlight the text in A1:A10.
5. On the *Data* tab in the Data Tools group, select *Text to Columns*.
6. A screen appears that states that your data is delimited; click *Next*.
7. A screen displays that allows you to see how your text will look when you select a particular type of delimiter. Click the box in front of *Space*. If there are checks in any other boxes, click them to clear them. Click *Next*.
8. Change the Column data format to *Text*; click *Finish*. The last names should have been moved into column B.
9. Convert the text in cells C1:C10 to two columns (C and D) using the same Text to Columns procedure as in steps 5–8, but using the comma between the city and state as the delimiter.
10. **Save as:** *78f convert*.

Change Text and Worksheet Orientation

Home tab > Cells >
Format > Format Cells >
Special

1. Open *df 78g worksheet*.
2. In column B, use *AutoFill* to complete assigning consecutive payroll numbers (127–134).
3. Angle column heading text clockwise.
4. Make rows 2 through 9 a height of 32 pts.
5. Format column C numbers as Social Security numbers.
6. Display column D numbers as dates in the March 14, 2012 format. You will need to increase the width of the column to accommodate the new date format.
7. Display column E numbers as phone numbers.
8. Add a new column between columns A and B. Separate the text in column A into two columns (first name in column A; last name in column B).
9. Merge and center *Employee* in cells A1:B1. Adjust width of columns to fit contents.
10. Change orientation to landscape.
11. Rename Sheet 1 **Employee Data** and Sheet 2 **Payroll**. Color each tab.
12. Delete the Sheet 3 tab.
13. **Save as:** *78g worksheet*.

Format Worksheet

 TIP Use the *Format Painter* (Home tab, Clipboard group) to quickly copy formatting from one cell to another cell or cells.

1. Open a new blank worksheet.
2. Specify height of rows 1–27 at 18 and row 28 at 54.
3. Specify column widths as follows: A and C at 4, B and D at 10, E at 2, and F at 50.
4. Merge cells A1 to F1, and key **ANSWER SHEET**, centered in 16-pt. font.
5. Key **Item** in cells A2 and C2 and **Answer** in cells B2 and D2 using Center alignment.
6. In cell F2, key **SHORT ANSWER RESPONSES**, centered.
7. Merge the following cell ranges: F3:F10, F11:F18, F19:F27, and E2:E28.
8. Merge cells A28 to D28, and key **Student Name**, using Center and Top Align. Key **Subject and Period** in cell F28 with the same alignment.
9. Use AutoFill to enter numbers 1–25 in cell range A3:A27 and 26–50 in cell range C3:C27.
10. Key **ANSWER 1, ANSWER 2,** and **ANSWER 3** in the three large merged cell areas in column F, with ANSWER 1 being in the first merged cell. Use Center and Top Align for the text.
11. Center the worksheet vertically and horizontally on the page, and print with gridlines.
12. Compare the format of your worksheet to that shown in the figure on the next page.
13. **Save as:** *78h worksheet*.

ANSWER SHEET

	Item	Answers	Item	Answers	SHORT ANSWER RESPONSES
1					
2	Item	Answers	Item	Answers	
3	1		26		ANSWER 1
4	2		27		
5	3		28		
6	4		29		
7	5		30		
8	6		31		
9	7		32		
10	8		33		
11	9		34		ANSWER 2
12	10		35		
13	11		36		
14	12		37		
15	13		38		
16	14		39		
17	15		40		
18	16		41		
19	17		42		ANSWER 3
20	18		43		
21	19		44		
22	20		45		
23	21		46		
24	22		47		
25	23		48		
26	24		49		
27	25		50		
	Student Name				Subject and Period

LESSON 79 Cell References

- Use relative, absolute, mixed, and 3-D cell references

79B

Relative, Absolute, and Mixed Cell References

You have learned that spreadsheet software copies a formula across a row or up or down a column. As the formula is copied into new cells, its contents are automatically adjusted to reflect the new address and the addresses of other cells in the formula.

When formulas are copied in this manner, the software is using **relative cell referencing**. That is, the copy of the cell is related to its new address. For example, if cell D1 contains the formula =B1+C1, when this formula is copied to cell E2, it changes automatically to =C2+D2. Because cell E2 is down one row and one column over, the cells in the formula are also one row and one column over from the cells in the original formula.

Sometimes you do not want the software to change a formula to reflect its new address when copying it to other cells. In these instances, you use **absolute cell referencing**. Absolute cell referencing is used by keying a $ sign before the column and row reference in the cell address that is not to change. For example, if you want to divide all the numbers in column B by a number that is in cell A1, you would use absolute cell referencing in cell A1 by keying a $ before the A and a $ before the 1 ($A$1).

A **mixed cell reference** is one that maintains a reference to a specific row or column but not to both. For example, D$1 is a mixed cell address. The reference to column D is relative, and the reference to row 1 is absolute. When copied to other cells, the reference to column D will change, but the reference to row 1 will remain the same.

The chart below further summarizes the three different types of cell references.

Cell Reference	Example	Explanation
Relative	A1	Column A and row 1 *will change* when copied to a new cell.
Absolute	$A$1	Column A and row 1 *will not change* when copied to a new cell.
Mixed	A$1	Column A *will change* when copied to a new cell (relative), but row 1 will not change when copied (absolute).

1. Open **df 79b cell references**.
2. In cell D3, key **=A3+B3+C3** and then copy to cells D4:D7. Notice that the formula added the numbers in columns A–C across each row since relative cell referencing was used.
3. In cell E3, key **=$A$3+$B$3+$C$3** and then copy to cells E4:E7. Notice that the formula added the numbers in columns A, B, and C across the same row (row 3) because absolute cell referencing was used for the row.
4. In cell F3, key **=A$3+B$3+C3** and then copy to cells F4:F7. Notice that the formula always added the numbers in columns A and B, row 3, to each value in column C as the formula was copied to each row. Your worksheet should look like the one shown in Figure 16-20.
5. **Save as: 79b cell references**.

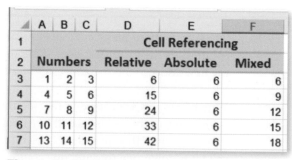

Figure 16-20 Relative, absolute, and mixed cell referencing

Application: Cell References

Home tab > Font > Fill Color drop-down arrow > Select desired color

Insert tab >Text > Header & Footer

1. Open *df 79c candy sales*.
2. Use the Auto Fill feature to complete cells A5:A14 with the room numbers. The first two room numbers have been entered.
3. Key the main heading as shown in the table below in row 1. Merge & Center the heading over cells A1:K1. Select *Heading 1* for the Cell Style.
4. Key row 2 as shown in the table on the next page, using the Fill Handle to add the days of the week after MON and TUE. Select *Heading 2* Cell Style for row 2. Select *Center* and *Middle* alignment.
5. Select the *Total* Cell Style for cells A15:K15.
6. Merge & Center cells A16:B16.
7. Select *Heading 2* Cell Style for A16:B16 and A17.
8. Calculate the total sales (Tot) for each room in column I and the sales for each day of the week in row 15.
9. Set column A width at **8**, columns B–I at **9**, and J at **10**.
10. Set row 1 height at **30**, row 2 at **20**, and rows 3–15 at **18**.
11. In cell I3, calculate the total number of candy bars sold by Room 101; copy the formula to cells I4:I14.
12. Calculate the total revenue ($Rev) in column J by multiplying column I values (relative) by cell A17 (absolute). Format column J as Currency .
13. In cell B15, calculate the total number of candy bars sold on Monday, and copy the formula to cells C15:I15. In cell J15, calculate the total $Rev.
14. In column K, add the heading **% OF REV**; set its width at **12**.
15. Calculate each room's percentage of the total revenue (cell J15; absolute) and display it in the % of Rev column. Format it as Percent with two decimal places.
16. Use a Fill Color of *Blue, Accent 1, Lighter 80%* for cells A1:K1 and *Blue, Accent 1, Lighter 40%* for cells A2:K2.
17. Change the orientation to *Landscape*; center the worksheet horizontally and vertically on the page.
18. Using the path shown at the left, include the headers shown below. Refer to the Application Guide if needed.

79c candy sales	Week of March 12-18	Blue Team

19. Print a copy of the worksheet.
20. **Save as:** *79c candy sales*.

	A	B	C	D	E	F	G	H	I	J
1	CANDY BAR SALES BY HOMEROOM									
2	ROOM	MON	TUE	WED	THU	FRI	SAT	SUN	TOT	$ REV
3	101	23	45	32	66	66	72	23		
4	103	45	65	82	45	45	56	33		
5	105	45	23	10	75	75	63	77		
6	107	34	23	15	34	56	45	23		
7	109	23	35	46	53	53	49	66		
8	111	22	33	55	88	88	46	23		
9	113	24	57	80	76	76	62	54		
10	115	23	56	80	55	55	65	29		
11	117	78	67	56	46	61	33	60		
12	119	35	65	73	59	92	47	59		
13	121	44	56	71	48	98	32	45		
14	123	35	58	56	59	84	15	38		
15	TOT									
16	CANDY BAR PRICE									
17	$1.25									

79D

Use 3-D Cell References

Sometimes you want to insert a reference from a different worksheet, such as inserting a reference to a cell in Sheet 1 on Sheet 2. A **3-D cell reference** refers to a cell or range of cells in another worksheet. A 3-D cell reference contains the cell or range name preceded by the worksheet name and the exclamation (!) mark. As shown in Figure 16-21, a 3-D reference in cell B2 in Sheet 2 to cell B6 in Sheet 1 would appear as =Sheet1!B6 in the Formula Bar when cell B2 in Sheet 2 is selected.

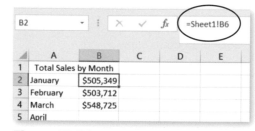

Figure 16-21 3-D cell reference

To insert a 3-D reference:

1. Click the cell that is to contain the reference.
2. Key an = sign.
3. Click the tab for the worksheet that has the cell or range of cells you want to reference.
4. Select the cell or range of cells to be referenced. Tap *Enter*. The display goes back to the original worksheet and shows the referenced value or formula.

To confirm the 3-D cell reference:

1. Activate the worksheet and then the cell where the reference was entered.
2. Read the information in the Formula Bar to verify it has been referenced correctly.

1. Open *df 79d 3-d references*. Verify that cell B2 in Sheet 2 contains a 3-D cell reference to cell B6 in Sheet 1.

2. Enter a 3-D cell reference so cell B3 (February sales) in Sheet 2 references the value in cell C6 (Total Sales for February) in Sheet 1.

3. Enter a 3-D cell reference so cell B4 (March sales) in Sheet 2 references the value in cell D6 (Total Sales for March) in Sheet 1.

4. **Save as:** *79d 3-d references*.

79E

Application: Cell References

Home > Alignment > Increase Indent

% of Net Revenues = Each value in column B/Net Revenues.

1. Using the worksheet skills you have learned, key and format the worksheet shown below. Utilize headings, column width and height, and fill color to make it easy for the user to comprehend the content of the worksheet. Use the *Increase Indent* feature using the path shown at the left to indent lines. If necessary, refer to the Application Guide at the beginning of this chapter for additional information on the Increase Indent feature.

2. Calculate the % of Net Revenues for each item (use two decimal places).

3. Print centered vertically and horizontally on the page.

4. **Save as:** *79e revenues*.

Jones Electric

	12/31/20--	% of Net Revenues
Revenues	$2,257,650	
Returns and Allowances	$ 1,568	
Net Revenues	$2,256,082	
Cost of Goods Sold		
Beginning Inventory	$ 125,612	
Purchases	$ 834,972	
Cost of Goods Available for Sale	$ 960,584	
Ending Inventory	$ 126,829	
Cost of Goods Sold	$ 833,755	
Gross Profit	$1,422,327	
Expenses	$1,165,750	
Net Profit	$ 256,577	

79F

Application: 3-D References

1. Open *df 79f loans*.

2. In the Loans worksheet, enter a 3-D reference in cell C3 that refers to the value in cell G3 in the Bates worksheet.

3. Insert the same 3-D reference in cells C4, C5, and C6 for Evans, Martinez, and Pope, respectively.

4. **Save as:** *79f loans*.

GaudiLab/Shutterstock.com

Digital Citizenship and Ethics Online auction sites such as eBay, uBid, and Bidz.com enable individuals and companies to buy and sell products using electronic bidding. While this form of digital commerce can be convenient, you should understand all sides of these transactions.

- Researching online merchants will help you identify the "best deal" and minimize the risk of making an unwise purchase
- Online purchases can run up credit card debt. If you cannot pay your bills, you can ruin your credit rating
- Providing personal information to insecure sites can make you vulnerable to Internet scams and identity theft

As a class, discuss the following:

1. How can irresponsible online purchasing practices lead to poor credit ratings?
2. How can you use an online auction site as a tool for comparison shopping?

COLLABORATION

LESSON 80   "What If" Questions, IF Function, and Formatting

OUTCOME

- Answer "what if" questions and use the IF function, apply conditional formats, and apply specialized conditional formats

80B

Prepare to Learn

1. Open *df 80b quotas*.
2. Calculate Next Year's Quota by multiplying column B values by cell A2. Enter A2 as an absolute reference address in the formula.
3. You decide all formatting features.
4. **Save as:** *80b quotas*.

80C

Answer "What If" Questions

An advantage of spreadsheet software is its ability to show the effects on all cells of a change in one cell. For example, in the worksheet you created in the above activity, you determined next year's quota for each salesperson if the company were to make next year's quota 1.05 (105 percent) of this year's quota. By changing the 1.05 in cell A2 to other numbers representing other possible changes, the effect of the change on the quotas for all salespersons can be computed at the same time.

1. Using the **80b quotas** worksheet, answer the following three "what if" questions. Unless directed otherwise, print the worksheet after each question is answered.
   a. What is each salesperson's quota if the goal is decreased to 95 percent of this year's quota?
   b. What is each salesperson's quota if the goal is increased to 105.5 percent of this year's quota?
   c. What is each salesperson's quota if the goal is decreased to 110 percent of this year's quota?

2. See if you can figure out on your own how to show the impact of the percentage changes for steps 1a, 1b, and 1c in the same worksheet as shown in Figure 16-22. Hint: Use copy and paste, change the cell location for A2, and recopy and paste the formula for the entries below it.

3. **Save as: *80c what if*.**

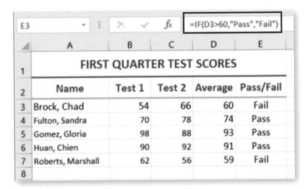

Figure 16-22 "What If"

80D

Use the IF Function

Formulas tab > Function Library > Logical > IF

The **IF function** compares the contents of two cells. Conditions that contain logical operators (shown at the left) provide the basis for the comparison. For example, an instructor could use an IF function (see the highlighted formula in Figure 16-23) to determine whether a student passed or failed.

	A	B	C	D	E
1	FIRST QUARTER TEST SCORES				
2	Name	Test 1	Test 2	Average	Pass/Fail
3	Brock, Chad	54	66	60	Fail
4	Fulton, Sandra	70	78	74	Pass
5	Gomez, Gloria	98	88	93	Pass
6	Huan, Chien	90	92	91	Pass
7	Roberts, Marshall	62	56	59	Fail
8					

E3 = IF(D3>60,"Pass","Fail")

Figure 16-23 IF function

Logical Operators
= (value of two cells are *equal*)
< (value of one cell is *less than* the other)
> (value of one cell is *greater than* the other)
<= (value of one cell is *less than* or *equal* to the other)
>= (value of one cell is *greater than* or *equal* to the other)
<> (values are *unequal*)

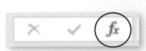

Insert Function button

The IF function involves three arguments. The first is the comparison of the scores in column D to the criterion (a score that is greater than [>] 60 in the formula entered in cell E3 in the example). The second argument is the text or value ("Pass" in the formula entered in cell E3) that is to be displayed in cell E3 if the comparison is true. The third argument is the text or value ("Fail") that is to be displayed in cell E3 if the comparison is false.

As shown in the formula for cell E3, the arguments of the IF function are keyed inside parentheses and are separated from each other with commas. If text is to be displayed for argument 2 or 3, the text should be keyed inside quotation marks. Quotation marks are not used if values are to be displayed. You can use the Formulas Function Library to enter these arguments (see Figure 16-24).

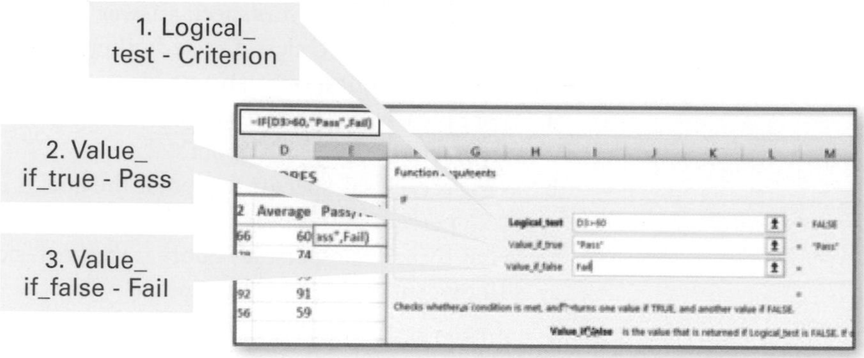

1. Logical_
   test - Criterion

2. Value_
   if_true - Pass

3. Value_
   if_false - Fail

Figure 16-24 Formula entered using Formulas >
Function Library > Logical > IF

★TIP ▶ You can also
click the *Insert
Function (fx)*
button in the Formula
Bar and select *IF* from
the function list to open a
dialog box where you can
enter function arguments.

1. Open **df 80d if function**.
2. Enter the function arguments using the IF function in E3 so that the software automatically displays whether a student passed or failed during the first quarter. (The Average must be greater than 60 to pass.) Once entered in E3, copy and paste the formula in E3 to E4:E7.
3. Chad Brock's Test 1 Score should have been 64 rather than 54. Make this correction. After you enter the correct score, the worksheet should show he passed the class.
4. Key **25** in cell A11 and **35** in cell B11. In cell C11, key an IF function that prints EQUAL if cell A11= cell B11 or UNEQUAL if cell A11 and cell B11 are unequal. Hint: Formula: =IF(A11=B11,"EQUAL","UNEQUAL")
5. In cell D11, key an IF function that prints HELP if the sum of cell A11+B11 is less than 75 and NOHELP if the sum is 75 or greater. Hint: Formula: =IF(A11+B11<75,"HELP","NO HELP")
6. In cell A15, key **25**; key **30** in cell B15; key **35** in cell C15; and key **45** in cell D15. In cell E15, key an IF function that prints NO Bonus if the sum of cells A15:D15 is less than 150 and BONUS if the sum of cells A15:D15 is greater than 150. Hint: Formula: =IF(SUM(A15:D15)<150,"NO Bonus","BONUS")
7. Change A1 to **45** and tap *Enter*; notice how D15 changes from No Bonus to BONUS.
8. **Save as:** **80d if function**.

80E

Application:
IF Function

1. Open **df 80e grade book**.
2. Enter the scores for TEST 4 as shown on the next page.
3. In column F, calculate the average score to the nearest whole number.
4. In column G, key an IF function that compares the scores in column F to a score of 75. If the score is less than 75, print **YES** in column G. If the column F score is 75 or more, print **No**.
5. You decide all formatting features.
6. **Save as:** **80e grade book**.

	A	B	C	D	E	F	G
1	GRADE BOOK						
2	NAME	TEST 1	TEST 2	TEST 3	TEST 4	AVG	NEEDS TUTORING
3	ABEL	78	85	72	78		
4	BOGGS	64	66	71	73		
5	CARR	78	82	86	75		
6	FRYZ	90	93	88	86		
7	GOOD	95	82	86	92		
8	MILLS	71	75	73	76		
9	POPE	62	71	73	66		
10	SIA	75	76	81	71		
11	TODD	66	65	50	61		
12	WILLS	75	64	75	70		
13	ZEON	81	74	65	60		

80F

Apply Conditional Formatting

Home tab > Styles > Conditional Formatting

Conditional formatting enables you to quickly apply formatting features in a cell when the data in the cell meet specified conditions. For example, your teacher can apply conditional formatting to change the font color and cell fill color to quickly identify students who have (1) scores above, below, or equal to a specific value; (2) the top and bottom score(s); and (3) scores above or below the average score on a test.

Conditional formats remain until they are cleared. Also, revisions that cause cell data to meet the specified condition will display the conditional formats, and revisions that cause cell data to not meet the specified condition will not display the conditional formats.

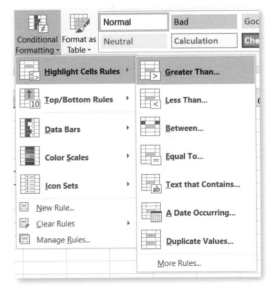

Figure 16-25 Highlight Cells Rules options

In this activity, you will use conditional formatting within the Highlight Cells Rules options (see Figure 16-25) and the Top/Bottom Rules.

1. Open *df 80f test scores*.
2. Highlight the scores C2:G24 and apply conditional formatting (Highlight Cells Rules) so that all test scores above 93 are highlighted with green fill and dark green text.
3. **Save as:** *80f test scores 1*.
4. Clear the rules. Apply conditional formatting (Top/Bottom Rules) to display the Top 10 percent of the scores in column G with a red border.
5. **Save as:** *80f test scores 2*.

Home tab > Styles >
Conditional Formatting >
Clear Rules from
Selected Cells
or
Home tab > Editing >
Clear > Clear Formats

6. Clear the rules. Apply conditional formatting (Top/Bottom Rules) to display scores in column G that are below the average score with formatting you choose.

7. **Save as:** *80f test scores 3*.

8. Clear the rules. Apply conditional formatting (Highlight Cells Rules) to highlight all scores of 100 with formatting you choose.

9. **Save as:** *80f test scores 4*.

10. Clear the rules. Apply conditional formatting (Highlight Cells Rules) to highlight all duplicate test scores in column D with formatting you choose.

11. **Save as:** *80f test scores 5*.

80G

Application: Conditional Formatting

1. Open *df 80g swim*. Apply conditional formatting using the following criteria. You choose the format to apply and clear the rules as needed.

   a. Highlight all boys and girls whose club is Seneca.

   b. **Save as:** *80g swim 1*.

   c. Highlight the scores of all boys who earned between 350 and 400 points.

   d. **Save as:** *80g swim 2*.

   e. Highlight the times of the girls whose time was below 101.

   f. **Save as:** *80g swim 3*.

   g. Format the points of the boys who earned more than the average points.

   h. **Save as:** *80g swim 4*.

80H

Conditional Formatting with Graphics

Home tab > Styles >
Conditional Formatting >
Select option

You can use data bars, color scales, and icon sets as specialized conditional formats as shown in Figure 16-26. A **data bar** shows the value of a cell relative to other cells—larger values have a longer data bar.

A **color scale** uses a two- or three-color gradient to show how values vary—the shade of the color represents the value in the cell.

	A	B	C	D	E	F
1	First	Data Bar	Color Scale	Icon Set	Icon Set	Icon Set
2	MELANIE	75	82	89	91	76
3	KYLE	80	75	88	89	75
4	CONNOR	67	68	78	98	84
5	DEREK	98	79	68	97	94
6	KATHERINE	87	88	86	79	83
7	BRETT	68	82	79	95	72
8	DENISE	98	74	97	75	74
9	RYAN	88	68	84	93	84
10	CAROLINE	84	70	81	78	94

Figure 16-26 Conditional Formatting with graphics

An **icon set** can classify data into three to five categories—each icon represents a value in the cell.

These specialized conditional formats can be accessed by selecting the desired format type from the Conditional Formatting drop-down list.

1. Open *df 80h formatting*.

2. Apply a Data Bars conditional format to values in column B.

3. Apply a Color Scales conditional format to values in column C.

4. Apply an Icon Sets conditional format to values in column D.

5. **Save as:** *80h formatting*.

Your formatted worksheet should look similar to this:

CANDY BAR SALES

ROOM	MON	TUE	WED
101	23	45	32
103	45	65	82
105	45	23	10
107	34	23	15
109	23	35	46
111	22	33	55
113	24	57	80
115	23	56	80
117	78	67	56
119	35	65	73
121	44	56	71
123	35	58	56

80I

Freeze/Unfreeze Columns and Rows

View tab > Window >
Freeze Panes >
Freeze Top Row

Freeze
Panes ▾

Often an entire worksheet cannot be seen on the screen because when you scroll through the worksheet, the information in the column and row headings disappears from the screen. When this takes place, you can freeze the column and row headings to keep them visible as you scroll to other cells of the worksheet.

1. Open **df 80i grades - all sections**.
2. Activate the *Freeze Top Row* feature to keep the top row visible as you scroll through the worksheet.
3. **Save as:** **80i grades - all sections**.

iStock.com/Jacob Wackerhausen

21st Century Skills: Financial Literacy

Managing your money and making smart economic choices are critical to your financial success. Credit cards are a tool you can use to help manage your finances.

A credit card is like a loan—you make a purchase using the card and agree to pay for it at a later date. By law, you must be 18 years of age to apply for a credit card and you must have a steady source of income in order to qualify. Credit cards are convenient in that you do not need to have enough money to pay at the time of the purchase.

But if you do not have the funds to pay in full when your credit card bill is due, you will have to repay the full amount plus interest, which is a percentage of the amount you owe. Interest can accrue quickly and significantly increase the balance due on your credit card. It is best to pay off your bill completely every month.

Think Critically

Cameron is a full-time college student and also works part-time at a local restaurant. He makes about $350 a week. He was recently approved for a credit card and just activated it for use. In the first few weeks, Cameron uses the card to buy some new clothes, a flat-screen TV, and gas for his car. He also charges several meals at restaurants to the card. When the first bill arrives, Cameron owes more than $1,500! What should he do? In a *Word* document, write an ending to the story in which you advise Cameron on how he should handle the first bill and how to be a more responsible user of his credit card.

LESSON 81 Integrating Worksheet and Word Processing Documents

OUTCOME
- Copy and link a worksheet to a word processing document

81B

Copy a Worksheet into a Word Processing Document

Home tab > Clipboard > Copy or Paste

> **NOTE** The *Excel* file that is to become a source copy for an activity will be saved with a filename that ends in "source." For example, the source file for this activity is named *81b source*. The *Word* file into which the worksheet will be pasted ends in "destination."

Worksheets can be copied into word processing documents by using Copy and Paste (or Paste Special) commands to avoid rekeying the information. A worksheet can be pasted in a variety of ways: with or without a link to the source document; with source file or destination file formatting; as a *Word* table, *Excel* worksheet, text, picture, hyperlink, and so on.

In this activity, the worksheet will be pasted into *Word* as a table by using Copy and Paste using the Picture paste option. See Figure 16-27.

1. Open the word processing document **df 81b destination**.
2. Open the worksheet **df 81b source** and save it as **81b source**.
3. Select cells A1:F20 and copy them to the Clipboard. Copy the worksheet cells into the word processing document using the Picture paste option (see Figure 16-27), placing it about a DS below the last line of the memo body. Leave about one blank line after the table, and then key your initials.
4. Center the table between the left and right margins with gridlines.
5. **Save as:** **81b destination**.

Paste Options:

Figure 16-27 Picture paste option

81C

Link a Worksheet to a Word Processing Document

Home tab > Clipboard > Copy

Home tab > Clipboard > Paste Special > Microsoft Excel Worksheet Object > Paste or Paste Link

If the data in the worksheet is likely to change, establishing a link between the *Word* document and the *Excel* worksheet eliminates the need to rekey the changes in the *Word* document each time the worksheet data changes. When you paste the worksheet into the *Word* document, use the *Link & Keep Source Formatting* Paste option shown in Figure 16-28.

If the worksheet data is not likely to change, the worksheet can be pasted without a link.

In this activity, you will use Copy/Paste Special to paste a worksheet (source file) into a *Word* document (destination file) and establish a link between them. In the next activity, you will update the source file and then the destination file.

Figure 16-28 Link & Keep Source Formatting

1. Open the word processing document **df 81c destination** and save it as **81c destination** but do not close it.
2. Open the worksheet **df 81c source** and save it as **81c source** but do not close it.
3. Copy the worksheet.
4. Use the Paste option *Link & Keep Source Formatting* to paste the worksheet into the document.
5. Place the worksheet below the last line of the memo body. Leave about one blank line before and after the worksheet and then key your initials.
6. Center the worksheet between the left and right margins. With the worksheet selected, use the path shown at the left to add *All Borders* to the worksheet.

Home tab > Paragraph > Borders > All Borders

7. **Save as:** **81c destination** and **81c source**.

81D

Update a Worksheet and Linked Word Processing Document

After you change a source file (**81c source**), the destination file (**81c destination**) can be updated when you open it by clicking *Yes* in the dialog box that appears when the destination file is opened (see Figure 16-29).

Figure 16-29 Updating *Word* file linked to *Excel* file

1. Open **81c source** and change the numbers to those given below:

Increase in net assets	
Operations	
Net investment income	$ 415,676
Net realized gain	$ 3,297,811
Change in net unrealized appreciation (depreciation)	$ 2,877,590
Net increase in net assets resulting from operations	$ 6,591,077
Distributions to shareholders	
From net investment income	$ (399,456)
From net realized gain	$(2,195,315)
Total distributions	$(2,594,771)
Share transactions	
Net proceeds from sales of shares	$ 897,120
Reinvestment of distributions	$ 2,987,407
Cost of shares redeemed	$10,976,866
Net increase in net assets resulting from share transactions	$ 897,120
Total increase in net assets	$10,082,968
Net assets	
Beginning of period	$48,595,195
End of period	$58,678,163

2. Save the changes to **81c source** and close the file.
3. Open **81c destination**, click *Yes* in the *Word* dialog box, and note that the numbers in the financial report have been updated automatically when the destination file opens.
4. **Save as:** **81d destination** and close the file.

81E

Application: Copy and Paste a Worksheet

1. Open word processing file *df 81e destination* and save it as *81e destination*. Do not close it.
2. Open a new blank workbook and create a worksheet from the data given below; save it as *81e source* but do not close it.

Business	Address	Points	Amount
Avenue Deli	309 Franklin Avenue	92	$15,000
Ford's Newsstand	302 Franklin Avenue	88	$15,000
Hannon Shoes	415 Shefield Avenue	86	$10,000
Unger Appliances	525 Station Street	83	$10,000
Best Food Market	311 Franklin Avenue	76	$ 5,000
Avenue Restaurant	376 Franklin Avenue	76	$ 5,000

3. Paste *81e source* using the Paste option *Keep Source Formatting* into *81e destination* between the paragraphs.
4. Format the destination file as needed, save it as *81e destination*, and close both files.

81F

Application: Update a Linked Worksheet

In this activity you will revise a worksheet that has been linked to a *Word* file and then open the *Word* file, update it, and save it.

1. Open the worksheet *df 81f source* and save it as *81f source*.
2. Delete values in the worksheet file *81f source* for Last Year; move the values for This Year to Last Year; and move the values for Next Year to This Year.
3. Key these new numbers for Next Year from left to right, formatting as necessary:

   6     $68,217   104 $47,248   15 $49,017
4. Save changes to *81f source* and close it.
5. Open *df 81f destination*, update it, and save it as *81f destination*.

LESSON 82   Spreadsheet Applications

OUTCOME   • Apply the spreadsheet features learned in this and the previous spreadsheet unit

82B

Integrate Word and Excel and Charting

1. Open the *Word* file **df 82b report table**.
2. Open a new worksheet file and copy the table into a blank worksheet; make formatting adjustments similar to the one shown below. Rename the Sheet1 tab to **Report**.

CORRESPONDENCE REPORT					
TYPE	MON	TUE	WED	THU	FRI
U.S. Postal Service	10	12	11	10	9
Interoffice	14	12	10	8	11
Email	24	18	15	14	12
Fax	8	7	10	11	6
Private carrier	9	11	10	13	8

3. Create a column chart with title, legend, and other features you choose. Key **Correspondence Type** as the chart title.
4. Move the chart to Sheet2. Change the tab name from Sheet2 to **Chart**.
5. Save the worksheet as **82b correspondence report** and close both files.

82C

Worksheet with Calculations and Conditional Formatting

1. Open **df 82c worksheet**. Review Lessons 79 and 80 as needed to complete the following steps.
2. Calculate the hours worked by each employee in column G.
3. Write an IF function for calculations in column H so that all hours worked up to and including 40 are paid at the hourly rate in cell D17.
4. Write an IF function for column I to calculate overtime pay that is paid at 1.5 times the hourly rate in D17 for all hours worked over 40.
5. In column J, calculate each employee's gross pay and apply conditional formatting to highlight those who earned more than $425.
6. Calculate totals for cells G15–J15.
7. Calculate the average pay in cell D18, the minimum pay in D19, and the maximum pay in D20.
8. Use two decimal places for currency.
9. Use data bars in column I (cell I4:I14) to show different levels of overtime pay.
10. **Save as: 82c worksheet**.

82D

What If

1. If needed, open **82c worksheet** and answer this question: What is the total payroll if the hourly rate is increased to $10.75?
2. Clear the conditional formatting in column J, and then reapply conditional formatting to highlight those who would earn more than $430.
3. **Save as: 82d worksheet**.

**Multiple Worksheets
and 3-D References**

> **★TIP** Enter long formulas in the Formula Bar rather than in the cell. It is easier to edit the formula and you are less likely to enter something you don't want.

Rebecca and her friends Sandra, Maria, and Midori have signed up for the *Steps to Good Health* program at their place of employment. Rebecca would like you to use your worksheet skills to keep track of how many steps they take each day and each month so she can submit them to Michael, who is in charge of the program.

Rebecca provided you with a file (*df 82e steps challenge*) that contains a worksheet for each person showing the steps taken for each day in January. First, you need to enter formulas to complete the worksheet for each individual. Column D (+/- from goal) calculates how many steps each person was over or under her goal. Column E (% of goal) shows the percent of the 7861-step goal they achieved each day. Row 35 should show the totals for columns B–E. Use Conditional Formatting to show each day each participant achieved greater than 150 percent of the goal in column E.

The fifth worksheet (Totals) is a summary sheet showing the totals for each participant. Use 3-D references to pull these total amounts from each person's worksheet.

Your final task is to complete row 34 of the Totals worksheet. Rebecca wants to know which day of the week her group took the most steps and which day of the week they took the fewest steps so they can work as a team to improve on that day of the week during February.

Rebecca would like you to get the information back to her as soon as possible so she can submit it to Michael and use it to motivate her team members to do even better in February.

Save as: *82e steps challenge.*

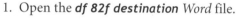

82F

Letter with Linked Worksheet

1. Open the *df 82f destination* Word file.
2. Open *df 82f source*; save the file as *82f source*.
3. Copy the table in cells A1:E6 from *82f source*.
4. Paste the cells into the Word document between the first two paragraphs using the *Link & Keep Source Formatting* Paste option. Center the table horizontally.
5. Save the Word file as *82f destination* and close both files.

82G

Update Letter with Link

1. Open worksheet *82f source* and increase each amount by $2.00. Save as *82f source* and close the file.
2. Open Word file *82f destination*, which will update the letter with the new amounts. Recenter the table horizontally. Use today's date and change the name and address to:

   > Dr. Patricia Kurtz
   > 1246 Warren Drive
   > Denver, CO 80221-7463

4. **Save as:** *82g destination.*

Assessment 9 — Enhanced Worksheets

Warmup

Key each line twice.

Alphabet

1 Al criticized my six workers for having quick tempers on the job.

Space Bar

2 Jo and I may go to the city to work for two days to help the man.

Speed

3 Jana may work with us to make a profit for the eighty city firms.

Activity 1
Assess Straight-Copy Skill

A all letters used

gwam 3'

Attitude is the way people communicate their feelings   4
or moods to others. Individuals who have a positive attitude   8
tend to think they will have successful experiences. A person   12
such as this is said to be an optimist. They expect the best   16
possible outcomes, and they view the world as a great place.   20
Good is found in even the worst situation.   22

People who often expect failure are described as having   26
negative attitudes. A pessimist is the name given to an individual   31
with a bad view of life. Pessimists usually emphasize the adverse   35
aspects of life and expect the worst possible outcome. They expect   39
to fail even before they start the day . You can plan on them to   44
find gloom even in the best situation.   46

Only you can determine whether your attitude is going to be   50
good or whether your attitude is going be bad. Keep in mind that   54
people generally are attracted to those who have a good attitude   59
and tend to shy away from those with a bad attitude. Your attitude   63
quickly determines just how successful you are in all your personal   68
relationships as well as in your professional relationships.   72

gwam 3' | 1 | 2 | 3 | 4 |

Activity 2
Worksheet

You have been hired as the payroll clerk at Anderson Graphics. Complete the February payroll using *df assessment9 activity2*. Finish entering the information and formulas to complete the payroll using the following information:

- Use Accounting Number Format for columns E:N (starting at row 4)
- Employees are paid time and one-half for overtime hours
- Calculate each type of tax by multiplying the tax rate by the gross salary
- Anderson, the CEO, receives a monthly salary of $10,000. Place her salary information on row 4; leave a blank row and enter the hourly employee information on rows 6–12
- Gross pay is before taxes are deducted; net pay is after taxes are deducted
- Use the Sort feature to alphabetize the names of the employees

Leave one blank row and calculate the payroll totals for all columns except Last Name, First Name, and Pay Rate.

Last Name	First Name	Federal Tax Rate	Regular Hours	Overtime Hours	Pay Rate
Porter	Leslie	12%	160		$10.50/hr.
Scott	Reed	12%	158		$10.50/hr.
Nicholson	Karlie	12%	160	12	$12.75/hr.
Thorn	Hunter	12%	80		$10.50/hr.
Sanchez	Felipe	12%	120	16	$13.00/hr.
Neagle	Sterling	12%	160		$10.50/hr.
Franco	Miguel	12%	160	8	$11.25/hr.
Anderson	Jill	22%			$10,000/month

Miscellaneous Tax Rates	
Federal Insurance Contribution Act (FICA)	6.2%
Medicare	1.45%
State Tax Rate	5.94%

Save as: *assessment9 activity2*.

Activity 3
Workbook

The Investment Club at your school has entered two teams (Charla/Glen – "Blue" stocks and Lindsay/Miguel – "Gold" stocks) in the annual state investment club competition. The club would like you to create a spreadsheet that provides the competitors with their status at the end of each week. Your first report will be completed on March 1.

Your workbook should have a summary sheet (see Figure 16-30) for worksheet 1. After creating worksheets 2 through 9, use 3-D Cell references to bring the information from worksheets 2-9 into the summary sheet.

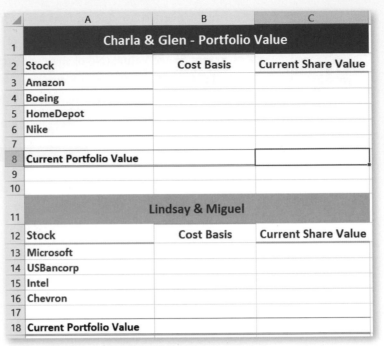

Figure 16-30 Portfolio summary worksheet

Worksheets 2 through 9 will be separate worksheets for each of the eight stocks. The tabs should be color coded blue and gold for each team's stocks (see Figure 16-31) and include the name of the stock with NO SPACES (see Tip).

Figure 16-31 Worksheet tab names and colors

The worksheet for Amazon has been started in *df assessment9 activity3*. You will need to key the formulas needed to complete the worksheet as shown in Figure 16-32. Once it is complete, you can use copy and paste to provide the basis for the other seven worksheets.

	Date Purchased	No. of Shares	Price Paid per Share	Cost Basis for Shares Purchased	Current Price per Share	Current Share Value	Dollar Gain/Loss	Percentage Gain/Loss
1				**Amazon**				
3	1/8/2018	5	$ 1,235.84	$ 6,179.20	$1,513.60	$ 7,568.00	$ 1,388.80	122.48%
4	2/1/2018	5	$ 1,431.50	$ 7,157.50	$1,513.60	$ 7,568.00	$ 410.50	105.74%
5	2/5/2018	5	$ 1,395.00	$ 6,975.00	$1,513.60	$ 7,568.00	$ 593.00	108.50%
6								
7	**Totals**	15		$ 20,311.70		$ 22,704.00	$ 2,392.30	111.78%

Figure 16-32 Stock worksheet

The formulas needed for calculations are as follows:

- **Cost Basis for Shares Purchased:** (No. of shares * Price Paid per Share)
- **Current Share Value:** (No of shares * Current Price per Share)
- **Dollar Gain/Loss:** (Current Share Value - Cost Basis for Shares Purchased)
- **Percentage Gain/Loss:** (Current Share Value/Cost Basis for Shares Purchased)

The information for each worksheet is shown in Figure 16-33.

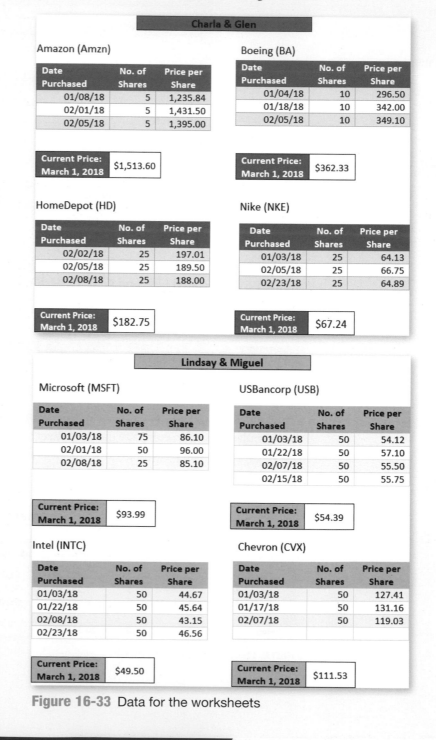

Figure 16-33 Data for the worksheets

Skill Builder 15

A

Warmup

Key each line twice.

alphabet 1 Jack Lopez will attend the quality frog exhibits over the summer.

un/nu 2 Our unique unit may not have its annual bonus numbers until June.

speed 3 Helena may blame the men for the problem with the neighbor's dog.

gwam 1' | 1 | 2 | 3 | 4 | 5 | 6 | 7 | 8 | 9 | 10 | 11 | 12 | 13 |

B

Keying Skill: Speed

Key each line twice.

Balanced-hand words of 2-5 letters

1 if me go he so us to am or by an of is to row she box air pay the

2 dig got due map jam own she box ant busy when city fish half rush

3 goal down dial firm keys pens rock odor sick soap tubs wish title

4 to do|to us|by the|if they|held a|the pen|their dog|is it|to make

5 a big fox|do the work|the gown is|when is it|he may go|a rich man

6 by the chair|he may make|did he spend|for the girls|for the firms

7 The maid may make the usual visit to the dock to work on the map.

8 Dick and Jay paid the busy man to go to the lake to fix the dock.

9 The girls may visit them when they go to the city to pay the man.

gwam 1' | 1 | 2 | 3 | 4 | 5 | 6 | 7 | 8 | 9 | 10 | 11 | 12 | 13 |

C

Key Mastery

Key each line twice.

Alphabetic sentences

1 Oki and Quin have just solved the exciting new puzzle from Bryan.

2 Val and Judith quickly mixed the prizes, baffling one wise judge.

3 Owen Jack even dozed off as he quietly prepared for his big exam.

4 Mickey and Alex gave Quinton six jigsaw puzzles for his birthday.

5 Carter Jung quickly baked six pizzas for the film festival crowd.

6 Jacki and Marvin will buy the guy six unique prizes for his dogs.

D

Speed Forcing Drill

Key each line once at top speed for 15". If you finish the line before time is called, key it again, trying to go faster.

Emphasis: high-frequency balanced-hand words

| | 4 | 8 | 12 | 16 | 20 | 24 | 28 | 32 | 36 | 40 | 44 | 48 |

Nancy and Helen may make the eight signs for them.
Bob and I paid the man for the shanty by the dock.
Helen paid the man to fix the signals down by the lake.
Rodney kept the box with the bugle for the man by the chair.
Nancy and Glen may hang the signs by the door of the shanty.

gwam 15" | 4 | 8 | 12 | 16 | 20 | 24 | 28 | 32 | 36 | 40 | 44 | 48 |

E

Timed Writing

1. Key a 1' timing on each ¶; determine *gwam*.

2. Add 2–4 *gwam* to the rate attained in step 1, and note quarter-minute checkpoints from the chart below.

3. Key two 1' guided timings on ¶ 1 to increase speed.

4. Practice ¶ 2 and ¶ 3 in the same way.

5. Key two 3' timings on ¶s 1 and 2 combined; count *gwam* and determine errors.

Quarter-Minute Checkpoints				
gwam	1/4'	1/2'	3/4'	1'
24	6	12	18	24
28	7	14	21	28
32	8	16	24	32
36	9	18	27	36
40	10	20	30	40
44	11	22	33	44
48	12	24	36	48
52	13	26	39	52
56	14	28	42	56
60	15	30	45	60

A all letters used   gwam 3'

When you talk about famous Americans, it doesn't take long   4
to come up with a long list. However, some individuals would   8
appear on nearly everyone's list. George Washington would be   12
one of those on most people's list. He is often referred to as   16
the Father of our Country because of the role he played in   20
the American Revolution and being our first president.   24

Abraham Lincoln would also be included on most lists. He   28
is often referred to as Honest Abe. He always gave the extra   32
effort. Because of this, he was successful. Whether the job   36
was splitting logs, being a lawyer, or being president,   39
Lincoln gave his best. Managing the Civil War required a   44
president who gave his best.   46

Harriet Tubman is recognized as another prominent   49
individual. She risked her own life for the freedom of others.   53
After becoming a free woman in the North, she returned to the   57
South to assist several hundred slaves escape. She was also   61
involved in the Civil War, serving her country as a Union spy   65
and scout.   66

gwam 3' | 1 | 2 | 3 | 4 |

Planning for Your Career 6

Understanding Employer Expectations

OUTCOMES

- Learn what employers expect of employees
- Learn the Framework for 21st Century Learning
- Learn about Digital Age literacy skills
- Learn the importance of inventive thinking skills
- Learn the importance of effective communication skills
- Learn the high productivity skills

Need for Effective Employees

aastock/Shutterstock.com

Employers attempt to hire employees who can demonstrate that they are prepared to be productive workers within their workforce. Productive employees are needed so employers can compete at the highest level within the market they serve. If an employee who is not adequately prepared is hired, the employer's orientation, training, and retraining costs are likely to be greater, which increases the employer's expenses, lowers the employer's profits that are needed to sustain or expand a business entity, and lessens the chances that the employee will be successful.

Businesses, government agencies, and educational institutions have conducted many studies, independently and collectively, to identify specific skills and knowledge that employers expect of workers, regardless of the job held or the career path being pursued. The results of these studies help schools design appropriate curriculum and activities, assist individuals in improving the likelihood of securing and being successful in a job and career they desire, and aid employers in identifying prospective candidates who have the needed skills and knowledge.

In 2007, The Partnership for 21st Century Learning developed a framework for the knowledge, skills, expertise, and support systems that students need to succeed in work, life, and citizenship. The **Framework for 21st Century Learning** was developed with input from teachers, education experts, and business leaders. It continues to be used by thousands of educators and hundreds of schools in the United States and abroad to ensure 21st-century readiness for every student.

Workers who develop the necessary competencies, foundation skills, and personal qualities are more likely to be successful workers and enjoy fulfilling careers. The Framework for 21st Century Skills is still highly relevant for workplace readiness for today's students. As you complete the activities in this module, try to make connections between the framework of competencies, foundation skills, and personal qualities with what is expected of you in order to be successful in your studies and school activities. These skills are also highlighted in the *21st Century Skills* and *Digital Citizenship and Ethics* features throughout this textbook.

1. Open a new *Word* document.
2. Compose a paragraph that states why employers try to hire employees who are adequately prepared for the workplace and why it is in your best interest to demonstrate that you are prepared to enter the workplace.
3. Save as: ***pc6 effective employees***.

Key Subjects and 21st Century Themes	The Framework for 21st Century Learning includes four major skill areas, briefly outlined here.

Mastery of key subjects and 21st-century themes is essential to student success. Key subjects include English, reading or language arts, world languages, arts, mathematics, economics, science, geography, history, government and civics. In describing the 21st-century framework, the term *literacy* is used to describe a person's knowledge of a particular subject or field and being able to apply or adapt that knowledge in a variety of contexts.

In addition, schools must promote an understanding of academic content at much higher levels by weaving 21st-century interdisciplinary themes into key subjects:

- Global awareness
- Financial, economic, business, and entrepreneurial literacy
- Civic literacy
- Health literacy
- Environmental literacy |
| **Learning and Innovation Skills** | Learning and innovation skills are what separate students who are prepared for the increasingly complex life and work environments in today's world and those who are not. These skills include:

- Creativity and innovation
- Critical thinking and problem solving
- Communication
- Collaboration |
| **Information, Media, and Technology Skills** | We live in a technology- and media-driven environment, marked by access to an abundance of information, rapid changes in technology tools, and the ability to collaborate and make individual contributions on an unprecedented scale. Effective citizens and workers must be able to exhibit a range of functional and critical thinking skills, such as:

- Information literacy
- Media literacy
- ICT (Information, Communications and Technology) literacy |
| **Life and Career Skills** | Today's students need to develop thinking skills, content knowledge, and social and emotional competencies to navigate complex life and work environments. These essential skills include:

- Flexibility and adaptability
- Initiative and self-direction
- Social and cross-cultural skills
- Productivity and accountability
- Leadership and responsibility |

The Framework's knowledge, skills, and qualities are explained further in the next sections. These framework skills will be organized in this text into four broad categories: Digital-Age Literacy, Inventive Thinking, Effective Communication, and High Productivity. To read more about the Partnership for 21st Century Learning, follow this link: http://www.p21.org/our-work/p21-framework.

1. Open a new *Word* document.
2. Select one of the bulleted skill sets within each of the four competency areas and write a report that describes at least one situation in which you successfully demonstrated that you possess the competency. Include an appropriate title and side headings to make your report attractive and easy to understand.
3. **Save as: *pc6 competencies 1*.**

Digital-Age Literacy

As society changes, the skills needed to negotiate the complexities of life also change. In the early 1900s, a person who had acquired simple reading, writing, and calculating skills was considered literate. To achieve success in the 21st century, students also need to attain proficiency in science, technology, and culture, as well as gain a thorough understanding of information in all its forms. **Digital-age literacy** includes the following:

- **Basic literacy:** Language proficiency (in English) and numeracy at levels necessary to function on the job and in society to achieve one's goals and to develop one's knowledge and potential in this digital age
- **Scientific literacy:** Knowledge and understanding of the scientific concepts and processes required for personal decision making, participation in civic and cultural affairs, and economic productivity
- **Economic literacy:** The ability to identify economic problems, alternatives, costs, and benefits; analyze the incentives at work in economic situations; examine the consequences of changes in economic conditions and public policies; collect and organize economic evidence; and weigh costs against benefits
- **Technological literacy:** Knowledge about what technology is, how it works, what purposes it can serve, and how it can be used efficiently and effectively to achieve specific goals
- **Visual literacy:** The ability to interpret, use, appreciate, and create images and video using both conventional and 21st-century media in ways that advance thinking, decision making, communication, and learning
- **Information literacy:** The ability to evaluate information across a range of media; recognize when information is needed; locate, synthesize, and use information effectively; and accomplish these functions using technology, communication networks, and electronic resources
- **Multicultural literacy:** The ability to understand and appreciate the similarities and differences in the customs, values, and beliefs of one's own culture and the cultures of others
- **Global awareness:** The recognition and understanding of interrelationships among international organizations, nation-states, public and private economic entities, socio-cultural groups, and individuals across the globe

1. If needed, open *pc6 competencies 1*.
2. Complete your report by selecting two of the "literacies" above and describe at least one situation in which you successfully demonstrated that you possess this knowledge or competency.
3. Save as: *pc6 competencies 2*.

Inventive Thinking

As technology becomes more prevalent in our everyday lives, cognitive skills become increasingly critical. These capabilities are "life skills" formulated in the context of digital-age technologies. **Inventive thinking** is comprised of the following life skills:

- **Adaptability and managing complexity:** The ability to modify one's thinking, attitude, or behavior to be better suited to current or future environments; and the ability to handle multiple goals, tasks, and inputs, while understanding and adhering to constraints of time, resources, and systems (such as organizational and technological systems)
- **Self-direction:** The ability to set goals related to learning, plan for the achievement of those goals, independently manage time and effort, and independently assess the quality of learning and any products that result from the learning experience
- **Curiosity:** The desire to know or the spark of interest that leads to inquiry
- **Creativity:** The act of bringing something into existence that is genuinely new and original, whether personally (original only to the individual) or culturally (where the work adds significantly to a domain of culture as recognized by experts)
- **Risk taking:** The willingness to make mistakes, advocate unconventional or unpopular positions, or tackle extremely challenging problems without obvious solutions, such that one's personal growth, integrity, or accomplishments are enhanced
- **Higher-order thinking and sound reasoning:** The cognitive processes of analysis, comparison, inference and interpretation, evaluation, and synthesis applied to a range of academic domains and problem-solving contexts

1. Open *df pc6 inventive skills* and rate your competence on each of the inventive thinking skills as directed in the appraisal form.
2. Save as: *pc6 inventive skills assessment*.

Effective Communication

Effective communication skills are essential for success in today's knowledge-based society. Information technology can play a facilitative role in effective communication, but emerging technologies also can present ethical dilemmas. As information and communication technologies become more pervasive in society, citizens will need to manage the impact on their social, personal, professional, and civic lives. Effective communication involves:

- **Teaming and collaboration:** Cooperative interaction between two or more individuals working together to solve problems, create novel products, or learn and master content
- **Interpersonal skills:** The ability to read and manage the emotions, motivations, and behaviors of oneself and others during social interactions or in a social-interactive context

- **Personal responsibility:** Depth and currency of knowledge about legal and ethical issues related to technology, combined with one's ability to apply this knowledge to achieve balance, integrity, and quality of life as a citizen, a family and community member, a learner, and a worker
- **Social and civic responsibility:** The ability to manage technology and govern its use in a way that promotes public good and protects society, the environment, and democratic ideals
- **Interactive communication:** The generation of meaning through exchanges using a range of contemporary tools, transmissions, and processes

1. Open *df pc6 effective communication skills* and rate your competence on each of the effective communication skills as directed in the appraisal form.
2. Save as: *pc6 effective communication skills assessment*.

High Productivity

Den Rise/Shutterstock.com

High productivity skills currently are not a high-stakes focus of academic assessments, yet the skills involved in this cluster often determine whether a person succeeds or fails in academics and the workforce:

- **Prioritizing, planning, and managing for results:** The ability to organize to efficiently achieve the goals of a specific project or problem
- **Effective use of real-world tools:** The ability to use real-world tools—the hardware, software, networking, and peripheral devices used by information technology (IT) workers to accomplish 21st-century work—to communicate, collaborate, solve problems, and accomplish tasks
- **Ability to produce relevant, high-quality products:** The ability to produce intellectual, informational, or material products that serve authentic purposes and occur as a result of students or employees using real-world tools to solve or communicate about real-world problems. These products include persuasive communications, synthesis of resources into more usable forms, or refinement of questions that build upon what is known to advance one's own and others' understanding

1. Open *df pc6 high productivity skills*. Assume you are the employee and your teacher is your employer. Indicate how your teacher would rate you on each of the high productivity skills as directed in the appraisal form.
2. Save as: *pc6 high productivity skills assessment*.

Before You Move On

Use the following words to complete the sentences:

AutoFill   worksheets   IF function

Copy and Paste   link   3-D cell reference

Convert Text to Columns   Normal View   data bars

rotated

1. When a new worksheet is opened, it is displayed in _____. Application Guide

2. The _____ compares the contents of two cells. LO 80D

3. Text can be _____ to various diagonal or vertical angles to change the orientation. LO 78C

4. Each workbook contains one or more _____. LO 78D

5. The _____ feature helps you separate information entered in cells in one column into cells in multiple columns. LO 78F

6. Information can be quickly copied to adjacent cells by using the _____ feature. LO 78B

7. A _____ refers to a cell or range of cells on another worksheet. LO 79D

8. You can use _____ as a specialized conditional format. LO 80H

9. If the data in a worksheet copied to a *Word* document is likely to change, establishing a _____ between the *Word* document and the *Excel* worksheet will eliminate the need to rekey the changes in the *Word* document each time the worksheet data changes. LO 81C

10. Worksheets are copied into a word processing document by using _____ commands to avoid rekeying the information. LO 81B

CHAPTER 17

Using a Database to Create, Analyze, and Distribute Information

Lesson 83   Database Review and Reinforcement

Lesson 84   Data Mining and Analysis Using Computed Fields

Lesson 85   Using a Database to Create a Mail Merge

Lesson 86   Data Mining and Analysis Using Computed Fields and Column Totals

Lesson 87   Using Queries Created from Multiple Tables to Create Word Documents

Lesson 88   Using a Database to Create Form Letters, Envelopes, and Labels

Assessment 10   Enhanced Database Skills

Application Guide

The **Expression Builder** in the Query feature is used to perform calculations on existing fields in a database. The Expression Builder shown in Figure 17-1 shows the expression (formula) entered to calculate the Total Sales for the Quarter by adding July Sales + August Sales + September Sales.

Expression Builder

Query Tools Design tab > Query Setup > Builder

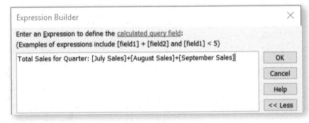

Figure 17-1 Expression Builder

Figure 17-2 shows the results when the query is run after the fields and the expression are entered into the query.

July Sales	August Sales	September Sales	Total Sales for Quarter
$45,351.00	$37,951.00	$42,819.00	$126,121.00
$53,739.00	$49,762.00	$54,829.00	$158,330.00
$33,371.00	$38,978.00	$42,561.00	$114,910.00
$39,371.00	$40,790.00	$50,096.00	$130,257.00
$42,173.00	$65,386.00	$55,142.00	$162,701.00
$17,219.00	$29,737.00	$33,890.00	$80,846.00

Figure 17-2 Computed field using Expression Builder

Mail Merge

External Data tab > Export > Word Merge

The Mail Merge feature in *Access* (see Figure 17-3) is valuable when you want to send the same document to multiple individuals. The *Word* Merge feature links to the Microsoft *Word* Mail Merge Wizard to add in variable information from a database, making it appear as though the document was specifically created for each individual person receiving the document. Email messages, envelopes, and labels are also often created using the Mail Merge feature.

NOTE The Mail Merge feature in *Word* was covered in Chapter 12.

Figure 17-3 Start Mail Merge from *Access*

Mail Merge merges two files: a word processing file, such as a form letter, and a data file, such as an *Access* table or query. The word processing file contains the text of the document (constant information) plus the merge field names (variable information). The merge field names are positioned in the document where the variable information from the database is to appear.

The data file contains a record for each recipient. Each record contains field(s) of information about the person such as the first name, last name, address, city, state, and ZIP code. You can start a Mail Merge from *Access* that brings up the *Word* Mail Merge Wizard to step you through the process.

Query from Two Tables

Information that is needed is often stored in different tables and queries. Within a database you can combine information from different sources. For example, one table might include the address for each member while another table includes payment of monthly fees. By establishing a relationship between the two tables on the Last Name field that occurs in both tables (as shown in Figure 17-4), the two tables can be connected and a query used to pull information from both tables.

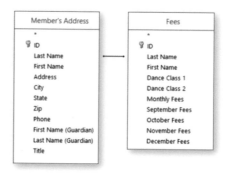

Figure 17-4 Establishing table relationship in a query

Totals Feature

The *Totals* feature (Figure 17-5) is used to insert totals at the bottom of a table or query. The feature will be used to calculate sums and averages in this chapter, but it can also be used to perform other mathematical calculations as well (see Figure 17-6). The feature is particularly useful when working with a database with a large number of records.

Figures 17- 5 Totals feature

Figure 17-6 Totals feature options

Saving Database Objects

Click object's Close button > Yes > Key object name > OK

TIP Another way to save a database object is to right-click the tab of the object you want to save and click *Save* on the shortcut menu to bring up the Save As dialog box.

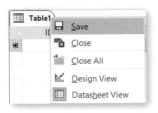

When an *Access* database object (table, form, query, or report) is created, it can be saved by clicking its Close button. Clicking the Close button brings up a dialog box asking, *Do you want to save changes to the design of object 'Object 1'?*

When you click *Yes*, the Save As dialog box appears (see Figure 17-7) where you key the object name, such as Class Roster.

Figure 17-7 Save As

After keying the name of the table, click *OK*. This changes the name on the tab above the table from Table 1 to Class Roster as shown in Figure 17-8.

Figure 17-8 Object (Table) names

You can use this procedure for saving all *Access* database objects (tables, queries, forms, and reports).

LESSON 83 Database Review and Reinforcement

OUTCOME

- Review database application skills

83A

Create a Table

TIP If the message "Security Warning: Some active content has been disabled" is displayed when you open a database, click the *Enable Content* button. Depending on your virus protection software, you might have to enable content every time you open a database.

Before starting these lessons, you will need a basic understanding of the following database concepts covered in Chapter 10:

- Creating a database
- Adding and editing records
- Sorting records
- Creating a table with Design View
- Editing records
- Creating forms, queries, and reports

Eastwick School of Dance has a database with a table with address information for its students. The school would like you to create another table in the database to keep track of student fees using the field names and data types shown here.

Last Name (Short Text)
First Name (Short Text)
Dance Class 1 (Short Text)
Dance Class 2 (Short Text)
Monthly Fees (Currency)

1. Open the *df 83 Eastwick School of Dance* database, and save it as *83 Eastwick School of Dance*.
2. Create and save a new table using the name *83a Fees*.

3. Key the information from the records on the next page into the table. If the monthly fee is not given, use the Fee Schedule information shown at the left to calculate the fee.
4. Save and close the database.

Fee Schedule	
Beg. Ballet	$28
Beg. Tap	$25
Beg. Jazz	$27
Inter. Ballet	$30
Inter. Tap	$29
Inter. Jazz	$29
Adv. Ballet	$34
Adv. Tap	$33
Adv. Jazz	$32

Eastwick School of Dance

Name	Dance Class 1	Dance Class 2	Monthly Fees
Julie Stewart	Beg. Ballet	Beg. Jazz	$55
Julie Vaughn	Adv. Ballet		$34
Lauren Martin	Beg. Ballet	Beg. Tap	$53
Jacqueline Finley	Inter. Ballet		$30
Angela Garcia	Beg. Jazz	Inter. Ballet.	
Kirsten Edmonds	Beg. Tap	Adv. Ballet	
Camille Ramirez	Inter. Tap	Inter. Jazz	$58
Stacy Rice	Inter. Jazz		
Loren Rizzo	Beg. Ballet		$28
Judy Higgins	Beg. Jazz		
Jill Giani	Beg. Ballet		$28
Anne Griffith	Inter. Ballet	Inter. Jazz	$59
Jayne Boyer	Beg. Tap	Beg. Jazz	$52
Diane Bunnell	Inter. Ballet		
Brook Byrns	Beg. Jazz	Inter. Ballet	$57
Alison Koosman	Adv. Ballet	Adv. Jazz	$66
Tasha Lang	Beg. Ballet	Inter. Tap	$57
Kayla Maas	Beg. Tap		$25
Carolyn McDowell	Beg. Ballet		

83B

Add Fields and Input Data

1. Open the ***83 Eastwick School of Dance*** database and the *83a Fees* table.
2. Add these fields using Currency for the Data Type:

   September Fees
   October Fees
   November Fees
   December Fees

3. Expand column headings to fit the text.
4. Update the records in the database table to include the new information shown below.
5. Print the revised table in landscape orientation.
6. Save and close the database.

Eastwick School of Dance

Name	Sept. Fees	Oct. Fees	Nov. Fees	Dec. Fees
Stewart	55	55	55	
Vaughn				
Martin	53	53		
Finley				
Garcia	57	57		
Edmonds	59	59		
Ramirez	58	58		
Rice				
Rizzo				
Higgins	27			
Giani	28	28		
Griffith	59	59		
Boyer	52	52		
Bunnell				
Byrns	57	57	57	
Koosman	66	66		
Lang				
Maas	25	25	25	
McDowell	28	28		

83C

Update Table

1. Open the **83 Eastwick School of Dance** database and the *Eastwick Fees* table.
2. Input the following records in the *83a Fees* table.
3. Save and close the database after you key the information.

Name	Dance Class 1	Dance Class 2	Monthly Fees	Sept. Fees	Oct. Fees	Nov. Fees	Dec. Fees
Tarin Chan	Inter. Ballet	Adv. Jazz	$62	$62	$62		
Marcia Moreno	Inter. Jazz		$29	$29			
Elizabeth Pingel	Beg. Tap		$25	$25	$25		
Sonja Phelps	Inter. Jazz	Adv. Tap	$62	$62	$62	$62	
Charlotte Ross	Beg. Ballet		$28	$28	$28		
Lynda Sackett	Inter. Ballet	Adv. Tap	$63	$63			

83D

Edit Records

1. Open the **83 Eastwick School of Dance** database and the *Eastwick Fees* table.
2. Make the following changes to the *Fees* table.
   a. Stacy Rice is enrolled in Inter. Jazz and Inter. Ballet (be sure to change fees).
   b. Byrns should be spelled **Burns**.
   c. Tasha Lang should be **Trisha Lang**.
   d. Diane Bunnell is enrolled in Adv. Ballet, not Inter. Make the necessary adjustments.
   e. Lynda Sackett decided not to take Adv. Tap. Make the necessary adjustments to reflect this change. The September Fees will stay at $63.00; however, change the Monthly Fee to $30.00 to reflect this change for future months.
3. Save and close the database.

83E

Edit Records

1. Open the **83 Eastwick School of Dance** database and the *Address* table.
2. Make the following changes.
   a. Diane Bunnell has a new address and telephone number:

   380 Innsbruck Drive
   St. Paul, MN 55112-8271
   612-329-7621

   b. Jackqueline Finley's name should be spelled **Jacqueline**. Her phone number should be **715-386-6764**.
   c. Make sure you change the spelling of Brook Byrns (**Burns**) and Tasha Lang (**Trisha**).
   d. Change Judy Higgins's mother's name to **Ms. Erin Schultz**.

e. Kayla Maas has a new address and telephone number:

1125 Westbrook Lane
Minneapolis, MN 55436-2837
612-348-8211

3. Save and close the database.

83F

Sort Information

1. Open the **83 Eastwick School of Dance** database.
2. Use the *Selection* feature in the Sort & Filter group of the Home tab to answer the following questions.
3. Open **df 83f Eastwick School of Dance** and record your answers.
4. **Save as:** **83f Eastwick School of Dance**.

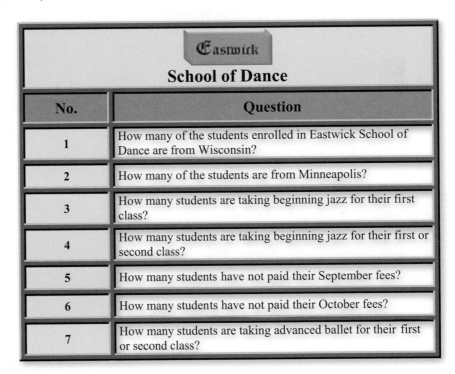

No.	Question
1	How many of the students enrolled in Eastwick School of Dance are from Wisconsin?
2	How many of the students are from Minneapolis?
3	How many students are taking beginning jazz for their first class?
4	How many students are taking beginning jazz for their first or second class?
5	How many students have not paid their September fees?
6	How many students have not paid their October fees?
7	How many students are taking advanced ballet for their first or second class?

83G

Create a Query in Design View

> **NOTE** If needed, refer to Lesson 58A in Chapter 10 to review creating a query.

Create a query in Design View using the *Address* table to display only students who live in Minnesota. Include these fields in the query:

- Last Name
- First Name
- Address
- City
- State
- ZIP

Save as: **Minnesota student addresses** and close the database.

OUTCOMES

- Create computed fields using the Expression Builder
- Create computed fields and analyze information extracted through queries with computed fields

84A

Expression Builder

Query Tools Design tab >
Query Setup > Builder

Queries are used for mining data that can be analyzed to answer questions. Queries can be used to extract (mine) information from a database table and display it in a datasheet that is a smaller table containing the record set (limited information) from the table.

The Expression Builder can be used to perform calculations on existing fields in a database. In Figure 17-9, *Total Sales* were calculated for each Rockwell Technologies sales representative.

Last Name	First Name	July Sales	August Sales	Total Sales
Carter-Bond	Mary	$45,351.00	$37,951.00	$83,302.00
Hull	Dale	$53,739.00	$49,762.00	$103,501.00
McRae	Jessica	$33,371.00	$38,978.00	$72,349.00

Figure 17-9 Calculated field in a query

1. Open *df 84a Rockwell Technologies*.
2. Create a query from the *Sales Reps – District 13* table of the *Rockwell Technologies* database using Query Design to include the following fields, shown in Figure 17-10:

Create tab > Queries >
Query Design >
Select table > Add

- Last Name
- First Name
- July Sales
- August Sales

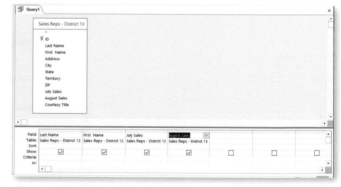

Figure 17-10 Query design

3. While still on the Query Tools Design tab, place the insertion point in the column to the right of *August Sales* and click *Builder* in the Query Setup group on the Design tab (see Figure 17-11). This opens the Expression Builder and places the insertion point in the Enter an Expression box.

Figure 17-11 Expression Builder icon

TIP If you need to revise the expression you created, place the insertion point in the column containing the expression and click *Builder*.

4. In the Enter an Expression box, key **Total Sales: [July Sales]+[August Sales]** (see Figure 17-12). Click *OK*.

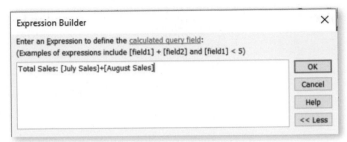

Figure 17-12 Expression entered in Expression Builder

5. Click *Run* in the Results group. Notice that the resulting table now includes a column labeled *Total Sales*.

6. **Save query as: *84a Total Sales*.**

84B

Create Computed Fields Using the Expression Builder

1. Open *df 84b Software Professionals*.

2. Create a query using Query Design with these five fields from the Software Professionals Inventory table: Stock Number, Software, Beginning Inventory, Purchases, and Sales (Figure 17-13).

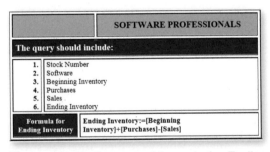

Figure 17-13 Query and formula for Ending Inventory

3. The field names can be quickly inserted into the table beneath the box displaying the field names by double-clicking the field names you want to appear in the table. After you double-click *Stock Number*, double-click *Software* and it will appear in the next column of the table.

4. Use the Expression Builder to create the formula shown in Figure 17-13 to calculate the Ending Inventory.

TIP The size of the box with the field names can be increased to show all the field names (see Figure 17-14) by positioning the pointer on a border or corner of the box to bring up a double-headed arrow and dragging.

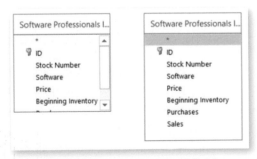

Figure 17-14 Increase size of field name box

5. Click *Run*.

6. **Save query as: *84b Ending Inventory*.**

Use Expression Builder to Calculate Total Fees

1. Open the **83 Eastwick School of Dance** database that you worked on in Lesson 83.
2. Use the *83d Fees* table to create a query with the following six fields:
   a. Last Name
   b. First Name
   c. September Fees
   d. October Fees
   e. November Fees
   f. December Fees
3. Use the Expression Builder to create a formula to calculate the Total Fees paid for September through December.
4. When you run the query, Total Fees appears in the query table, but no amounts. Go back into the query and key a 0 (zero) into each month where no fees have been paid. Once you have an amount in each month of the row, the Total Fees column will calculate the amount that the student has paid. When the student pays the fee for the month where a zero appears, the amount can be recorded and the Total Fees will reflect the new amount.
5. Save query as: **Total Fees: September-December**.

Query Table Analysis

Open **df 84d analysis** and respond to these questions, using the Eastwick School of Dance, Rockwell Technologies, and Software Professional databases from the previous lessons.

1. Who are the students who have paid no fees from September through December? Use the *Selection* feature of the *Sort & Filter* group on the Home tab. Remember to click the *Toggle Filter* button once you have recorded your answers.
2. What would you recommend that the owner of Eastwick School of Dance do with these students?
3. Who were the top three sales people at Rockwell Technologies for the months of July and August; what were their Total Sales? Use the *Sort* feature of the *Sort & Filter* group. Don't save the changes after sorting the query.
4. Are there any software inventories at Software Professional that need to be replenished right away?
5. Does any of the software have an Ending Inventory higher than the Beginning Inventory?

Save as: **84d analysis**.

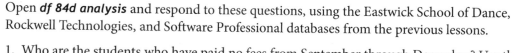

LESSON 85   Using a Database to Create a Mail Merge

OUTCOMES

- Modify a database to include additional fields for a merge document
- Create a mail merge using a form letter and database fields

Review: Merge Feature: Create Database File

The Merge feature merges a word processing file (form letter) with a database file. For example, if you wanted to send a letter to all Rockwell Technologies sales representatives, it would be easy to create a form letter that would be merged with the database file containing their addresses. The Merge feature allows you to personalize each letter without having to key a separate letter to each person, thus saving a lot of time and effort.

NOTE | **Review Chapter 12, Lessons 64, 65, and 66 on the basics of Mail Merge using Microsoft *Word*.**

The database file contains a record for each recipient. Each record contains field(s) of information about the person such as first name, last name, address, city, state, ZIP, etc.

The word processing file contains the text of the document (constant information) plus the merge field names (variable information), as shown in Figure 17-13. The merge field names are positioned in the document where the variable information from the database is to appear. A personalized letter to each recipient is the result of merging the two files.

In this activity you will create a query that selects the fields you want to appear in the form letter shown in Figure 17-15.

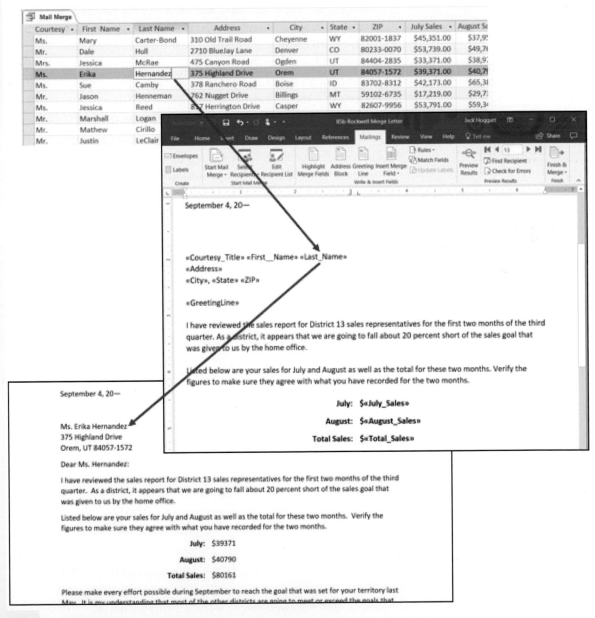

Figure 17-15 Mail Merge using *Access* data source and *Word* form letter

1. Open the *Sales Reps – District 13* table in the **Rockwell Technologies** database.
2. Create a query that selects the following fields: Courtesy Title, First Name, Last Name, Address, City, State, ZIP, July Sales, August Sales, and a calculated Total Sales field. If needed, review using the Expression Builder to create a calculated field in Lesson 84A. The Greeting Line will be specified in the *Word* part of the merge in 85B.
3. **Save the query as:** *Mail Merge*.

85B

Mail Merge: Create Form Letter

(In *Access*)
External Data tab > Export > Word Merge

(In *Word*)
Mailings tab > Write & Insert Fields > Insert Merge Field

1. If necessary, open the *Mail Merge* query you created in Lesson 85A. Click the *External Data* tab, then click the *Word Merge* button in the Export group to start the *Word* Mail Merge Wizard.
2. Select *Create a new document and then link the data to it* and click *OK*. Microsoft *Word* opens to a blank document with the Mail Merge pane displayed at the right. If the Mail Merge *Word* document doesn't appear on your screen after the *Mail Merge Wizard* disappears from the screen, minimize the *Access* file screen.
3. In the Mail Merge pane, the *Letters* document type should be selected. Click *Next: Starting document* at the bottom of the pane (Step 1 of 6).
4. Under Select starting document, choose *Use the current document, if not already selected*, and click *Next: Select recipients* (Step 2 of 6).
5. Under Select recipients, choose *Use an existing list*, if not already selected. Click *Edit recipient list*. In the Mail Merge Recipients dialog box, click the check mark at the top of the column to the right of Data Source to deselect (clear) all check marks. Then put check marks in the boxes for *Hernandez, Tapani,* and *Butler*. Click *OK*. Click *Next: Write your letter* (Step 3 of 6).
6. That brings up *Write your letter*. Key the merge letter (form letter), inserting merge fields as shown in the following letter. Use the *Greeting Line* button in the Write & Insert Fields group on the Mailings tab to insert the greeting line.
7. After the letter is keyed, click *Next: Preview your letters* (Step 4 of 6) in the Mail Merge pane.
8. Use the >> and << buttons in the Preview Results group to scroll through the letters.
9. Click *Next: Complete the merge* (Step 5 of 6) to complete the merge.
10. Under Merge, click *Edit individual letters* and choose *All* (Figure 17-16). Click *OK* to create a *Word* document with all three letters (Step 6 of 6).

Figure 17-16 Merge to New Document

11. **Save as** *85b Rockwell merge letters*. Print the letters.

September 4, 20—

«Courtesy_Title» «First_Name» «Last_Name»
«Address»
«City», «State» «ZIP»

«GreetingLine»

I have reviewed the sales report for District 13 sales representatives for the first two months of the third quarter. As a district, it appears that we are going to fall about 20 percent short of the sales goal that was given to us by the home office.

Listed below are your sales for July and August as well as the total for these two months. Verify the figures to make sure they agree with what you have recorded for the two months.

July:	$«July_Sales»
August:	$«August_Sales»
Total Sales:	$«Total_Sales»

Please make every effort possible during September to reach the goal that was set for your territory last May. It is my understanding that most of the other districts are going to meet or exceed the goals that were given to them.

If I can provide additional assistance to you to help you meet your goal, please contact me.

Sincerely,

Paul M. Vermillion
District Sales Manager

xx

OUTCOMES

- Create queries with computed fields
- Calculate column totals
- Analyze information extracted through queries

86A

Create Queries with Computed Fields

View tab > Design View > Query Setup > Builder

1. Open **df 86a Rockwell Technologies** database, and save it as **86a Rockwell Technologies**.
2. Review using the Expression Builder in a query to compute fields in Lesson 84.
3. Use Query Design to create a query that shows Total Sales for Quarter (July through September) and Average Monthly Sales for the quarter for each of the sales reps in District 13. Use the fields shown in Figure 17-17 in the query and to verify the accuracy of the query when completed.

Last Name	First Name	Territory	July Sales	August Sales	September Sales	Total Sales for Quarter	Average Monthly Sales
Bell	Scott	Colorado	$39,200.00	$43,286.00	$47,804.00	$130,290.00	$43,430.00
Butler	Warren	Arizona	$35,975.00	$46,873.00	$50,980.00	$133,828.00	$44,609.33
Camby	Sue	Idaho	$42,173.00	$65,386.00	$55,142.00	$162,701.00	$54,233.67
Carter-Bond	Mary	Wyoming	$45,351.00	$37,951.00	$42,819.00	$126,121.00	$42,040.33
Chi	Karrie	Arizona	$39,750.00	$48,621.00	$50,805.00	$139,176.00	$46,392.00
Cirillo	Mathew	Idaho	$29,731.00	$37,956.00	$39,885.00	$107,572.00	$35,857.33

Figure 17-17 Total Sales for Quarter query

> **NOTE** The Average Monthly Sales for the three new sales reps (Sanchez, Hayes, and Phipps) is computed as though they were with the company for all three months of the quarter. Thus, their Average Monthly Sales is not a fair representation of their actual performance.

4. The formula for Total Sales for Quarter is:

$$[July\ Sales]+[August\ Sales]+[September\ Sales]$$

5. The formula for Average Monthly Sales is:

$$([July\ Sales]+[August\ Sales]+[September\ Sales])/3$$

or

$$[Total\ Sales\ for\ Quarter]/3$$

6. Run the query. Note that the Average Monthly Sales comes up with a lot of ####'s in many of the cells. Widen the field to show the numbers.

7. To change the format of the field to Currency, with the pointer still in the field display the Property Sheet using the path shown at the left. See Figure 17-18.

Query Tools Design tab > Show/Hide > Property Sheet

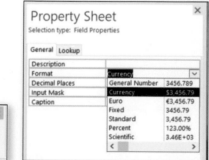

Figure 17-18 Property Sheet

8. In the Property Sheet, click in the box to the right of Format to bring up the down arrow. Click the down arrow and select *Currency* (Figure 17-18).

9. Run the results again to verify that the field is now displayed with Currency format.

10. **Save the query as: *86a Total Sales for Quarter*.**

Calculate the following District Totals:

- Total District Sales for July
- Total District Sales for August
- Total District Sales for September
- Total District Sales for the Third Quarter
- Average District Sales for Quarter

Use the following procedure to do the calculations using the **86a Rockwell Technologies** database.

1. Open the **86a Total Sales for Quarter** query, if it isn't still open.

2. On the Home tab in the Records group shown in Figure 17-19, click *Σ Totals*. This inserts the Total row at the bottom of the query. (To remove the *Total* line, click *Σ Totals* again.)

Figure 17-19 Totals feature

3. Click the Total row cell for July Sales. A down arrow should appear.

4. Click the drop-down list arrow and select the function (*Sum*) you want performed (Figure 17-20). Once the function has been clicked, the total for July ($1,016,039.00) appears in the *Total* line.

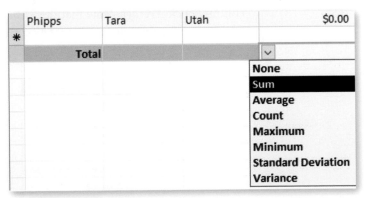

Figure 17-20 Total line functions

5. If the field isn't wide enough to allow the total to appear, double-click (or click and drag) the right-side line of the cell of the column heading to expand the column width.

6. Click the down arrow in the rest of the fields where calculations are to be performed and click the desired function to complete the calculations and expand column widths as needed (Figure 17-21).

$35,975.00	$46,873.00	$50,980.00	$133,828.00	$44,609.33
$56,730.00	$46,720.00	$54,560.00	$158,010.00	$52,670.00
$0.00	$0.00	$23,891.00	$23,891.00	$7,963.67
$0.00	$0.00	$19,799.00	$19,799.00	$6,599.67
$0.00	$0.00	$25,882.00	$25,882.00	$8,627.33
$1,016,039.00	$991,734.00	$1,178,635.00	$3,186,408.00	$40,851.38

Figure 17-21 Total line

7. Open **df 86 analysis form** and record your answers to questions 1–4. Save as: **86 analysis form**.
8. Keep the form open to answer questions 5–8 as you complete 86C.

86C

Calculate Average District Sales

Calculate the District 13 averages and record your answers on the **86 analysis form**:

- Average District Sales for July.
- Average District Sales for August.
- Average District Sales for September.
- Average District Sales for Quarter.

Use the procedure shown below to do the calculations to get the averages.

1. Open the *86a Total Sales for Quarter* query, if it isn't still open.
2. Click the Total cell for July Sales (Figure 17-22).

Phipps	Tara	Utah	$0.00
Total		⌄	**$1,016,039.00**

Figure 17-22 Total July Sales

3. Click the down arrow that appears when you click in the cell.

   The figure that currently appears is the sum of the column. To calculate the Average of the column, click *Average*. Note that the $1,016039.00 changes to $39,078.42, which represents the average for the column (Figure 17-23).

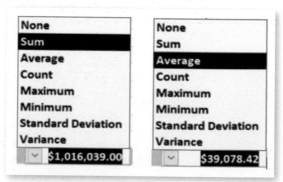

Figure 17-23 Change Totals from Sum to Average

4. Follow the same procedure to calculate the Averages for the remaining columns and record your answers on the form.
5. Save as: **86 analysis form.**

Use the information gathered for the **86 analysis form** and the *86a Total Sales for Quarter* query to answer the following questions. Record your answers on **df 86d Analyze Information Form**. After you complete the form, save the form as **86d analyze information form** and print a copy of it.

1. Which month generated the greatest sales revenue?
2. Which month generated the least sales revenue?
3. What impact did the new employees have on *Total Sales for the Quarter*?
4. What impact did the new employees have on *Average Monthly Sales* when they were included in the calculation?
5. How many sales reps had average monthly sales that were 20 percent higher than the average of all sales reps? To answer this question, create and run a query using the *Total Sales for Quarter* query with the Last Name, First Name, and Average Monthly Sales. Using the calculator feature on your computer, calculate what 120 percent of the Average Monthly sales is and use that amount for the Criteria for the Average Monthly Sales column in Design View of the query.
6. Save the query as: **86d Sales 20% Higher than Average for Quarter**.
7. How many sales reps had average monthly sales that were 20 percent lower than the average of all sales reps? Run a query using the *Total Sales for Quarter* query that includes the *Last Name, First Name*, and *Average Monthly Sales* fields. Calculate what 80 percent of the Average Monthly Sales is and use that amount as the Criteria for the Average Monthly Sales column.
8. Save the query as: **86d Sales 20% Lower than Average for Quarter**.

21st Century Skills: Civic Literacy

All of us are members of a community, whether it's a small town, suburban neighborhood, or large municipality. Being a member of any type of community comes with certain rights and responsibilities.

As a U.S. citizen, you have basic constitutional rights, such as freedom to practice any religion you choose or freedom to assemble and protest government policies. But you also have responsibilities as a citizen. These include obeying laws, paying taxes, and participating in elections. Even if you are not subject to paying taxes or old enough to vote or drive, you can show your civic-mindedness in other ways. For example, you can:

- Perform community service, such as picking up trash or planting trees
- Support political candidates and issues for which you feel strongly
- Identify ways to stay informed and understand governmental processes

Think Critically

1. In groups, brainstorm issues that affect your community. This could be a local issue, such as downsizing the police force or restricting the use of skateboards in public parks, or a national issue, such as changing the federal income tax rate.
2. As a group, select the issue that you think is most important. Then create a plan of action for how you would support the issue or bring about change. Would you organize a rally or protest? Send letters to your congressional representatives? Hand out flyers? Present your plan to the class.

COLLABORATION

LESSON 87

Using Queries Created from Multiple Tables to Create Word Documents

OUTCOMES

- Analyze sales information by territory
- Create a query from two tables
- Create a *Word* table from a database query

87A

Analyze Total Sales Information by Territory

The *Total Sales for Quarter* query can be used to provide more information. The query can be structured so that each of the territories can be evaluated individually rather than viewing the district as a whole.

Create queries (using the *86a Total Sales for Quarter* query in the **86 Rockwell Technologies** database.) showing the totals for each of the seven territories. Include the following fields with each query and save them with the query names shown below:

- Last Name
- First Name
- Territory
- July Sales
- August Sales
- September Sales
- Total Sales for Quarter
- Average Monthly Sales

- *Total Sales for Quarter - Arizona*
- *Total Sales for Quarter - Colorado*
- *Total Sales for Quarter - Idaho*
- *Total Sales for Quarter - Montana*
- *Total Sales for Quarter - South Dakota*
- *Total Sales for Quarter - Utah*
- *Total Sales for Quarter - Wyoming*

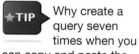 **★TIP** Why create a query seven times when you can copy and paste the first one and change the criteria?

1. Create the query with the fields using *Arizona* for the *Criteria* in the Territory column.
2. Run the query.
3. Use the *Totals* feature to insert the Totals line.
4. Click the down arrow on each sales column and select *Sum* except for the Average Monthly Sales column, where you will select *Average*.
5. You query should look like Figure 17-24.

Last Name	First Name	Territory	July Sales	August Sales	September Sales	Total Sales for Quarter	Average Monthly Sales
Chi	Karrie	Arizona	$39,750.00	$48,621.00	$50,805.00	$139,176.00	$46,392.00
Finley	Ann	Arizona	$19,765.00	$35,765.00	$23,800.00	$79,330.00	$26,443.33
Reese	Jay	Arizona	$67,890.00	$45,780.00	$50,775.00	$164,445.00	$54,815.00
Butler	Warren	Arizona	$35,975.00	$46,873.00	$50,980.00	$133,828.00	$44,609.33
Hulett	Sandra	Arizona	$56,730.00	$46,720.00	$54,560.00	$158,010.00	$52,670.00
Sanchez	Rey	Arizona	$0.00	$0.00	$23,891.00	$23,891.00	$7,963.67
Total			**$220,110.00**	**$223,759.00**	**$254,811.00**	**$698,680.00**	**$38,815.56**

Figure 17-24 Total Sales for Quarter – Arizona

6. Save the query as **Total Sales for Quarter - Arizona** and close the query.
7. In the left-hand column, click the *Arizona* query and Copy and Paste. This brings up the Paste As dialog box. Delete *Copy of* and change *Arizona* to **Colorado** as shown in Figure 17-25.

Figure 17-25 Copy and Paste a query

8. Click *OK*.

9. Click *Paste* again to bring up the Paste As dialog box again. Edit the query name to change it to Total Sales for Quarter – **Idaho**. Repeat this procedure for each of the seven territories.

10. Open the *Colorado* query.

11. Change the View to *Design View*.

12. Change the *Criteria* from *Arizona* to *Colorado*.

13. Run the query to verify that the query now includes the Colorado sales reps with totals automatically changed as shown in Figure 17-26.

Last Name	First Name	Territory	July Sales	August Sales	September Sales	Total Sales for Quarter	Average Monthly Sales
Hull	Dale	Colorado	$53,739.00	$49,762.00	$54,829.00	$158,330.00	$52,776.67
LeClair	Justin	Colorado	$63,212.00	$40,321.00	$50,705.00	$154,238.00	$51,412.67
Donovan	Kellee	Colorado	$37,198.00	$45,865.00	$49,814.00	$132,877.00	$44,292.33
Rivera	Jose	Colorado	$55,400.00	$37,751.00	$50,880.00	$144,031.00	$48,010.33
Bell	Scott	Colorado	$39,200.00	$43,286.00	$47,804.00	$130,290.00	$43,430.00
Hayes	Jackson	Colorado	$0.00	$0.00	$19,799.00	$19,799.00	$6,599.67
Total			$248,749.00	$216,985.00	$273,831.00	$739,565.00	$41,086.94

Figure 17-26 Total Sales for Quarter – Colorado

14. Repeat the procedure for each of the remaining territories.

15. Open *df 87 analysis form* and answer the following questions:

- What are the total Sales for July for each state?
- What are the total Sales for August for each state?
- What are the total Sales for September for each state?
- What are the total Sales for the third Quarter for each state?
- What are the total Average Monthly Sales for the third quarter for each state?

16. Save as: *87 analysis form*.

Copy Access Table to Word Document

Tables and queries created in *Access* can be copied and pasted in a *Word* document. Create a table of quarterly sales for the Arizona reps of Rockwell Technologies by following these steps.

1. Open the **86 Rockwell Technologies** database.
2. Right-click the *Total Sales for Quarter - Arizona* query (Figure 17-27).
3. Copy the query. (You don't have to open the query; just click and copy the query name.)
4. Open a new *Word* document.
5. Paste the query in the *Word* document as shown in Figure 17-28.

Figure 17-27 Total Sales for Quarter - Arizona

Total Sales for Quarter - Arizona							
Last Name	First Name	Territory	July Sales	August Sales	September Sales	Total Sales for Quarter	Average Monthly Sales
Chi	Karrie	Arizona	$39,750.00	$48,621.00	$50,805.00	$139,176.00	$46,392.00
Finley	Ann	Arizona	$19,765.00	$35,765.00	$23,800.00	$79,330.00	$26,443.33
Reese	Jay	Arizona	$67,890.00	$45,780.00	$50,775.00	$164,445.00	$54,815.00
Butler	Warren	Arizona	$35,975.00	$46,873.00	$50,980.00	$133,828.00	$44,609.33
Hulett	Sandra	Arizona	$56,730.00	$46,720.00	$54,560.00	$158,010.00	$52,670.00
Sanchez	Rey	Arizona	$0.00	$0.00	$23,891.00	$23,891.00	$7,963.67
			$220,110.00	$223,759.00	$254,811.00	$698,680.00	$38,815.56

Figure 17-28 Query copied and pasted in a *Word* document

6. In the *Word* document, make the modifications shown below. The modified table should be similar to the one shown in Figure 17-29.

Modification	Path or Quick Keys
Delete main title	Table Tools > Layout > Rows and Columns > Delete > Delete Column
Change shading	Table Tools > Design > Table Styles > Shading > Select Color
Use Center Align for the Territory column	Ctrl + E
Delete the *First Name* column	Table Tools > Layout > Rows and Columns > Delete > Delete Column
Adjust column width	Table Tools > Layout > Cell Size > Distribute Columns or Click and drag column borders
Merge cells	Table Tools > Layout > Merge > Merge Cells

7. **Save as:** *87b Arizona*.

Last Name	Territory	July Sales	August Sales	September Sales	Total Sales for Quarter	Average Monthly Sales
Chi	Arizona	$39,750.00	$48,621.00	$50,805.00	$139,176.00	$46,392.00
Finley	Arizona	$19,765.00	$35,765.00	$23,800.00	$79,330.00	$26,443.33
Reese	Arizona	$67,890.00	$45,780.00	$50,775.00	$164,445.00	$54,815.00
Butler	Arizona	$35,975.00	$46,873.00	$50,980.00	$133,828.00	$44,609.33
Hulett	Arizona	$56,730.00	$46,720.00	$54,560.00	$158,010.00	$52,670.00
Sanchez	Arizona	$0.00	$0.00	$23,891.00	$23,891.00	$7,963.67
Totals		$220,110.00	$223,759.00	$254,811.00	$698,680.00	$38,815.56

Figure 17-29 Modified table

87C

Create a Query from Two Tables

Data from two different tables can be merged in a query when the two tables have a common field (a field that exists in both tables that is exactly the same). The common field allows the program to match records from one table with records in another table.

Baxter International has a table for address information and a table for recording subscription fees. Each month they send out a reminder to customers who are behind in paying their subscription fee. The reminder is sent on the 15th of the following month when fees were not paid. For example, if no fees were paid in February, a reminder would be sent on March 15. In order to send out such a reminder, information from both tables is required. Create a query to determine who is behind with their payments to use for mailing reminders. Use the following steps to complete the query.

1. Open **df 87c Baxter International** database and save it as **87c Baxter International**.
2. Use the *Query Design* feature to create a query. Add both tables to the Query dialog box.
3. Establish the relationship between the two tables by clicking on *Last Name* in the *Fees* table and dragging it a little beneath Last Name (not on top) in the *Member's Address* table. You should see an arrow connecting Last Name in the *Fees* table to Last Name in the *Member's Address* table as shown in Figure 17-30. If it connects to a field name other than Last Name, click the line between the two tables, tap the *Delete* key, and click and drag again.

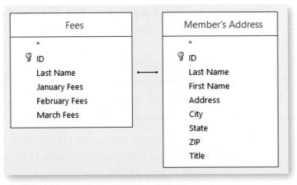

Figure 17-30 Establish a relationship between two tables

4. Include the following fields from the *Member's Address* table, except those indicated as from the *Fees* table in the query:

- Last Name (*Fees* table)
- First Name
- Address
- City
- State
- ZIP
- February Fees (*Fees* table)

5. For the criteria in the *February Fees* field, key **Is Null**. Your query should look similar to Figure 17-31.

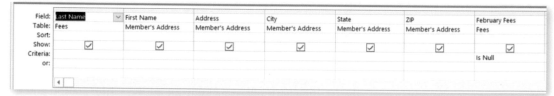

Figure 17-31 Query Design with fields and criteria

6. Run the query.
7. Save as: **87c February fees past due.**
8. Edit the query to include *Title* field. The query should look like Figure 17-32.

Last Name	First Name	Address	City	State	ZIP	February Fee	Title
Sessions	Jon	218 Woodland Way, SE	Portland	OR	97267		Mr.
Murphy	Shawn	488 Everett Street, NE	Portland	OR	97232		Mr.
Sabo	Kent	77 Hampton Street, SW	Portland	OR	97223		Mr.
Gonzalez	Felipe	8800 Hancock Court, NE	Portland	OR	97220		Mr.
Van Pelt	Jordan	1440 Duke Street, SE	Portland	OR	97202		Mr.

Figure 17-32 Query of members who haven't paid February fees

LESSON 88 — Using a Database to Create Form Letters, Envelopes, and Labels

OUTCOMES
- Create a form letter
- Create envelopes
- Create labels

88A

Create a Mail Merge

1. Use the *Mail Merge* feature to create the form letter shown on the next page to send to the individuals who have not paid their February fees at Baxter International. If needed, refer to Lessons 85A and 85B to review the steps for creating a Mail Merge.

2. Use the *87c February Fees Past Due* query for the database file in the merge. Print a copy of the form letter.

3. Save as: **88b Baxter merge letter.**

4. Use the *Find Recipient* feature to find the letter being sent to Felipe Gonzalez; print a copy of the letter.
5. **Save as:** *88b Gonzalez*.

March 15, 20—

«Title» «First_Name» «Last_Name»
«Address»
«City», «State» «ZIP»

Dear «First_Name»,

I hope you are enjoying your subscription with Baxter International. As of today, March 15, we have not received your February or March subscription fees. Please send us a check today for $50 to cover the fees for these two months.

If you have questions about your fees, please call me at 503.829.1590.

Sincerely,

Jane R. Delgado
Subscription Manager

xx

88B

Create Envelopes

Mailings tab > Start Mail Merge > Start Mail Merge > Envelopes

Use the Mailings feature in *Word* to create envelopes for the letters created in 88A by following these steps.

1. Open a blank document in *Word*.
2. Click *Start Mail Merge* in the Start Mail Merge group on the Mailings tab.
3. Click *Envelopes*.
4. In the Envelope Options dialog box, select *Size 10* for the Envelope size. If Size 10 doesn't appear automatically, click the down arrow beneath Envelope size and click *Size 10*.
5. Click *OK*.
6. Key the return address starting at the insertion point:

> Baxter International
> 8076 Majestic Lane, SW
> Portland, OR 97224

7. Select the recipients by clicking *Select Recipients* and then clicking *Use an Existing List*. See Figure 17-33.

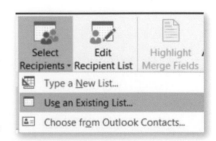

Figure 17-33 Select Recipients

8. Locate and double-click *87c Baxter International* database; then click the object (*February Fees Past Due*) containing the list of the recipients and click *OK*.

9. Click at the bottom/middle of the envelope to bring up the box and use the *Insert Merge Field* feature to insert the fields as illustrated in Figure 17-34. Be sure to add spaces between fields where needed.

Baxter International
8076 Majestic Lane, SW
Portland, OR 97224

«Title» «First_Name» «First_Name»
«Address»
«City», «State» «ZIP»

Figure 17-34 Envelope with merge fields

10. Click *Preview Results*. Make sure you have inserted the spaces and the comma after the City.

11. Use *Find Recipient* to locate and then print an envelope for Felipe Gonzalez.

12. **Save as:** ***88b Baxter envelopes***. Close the file.

88C

Mailing Labels

The Mailings feature can also be used to create and print labels. Create mailing labels for all of Baxter International's members using the *Member's Address* table by following these steps.

1. Open a blank document in *Word*.

2. Click *Start Mail Merge* in the Start Mail Merge group of the Mailings tab.

3. Click *Labels*.

4. In the Label Options dialog box as shown in Figure 17-35:

Select *Continuous-feed printers* for the Printer information.

Select *Avery A4/A5* for the Label information.

Select *4423/3* for the Product number.

Click *OK*.

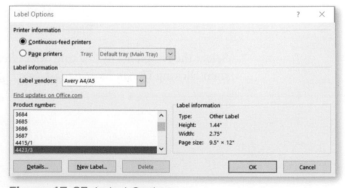

Figure 17-35 Label Options

5. Click *Select Recipients*; click *Use an Existing list*.

6. Locate and select *Member's Address* table from the *87c Baxter International* database. Click *OK*.

7. Use the *Insert Merge Field* feature to insert the fields, as shown in Figure 17-36. Be sure to insert the spaces between field names on the same line and the comma following the city field.

Figure 17-36 Inserted merged fields

8. Click *Update Labels* to place the fields in each label, as shown in Figure 17-37.

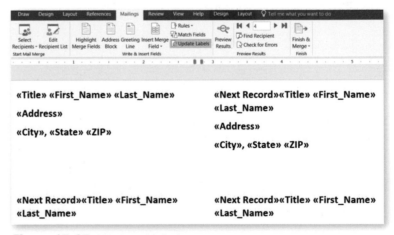

Figure 17-37 Updated labels

9. Click *Preview Results* to see merged labels. This replaces the merged fields with data from the recipient list as shown in Figure 17-38.

Figure 17-38 Preview results

10. Print a copy of the labels.
11. **Save as:** *88c Baxter mailing labels.*

Assessment 10   Enhanced Database Skills

Activity 1
Input Data into Form

Open *df a10 activity1* and save it as *a10 activity1*. Enter the information shown below into the *Sales Reps – District 14* form for the two new sales reps as records 31 and 32.

Title	Mr.
Last Name	Montessa
First Name	Carlos
Address	852 Lake Grove Court
City	San Diego
State	CA
ZIP	92131-3321
Territory	California

Title	Ms.
Last Name	McGraw
First Name	Katherine
Address	673 Union Street
City	San Francisco
State	CA
ZIP	94133-8634
Territory	California

Activity 2
Editing Records

Make the following changes to the records in the *Rockwell Technologies - District 14* table.
1. Change *Winters'* address to **1472 Prescott Street**.
2. Change the ZIP for *Culver* to **97301-8824**.
3. Change *Phillips'* address to **387 Ferguson Avenue, Modesto, 95354-3210**.

Activity 3
Input Data into Form

The third-quarter sales figures for Washington just arrived. Please enter them in the *Sales Reps - District 14* form.

Last Name	First Name	July Sales	August Sales	September Sales
Beckwith	Kent	$68,524	$62,566	$66,750
Bushlack	Michael	$70,500	$75,306	$72,906
Davis	Isiah	$39,763	$48,655	$51,402
Hughes	Justin	$55,671	$63,339	$60,113
Sherman	Karen	$80,754	$54,354	$75,385

Activity 4
Run a Query

1. Using the *Sales Reps - District 14* table create a query called *Total Sales for Quarter*. Include Last Name, First Name, Territory, July Sales, August Sales, and September Sales.
2. Add a new column for **Total Sales for Quarter**. Use the Expression Builder to compute the total sales.
3. Sort the query by *Total Sales* in descending order. Print a copy of the query.

Activity 5
Use Total Feature

Use the Σ Totals feature to calculate the following for District 14 sales reps. The new sales reps will be included in the figures. Record your answers on the **df a10 activity5 form**:

- Average District Sales for July.
- Average District Sales for August.
- Average District Sales for September.
- Average District Total Sales for Quarter.

Save as: **a10 activity5 analysis form**.

Activity 6
Create Mailing Labels

Prepare a set of mailing labels similar to the ones shown below for District 14 sales reps using the *Sales Reps - District 14* table. Use Avery A4/A5 for the Label vendor and Avery 4423/3 labels. Print the labels.

Save as: **a10 activity6 labels**.

Mr. Justin Hughes
313 Glenwood Drive
Vancouver, WA 98662-1148

Ms. Rose Winters
1472 Prescott Street
Portland, OR 97217-8755

Mr. Chad Chambers
2317 Silver Dollar Avenue
Las Vegas, NV 89102-9964

Mrs. Harriet Hanson
1890 Rancho Verde Drive
Reno, NV 89511-2221

Mrs. Mai Yang
2187 Klamath Street
Salem, OR 97306-9031

Mr. Albert Zimmer
330 Van Ness Avenue
Los Angeles, CA 90020-3341

Prepare a mail merge letter from the information below for *Rockwell Technologies - District 14* sales reps with Quarterly sales greater than $200,000. Use Courier New 12 pt. font and a 2" top margin for the merge letter. You will need to create a query to determine those sales reps with sales greater than $200,000. Be sure to include all the fields in the query that you will need to complete the mail merge. To do this you will need to use the *Sales Reps - District 14* table and the *Total Sales for Quarter* query and establish a relationship between the two in the query you create. Save the query as ***Reps > $200,000 sales***. Print a copy of the letter to Greg Stockton.

Date the letter **October 16, 20—**

The letter is from **Leslie R. Fenwick, President**

Save as: *a10 activity7 form letter*.

«Title» «First_Name» «Last_Name»
«Address»
«City», «State» «ZIP»

Dear «Title» «Last_Name»:

Congratulations! The sales report I received from your district manager lists your name as one of the five sales representatives in District 14 with sales over $200,000 for the quarter.

July-September was a very good quarter for District 14 sales representatives. They averaged just over $160,000 of sales during the quarter. This was an increase of approximately 8.38 percent over 2nd quarter sales. This increase is due in large part to your efforts during the quarter.

We appreciate your hard work to make this the best year ever at Rockwell Technologies.

Sincerely,

Skill Builder 16

A

Warmup

alphabet 1 Maxine Pelzer has flown the big jet over the quaint, dark canyon.

Shift key 2 Jay Reyes is in New York; Sara Jones is in San Diego or San Jose.

speed 3 Enrique lent the field auditor a hand with the work for the firm.

gwam 1' | 1 | 2 | 3 | 4 | 5 | 6 | 7 | 8 | 9 | 10 | 11 | 12 |

B

Technique: Letter Keys

Key each line twice.

One-hand words of 2–5 letters

1 be no up we at in ax my as on add bag car dad war tax sat saw see
2 dad oil egg lip cab joy fee pop art you age him sad mom seat look
3 save milk race pull star pink grade onion grass polio serve pupil

4 as my | at a rate | we are | no war | get set | at my best | you were | a great
5 as few | you set a date | my card | water tax | act on a | tax date | in case
6 my only date | water rate | my tax case | tax fact | my best date | my card

7 No, you are free only after I act on a rate on a state water tax.
8 Get him my extra database only after you set up exact test dates.
9 You set my area tax rate after a great state case on a water tax.

gwam 1' | 1 | 2 | 3 | 4 | 5 | 6 | 7 | 8 | 9 | 10 | 11 | 12 | 13 |

C

Speed Forcing Drill

Key each line once at top speed. If you finish all lines before time is called, key them again, trying to go faster.

Emphasis: high-frequency balanced-hand words

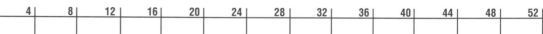

| 4| | 8| | 12| | 16| | 20| | 24| | 28| | 32| | 36| | 40| | 44| | 48| | 52|

Jay and I may make a bid for the antique pen.
Clem may make a big profit for the six firms.

Pamela may pay for the eight pens for the auditor.
Nancy bid for the antique chair and antique rifle.

If the pay is right, Sue may make their gowns for them.
When did the auditor sign the audit forms for the city?

Laurie kept the men busy with the work down by the big lake.
Diana may go with us to the city to pay them for their work.

Did the firm bid for the right to the land downtown by city hall?
Jay may suspend the men as a penalty for their work on the docks.

gwam 15" | 4| | 8| | 12| | 16| | 20| | 24| | 28| | 32| | 36| | 40| | 44| | 48| | 52|

D

Reading/Keying Response Patterns

1. Key each line three times (slowly, faster, top speed).
2. Key two 1' timings on lines 7–9; determine *gwam* on each timing.

Emphasize quick finger reaches, wrists low and relaxed.

balanced-hand words

1 is by do if go he so us to me of jam row rug she bus air but city
2 both also busy held duck dial form make rush sick soap when towns
3 visit widow theme title ivory proxy quake shape amend burnt chair

Emphasize high-speed phrase responses.

balanced-hand phrases

4 He owns it | make the signs | paid the man | go to work | if they fix the
5 Go to the | they may make | to the problem | with the sign | and the maps
6 With the city | the eighth neighbor | social problem | the big ornament

Emphasize high-speed, world-level response; quick spacing.

balanced-hand sentences

7 Pamela paid the man by the city dock for the six bushels of corn.
8 Keith may keep the food for the fish by the big antique fishbowl.
9 The haughty girls paid for their own gowns for the island social.

gwam 1' | 1 | 2 | 3 | 4 | 5 | 6 | 7 | 8 | 9 | 10 | 11 | 12 | 13 |

E

Timed Writing

1. Key a 1' timing on ¶ 1; determine *gwam*.
2. Add 2–4 *gwam* to the rate attained in step 1, and note quarter-minute checkpoints from the chart below.
3. Key two 1' guided timings on ¶ 1 to increase speed.
4. Practice ¶ 2 in the same way.
5. Take two 3' timings on ¶s 1 and 2 combined; determine *gwam* and number of errors.

Quarter-Minute Checkpoints				
gwam	1/4'	1/2'	3/4'	1'
24	6	12	18	24
28	7	14	21	28
32	8	16	24	32
36	9	18	27	36
40	10	20	30	40
44	11	22	33	44
48	12	24	36	48
52	13	26	39	52
56	14	28	42	56
60	15	30	45	60

A all letters used

gwam 3' | 5'

One of the great statesmen of our nation was Benjamin
Franklin. Among other things, the man is quite well known for his
work as an author, as a philosopher, as a scientist, and as a
diplomat and representative of our country. Recognized as one of
the excellent leaders of the Revolution, he is considered a founding
father of the United States. His name can be seen on the
Declaration of Independence as well as the United States
Constitution.

4 | 2
8 | 5
12 | 7
16 | 10
21 | 12
25 | 15
28 | 17
29 | 17

Some of the things that Franklin is given the credit for
include the Franklin stove, the lightning rod, bifocals, and many,
many witty quotes in his almanac. Franklin once said, "If you
would not be forgotten as soon as you are dead, either write
something worth reading or do things worth the writing." Because
of his many personal accomplishments and the written documents
that his signature appears on, Mr. Franklin will not likely be
forgotten very soon! He is a role model that all Americans should
try to model their life after.

33 | 20
37 | 22
41 | 25
45 | 27
49 | 30
54 | 32
58 | 35
62 | 37
64 | 38

gwam 3' | 1 | 2 | 3 | 4 | 5
5' | 1 | 2 | 3

Planning for Your Career 7

Being Effective and Advancing Your Career

OUTCOMES

- Understand the performance review process
- Learn the importance of continuous improvement
- Set priorities and develop plans for the present, near future, and long term
- Identify a mentor
- Learn how to project professionalism
- Learn important ways to advance your career

Performance Reviews

Most employees have their job performance reviewed annually by their supervisors. Some employees are evaluated more frequently, including those employees who have been recently hired. Newly hired employees may be assigned a conditional, provisional, or probationary status that may last until the performance review results warrant reclassification either to a regular status or dismissal from the position.

The performance review process often requires an employee to complete a self-appraisal that the supervisor will consider when completing her appraisal of the employee's performance (see Figure PC7-1). Additionally, the review process may require the employee to achieve specific goals during the next performance review period. The results of an employee's job performance review may be used to determine such matters as:

- If an employee's employment will be continued or terminated
- If an employee is ready to accept additional duties and responsibilities within his present position
- If an employee deserves a raise in pay and/or a bonus and the size of the raise or bonus
- If an employee will be promoted to a more responsible position
- Professional development activities for the employee

Figure PC7-1 Performance review form

Performance reviews are usually based on criteria stated on a form provided by the employer. The criteria describe the components of the position that will be evaluated and a rating scale that describes various levels of performance. Employees typically have access to the performance review form so they know the criteria against which their performance is being judged. Also, the same form is typically used to evaluate all employees within similar job classifications to increase the likelihood that employees are assessed similarly.

In this activity you will complete a self-appraisal form for recently hired employees. Your supervisor would consider your self-appraisal when completing her review of your performance in your new job.

Assume that this class is your new job and that you are to complete the requirements of this class to the best of your ability. Your teacher is your supervisor and is required to assess your performance in this class. As part of the performance review process for a new employee, you are required to complete a self-appraisal of your performance every three months. Your supervisor will consider your self-appraisal when assessing your performance. Your supervisor's assessment will determine if you will continue in a probationary status, must reach specific goals during the next review period to retain your employment, or will be reclassified as a regular employee.

1. Open *df pc7 self-appraisal*. Note: As you key text into the document in the following steps, you should adjust the vertical spacing as needed to make the form attractive and easy to read and understand. If needed, the form can be more than one page.

2. Complete the first part of the form using your name, *Student* as the position, the date you began the class as the start date, the last three months as the review period, and your teacher's name as your supervisor.

3. Read the description for each Performance Rating and identify the points assigned to each rating.

4. Complete the six items in the Performance Component section. Include the number of the rating you believe you deserve in the Rating column. Key statements and/or identify evidence that supports your rating. For example, you could cite specific assignments that serve as evidence of the quality of your work. Or you could state that you have missed no classes to support your work habits rating.

5. Print the completed form, sign and date it.

6. Save as: *pc7 self-appraisal*.

Continuous Improvement

It is important that you be able to demonstrate that you possess the competencies, skills, and personal qualities that are expected of all employees. In this module, the focus is on continuously developing your competencies, skills, and personal qualities to higher levels and expanding them as new knowledge and technology impact your workplace. Through continuous improvement, you will increase your effectiveness in your present position and the likelihood that you will have opportunities to advance to higher-level positions during your career. Continuous improvement is also important for those who own their own business because the higher-level and expanded skills and knowledge will increase the chances that the owner will be able to sustain or grow the business.

Leremy/Shutterstock.com

1. Open *df pc7 effectiveness report*. Review the information requested in the Continuous Improvement section of the form.

2. Working with one or more classmates, identify at least five new products or product enhancements that have become available during the past five years and briefly describe how each has affected the way people work.

3. Record your findings in the space provided in *df pc7 effectiveness report*.

4. Save as: *pc7 effectiveness report 1*.

Planning

Effective employees begin every endeavor with an end in mind; that is, they plan and set priorities.

- They plan and set priorities for the day—What do I need to accomplish during this workday and how will I get it done?
- They plan and set priorities for the near future—What do I need to do to increase my chances for a promotion this year?
- They plan and set priorities for the long-term future—What do I need to do within the next five years to obtain the position I aspire to?

StockLite/Shutterstock.com

Planning and prioritizing take on more importance in today's world since most people no longer stay with one employer or in one career during their working years. Technology advances and the need to compete in a global environment have caused changes in the workplace that have both positively and negatively affected employees. In today's environment, many employers expect their employees to plan and pursue their own professional development so they will be able to take advantage of employment opportunities that arise with the present employer, with a different employer, or as an entrepreneur.

1. Open *pc7 effectiveness report 1* and preview the information requested in the Planning section and then key the following information in the appropriate space.

- Identify your priorities for today and describe your plan for accomplishing them
- Identify special projects, tasks, and/or activities you need to accomplish within the next four weeks and describe your plan for accomplishing them
- Identify what major priorities you want to accomplish this summer and describe your plan for accomplishing them

2. Save as: *pc7 effectiveness report 2*.

Selecting a Mentor

A mentor is someone who is willing to share experiences and knowledge that you can consider when making a decision or solving a problem relating to your present job or career opportunities.

Michal Kowalski/Shutterstock.com

A mentor may be someone who works for the same or a different employer, a family member, a teacher, a coach, and so on. An effective mentor will be available as needed to provide you with information, make positive suggestions, point out possible consequences of different actions, and provide the guidance needed so you can make a decision or solve a problem. As your career advances and your responsibilities change, you may need to establish a relationship with a different mentor who has the experience and knowledge appropriate for your present circumstances.

Mentors usually know your abilities, strengths and weaknesses, interests, and career goals and will oftentimes spread the "good word" about you to their colleagues when they know of opportunities for career advancement that could benefit you.

1. Open *pc7 effectiveness report 2* and preview the information requested in the Selecting a Mentor section.

2. In the space provided, name one person you would want to serve as your mentor when you are graduated from high school and begin to pursue your career via pursuing further education, entering the workforce, or serving in the military. Identify your relationship with this person and the experience and knowledge he or she has that you believe will be helpful to you as you embark on your career or preparation for your career.

3. Save as: *pc7 effectiveness report 3*.

Professionalism

One important aspect of being an effective employee and enjoying a rewarding career is to act professionally at all times. You should strive to earn a reputation for being dependable, believable, honest, cooperative, and eager to learn. While professionalism has many dimensions, the following are practical actions that project a professional image.

- Always be on time, respect the time of others, and don't be known for rushing to leave at the end of the workday
- Dress professionally, neatly, and appropriately for the situation
- Display a positive attitude, especially during difficult situations when others may be negative
- Don't whine, make excuses, or blame others when things don't go your way
- Ask questions when you are not sure what to do or how to do something
- Be flexible, take chances to grow, and try to make things work
- Show initiative and don't be afraid to volunteer to do something that may be new or different or will help you expand the scope of your position
- Follow through to complete the duties and responsibilities of your position
- Always try to create a favorable impression with all people you meet and work with as you cannot predict who may affect your career opportunities

1. Open *pc7 effectiveness report 3* and in the Professionalism section, describe at least five situations in which you demonstrated one or more of the above actions that help project a professional image. You may include activities related to school, community, church, work, or home.
2. Save as: *pc7 effectiveness report 4*.

Advancing Your Career

If you are like most working individuals, you will strive to advance to higher-level positions. This is especially true during the early years when you aspire to advance beyond entry-level positions to ones that have expanded duties and responsibilities. Advancements usually result in higher earnings and greater recognition from your peers, family, friends, and acquaintances. Unfortunately, each advancement may not bring with it job satisfaction. If job dissatisfaction becomes a concern in your career, you should consider taking a different path in your career to regain the level of job satisfaction you desire. There are many paths that individuals can follow to advance their career. Among them are:

- Working for the same employer while seeking promotions or transfers that will advance your career
- Changing employers to obtain promotions or transfers that will advance your career
- Seeking a position that will enable you to remain employed while pursuing concurrent self-employment opportunities
- Becoming self-employed on a full-time basis

Other avenues you can use to advance your career include such things as continuing your educations, getting involved in professional and trade associations, and networking.

Education. Once you have achieved the level of education that is needed for entry into your chosen career field, it is good to plan to complete additional education that will help you be more effective and advance your career or is required to maintain a professional license, certification, or designation. Trade schools, colleges and universities, professional and trade associations, and government agencies usually offer educational opportunities in a variety of formats, including distance learning, to meet the educational needs of workers. Some employers will pay part or all of the tuition if the additional education is of value to their business. The desired education can usually be completed as a part-time student allowing you to continue your employment. The educational objectives of workers are varied and may include learning in one of the following formats:

- Complete one or a series of courses that will provide the content you want. For example, if you are working in information technology and want to learn a new programming language, you could complete that programming course at a trade school, community college, or college or university.

- Complete the course requirements to earn or maintain a license or certification. For example, if you are an English teacher and want to be able to also teach social studies, you could complete the required courses at a college or university that certifies social studies teachers. Or, if you are a certified financial planner and need to complete continuing education to maintain your certification, you could complete approved course work offered by the professional association that awards the certification.

- Complete a program of studies that will lead to an undergraduate or graduate degree. For example, you may have a bachelor's degree in engineering but want to complete a master's degree program in business to enhance your opportunities to move into a position where you might supervise engineering or engineering functions of the business. Or, if you completed an undergraduate major in business and wish to become a registered nurse, you could complete a nursing program of study that leads to licensure or one that leads to licensure and a two- or four-year nursing-related degree.

iStock.com/skynesher

Professional, Trade, and Service Associations. Another avenue for increasing your job performance or advancing your career is to become a member of professional, trade, and service associations that are important in your career field.

These associations often operate at the local, state, regional, national, and/or international level. As a member, you will have continuous access to valuable information that will keep you informed about issues, trends, conditions, and new developments within the industry, profession, or community served by the association. You can keep informed by accessing the association's website, reading the association's research and publications, and attending association meetings, conferences, and conventions.

The associations may also provide you with many opportunities to develop and refine your organizational and leadership skills by serving on or chairing committees or serving as an officer. Some of the professional associations sponsor student organizations that provide high school and college students the opportunity to develop and practice important career skills while they are in school.

Networking. Networking is the practice of establishing and maintaining associations with persons to support mutually beneficial relationships. Networking is an excellent means to find jobs because those who make the actual hiring decisions would much rather consider hiring someone who has been recommended by someone they know and trust. Not only does the recommendation serve as a reference check, it saves the employer the time and effort he would spend sorting through the resumes a position advertisement is likely to generate.

Networking is done through interactions with people in a wide variety of venues. You are networking when you develop meaningful connections with people at school, professional meetings, conferences, seminars, sporting events, church, and so on. A meaningful connection is usually developed when the person knows your name, remembers positive things about you, and is likely to refer you to others at appropriate times.

Your neighbors, teachers, classmates, relatives, and friends with whom you have a meaningful connection are also in your network. In other words, your network can be as large as the number of people you interact with in meaningful ways and the number of people with whom they have meaningful interactions. However, it is important to remember that an effective network is built upon a relationship that will benefit the other person as well as yourself. You should always think of ways you can help those in your network as well as how they can help you.

In addition to networking face-to-face with people, you can use web tools to network online. For example, you can use blogs or videoconferencing to carry on conversations with those who have similar interests and social networking sites to develop professional linkages.

1. Open *pc7 effectiveness report 4* and in the appropriate place in the Advancing Your Career section:

   - Identify at least five individuals from your school (teachers, coaches, counselors, principals, classmates, etc.) you would include in your professional network and briefly state why.
   - Identify the position you aspire to hold within 10 years from now and describe the education that you need for the position and a career path that will enable you to attain the desired position.

2. Save as: *pc7 effectiveness report 5*.

Communication Skills 9

ACTIVITY 1: Internal Punctuation - Quotation Marks and Hyphens

1. Study each of the 6 rules.
   a. Key the *Learn* line(s) beneath each rule, noting how the rule is applied.
   b. Key the *Apply* lines, using quotation marks and hyphens correctly.

Internal Punctuation: Quotation marks

Rule 1: Use quotation marks to enclose direct quotations. Note: When a question mark applies to the entire sentence, place it outside the quotation marks.

Learn	1	Dr. Vang asked, "Did you enroll in the global marketing program?"
Learn	2	Who said, "Impossible is just an opinion"?
Apply	3	Did Mark Twain say, The secret of getting ahead is getting started?
Apply	4	Mee Yang asked, Will you be my partner in the biology lab?

Rule 2: Use quotation marks to enclose titles of articles, poems, songs, television programs, and unpublished works, such as theses and dissertations.

Learn	5	She found the poem "Invictus: The Unconquerable" in the *Book of Verses*.
Apply	6	The song The Music of the Night is from *The Phantom of the Opera*.
Apply	7	His thesis title is Data Security: Where Do We Go from Here?

Rule 3: Use quotation marks to enclose special words or phrases used for emphasis or for coined words (words not in dictionary usage).

Learn	8	She was happy to describe her co-worker as "honest and ingenious."
Apply	9	In an interview, avoid the use of umm, ya know, and like.
Apply	10	Jake described the play as awesome; Julie described it as terrible.

Rule 4: Use a single quotation mark (the apostrophe) to indicate a quotation within a quotation (including titles and words as indicated in Rules 2 and 3, above).

Learn	11	She said, "I loved 'Cats', but I think I loved 'Chicago' even more."
Apply	12	I say, "Enjoy life, as Chaplin said, A day without a laugh is a wasted day."
Apply	13	Felipe said, "I enjoy watching reruns of Monk and Law and Order."

Internal Punctuation: Hyphen

Rule 5: Use a hyphen to join compound numbers from twenty-one to ninety-nine that are keyed as words.

Learn	14	Only twenty-two of the ninety-six students received academic honors.
Apply	15	Fifty two employees attended the convention; forty one did not.
Apply	16	There were twenty one candles on each of the twenty one cakes.

Rule 6: Use a hyphen to join compound adjectives preceding a noun they modify as a unit.

Learn	17	The dresses made by the well-known designer sold out quickly.
Apply	18	The most up to date itinerary will be posted early tomorrow.
Apply	19	The sleek cellphone offers state of the art hardware and software.

(continued on next page)

2. Key Proofread & Correct, using quotation marks and hyphens correctly.
   a. Check answers.
   b. Using the rule number(s) at the left of each line, study the rule relating to each error you made.
   c. Rekey each incorrect line, using quotation marks and hyphens correctly.

Save as: **CS9 ACTIVITY1**

Proofread & Correct

Rules

1	1	President Sax asked, Are you are ready to vote on the proposal?
1	2	The manager said, Is anyone interested in working overtime this week?
2	3	Why didn't you watch America's Got Talent this week?
2	4	My favorite column, It's About Time, is written by Judy J. Cagel.
3	5	All those in favor say aye; all those opposed say nay.
1,4	6	I asked, Who said, Ask not what, Four score, and This day will live?
5	7	John F. Kennedy was forty three when he was inaugurated, not forty four.
6	8	The self confident teacher told us to stop being under achieving students.
6	9	They ordered state of the art equipment for their recordings studio.
1,6	10	The hard working clerk said, Over the counter sales decreased significantly.

ACTIVITY 2: Word Choice

1. Study the definitions of the words.
2. Key the *Learn* line(s), noting the correct usage of each word.
3. Key the *Apply* line(s), inserting the correct word(s).

Save as: **CS9 ACTIVITY2**

desert (n) a region rendered barren by environmental extremes	**miner** (n) one who removes minerals/ore from the earth; machine used for that purpose
dessert (n) the last course of a lunch or dinner	**minor** (adj/n) lesser/smaller in amount, extent, or size; under legal age

Learn 1 The diner will keep the **dessert** to eat as a snack in the **desert**.

Apply 2 April is planning to serve apple pie for (desert/dessert) today.

Apply 3 The men filled six water bottles for the (desert/dessert) trip.

Learn 4 The injury to the copper **miner** is no **minor** legal matter.

Apply 5 The law states that a (miner/minor) can't work as a (miner/minor).

Apply 6 This is a (miner/minor) point, but the (miner/minor) will retire soon.

ACTIVITY 3: Writing

Complete as directed.

Save as: **CS9 ACTIVITY3**

Write a paragraph or two explaining how you would respond during a job interview to the following question:

Describe a situation where you set a goal and what you did to achieve it.

ACTIVITY 4: Speaking

COLLABORATION

Save as: **CS9 ACTIVITY4**

Listed on the next page are suggestions for overcoming the fear of speaking in front of an audience. With three of your classmates, develop a presentation on "Overcoming Your Public Speaking Fears" to share with your class. Each person in your group will deliver part of the presentation. One person will give the introduction and the conclusion to the presentation. The other three members will each suggest two ideas for overcoming the fear from the list below or others that your group come up with.

1. Know your topic—view yourself as the expert on the subject.
2. Memorize your first sentence to get off to a good start, but practice it so that it doesn't come off as being memorized.
3. Be organized.
4. Include visual aids to take the focus off you.
5. Focus on the material rather than your audience.
6. Slow down; plan pauses.
7. Use effective gestures.
8. Recognize that being nervous is natural; you should be more worried if you aren't nervous.
9. Practice, preferably in the room where you will be presenting.

Before You Move On

Use the following words to complete the sentences:

common field	query	data
Expression Builder	Mail Merge	computed fields
relationship	Totals	envelope
variable		

1. The _____ is used to perform calculations on existing fields in a database. Application Guide

2. In a mail merge, the database contains the _____ information. Application Guide

3. When you want information from two database tables, you can establish a(n) _____ between the two tables and create a query. Application Guide

4. The feature in a database that automatically calculates sums and averages is called the _____ feature. Application Guide

5. *Access* uses the *Word* _____ feature to replace fields in a form letter with information from a database. LO 85B

6. In a mail merge, an *Access* database or query can serve as a(n) _____ file. LO 85A

7. The Expression Builder is used to create _____. LO 84B

8. When a table contains all the sales reps in a district, you create a(n) _____ to show only the sales reps working in Colorado. LO 87B

9. To merge data from two different tables in a query, you have to have a(n) _____. LO 87C

10. In a mail merge, Size 10 refers to the _____ size. LO 88B

HPJ Communication Specialists

Work Assignment

Ms. Natasha Parker
President & CEO

Ms. Helen St. Claire
Administrative Assistant

HPJ Communication Specialists prepares, organizes, and delivers communication training seminars. Three partners—Stewart **H**errick, Natasha **P**arker, and Spencer **J**orstad—founded the company in 1991. In 1998, Ms. Parker bought out the other two partners. Today the company has five branches located in Dallas, Denver, Minneapolis, New York, and San Francisco. Company headquarters are located in Minneapolis, Minnesota.

You have been hired by HPJ to work part-time on some of the projects that have been assigned to Helen St. Claire. Ms. St. Claire is an administrative assistant for the president and CEO, Natasha S. Parker, as well as for Erika Thomas, the Minneapolis branch manager.

In this position you will be required to use:

- *Word* to prepare letters, memos, reports, agendas, etc.
- *Outlook* for email communication and to manage contact information
- *Access* to create and maintain a database of employee information
- *Excel* to construct a worksheet to calculate salary increases
- *PowerPoint* to design slide presentations for meetings

Photo Courtesy of the Author.

HPJ Communication Specialists
3251 Wayzata Blvd.
Minneapolis, MN 55461-4533
Telephone (612) 555-0418

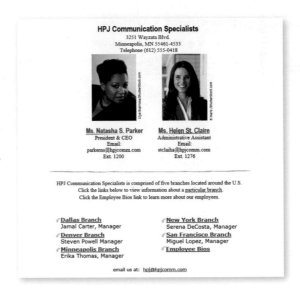

HPJ Company Directory

The company has a directory (see **df hpj directory**) containing the following information:

- HPJ branch locations
- Address and phone number for each branch
- Contact information and bios for each branch manager
- Contact information and bios for each communication specialist

Dallas Branch
Jamal Carter, Manager

Denver Branch
Steven Powell Manager

Minneapolis Branch
Erika Thomas, Manager

New York Branch
Serena DeCosta, Manager

San Francisco Branch
Miguel Lopez, Manager

Employee Bios

You will need the directory to gather information to complete some of the projects you are working on for Ms. St. Claire.

Data Files

Some of the projects you will be working on have already been started or require information from previously created documents. You will need to access the company data files to complete these projects.

File Naming

In order to quickly access information, HPJ has established a *file-naming* system that is used by company employees. It is very simple. All files you create should be named with *hpj*, followed by the project number (*hpj project1*, *hpj project2*, etc.).

Document Formats

During your training program, you were instructed to use block format for all company letters and the unbound format for company reports. Additional general instructions will be attached to each document you are given to process. Use the date included on the instructions for all documents requiring a date.

As with a real job, you will be expected to work independently and learn on your own how to do some things that you haven't previously been taught using resources that are available to you. You will also be expected to use your decision-making skills to arrange documents attractively whenever specific instructions are not provided. Since HPJ has based its word processing manual on the *Century 21* textbook, you can refer to this text in making formatting decisions. In addition to your textbook, you can use the Help feature of your software to review a feature you may have forgotten or to learn new features you may need.

HPJ is extremely concerned about the image it presents to the public. You are expected to produce error-free documents, so check spelling, proofread, and correct your work carefully before presenting it for approval. Errors are unacceptable.

NOTE Appendix C, on the student companion website, includes a formatting reference guide.

Use the following formatting guides in Figures IP3-1 through IP3-4 to prepare memos, letters, reports, and emails. If you have additional questions about format, refer to your textbook.

Figure IP3-1 Format Guide: Memo

Signature Block

Multiple Enclosure Notation

Note: If a letter or memo is longer than one page, a header is placed on all pages except the first using the Header feature. The header consists of three lines blocked at the left margin. Line 1 contains the addressee's name, line 2 contains the word *Page* and the page number, and line 3 contains the date.

Ms. Charla Ramirez
Page 2
May 28, 20—

Figure IP3-2 Format Guide: Letter

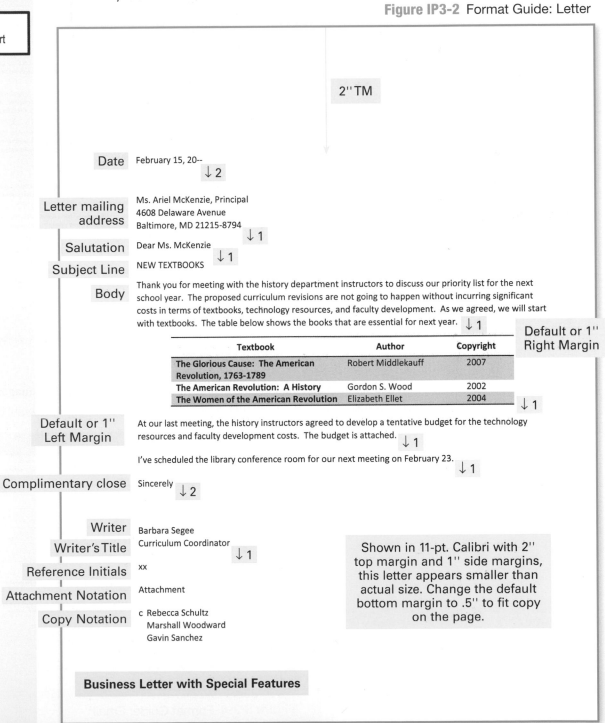

2" TM

Date   February 15, 20--
↓ 2

Letter mailing address
Ms. Ariel McKenzie, Principal
4608 Delaware Avenue
Baltimore, MD 21215-8794
↓ 1

Salutation   Dear Ms. McKenzie
↓ 1

Subject Line   NEW TEXTBOOKS

Body   Thank you for meeting with the history department instructors to discuss our priority list for the next school year. The proposed curriculum revisions are not going to happen without incurring significant costs in terms of textbooks, technology resources, and faculty development. As we agreed, we will start with textbooks. The table below shows the books that are essential for next year.   ↓ 1

Default or 1" Right Margin

Textbook	Author	Copyright
The Glorious Cause: The American Revolution, 1763-1789	Robert Middlekauff	2007
The American Revolution: A History	Gordon S. Wood	2002
The Women of the American Revolution	Elizabeth Ellet	2004

↓ 1

Default or 1" Left Margin   At our last meeting, the history instructors agreed to develop a tentative budget for the technology resources and faculty development costs. The budget is attached.   ↓ 1

I've scheduled the library conference room for our next meeting on February 23.   ↓ 1

Complimentary close   Sincerely   ↓ 2

Writer   Barbara Segee

Writer's Title   Curriculum Coordinator   ↓ 1

Reference Initials   xx

Attachment Notation   Attachment

Copy Notation   c Rebecca Schultz
                                     Marshall Woodward
                                     Gavin Sanchez

Shown in 11-pt. Calibri with 2" top margin and 1" side margins, this letter appears smaller than actual size. Change the default bottom margin to .5" to fit copy on the page.

Business Letter with Special Features

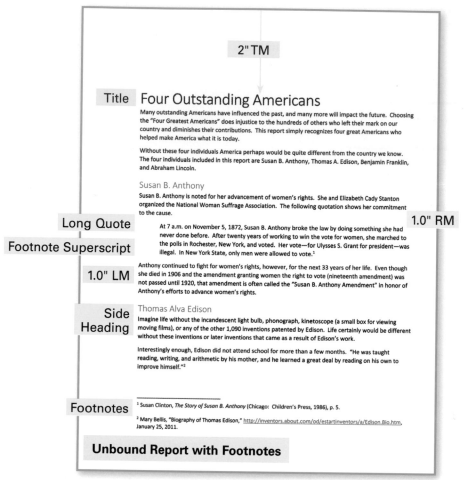

Figure IP3-3 Format Guide: Report

When sending an email to all five branch managers, use **Branch Managers** for the opening line and **Natasha** for the closing line of the email message, as shown in Figure IP3-4.

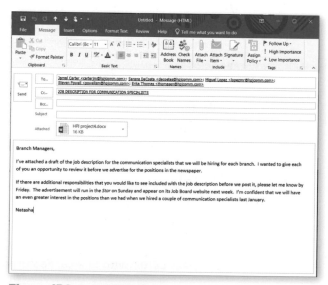

Figure IP3-4 Format Guide: Email

Project 1

HPJ From the Desk of
Helen St. Claire

You will be corresponding with the branch managers frequently. Create an HPJ Branch Managers contact folder, and key contact information for each of the branch managers as shown at the right. You will need to get the information for the other three managers from the company directory (*df hpj directory*). Save as shown in the Work Assignment instructions.

June 5   HSC

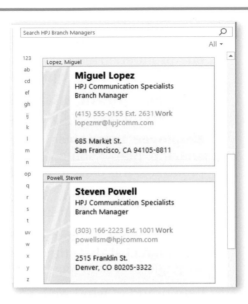

Project 2

HPJ From the Desk of
Helen St. Claire

Ms. Parker wants the attached letter sent to each branch manager. Use the mailing addresses from your contacts to create a database table with the information needed to do a mail merge with form letters and memos you create. Call the database *HPJ Communication Specialists* and the table of addresses *Addresses for Branch Managers*.

June 5   HSC

Dear

Each of you has indicated a need for additional personnel. I've heard your requests. With this quarter's increase in seminar revenues, I am now in a position to respond to them. Five new communication specialist positions, one for each branch, have been added.

Since training for the positions takes place here at the home office, it is more cost effective to hire communication specialists from this area. I will take care of recruitment and preliminary screening. However, since each of you will work closely with the individual hired, I think you should make the final selection.

When you are here for the annual meeting, I'll schedule time for you to interview eight individuals. If you are not satisfied with any of the eight, we will arrange additional interviews. I should have a job description created within the next week. When it is completed, I'll send it to you for your review.

Technology. The changed marketplace is demanding that we explore new ways of delivering our seminars. How can we better use technology to deliver our product? This may include putting selected seminars online, inter- and intra-company communication, etc.

Company growth. What steps can we take to increase company growth? Last year revenues grew by 15 percent; our expenses grew by 8 percent.

Employee incentives. Last year we implemented a branch manager profit-sharing plan. Some of you have indicated that we need to expand this profit-sharing plan to include our communication specialists.

Regional expansion. Some of the regions have been very successful. How do we capitalize on that success? Is it time to divide the successful regions?

International expansion. HPJ has put on several seminars overseas—at a very high cost. Is it time to start thinking about creating a branch of **HPJ** at a strategic overseas location?

I am proud of what we have been able to accomplish this year. The foundation is in place, and we are ready to grow. Each of you plays a critical role in the success of **HPJ**. Thank you for your dedication and commitment to making our company the "leader in providing corporate and individual communication training." Best wishes for continued success. I'm looking forward to discussing **HPJ's** future at this year's annual meeting. If you have additional items that you would like included on the agenda, please get them to me before June 15.

Job Description
HPJ Communication Specialist

HPJ Communication Specialists work cooperatively with other branch members to develop and deliver communication seminars throughout the United States.

Position Requirements

a. College degree
b. Excellent oral and written communication skills
c. Excellent interpersonal skills
d. Technology skills
e. Knowledge of business concepts

Duties and Responsibilities

a. Research seminar topics
b. Develop seminars
c. Prepare electronic presentations for seminars
d. Prepare seminar manual
e. Present seminars

Project 5

SUBJECT: JOB DESCRIPTION FOR COMMUNICATION SPECIALISTS

I've attached a draft of the job description for the communication specialists that we will be hiring for each branch. I wanted to give each of you an opportunity to review it before we advertise for the positions in the newspaper.

If there are additional responsibilities that you would like to see included with the job description before we post it, please let me know by Friday. The advertisement will run in the *Star* on Sunday and appear on its Job Board website next week. I'm confident that we will have an even greater interest in the positions than we had when we hired a couple of communication specialists last January.

Project 6

New Seminar Descriptions

Seminar Title	Seminar Description	Cost per Person
Business Etiquette: You Cannot Not Communicate!		$99
Gender Communications: "He Says, She Says"		$75
International Communication		$75
Listen Up!		$99
Technology in the Workplace		$125

Project 7

I just got the following job description today; include it with the table. If necessary, adjust the top and bottom margins to fit it on one page.

Title: Enhance Your Communication Skills

Cost: $219

Description: Executives with excellent oral and interpersonal communication skills have a decisive advantage over their competitors. After completing this two-day seminar, your oral and interpersonal communication skills will have a greater impact

Project 8

HPJ From the Desk of
Helen St. Claire

Ms. Parker would like you to add a table for *Employee Information* to the HPJ Communication Specialists database with the fields that are shown at the right. Create a form to key the information for all employees into the database.

In addition to the information at the right, you will need the following to complete the project:

df hpj project8 notes (start with this file)
df hpj directory (company directory)
df hpj project8 (employee information)
df hpj project8 worksheet (worksheet for gathering data)

June 6   HSC

Project 9

HPJ From the Desk of
Helen St. Claire

Correct Serena DeCosta's email address in the HPJ Directory and contacts file you created for Project 1. It should be decostsl instead of decostas. You will need to make that correction in the contacts file you created for Project 1.

June 6   HSC

Employee Information

ID	1	E-mail Address	parkerns
Last Name	Parker	Work Phone Number	(612) 555-0418
First Name	Natasha	Extension	1200
Middle Initial	S.	Date of Birth	June 15, 1970
Branch	Headquarters	Employee ID	547-18
Job Title	President and CEO	Gender	Female
		Employment Start Date	9/1/1991

Employee ID Numbers

Employee	ID No.	Employee	ID No.
Ammari, Ann	382-49	Morina, Jarrod	302-18
Ashley, David	497-23	Morneau, Betty	279-43
Black, Virginia	127-88	Parker, Natasha	547-18
Carter, Jamal	385-61	Polacheck, Jan	675-66
Casey, Shawn	420-29	Poquette, Rae	150-32
Cey, Donald	303-61	Powell, Steven	576-39
Cody, William	569-17	Redford, Jason	295-36
DeCosta, Serena	202-57	Ryan, Carlos	129-54
Dent, Marsha	801-74	St. Claire, Helen	350-32
Gibbons, Tracy	245-71	Thomas, Erika	465-01
Gray, Stephon	908-17	Thomasson, Ed	394-29
Logan, Kay	570-45	Van Horn, Ron	616-89
Lopez, Miguel	129-06	Wright, Syd	545-11
McCain, Beau	609-40		

Format the attached agenda for the Branch Manager Annual Meeting that Ms. Parker will be facilitating. Use the agenda template (*df hpj project10 template*). You will need to modify the template to fit the agenda items. The meeting will start at 9 a.m. on June 26. All branch managers will be invited to attend the meeting.

June 8   HSC

Agenda

- I. Call to order
- II. Greetings
- III. Roll call
- IV. Approval of minutes from last meeting
- V. Discussion items
    - a) Seminars
        1. Enhancement
        2. Expansion
        3. Client base
    - b) Leadership
    - c) Company growth
        1. Regional expansion
        2. International expansion
    - d) Employee incentives
        1. Branch managers
        2. Communication specialists
    - e) Technology
- VI. Miscellaneous
- VII. Adjournment

Ms. Parker would like the attached letter sent to the branch managers. Enclose a copy of the agenda and the hotel confirmation (when it's available) with the letter.

June 8   HSC

Attached is the agenda for the annual meeting. I didn't hear from any of you about additions to the agenda; however, if you have items to discuss, we can include them under Miscellaneous.

Your accommodations have been made for the McIntyre Inn. Your confirmation is enclosed. A limousine will pick you up at the Inn at 8:30 a.m. on Monday. Activities have been planned for Monday and Wednesday evenings. Tuesday and Thursday mornings have been left open. You can arrange something on your own, or we can make group arrangements. We'll decide on Monday before adjourning for the day.

I'm looking forward to seeing you on the 26th.

Project 12

HPJ Communication Specialists
Interview Schedule for **Miguel Lopez**
June 29, 20--, Room 104

Time	Name of Interviewee
1:00–1:15	Olga Novak
1:20–1:35	Christian Cey
1:40–1:55	Joan Langston
2:00–2:15	Tim Wohlers
2:20–2:35	Mitch Hughes
2:40–2: 55	Hideki Rusch
3:00–3:15	Jana Parker
3:20–3:35	Katarina Dent

Project 13

Seminar Objectives for: (Use *Heading 1* style and apply bold)
Technology in the Workplace (Use *Title* style)
Minneapolis Branch (Use *Heading 1* style, do not bold; leave 1 blank line after heading; use 12-pt. font for remainder of the text)

1. Discuss the role of communication technology in today's business environment and how it has changed over the past ten years.
2. Inform participants of various technological communication tools presently available.
3. Highlight the advantages/disadvantages of these tools presently available.
4. Demonstrate:
   - Videoconferencing
   - Teleconferencing
   - Data conferencing
   - GroupSystems
   - Internet resources
5. Inform participants of various technological communication tools that are in development.
6. Discuss Internet resources available to participants.
7. Discuss how using high-speed communication in today's business environment can give a firm a competitive advantage in the global marketplace.

Here is an update on recent progress of the Minneapolis Branch.

Seminar Bookings

We are fully booked through April and May. Additional communication specialists are desperately needed if we are going to expand into other states in our region. Most of our current bookings are in Minnesota, Iowa, and Wisconsin. We will be presenting in Illinois for the first time in May. I anticipate this will lead to additional bookings that we won't be able to accommodate. This is a problem that I enjoy having. Michigan, Indiana, and Ohio provide ample opportunities for expansion, when resources are made available.

New Seminar

A lot of progress has been made on the new seminar we are developing, "Technology in the Workplace" (see attachment for seminar objectives). Our branch will be ready to preview the seminar at our annual meeting. Not only will the seminar be a great addition to our seminar offerings, but also I believe HPJ can use it to communicate better internally. I will present my ideas when I preview the seminar. The seminar covers:

- Videoconferencing
- Teleconferencing
- Data conferencing
- GroupSystems
- Internet resources

Graphic Designer

A graphic artist has been hired to design all of the materials for the new seminar. He will design promotional items as well as content-related items. Currently he is working on the manual cover and divider pages. These items will be coordinated with the emblems used in the slide show portion of the presentation, along with name tags, promotional paraphernalia, and business cards.

This should give our seminar a more professional appearance. If it works as well as I think it is going to, we will have the designer work on materials for our existing seminars to add the "professional" look.

HPJ From the Desk of
Helen St. Claire

Format the text as an unbound report with footnotes (shown at bottom of attached copy). Format the side headings using Heading 1 style; format the paragraph headings using Heading 3 style. The report will be a handout for the "Listen Up!" seminar.

June 12   HSC

LISTEN UP!

According to Raymond McNulty, "Everyone who expects to succeed in life should realize that success only will come if you give careful consideration to other people." To acomplish this, you must be an excellent listener. One of the most critical skills that an individual acquires is the ability to listen. studies indicate that a person spends 80 percent of their his or her time communicating, of which 45 to 50% is spent listening. The following breakdown is the average individual of time spent as communicating.[2]

- Writing 9%

- Reading 16%

- Speaking 30%

- Listening 40-50%

Since a great deal of the time spent communicating is spent listening, it is important to overcome any obstacles that obstruct our ability to listen and to learn new ways to improve our listening ability.

Barriers to Listening

Anything that interferes with our ability to listen is classified as a barrier to listening. These barriers that obstruct our ability to listen can be divided into two basic categories--external and internal barriers.

Internal barriers. Internal barriers are those that deal with the mental or psychological aspects of listening. The perception of the importance of the message, the emotional state, and the tun running in and out of the speaker by the listener are examples of internal barriers.

External Barriers. External barriers are barriers other than those that deal with the mental and psychological makeup of the listener that tend to keep the listener from devoting full attention to what is being said. Telephone interruptions, uninvited visitors, noise, and the physical environment are examples of external barriers.

(Report continued on next page)

Ways to Improve Listening

Barrier**s** to listening can be over come. However**,** it does take a
sincere e**f**ort on the part of the ~~speaker~~ *listener*. Neher and Waite suggest
the following ways to improve listening skills.[3]

* Be aware of the barriers that are especially troublesome for you.
  Listening difficulties are individualistic. Developing awareness
  is an important step in overcoming *such barriers*.

* Listen as though you will have to paraphrase what is being said.
  Listen for ideas rather than for facts.

* Expect to work **a**t listening. **work** at overcoming distractions, such
  as the speaker's delivery or nonverbal mannerisms.

* Concentrate on summarizing the presentation as you listen. If
  possible, think of additional supporting material that would fit
  with the point that the speaker is making. Avoid trying to refute
  the speaker. Try not to be turned off by remarks *you* disagree with.

[1]H. Dan O'Hair, James S. O'Rourke IV, and Mary John O'Hair,
Business Communication: A Framework for Success (Cincinnati:
South-Western Publishing, 2001), p. 211.

[2]The Listening Center. "The Sacred Art of Listening." http://www.
sacredlistening.com/tlc_listening101.htm, (23 April 2018).

[3]William W. Neher and David H. Waite, *The Business and Professional
Communicator* (Needham Heights, MA: Allyn and Bacon, 1993), p. 28.

Project 16

Ms. Parker wants an update
on the registration numbers for
the *Like a Pro Seminars* to be
held in Denver on August 6-10.
Prepare a worksheet similar to
the one I attached from the *Like
a Pro Seminars* held in New York
earlier this summer. I ran queries
to get the numbers (*df hpj
project16 - denver*).

Like a Pro Seminars - New York			
May 15-19			
	No. Registered	Registration Fee	Revenue
Speak Like a Pro	22	259	$5,698.00
Write Like a Pro	18	319	$5,742.00
Dress Like a Pro	23	129	$2,967.00
Dine Like a Pro	33	179	$5,907.00
Attending all Four Seminars	26	750	$19,500.00
Totals	122	1636	$39,814.00

The company organizational chart needs updating. Print a copy of the most recent master file of the organizational chart (*df hpj project 17*) and verify the information against the information included in the HPJ Directory. Mark the changes on the printed copy and then update the master file with the changes, using June 12 for the date.

HPJ From the Desk of
Helen St. Claire

See the note attached at the right.

June 12   HSC

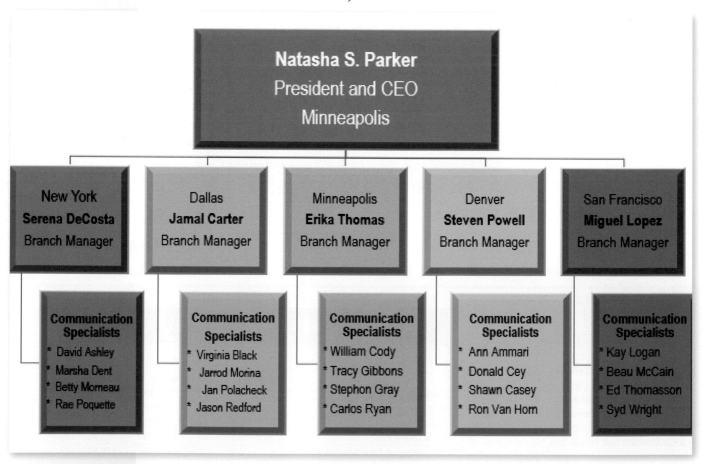

HPJ From the Desk of
Helen St. Claire

Prepare (don't send) this message as an email to the communication specialists in the Minneapolis branch from Erika Thomas. You will need to get the email addresses from the HPJ Directory. **New Communication Specialist** is the subject.

June 13   HSC

William, Tracy, Stephon, and Carlos,

Good news!

Stewart Peters will be joining our branch as a Communication Specialist on Monday, July 15.

Stewart grew up in New York, where he completed an undergraduate degree in organizational communication at New York University. He recently completed his master's degree at the University of Minnesota.

Stewart's thesis dealt with interpersonal conflict in the corporate environment. Since we intend to develop a seminar in this area, he will be able to make an immediate contribution.

Please welcome Stewart to HPJ and our branch when he arrives on the 15th.

Erika

HPJ From the Desk of
Helen St. Claire

I've started an electronic slide presentation for the annual meeting (*df hpj project19*). Please insert slides 2–9. I've attached sketches of slides 2, 3, and 4. Slides 5–9 will be similar to slide 4, showing a description of each of the new seminars. Get the information for the slides from the Organizational Chart (Project 17) and from the New Seminar Descriptions table (Project 7) that you completed earlier.

June 13   HSC

Slide 2

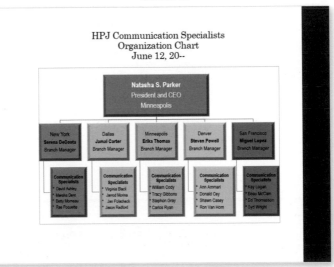

Slide 3

New Seminars

Business Etiquette: You Cannot Not Communicate!

Gender Communication: "He Says, She Says."

International Communication

Listen Up!

Technology in the Workplace

Enhance Your Communication Skills

Slide 4

Business Etiquette: You Cannot Not Communicate!

· If business etiquette is important to you, don't miss this seminar. Learn what's acceptable—and what's not—in formal business settings.

Project 20

1	Present and Proposed Salaries for HPJ Communication Specialists						
2	Name	Present Salary	PRP (Performance Review Points)	Base Raise	Merit Raise	Proposed Salary	% Increase
3	Ammari, Ann	$46,320	71				
4	Ashley, David	$48,240	58				
5	Black, Virginia	$42,562	47				
6	Casey, Shawn	$47,212	65				
7	Cey, Donald	$38,568	69				
8	Cody, William	$52,643	58				

HPJ From the Desk of
Helen St. Claire

I need to give Ms. Parker information about our Communication Specialists' present and proposed salaries. The proposed salary is based on an across-the-board raise for all specialists meeting expectations and a merit raise for those exceeding expectations. Find the worksheet named *df hpj project20*, which has the present salaries and the performance review points (PRP). Use the directions at the right to complete the worksheet. Also, this is very sensitive data, so please keep it secure and confidential.

June 14   HSC

1. After the Name column insert a column for the branch where the employee works.
2. Delete Jan Polacheck from the list; she will be leaving the company at the end of the month.
3. In the *Base Raise* column, write and key a formula that provides everyone with more than 45 performance review points (PRP) a 2% salary increase (round to nearest dollar). Key **0** for those employees not getting a base raise. Format all amount columns as *Accounting*.
4. Apply conditional formatting so that all PRP scores greater than 66 are highlighted with *Light Red Fill with Dark Red Text*. Apply conditional formatting for all PRP scores of at least 45 but not more than 66 so they are highlighted with *Yellow Fill with Dark Yellow Text*.
5. In the *Merit Raise* column, key **$1,500** for each employee with more than 66 PRP.
6. In the *Merit Raise* column, key **$750** for each employee with at least 45 PRP but not more than 66 PRP. Key **0** for those employees not getting a merit raise.
7. In the *Proposed Salary* column, compute the proposed salary for each employee.
8. Format the % Increase column as a *Percentage* and compute the percent that each person receives as a raise.
9. In the second row beneath the last employee, compute a sum for each column that contains dollar amounts. Label the row appropriately.
10. In the row below the totals, compute an average for each column that contains a value. Round the PRP average to the nearest whole point.
11. In the next row, display the maximum for each column that contains dollars or percent.
12. In the next row, display the minimum for each column that contains dollars or percent.
13. Format the spreadsheet attractively.
14. Change the *Orientation* to *Landscape* to fit all columns on one page. Print the worksheet.

Project 21

HPJ From the Desk of
Helen St. Claire

Ms. Parker approved the proposed salaries for the Communication Specialists. She would like you to update the database by adding a field for **Salary**. Using the *Proposed Salary* column from the Project 20 worksheet, input the salaries for the communication specialists. The salaries for the remaining company employees are shown at the right.

June 16   HSC

Employee	Present Salary
Parker, Natasha	$104,958
St. Claire, Helen	$37,650
Carter, Jamal	$78,728
DeCosta, Serena	$75,389
Lopez, Miguel	$79,539
Powell, Steven	$73,899
Thomas, Erika	$83,762

1. HPJ is an equal opportunity employer. Ms. Parker would like you to do a query to determine if men and women have received equal opportunities in upper-level positions within the organization. Create a query with the following fields:

> Last Name
> First Name
> Branch
> Job Title
> Gender

You will need to set the "Criteria" for Job Title to "***Branch Manager***" to show only those at the branch manager level.

> Query Name: **M/F Branch Managers**

2. Create a query for Ms. Parker showing first and last name, job title, branch, and salary. She would like the query sorted by job title in ascending order before you print a copy of the query for her.

> Query Name: **Salary by Job Title**

GLOSSARY

A

3-D cell reference   Refers to a cell or range of cells on another worksheet

absolute cell referencing   In a spreadsheet, when a cell is copied, the copy of the cell maintains a reference to a specific row and column

active cell   Current location of the insertion point that is highlighted with a thick border; stores information that is entered

Align Left   Software feature that starts all lines of the paragraph at the left margin; default paragraph alignment

Align Right   Software feature that ends all lines at the right margin

Animation schemes   Preset animation options that range from very subtle to very glitzy

application   Software that allows a person to complete a specific task such as creating a report, browsing the Internet, editing a multimedia video, or calculating a math problem

application form   Applicants often fill in forms at the company, using a pen to write on a printed form or keying information into an online employment application form

AutoCorrect   Software feature that detects and corrects *some* typing, spelling, and capitalization errors automatically

AutoFit Contents   Option in the AutoFit feature that adjusts column widths to be just wide enough for all contents to fit within the cells

AutoFit Window   Option in the AutoFit feature that adjusts column widths to fit within the left and right margins of a document

B

Back button   Button located on the browser toolbar that returns the user to the previous page

Backspace   Key used to delete characters to the left of the insertion point

Bar and Column graph   Type of graph that compares item quantities

bar chart   Graph that compares values across categories of data

block letter format   Commonly used format in which all letter parts begin at the left margin

blog   Internet site that allows a person to post messages for others to read, usually organized around a particular topic such as music or sports

Bold   Software feature that prints text darker than regular copy

borders   Printed line around cells in a table or around graphic objects such as text boxes or pictures

bullets   Special characters used to add visual interest or emphasis to text in a list

business letter   Letter typically printed on letterhead stationery (stationery that has a preprinted return address)

C

Calendar   PIMS feature for keeping track of schedules

Caps Lock   Key used to create a series of capital letters

career portfolio   A place to store items and information that show off your best work abilities

carpal tunnel syndrome (CTS)   Form of repetitive stress injury (RSI) that affects keyboard users, causing numbness or pain in the hand, wrist, elbow, or shoulder

cell phone   A mobile telephone that uses radio waves to transmit calls

cells   Place where a row and a column cross each other in a table; text, numbers, and formulas for calculating amounts can be entered in a cell

Center   Software feature that places an equal (or nearly equal) space between the text and each side margin

chart title   Identifies chart contents

Chat tools   Provide communication over the Internet using software or apps such as an instant messenger

citation   Note placed in a report body to mark material taken from other sources

clip art   Ready-made drawings and photography that can be inserted or copied into a document

Clipboard   When you Cut or Copy in *Office*, the contents are saved to the Clipboard

Close button   Closes a window and shuts down the open application

cloud   Location on the web where information or applications may be stored

cloud computing   Software and files are stored on remote computers and accessed through the Internet rather than residing on an individual user's computer

color scale   Uses a two- or three-color gradient to show how values vary—the shade of the color represents the value in the cell

column chart   Graph that compares values across categories of data

column heading   Appears in a cell at the top of a range of data in a column and describes the data

columns   Information arranged vertically in a table

complimentary close   The farewell portion of a letter

computer virus   Destructive program that destroys or harms data on a computer; can be loaded onto a computer and run without the computer owner's knowledge

Contact Group   Allows you to work more efficiently when emailing because you can send a message to a group rather than to each contact individually

Convert Table to Text   Feature that can be used to convert a table into text that is separated by tabs, commas, or other separators

Convert Text to Table   Feature that can be used to convert lists or other data that are separated by tabs into a table

Copy   Software command that copies selected text so it can be pasted to another location; original text is unchanged

copyright   Form of protection for certain works (books, articles, music, plays, movie scripts, artwork) granted by the U.S. government that states how the work may be legally used or copied

CPU (central processing unit)   Another name for a microprocessor

Custom animation   Allows several different animations to be included on each slide

Cut   Software command that removes selected text from a document

cyber predator   Someone who uses the Internet to hunt for victims whom they take advantage of in many ways

cyberbullying   Using online communications to harass or upset someone by sending hateful, humiliating, or threatening messages or photos

D

data   Facts and figures such as words, pictures, and numbers

data bar   Shows the value of a cell relative to other cells—larger values have a longer data bar

data type   Determines the kind of data in a database that a field can hold, such as text, currency, date, etc.

database   Organized collection of facts and figures

design theme   Software feature that provides a consistent, attractive look to a presentation

Designer   *PowerPoint* software feature that provides design suggestions and ideas for presentations

desktop   On-screen work area where windows, icons, tools, gadgets, and images appear

digital certificate   An attachment to a document that verifies the identity of a person sending a message or indicates the security of a website

digital collaboration tools   Digital applications that allow individuals to have conversations and share ideas with others from anywhere

digital communication   The electronic exchange of information

digital footprint   Every string of text you write and photo or video you post leaves a trail of information about you for millions of other digital users to read and view

DigiTools   Another name for digital communication tools

distribution   Involves sending and sharing information with the people who want or need it

domain names   Internet address in alphabetic form, such as .gov or .edu, that can provide some insight into the purpose of the site

double-space (DS)   To tap the Enter key twice to move the insertion point down two lines

E

e-commerce   Conducting business online

edits   Changes and corrections made to a database or another document

electronic presentations   Computer-generated visual aids (usually slide shows) that can be used to help communicate information

email   Electronic transfer of messages

employment application letter   Letter that accompanies a resume, whether print or digital; includes three topics: the position you are applying for, the evidence that you qualify for the position, and a request for an interview

Envelopes   *Word* feature used to create envelopes

ethics   Moral standards or values that describe how people should behave

Expression Builder   Part of the Query feature that be used to perform calculations on existing fields in a database

F

fair use doctrine   Rules pertaining to the use of a small portion of a copyrighted work for educational purposes

Favorites   Browser feature that allows a person to create a list of links for sites

field   Contains one piece of information about a person or item in a database, displayed as a column in a database table

filter   Database feature that hides records in a table that do not match the set criteria

Find and Replace   Feature used to search for a word or phrase in a document and then replace the text with other words

firewall   Hardware and software used to help prevent unauthorized users from accessing a person's data

flaming   Hostile and overly harsh arguments made via Internet forums, chat rooms, video-sharing websites, and game servers

flash memory   Type of memory storage that is often used in portable devices such as USB flash drives, laptops, and smartphones; it is relatively inexpensive and characterized by quick read access time

folders   Used by *Windows* operating systems to organize computer files

format   To place text on a page so it looks good and is easy to read

Format Painter   Software feature that quickly copies formatting from one place to another

forms   Object used to enter or display data in a database

formula   Equation that performs calculations on values in a worksheet

Forward button   Button in an application window that allows a user to return to the page he or she just left

function   Predefined formula that can be used to perform calculations

G

graphical user interface (GUI)   Computer interface that displays pictures, icons, and other images; allows the user to give commands and navigate by clicking the mouse or tapping a digital pen rather than keying commands

graphics Images that can enhance a message and help convey ideas; can include clip art, photos, or scanned original artwork

grids Lines that extend from tick marks to make it easier to see data values

gwam Number of standard words keyed in one minute

H

hacker Person who accesses computers or networks without proper permission

hacking Accessing computers or networks without proper permission

hanging indent Software feature that begins all lines except the first line away from the left margin

hard drive Most common storage device inside a computer

hard page breaks The end of a page and the beginning of a new page; inserted manually at any point where a new page must begin before the current one is full

hardware Physical parts of a computer that a person can touch with his or her hands

Help Software component that provides a user's manual on how to use the application

History Browser feature that shows the user a list of links for sites he or she has visited recently

Home button Button that allows the user to return to the home page or starting point

home keys Keys on which the keyboarder places his or her fingers to begin keying: **a s d f** for the left hand and **j k l ;** for the right hand

hyperlink Text, button, or graphic in an electronic document that, when clicked, takes the user to a new location

hyphenation Software feature that automatically divides (hyphenates) words that would normally wrap to the next line; this evens the right margin, making the text more attractive

I

icon set Classifies data into three to five categories—each icon represents a value in the cell

identity theft Finding out personal information about a person so as to impersonate that person by using his or her credit cards and damaging that person's good name

IF function Compares the contents of two cells in a spreadsheet

information processing Putting words, pictures, facts, or numbers into a meaningful form that can be used and understood

input Refers to the way a user puts data into a computer

Insert Default insertion method for keying text in a document; newly keyed text appears at the position of the insertion point and existing text moves to the right

Insert Date & Time Software feature that inserts the date and/or time in a document

instant messaging A system for exchanging messages in real time—or instantaneously—via the Internet or a shared network

Internet The global network of computers that connects millions of networks and computers around the world

Internet service provider (ISP) Company that provides a connection to the Internet on a user's computer

interview follow-up letter Letter sent to the person(s) interviewing you to thank them for the time given and courtesies extended to you during the job interview

Italic Software feature that prints letters that slope up toward the right

J

Justify Software feature that starts all lines at the left margin and ends all full lines at the right margin

K

keyword Word that a person types into a search text box to search for information on the web or on a single site

L

labels Letters and/or symbols (with or without numbers) that are keyed into a spreadsheet cell; the label status is assigned automatically and the data is left-aligned; also, the names used to identify parts of a graph

LAN (local area network) Network that connects computers that are close to each other, usually in the same building

landscape orientation Orientation in which the long side of the paper is positioned at the top

layout The way text and graphics are arranged

left indent Moves the first line of a paragraph one tab stop to the right, away from the left margin

Left tab Align all text evenly at the left by placing it to the right of the tab setting

legend Key used to identify a chart's data categories; usually contains different colors or patterns

Line and Paragraph Spacing Software feature that sets the amount of space between lines or paragraphs.

line graph Type of graph that shows changes in quantity over time or distance

login name Series of letters and/or numbers that identifies the user to the computer

M

Mail Merge Used to combine information from two files, such as a letter and an address list, into a third merged file

Mail Merge Wizard Software feature that guides you through the mail merge process

margin Blank space between the edge of the paper and the print

Maximize Button that removes an application window from the taskbar so as to fill the entire screen

meeting An appointment that includes others to whom you send an invitation

meeting organizer Person who creates the meeting and sends the invitation

memory Computer data storage for the operating system, applications, and data when a computer is on

Merge Cells Software feature that joins two or more adjacent table cells in the same row or column into one cell

merge fields Placeholders where information will be inserted in a merge file

merged file The result of a mail merge

microprocessors Small circuit board that controls all of the work done by a computer; most important part of a computer

Minimize Button that sends an application window to the taskbar to hide it from the screen

mixed cell reference In a spreadsheet, when a cell is copied, the copy of the cell maintains a reference to a specific row or column but not to both

mixed punctuation A colon after the salutation and a comma after the complimentary close

N

netiquette Rules for proper online behavior

network Two or more computers connected by either a cable or a wireless connection

Notes PIMS feature for recording reminders

Notes pane Window that allows the user to key notes about a slide

O

OneDrive Microsoft's cloud storage feature

online apps Applications that run over the Internet inside a web browser that permit completion of specific tasks such as sending email, creating reports, and viewing multimedia

online employment application form Employment application form that is filled out and submitted online

open punctuation No punctuation after the salutation or complimentary close

operating systems (OSs) Software that controls the basic operations of a computer

organic results Main list of results returned after an online search that is not influenced by advertising dollars

orphan line The first line of a paragraph that appears at the bottom of a page by itself

outline Document that organizes facts and details by main topics and subtopics

output Way in which the user obtains data from a computer, such as reading a text message, printing a report, or viewing photos on a monitor

Overtype Insertion method that allows you to replace (type over) current text with newly keyed text

P

paragraph Any amount of text that is keyed before the Enter key is tapped; can be one word or several words or lines

password Series of letters and/or numbers and symbols that a person keys to gain access to a computer

Paste Software command that places text that has been cut or copied into a document

path Drive and series of folders and subfolders that describe the location of a computer file, such as Documents\Computers\ Chapter 2\<Name>Moon Project 2

People (Contacts) PIMS feature for maintaining information needed to contact others

peripherals Device that works with a computer, such as a printer, digital tablet, scanner, or headset

personal-business letter Letter written by an individual to deal with business of a personal nature; typically printed on personal stationery that does not have a preprinted return address

personal computer (PC) Small computer designed for an individual user

personal interview Part of the employment process that provides the employer an opportunity to assess your personal attributes, demeanor, job qualifications, etc. in a formal setting to assist them in selecting the best person for the position; it also provides you with an opportunity to demonstrate that you are the best candidate and to gather information that will help you decide if you want the position

phishing Computer scam in which the victim receives an official-looking email that appears to be from a bank or other financial institution; the email says there is a problem with an account and asks the user to provide an account number, Social Security number, password, or some other personal information

phrase searching Turning individual words into exact phrases, such as "big cottonwood canyon," by using quotation marks when conducting an online search

pie chart Type of graph that shows parts of a whole; the proportional relationship of one set of values

placeholder Box with dotted borders that is part of most slide layouts; holds title and body text or objects such as charts, tables, and pictures

plagiarism Using material created by another person and claiming it as one's own

podcasting Form of audio broadcasting on the Internet

portrait orientation Orientation in which the short side of the paper is positioned at the top

Presenter View Presentation software feature that projects the presentation onto a larger screen for the audience while putting a "speaker view" with notes for the presenter on a smaller laptop screen

primary key   Field that uniquely identifies each record in a database table

primary sort   The first or major field by which a table will be sorted

Print Preview   Software feature that shows what a document will look like when it is printed

print resume   Resume printed on paper and mailed to prospective employers

privacy policy   Document that tells how personal data collected by a company will be used

private cloud   Cloud computing in which only a limited number of people have permission to access the server, usually employees in a company or members of a team

processing   Refers to how data is changed or used

processor   Another name for a microprocessor

productivity   Measure of how much work can be done in a certain amount of time

proofreaders' marks   Letters and symbols used to show the errors or changes needed in a document

public cloud   Cloud computing in which the server and its files are open to the public

Q

query   (1) A search you make on the Internet; (2) database object that displays certain data that meet the set criteria

R

RAM (random access memory)   Temporary memory used by a computer to store information currently being used by the computer

range   Group of two or more cells on a worksheet

ransomware   Type of malware that blocks access to a computer system or files or makes other threats until a sum of money is paid

record   Contains all of the information about one person or item in a database, displayed as a row in a database table

Redo   Software feature that reverses the last Undo action

redundant   System in which components are duplicated so if any fail, there will be a backup

relative cell referencing   In a spreadsheet, when a cell is copied, the copy of the cell is related to its new address

repetitive stress injury (RSI)   Condition that is a result of repeated movement of a particular part of the body, such as tennis elbow

report   (1) Document that gives facts, ideas, or opinions about one or more topics; (2) database object that is used to format and display data from tables or queries

Restore Down   Button used to restore an application window to its previous size

results   Answer to a query

resume   An honest summary of your experiences and qualifications for the position you are seeking

Ribbon   Location in a Microsoft *Office* application where all of the commands are displayed

Ribbon tabs   The Ribbon is organized by tabs that include icons for commands relating to a particular feature or task

Right tab   Align all text evenly at the right by placing it to the left of the tab setting

rows   Information arranged horizontally in a table

S

scale   Numbers on the Y- or X-axis representing quantities

scam   Scheme used to take money under false pretenses or for a product that does not work as advertised

Screen Clipping   Software feature that allows you to take "snapshots" or clippings of on-screen items

search   Browser feature that allows a person to look for information related to a word or term

search box   Location where a user can key keywords to conduct a search

secondary sort   The second or minor field by which a table will be sorted

section break   Software feature that allows you to divide a document into separate sections

servers   Hardware that houses large amounts of information in a network

shading   Colored fill or background that can be applied to cells in a table or objects such as shapes or text boxes

sheet tab   Each worksheet in an *Excel* workbook appears as a sheet tab at the bottom of the screen

single-space (SS)   To tap the Enter key once to move the insertion point down one line

sizing handles   One of the small squares or circles that appear on the border of a selected graphic

Slide pane   Displays the current slide or the slide clicked on the Slides tab

SmartArt   Software feature that is used to present ideas in graphic form with text

smartphone   A cell phone offering advanced capabilities with computer-like functionality

social networking sites   Provide an online venue for individuals or organizations with common interests

soft page break   The end of a page and the beginning of a new page; automatically inserted by the software when the current page is full (when the bottom margin is reached)

software   Programs that give instructions to a computer

solid state drives (SSDs)   Storage device that uses non-volatile solid-state (flash) memory, faster but more expensive than magnetic hard drives

sort   To arrange or group items in a particular order; *Access* feature that is used to arrange the information in a table or query in a certain order

source document   A paper form from which data is keyed

Space Bar   Key used to place a space between words

spam   Unsolicited email messages sent to many addresses; "junk" email

Spelling & Grammar Check   Software feature that checks a document for misspellings and grammar errors

Split Cells   Software feature that divides adjacent table cells into multiple cells and columns

sponsored links   Advertising links returned from an online search that are located at the right side (or sometimes at the top) of the results; sponsored by companies that want to sell products

spreadsheet software   Computer program used to record, report, and analyze data in worksheets

standard format   Criteria used when creating reports pertaining to such items as margins, spacing, styles, and references

standard word   In keyboarding, five characters (letters, numbers, symbols, and/or spaces)

Start screen   The tiled interface that displays when a user opens *Windows* and clicks the Start button

stem   Main part of a search word (*ski*) that is referenced when related words with different endings or tenses are included in the search (*skis, skiing, skier, skied*)

storage   Refers to saving data for later use

style   Collection of format settings for font, font size, color, paragraph spacing, alignment, and so on that are named and stored together in a style set

subfolder   Folder stored inside another folder

system administrator   Expert who manages a computer network

T

Tab   Key used to move the insertion point to a specific location on the line

table   Information arranged in rows and columns so readers can easily understand the information; database object used for organizing and storing data

table grid   Software feature used to create tables in a word processing document

tabs   Set locations at which text can be placed

taskbar   *Windows* feature that displays icons for open applications and files

Tasks   PIMS feature for recording items that need to be done

template   Master copy of a set of predefined styles for a particular type of document

text box   Container or drawing object for text or graphics

thesaurus   Software feature that finds synonyms or antonyms for a selected word

Thumbnail pane   Pane at the left side of the *PowerPoint* window in which you can click small thumbnails of slides to select them

tick marks   Coordinate marks on the graph to help guide the reader

transition   How a presentation changes from one slide to the next

Trojan   Malicious program disguised as a legitimate file that the user downloads or opens

trolling   Planting stories and making misstatements on the Internet or social media to push a particular ideology or provoke extreme emotions on a topic

U

unbound reports   Short report that is often prepared without covers or binders

Underline   Software feature that underlines text as it is keyed

Undo   Software feature that reverses the last change made

uniform resource locator (URL)   Address for a website

USB flash drive   Peripheral device commonly used to store computer files

user interface (UI)   Allows users to give commands to a computer

V

video and web conferencing   Transmitting and receiving images and voice in real time over the web, sharing documents and applications and communicating as if face-to-face with individuals anywhere in the world

W

web browser   Program that lets the user find and view webpages

widow line   The last line of a paragraph that appears by itself at the top of a page

wiki   Online encyclopedia that can be edited by nearly anyone in the world, allowing people with different backgrounds and knowledge to collaborate and research together

window   Framed screen in which an application opens

workbook   Spreadsheet file that may contain one or more worksheets, usually with related data

worksheet   Section in a workbook (spreadsheet file) where the user can enter data

worksheet title   Describes the content of a worksheet table

World Wide Web   The system of sites, documents, and graphical content hosted on Internet servers; commonly called the web

X

X-axis   The horizontal axis; usually for categories

Y

Y-axis   The vertical axis; usually for values

Z

Zoom   Software feature that increases or decreases the amount of the page appearing on the screen

A

Absolute cell referencing, 16-10–16-11
Acceptable-use policies (AUPs), 2-17–2-18
Access point, 2-21
Accuracy, 6-34
Adaptability and managing complexity, 16-35
Align left, paragraph alignment, 6-2
Alignment
    paragraph, 6-2
    table, 7-14–7-15
Align right, paragraph alignment, 6-2
Animation(s)
    custom, 15-1
    design tips, 15-2
    schemes, 15-1
' (apostrophe) key, learning, 1-73–1-74
Apple PCs, 1-19
Application(s)
    conditional formatting, 16-18–16-19
    copy and paste worksheet, 16-23
    IF function, 16-17–16-18
    software, 1-34
    3-D cell reference, 16-14
    update a linked worksheet, 16-23
Application forms, 15-36–15-38
Application letters, 13-21
    employment, 13-20–13-21
Ascending order, in sort, 9-22
Attachment/enclosure notations, in personal-business
    letter, 5-3
AUPs (acceptable-use policies), 2-17–2-18
Authority, 34
AutoCorrect, 1-16
AutoFill, 16-4–16-5
AutoFit Contents feature, 7-8
AutoFit Window feature, 7-8
AVERAGE function, 14-4, 14-12
    in spreadsheets, 9-15, 9-16

B

Back button, browser window, 2-23
Backspace key, learning, 1-69–1-71
Bar charts, 9-25–9-26
Bar graphs, in Microsoft *PowerPoint,* 8-21–8-22
Basic literacy, 16-34
Bibliography, 13-3
b key, learning, 1-41–1-42
Block letter format, 5-1–5-2
    assessment of, 5-22
    with open punctuation, 5-16

Block paragraphs, 1-57
Blog, 2-19, 9-37
Body, personal-business letter, 5-2
Bold, word processing applications, 1-17
Bound reports, 13-1
    collaborative report with footnotes, 13-12–13-14
    with footnotes, 13-8–13-11
    standard margins, 13-1
Browsers, web, 2-21
Bulleted lists, 6-15, 8-9, 14-2, 14-6
Bullets, 5-8
Business letter, 5-1
    block format with open punctuation, 5-16
    envelopes, 5-16–5-17
    from model copy, 5-14–5-15

C

Calculator, accessing, 2-2–2-6
Calendar, for personal information management software,
    4-4, 4-14
Capitalization, 1-84–1-85
Capital letters, 3-10
Caps Lock key, learning, 1-67–1-68
Career
    employment documents, 11-18
    personal reference list, 11-20
    portfolio and reference list, 11-18–11-20
    reference list, 11-19
Career, effective, 17-32–17-37
    advancing career, 17-35–17-37
    continuous improvement, 17-33
    performance reviews, 17-32–17-33
    planning, 17-33–17-34
    professionalism, 17-35
    selecting a mentor, 17-34
Cell(s), 9-2
    clearing content of, 9-19
    deleting content of, 9-19
    editing content of, 9-17–9-20
Cell margins, in tables, 14-3, 14-10
Cell phone, 9-36
Cell references
    absolute, 16-10–16-11
    application, 16-12–16-13, 16-14
    mixed, 16-11
    relative, 16-10
    3-D, 16-13–16-14
Centering tables, 7-6
Center, paragraph alignment, 6-2
Central processing unit (CPU), 1-32

Central Valley Education Foundation (CVEF), CVEC-1–CVEC-10
  correspondence, CVEC-2
  data source, CVEC-10
  donation form, CVEC-9–CVEC-10
  email, CVEC-3, CVEC-5
  file names, CVEC-2
  letter, CVEC-8
  presentation, CVEC-4, CVEC-7, CVEC-8
  promissory note, CVEC-8
  reports, CVEC-2, CVEC-4, CVEC-5
  scholarship tables, CVEC-3
  tables and charts, CVEC-2, CVEC-6
  work assignment at, CVEC-1–CVEC-2
  worksheets, CVEC-3–CVEC-4, CVEC-5, CVEC-7
Century 21 skills
  access information, 3-8
  communicate clearly, 4-7
  creativity and innovation, 14-15
  evaluate information, 3-8
  judgments and decisions, 13-8
  leadership, 7-20
Chart(s), 9-25–9-29. *See also* Graphs/charts
  adding, 9-28–9-29
  bar, 9-25–9-26
  column, 9-25–9-26
  layout and styles, changing, 9-27–9-28
  pie, 9-25–9-26
  type, changing, 9-27
Chat tools, 9-37
Citations, 6-18–6-19
c key, learning, 1-37–1-38
Clip art, 6-6
Clipboard, 3-5
Close button, 3-2
Cloud, 1-78
Cloud computing
  advantages of, 8-39
  definition of, 8-38
  drawbacks of, 8-39–8-40
  sharing information online, 8-42–8-43
  working with online applications, 8-40–8-42
Collaborative blogs, 9-37
Collaborative reports, 12-14
: (colon) key, learning, 1-65–1-66
Color scale, 16-19
Column(s), 9-2
  charts, 9-25–9-26
  deleting, 9-21
  graphs, in Microsoft *PowerPoint,* 8-21–8-22
  headings, for worksheets, 9-7–9-8, 9-11
  inserting, 9-21
, (comma) key, learning, 1-55–1-56
Communications and schedules, managing, 11-1–11-5
  career portfolio and reference list, 11-18–11-20

contact groups, 11-4–11-9
create and edit contact groups, 11-9
organize and manage emails, 11-10–11-11
schedule meetings with calendars, 11-12–11-15
Communication skills
  capitalization, 1-84–1-85
  composing, 1-85, 4-26
  internal punctuation, 14-28–14-29
  number expression, 4-25–4-26
  pronoun agreement, 6-36–6-37
  speaking, 1-85, 4-27, 6-38, 10-46, 14-29
  terminal punctuation, 10-45
  word choice, 1-85, 4-26, 6-37, 10-46, 14-29
  writing, 6-38, 10-46
Complimentary close, 5-2
Composing skills, 1-85, 4-26
Computer(s)
  daily life and, 1-21–1-22
  as DigiTools, 1-32
  early history of, 1-18–1-20
  hardware, 1-32
  keying position, 1-3
  microprocessor, 1-32
  peripherals, 1-33
  processor, 1-32
  productivity and, 1-20–1-21
  turning off, 1-49–1-50
Computer crime, 4-19–4-21
  hackers, 4-19
  identity theft, 4-20
  scams, 4-21
  virus, 4-19
Computer virus, 4-19
Computer vision syndrome, 10-42
Conditional formatting
  application, 16-18–16-19
  with graphics, 16-19–16-20
  worksheet with calculations and, 16-24
Contact group, email, 11-2
  add members, 11-7–11-8
  create and modify, 11-9
  create new contacts, 11-7
  edit contacts, 11-6–11-7
  remove members, 11-8–11-9
  warmup, 11-6
Contacts, for personal information management software, 4-4–4-6, 4-11–4-13, 4-15
Content slide, in Microsoft *PowerPoint,* 8-9–8-10
Copy notation, in personal-business letter, 5-3
Copyright, 4-24
Copy, word processing applications, 1-31
Corporate blogs, 9-37
COUNT function, 14-4, 14-12
  in spreadsheets, 9-15, 9-16

Coverage, 6-34
Cover page, 14-19
  collaborative report with footnotes, 13-14
  feature, 6-11
  reporting with styles, 13-4
  unbound reports with footnotes, 13-11
CPU (Central processing unit), 1-32
Creativity, 16-35
Crimes, computer, 4-19–4-21
Critical defensive measures, 5-28–5-29
Crop design theme, in Microsoft *PowerPoint*, 8-11
Crypotoviral extortion, 4-19
Curiosity, 16-35
Currency, 6-34
Custom animation, 15-1
Cut, word processing applications, 1-31
Cyberbullying, 10-40–10-42
Cyber predators, 10-9

D

Data, 1-35, 1-77
  bar, 16-19
  safety, 4-22–4-24
  storage of, 1-77–1-78
Database(s), 10-1–10-46
  components of, 10-2
  create form letter, 17-29
  create mailing labels, 17-28
  creation of, 10-10–10-11, 10-36
  definition of, 10-1
  editing records, 17-27
  envelopes creation, 17-23–17-24
  expression builder, 17-1
  filter, 10-8–10-9
  input data into form, 17-27, 17-28
  mail labels, 17-24–17-26
  mail merge, 17-1–17-2, 17-10–17-13, 17-22–17-23
  modifying, 10-37
  query from two tables, 17-2
  review and reinforcement, 17-3–17-7
  run a query, 17-28
  saving database objects, 17-3
  sorting, 10-8
  total feature, 17-2, 17-28
Database forms
  creating, 10-19–10-20
  creating using Wizard, 10-21–10-22
  definition of, 10-5
  planning and creating database,
    10-17–10-18
Database query
  creating in design view, 10-27–10-29
  definition of, 10-5–10-6

filtering by selection, 10-29–10-30
  sorting records, 10-30
Database records
  methods for editing, 10-25–10-26
  reasons for editing, 10-25
Database report
  creating, 10-31–10-33
  creating query, 10-33–10-34
  creating report, 10-33–10-34
  definition of, 10-6–10-7
  Report Wizard, 10-32–10-33
Database review and reinforcement, 17-3–17-7
  add fields and input data, 17-5
  create a query in design view, 17-7
  create a table, 17-3–17-4
  edit records, 17-6–17-7
  sort information, 17-7
  update table, 17-6
Database software, 10-1
Database table, 10-2–10-3
  adding records to, 10-14–10-16
  creating and saving, 10-11–10-13
  data types, 10-12
  defining and sequencing fields, 10-3–10-4
  modified table or form, 10-8
  modifying, 10-27
  previewing, 10-16–10-17
  primary key, 10-12–10-13
  printing, 10-16–10-17
  records, 10-2
  table design, 10-12
Database table fields, 10-2
  adding, 10-22–10-25
  deleting, 10-22–10-25
Data mining and analysis
  analyzing information, 17-17
  average district sales calculation, 17-16
  copy access table to word document, 17-20–17-21
  create queries with computed fields, 17-14–17-15
  create query from multiple tables, 17-18–17-22
  creating computed fields, 17-9
  creating query from two tables, 17-21–17-22
  Expression Builder, 17-8–17-9
  query table analysis, 17-8–17-9
  sales information by territory, 17-18–17-19
  total district sales calculation, 17-15–17-16
  using computed fields and column totals,
    17-14–17-17
Data source file, 12-1
  create, 12-4–12-6
  edit, 12-7–12-8
Data types, 10-12
Date, in personal-business letter, 5-2

Date & Time feature, 5-6
Decimal tabs, 14-2, 14-5–14-6
Deleting
    cells, 9-19
    columns, 7-6–7-7, 7-18–7-19, 9-21
    rows, 7-6–7-7, 7-18–7-19, 9-21
Descending order, in sort, 9-22
Designer, in Microsoft *PowerPoint,* 8-5
    enhancing slides with, 8-25–8-26
    generating slides with, 8-26
Design theme, in Microsoft *PowerPoint,* 8-2–8-3, 8-11
Desktop, 1-47
Different First Page feature, 6-3, 6-20
Digital behavior, responsible, 10-40
Digital certificate, 4-22–4-23
Digital citizenship and ethics, 3-3, 4-15, 5-14, 6-20, 7-23, 11-9,
    12-5, 14-16, 16-15
    cyber predator, 10-9
Digital collaboration tools, 9-35–9-37
Digital communication
    basic tools, 9-35
    collaboration tools and, 9-36–9-37
Digital etiquette, 10-40
Digital footprint, 10-43
Digital resumes, 12-27–12-29
    personal, 12-29
DigiTools, 1-32
Disaster recovery, 5-31
Distribution, information processing, 1-36
Division, 2-8–2-9
Document
    multi-column, 6-6
    three-column, 6-28
Domain name, 2-21–2-22
Double-space (DS), 1-4

E

e-commerce, 2-20
Economic literacy, 16-34
Editing database records
    methods, 10-25–10-26
    records, 10-25
e key, learning, 1-9–1-11
Electronic presentations, 8-1–8-44. *See also* Microsoft
    PowerPoint
Electronic table of contents, 13-4
Ellipsis, 13-2
Email (electronic mail), 2-19
    adding attachments to contacts, 11-2
    additional calendars, 11-4
    attachments, 4-2
    body, 4-2
    contact group members, adding/removing, 11-2

contact groups, creating, 11-2
create new folder, 11-10
editing contacts, 11-2
heading, 4-2
inbox, 4-3
junk email filter and folder, 11-3, 11-10–11-11
managing messages, contacts, and calendars, 11-1
meeting request, replying to, 11-4
new email folders, 11-2
printing calendars, 11-4–11-5
proposing new meeting time, 11-4
Search and Arrange By, 4-3–4-4
Search People, 4-3
tags, 4-2–4-3
Email messages
    assessment of, 5-22
    creating, 4-9–4-10
    evaluating, 4-9
    formatting, 4-8–4-9
    tips for managing, 4-11
Employee, effective, 16-32–16-36
    digital-age literacy, 16-34–16-35
    effective communication skills, 16-35–16-36
    high productivity skills, 16-36
    information, media and technology skills, 16-33
    inventive thinking, 16-35
    key subjects and 21st century themes, 16-33
    life and career skills, 16-33–16-34
    need for, 16-32
    understanding employer expectations,
        16-32–16-36
Employer expectations, 16-32–16-36
    digital-age literacy, 16-34–16-35
    effective communication skills, 16-35–16-36
    high productivity skills, 16-36
    information, media and technology skills, 16-33
    inventive thinking, 16-35
    key subjects and 21st century themes, 16-33
    learning and innovation skills, 16-33
    life and career skills, 16-33–16-34
    need for effective employees, 16-32
Employers, researching, 14-25
Employment
    application forms, 15-36–15-38
    application letter, 13-20–13-21
    interview follow-up letter, 15-38
End-of-class routine, 1-8
Enter key, 1-4, 1-5, 1-7, 1-15, 1-30, 1-42
Envelopes
    in business letter, 5-16–5-17
    in personal-business letter, 5-3, 5-17
    in word processing (WP) applications, 5-7–5-8
Ergonomic mouse, 1-49

Ethics, 4-18–4-19
Expression Builder, 17-1, 17-8–17-10
    to calculate total fees, 17-10
    create computed fields using, 17-9

F

Facebook, 1-18
Fair use doctrine, 4-24
Favorites features, of Internet browsers, 3-11–3-13
Fields, in database table, 10-2
File(s)
    following path to, 1-83
    navigating, 1-79–1-80
    password-protecting, 5-27–5-28
    safeguarding, 5-27–5-28
File Explorer
    folders in, 1-79–1-80
    navigating files, 1-79–1-80
Filter, in database, 10-8–10-9
Financial worksheets, preparing and analyzing,
    16-1–16-37
    cell references, 16-10–16-15
    changing views of, 16-1
    formatting and worksheet skills, 16-4–16-10
    freeze/unfreeze columns and rows, 16-1
    function and formatting, 16-15–16-18
    increase/decrease cell indents, 16-2
    insert headers and footers, 16-2
    set print area, 16-3
    spreadsheet applications, 16-24–16-25
    vertical cell alignment, 16-3
    worksheet and word processing documents, integrate,
        16-21–16-23
    zooming the view, 16-3
Find feature, 5-4
Firewalls, 4-23
Flaming, 10-40–10-42
Flash memory, 1-50
Folder(s), 1-79
    copying, 1-82–1-83
    copy using Ribbon commands, 1-83
    creating, 1-80–1-81
    deleting, 1-81
    in File Explorer, 1-79–1-80
    following path to, 1-83
    move using Ribbon commands, 1-83
    moving, 1-82–1-83
    moving by dragging, 1-82
    renaming, 1-81
Font group, 5-4–5-5
Footnotes, 13-2
    bound reports with, 13-8–13-11

    collaborative report with, 12-14
    MLA report with, 13-6–13-7
    unbound reports with, 14-18–14-19
Format, 6-1
Format Painter command, 3-5
Formatting
    MLA reports, 6-1, 6-2
    numbers, 9-12–9-13
    pictures, 6-6
    standard, 6-3–6-4
    table with, 14-21
    text box, 6-5
    worksheets, 9-8–9-12
    worksheet skills and, 16-4–16-10
Forms, database, 10-5
Formulas, 9-13–9-15, 14-13
    recalculate, 14-4, 14-13
    SUM function, 14-3–14-4, 14-12
    table with, 14-20–14-21
    writing, 14-4, 14-13
Form Wizard, 10-21–10-22
Forward button, browser window, 2-23
Framework for 21st Century Learning, 16-32
FTC (U.S. Federal Trade Commission), 4-20
Functions, 9-15–9-16

G

g key, learning, 1-25–1-26
Global awareness, 16-34
Google *Chrome,* 2-21
Grammar & Spelling feature, 5-5
Graphical user interface (GUI), 1-47
Graphics
    inserting in Microsoft *PowerPoint,* 8-12
    presentation (slide show) with, 15-15–15-22
Graphs/charts, 8-20–8-24. *See also* Chart(s)
    bar, 8-21–8-22
    column, 8-21–8-22
    grids, 8-21
    labels, 8-21
    legend, 8-21
    line, 8-23
    pie, 8-23–8-24
    scale, 8-20
    tick marks, 8-20
    X-axis, 8-20
    Y-axis, 8-20
Gridlines, 9-7
Grids, in graphs and charts, 8-21
Gross words a minute (gwam), 1-42
Group blogs, 9-37
GUI (Graphical user interface), 1-47

Guided (Paced) timing Procedure, 6-31
Guided writing, 8-37
gwam (Gross words a minute), 1-42

H

Hackers/Hacking, 4-19
Hanging indent, in paragraphs, 6-8–6-9
Hard drive, 1-32
Hard page breaks, 6-7
Hardware
    computer, 1-32
    maintenance, 7-36–7-37
Headings, column, 9-7–9-8, 9-11
Help
    about screen tips, 3-5
    accessing, 3-2
    basics, 3-1
    examining Office 365 online resources, 3-6
    exploring, 3-4
    online training, 3-7–3-8
    pop-up description, 3-5–3-6
    using panel, 3-3–3-4
    using screen tips, 3-6
Hide/Show feature, 5-10
Higher-order thinking and sound reasoning, 16-35
High productivity skills
    ability to produce relevant, high-quality products, 16-36
    effective use of real-world tools, 16-36
    prioritizing, planning, and managing for results, 16-36
History feature, of Internet browsers, 3-11–3-13
h key, learning, 1-9–1-11
Home button, browser window, 2-23
Home, computers and, 1-21
Home-key position, 1-3, 1-6
Home keys (asdf jkl;), 1-2–1-5
Hotspots, 2-21
HPJ Communication Specialists, HPJ-1–HPJ-18
    company directory, HPJ-2
    data files, HPJ-2
    document formats, HPJ-3–HPJ-17
    file naming, HPJ-2
HTML (Hypertext Markup Language), 2-19
Hyperlinks, 2-23, 15-2
Hypertext Markup Language (HTML), 2-19
Hyphenation, 5-5
- (hyphen) key, learning, 1-73–1-74

I

IBM PCs, 1-19
Icon set, 16-19
Identity theft, 4-20
IF function, 16-15–16-18
i key, learning, 1-12–1-13
Indentation

hanging, in tables, 14-2, 14-5–14-6
    paragraph, 6-17
    word processing applications, 6-8–6-9
Information
    data mining, 17-1–17-17
    literacy, 16-34
    processing, five-step process of, 1-35–1-36
Initiative skill, 1-8
Input, information processing, 1-36
Insert Date and Time, 5-6
    in modified block personal-business letter, 5-18
Insert endnote/footnote feature, 6-10
Inserting
    columns, 7-6–7-7, 9-21
    rows, 7-6–7-7, 9-21
    table, 7-2–7-4
    in word processing application, 1-16
Insert text from file feature, 6-10
Insert Time and Date, 5-6
    in modified block personal-business letter, 5-18
Instagram, 1-19
Instant messaging, 2-19
Interactive communication, 16-36
Internal punctuation, 14-28–14-29
Internet, 2-19–2-23
    browsers for, 2-21
    connecting to, 2-20–2-21
    domain names, 2-21–2-22
    hyperlinks on, 2-23
    safety, 4-21–4-24
    web addresses on, 2-21–2-23
Internet research skills
    evaluating search results, 6-33–6-34
    improving search results, 6-32–6-33
    understanding needs, 6-32
    validating and fact-checking research results, 6-35–6-36
Internet service provider (ISP), 2-20
Interpersonal skills, 16-35
Interview
    asking questions, 14-26
    creating impression, 14-26–14-27
    responses to questions, 14-25–14-26
Interview follow-up letter, 15-38
iPhones, 1-19, 1-20
ISP (Internet service provider), 2-20
Italic, word processing applications, 1-17

J

Junk email
    create meeting, 11-4
    filter, 11-3-11-4, 11-11
    filter lists, 11-3–11-4
    folder, 11-3, 11-10–11-11
Justify, paragraph alignment, 6-2

K

Keep with next feature, 6-7
Key block paragraphs, 1-66, 1-68
Keying
    handwritten (script) copy, 2-10
    position, 1-3, 1-6
    rough draft, 7-32
    skill building, 10-38–10-39
    speed, 1-30, 1-44, 1-58, 1-71, 4-17, 7-33
    technique, 1-4, 1-7, 2-10, 4-16, 8-36, 14-24
Keystroking, 1-4
Keywords, 1-8, 3-13

L

Labels, in graphs and charts, 8-21
LAN (local area network), 1-77
Landscape orientation, 7-8
Layout, 8-3–8-5
Leadership, 7-20
Learning keys
    standard plan for, 1-9–1-10
    techniques check, 1-10
Left indent, in paragraphs, 6-8–6-9
Left Shift key, learning, 1-27–1-28
Left tabs, 1-75
Legend, in graphs and charts, 8-21
Letter. *See* Business letter; Personal-business letter
Letter address, in personal-business letter, 5-2
Letter keys, 13-18, 14-22
Letter with table, 7-19–7-20
Line breaks, 6-7–6-8
Line graphs, in Microsoft *PowerPoint*, 8-23
Line spacing, 1-59
    standard format, 6-3
Links, sponsored, 3-17
Lists
    bulleted, 6-15, 8-9, 14-2, 14-6
    modified block personal-business letter with,
      5-19–5-20
    numbered, 2-17–2-18, 14-2, 14-6
Local area network (LAN), 1-77
Logging off, 1-49–1-50
Logical operators, 16-16
Login names, 1-46

M

Mail merge, 12-1, 17-1–17-2, 17-10–17-13,
    17-22–17-23
    applications, 12-10–12-11
    create form letter, 17-12–17-13
    feature, create database file, 17-10–17-12
    labels and directories, 12-13–12-15

    letters to selected recipients, 12-11–12-12
    management and main document files, 12-9–12-12
Mail Merge Wizard, 12-1
Manual table of contents, 13-3
Margin, 1-4, 1-59
    standard format, 6-3
Math problems, 2-6, 2-7, 2-9
MAX function, 14-4, 14-12
    in spreadsheets, 9-15, 9-16
Maximize button, 1-62–1-63
Meeting, 11-4
    organizer, 11-4
Memory, 1-50
Mental health issues, 10-42–1043
Merge Cells feature, 7-7
Merged file, 12-1
Microprocessors, 1-32
Microsoft *Edge,* 2-21
Microsoft *Excel,* 9-1
    features of, 9-3
    worksheet window, 9-3
Microsoft *OneDrive,* 8-40–8-41
Microsoft *PowerPoint*
    bar graphs, 8-21–8-22
    changing design theme, 8-11
    column graphs, 8-21–8-22
    creating presentation, 8-28–8-31
    Crop design theme, 8-11
    defined, 8-1
    delivering presentation, 8-32
    designer, 8-5
    design theme, 8-2–8-3
    enhancing slides with Designer, 8-25–8-26
    fcatures, 8-2
    generating slides with Designer, 8-26
    graph elements, 8-20–8-21
    graphics, inserting, 8-12
    line graphs, 8-23
    photos, inserting, 8-13
    pictures, creating slides with, 8-17
    pie chart, 8-23–8-24
    shapes, creating slides with, 8-16
    shapes, inserting, 8-14–8-15
    slide layout, 8-3–8-5
    Slide Show assessment, 8-33–8-34
    SmartArt, creating slides with, 8-18–8-19
    tables, creating, 8-20
    title and content slide, creating, 8-9–8-10
    Vapor Trail design theme, 8-11
    variants, 8-3
    view presentation, 8-8
    view slides, 8-5–8-7
    Wisp design theme, 8-11

Microsoft *Word*
    inserting *Excel* worksheets in, 9-24–9-25
    key and edit text in, 2-13–2-14
    numbered lists, 2-17–2-18
    opening files in, 2-15–2-16
    preview in, 2-16–2-17
    printing document in, 2-16–2-17
    Ribbon feature of, 2-12–2-13
    saving files in, 2-14–2-15
MIN function, 14-4, 14-12
    in spreadsheets, 9-15, 9-16
Minicomputers, 1-19
Minimize button, 1-62–1-63
Mixed cell reference, 16-11
Mixed punctuation, 5-3
m key, learning, 1-51–1-52
Modern Language Association (MLA) reports, 6-1, 6-2,
    7-27–7-28
    bulleted lists, 6-15
    composing, 6-15
    font settings, 6-12
    with footnotes, 13-6–13-7
    line spacing and selecting text, 6-11–6-12
    outline using numbering feature, 6-15–6-16
    page numbers, headers and footers, 6-13
    paragraph alignment, 6-12
    paragraph indents, 6-17
    with textual citations, 13-7
    unbound report, 6-13–6-14
    works cited page, 6-18–6-19
Modified block format, 5-1–5-2
Modified block personal-business letter, 5-1–5-2, 5-18–5-20
    assessment of, 5-23
    inserting Date and Time, 5-18
    with list, 5-19–5-20
    setting tabs, 5-18
Money transactions, computers and, 1-21
Mouse, 1-48–1-49
    safety tips for, 1-49
Multi-column document, 6-6, 6-26–6-27
Multicultural literacy, 16-34
Multiplication, 2-6–2-8

N

Name of the writer, in personal-business letter, 5-3
Narrow search, 3-16–3-17
Netiquette, 4-18–4-19
Network/Networking, 2-19, 17-36–17-37
Neuromorphic chips, 1-19
Newhouse Realty, Newhouse-1–Newhouse-14
    client information, Newhouse-2
    company email, Newhouse-2
    data files, Newhouse-2
    emails, Newhouse-2
    file names, Newhouse-2
    letter format, Newhouse-2–Newhouse-3
    processing instructions, Newhouse-1–Newhouse-2
    work assignment at, Newhouse-1
Newsletter, 14-19–14-20
n key, learning, 1-25–1-26
Normal View, 16-1
    in Microsoft *PowerPoint,* 8-5, 8-6
Notes, for personal information management
    software, 4-7, 4-14
Notes Page View, in Microsoft *PowerPoint,* 8-6
Notes pane, Microsoft *PowerPoint,* 8-2
Numbered lists, 2-17–2-18, 14-2, 14-6
Number expression, 4-25–4-26
Numbering, 5-8
    formatting, 9-12–9-13
Numeric keypad, learning, 2-1–2-6
    division, 2-8–2-9
    multiplication, 2-6–2-8
    subtraction, 2-6–2-8

O

Objectivity, 6-34
o key, learning, 1-23–1-24
OneDrive, 1-78
Online applications
    sharing information, 8-42–8-43
    working with, 8-40–8-42
Online apps, 1-34–1-35
Online safety, 5-31
Open punctuation, 5-3
    block letter format, 5-16
Operating systems (OSs), 1-34, 1-46
    mouse devices for, 1-48–1-49
Organic results, 3-17
Organizational blogs, 9-37
Orphan line, 6-7
OSs (Operating systems), 1-34, 1-46, 1-48–1-49
Outline, 6-2
    using numbering feature, 6-15–6-16
    View, in electronic presentations, 8-5, 8-6
Output, information processing, 1-36
Overtype, 1-16

P

Page Break Preview, 16-1
Page breaks, 6-7–6-8
Page Layout View, 16-1
Page numbers
    headers and footers, MLA reports, 6-13
    standard format, 6-3
    word processing applications, 6-8

Paragraph(s)
    alignment, 6-2
    block, 1-57
    hanging indent, 6-8–6-9
    headings, 13-1
    indents, 6-17
    key block, 1-66, 1-68
    keying speed check, 6-31
    left indent, 6-8–6-9
    spacing, 1-59
    speed check, 1-74
Passwords, 1-46
    protection in files, 5-27–5-28
    in system security maintenance, 5-29–5-30
Paste, word processing applications, 1-31
Path, 1-83
PC (personal computer), 33
PDAs, 1-19
. (period) key, learning, 1-27–1-28
Peripherals, computers, 33
Personal blogs, 9-37
Personal-business letter, 5-1–5-4, 5-10–5-13
    in block letter format, 5-1–5-2
    envelopes, 5-3, 5-17
    Find and Replace, 5-4, 5-13
    letter parts, 5-1–5-3
    in modified block format, 5-1–5-2
    open and mixed punctuation, 5-3
Personal computer (PC), 33
Personal digital resumes, 12-29
Personal digital safety, 10-43
Personal information management (PIM)
    create and edit contact groups, 11-9
    manage contact list, 11-4–11-9
    organize and manage emails, 11-10–11-11
    schedule meetings with calendars, 11-12–11-15
Personal information manager software (PIMS), 4-1–4-7
    Calendar, 4-4
    Contacts, 4-4–4-6
    Email, 4-1–4-4
    Notes, 4-7
    Tasks, 4-6
Personal interview
    asking questions, 14-26
    creating impression, 14-26–14-27
    definition of, 14-25
    interview questions, responses to, 14-25–14-26
    researching employers, 14-25
Personal print resumes, 13-21
Personal responsibility, 16-36
Personal safety, 4-21–4-22
Phishing, 3-3
Photos, inserting in Microsoft *PowerPoint*, 8-13
Phrase searching, 3-18

Physical health issues, 10-42–1043
Pictures, 6-6, 6-25–6-26, 6-28–6-29
    in two-columns report, 13-15–13-17
Pie chart, in Microsoft *PowerPoint*, 8-23–8-24
Pie charts, 9-25–9-26
PIMS. *See* Personal information manager software
p key, learning, 1-53–1-54
Placeholders, 12-4
    in Microsoft *PowerPoint*, 8-2
Plagiarism, 4-24
Podcasting, 9-37
Pointers, 1-63–1-64
Pointing devices, 1-48–1-49
Portrait orientation, 7-8
Preformatted text box, 6-5, 6-24
Presentation
    creating, 8-28–8-31
    delivering, 8-32
    Slide Show assessment, 8-33–8-34
Presentation (slide show), 15-2
    animations, 15-1, 15-15–15-22
    assessment, 8-33–8-34
    audio, 15-5, 15-22–15-27
    create with hyperlink, 15-10–15-13
    create with pictures and screen clippings, 15-8–15-10
    creating, 8-28–8-31
    deliver an effective presentation, 15-27–15-28
    delivering, 8-32
    design tips, 15-2
    with graphics, animations, and transitions, 15-15–15-22
    hyperlinks, 15-2
    insert screen clippings, 15-7–15-8
    insert slides in, 15-13–15-14
    navigation shortcuts, 15-3
    pictures and videos, 15-4
    Presenter view, 15-3–15-4
    screen clipping, 15-5
    with screen clippings, 15-7–15-14
    timing, 15-5–15-6
    transitions, 15-6
Presentation software. *See* Microsoft *PowerPoint*
Preview/Previewing
    in database table, 10-16–10-17
    in Microsoft *Word*, 2-16–2-17
Primary key, 10-12–10-13
Primary sorting, 10-8
Print Preview, 1-45
Print/printing, 1-45
    in database table, 10-16–10-17
    in Microsoft *Word*, 2-16–2-17
    personal resumes, 13-21
    word processing applications, 1-45
    worksheets, 9-8–9-12

Print resumes, 12-25–12-26
Privacy policy, 4-23
Privacy statement, 4-22–4-23
Private clouds, 8-38. *See also* Cloud computing
Processing, information processing, 1-36
Processor, computers, 1-32
Productivity, computers and, 1-20–1-21
Professional, Trade, and Service Associations, 17-36
Pronoun agreement, 6-36–6-37
Proofreaders' marks
    definition of, 6-21
    standard, unbound report with, 6-22–6-23
Public clouds, 8-38. *See also* Cloud computing
Public safety, computers and, 1-21
Punctuation
    mixed, 5-3
    open, 5-3

Q

q key, learning, 1-55–1-56
Query, 3-14. *See also* Database query
? (question mark) key, learning, 1-67–1-68
" (quotation mark) key, learning, 1-69–1-71

R

Random access memory (RAM), 1-50
Range, of cells, 9-10
Ransomware, 4-19
Reading View, in Microsoft *PowerPoint,* 8-6, 8-7
Record(s), 12-4
    in database table, 10-2
Redo, word processing applications, 1-45
Reference(s)
    collaborative report with footnotes, 13-14
    initials, in personal-business letter, 5-3
    list, standard format, 6-3
    reporting with styles, 13-3
    unbound reports with footnotes, 13-11
Relative cell referencing, 16-10
Remove Space After Paragraph feature, 5-7
Replace feature, 5-4
Report(s), 6-1–6-42
    composing, 6-15
    database. *See* Database reports
    definition of, 6-1
    Different First Page feature for, 6-3, 6-20
    MLA report, 7-27–7-28
    multi-column document, 6-6, 6-26–6-27
    outline, 6-2
    paragraph alignment, 6-2
    pictures, 6-6
    proofreaders' marks, 6-21
    standard, 6-21, 7-29

    styles, 6-9, 6-20
    with table of contents, 14-19
    three-column, 6-28
    two-column, 13-15–13-17
    unbound, 6-3–6-4, 6-21, 7-29
    Wizard, 10-32–10-33
Reporting with styles
    bibliography, 13-3
    cover page, 13-4
    documentation, 13-2
    ellipsis, 13-2
    internal spacing, 13-1
    page numberings, 13-1
    references, 13-3
    table of contents, 13-3–13-4
    template, 13-4
    titles and headings, 13-1
    works cited pages, 13-3
Researching employers, 14-25
Response pattern, reading/keying, 17-31
Restore Down button, 1-62–1-63
Results, 3-14
    organic, 3-17
Resume, 12-25
    tools, 12-29
Return address, in personal-business letter,
    5-1–5-2
Ribbon, 1-61
    in Microsoft *Word,* 2-12–2-13
    tabs, 2-12
Right Shift key, learning, 1-39–1-40
Right tabs, 1-75
Risk taking, 16-35
r key, learning, 1-12–1-13
Rough draft (keying), 7-32
Row(s), 9–2
    deleting, 9-21
    headings for worksheets, 9-7–9-8
    inserting, 9-21

S

Safeguarding files, 5-27–5-28
Safety
    of data, 4-22–4-24
    Internet, 4-21–4-24
    online, 5-31
    personal, 4-21–4-22
    survey, creating, 10-44
    workplace, 5-32
Salutation, in personal-business letter, 5-2
Saving, in Microsoft *Word,* 2-14–2-15
Scale, in graphs and charts, 8-20
Scams, 4-21

Schedule meetings and print calendars
    create additional calendars, 11-14–11-15
    create meetings, 11-12–11-13
    print calendars, 11-15
    propose a new meeting time, 11-13–11-14
    reply to a meeting request/invitation, 11-13
    share and print calendars, 11-13
School, computers and, 1-21
Scientific literacy, 16-34
Screen tips
    in Help, 3-6
    learning, 3-5
Search feature
    analyzing results, 3-17
    improving, 3-18
    narrow, 3-16–3-17
    techniques, 3-18–3-20
    on websites, 3-13–3-15
    for World Wide Web, 3-15–3-17
Searching, phrase, 3-18
Secondary sorting, 10-8
Section break, 13-4
Select text, word processing applications, 1-31
Self-direction, 1-8, 16-35
Sentences, speed check, 1-74, 5-24, 6-30–6-31, 8-35
Servers, 2-19
Shading and Borders feature, 7-9–7-10, 7-22–7-23
Shapes, inserting in Microsoft *PowerPoint*, 8-14–8-15
Sheet tabs, 9-2
Show/Hide feature, 5-10
Shutting down, 1-49–1-50
Side headings, 13-1
Signing out, 1-49–1-50
Single-space (SS), 1-4
Slide layout, in Microsoft *PowerPoint*, 8-3–8-5
Slide pane, Microsoft *PowerPoint*, 8-2
Slide Show, in Microsoft *PowerPoint*, 8-6, 8-7
Slide Sorter View, in Microsoft *PowerPoint*, 8-6, 8-7
SmartArt, creating slides with, 8-18–8-19
Smartphone, 9-36
Social and civic responsibility, 16-36
Social networking sites, 9-37
Soft page breaks, 6-7
Software
    applications, 1-34
    definition of, 1-34
    types of, 1-34
Software maintenance
    keeping other programs updated, 7-36
    viruses and spyware, 7-35–7-36
Solid state drives (SSDs), 1-77
Sorting, 7-10
    in database, 10-8

database records, 10-30
    table, 7-24–7-25
Space Bar, 1-4, 1-5, 1-7
    shift keys and, 1-43
    technique, 1-14, 1-42
Space program, 1-21–1-22
Spacing
    double, 1-4
    line, 1-59
    paragraph, 1-59
    with punctuation, 1-40, 1-52
    single, 1-4
    technique, 1-4, 1-7
Spam, 4-18, 11-3
Speaking skills, 1-85, 4-27, 6-38, 10-46, 14-29
Speed forcing drill, 2-11, 3-9, 3-10, 4-17, 13-19, 14-24, 17-30
Spelling & Grammar feature, 5-5
Split Cells feature, 7-7
Sponsored links, 3-17
Spreadsheet(s), 9-1
    applications, 16-24–16-25
    AutoFill, 16-4–16-5
    conditional formatting, 16-24
    freeze/unfreeze columns and rows, 16-20
    functions in, 9-15–9-16
    integrate word and excel and charting, 16-24
    keying skill, 16-30
    key mastery, 16-30
    letter with linked worksheet, 16-25
    speed forcing drill, 16-31
    timed function, 16-31
    worksheet into *Word*, 16-21–16-22
    worksheet linked to word processing document, 16-21–16-22
Spyware, 7-35
SSDs (solid state drives), 1-77
Standard format, 6-3–6-4, 6-21
Standard reports, 7-29
Standard word, 1-42
Status bar, 16-1
Stem, word, 3-18
Storage, information processing, 1-36
Storage spaces, 1-77–1-78
Styles, 6-9, 6-20
    standard format, 6-3
Subfolders, 1-79
Subtraction, 2-6–2-8
SUM function, 14-3–14-4, 14-12
    in spreadsheets, 9-15
System administrators, 1-77
System maintenance
    schedule, 7-37
    understanding, 7-34

System security maintenance
    commonsense security practices, 5-30
    critical defensive measures, 5-28–5-29
    disaster recovery, 5-31
    permissions and passwords, 5-29–5-30

T

Tab key, learning, 1-69–1-71
Table(s), 7-1–7-39, 14-1–14-22
    adjusting column width and row height, 7-8
    alignment, 7-14–7-15
    analyzing, 14-14–14-15
    AutoFit Contents feature, 7-8
    AutoFit Window feature, 7-8
    AVERAGE function, 14-4, 14-12
    borders and shading, 7-22–7-23
    bulleted lists, 14-2, 14-6
    with calculations, 14-22
    cell content, selecting and formatting, 7-4–7-5
    cell margins, 14-3, 14-10
    centering, 7-6
    column widths, changing, 7-12–7-13
    converting text from, 7-2, 7-25
    converting text to, 7-2, 7-25
    COUNT function, 14-4, 14-12
    creating, 7-11–7-12
    decimal tabs, 14-2, 14-5–14-6
    definition of, 7-1
    designing basic, 7-14
    Format Painter, 7-5
    formatting with, 14-21
    with formulas, 14-20–14-21
    hanging indents, 14-2, 14-5–14-6
    heading styles, changing, 7-14
    inserting, 7-2–7-4
    insert space after, 14-3, 14-10
    keying and converting text to, 7-25–7-26
    keying around, 7-3–7-4
    landscape orientation, 7-8
    letter with, 7-19–7-20
    MAX function, 14-4, 14-12
    merge cells, 7-7, 7-16–7-18
    in Microsoft *PowerPoint*, 8-20
    MIN function, 14-4, 14-12
    moving around, 7-3–7-4
    numbered lists, 14-2, 14-6
    portrait orientation, 7-8
    presenting information, 14-8
    properties, 7-6
    repeat headers, 14-2, 14-10
    research and design, 7-26
    reviewing, 14-5
    row height, changing, 7-21–7-22

    rows and columns, adding/deleting, 7-18–7-19
    select cells, 7-16–7-18
    shading and borders, 7-9–7-10, 7-22–7-23
    sorting, 7-10, 7-24–7-25
    split cells, 7-7, 7-16–7-18
    styles, 7-9, 7-13–7-14
    SUM function in formula, 14-3–14-4, 14-12
    text direction, changing, 14-2, 14-8–14-9
    vertical alignment, 7-8–7-9, 7-21–7-22
Table grid, 7-2
Table of contents, 13-3–13-4
    collaborative report with footnotes, 13-14
    electronic, 13-4
    manual, 13-3
    report with, 14-19
    unbound reports with footnotes, 13-11
Tablet PCs, 1-19
Tabs, 1-75
    decimal, 14-2, 14-5–14-6
    in modified block personal-business letter, 5-18
    in word processing applications, 5-9
Tasks, for personal information management software,
    4-6, 4-14
Teaming and collaboration, 16-35
Technological literacy, 16-34
Template, 13-4
Terminal punctuation, 10-45
Text box
    drawing, 6-5, 6-24–6-25
    formatting, 6-5, 6-25
    preformatted, 6-5, 6-24
Textual citations, 13-2
    MLA report with, 13-7
    standard format, 6-3
Text wrapping, 6-28–6-29
Text Wrapping Break feature, 5-7
Thesaurus, 5-6
Three-column document, 6-28
3-D cell reference, 16-13–16-14
    application, 16-14
    multiple worksheets and, 16-25
Thumbnail pane, Microsoft *PowerPoint*, 8-2
Tick marks, in graphs and charts, 8-20
Time & Date feature, 5-6
Timed writings, 2-11, 3-10, 5-26, 10-35,
    14-17, 17-31
Title and content slide, in Microsoft
    PowerPoint, 8-9–8-10
t key, learning, 1-23–1-24
Track pad, 1-48–1-49
Transportation, computers and, 1-21
Trojan, 4-19
Trolling, 6-35

Twitter, 1-18
Two-columns reports, 13-15–13-17
Two-page unbound report, 13-5

U

UI (User interface), 1-47
u key, learning, 1-37–1-38
Unbound reports, 6-3–6-4, 6-13–6-14, 6-21, 7-29
    cover page, 13-6
    with footnotes, 14-18–14-19
    MLA report with footnotes, 13-6–13-7
    MLA report with textual citations, 13-7
    two-page, 13-5
Underline, 1-17
Undo, word processing applications, 1-45
Uniform resource locator (URL), 2-21–2-22
USB flash drives, 1-77
User interface (UI), 1-47
U.S. Federal Trade Commission (FTC), 4-20

V

Vapor Trail design theme, in Microsoft *PowerPoint,* 8-11
Variants, in Microsoft *PowerPoint,* 8-3
Vertical alignment, tables, 7-8–7-9
Video conferencing, 9-37
View presentation, 8-8
View tab, 16-1
Viruses, software, 7-35–7-36
Visual aids, 8-1
Visual literacy, 16-34
v key, learning, 1-53–1-54

W

Web browser, 2-21
Web conferencing, 9-37
Webpages, accessing and navigation, 2-21–2-23
Websites
    addresses for, 2-21–2-23
    certificate, 4-23
    History and Favorites, 3-11–3-13
    hyperlinks in, 2-23
    privacy statement, 4-22–4-23
    Search feature on, 3-13–3-20
Widow line, 6-7
Window, 1-61
Windows 10, 1-19, 1-47
Windows Defender Firewall, 5-29
Windows OS, 1-60–1-64
    maximizing/minimizing windows in, 1-62–1-63
    open applications, 1-60
    parts of *Windows* application, 1-61–1-62
    pointers and, 1-63–1-64

resizing and restoring windows in, 1-62–1-63
Windows Start screen, 1-47–1-148
Wisp design theme, in Microsoft *PowerPoint,* 8-11
w key, learning, 1-39–1-40
Word choice, 1-85, 4-26, 6-37, 10-46, 14-29
Word processing (WP) applications
    adjusting column width and row height, 7-8
    AutoCorrect, 1-16
    bold, 1-17
    bullets, 5-8
    cell content, selecting and formatting, 7-4–7-5
    centering tables, 7-6
    cover page feature, 6-11
    cut, copy, and paste, 1-31
    deleting rows and columns, 7-6–7-7
    envelopes, 5-7–5-8
    Font group, 5-4–5-5
    Format Painter, 7-5
    hyphenation, 5-5
    indentations, 6-8–6-9
    insert, 1-16
    Insert Date & Time feature, 5-6
    insert endnote/footnote, 6-10
    inserting rows and columns, 7-6–7-7
    insert table, 7-2–7-4
    insert text from file feature, 6-10
    italic, 1-17
    landscape orientation, 7-8
    left tabs, 1-75
    line breaks, 6-7–6-8
    line spacing, 1-59
    margin, 1-59
    Merge Cells feature, 7-7
    numbering, 5-8
    overtype, 1-16
    page breaks, 6-7–6-8
    page numbers, 6-8
    paragraph spacing, 1-59
    portrait orientation, 7-8
    print preview, 1-45
    redo, 1-45
    Remove Space After Paragraph feature, 5-7
    right tabs, 1-75
    select text, 1-31
    shading and borders features, 7-9–7-10
    Show/Hide feature, 5-10
    sort feature, 7-10
    Spelling & Grammar feature, 5-5
    Split Cells feature, 7-7

Word processing (WP) applications (*Continued*)
 styles, 6-9
 table properties, 7-6
 table styles, 7-9, 7-13–7-14
 tabs, 5-9
 Text Wrapping Break feature, 5-7
 thesaurus, 5-6
 underline, 1-17
 undo, 1-45
 vertical alignment, 7-8–7-9
 zoom, 1-45
Work-area arrangement, 1-2, 1-5
Workbooks, 9-2
Workplace, preparing for
 digital resumes, 12-27–12-29
 personal digital resumes, 12-29
 print resumes, 12-25–12-26
 resume tools, 12-29
Workplace safety, 5-32
Works cited page, 6-18–6-19, 13-3
Worksheets, 9-2
 aligning, labels and values, 9-5–9-7
 basic parts of, 9-2, 9-4
 centering, 9-10
 change text orientation, 16-5–16-6
 with charts, 9-24–9-29
 clearing cells in, 9-19
 column headings for, 9-7–9-8, 9-11
 column width, changing, 9-17–9-18
 convert text to columns, 16-8
 copy and paste, 16-23
 creating, 9-12
 deleting cells in, 9-19
 editing, 9-17–9-20
 editing cell content in, 9-17
 entering labels and values, 9-5–9-7
 format, 16-9–16-10
 formatting, adding chart and, 9-28–9-29
 formatting content of, 9-10–9-12
 formatting numbers, 9-12–9-13
 formulas, 9-13–9-15
 insert and delete, 16-7
 inserting, in *Word* document, 9-24–9-25
 margins, 9-9
 modifying, 9-19–9-20, 9-24
 moving around in, 9-4–9-5
 organize sheets, 16-7
 orientation, change text and, 16-9
 page orientation, 9-9
 preview, 9-8–9-9
 printing, 9-8–9-12
 range of, 9-10
 row headings for, 9-7–9-8
 row height, changing, 9-17–9-18
 sorting data, 9-22–9-23
 update a linked, 16-23
World Wide Web, 1-19, 2-19
 Search feature, 3-15–3-17
Writing skills, 6-38, 10-46
Written communication, 12-1–12-29
 business and personal-business letters and memos,
  12-2–12-3
 data source files, 12-3–12-8
 mail merge, 12-1, 17-10–17-13
 main document files, 12-9–12-15

X
X-axis, in graphs and charts, 8-20
x key, learning, 1-51–1-52

Y
Y-axis, in graphs and charts, 8-20
y key, learning, 1-41–1-42

Z
z key, learning, 1-65–1-66
Zoom, word processing applications, 1-45